Photographing CUSTER'S BATTLEFIELD

Photographing CUSTER'S BATTLEFIELD

The Images of KENNETH F. ROAHEN

Sandy Barnard

University of Oklahoma Press | Norman

Also by Sandy Barnard

(and James S. Brust and Brian C. Pohanka) *Where Custer Fell: Photographs of the Little Bighorn Battlefield Then and Now* (Norman, Okla., 2005)

LIBRARY OF CONGRESS CATALOGING-IN-PUBLICATION DATA

Roahen, Kenneth F., 1888–1976, photographer.

Photographing Custer's battlefield : the images of Kenneth F. Roahen / Sandy Barnard.

pages cm

Includes bibliographical references and index.

ISBN 978-0-8061-5159-5 (hardcover) ISBN 978-0-8061-9208-6 (paper)

1. Roahen, Kenneth F., 1888-1976—Photograph collections. 2. Little Bighorn Battlefield (Mont.)—History—Pictorial works. 3. Little Bighorn Battlefield (Mont.)—Pictorial works. 4. Little Bighorn Battlefield National Monument (Mont.)—Pictorial works. 5. Little Bighorn, Battle of the, Mont., 1876. I. Barnard, Sandy, author, photographer. II. Title.

E83.876.R628 2016

973.8'2—dc23

2015030119

The paper in this book meets the guidelines for permanence and durability of the Committee on Production Guidelines for Book Longevity of the Council on Library Resources, Inc. ∞

Interior layout and composition: Alcorn Publication Design

To John H. Boyd, Jr., my mentor in journalism and a friend for more than forty-six years

Contents

List of Maps ix

Preface xi

Acknowledgments xv

PART 1: THE LITTLE BIG HORN

1. Researching the Custer Battlefield Story 3
2. Roahen Biographical Sketch 9
3. Little Big Horn Battle Historical Background 29

PART 2: KENNETH F. ROAHEN'S PHOTOGRAPHS

4. The Crow's Nest 43
5. Walter Camp's Marker on the Divide 56
6. From the Divide to Reno Creek 59
7. The Morass 61
8. Girard's Knoll 67
9. Major Reno's First Crossing 74
10. Reno's Advance Down the Valley 81
11. Reno Valley Fight and Retreat Crossing 86
12. Aerial Photos of the Reno Retreat Crossing 112
13. Reno-Benteen Defense Site 115
14. Weir Point to Medicine Tail Coulee 135
15. Calhoun Hill, Finley-Finckle Ridge, and Battle Ridge 153
16. Keogh Sector 160
17. Below Custer Hill 165
18. Last Stand Hill 182
19. Entering the Main Battlefield 200
20. Visitor Center Dedication, June 25, 1952 225
21. Roahen's 1951 Aerial Photos of the Seventy-Fifth Anniversary 229

Notes 239
Bibliography 245
Index 251

Maps

Map 3.1. Little Big Horn campaign map 32

Map 4.1. Crow's Nest area 44

Map 7.1. The Morass, Girard's Knoll, and Reno's first crossing 61

Map 11.1. Reno valley fight and retreat crossing 87

Map 13.1. Reno-Benteen Defense Site 116

Map 14.1. Weir Point vicinity 135

Map 14.2. Medicine Tail Coulee vicinity 139

Map 15.1. Calhoun Hill, Finley-Finckle Ridge, and Battle Ridge 153

Map 16.1. Keogh Sector 160

Map 17.1. Below Custer Hill 165

Map 18.1. Custer Hill 184

Map 19.1. Stone House, Custer National Cemetery, and vicinity 201

Preface

IN 2009, I HAD READ about the donation of a collection of 10,000 Kenneth F. Roahen photographs by his niece, Elaine Ooley, to the Big Horn County Historical Museum in Hardin, Montana.[1] As a youngster, Mrs. Ooley had frequently visited her uncle and his wife at their Billings, Montana, home and was intimately familiar with his love of photography. She often accompanied him on his assignments and handled tasks for him in his photographic workspace in the basement of the house. She would crank a large drum to turn out her uncle's photographs. For assisting him, he would reward her with a large silver dollar. Ooley also recalls meeting such well-known photographers at the house as Ansel Adams and Frank Haynes.

> In the early 1970s, her uncle called her early one morning and bluntly asked, "What are we going to do with these god-damned pictures?"
>
> "I said I would take the god-damned pictures," said Ooley, who turned 102 in January 2016.
>
> Roahen replied, "Are you sure?" She told him, "Yes," and he hung up, the matter settled.

After his death in 1976, she spent more than twenty-five years organizing his collection and his other materials, but she realized they would be better protected in a museum or archive. "The manner in which Kenneth Francis Roahen catalogued this collection is a reminder that it was to be shared and enjoyed," she told newspaper reporters.

She and her late husband, Jack, considered various options over the years. Key was to locate a facility that would accept the entire collection, keep it intact, and display it appropriately. Finally, in 2009, Ooley reached an agreement with museum director Diana Scheidt. At the time, Scheidt said, "The collection will be an asset to Big Horn County Historical and Montana, as Kenneth F. Roahen was a true historian who preserved history through his documents and the eye of a lens."

Soon after reading about Mrs. Ooley's gift in 2009 to the Hardin museum, I explored the possibility of using Roahen's Little Big Horn images in a follow-up to an earlier photo-history book, *Where Custer Fell: Photographs of Little Bighorn Battlefield Then and Now*, which I had coauthored in 2005 with Dr. James S. Brust and the late Brian C. Pohanka. After more than thirty years researching the Battle of Little Big Horn, the life and career of Lt. Col. George Armstrong Custer, and related issues and personalities, I was greatly familiar with Roahen's reputation as a photographer of the then Custer Battlefield National Monument from the early 1930s to the early 1970s. He also was one of fifteen "historical" photographers whose Little Big Horn images my colleagues and I had featured in our book. Roahen had been active as a photographer in

Montana from 1930 to near the time of his death in early 1976, and his photos were the most modern that we published in *Where Custer Fell.*

In June 2009, I discussed the prospects for a new book focused on Roahen's images with Scheidt. Though she expressed interest in such an undertaking, her staff was still assessing what is now called the Kenneth F. and Sandae Woodworth Roahen Collection. Besides images in print, negative, and slide form of Custer Battlefield National Monument and the greater battlefield, his photos included such subjects as wildlife, Crow Reservation life, Yellowstone Park, and various public events.

My task would have to wait for at least another year. Unfortunately, in 2010 I was laid up by kidney disease and the need for a kidney transplant. After a successful transplant in late 2010, I was ready by the summer of 2011 to launch my Roahen project. Scheidt agreed, and that September I returned to the museum and scanned some 140 Roahen images for possible use. In June 2012, I selected seventy more images in negative or transparency form in the collection. That summer Scheidt had those images professionally scanned for me.

In late September and early October 2012, my wife, Betty, and I spent ten days trekking about the greater Little Big Horn battlefield—from the back country in the Wolf Mountains down Reno Creek into the Little Big Horn Valley, across the area of the Reno valley fight and retreat crossing, and, finally, over the major battlefield segments on the bluffs above the Little Big Horn River that are under the jurisdiction of the National Park Service. We located each site where Roahen had shot an original photograph and attempted to match his image with the modern view. In June 2013, we returned to finish our photography task by reshooting the remaining images. In a few cases we successfully confirmed sites that had escaped our notice the previous fall. We also determined that some images anonymously listed in the battlefield's archives actually were Roahen's.[2] This volume is the result of that research and those hikes.

My review of Roahen's Little Big Horn photographs in the museum collection proved surprising in one important way. My research had disclosed that Roahen shot and reshot the Little Big Horn battlefield every year or two for renowned park superintendent Edward S. Luce in the 1940s and continued his work deep into the 1960s, if not the early 1970s. Through his photographs he had sought to document changes occurring to the field. In the end only about 175 to 200 unique images of the field were found. The vast majority of his photographs deal with countless other subjects, especially landscapes and animals. Whether his numerous other Custer battlefield images had simply been lost, given away, or sold remains a mystery.

Research into Roahen's life does allow for some tentative conclusions. As a decade, the 1930s seem to be missing in action as far as Roahen battlefield photographs are concerned. It appears likely that he remained busy as a U.S. Fish and Wildlife agent, which required considerable travel. For example, in 1934 a rostrum was built in the Custer Battlefield National Cemetery that functioned for several decades as a speakers' platform during special events, including Memorial Day observances. Roahen's collection lacks any photos of its construction or use during that decade, suggesting that he did not attend the dedication event or others.

Sometime in the period 1960–63, probably 1963, Roahen wrote a letter to Conrad L. Wirth, then the director of the National Park Service, that addresses both the issue of the number of photos he shot as well as his own activities during the 1930s. First, Roahen explained that he was kept busy early in his years in Montana on investigations, especially in Yellowstone Park. He also photographed that park's backcountry range conditions about every three years.[3] Roahen added, "I have been around Custer Battlefield for 32 1/2 years, and shot pictures for about every supt. and historian since."

In any case, I found this more limited number of battlefield images to be more than sufficient for the purposes of this book. Indeed, Roahen images may be found in other archival collections, including Little Bighorn Battlefield National Monument, or in personal collections. But casting a wider net for additional, perhaps unique, publishable images did not seem practical, and, again, the 175 to 200 images I did find in his collection do cover much of the field.

Some caveats in matching Roahen's photos with my modern reshoots must be mentioned here. Although the Hardin museum's Roahen collection contains many of his cameras, we have little idea about what kind of equipment he used in the field at any specific time across the more than four decades he labored as a battlefield photographer. Too, he often carried with him a six-foot stepladder that allowed him greater access over fences and other obstacles. I did not. Finally, compared to today's extended battlefield, in most instances when he took his photos vegetation was less abundant or much shorter. Similarly, modern changes made reshooting a few of his images difficult, if not impossible. A good example is a photograph that he took from the fence line of the national cemetery up toward Last Stand Hill. Today, standing at that spot, one merely obtains a good shot of the west wall of the Visitor Center.

It should be noted, as well, that images Roahen published in the media of his day reveal that he could produce high-quality work. However, among his battlefield photographs in the museum I found some that are poorly focused and poorly composed. Nevertheless, several are included here because subject matter must trump quality.

When Betty and I walked over the battlefield in 2012 and 2013, we were, as Jim Brust stated in our 2005 book, "looking and learning" as we went. In that sense I offer these Roahen photos to readers, but with a caution. Roahen was a product of his times—the middle third of the twentieth century—and the often one-sided thinking about the glorious Custer and his regiment then associated with the Little Big Horn struggle. As is true with all students of the Custer fight, he undoubtedly had evolved his battle theories over many years and had spent countless hours discussing the myriad subjects with his well-learned friends, including such professionals as Superintendent Luce, battlefield historian Don Rickey, author Jesse W. Vaughn, as well as Billings, Montana, friends George C. Osten and William H. Bellingham. Did Roahen's interpretations make him "right?" That is up to future researchers to determine—or at least to argue about. Roahen did possess one advantage over most of his peers as well as modern historians: he documented his theories through his photographs. A photograph, it can be argued, may be more objective in what it sees, but what appears in his camera's view finder depends on the photographer and his own beliefs.

In *Where Custer Fell*, we focused on fifteen "historic photographers" whose work captured the Custer battlefield during the first fifty years after the general's defeat in 1876.[4] Their work documented the evolution of the site from a military and Indian tragedy on a bone-strewn ridge above the Little Big Horn River to a national historic landmark. With an extended focus on photographs of one of them, Kenneth F. Roahen, this book expands that coverage of the battlefield for another five decades, moving us from the 1930s to the mid-1970s.

Acknowledgments

SUCH A PROJECT could not be attempted, much less successfully completed, without the assistance of many individuals. Foremost, I must acknowledge my significant debt to Diana Scheidt and the Big Horn County Historical Museum staff for their able assistance in making the Roahen photographs available to me for review and scanning. Scheidt also introduced me to Mrs. Elaine Ooley, who has worked tirelessly for decades to preserve her uncle's legacy and his work. She provided me with countless details about her uncle's life and career.

Next would be National Park Service personnel at the Little Bighorn Battlefield National Monument. Foremost was then interim superintendent David Harrington was well as chief of interpretation Ken Woody and law enforcement officer Michael Stops. Seasonal ranger Michael N. Donahue was especially helpful, both at the battlefield in his formal Park Service role and as a longtime friend with an equally strong interest in the history of the Indian wars and the Battle of Little Big Horn.

For many years, Kenneth F. Roahen was a game agent with the U.S. Fish and Wildlife Service. Several members of its archival staff at the service's National Conservation Training Center in Shepherdstown, West Virginia, were immensely helpful to me in locating pertinent letters, documents, photographs, reports, and magazines associated with Roahen's career. I owe a special thanks to Fish and Wildlife Museum curator Jeanne M. Harold, historian Mark Madison, and associate Andy White.

Beverley Komarek, director of the Barton County Historical Society in Great Bend, Kansas, and research assistant Karen Neuforth provided me with much information about the area in which Kenneth Roahen grew up. Linda Colle scoured reels of microfilm of Kansas newspapers to find pertinent articles related to Roahen and his family.

Former Park Service scientists, rangers, and historians, all of whom are longtime friends, provided invaluable insights into the battlefield's history as well as their own recollections of Roahen. No two men are more respected as historians of the Indian wars than Robert M. Utley and Jerome Greene. Additionally, Douglas D. Scott, former Park Service archaeologist, frequently answered my questions about the battle itself and the history of archaeological efforts at the site. Author-historian Paul Hedren offered much insight into the army's organizational structure and the Indian wars.

Several longtime residents of Hardin, Crow Agency, and Garryowen, Montana, provided insights into the battle history and the historic sites that surround them. Among them are Christopher Kortlander, owner of the Garryowen property; Mark Real Bird, Gilbert Bird In Ground, Jr., and Wilford Bird In Ground, who provided me with access to the historic sites at Medicine Tail

Coulee and the area of Reno's retreat crossing; Patrick Hill; Putt Thompson; and Rhonda and Glen Elhard. Glen performed double-duty for me. First, he guided me across his Little Big Horn Valley property where the river meanders, first by truck and then on foot, near to the point where Deep Ravine empties into the Little Big Horn River. When a deep feeder creek blocked our path, I feared the Roahen image would have to go unmatched with a modern photo; with a suppressed immune system, I could not risk a bath in the dank creek waters. Glen took my camera in hand, crossed a beaver dam, and made his way through heavy undergrowth to the site. Technically the modern image may be mine, but, rest assured, it exists only through Glen's efforts on my behalf. James Court, former Battlefield superintendent and director of the Custer Battlefield Preservation Committee, provided me with complete access to the organization's properties in the valley and on the bluffs.

No one may have helped me more than Hardin resident and my longtime friend Dennis Fox. For one, he provided me with copies of his own Roahen images. He also offered his personal insights into battlefield sites, drawn from an entire lifetime spent in the battlefield's vicinity. Most important, he gave up a full day ferrying Betty and me into the Little Big Horn backcountry and climbing with us to the high point on the divide between Rosebud Creek and the Little Big Horn River that Kenneth Roahen believed was the historic Crow's Nest. We followed Reno Creek down the road bearing its name through the area of the Morass to the area where Major Reno first crossed the Little Big Horn River.

During my more than thirty-five years studying the Civil and Indian wars, I have enjoyed the friendship of many people who share my interests in military history. Many of them have developed unparalleled knowledge of the historical events of 1876 that cannot be equaled by the fanciest of degrees. Once again, at the top of the list is my "pard," Dr. James S. Brust, who coauthored *Where Custer Fell* with me in 2005. Though his medical practice did not afford him the considerable time necessary to join me in the field for this project, except for one memorable Sunday morning in June 2013, he has patiently reviewed my manuscript and across many months responded to my thoughts and questions with information drawn from his immense knowledge of battlefield photographs. He urged me to pursue the Roahen project and provided encouragement all along the way. He also has readily made available several of his own photographs pertinent to the Roahen study.

Equally helpful to my project has been author Bruce Liddic. I believe no one today is better read or more knowledgeable about the events of the Little Big Horn than Bruce. Countless times I emailed or phoned him with questions. He never failed to respond with information drawn from his superb insights on the Little Big Horn battle and the battlefield itself. He also reviewed snippets of the manuscript at various points as well as the entire final draft.

Within what I call the Custer/Little Big Horn research community, numerous other people gave me information or guidance along the way. They include Dale Kosman, Kevin Connelly, C. Lee Noyes, Thomas Bookwalter, W. Donald

Horn, the late Frank Mercatante, Norvelle Wathen, Richard Upton, and Jim Mundie. Ron Nichols, Dale Kosman, and Francis Taunton also reviewed early drafts of my manuscript. Father Vince Heier's book, *Little Bighorn*, which is a study of the Little Big Horn battlefield through postcard images, was especially helpful. At least two modern reshoots in this book were made possible only through, shall I say, the unique efforts on that memorable Sunday morning of my good friend from the United Kingdom, retired British Army major Kevin Galvin.

Once again, artist-historian Gary Raham has drawn the maps for one of my books. I am greatly indebted to Gary for his patience, for I sometimes fail to provide him with the clearest of directions.

Finally, as always, one person deserves the lion's share of the credit for enabling me to bring a book to publication. My wife, Betty, accompanied me on every one of my Roahen-related trips to the Little Bighorn Battlefield and proved her keen eye for picking up details on the ground. Over the years, she has evolved into my primary research assistant. On the personal level, it would have been impossible for me to complete this manuscript so quickly without Betty's incomparable assistance, love, and understanding. We have been married for nearly fifty years, and George Custer has been a part of our lives for some thirty-five of those years.

At this point, an author must say he accepts all blame for any errors in facts or interpretation that readers may find in his book. Of course, that must be true. After all, the name on the cover is no one else's but my own.

PART 1

The Little Big Horn

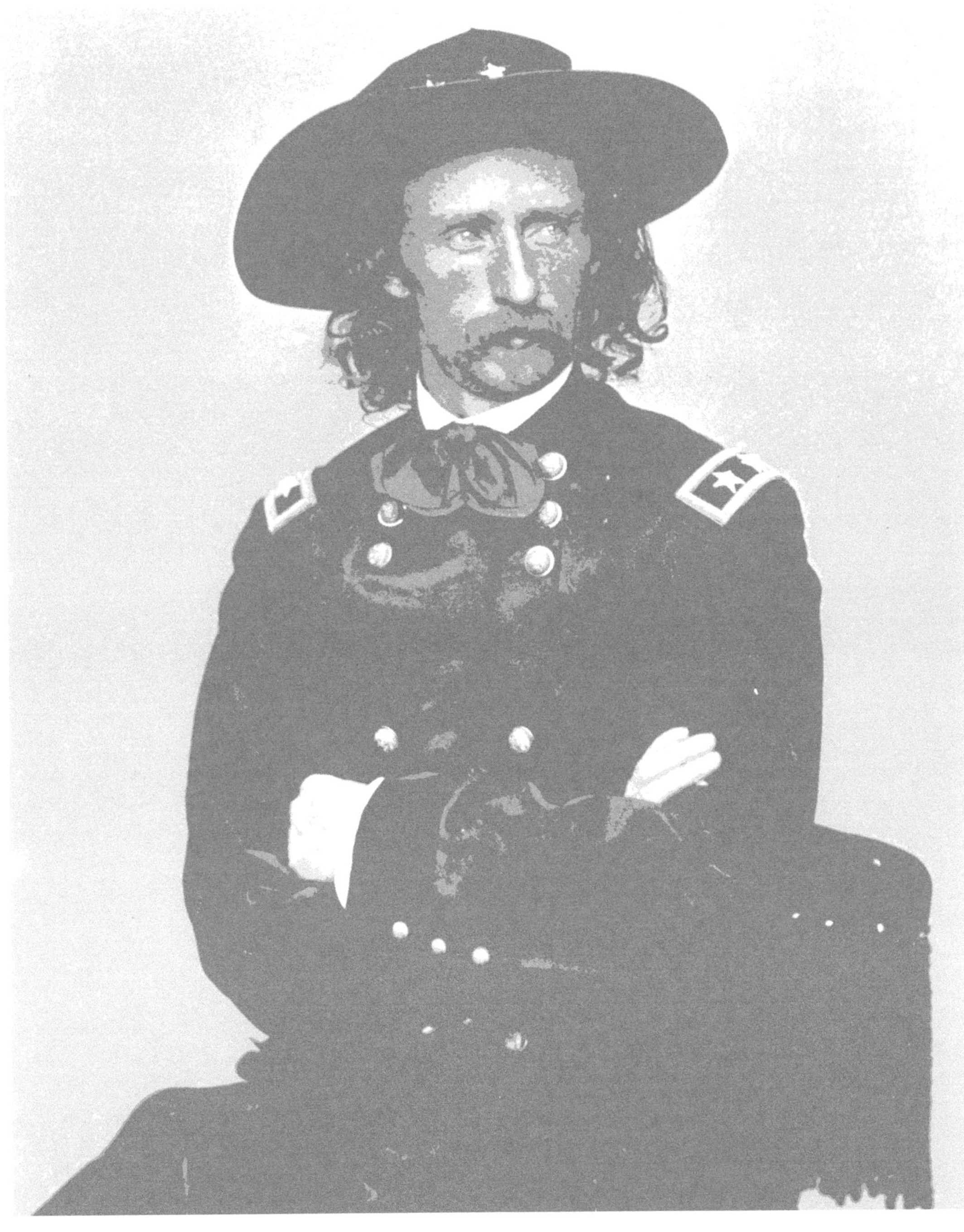

CHAPTER 1

Researching the Custer Battlefield Story

In its March 2010 newsletter, the U.S. Fish and Wildlife Service paid tribute to one of its most storied game agents, Kenneth F. Roahen. It noted that "he was small and scrappy, and . . . you wouldn't want to mess with him!"[1]

For some forty years as a game agent, Roahen had dedicated himself to protecting wildlife, sometimes at the risk of his own life. Yet today he is better remembered as a photographer, equally as dedicated to researching the last battle of Lt. Col. George Armstrong Custer and preserving the Custer Battlefield National Monument (today's Little Bighorn Battlefield National Monument).

As early as 1930, Roahen launched his own research and photography efforts at what was then known as Custer Battlefield. In so doing, he was following in the footsteps of numerous researchers and photographers who had preceded him. On the research side, within the first twenty-five years after Custer fell on a ridge above the Little Big Horn River on June 25, 1876, a cottage industry of battle study arose among devotees of his last fight, an effort that continues unabated today. Foremost among that first generation of researchers seeking to unravel the mysteries behind Custer's death was Walter Mason Camp, a Chicago-based editor of a professional railway publication. For the first two decades of the twentieth century, Camp visited and revisited the Little Big Horn battlefield and other Indian wars battlefields, seeking out yet another elusive tidbit of information. As part of his Custer battle research efforts, he tracked down and interviewed some two hundred Little Big Horn survivors among both whites and Indians. Alas, on August 3, 1925, he died suddenly of kidney disease and left unfinished his epic inquiry into the 1876 military disaster at the Little Big Horn.

In the next ten to fifteen years, Camp was succeeded by such men as Earl A. Brininstool, Dr. Charles W. Kuhlman, Fred Dustin, Robert Ellison, William J. Ghent, Gen. William Carey Brown, and Col. William A. Graham. Ellison and Brown made certain that Camp's materials would be preserved for future researchers by buying a large portion of his notes and other materials from Camp's widow. Brininstool, Kuhlman, and Graham all wrote major books about the battle that modern researchers still consult.[2] Beginning in the early 1940s, a third generation of researchers coalesced around the dynamic, colorful personality of Capt. Edward S. Luce, the superintendent of Custer Battlefield from 1941 to 1956.[3] Not only was Ken Roahen among them, but so were two of his Billings, Montana, friends, George C. Osten and William H. Bellingham. According to today's labels, their activities tended to mark them

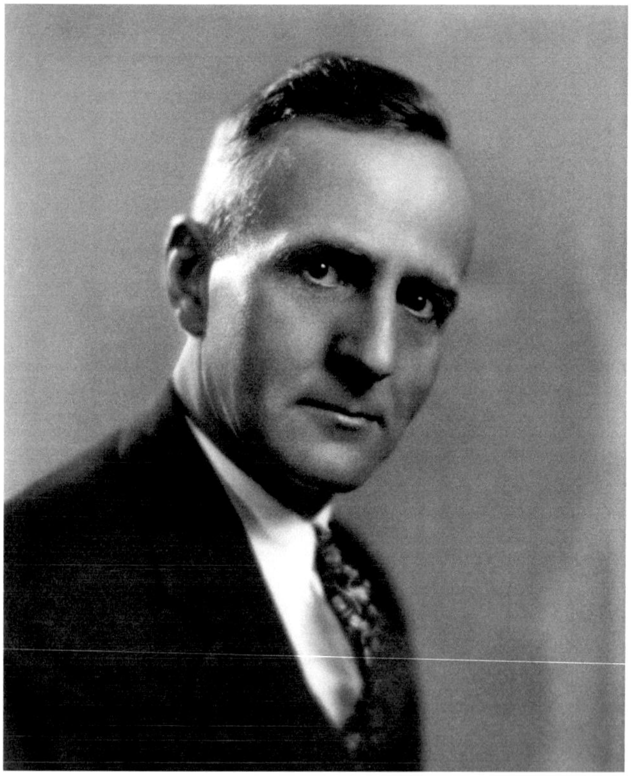

Figure 1.1. (*left*) Kenneth F. Roahen. Courtesy of Big Horn County Historical Museum.

Figure 1.2. (*below*) Walter M. Camp. Courtesy of John Husk.

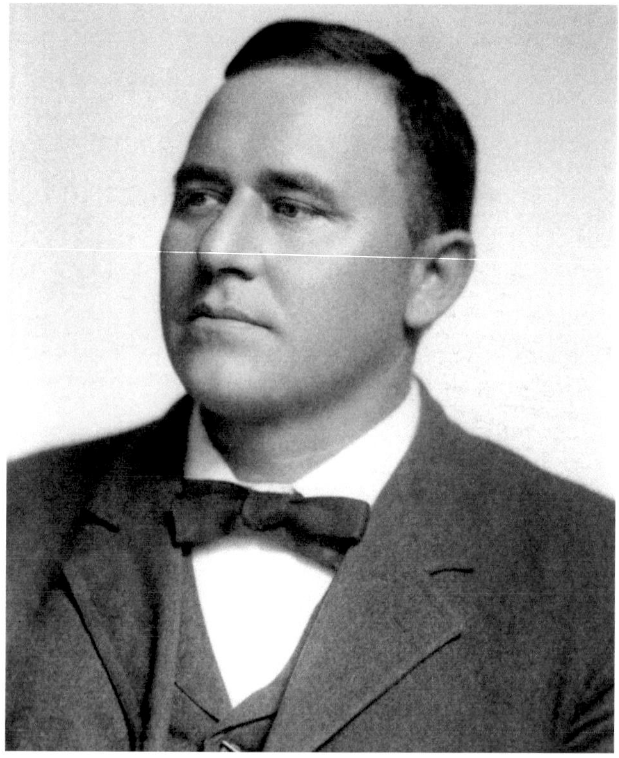

as Custer buffs. Their findings and theories seldom were formally published, but they did make one distinctive contribution to battlefield study: they were active early members of the Custer Battlefield Historical and Museum Association (CBHMA), founded in January 1953, out of which many of today's more influential students and scholars of the Little Big Horn battle have come.[4] Osten served on its founding board of directors, and later Roahen and Bellingham were board presidents.

Among these Luce-era men, Roahen, through his photography, probably has had the most lasting impact on battlefield research across several decades. He also became a recognized artist in scenic, wildlife, and American Indian photography, amassing a collection of some 10,000 images. Throughout his lifetime and after his death, Roahen's photographs have been published internationally. They have also appeared in many news features, books, magazines, and motion pictures.

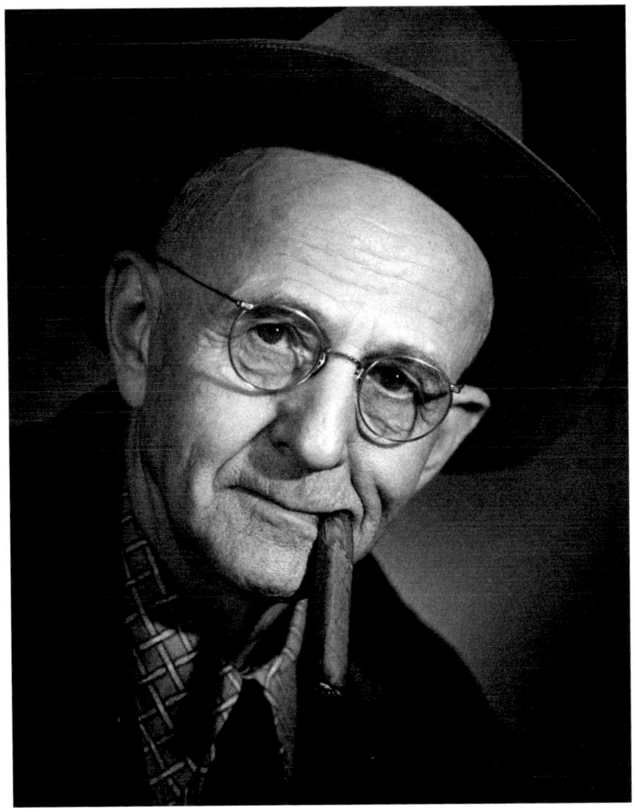

Figure 1.3. (*below*) Captain Edward S. Luce. Courtesy of Big Horn County Historical Museum.

Figure 1.4. (*right*) Kenneth F. Roahen. Courtesy of Big Horn County Historical Museum.

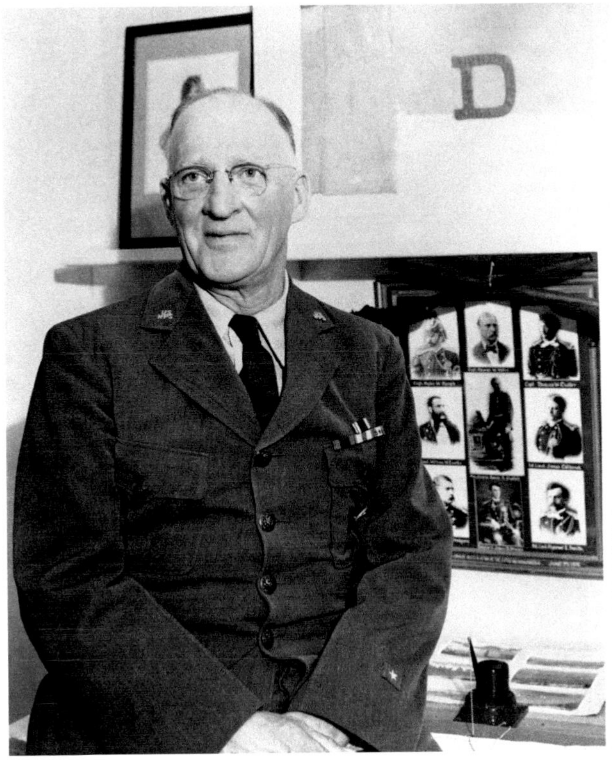

As a photographer, Roahen also stands among a long line of renowned and lesser known men and women who have aimed their cameras at features on the battlefield and captured on film further evidence that students of the fight could consider in determining why Custer's command fell on June 25, 1876. Among the famous photographers whose work was published in *Where Custer Fell* are John H. Fouch, Laton A. Huffman, Stanley J. Morrow, David F. Barry, Frank Jay Haynes, Lee Moorhouse, and Edward S. Curtis. Other men and the one woman are Christian Barthelmess, Richard Throssel, Fred E. Miller, H. R. Locke, William R. Cross, Elsa Spear, and Walter Camp.

Roahen is just the latest personality with Custer/Little Big Horn ties on whom I have focused my research and writing since my first visit to Little Big Horn on July 29, 1980.[5] With my ever-evolving expertise, I have found myself with countless opportunities to speak to historical groups in both the United States and England, community groups, Civil War round tables, and

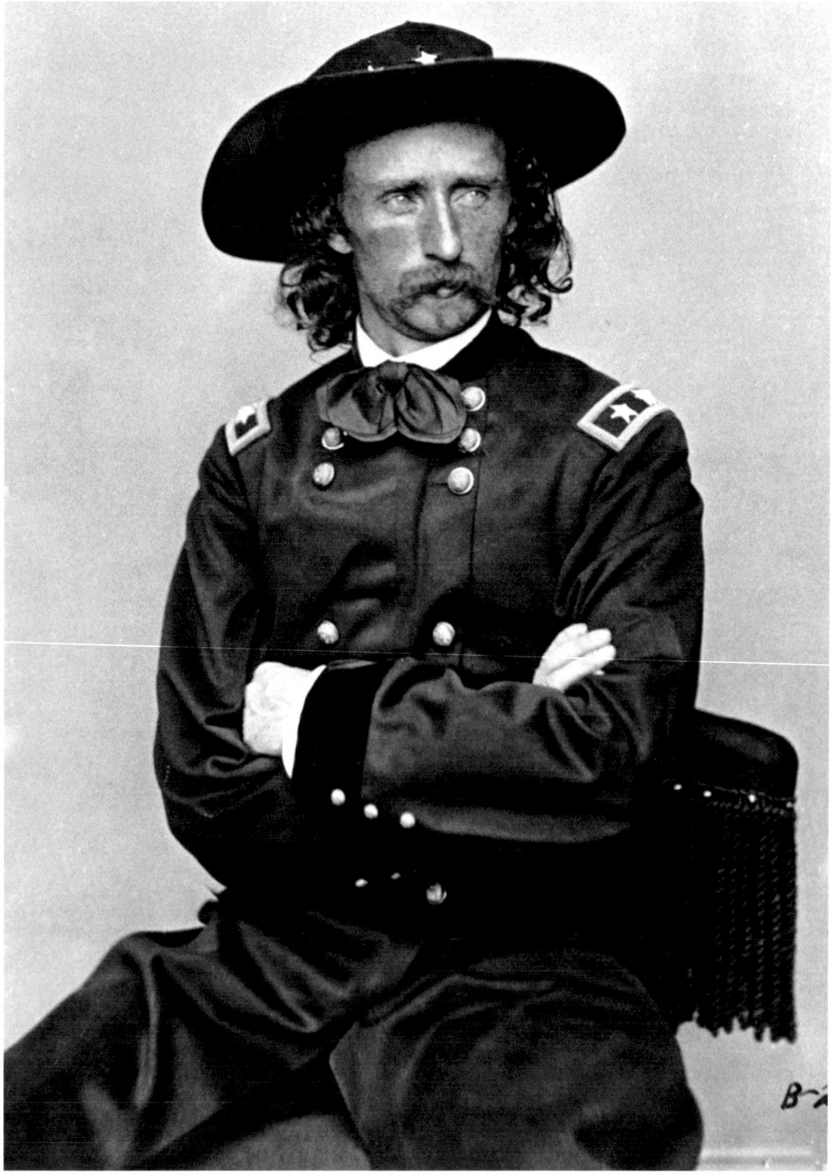

Figure 1.5. Custer, 1865, by Mathew Brady. Courtesy of Little Bighorn Battlefield National Monument.

schools and universities, including the U.S. Military Academy at West Point, Temple College in Texas, Colorado State University, and Valparaiso University. Inevitably, I tell my audiences that I can vouch for only three facts about the Little Big Horn battle and Custer's Last Stand: Custer came, Custer saw, Custer got his derriere whipped! Almost everything else in the story is fair game for speculation and interpretation.

I am, however, just one more individual taking part in a long-standing historical debate about the Little Big Horn. Beginning with the survivors of the 7th U.S. Cavalry Regiment as well as the relief troops under Brig. Gen. Alfred H. Terry in 1876, countless folks have traveled the Custer trail while speculating about what actually occurred that June 25 to cause the annihilation of five companies under Custer's immediate command. In many cases I have disagreed with the conclusions of other researchers. Some often remind me of journalism students whom I taught during a thirty-year career at Indiana State University. Journalism students or Little Big Horn aficionados frequently have difficulty differentiating between facts and opinions. Why focus on "just the facts" when what you believe in your head can be just as "accurate"—or not?

So it is with Custer's last fight. An old-timey theory, equally popular with white researchers as well as Indians, maintained that Custer died at the river crossing in Medicine Tail Coulee. Only in that way could they explain his defeat at the hands of uncivilized Indians. Even today, many writers foolishly theorize that Custer's defeat flowed from his presumed academic incompetence as a West Point cadet fifteen years before his last battle. Or, he fell because he was arrogant and vain, or he was outrageously ambitious, a glory hunter.

Another theory that has existed almost since the day Custer's body was found on Last Stand Hill (also popularly known as Custer Hill) blames his death on the military incompetency of his two highest-ranking subordinates, Maj. Marcus A. Reno and Capt. Frederick W. Benteen. The two men supposedly felt great personal hatred for their commander. According to such accounts, Reno, wrongfully and cowardly, curtailed his charge down the Little Big Horn Valley toward the Indian encampment and later fled from the timber to the bluffs, releasing scores of warriors to focus on Custer's approaching column. Reno also is cited for alleged drunkenness, for poor tactics in fleeing the valley after being repulsed by the Indians, for cowardly behavior in not advancing immediately to Custer's aid, and for suggesting that surviving 7th Cavalry troops abandon the regiment's wounded on the bluffs above the Little Big Horn River and flee to safety under the cover of darkness.

For Benteen's part, after Custer dispatched a messenger to the captain, recalling him from his scout of rugged bluffs to the southwest to join in the fight, he failed his commander by dawdling on the back trail. He also disobeyed Custer's last order to come to his aid with extra ammunition from the regiment's pack train. A version of the theory blames Benteen's actions on his absurd desire to see his hated commander defeated.

If such opinions overrule the facts involving the major players in the battle, we should not be surprised to encounter a similar situation when trying to locate major landmarks associated with Custer's actions on his last day. For example, the Crow's Nest is familiar to generations of Little Big Horn students, except when they try to pin down the historic site's exact spot from which Custer viewed the Indian encampment some ten miles in front of him on the morning of June 25. Other landmarks on Custer's route down Reno Creek are similarly lacking in specificity. Though the site of the Morass is generally well accepted today, other landmarks, such as the Lone Tepee and Girard's Knoll, depend on one's interpretation of who said what, when, and from where. Some researchers place them several miles up Reno Creek; others pinpoint them a mere three-quarters of a mile from the Little Big Horn River. Opinions usually trump facts.

Fortunately, photographs can assist us in unraveling the mysteries that still surround the Little Big Horn fighting. In the preface to *Where Custer Fell*, coauthor James Brust noted how superficially most readers view photographs they see in history books: "Going from book to book, I might find the same early battlefield picture marked with three different dates and labeled as the work of two different photographers. I had not paid much attention before because these pictures were mere window dressing, with little analysis in the captions and no discussion of them in the text." He pointed out that a camera records exactly what it sees, "making a photograph the most objective and literal of historical documents. One early picture of a battlefield ought to be worth a thousand words of years-later reminiscence, but most historians and authors pay scant attention to the photographic record."[6]

Fortunately, our original decade-long task of researching and reshooting Custer Battlefield photographs proved the value of comparing historical images to their modern counterparts. In concluding the preface, Brust described the photographic efforts of the trio of authors as "a never-ending project, as previously unknown early battlefield photos continue to surface, presenting new opportunities to walk the field and find the sites where they were taken, looking and learning as we go."[7] In preparing this book as well as reshooting Kenneth Roahen's historic battlefield images, I realized anew how true my colleague's words remain today.

CHAPTER 2

Roahen Biographical Sketch

From 1924 to 1955, Kenneth F. Roahen worked as a fish and game warden and photographer, first in Illinois and later in Montana, for what is today's U.S. Fish and Wildlife Service. As a resident of Billings, Montana, for the last forty-six years of his life, he often could be seen on the city's streets outfitted in his customary outdoorsy way: military-style canvas jacket and topped by a brown slouch hat. Hanging from his lower lip was a large cigar that he chewed but seldom smoked. As a newspaper reporter once wrote, "Even more familiar is the ever-present cigar that dangles from his lower lip as though looking for a spot to land."[1]

Addison Bragg, a newspaper columnist for the *Billings Gazette*, once commented on Roahen's habit: "One of my favorite chewers is Ken Roahen who in the 25 years I have known him has never been without a drooping cigar (White Owl) in his mouth. He will, on occasion, touch a match to it—But I've long suspected this is only to satisfy some purists in the crowd who hold to the belief that a cigar is for smoking."[2]

A 1964 newspaper feature story described Roahen as "a wiry man with a light stubble of a beard . . . [who] barely moves his mouth around as he talks around an ever-present cigar dangling from one corner." In the article, Roahen explained how he managed to hang onto his cigar: "I've got a high tooth that holds it. Sometimes when I am talking to people they just keep bending closer and closer watching it."[3]

Roahen Vital Statistics

Born August 28, 1888, on a farm in Dighton, Kansas,[4] Roahen grew to adulthood in Claflin, Kansas, a small community that sits at the state's geographic center about 15 miles northeast of Great Bend. Not only does the Arkansas River flow close by, but the surrounding countryside abounds with creeks, wetlands, woods, and rolling fields. It undoubtedly offered the youth great opportunities for hunting and fishing and helped point him toward his primary life's work protecting wildlife and the environment, decades before Americans gave much consideration to such causes.

Similarly, Claflin and surrounding Barton County sit near the center of some of the most interesting frontier history of the nineteenth century. They are located close to the historic Santa Fe Trail, an area often crisscrossed by elements of George Custer's 7th U.S. Cavalry in the late 1860s. Growing up in Claflin some twenty-five years later, Roahen surely would have appreciated all this history. It is equally unsurprising that as an adult in Montana after

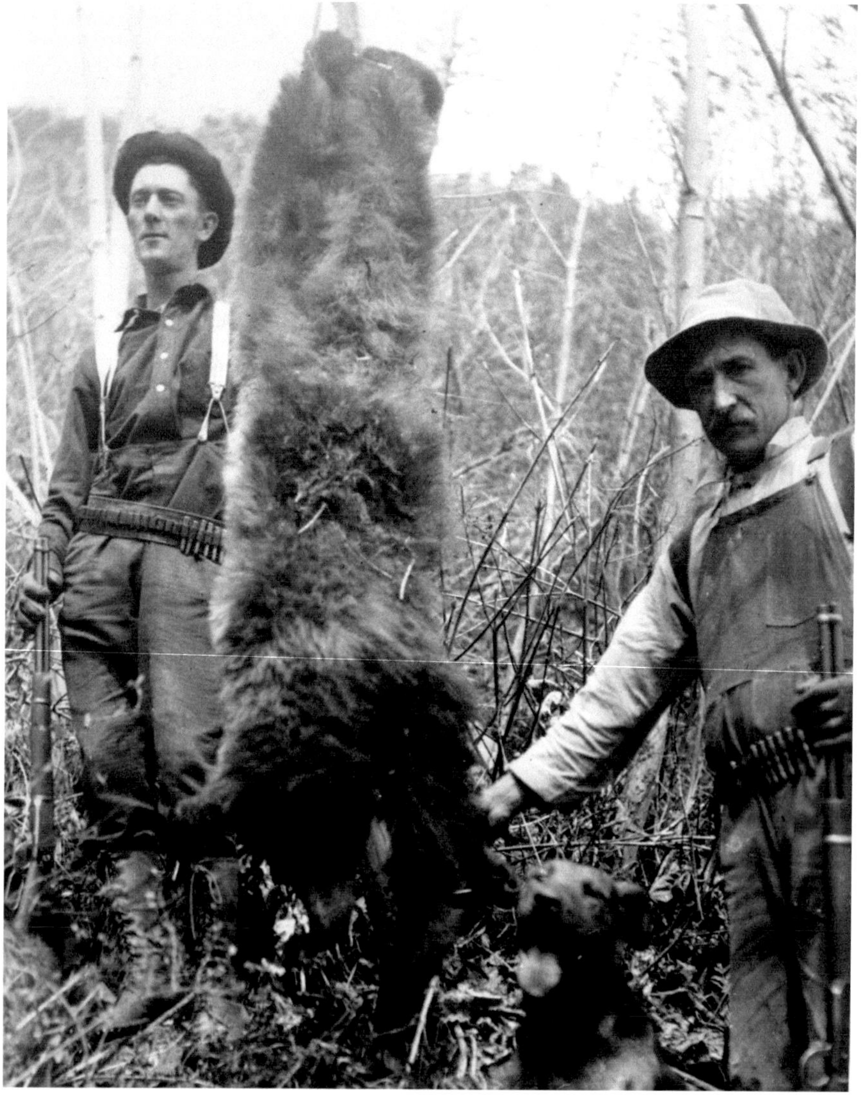

Figure 2.1. Roahen (*on left*) with grizzly and Bruce Neal. Courtesy of U.S. Fish and Wildlife Service.

1930 Roahen combined his love of the outdoors with that of frontier history.

Roahen's parents were Daniel L. and Susan M. Roahen, both originally of Ohio. His father was born on December 21, 1850, in Springfield.[5] On December 20, 1876, in London, Ohio, Daniel married Susan M. Osburn, who had been born on November 22, 1854, in that town.[6] Two years later, Susan gave birth to their first son, Ernest E. Roahen. Records for Ernest indicate that the family remained in Ohio at the time of his birth.[7] However, about 1884 they relocated to Kansas, stopping for a year in El Dorado, then moved to a homestead near Ness City. There their attempts at eking out a living on a farm proved unsuccessful. They could find no water and could raise no crops.[8]

Eventually, they packed everything up again for a move to Lane County, where they lived for three years at Dighton and where their second son, Kenneth, was born in August 1888. Within six months of his birth, the family had decided to move to Claflin.[9] "The Dighton venture was not a success and soon we were forced to give it up," Mrs. Roahen recalled in a 1937 interview.

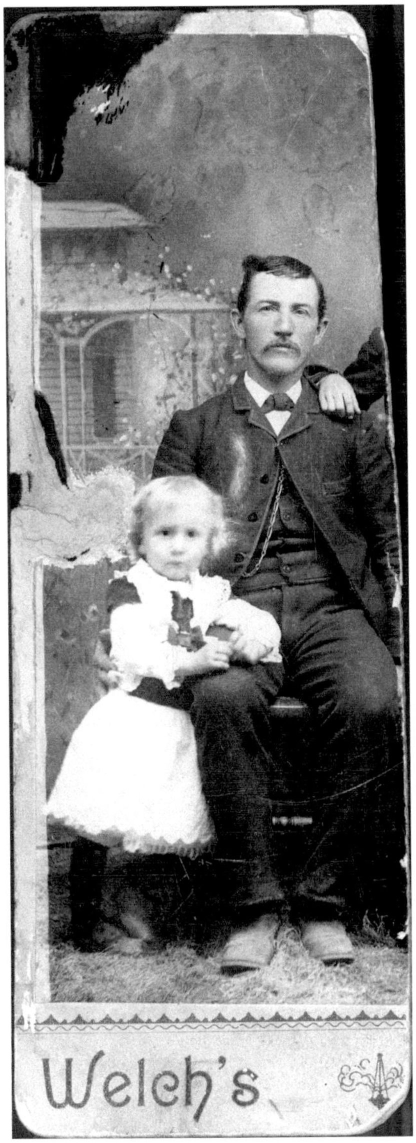

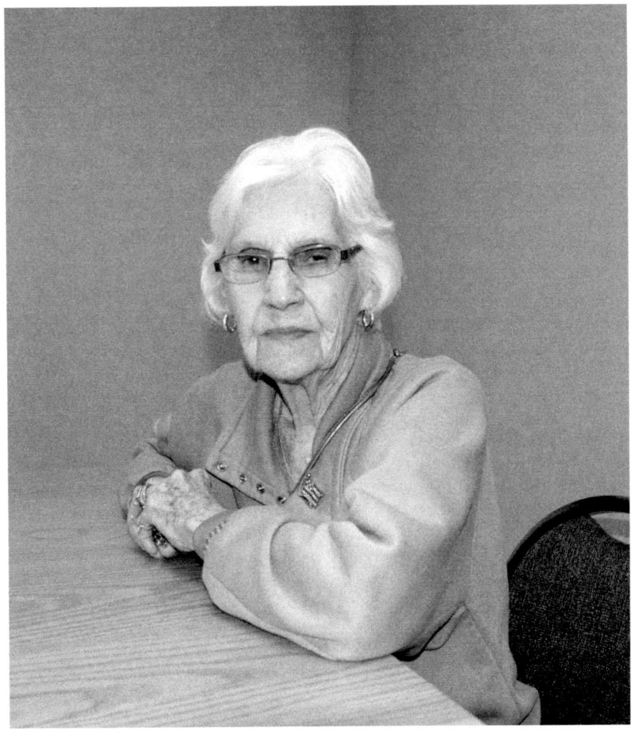

Figure 2.2. Daniel and Kenneth Roahen. Courtesy of U.S. Fish and Wildlife Service.

Figure 2.3. Elaine Ooley. Author's photograph.

"Mr. Roahen set out toward the east to sell our wagon and team for enough cash to buy a ticket home [Ohio]. When he got as far as Claflin he was offered a job with the team. We then decided to move to Claflin, tore down our frame house in Dighton and shipped it to Ellinwood on the Santa Fe, hauling it by team to Claflin. A few new shingles on the roof and repairs where the sections joined were the only alterations needed when the house was set up again in Claflin."[10]

Roahen wrote to relatives in 1960 that his "father and mother built the third house in Claflin. Now there is a big oil field within a mile of the town, even on some of the land Father had."[11] The senior Roahen tackled a variety of jobs, including initially farming, as outlined in his 1932 obituary: "Mr. Roahen broke up the land just south of Claflin, known then as the Giles land and later the Casey farm, and farmed it for several years." He next went into the feed, coal, and machinery business for fifteen years. "Since then he has been living here, looking after his property."

Roahen's niece, Elaine Ooley, recalled in an interview that in those days Claflin lacked public schools. "He and his brother, Ernest, were tutored by their mother. She had been a former high school English teacher."[12] The 1937 newspaper interview with Mrs. Roahen noted that they "went to college directly from their mother's teaching at home."

Kenneth's love of photography developed early in his life, Mrs. Ooley said. About 1901, when he was age thirteen, he received a stereoscope for Christmas, and he accumulated cards for it that depicted Indians, wild game, government officials, and important buildings such as the White House. By his fourteenth birthday, the young entrepreneur was ordering more stereo views that he could sell to friends and others. He poured his profits into buying more cards.

In 1902, he advanced his photography interests by buying his first inexpensive camera and soon was making prints from glass plate negatives.[13] In a 1964 interview with the *Billings Gazette*, he told the reporter, with a grin, "When I started making pictures there wasn't a lens on the camera." In a biographical letter to distant relatives in 1960, Roahen revealed, "As a young kid, I had a failing for photography, and back in 1910, won some pretty high returns, but it was only a sideline then."[14]

The 1905 Kansas census lists the then sixteen-year-old Roahen as living with his parents in Barber County. The 1909 Kansas City, Missouri, city directory shows him working as a clerk in that city, probably for his brother, Ernest.[15] The same city directory has Ernest operating the Roahen-Cary Grain Co. in the Board of Trade Building. Presumably the younger man was staying with his brother and his family, who had lived there since earlier in the decade.

By the 1910 census, Roahen was living on his own in Great Bend, not far from Claflin, where his parents were listed. It lists him as a boarder and his occupation as a bookkeeper for a hardware store. That same year, the Wichita, Kansas, city directory lists him as a student there. In 1911, Roahen graduated from Wichita Business College as a certified public accountant.[16] Later, Elaine Ooley reported, he attended the College of Salina, Kansas, and the University of Kansas.

The year 1910 proved personally important in another way for Roahen. On December 26, 1910, he married Frances Moses of Great Bend. According to the *Great Bend Tribune* wedding announcement, "One of the prettiest home weddings took place Monday night at the R. H. Moses home when Miss Frances Moses was united in marriage to Mr. Kenneth Roahen. The ceremony took place in the living room of the Moses home beneath a beautifully decorated arch. . . . About 50 guests, the majority of them relatives, were present."[17] The *Tribune* added about Frances: "The bride is the eldest daughter of Mr. and Mrs. R. H. Moses and one of the most popular young ladies of the city. She is an accomplished musician and a general favorite."

Frances was about nineteen when they married. The 1910 census misspells her name as "Francis" and has her living with her parents, Reuben H. and Louise A. Moses, in Great Plains. Her father, then seventy-two, was originally a New Yorker, and her mother, age forty-six, had been born in Missouri.

Frances herself had been born in Missouri, and no occupation was listed for her. She had a younger sister named Louise.[18]

As for Roahen himself, the *Tribune* noted, "The groom is a young man of worth, the son of Mr. and Mrs. D. L. Roahen of Claflin and popular with all who know him. For some time he has been book-keeper and cashier for the F. R. Moses Mercantile Co."

Not much is known about their life together or even how long the couple remained married. Evidence suggests that by 1920 the marriage had ceased to function. When an actual divorce may have occurred is unknown, but likely it was finalized by 1927. Roahen would remarry in 1928.

Roahen's World War I draft card, dated August 5, 1917, gives his age as twenty-nine and his residence as Cashmere, Washington. His birth date is inaccurately cited as August 27, 1888, but his birthplace of Dighton is correct. According to the card, he was working as a box agency manager for the Wenatchee Valley Box Co. in Wenatchee, Washington. Of special interest, the form indicates that he was married and claimed exemption from the draft because of marriage.[19] That status failed to help him avoid a few months of army service. His Veterans Affairs file reveals that he served from August 14 to November 26, 1918. According to the draft card, he was of medium build and medium height and had gray eyes and brown hair. Additionally, he was described as "slightly bald."[20]

Elaine Ooley reported that he worked as an instructor for an army detachment stationed at the State College of Pullman, Washington. In 1960, Roahen revealed, "When I came out of the army [I] was in pretty tough shape." He failed to mention any actual ailments, or whether they were physical or emotional, either leading to or caused by the soon-to-come breakup with his wife Frances.[21]

Frances herself survived until February 24, 1946, when after a two-week illness she died that morning at age fifty-five in the General Hospital in Ellensburg, Washington. She had been an assistant dietician for the hospital. According to her obituary published in the *Great Bend Tribune*, at some point she had remarried a man named Swan Burnett, who apparently had died earlier. They had a seventeen-year-old son, also named Swan, who was a freshman in college in 1946 when his mother died. The obituary notes that she had moved from Great Bend some thirty years earlier.[22] At the time of her death, she and Roahen had been divorced for at least two decades.

According to a 1914 city directory for Chelan, Washington, Roahen worked as a manager for the Lamb-Davis Lumber Co. He also was still married to Frances. Another source says that as early as 1912 he was working as a county game warden in Chelan County.[23] The 1920 census still listed the couple as married but apparently no longer living together. Roahen, then thirty-one, was living in Portland, Oregon, working as a truck salesman. He is listed as a lodger and married. The census fails to mention his wife under either her maiden or her married name. Some time after his discharge from the army, or certainly by the early 1920s, Roahen had gone to work for the Washington State Game Department as its only game warden.[24]

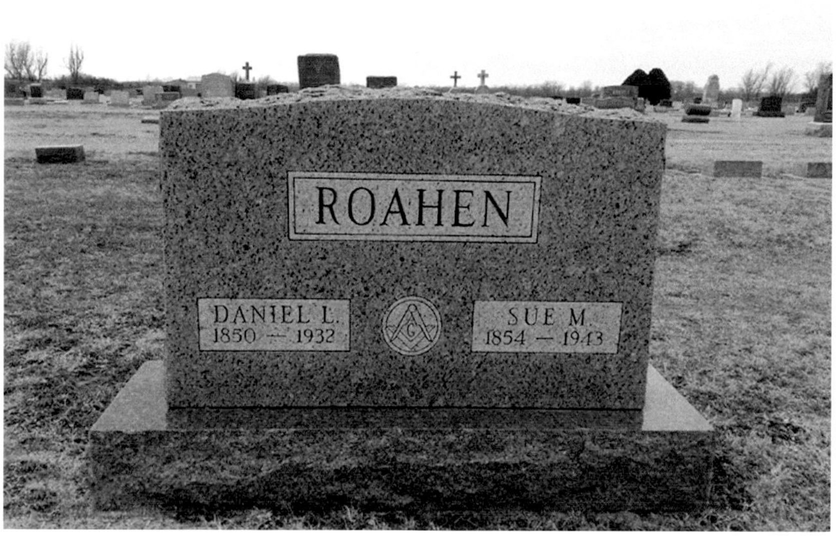

Figure 2.4. Grave of Daniel and Susan Roahen in Pleasant View Cemetery, Claflin, Kansas. Courtesy of Linda Colle.

On March 9, 1923, Roahen's brother, Ernest, died of pneumonia at age forty-five in Kansas City. When Ernest was twenty-five, on June 3, 1903, he had married Elsie L. Ozenberger in Claflin. She was about the same age as her husband as she, too, had been born in 1878.[25] At the time of Ernest's death, Kenneth Roahen said, his brother owned the third-largest grain house on the Kansas City Board of Trade.[26]

Roahen's parents were still living when Ernest died. Father Daniel survived until October 31, 1932, when he died at age eighty-one in Claflin. His obituary notes that among his survivors were not only his daughter-in-law, Elsie, but also a grandson, Richard L. Roahen, a professor at the State Teachers College in Emporia, Kansas.[27] The *Billings Gazette* reported on Thursday, November 3, 1932, that Kenneth Roahen had flown the previous day to Kansas for the funeral.[28] Kenneth's mother, Susan, survived until November 21, 1943, when at age eighty-nine she, too, died in Claflin. Both parents are buried in the town.[29]

In 1924, Roahen made perhaps the most significant career decision in his life, when he joined the U.S. Department of Agriculture's Biological Survey as a federal game warden (later game agent), assigned to its Illinois District, headquartered in Peoria, Illinois. Later, when the survey was transferred to the U.S. Department of the Interior, it was renamed the U.S. Fish and Wildlife Service. Roahen and twenty-one other game wardens were redesignated as agents.[30] His area of authority included Indiana, Illinois, parts of Kentucky and Wisconsin, Michigan, Iowa, and Missouri. On occasion he had special assignments in Maryland and Virginia.

At that time Peoria was the center for widespread bootlegging of ducks and furs, often carried out by mobsters associated with Chicago gangsters, including Al Capone. In describing Roahen's district, a 1964 newspaper stated, "Populating the district were some of the most rapacious duck 'bootleggers' ever assembled."[31] The mob crews relied on traps of all kinds, large and small, to

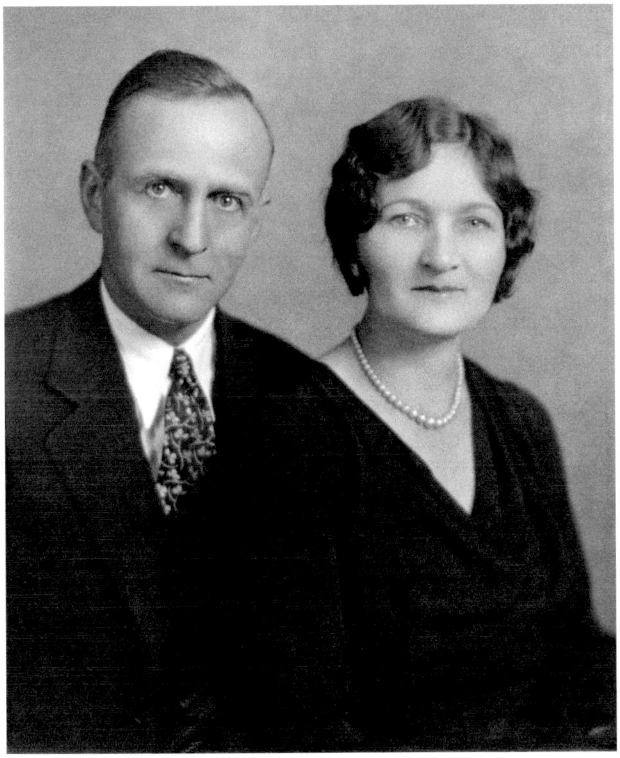

Figure 2.5. Kenneth and Sandae Roahen. Courtesy of U.S. Fish and Wildlife Service.

steal the birds out of the wild for the dinner tables of Prohibition-era Chicago. The ducks, sometimes as many as 5,000 in a day, would bring as much as $1.50 apiece when sold to nightclubs in the city.

Roahen patrolled the marshes, often alone, and his dangerous exploits read as exciting as any undertaken by federal agent Eliot Ness and his so-called Untouchables of that era. During his first five years as a federal game agent, Roahen was hospitalized a half dozen times after being beaten and shot. Across his thirty years as an agent, he underwent eighteen operations related to shootings and beatings. According to one surgeon who knew Roahen, "They can't kill this guy by shooting at him, although he should have been dead long ago, with all the slugs he has in him. Some day, though, he might fall off a chair and break his neck."

But Roahen proved undaunted in upholding federal game laws. "They've taken a lot of lead out of me. I used to have some of it I kept as relics."

Roahen was so much at risk from gangsters that eventually the government had to move him out of harm's way, reassigning him in 1930 to Montana. But first, while still in Illinois, Roahen remarried. On January 3, 1928, at age thirty-nine, he married Olathe Susanne Woodworth Gouker, also known as Sandae, in either Decatur, Illinois, where she had lived for some years, or Peoria. City directories for Peoria show the couple living there for their first two years together.[32]

Throughout most of her life prior to marrying Roahen, Susanne had gone by her first name, Olathe, but in her forty-eight years of marriage to Roahen she relied on her middle name or its variation, Sandae. She had been born on

February 4, 1895, in Arthur, Illinois, to William Horace Woodworth (1854–1922) and Malissa Douglas Taylor (1859–1916).[33]

When she married her first husband, Chester A. Gouker, is unclear. The 1910 census lists Gouker, then seventeen, as living with his parents in Decatur. By June 5, 1917, when Gouker signed his World War I draft registration card, he was listed as married. His birthdate was listed as June 12, 1893, and his occupation as steamfitter. According to the card's physical description of him, he was tall, stout, and had light blue eyes and dark brown hair. The Social Security Death Index reveals that he died in March 1964 in Missouri.[34]

Of significance, genealogical information about the couple on Ancestry.com suggests that they had an unnamed son, listed simply as male Gouker, but that remains unconfirmed. We can conclude only that any possible child may have died soon after birth. No later records include a child or young man living with either parent.

All during their marriage the Goukers remained in Decatur, which would not have been far from Roahen, who had moved to the area in 1924.[35] According to the 1929 city directory, Gouker was now single, which agrees with historical records that show Roahen marrying Susanne Gouker in 1928. Unfortunately, history is silent about how all of this came about. We know no more about Susanne's first marriage than Roahen's own.[36]

"Two-Gun Roahen"

As mentioned earlier, in 1930 the government hurriedly moved Roahen and his wife out of Illinois to Montana for their safety. Roahen would find both his career and life in Montana agreeable, and he would reside there for the remaining forty-six years of his life. He served as a game agent from early December 1930 until retiring in early 1955. As he wrote to R. W. Caldwell of Omak, Washington, on November 27, 1931, "I came to Montana last December [1930] but do not know how long I will be here. To be frank I was sent out on really a vacation for my health, as [I] was getting in pretty bad shape, as you know after you been on the operating table 18 times it kinda gets your strength, and I still have a few chunks of lead in my system from the duck bootleggers on the Illinois River, and Montana District is about the lightest we have."[37]

In his 1960 letter to his distant relatives, Roahen mentions that "possibly during [19]24- to 30, and for sometime after, you may have seen various newspaper and magazine articles under the heading: Two-Gun Roahen, and some of the gun fights I had around Chicago, etc., well, that happened to be me. From the time I was just a kid, I always had guns, and really became pretty well known for handling a six-gun, except I trained for either hand or both, that was the reason I was assigned the Illinois District [of the then Biological Survey], although they did not tell me that when they sent me there."[38]

Early in his time in Illinois, Roahen worked out of Havana and later Peoria, which was the government's headquarters for its efforts to quell gangs engaged in duck and fur bootlegging. Midwest marshes, rich in ducks, required almost

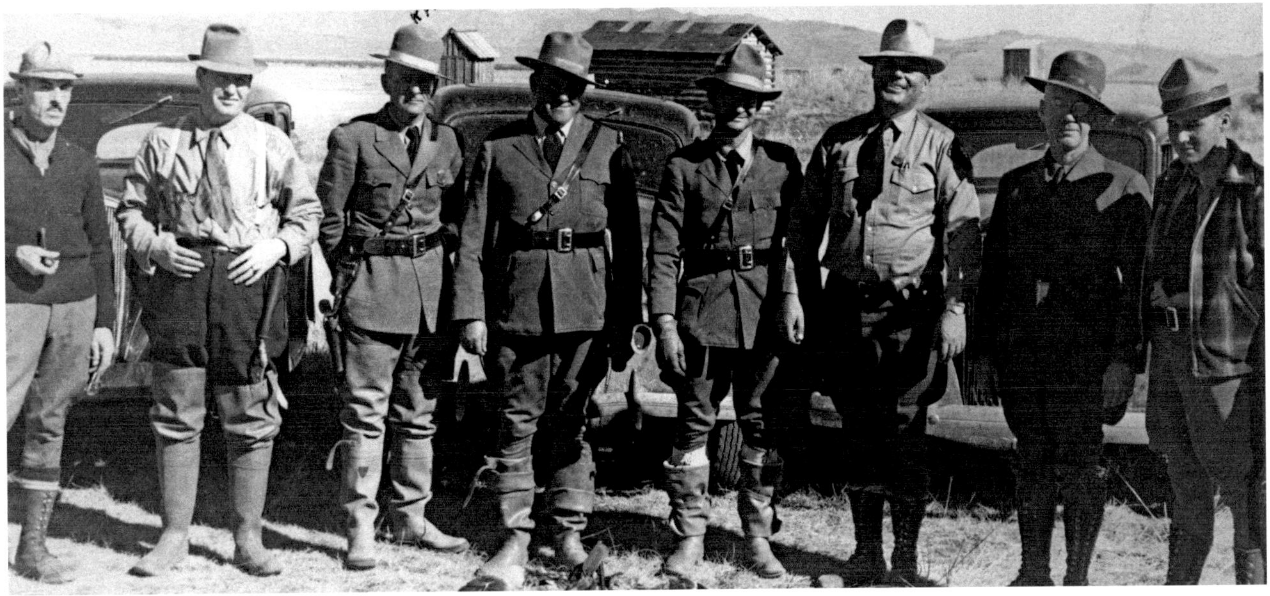

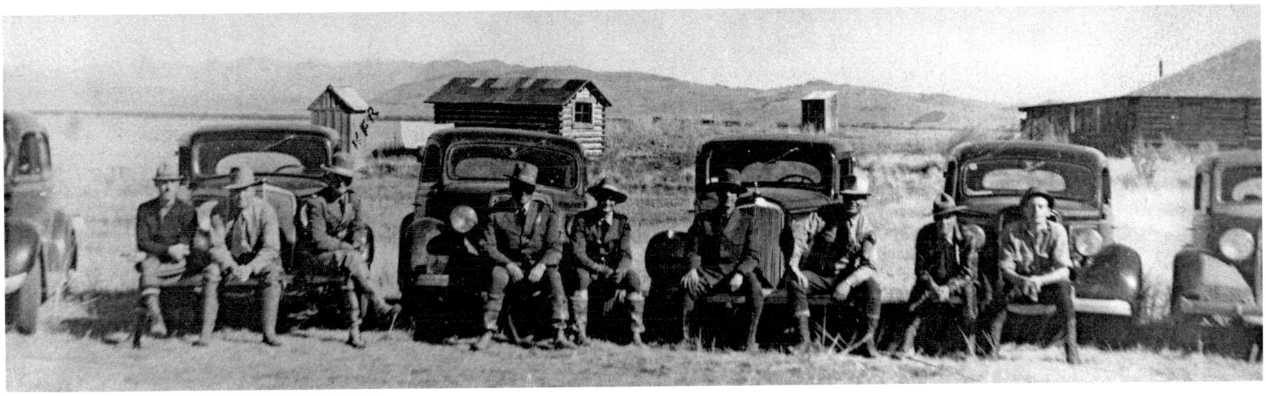

Figure 2.6. Roahen's fish and game field group. *Top*: Roahen third from left; *bottom*: Roahen third from left. Courtesy of U.S. Fish and Wildlife Service.

constant patrolling by Roahen and his comrades to combat the gangs of "goons," as he called them, who relied on sophisticated equipment and weapons. That made the game agents' job more dangerous, for they frequently faced ambushes in the marshes. Reportedly the poachers, often labeled "market hunters," played a popular game called "Kill the Game Agent."[39]

After one beating, Roahen was left unconscious on the roadway and almost died before help arrived. Another time, he took a charge of buckshot in his face, fortunately from too far away to do significant damage. Surgeons still had to dig three pellets out of his forehead. "I still have one buried in the bone just above my teeth, which took a chunk out of my nose, and I was also hit in the thigh, from which I have about a three inch scar," he said.

In yet another ambush, Roahen was shot in the face with a revolver, the slug coming out of his mouth. Attempts were made to dynamite Roahen's patrol boats. He had a 26-foot speed boat for his patrols on the Illinois River, which the gangs attempted to blow up one night while he slept on board by floating a bunch of explosives, like a naval mine, toward his boat. "However, at the time I had an Airedale dog, and he slept on the deck, and he was trained not to bark, but if he heard any noise, he was down to the [bunks] right now pulling

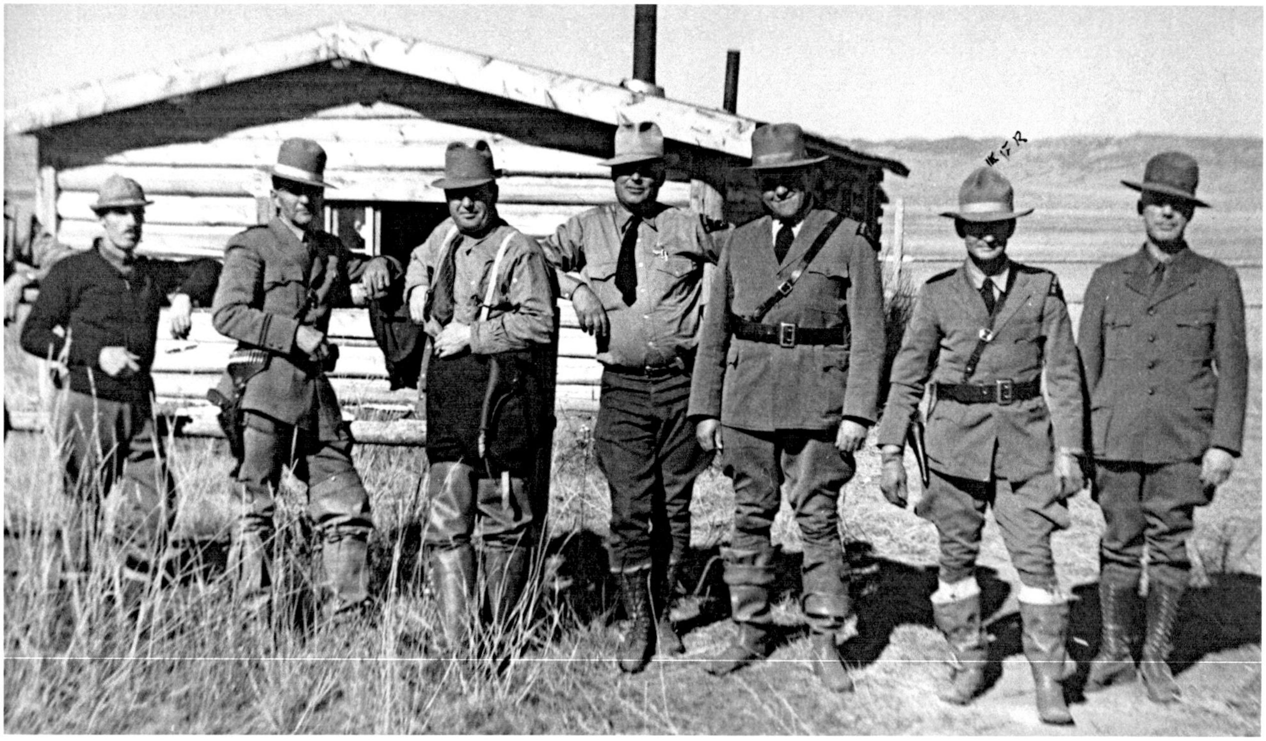

Figure 2.7. Roahen (*second from right*) and armed fish and game agents. Courtesy of U.S. Fish and Wildlife Service.

at the bed covers to get me up," he recalled. "This is what saved the deal that night, as I got up on deck in time to ward off the contact of the float with the boat and it floated past the boat. I could hear the oarlocks as the [other] boat rowed away but it was too dark to see them."[40]

In a draft submitted to his regional supervisor in June 1954, Roahen recalled the unsuccessful attempts to blow up his boats. "On the second attempt, that guy made quite a splash when he hit the water from his boat owing to the force of a load of buckshot at midnight. Found his boat the next day, but not him, so his identity was unknown."[41]

Even when Roahen was off-duty and at home, mob gangs stalked him. One night in Peoria, he said, "I'd fooled them. They'd been watching the house to discover when I'd be home, but I took the train to Chicago after dark that night." His train trip turned out to be what a friend, Thornhill Broom of Chicago, termed a "lucky deal." Broom knew of the dangers the game agent faced. Without Roahen's knowledge, Broom had hired a private detective to tail the game agent and protect him. Unfortunately, Roahen's wife, Sandae, remained alone in the house. About 11 to 11:30 P.M., Roahen's next-door neighbor returned home and noticed a taxi parked in the couple's driveway, the driver still at the wheel. A second man was crawling across the lawn toward the house cradling a tommy gun. The neighbor's presence apparently spooked the two would-be assassins. The gunman jumped into the taxi, and the driver backed into the street. As other neighbors began to stir, the men drove away. Later, the cab was found abandoned about a block from the Roahens' house.[42] Roahen testified in a 1954 affidavit that this incident occurred about a month before he was transferred to Montana.

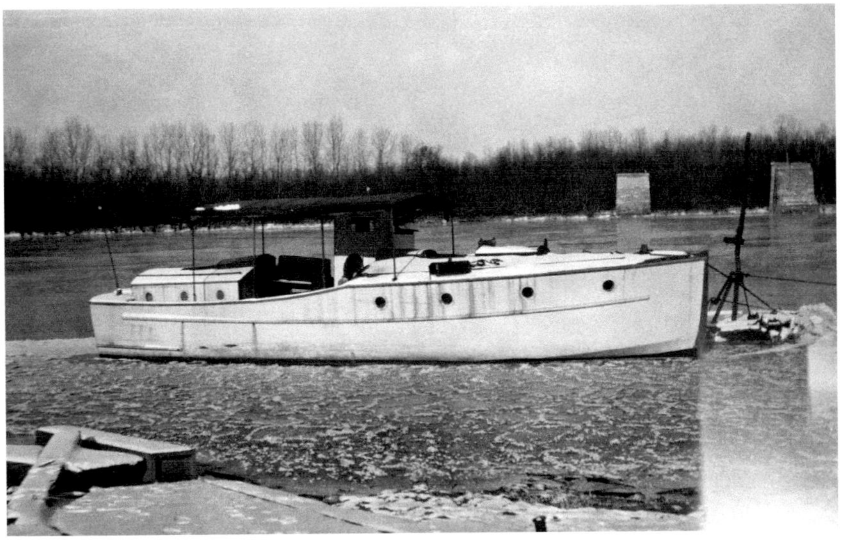

Figure 2.8. Roahen's patrol boat. Courtesy of U.S. Fish and Wildlife Service.

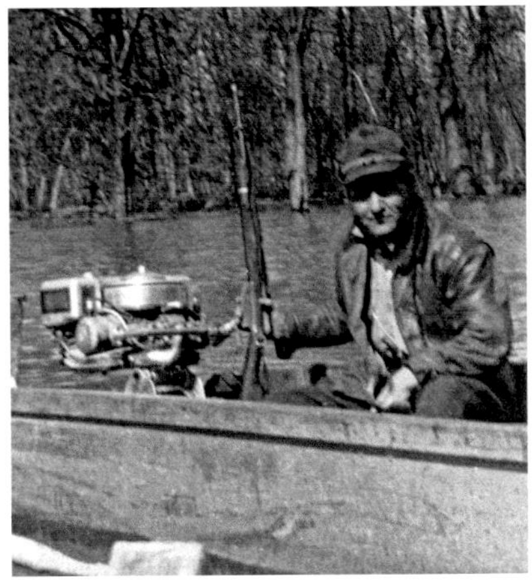

Figure 2.9. Roahen in open boat. Courtesy of U.S. Fish and Wildlife Service.

Despite his many injuries Roahen, dubbed Uncle Sam's "Bird Cop" in 1929 by Bob Becker of the *Peoria Star*, was not shy about fighting back. As he recalled in the newspaper account, many of his assailants had to be hospitalized. "And some were beyond hospital assistance."[43] According to Becker' report, Roahen had nearly been murdered in 1924–25. Roahen told the reporter that "the disadvantages an officer had was that he didn't know the bootlegger guards were around until they started shooting. In many of the swamps you couldn't see 50 feet, and the only thing that an officer had to shoot at was in the general direction the lead was coming from."[44] Roahen succinctly summed up the dangerous situation in a 1964 story: "When you left the house in the morning you never knew if you'd come back that night."

Another near-murder occurred on March 3, 1925, according to an undated draft document Roahen likely wrote in 1954, about a year before his retirement, as well as an official incident report in the records of today's Fish and Wildlife Service.[45] Roahen and his partner, game warden M. A. Charlton, who headed the Ohio District but was on special duty with Roahen, were working the bottomlands of the Sangamon River. After hearing firing, they came upon a full case of shells and two sheepskin-lined coats.

Almost immediately, a gunman, evidently a guard, began firing a shotgun at them from a hideout about 25 yards away among the trees. The two wardens returned fire, even though they remained unprotected in the open. The guard's two companions closed in on the two lawmen from another side.

The first gunman, who had been wounded by the agents' return fire, called out, saying that if Roahen and Charlton backed off no more shots would be fired.

According to the incident report, "As the wardens were practically surrounded, this was their only choice." Charlton bore at least six wounds in the arms, hands, hip, and a leg. Roahen also had been wounded in the hands, arms, stomach, and face. Each of the wardens had been struck by buckshot. "Following the shooting it was necessary for the wardens to walk back through the bottoms for five miles to their boat, row for some distance, and then drive to Havana [Illinois], 25 more miles, before they could receive medical attention."

Roahen stated that his boss, George Lawyer, complained whenever the agent submitted a report involving shootings and possible deaths: "Don't you know every time you kill one of those (so and so's) I have to get a clearance from the Secretary for you?" Roahen told Lawyer that he thought he needed to report such incidents. "George replied, throw the damn typewriter in the river and do more shooting. So accordingly no further 'written reports' were submitted."

In 1928, Roahen was honored by Agriculture secretary W. M. Jardine, who reportedly presented him with the only cabinet citation given to a U.S. game warden. According to the citation, "The incident in which you were involved on December 6 [1928], when in carrying out your enforcement work you encountered four violators of the Migratory Bird Treaty Act who held their guns on you for a considerable period while you were attempting to arrest them. The fact that you finally arrested two of the men while still covered by the gun of one of them speaks much for your coolness and tact in a very dangerous situation." The secretary further praised him for capturing the men without having to kill any of them.[46]

According to the 1964 *Billings Gazette* article and an affidavit Roahen completed on June 23, 1954, he had been visiting a large private club, the Clear Lake Hunting Club in Clear Lake, Illinois, near Springfield, when he spotted two men illegally chasing and shooting ducks from a kicker boat, or motorboat.[47] As Roahen rowed out from his hiding place in the timber to intercept them, the poachers raced for the other shore. When Roahen was within about 75 yards of the other boat, the hunter raised his gun and pointed it directly at the pursuing game agent. Roahen, using one of his specially made revolvers, fired a shot into the water next to the boat. "It splashed water all over them," but the criminals still escaped to the river.

Roahen had the son of a club member with him, whom he quickly deposited safely on shore. About that point either both poachers or one of them (the details vary in Roahen's several accountings) returned in their motorboat, while towing two other men in a second boat behind them on a 15-foot rope. Roahen placed one of his revolvers beside him on the seat of his boat.

The first boat came alongside Roahen's while the second boat pulled in behind him. "They stated they were going to blow me out of my boat."

According to his *Gazette* account, Roahen swung a leg over the side and clamped the second boat to his own. "They were two Chicago gangsters and they hired two river boatmen to help them. All four pulled guns," Roahen recalled.

Roahen flashed his federal agent's badge at them, and either two or three of the men immediately surrendered to him. But the remaining individual kept his shotgun pointed at Roahen. "He kept jabbing me in the back," Roahen said, so hard that he cracked the leather of the agent's jacket. Roahen, however, noticed the man did not have his gun's hammer pulled back. He grabbed his own gun and sat, his arms crossed. His own gun remained under his arm, inside his jacket pointing at the other man. "I wasn't worried. I knew I could shoot him before he could get his hammer back."

For almost an hour they floated around the lake in a standoff, but all of this was observed by hunting club members on the shore. Eventually the club's superintendent, a former Pinkerton detective, and a boat operator rowed out to assist Roahen. The gunman moved his shotgun from Roahen's back and toward the fast approaching ex-detective. Roahen whipped out his own pistol, forcing the mobster to surrender. Bystanders criticized Roahen for not killing the man holding the shotgun. They maintained that the game agent had many witnesses whose testimony would have supported his action.

At the bottom of an earlier draft of the affidavit for his superiors, he typed, "I really don't care about making these kind of reports, as someone might think I was putting out a bunch of bunk."[48]

On another occasion, Roahen refused a $50,000 bribe in a Chicago case that involved some forty-five prominent figures. He was warned, "If I didn't take the money I would not live very long." As he was driving home from Chicago, a car suddenly passed him. "Before I could even get their license number," Roahen recalled, "ten tommy gun holes were in or through my car." But he survived yet again a threat against his life. Apparently he must have been lucky. All the rounds missed him. All the men involved in his wildlife case went to court and paid fines. Roahen made no mention of whether his would-be assassins were caught and prosecuted.[49]

Roahen was once accused of accepting bribes, and Washington sent out an investigator, who quickly concluded, "I don't want to waste any more time on this frame up." In another episode, Roahen identified an attorney—a "Mr. Chipperfield" of Canton, Illinois, who later became a congressman—as having made promises to those Roahen termed the "Illinois river rats." The only Illinois congressman of that era with such a name was Republican Burnett Mitchell Chiperfield of Canton, who served in Congress from 1929 to 1933. According to Roahen's story, if the river rats (whiskey bootleggers, moonshiners, duck bootleggers, and black bass bootleggers) elected this lawyer, he would open the millionaire clubs to public shooting "and throw the federal warden out of Illinois." The lawyer complained that Roahen had shot a man out of his boat "without any provocation" and filed forty-one witness affidavits against the game agent. Roahen noted, "This was really amusing as some of the witnesses couldn't read nor write, yet these affidavits were all nicely written and signed in long hand. When the Solicitor Williams finished his investigation, I received a salary increase."[50]

When the gangs couldn't shoot Roahen or dynamite him, they tried to kill him in a car accident. One day his new Dodge coupe was broadsided about 15 miles from Decatur and rolled at least three times. Roahen thought he was unhurt and managed to seize the other driver, who clearly was affiliated with the gangs but would not squeal about who had hired him to kill the agent. Two months later, injuries to his stomach caused by the accident forced Roahen to undergo the first of six major operations. In his 1954 accounting, he wrote, "I never will recover fully from this deal."[51]

At the time of Roahen's retirement in early January 1955, Montana federal district judge Charles Perry praised him in a letter as "a competent and fearless officer." In another letter, Roahen quoted an unnamed federal judge's praise of him: "Mr. Roahen, I know when you appear in my court, that you have a case with sufficient evidence, or you would not be in court."[52]

Roahen apparently had a reputation as feisty and difficult to get along with, even as a younger man. In early 1955, E. L. Paynter, game commissioner for the Saskatchewan Department of Natural Resources, told him in a letter, "I don't suppose you particularly carried any charm around with you in order to keep a-rolling during those years, but I think you were too darned tough to admit it when you did get a sizzler."[53]

On April 19, 1929, in Chicago, the Izaak Walton League presented Roahen with a platinum watch and chain during its annual convention. The inscription on the watch read: "Presented to Kenneth F. Roahen, who repeatedly has risked his life in resisting the lawless destruction of wildlife, by the Chicago Chapter, Izaak Walton League."

Roahen and the Custer Battlefield

The government transferred Roahen to Montana in late 1930 to avoid retaliation against him by the gangs he had battled, but he put a different spin on the reasons. "I would have had to move anyway," Roahen said in the 1964 newspaper interview. "I got shot up and could not handle a six-shooter anymore. If you couldn't handle a six-gun you did not fool around with that Chicago bunch."[54]

The Roahens arrived in Billings, where he replaced George Mushbach, the former federal game warden. For his first six years, Roahen conducted surveillance and investigations over a wide area of not only Montana but also Wyoming, Idaho, Nebraska, and North and South Dakota. In time, with additional men hired, his jurisdiction was whittled down to Montana itself, including Yellowstone Park, but, as necessary, his investigative work often took him to other states. He also was named a Montana state game warden, which increased his investigatory powers within the state.

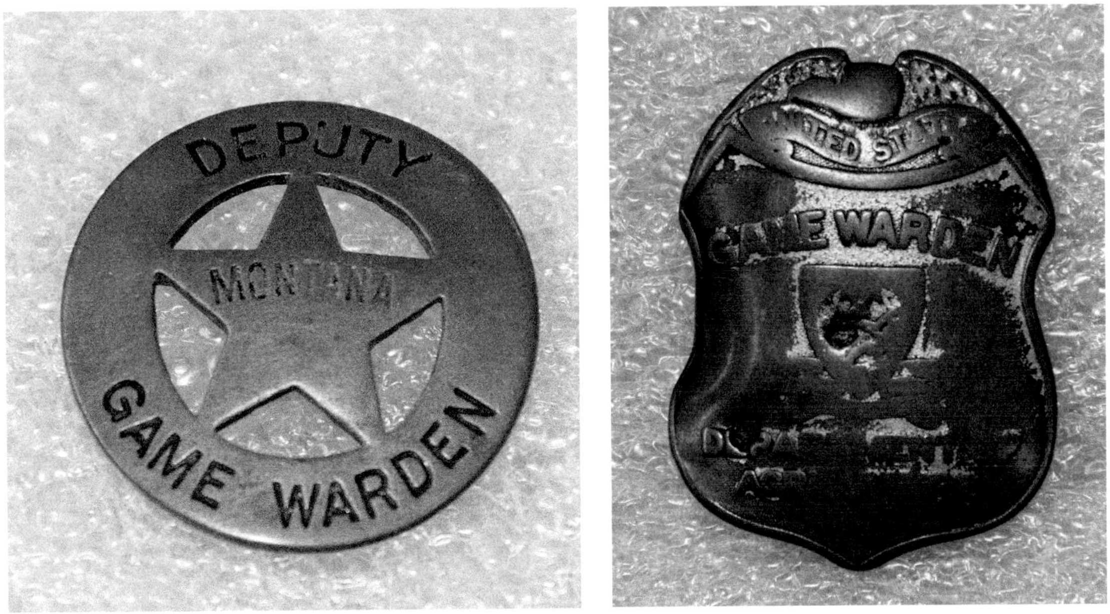

Figure 2.10. Roahen's Montana and U.S. game warden badges. Author's photos.

Much of his work was connected to fur smuggling and illegal trapping. Furs entered Montana from Canada and Alaska to be shipped east. Roahen told the *Billings Gazette*, "This used to be one of the hot spots for that business. But these outfits were small stuff compared to the big outfits in Detroit and elsewhere in the east."[55]

Soon after his arrival in Montana, Roahen took over temporarily as the acting superintendent of the National Bison Range at Moise, northwest of Missoula. Its previous supervisor was under investigation and would eventually be ousted. Roahen remained there for several months until he moved his headquarters into Billings.

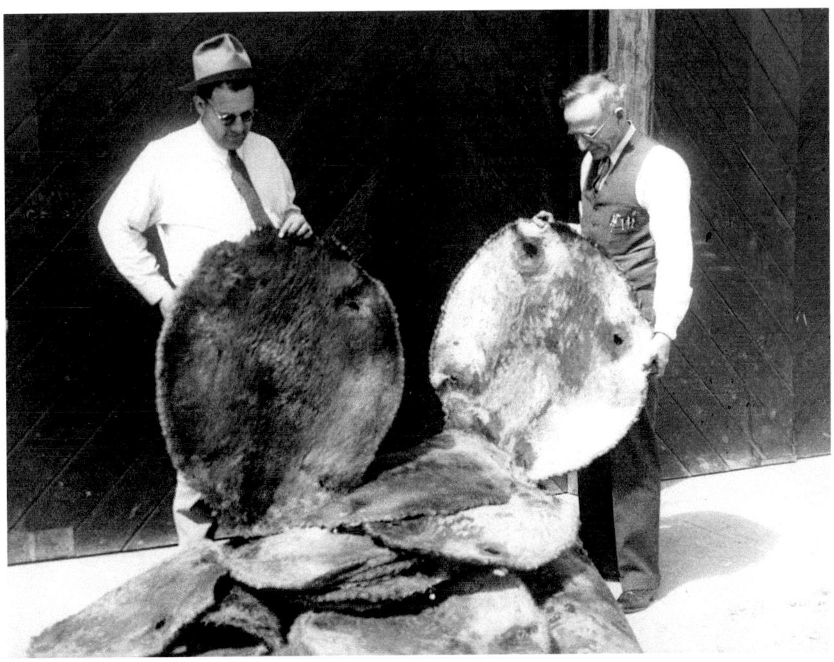

Figure 2.11. Montana furs bust: Roahen (*right*) and James Gerow, Idaho District Fish and Game agent. Courtesy of U.S. Fish and Wildlife Service.

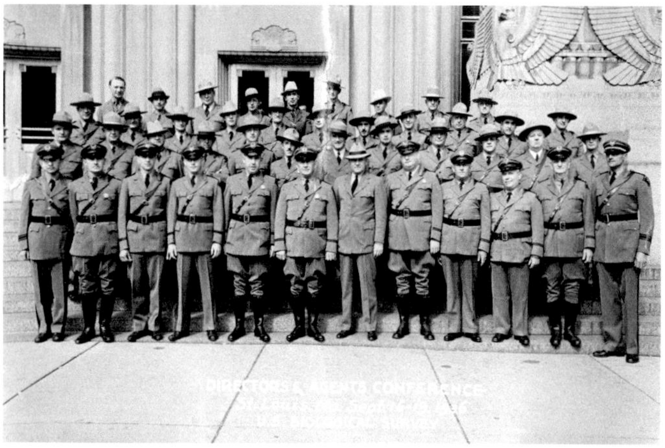

Figure 2.12. Fish and game agents, St. Louis, 1936. Roahen is second from right, back row. Courtesy of U.S. Fish and Wildlife Service.

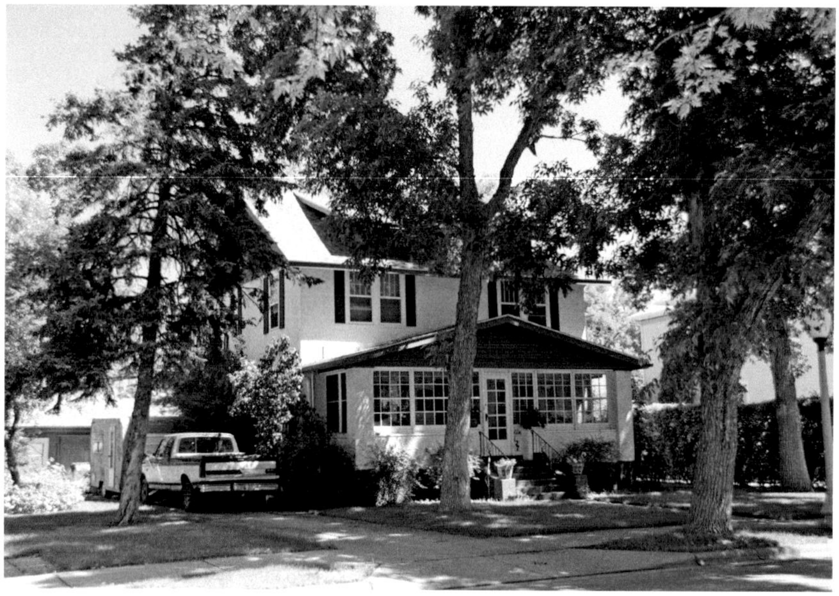

Figure 2.13. Roahen house, 27 Lewis Ave., Billings, Montana. Author's photo.

City directories for Billings in the early 1930s indicate that the couple initially lived in at least two locations in Montana's largest city: first, 341 Burlington Avenue, and, by early 1935, 535 Yellowstone Avenue. By 1937, their residence was listed as 27 Lewis Avenue, where they would spend the rest of their lives.[56] Roahen's occupation across the years was listed as game agent. After he retired in 1955, his occupational listing changed to commercial photographer.

In 1937, the Fish and Game Service came up with what might have appeared as a great idea but was one that just did not turn out well. Roahen's superiors brought him to the agency's Washington, D.C., headquarters and appointed him its chief photographer for the United States and Alaska. The experiment lasted just three months. Roahen, who preferred law enforcement field duties, successfully lobbied for a return to his Billings post. However, he continued to handle special photography assignments far and wide for the federal agency and others, as the need arose. He photographed not only wildlife but also federal lands, parks, dam construction, and other government projects.

One personal setback occurred on June 17 that year. Flood waters from the Yellowstone River destroyed some 1,000 feet of priceless movie film he had shot. The footage, stored in the basement of the Federal Building, covered his six years in the Midwest before his assignment to Billings.

In early 1941, an event occurred that greatly impacted both the Custer battlefield and Roahen's ties to the site and his photographic career. Edward S. Luce assumed the battlefield's superintendency, and he would hold his influential position for fifteen years.[57] Though correspondence between the two men often reflects the formality of their times (e.g., "Dear Mr. Roahen"), the two became close friends and enjoyed a satisfying professional relationship.

Soon after he met Luce, Roahen's commercial career as a photographer took off. He began converting his battlefield photos into picture postcards for sale at the battlefield Visitor Center, then located in the historic Stone House. Produced in thousands of copies, those postcards today are commonly found in antique malls, for sale on eBay, or in private collections. Western historian Robert M. Utley worked as a seasonal ranger under Luce during the late 1940s. "In our little office and reception center in the old Stone House we sold Ken's postcards. That was all that we had to sell and that was all the income the Association had." The Reverend Vincent A. Heier, an expert on Custer-themed memorabilia, noted in the same article that Roahen was "the most prolific maker of postcard images."[58]

By the early 1950s, Roahen was shooting not only his customary black-and-white film but also color images. In an October 1953 letter to 20th Century Photo Color Service, Boise, Idaho, he stated that he had already processed 35,000 prints for the battlefield that year, a figure that seems extraordinarily high.[59] He also sold photos to other dealers and individuals. As his government career was winding down in the early 1950s, his commercial photography business flourished. Roahen seemed more content to put his days as a take-no-prisoners law enforcement officer behind himself. Virtually all of the exciting game agent enforcement stories that he related in newspapers and magazines recall episodes from early in his career, mostly in Illinois.

Roahen was an expert in firearms, but he also had great concerns about children's use of them. He believed youngsters required proper training with weapons. In 1961, he wrote about his concerns to FBI director J. Edgar Hoover, who replied, "I deeply share the concern you express in easy accessibility of weapons for young people these days, and I am enclosing a statement which reflects my further views in this regard."[60]

At least in his early retirement years, Roahen remained active shooting for such regional and national magazines and newspapers as *Life*, *Look*, and *Saturday Evening Post* and various photographic distribution agencies.[61] A favorite assignment involved serving as the official photographer for the Dude Ranch Association, which operated dude ranches in eleven western states, Alberta, and Saskatchewan. He wrote to a friend, "So you can see I get around and mix up with the millionaires at the ranches." As the association's official photographer at its ranches, he was often absent from his Billings home from June to mid-September during his retirement years.

In early 1953, Luce received permission from the National Park Service to launch the Custer Battlefield Historical and Museum Association "for the furtherance of the interests in historical research and related subjects to Custer Battlefield National Monument." Judge Ben Harwood was the association's first president, and its seven-member board of directors included Roahen's friend George C. Osten as treasurer and Luce, now referring to himself as a major, as executive secretary. Another member was Crow tribal leader Joe Medicine Crow, who in 2016 remains the founding board's sole surviving member.

In 1962, Roahen began the first of three one-year terms as association president. His tenure as president would not always be easy. By that time, Luce had long since retired. He would die on November 8, 1963, at his home in San Diego, California. As president, Roahen found himself frequently clashing with then battlefield superintendent Thomas K. Garry, who had assumed the post in March 1959.

The most controversial issue at the center of the CBHMA's disputes with Garry concerned the future of the Stone House, built in 1894 as the superintendent's residence. In 1952, the present-day battlefield Visitor Center had been built and dedicated by Luce. By the early 1960s, the Stone House needed significant repairs and modernizing, steps that Garry opposed. He wanted it demolished so its site could be used to expand burial space in Custer National Cemetery. As CBHMA's president, Roahen led a successful fight to save the historic structure from demolition. Today it serves as the White Swan Library for research on the battlefield and its personalities.

For all of his good points, Roahen always had a prickly side to his personality. He clearly mixed well with people and made many friends, but he also could be feisty. After his retirement in January 1955, he wrote a scathing letter to Paul Quick, assistant regional director of the Fish and Wildlife Service in Portland, Oregon, effectively rejecting an award citation that had been prepared for him: "To be frank, I would not accept the present citation and award in the manner as written, and am returning same, and farther to be frank, I would not accept a 'Meritorious Award' at all."[62]

In Roahen's view, a meritorious award was "the lowest award just generally given to all employees retiring. I am not particularly interested in another award of the same category, and owing to what I have gone through with, at various times from being shot from ambush, auto machine gunned, attempted shooting in my home, and the injuries received from such, as well as other ways in line of duty, resulting in months spent in various hospitals, included eighteen operations (some major) for the removal of 'slugs' of various types and sizes . . ."

Earlier, he had told Quick that no employee currently in the regional office had been "associated in any manner with the waterfowl or enforcement activities back in the early twenties, so it [could] be readily understood why [his] citation was so grossly misrepresented and ridiculous."

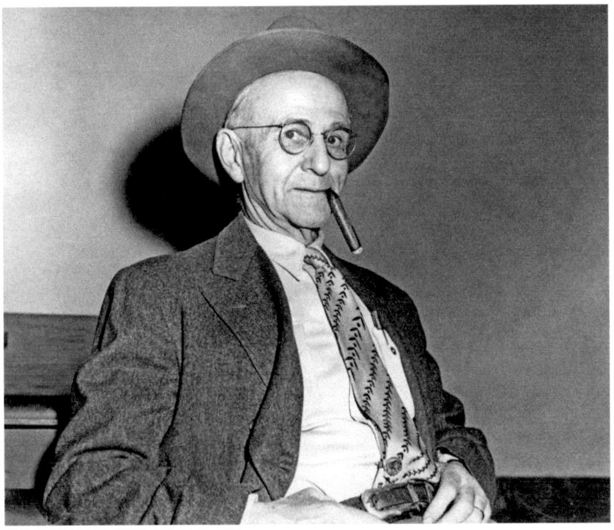

Figure 2.14. Roahen, late in life, with his cigar drooping, Mountainview Cemetery. Courtesy of U.S. Fish and Wildlife Service.

He concluded his frank diatribe to Quick: "Not only is it my opinion, but likewise the opinion of several prominent citizens of Billings and Federal officials who have known of my work, that I should receive an outstanding award, to which of course, you would not agree."

As he aged, this side of him became more obvious. In the summer of 1963, Roahen had a falling out with Superintendent Garry, who had told him, evidently with sarcasm, "You are a special privileged man" around the battlefield. In responding, an offended Roahen pointed out again that he had taken photographs at the behest of superintendents and historians for more than twenty-five years. "However," he stressed, "no invoice was ever sent to the battlefield for such pictures."[63] Additionally, he reminded Garry that every year or two he reshot previous photos to show changes as well as the growth of trees, especially around the cemetery. The question remains, what happened to all of the hundreds, if not thousands, of images he must have taken of the immediate Custer Battlefield National Monument and its related historic sites?

Roahen also clashed with battlefield historian Warren J. Petty between 1960 and 1963. In his letter to Park Service director Conrad Wirth in that early 1960s period, Roahen lambasted Petty: "Confidentially, I have never seen a Historian at the Battlefield, or other places, such as we now have at the Battlefield. He is now in his third year, and until just this last Decoration Day, he had never even been to the Reno Battlefield west of the river, at which time Geo. Osten took him over. Unless he has been up to Reno Creek, Crows Nest, Davis Creek Divide, important places in the Custer march, within the last couple of months, he has never seen that portion of the area."[64] Roahen had recommended to a California group seeking a guide that they contact Petty. "When they returned to Blgs [Billings], they called me and stated Petty wouldn't talk to them, and they had to hire a man for two days at Hardin. Of course he could not talk with them because he had not been over the battlefield."

Between 1967 and 1969, B. William Henry served as the battlefield's historian. Henry recalled Roahen as "a cranky old man" in that period.[65] Richard

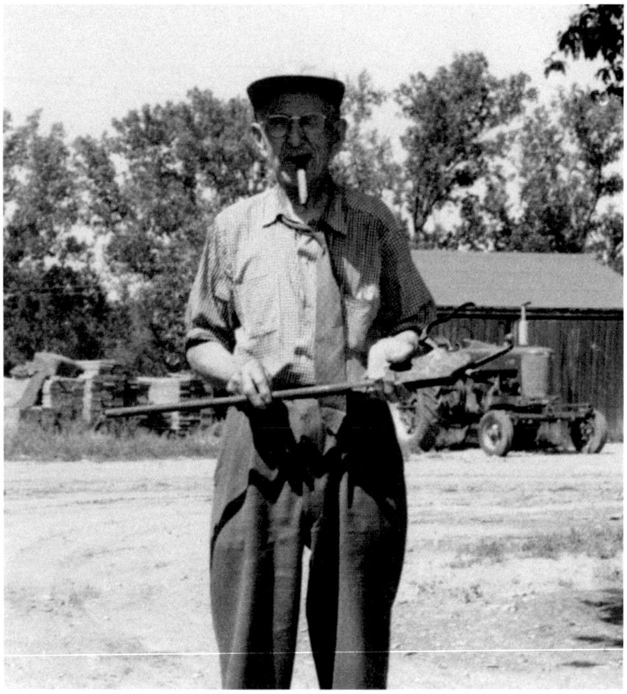

Figure 2.15. Elderly Roahen, Little Big Horn Valley, ca. 1970s. Courtesy of Big Horn County Historical Museum.

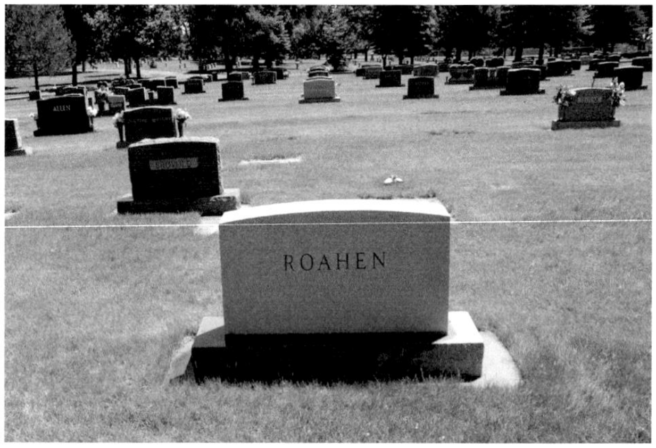

Figure 2.16. Roahen grave, Billings, Montana. Author's photo.

Upton, owner of Upton and Sons Publishers, knew Roahen from the late 1960s to the period close to the latter's death in 1976 and recalled him as an individual who could "rub people the wrong way." He last associated with Roahen in June 1975 when they sat near each other on a bus trip from the battlefield Visitor Center to the Rosebud Battlefield at the time of the annual CBHMA meeting. Roahen, despite his fragile state and advanced age, "was unaccompanied on the bus. He didn't look as if he should be unaccompanied. He wore a good suit of clothes, but it was well-worn."[66]

At the time, Roahen was eighty-seven years old, and he would live only until January 9, 1976. A committee formed to plan events for the centennial observance of the Little Big Horn battle listed Roahen as a member, but he likely played at best a minor role. His obituary in the *Billings Gazette* indicates that he died at the Western Manor nursing home, suggesting that his health had been failing that fall of 1975 after he attended the previous June's CBHMA meeting.[67]

His funeral took place January 13, 1976. His honorary pallbearers included his friends George C. Osten, attorney William H. Bellingham, Judge Ben Harwood, Montana artist J. K. Ralston, and author John A. Popovich. The burial was in Mountview Cemetery in Billings. His wife, Sandae, would survive him for a little more than four years. On June 3, 1980, she, too, died in Billings and was buried beside her husband.

CHAPTER 3

Little Big Horn Battle Historical Background

On June 25, 1876, the U.S. Army suffered one of its greatest defeats on the North American continent when Lt. Col. George Armstrong Custer and 267 members of his 7th U.S. Cavalry Regiment were killed in action in legendary combat with Sioux and Northern Cheyenne warriors in the valley of the Little Big Horn River and on the ridges above its banks in southeastern Montana Territory. Popularly dubbed "Custer's Last Stand," the Battle of the Little Big Horn remains a fascinating event for students of history. Though Custer was operating under the broad directives of the administration of President Ulysses S. Grant and the field orders of his immediate commander, Brig. Gen. Alfred H. Terry, his attack on what may have been the largest Indian village to gather on the Northern Plains remains steeped in controversy. Did Custer die because he failed to follow his orders? Did he die because he was an egotist consumed by ambition and a desire for personal glory? Was he a raving lunatic bent on committing genocide against a peaceful village of American Indians desirous only of maintaining their nomadic lifestyle on the Plains following the herds of bison? Or did Civil War hero Custer die in a glorious final stand, furthering the self-proclaimed mandate of white Americans to prosper and spread across the entire country?

Any answer depends on one's historical and cultural perspective, and no generally accepted conclusion about Custer likely will ever be agreed upon by all Americans. That no man in Custer's immediate five companies survived the fighting further guarantees that history will never unravel the entire story of what happened along the Little Big Horn that June 1876. Modern scholars and students engage in endless speculation and express countless personal opinions about the Little Big Horn and Custer's actions. Questions often center on why Custer lost, instead of why the Indians defeated him. As we wrote in our 2005 book, *Where Custer Fell*, "The event remains a fascinating challenge to those who pursue historical truth within a subject heavily mantled in mythology, recrimination, and dispute. . . . Indeed, during the century and more that has elapsed since warrior and soldier clashed on the sprawling landscape of southeastern Montana, many researchers have attempted to reconstruct the fate of Custer's command, but none can ever hope to know the actual sequence and course of events. . . . the enigmatic details of the general's last fight remain a fertile ground for the endeavors of amateur and professional historians alike."[1]

Custer's battle with the Lakota (Sioux) and Cheyenne tribes was not just an isolated event in 1876 but rather a part of a continuing series of struggles for dominance on the Plains. These clashes stretched back to the end of the Civil War in 1865, and certainly well before the war, as more and more white

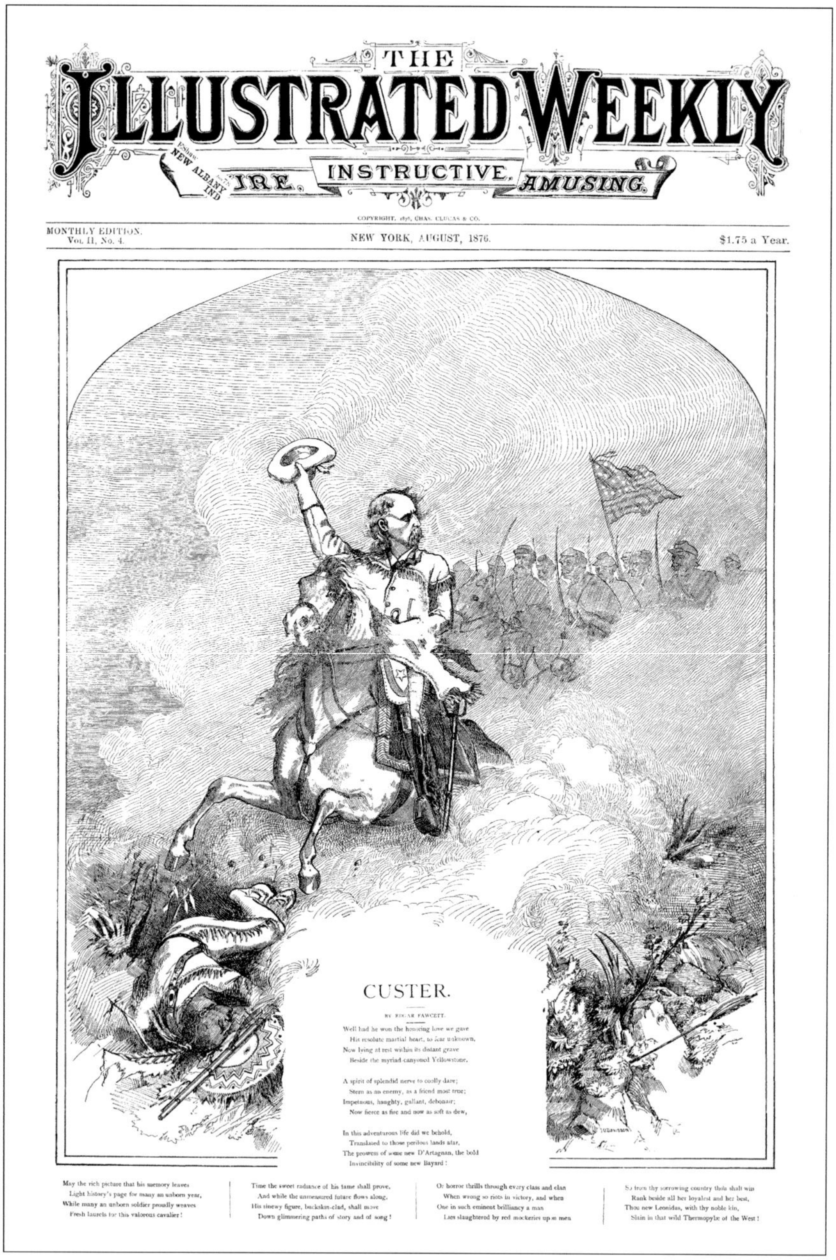

THE ILLUSTRATED WEEKLY

NEW ALBANY IND

INSTRUCTIVE, AMUSING.

COPYRIGHT, 1876, CHAS. CLUCAS & CO.

MONTHLY EDITION.
VOL. II, No. 4.

NEW YORK, AUGUST, 1876.

$1.75 a Year.

CUSTER.

BY EDGAR FAWCETT.

Well had he won the honoring love we gave
His resolute martial heart, to fear unknown,
Now lying at rest within its distant grave
Beside the myriad-canyoned Yellowstone.

A spirit of splendid nerve to coolly dare;
Stern as an enemy, as a friend most true;
Impetuous, haughty, gallant, debonair;
Now fierce as fire and now as soft as dew,

In this adventurous life did we behold,
Translated to those perilous lands afar,
The prowess of some new D'Artagnan, the bold
Invincibility of some new Bayard!

May the rich picture that his memory leaves
Light history's page for many an unborn year,
While many an unborn soldier proudly weaves
Fresh laurels for this valorous cavalier!

Time the sweet radiance of his fame shall prove,
And while the unmeasured future flows along,
His sinewy figure, buckskin-clad, shall move
Down glimmering paths of story and of song!

Or horror thrills through every class and clan
When wrong so riots in victory, and when
One in such eminent brilliancy a man
Lies slaughtered by red mockeries upon men

So from thy sorrowing country thou shalt win
Rank beside all her loyalest and her best,
Thou new Leonidas, with thy noble kin,
Slain in that wild Thermopylæ of the West!

Figure 3.1. A bald Custer, *Illustrated Weekly*, 1876. Author's collection.

Americans of European descent ventured west. Many were merely immigrants seeking new lives on lands that had been inhabited by American Indians for centuries. In the early 1870s, surveying crews of the Northern Pacific Railroad crossed Dakota Territory and entered Montana Territory, planning where to lay its tracks across wilderness lands considered the property of the tribal nations. In 1873, Custer's 7th Cavalry, part of a larger force authorized by the U.S. government to protect the rail crews working in Montana, twice engaged the Lakotas, repulsing the warriors in what amounted to little more than skirmishes. In 1874, Custer, again under government orders, ventured anew into Indian country, this time the Black Hills, which even today are considered the spiritual center of Lakota life. His mission: look for possible

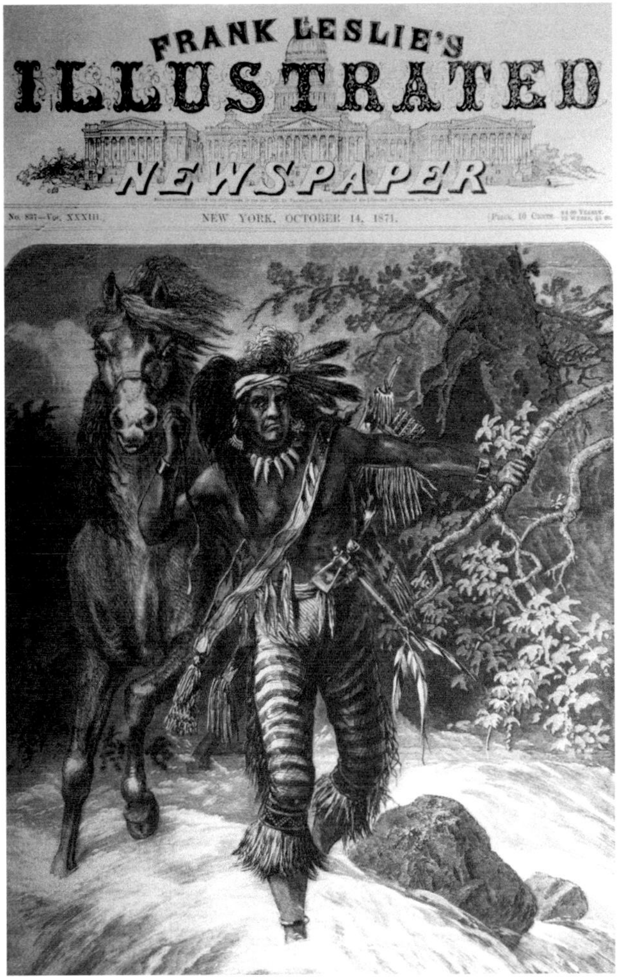

Figure 3.2. (*left*) Sitting Bull, *Leslie's Illustrated*, 1871. Author's collection.

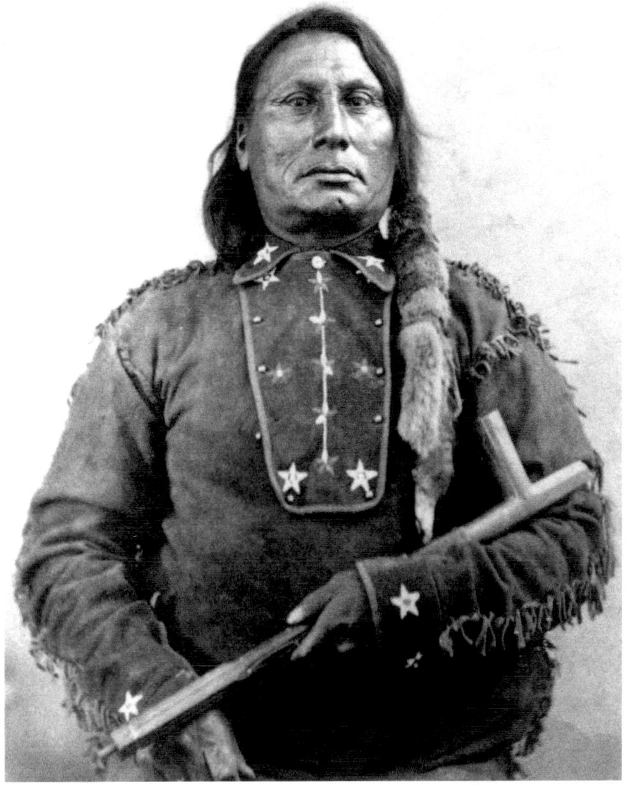

Figure 3.3. Gall. Courtesy of Glen Swanson.

locations to build forts. However, his large combined military and civilian force also included geologists who found gold.

By late 1875, as miners flocked into the Black Hills, President Grant's administration struggled uneasily with the resulting dilemma. The illegal presence of miners and settlers alike antagonized the Indians, who often responded with violence. Thus, Grant ordered roaming bands of Indians to abandon traditional hunting grounds that had been promised to them in the 1868 Fort Laramie Treaty and to join other bands of their people on reservations in western Dakota Territory. Instead, Lakota leaders, such as Sitting Bull, Gall, and Crazy Horse, vowed to protect their freedom. Even if the Indian leaders had been inclined to obey, a harsh winter clearly prevented their people from meeting the government's late January 1876 deadline for moving to the reservations. The army was ordered to compel these so-called hostiles—principally Lakotas and Northern Cheyennes—to forever abandon their traditional nomadic ways. No one in the government or the military could envision the disasters that would befall the army in 1876 in its attempts to carry out that task.

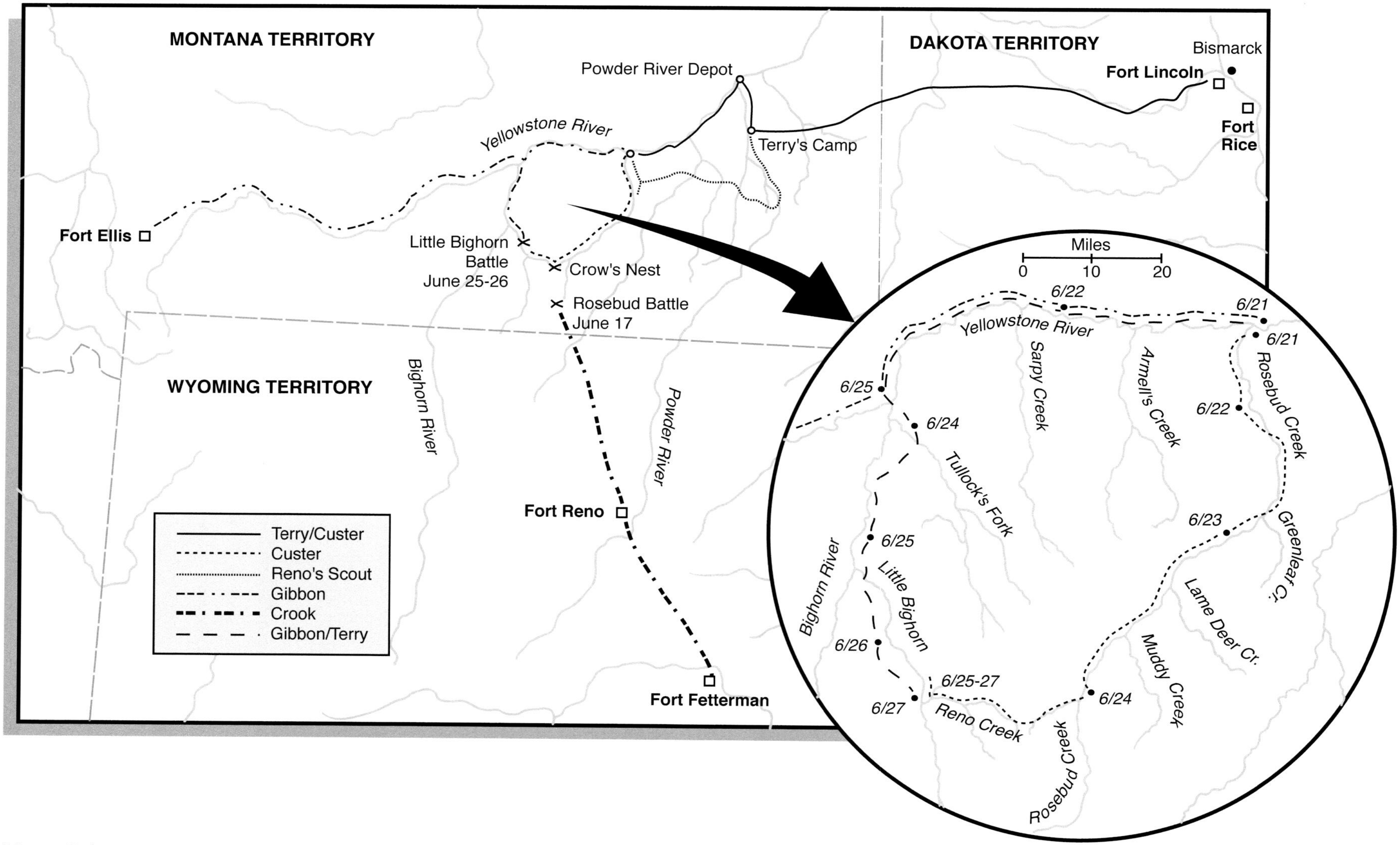

Map 3.1. Little Big Horn campaign map.
Map by Gary Raham.

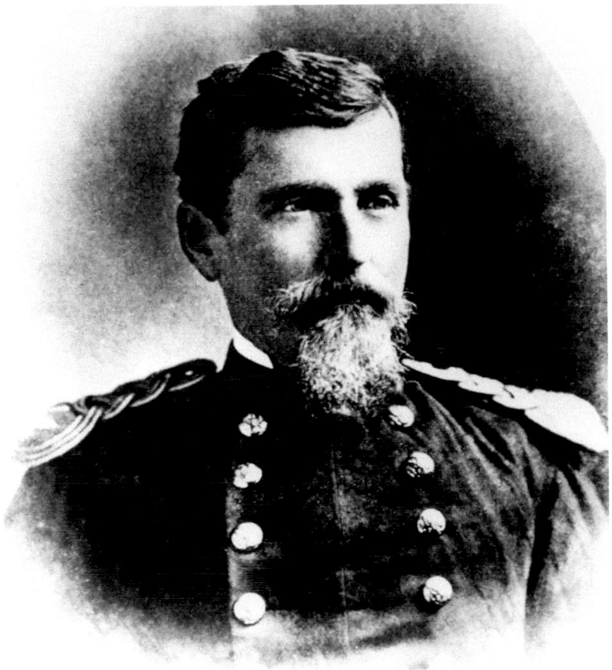

Figure 3.4. (*left*) John Gibbon. Courtesy of Little Bighorn Battlefield National Monument.

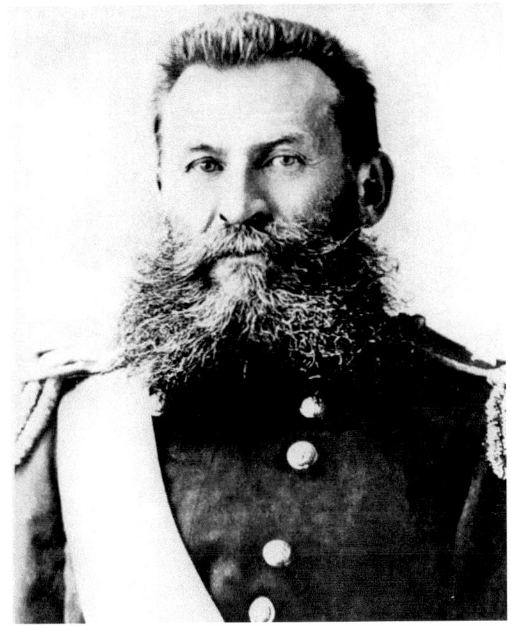

Figure 3.5. (*below*) George Crook. Courtesy of Little Bighorn Battlefield National Monument.

The 1876 campaign, or Great Sioux War (which stretched into 1877), called for three military columns to advance into the wilderness where these scattered bands lived—modern North and South Dakota and parts of Montana and Wyoming.[2] The army's senior leaders were all experienced veterans of the Civil War, but a decade on the Plains had made them no wiser in fighting Indians, whose methods of combat were far removed from the European style so prevalent during the Civil War and for which young cadets were still trained at the U.S. Military Academy at West Point. Too, as the war slipped from reality to memory, the army increasingly relied on often poorly motivated, poorly trained soldiers, many of whom were immigrants ill suited for long campaigns and Indian fighting.

In 1876, from Fort Ellis and Fort Shaw in western Montana Territory marched the Montana Column, commanded by Col. John Gibbon; from Fort Fetterman to the south came the Wyoming Column under Brig. Gen. George Crook, probably the army's most experienced Indian fighter; and from Fort Abraham Lincoln to the east, across the Missouri River from Bismarck, Dakota Territory, came the Dakota Column of Brigadier General Terry, which included some 650 men in twelve companies of Custer's 7th U.S. Cavalry. Setting out on May 17, 1876, Terry expressed his confidence for the campaign's success to Gen. Philip H. Sheridan: "I have no doubt of the ability of my column to whip all the Sioux whom we can find."[3]

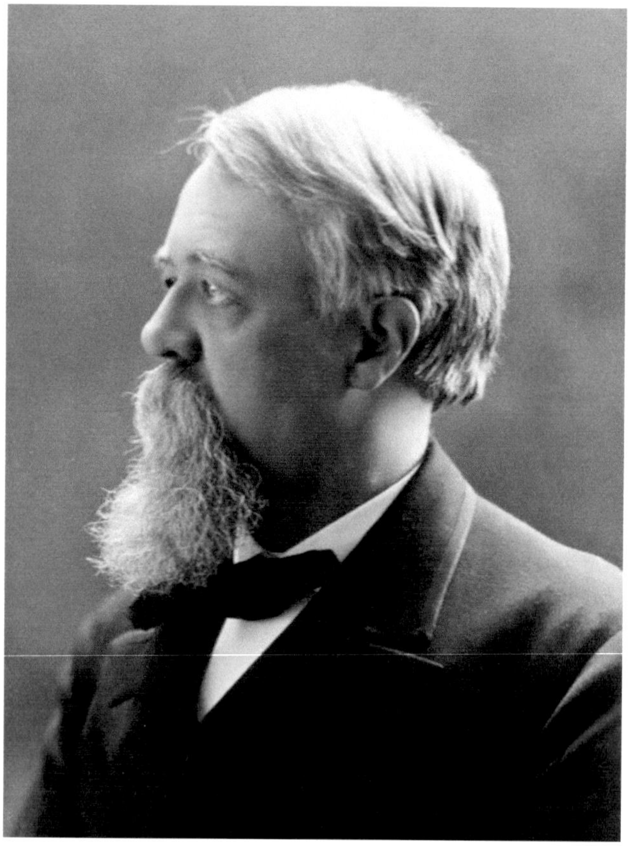

Figure 3.6. Alfred H. Terry as a civilian. Author's collection.

Ahead of the army were as many as 1,500 warriors, if not more, and their dependents, who may have numbered as many as 10,000 men, women, and children. They had gathered under the leadership of a charismatic Hunkpapa spiritual leader, Sitting Bull. The first action of the summer campaign occurred on June 17 but involved only Crook's force. Terry and Custer remained in camp near the confluence of the Tongue River and Yellowstone River, awaiting the results of a scout by a 7th Cavalry detachment under Maj. Marcus A. Reno, the regiment's second-in-command. Early on June 17, while Crook's 1,350 men were camped for morning coffee along the banks of Rosebud Creek, his column was unexpectedly attacked by as many as a thousand warriors led by Crazy Horse. Fighting raged throughout the day, but both sides sustained only light casualties. Their fighting done, the warriors chose to withdraw, leaving Crook in command of the field and claiming a rather hollow victory. However, instead of continuing his northward march toward the other military columns in the field, Crook opted to return south to encamp along Goose Creek in what is now Sheridan, Wyoming, to await resupplies. At a critical moment for the army's campaign, he chose to idle his troops for several weeks. Of greater concern, although his options were few, he made no effort to inform Terry, Gibbon, and Custer about his departure from the field or that the Indians were prepared to resist the troops with great confidence and resolve.

The next move for the army came four days later, June 21, while Terry, Custer, and Gibbon were camped at the mouth of the Rosebud by the Yellowstone

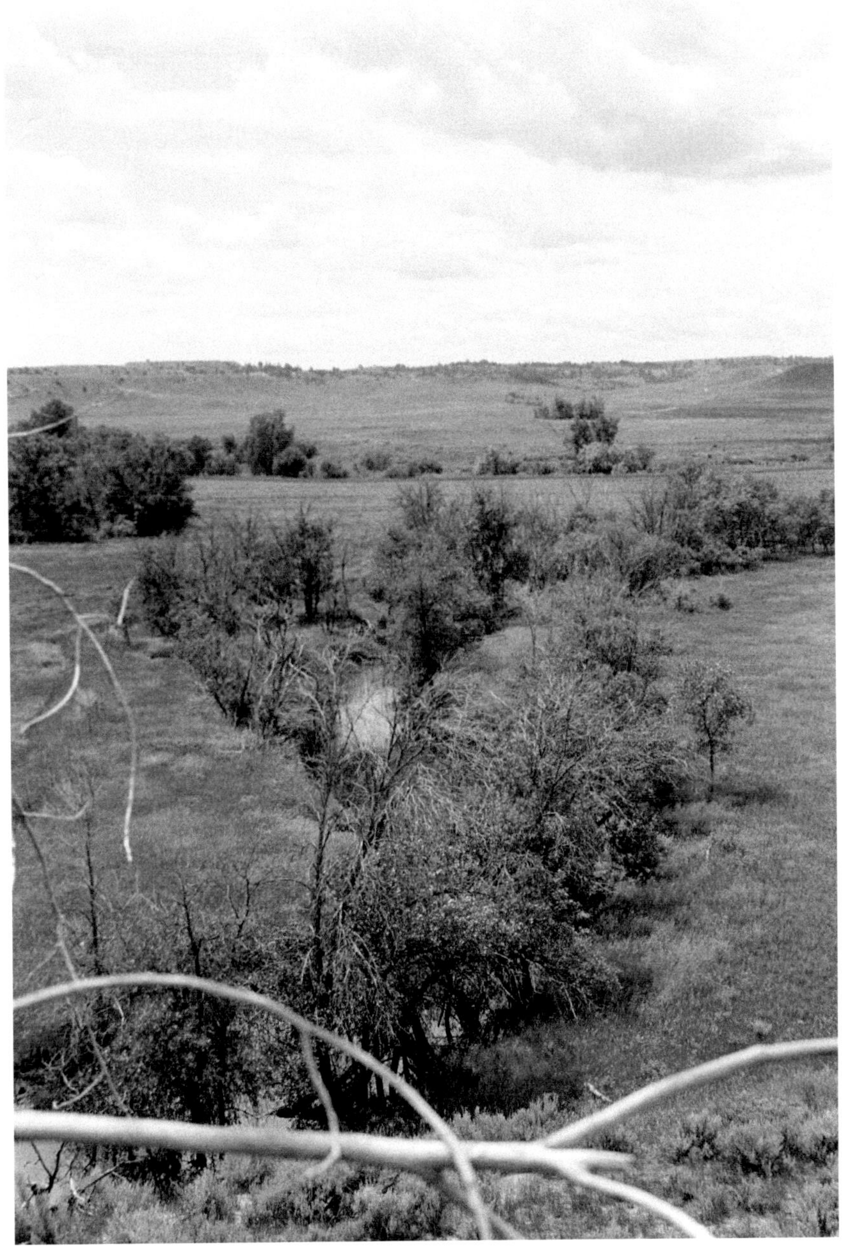

Figure 3.7. Rosebud Creek looking southwest. Author's photo.

River. Major Reno had returned from a nine-day scout with six companies of the 7th Cavalry during which he saw no action but brought Terry his first solid evidence of where his foe might be. Reno reported that at least eight hundred warriors appeared headed toward the Little Big Horn Valley. On June 22, Terry ordered Custer to take the 7th Cavalry's twelve companies south up Rosebud Creek in pursuit of the Indians, then move west to the Little Big Horn. In support, Terry and Gibbon would head west along the Yellowstone, then south along the Big Horn River to the mouth of the Little Big Horn. With luck, Terry would be in position on June 26 to entrap whatever Indians Custer forced to flee north. Unfortunately, in laying out their plans the army's leaders lacked one critical piece of intelligence about their enemy: throughout June, Indian strength had been growing steadily, and the tribal gathering along the Little Big Horn numbered at least 1,500 adult warriors, if not more.

For his advance up Rosebud Creek, Custer's regiment consisted of 597 soldiers plus fifty scouts and civilians. Only the mule-borne pack train prevented an even quicker move in the rugged backcountry of the Rosebud.[4] Custer kept his Crow and Ree scouts active for the next three days seeking signs of the enemy. By June 24, his scouts reported that the warriors were likely to be found on the lower reaches of the Little Big Horn. By dawn of June 25, they had scaled a ridge overlooking a bowl-like depression later known as the Crow's Nest and spotted unmistakable signs of a large Indian pony herd roaming in the Little Big Horn Valley, some 15 miles to the west. After a night march, Custer rode ahead of his column and joined his scouts at the Crow's Nest. Custer could make out neither the massive pony herd nor the smoke of the enemy camps, but he believed his scouts were correct. His first thought was to repeat his strategy from eight years earlier at the Battle of the Washita, when he had successfully struck a Cheyenne village at dawn from multiple directions. Now he would launch an early morning attack on June 26.

New information soon altered his thinking about when to attack and likely influenced the battle's outcome that afternoon. Custer feared outriding Indian hunting parties had spotted his regiment and that his elusive foe would flee before the army could corral them. Custer opted for a more dangerous midday attack on June 25.[5] After crossing the divide between Rosebud Creek and the Little Big Horn River and beginning his march down the valley of what is known today as Reno Creek, Custer halted his command.[6] He ordered Capt. Frederick W. Benteen and the 115 men of Companies D, H and K to ride southwest, over a series of rugged ridges and coulees toward the distant river valley, and attack whatever Indians or outlying villages they might discover. In 1868, in launching his attack at the Washita River, Custer had been unaware of other villages downstream and soon found himself engaged with their warriors. In 1876, he would take no chances.

According to his orders, if Benteen found no enemy he was to countermarch to rejoin the greater command. In a further division of the regiment, Custer also assigned three-company battalions to Reno (A, G, M) and Capt. Myles W. Keogh (C, I, L) and a two-company battalion to Capt. George W. M. Yates (E, F). Company B, under Capt. Thomas M. McDougall, would protect the slow-moving pack train.

Custer's next decision came two hours later and several miles closer to the Little Big Horn. Interpreter-scout Frederick Girard yelled to him from a small knoll near an abandoned camp on the lower reaches of Reno Creek, "Here are your Indians, running like Devils."

Ahead of the troops, Indian horsemen could be seen riding hard for the river. Custer responded, personally or through his adjutant, by ordering Major Reno with his 130 cavalrymen and twenty-four scouts to charge what the 7th's commander erroneously assumed were scattering warriors and their women and children.[7] Reno likely assumed—perhaps erroneously—that Custer would

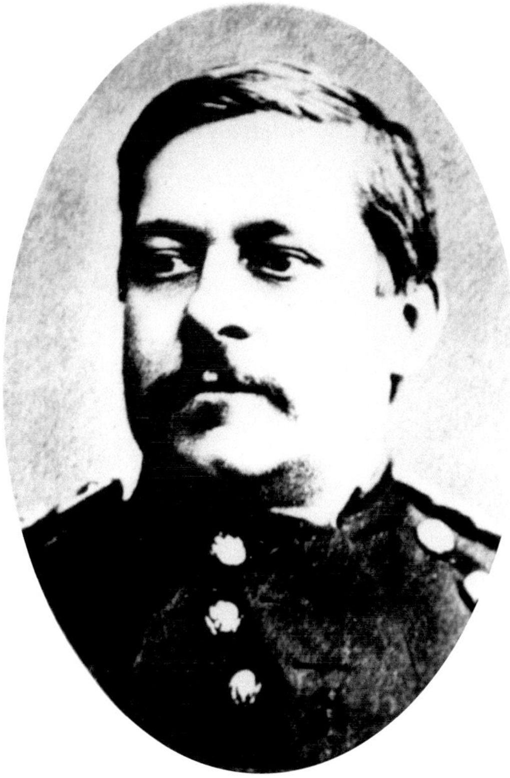

Figure 3.8. (*top left*) Marcus A. Reno. Courtesy of Little Bighorn Battlefield National Monument.

Figure 3.9. (*below*) Frederick W. Benteen. Courtesy of Little Bighorn Battlefield National Monument.

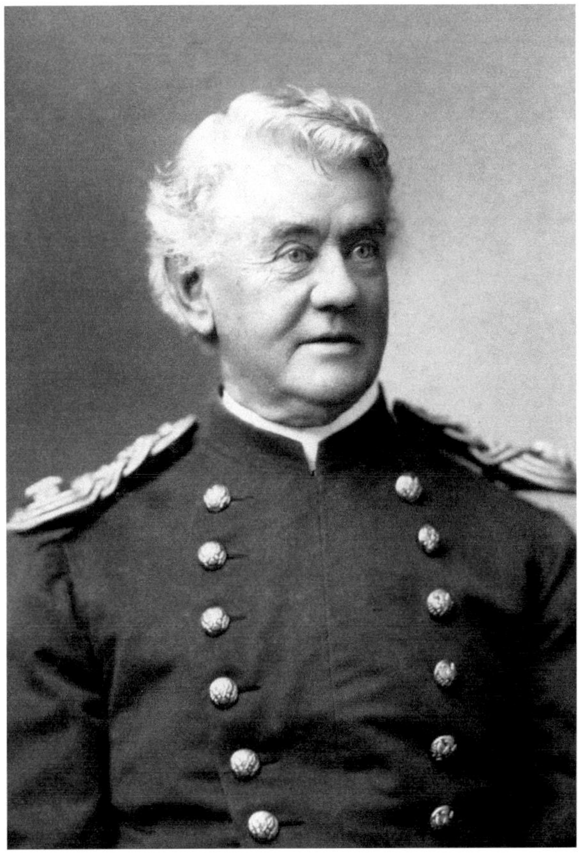

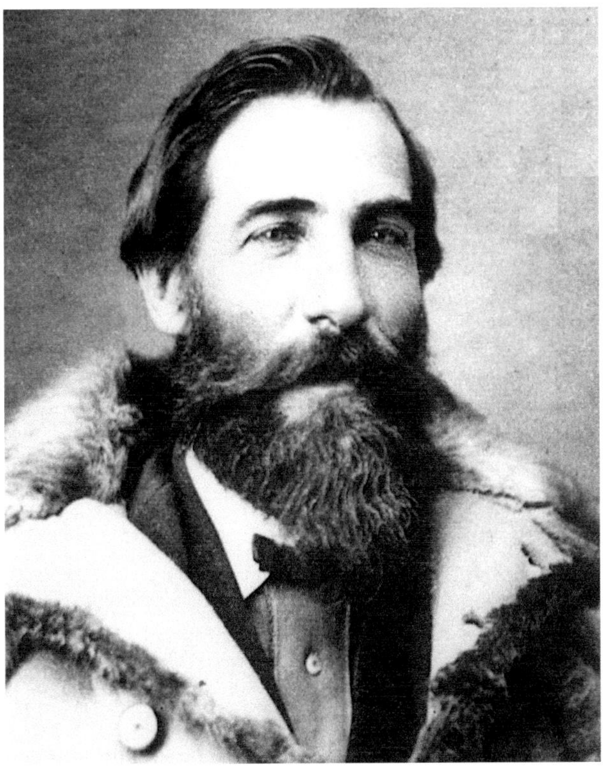

Figure 3.10. (*bottom left*) Fred Girard. Courtesy of Little Bighorn Battlefield National Monument.

support him from the rear. Instead, Custer with Keogh's and Yates's battalions—numbering 220 men prior to the dispatch of two couriers, the departure of four Indian scouts, and the straggling of at least four troopers whose horses gave out—turned to the north and mounted the high bluffs east of the river. Lagging far behind Custer and Reno on the regiment's back trail were the 135 men of Captain McDougall's reinforced Company B, escorting the pack train. McDougall would catch up only after the Indians had been engaged.

Whatever Custer was thinking when he turned to the north remains unclear. Sgt. Daniel Kanipe, who carried a message urging on the pack train, thought Custer reacted to the appearance of some fifty to one hundred warriors on the high ground to his front.[8] Perhaps Custer feared an Indian party was riding out to confront his soldiers, or he may have intended to follow the warriors into the village proper. Cheyenne accounts confirm the presence of a sizable band east of the Little Big Horn, among them the warriors Wolf Tooth and Big Foot. Likely other parties, of varying strength, were east of the river.[9] Some students of the battle believe Custer planned to hit the village at its northern end in a classic pincer movement. A more current theory holds that Custer was endeavoring to cut off the apparent flight of his enemy and seize the women and children, as he had done at the Washita nearly eight years before. Custer's fateful decision to head north remains a key point of controversy about the Little Big Horn fight.

In acting, Custer undoubtedly believed he controlled his combat situation, but from that moment on events would prove him wrong. Custer may have surprised the Indians when his soldiers first appeared on the edge of their camps, but hundreds of warriors rushed to defend their families. They quickly stalled Reno's advance down the valley. Reno grew evermore hesitant as increasing numbers of warriors surged forward on his front. How many more lay hidden in the huge Indian village beyond his view added to his concern. His orders were to charge the enemy and he had done that, but now his opponents appeared poised to overwhelm him. Reno halted his battalion, dismounted its three companies, and formed a skirmish line. Every fourth man seized the reins of his comrades' horses and led them into a timbered area along the river on Reno's right flank, thereby reducing his combat strength by a fourth.

As warriors swarmed about his command, Reno feared his slender line would be flanked or surrounded. After ten or fifteen minutes, warrior pressure forced Reno to retreat from his skirmish position to new lines in the timber. Despite Custer's earlier promise of support, and the major's own warnings relayed by two couriers he had dispatched to his commander that warriors were seriously resisting the cavalry's attack, Custer's own battalions were nowhere in sight. A few soldiers claimed to have seen Custer's own troops on the bluffs across the river.

Within thirty minutes of the retreat into the timber, Indians were again pressuring the major's fragile lines. Reno ordered his men to mount—his critics claim he panicked—and they dashed from the timber in a fighting retreat that quickly degenerated into a chaotic stampede. Desperate troopers galloped for the river and the 200-foot bluffs beyond with angry warriors in close pursuit. By the time Reno's exhausted survivors had scaled the high bluffs, nearly 40 percent of his men lay dead, wounded, or abandoned in the escape from the timber. In addition, some twenty Indian scouts had departed, placing Reno's overall loss at more than 50 percent.[10] With such losses, Reno's battalion no longer remained an effective fighting force.

Figure 3.11. Edward S. Godfrey. Courtesy of Little Bighorn Battlefield National Monument.

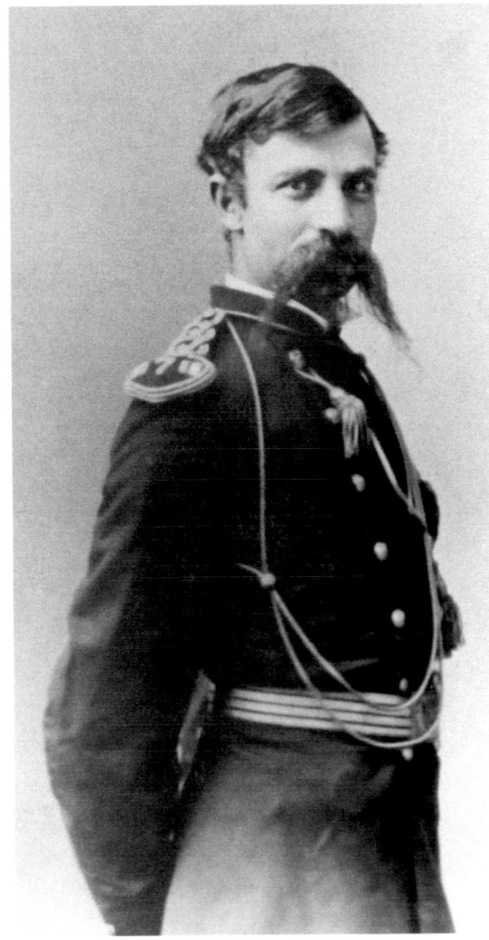

Elsewhere, Captain Benteen had ended his southwest maneuvers and followed the regiment's back trail; en route, he received two messages from Custer urging him to advance rapidly. Just as the final survivors of Reno's broken command reached the safety of the bluffs east of the Little Big Horn, Benteen's companies rode up. Some thirty minutes later, Captain McDougall's pack train began to arrive. While Reno and Benteen reorganized their commands and established a defensive perimeter, Indian pressure slowed. At the same time, heavy firing was apparent to the north. Clearly Custer was engaged.

One of Benteen's messages had instructed him to come quickly and bring the packs. Today he is still criticized for his failure to arrive as quickly as possible and without the pack train. Too, neither Reno nor Benteen showed any inclination to ride north toward the sound of the guns and determine the fate of their commander. Angered by their seeming inaction, Capt. Thomas B. Weir on his own rode north from the defensive site, followed by his own Company D. His unauthorized move prompted a poorly coordinated advance by the remaining companies, several joining Weir's troopers atop a conspicuous elevation known today as Weir Point. This stood one mile north of Reno's original position and three miles from the ridgeline where Custer would meet his death. Weir's men likely witnessed the last stages of Custer's battle, but from that distance the soldiers could not have realized what they actually were viewing.[11]

Soon, large groups of Indians rapidly approached the 7th's companies. The troops quickly retreated from Weir Point to their original position on the bluffs. Only one man, farrier Vincent Charley of Company D, was killed in this equally chaotic withdrawal. Only action by Lt. Edward S. Godfrey, who formed an effective rearguard with his dismounted Company K, probably ensured the troopers' escape. As the soldiers dug in for a protracted siege, some wondered about the whereabouts of Custer's command. Most believed he, too, had been besieged or had continued north to join Terry's forces.

For the rest of that day and most of the next, the seven companies endured deadly sniping fire that steadily added to the number of dead and wounded.[12] Acting assistant surgeon Henry R. Porter cared for the battalion's wounded in a makeshift hospital, partially sheltered from Indian fire by mules and horses, which he had set up in a swale at the center of the defensive site. Needed water could be obtained only by dangerous descents down the bluffs to the river. Only occasionally did warriors seek to engage the soldiers in their lightly fortified position. Captain Benteen personally led a charge that repulsed one such foray. Today he is given more credit than Reno for overseeing the successful defense.

By the evening of June 26, the Indians had ceased their attacks. Soon the surviving soldiers watched as a huge column of warriors and their families trekked southwest across the valley floor toward the distant Big Horn Mountains. By dawn on June 27, the valley was empty. About 11 A.M., Terry's and Gibbon's column were seen advancing through the abandoned village. Any joy at their rescue was short-lived among the besieged cavalrymen. Word soon followed that the bodies of Custer's dead had been discovered downstream.

On June 28, the 7th Cavalry buried its dead amid what Lieutenant Godfrey called "a scene of sickening, ghastly horror." Scattered over the sagebrush-covered ridges and coulees were the bodies of all 209 men who had ridden into the fight with Custer. Most were naked, bloated, and discolored; many had been terribly mutilated. Capt. Walter Clifford of Gibbon's 7th Infantry described the sight before him as "horrible in the extreme. . . . Here a hand gone, here a foot or a head, gaudy gashes cut in all parts of the body, eyes gouged out, noses and ears cut off, and skulls crushed in."[13]

In the conclusion to the historical background chapter of *Where Custer Fell*, we stated: "The abundant photographic record of the Little Bighorn Battlefield chronicles the timeless face of that historic landscape and the changes wrought by our ongoing endeavor to memorialize, interpret, and comprehend what transpired there. These images cannot solve the mystery, but they do elaborate upon it, and perhaps they can guide us a little closer to the unknowable truth."[14] That remains true today. Through the collection of photographs by Kenneth F. Roahen, we can learn that much more about this timeless historic landscape on which people of different cultures engaged in brutal combat designed to defend their respective ways of life.

PART 2

Kenneth F. Roahen's Photographs

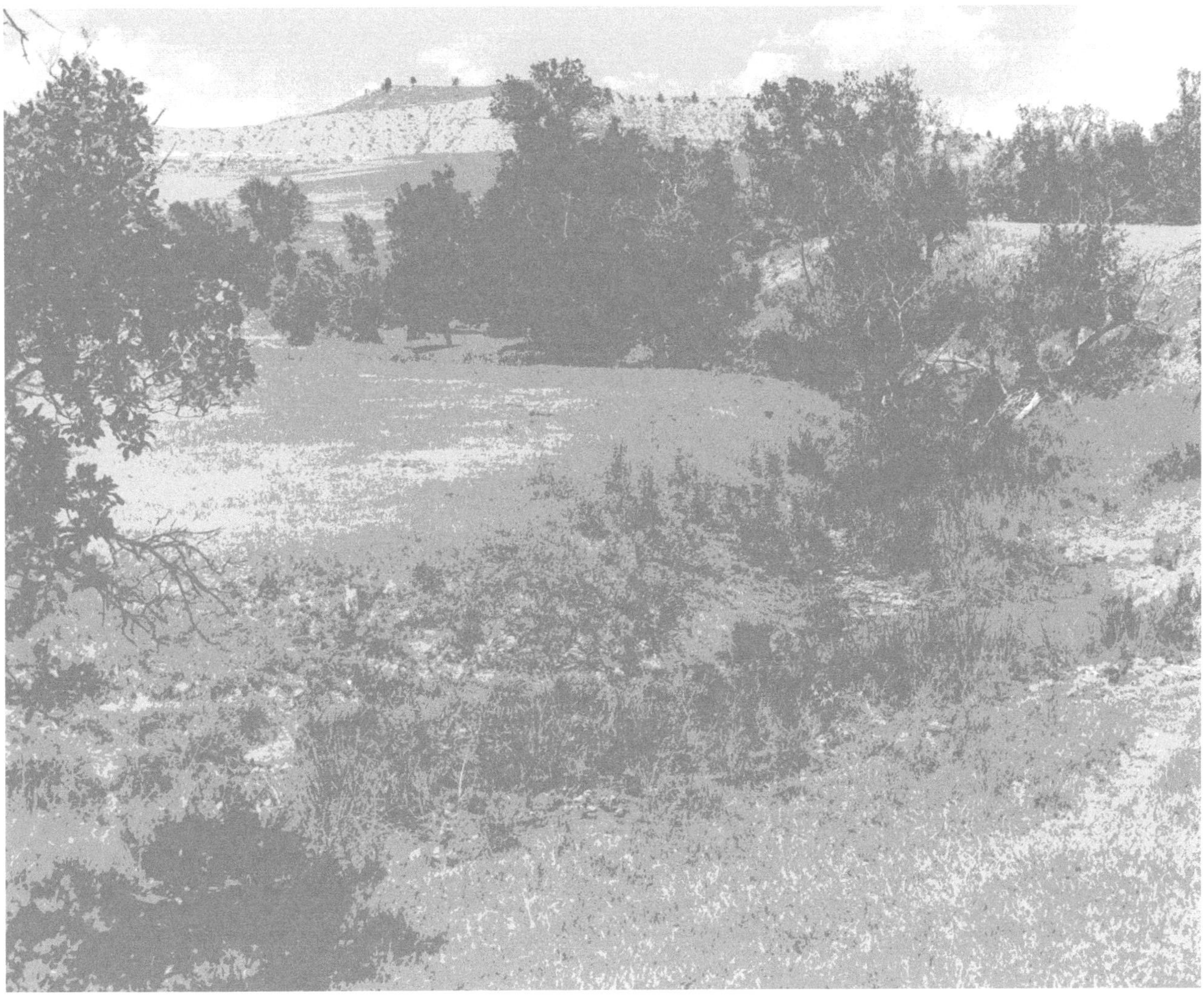

CHAPTER 4

The Crow's Nest

The Crow's Nest stands as one of the truly significant sites associated with the last day that Custer led his 7th U.S. Cavalry Regiment on the Little Big Horn campaign of 1876. The historical record substantiates that, on the morning of June 25, Custer climbed a high precipice in the Wolf Mountains that his Crow scouts had earlier reached. From this ridgetop, Custer looked west, seeking his first glimpse of his enemy's encampment on the distant Little Big Horn River. Try as he might, he failed to see it. Relying on the word of his scouts that the camp lay some ten miles or more to the west in the Little Big Horn Valley, he organized his regiment for its final movement to engage the enemy. In that sense, the Crow's Nest is the opening action in what was to become the Battle of the Little Big Horn, a gateway of sorts to what followed on that day.

Yet, despite the endless attention researchers have focused on the Crow's Nest, that geographic feature's physical location remains among the Little Big Horn landmarks most enshrouded in continuing mystery and debate. Author Bruce Liddic describes the vicinity as "a rough and broken land of elevations with sharp sides and deep narrow ravines." But, he adds, "this viewpoint's exact location is a source of puzzlement and debate among historians almost since the beginning."[1]

Beginning in the late 1890s early researcher Walter Camp spent more than twenty years researching the battle, while, in part, interviewing some two hundred participants and personally exploring the Reno Creek/Davis Creek backcountry. That search included seeking to unravel the mystery of the Crow's Nest's location. At one point he corresponded with Lt. Charles A. Varnum, who was chief of Custer's scouts in 1876. Varnum replied that the Crow's Nest was located "near the summit of a high ridge in the divide between the Rosebud and the Little Big Horn." Camp eventually concluded that the feature was close to the divide and at or near a site a local rancher would further identify in 1966. Camp stated: "Crow's Nest is about a mile east of the divide at the lowest point of the divide. Crow's Nest is a spur running 10 degrees west of N. The base of it is about 1/2 mile south of Custer's trail over the divide."

Accordingly, as Liddic notes, "Camp concluded after studying all the evidence, interviewing the participants, and personally traveling over the back country, the point where the scouts climbed in the early hours of the 25th was close to the divide and is what we know today as the Crow's Nest."

What we consider today as the Crow's Nest largely hinges on only one photograph that can be deemed historical, taken in 1919, and a decision in 1966 by a longtime Little Big Horn Valley rancher named Henry Weibert to erect

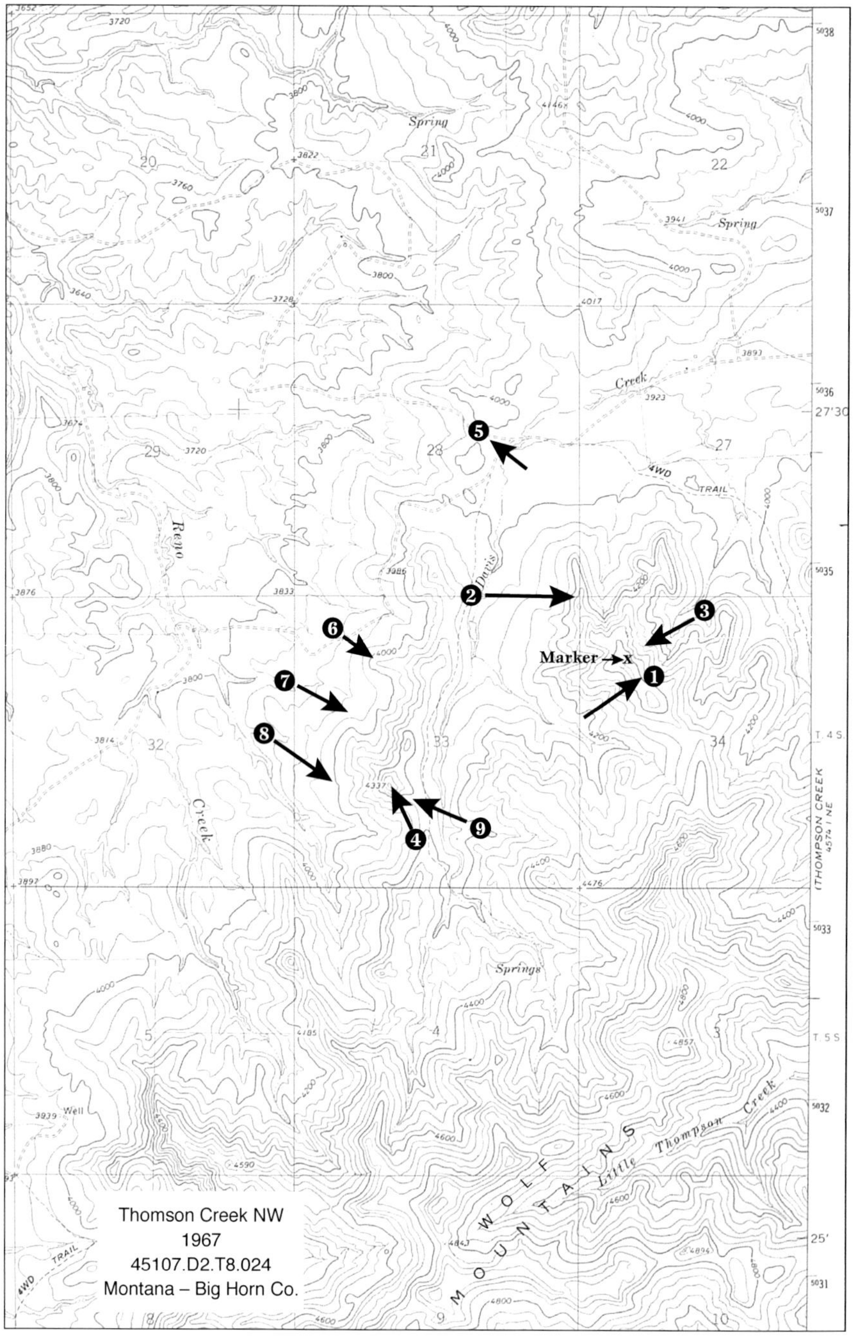

Map 4.1. Crow's Nest area. Map by Gary Raham, based on the 1967 USGS topographical map.

x = Camp marker

1. Fig. 4.2
2. Fig. 4.1
3. Fig. 4.3
4. Figs. 4.9–4.13
5. Figs. 5.1, 5.2, 5.3t
6. Fig. 4.5
7. Fig. 4.6
8. Fig. 4.7
9. Fig. 4.8

a marker on top of a ridge above the spot seen in that photograph.[2] Even that image fails to show the front of the ridgeline where Custer likely would have stood to look west toward the Little Big Horn. Instead, we see just the rear where Custer may have hidden his regiment to rest for its attack later that day. This amateur 1919 snapshot (fig. 4.2) shows Gen. Hugh Scott, a former 7th Cavalry regimental officer and later army chief of staff, standing on an overlook alongside Col. Tim McCoy, better known as a popular western film star. Standing to the general's right is White Man Runs Him, one of the Crow scouts who originally led Lieutenant Varnum to the Crow's Nest in 1876. Behind the group is a bowl-shaped depression where the troops may have

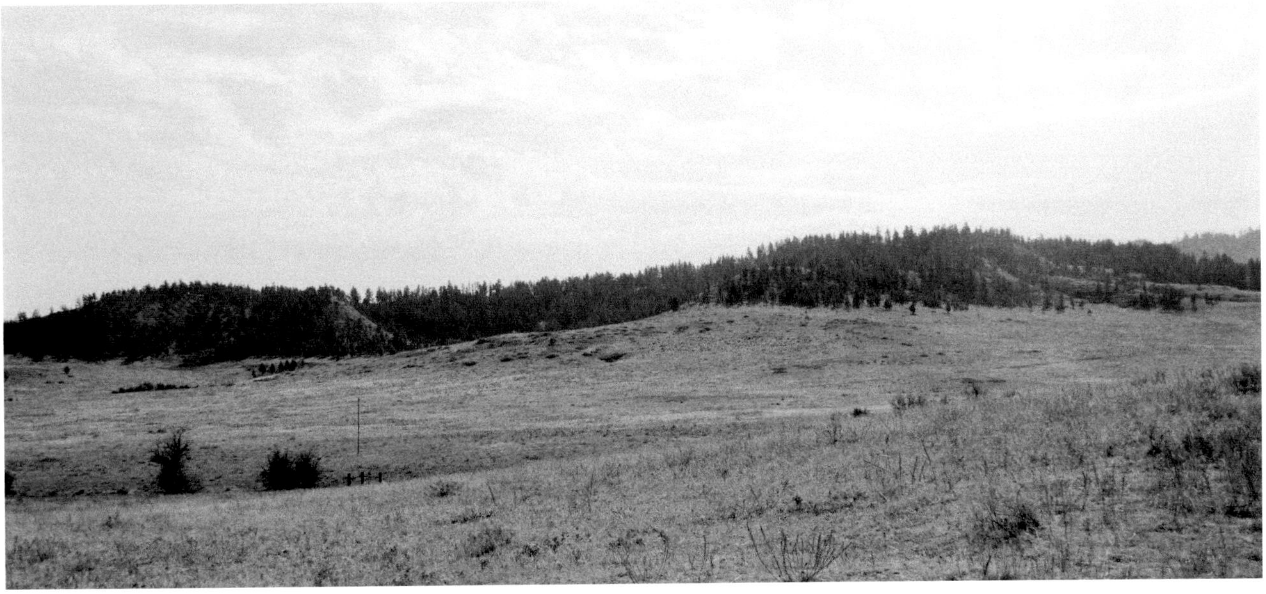

Figure 4.1. Modern view (2012) of the traditional Crow's Nest, first identified by Walter Camp and rediscovered in 1966 by Montana rancher Henry Weibert, who placed a marker atop the ridge (*right side in this photo*). Photo is looking east from the Davis Creek trail. Author's photo.

rested. The image first appeared in 1953 in Col. William A. Graham's classic book *The Custer Myth*.[3]

In 1966, Weibert relied on that photo to rediscover the location and to place a historical marker higher up and toward the front on the ridge.[4] The site in the photograph is clearly not the point from which Custer's scouts and later the general himself looked out upon the valley of the Little Big Horn. However, inasmuch as battle veteran White Man Runs Him guided the Scott party to that point, for almost fifty years battle students have valued that photo as solid evidence of the general location of the historic Crow's Nest.

A line of trees crosses the view in the low point of the depression. In the 1919 photo's upper left is Davis Creek, the route Custer's command followed on its way from the valley of the Rosebud (out of sight to the right of the photo) to the divide and onto the valley of the Little Big Horn. The divide itself, separating the Rosebud and Little Big Horn drainages, is about a quarter mile to the left and out of view. The term "Crow's Nest" refers to the depression itself seen in the middle background of the photograph and not to the Crow scouts themselves.

When Varnum wrote to Camp in 1909, he mentioned that the depression was on the Rosebud side of the Crow's Nest, and he estimated the distance from the observation point itself to the divide at a quarter to half a mile.[5] Though Varnum also recalled "quite a steep climb" to reach the top of the hill, he told Camp, significantly, "I can recall nothing particular to call your attention to just now." That suggests that prior to the battle he had paid little attention to the countryside, which loomed noteworthy only in the aftermath of the disastrous fighting later that day. This also underscores that prior to the battle most 7th Cavalrymen would have been unaware of their actual position in the surrounding wilderness.

In *Where Custer Fell*, we concluded that without the 1919 photograph the exact location of the Crow's Nest would remain uncertain. In reaching that

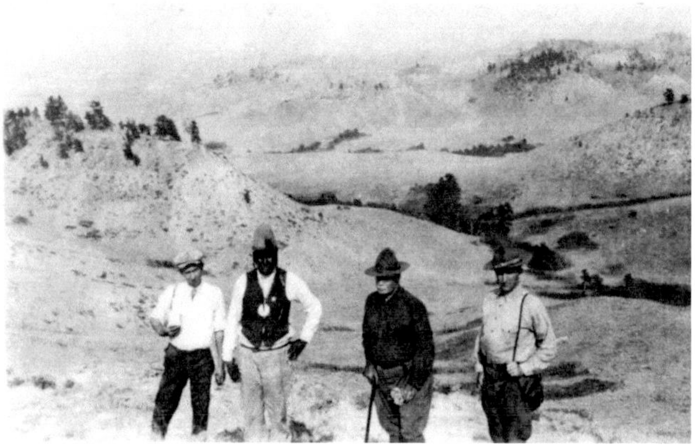

Figure 4.2. (*left*) General Hugh Scott at the Crow's Nest, 1919. Courtesy of Tim McCoy Collection and Glen Swanson.

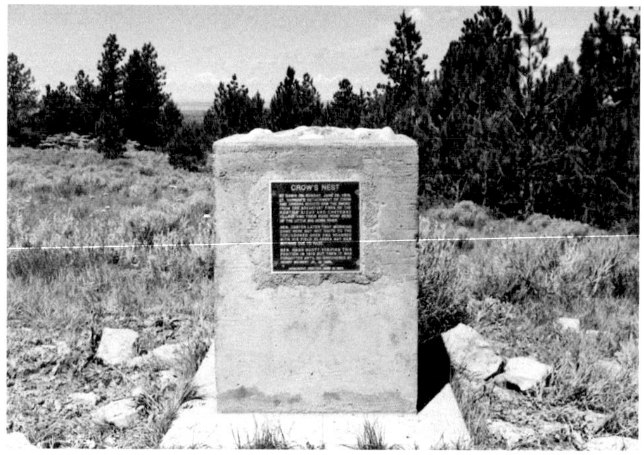

Figure 4.3. (*below*) Weibert's 1966 Crow's Nest marker, looking west, above the site where fig. 4.2 was taken. Courtesy of Dale Kosman.

decision, we overlooked the considerable efforts of a group of Montana residents—otherwise barely remembered Custer buffs—to pinpoint the Crow's Nest and numerous other sites associated with the 1876 campaign and battle. On May 30, 1961, about five years before Weibert's determination of the Crow's Nest, photographer Roahen and two Billings friends, George Osten and William Bellingham, trekked into the Reno Creek/Crow's Nest backcountry on a photo expedition. They repeated their efforts two years later, on October 18, 1963.

Roahen shot a series of photographs of a different high precipice that he labeled the "Crow's Nest," or the "Indian Crow's Nest"; if he took photos of the ridgeline White Man Runs Him pointed out in 1919, they are not contained in his collection at the Big Horn County Historical Museum. The two features are about a half mile apart. Roahen's site sits on the divide, whereas the ridge favored by Camp and Weibert as well as many modern researchers is about a quarter mile east of the divide. Weibert's exact site cannot be seen from the floor of the Davis Creek valley, but Roahen's so-called Indian Crow's Nest dominates the approach up Reno Creek. From its rocky top, one can view the headwaters of Davis Creek to the east and, just below and to its left front, the headwaters of Reno Creek.

Remember that Varnum could recall "nothing particular" about the site he had climbed. That would not be surprising to a modern researcher who visits Weibert's wide-ranging ridgetop, but Roahen's Crow's Nest is clearly a high

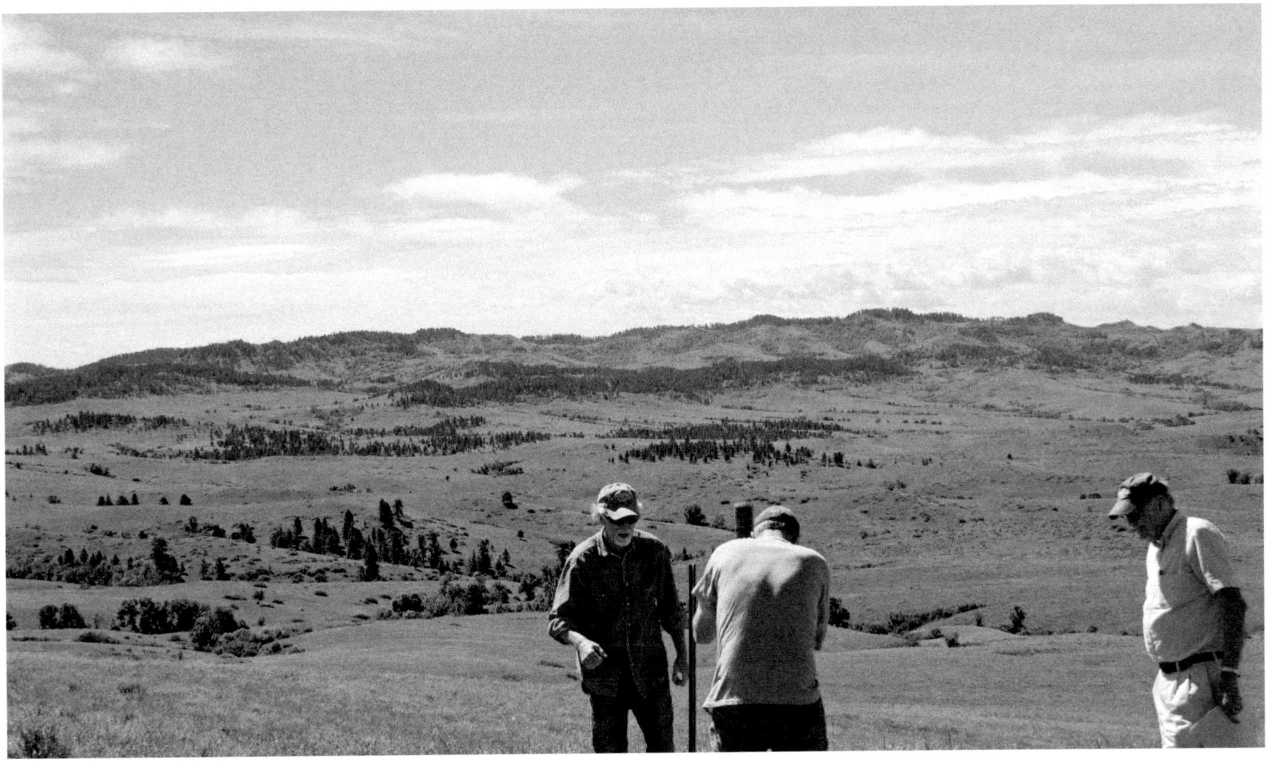

Figure 4.4. In this photo, taken a couple of miles from the respective Crow's Nest sites and looking east, both Weibert's and Roahen's choices can be seen. On the photo's left a grove of trees sits on a west slope of a lower ridge. Directly behind that ridge is another triangular tree-covered one. Above that area would be the Camp/Weibert Crow's Nest. This photo was taken June 26, 2013, when Don Horn, Jr. (*left, facing camera*), Lowell Smith (*middle, back to camera*), and Bruce Liddic (*right*) led a group of Little Big Horn Associates members who were prepping to lead a tour for attendees at the Associates' conference a few days later. Smith placed a steel post for members to use to locate Weibert Crow's Nest. By coincidence, straight above that post, in the center of the lower ridge, which is the Rosebud Creek–Little Big Horn divide, the rocky top of Roahen's Indian Crow's Nest can be seen.

spot, a virtual "crow's nest" from a seafarer's viewpoint. The depression below the Weibert site better fits the historical description of a secure place for hiding troops; behind Roahen's feature lies a wide open valley that could have held a regiment, but it may not have afforded as much cover and protection.

In other words, the historical record does not reconcile opposing theories about the Crow's Nest's true location. Certainly, Camp stands as a highly credible figure among battle researchers, and Weibert himself lived many decades in the Little Big Horn Valley. Weibert, who died in 1997, befriended several decades of battle students, including many members of the Little Big Horn Associates and CBHMA. His ranch on Reno Creek Road, above the place where Major Reno's battalion originally crossed the Little Big Horn River, often served as a way station for his visitors.[6] The 1919 photo with General Scott and White Man Runs Him that he relied on would seemingly be hard to dismiss.

Yet Kenneth Roahen and George Osten, as sleuths investigating the greater campaign and battle story, also cannot be dismissed, even if their names may be less familiar today. They, too, spent decades living with and researching the battle. Osten himself was born about 1888 in Iowa and appears in Billings in the 1920 federal census.[7] Researcher William Boyes wrote that Osten moved to Billings in 1913. Osten lived for seven decades in the Montana city, until his death in April 1983.[8] From 1931 to 1945, Osten was active in city government and served as Yellowstone County clerk. He also hosted the fiftieth anniversary observances at Custer Battlefield in 1926 and personally transported the now retired General Godfrey and his wife to various events.[9] Roahen arrived

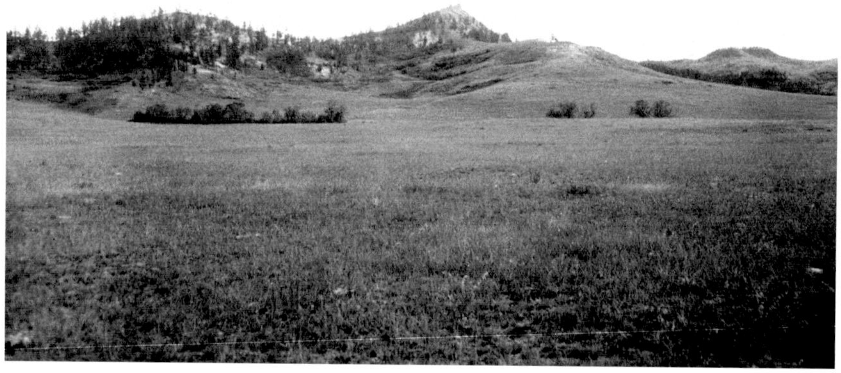

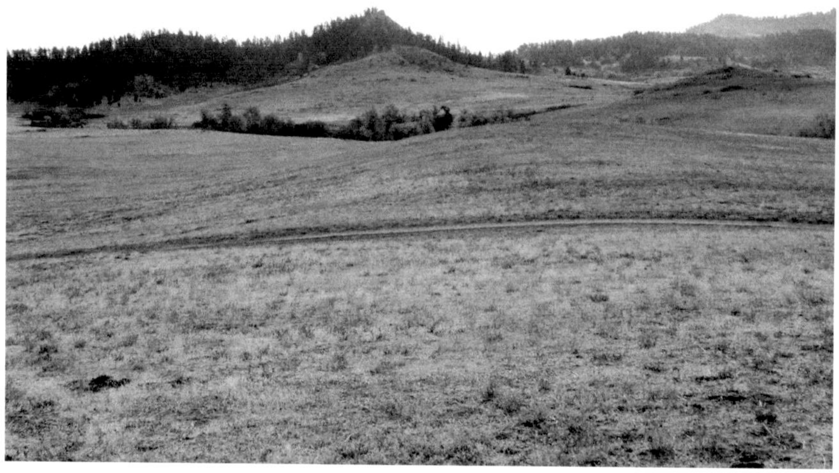

Figure 4.5. (*top*) Roahen's Indian Crow's Nest. The rocky peak he identified as the Indian Crow's Nest can be seen in the photograph's center. Courtesy of Big Horn County Historical Museum. (*bottom*) The peak in 2012 is more tree-covered. Both photos are looking east.

in Billings in late 1930 and may have photographed the Crow's Nest and other Little Big Horn sites almost immediately.[10]

In his early years in Billings, Osten could have met Walter Camp, and he certainly knew other early battle researchers such as Fred Dustin, E. A. Brininstool, Charles Kuhlman, and William A. Graham. After 1930, Roahen, too, would have been familiar with such men. Dustin, for one, may have been their source for believing the high point in Roahen's photographs was the actual Crow's Nest. In his classic book *The Custer Tragedy*, Dustin includes

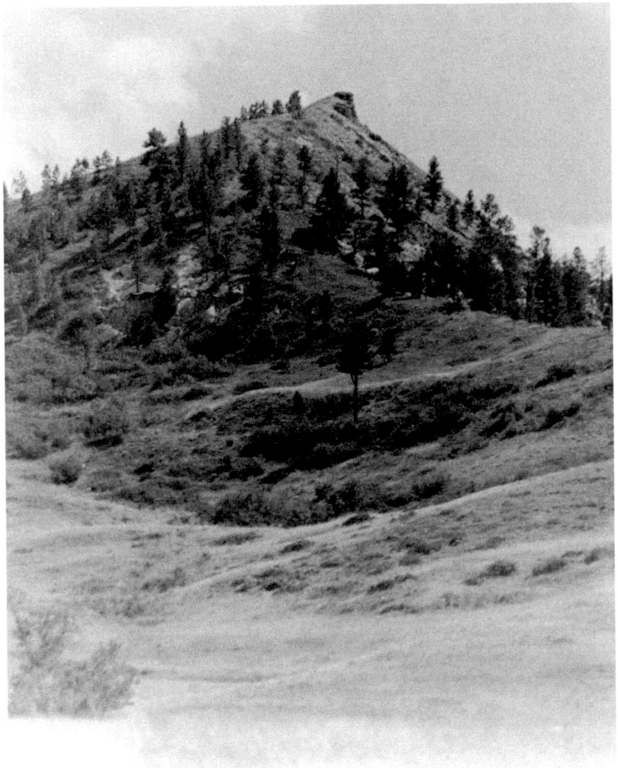

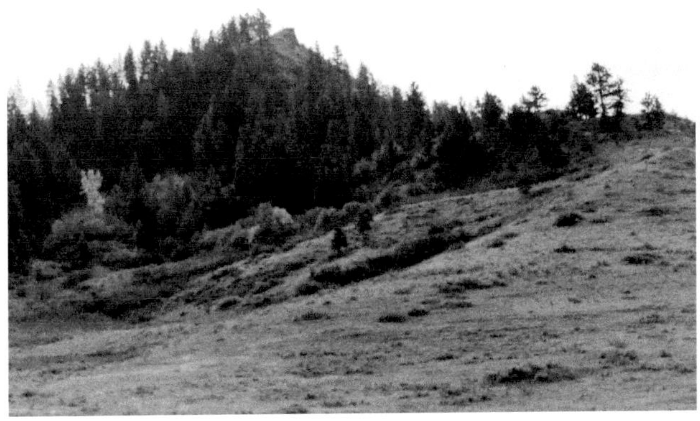

Figure 4.6. (*left*) Roahen close-up of his Indian Crow's Nest, looking east. Whether his comrades and he ascended the peak from its front or back is unknown. His photograph reveals that a frontal approach would have been possible in 1961 and 1963. Courtesy of Big Horn County Historical Museum. (*below*) The hill in 2012 is much more heavily vegetated. We drove around the Rosebud Creek–Little Big Horn divide and ascended the hill from its rear along Davis Creek.

a footnote with a physical description of the Crow's Nest: "The True Crow's Nest is a rounded, oval hill directly southeast of where the great trail crosses the divide, a half mile less from the Camp marker. This hill is exactly on the divide, and from it about everything of note that could be seen from the higher peak was observable from its summit. A few pine trees are growing on it, and were in 1876, forming a slight screen from observation from the Reno Creek Valley. It was easily ascended, especially from the trail where it crossed the divide, and from a little branch of Davis Creek that had its beginnings forty rods southeast."[11]

His description perfectly matches the physical location of Roahen's peak. In fact, on September 30, 2012, my party ascended Roahen's Crow's Nest from the trail to the rear, just above Davis Creek. The climb may not have been as easy as Dustin describes it, but we encountered no challenges in making our way to the top. Dustin refers to it as a peak, a descriptive term that does not fit the Weibert/Camp ridge near the 1919 photo site.

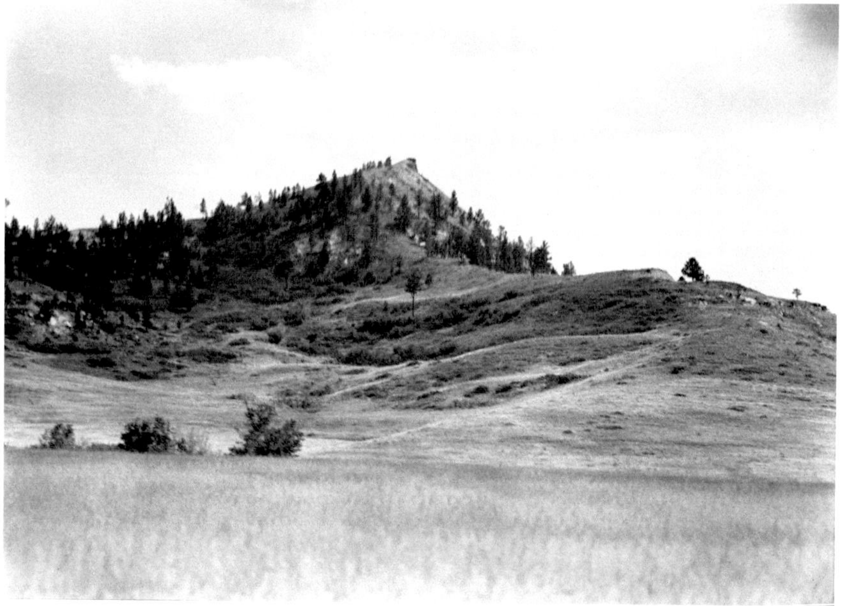

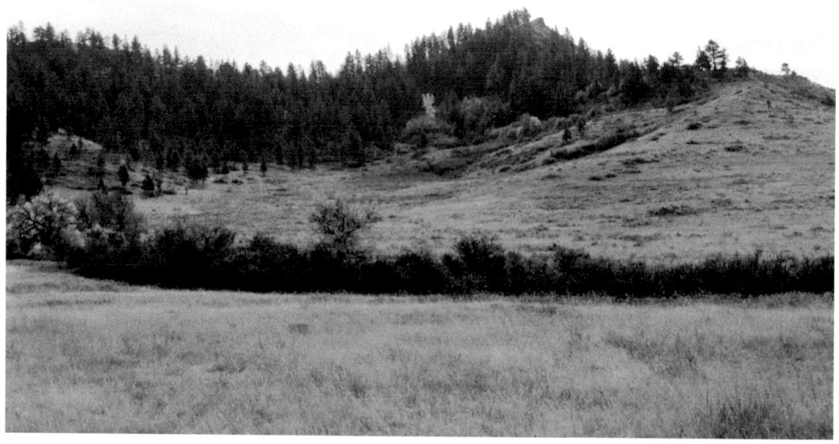

Figure 4.7. (*top*) Wider view of Roahen's fig. 4.6. It is unclear whether both were shot the same year, but vegetation on the hill appears to be about the same. Courtesy of Big Horn County Historical Museum. (*bottom*) Modern view (2012).

A much earlier description of the Crow's Nest can be found in the papers of renowned photographer Edward S. Curtis. In Volume 3 of his epic *The North American Indian*, Curtis described his visit to the site with three of the Crow scouts, including White Man Runs Him, in August 1907: "This outlook, which affords a splendid view of the entire region, is about fifteen miles from the encampment site and is at the head of Davis creek, which flows into the Rosebud, and Middle Reno creek, which empties into the Little Bighorn."[12] If Curtis was describing the Roahen site, that would seemingly call

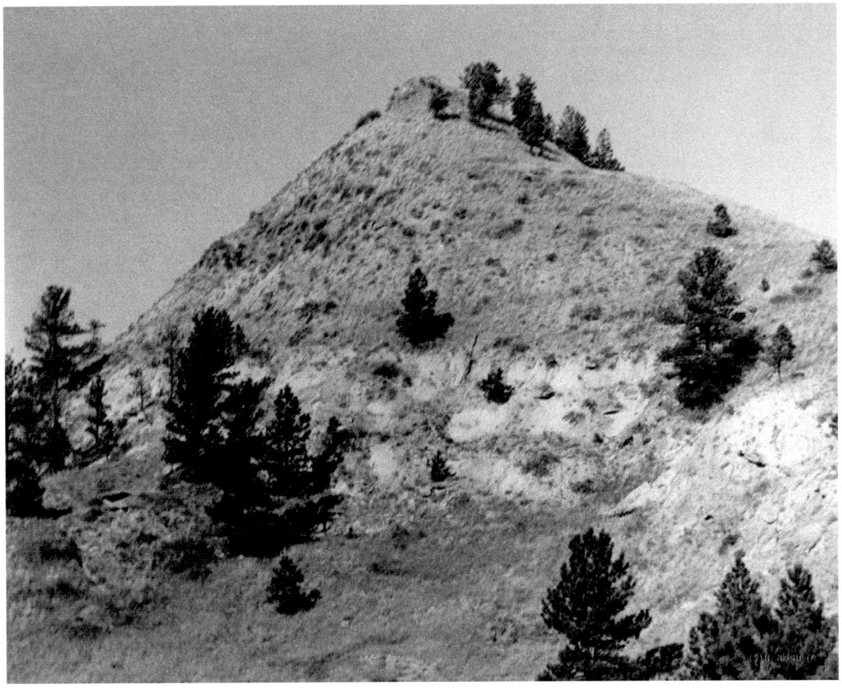

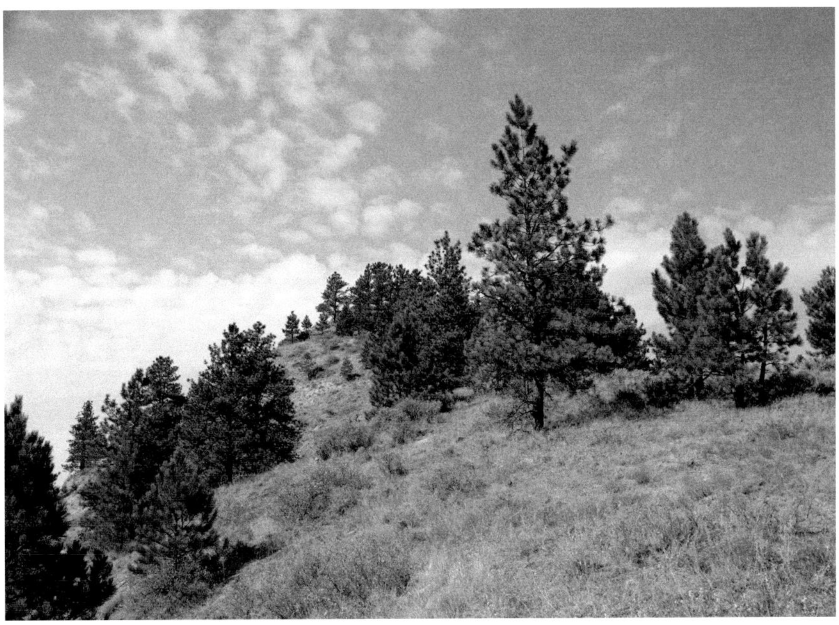

Figure 4.8. (*top*) Rear of the Indian Crow's Nest, October 18, 1963. This photo suggests that Roahen and his friends climbed to the top from the rear, or its east slope. Courtesy of Big Horn County Historical Museum. (*bottom*) Today's divide (2012) is more heavily forested than in Roahen's era, making a more accurate match for Roahen's original impossible.

into question the decision by White Man Runs Him in 1919 to take the Scott party to a different location.

Osten and Roahen's close friendship with Edward S. Luce, the battlefield's most historically influential superintendent, afforded the two men unfettered access to the battlefield for fifteen years. In the 1950s and 1960s, they enjoyed equally close ties with Don Rickey, one of the battlefield's significant historians. In that period, Roahen also photographed various battlefields for historian Jesse W. Vaughn, a Windsor, Colorado, attorney who wrote numerous books about the Indian wars. Vaughn, also an avocational archaeologist, was

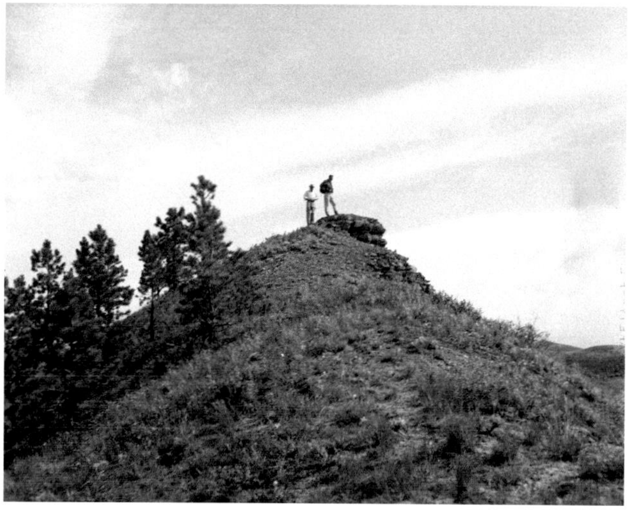

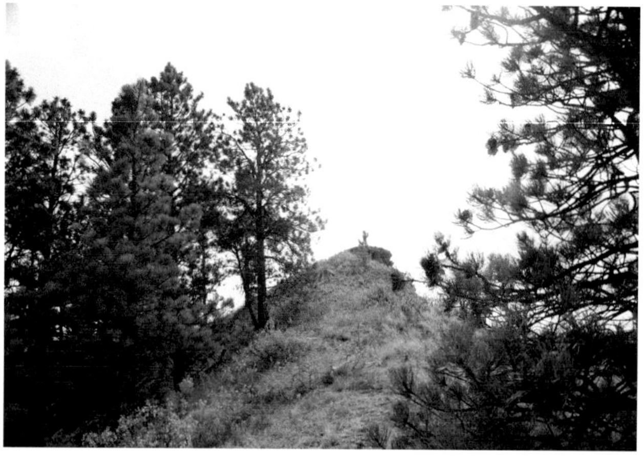

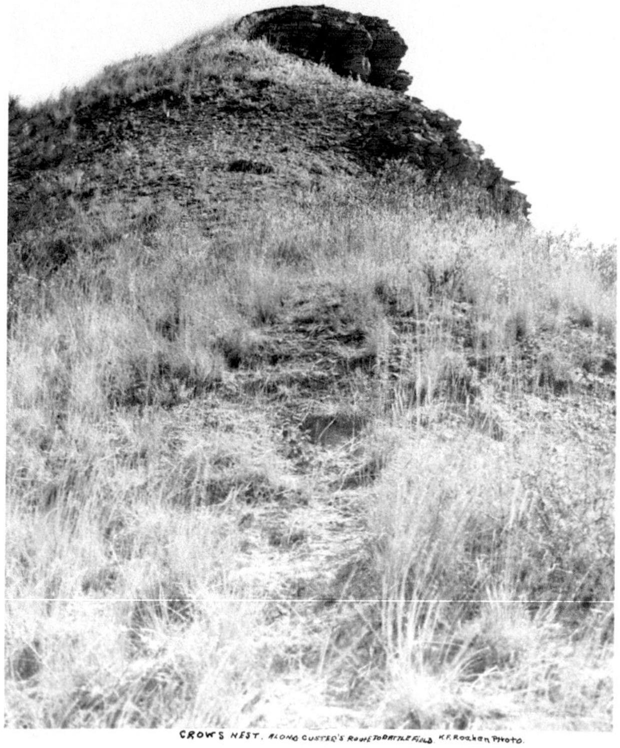

Figure 4.9. (*top left*) George Osten (*left*) and William Bellingham on top of the Indian Crow's Nest on May 30, 1961. To shoot this photograph of his friends, Roahen stood on the front slope aiming toward the peak. Courtesy of Big Horn County Historical Museum. (*bottom*) The 2012 photo is a nice match, but the hill today is more heavily tree-covered.

Figure 4.10. (*top right*) Crow's Nest, October 18, 1963, appears as a variant of fig. 4.9, minus the two men. Not only is this one dated, it also contains in Roahen's handwriting his important statement identifying this site as "Crow's Nest, along Custer's route to Battlefield." Courtesy of Big Horn County Historical Museum.

one of the first researchers to rely on advances in metal detector technology to support his battlefield surveys.[13]

In other words, Osten and Roahen's roots into the Custer story go deep. Their thoughts as well as Roahen's photographs stand as equally credible. Their own research makes equally good fodder for the continuing debate about the whereabouts of the Crow's Nest and other landmarks of the Little Big Horn battle. So who is right?

As Bruce Liddic noted, "All this is interesting for debate among historians but what effect did it have on the coming battle? What difference did it make if the scouts ascended this hill or 'Varnum's Lookout' or another unknown hill? The view reported would be the same and the actions of the regiment [were] based upon the scene described from whatever the viewpoint. Its location would not have changed anything on this Sunday."[14]

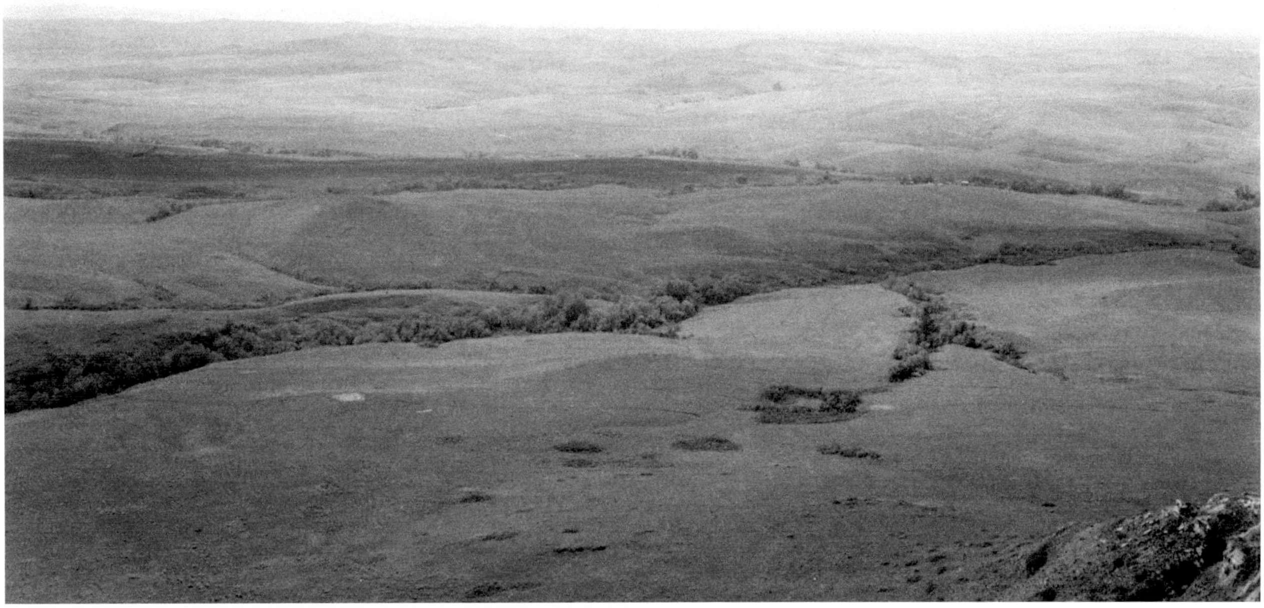

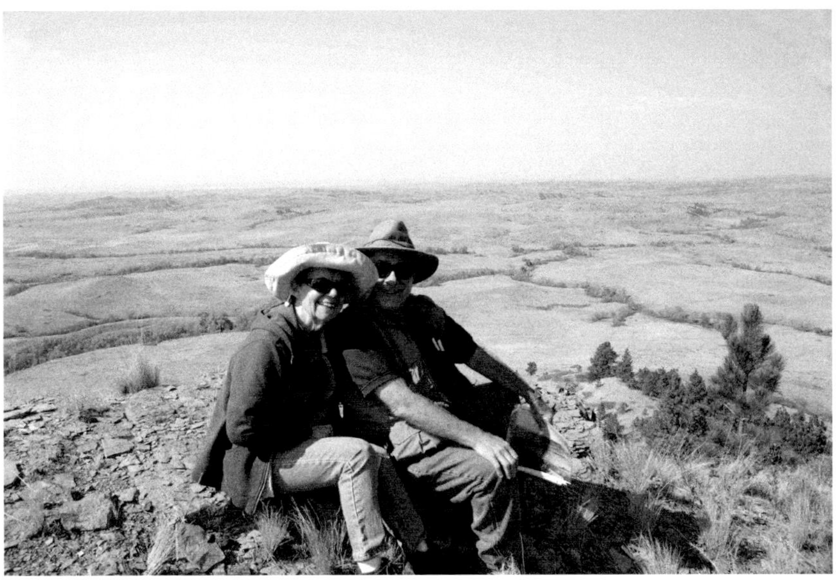

Figure 4.11. (*top*) Looking southwest at the headwaters of Reno Creek. Roahen stood on top of the Indian Crow's Nest to make this image. Courtesy of Big Horn County Historical Museum. (*bottom*) The 2012 reshoot reveals the creek's similar configuration today in a broader perspective. It also shows that the peak remains rocky and dominates the approach up the creek. Pictured are author Sandy Barnard and his wife, Betty.

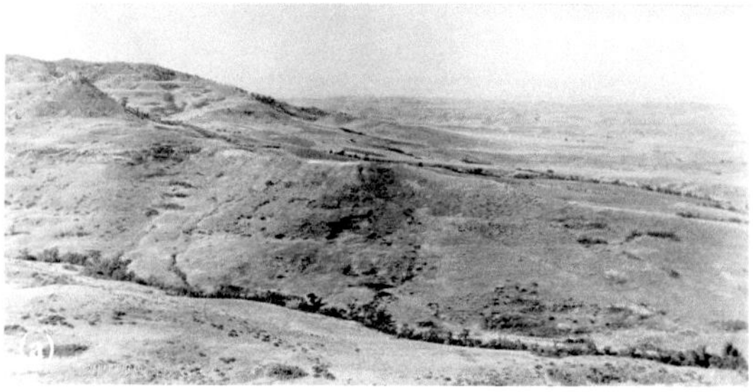

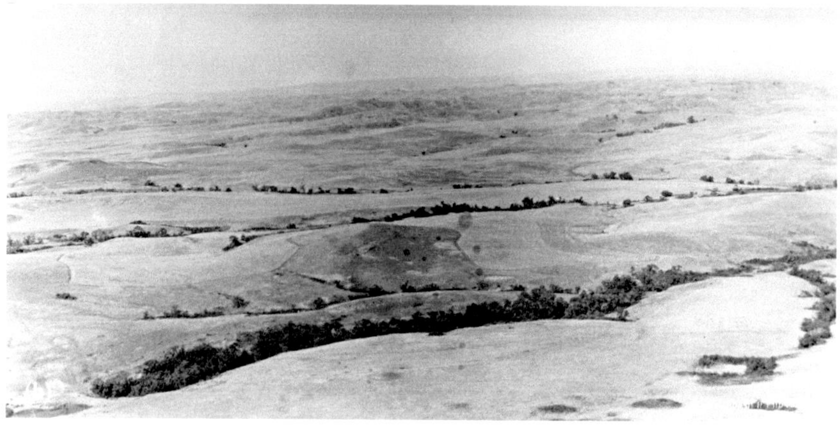

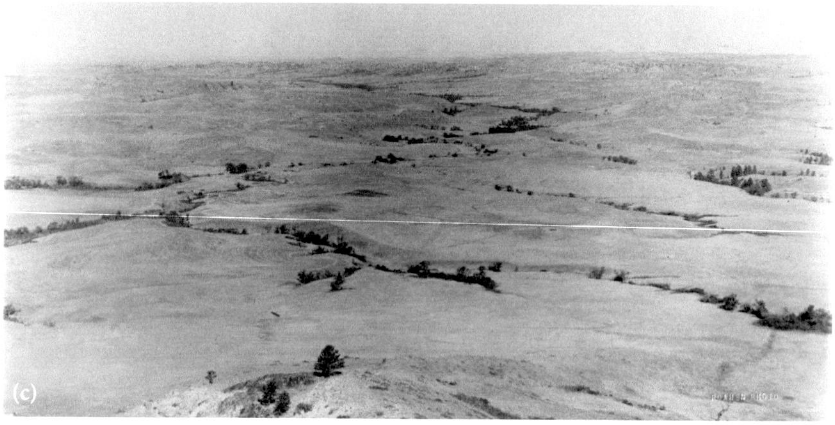

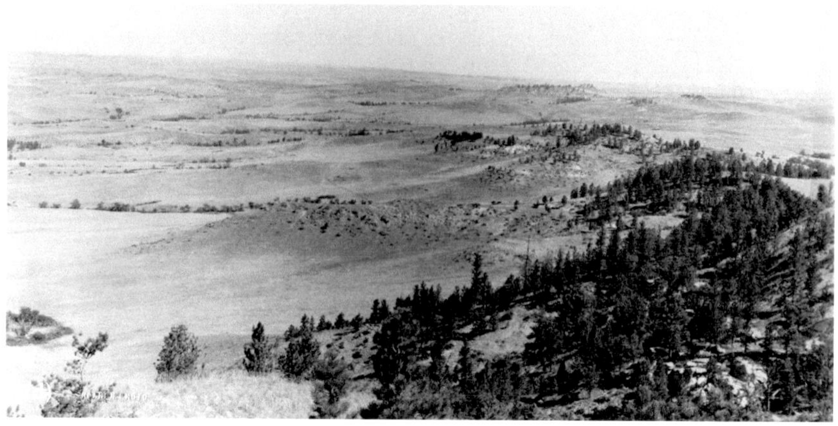

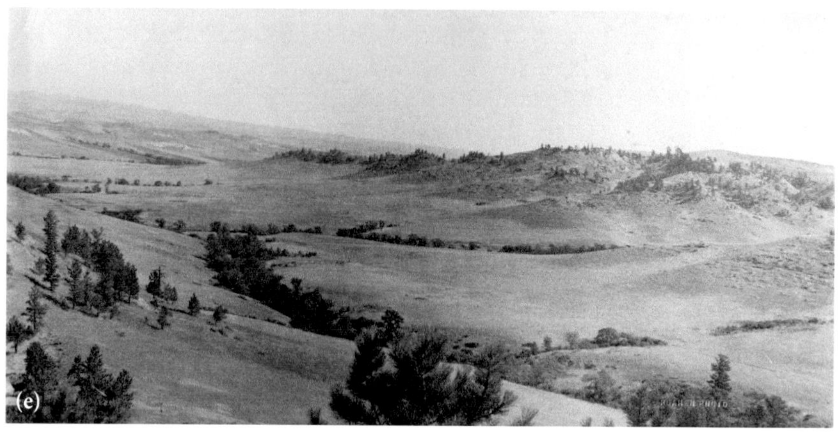

Figure 4.12. Roahen's west-looking panorama. Roahen shot five separate images but joined them with fabric tape to create a panoramic view of the Reno Creek valley below and the divide. (a) shows the headwaters of Reno Creek, which run between the Indian Crow's Nest and the next ridge. In (b), Reno Creek is in the foreground and Captain Benteen's scout area appears in the background, center to right. Photo (c) is looking down Reno Creek along the route to the Little Big Horn River. Reno Creek appears as the near creek on the left of the photo. It is joined by two other water courses, first from the right and then the left, before threading its way across the photo toward a gap in the ridges in the upper center. Photo (d) is to the right of center. The tree-lined ridge is the divide. Just behind the divide, toward the top of the photo's right side, can be seen Davis Creek. Photo (e) is looking down Davis Creek with the divide to the left. The creek runs immediately behind and at the base of the divide. All photos courtesy of Big Horn County Historical Museum.

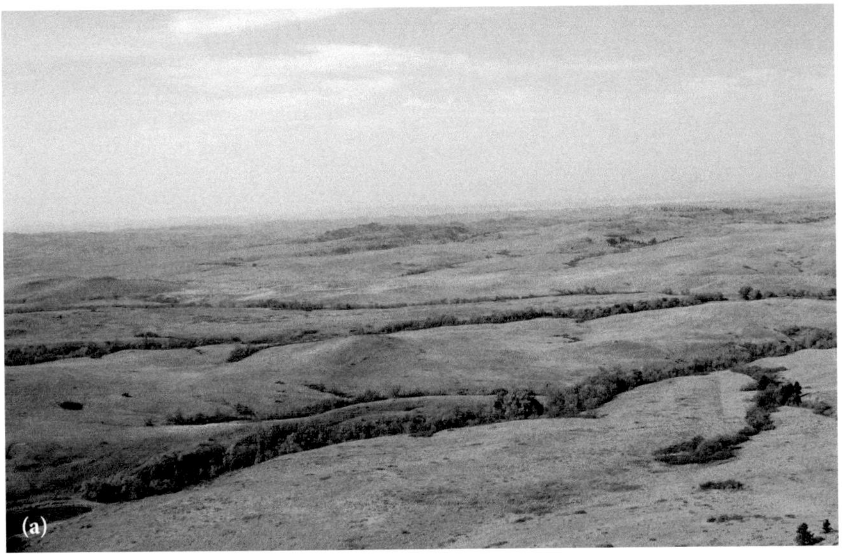

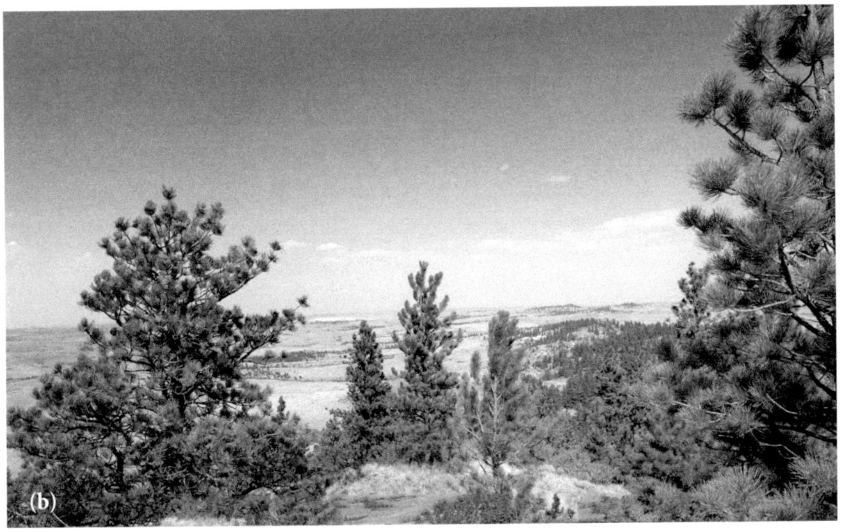

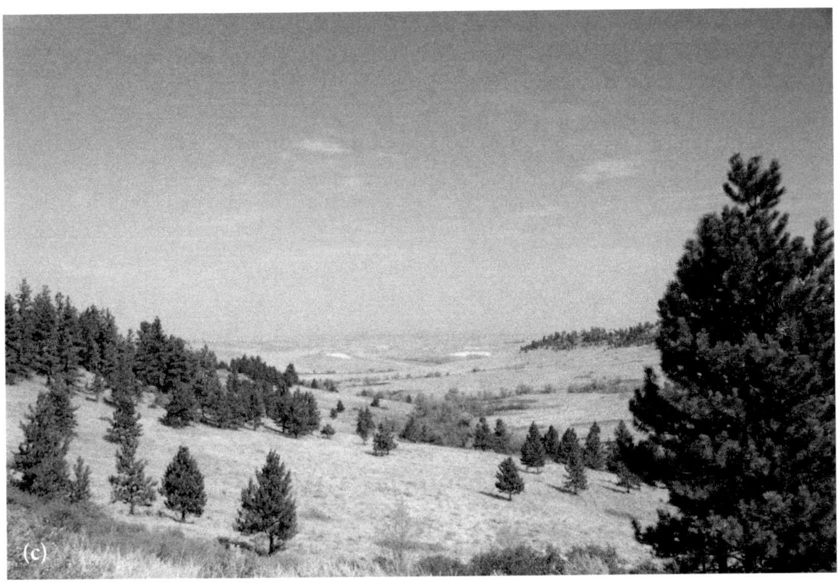

Figure 4.13. (a) This 2012 photo is essentially a match for Roahen's Reno Creek image (fig. 4.12b). Note how similar the countryside is. The dammed-up pond in this modern reshoot can be seen in the lower left corner of Roahen's original 1961 photo. (b) Two photographs were merged to create a match for Roahen's figs. 4.12c and d looking northwest. Heavy vegetation made creating a more accurate panorama from atop the Indian Crow's Nest impossible. Today's trees are more plentiful and taller than in Roahen's day more than sixty years ago. On the modern photo's far left, Reno Creek can be seen, although the tree soon blocks the view. On the photo's right side, beyond the tall tree, can be seen the slopes of the divide. Photo (c), looking north, provides a near match for Roahen's fig. 4.12e. The rear of the divide is on the left looking down Davis Creek, seen at the base. Roahen's photo 4.12a at left was not matched.

CHAPTER 5

Walter Camp's Marker on the Divide

By 1917, Walter M. Camp had spent nearly two decades researching the Little Big Horn battle and other Indian wars engagements.[1] He had previously befriended Peter Thompson, a Little Big Horn Medal of Honor recipient who may have been among the last soldiers to see Custer alive, and visited the battlefield with the ex-cavalryman.

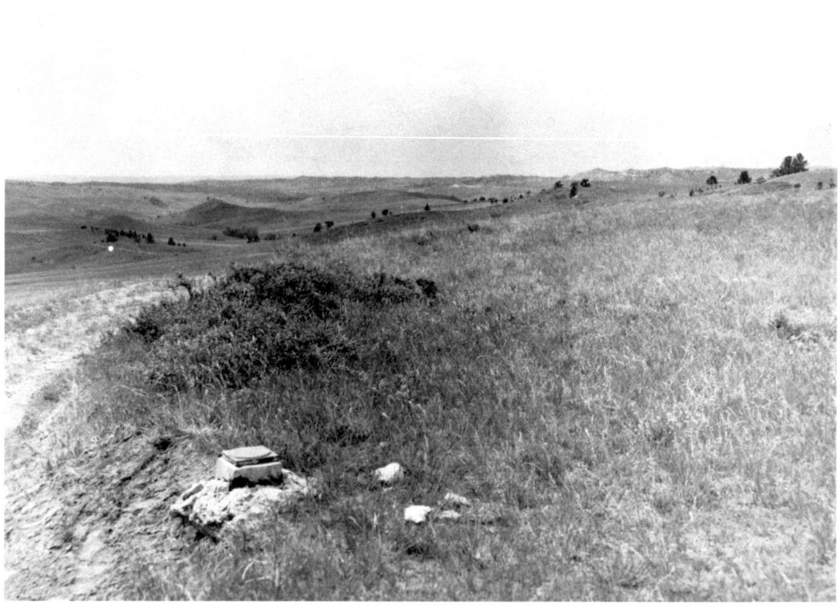

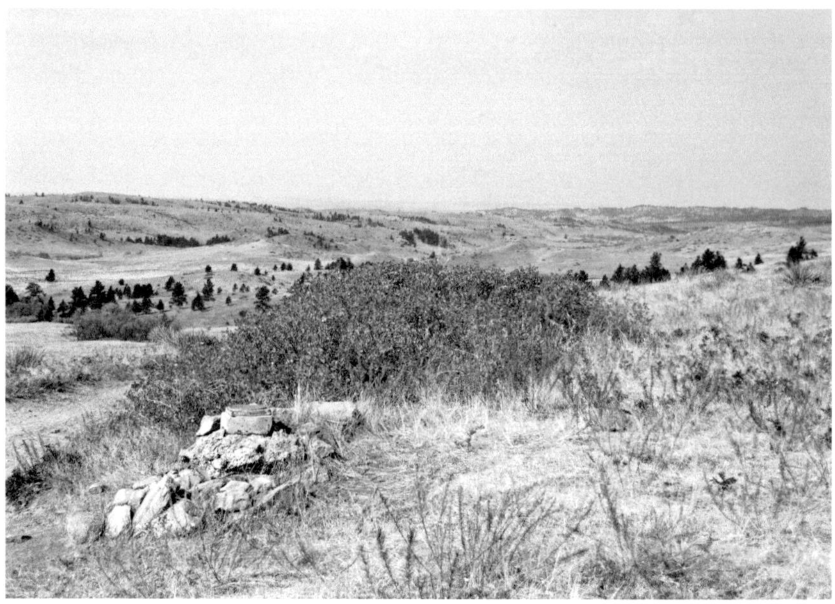

Figure 5.1. (*top*) Camp's divide marker in context. Courtesy of Big Horn County Historical Museum. (*bottom*) Today's Camp marker site, looking west, appears similar to when Roahen shot his photo in the early 1960s. On the distant hills a few more trees appear, and brush behind the marker has grown considerably. The dirt trail has deepened with the passage of time, which may have eroded the soil in front of the marker. As a result, people have piled up rocks to protect the marker and its base.

That year, Thompson invited Camp to accompany him on a hunting expedition into the Big Horn Mountains. By August 4, Camp had reached Sheridan, Wyoming, and planned to travel with Thompson for the next ten days. That schedule soon grew to eighteen days. By August 24, the men had reached a point on the divide between the valleys of the Rosebud and the Little Big Horn. With Camp was M. L. Wilson, a representative of the Montana Historical Society, which had asked the researcher to place a historic marker on the spot where Custer and his regiment had crossed on June 25, 1876. "This marker consisted of a circular brass tablet, eight inches in diameter, riveted to a square plate of cast-iron, one inch thick, the latter set three feet in the ground and projecting a foot above ground. The tablet laid horizontally on top of the pillar and had the following stamped inscription, 'General George A. Custer and the Seventh U.S. Cavalry Crossed the Divide at This Point, June 25, 1876.'"[2]

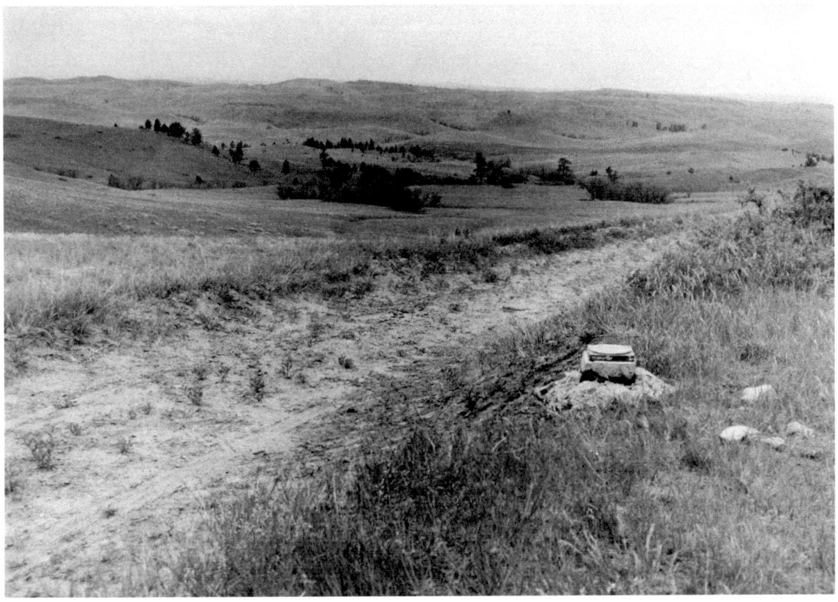

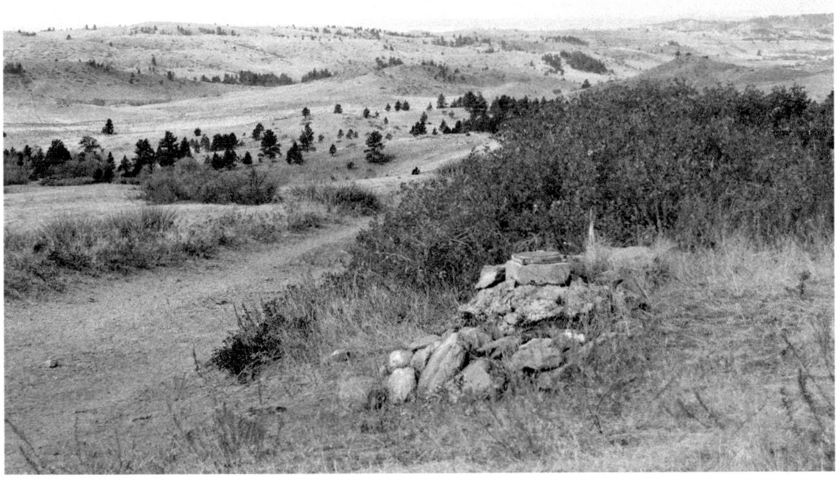

Figure 5.2. (*top*) Another view of the Camp marker; inasmuch as it was taken at some later date, it reveals more wear in front of the marker. Courtesy of Big Horn County Historical Museum. (*bottom*) The wear evident in Roahen's photo required building the rock support seen in this modern photo.

In his report to the Montana Historical Society, Camp noted that the crossing site had been pointed out to him by Crow scout Curly on August 4, 1909, and by another scout, George Herendeen, on July 27, 1910. After Camp placed the marker, Herendeen revisited the site and confirmed that it was in the proper location.

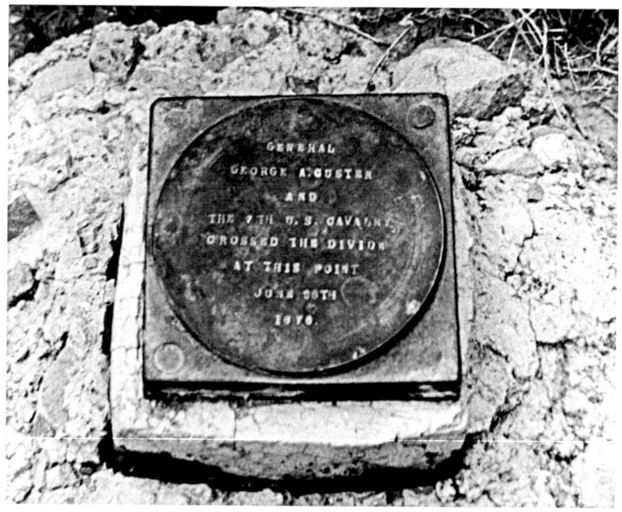

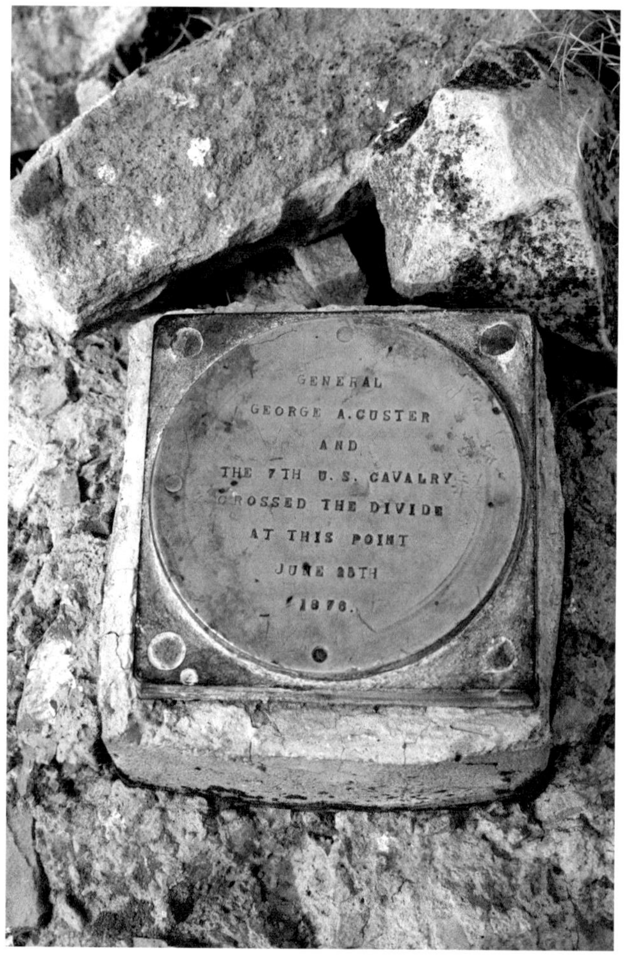

Figure 5.3. (*top*) Camp divide marker, presumably taken in either 1961 or 1963. Courtesy of Big Horn County Historical Museum. (*bottom*) Modern (2012) reshoot.

CHAPTER 6

From the Divide to Reno Creek

Two Roahen photographs (figs. 6.1 and 6.2) appear quite similar and likely were made at the same time on August 18, 1962. I first thought that they might have been taken from the top of Roahen's Crow's Nest, but modern reshoots failed to line up the land features properly. More likely, they were taken along the front of the divide itself, looking generally west, but from where could not be determined. Figure 6.2 strongly suggests Roahen's main objective is Reno Creek itself, which runs between the two high ridges that dominate that photo. The modern photo in figure 6.1, which was cropped to match the countryside in Roahen's image more closely, was taken about two hundred yards south of the ridge on which the Camp marker sits. Still, the exact sites remain unconfirmed.

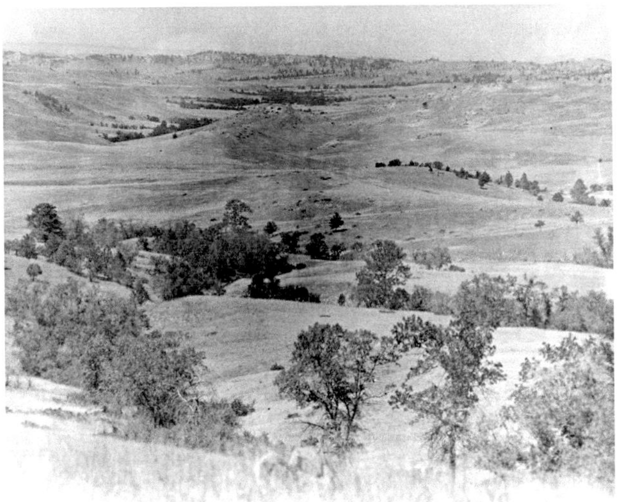

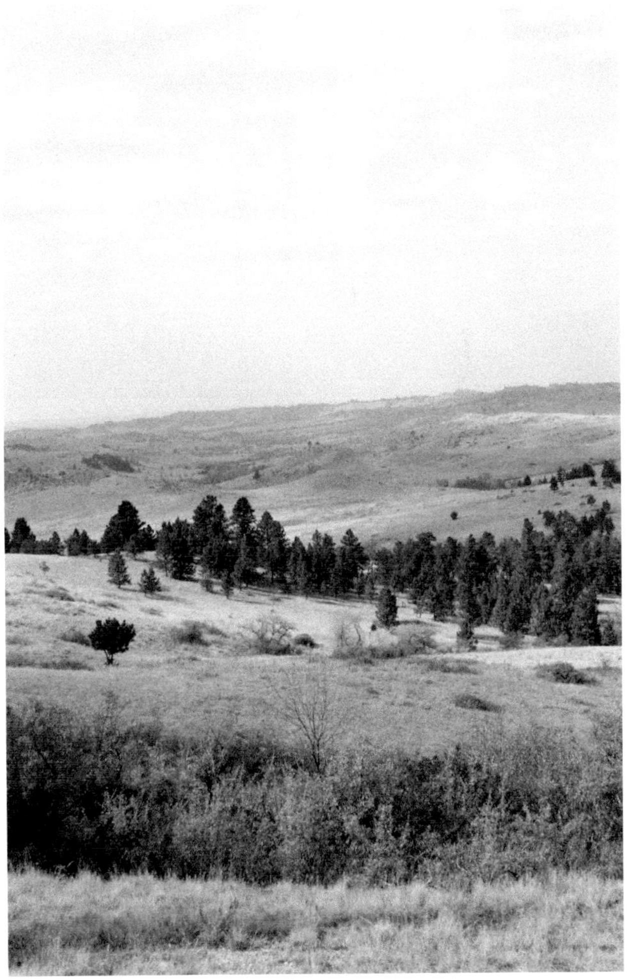

Figure 6.1. (*above*) From the Rosebud Creek–Little Big Horn divide to Reno Creek backcountry, looking west. Courtesy of Big Horn County Historical Museum. (*right*) Modern (2012) reshoot.

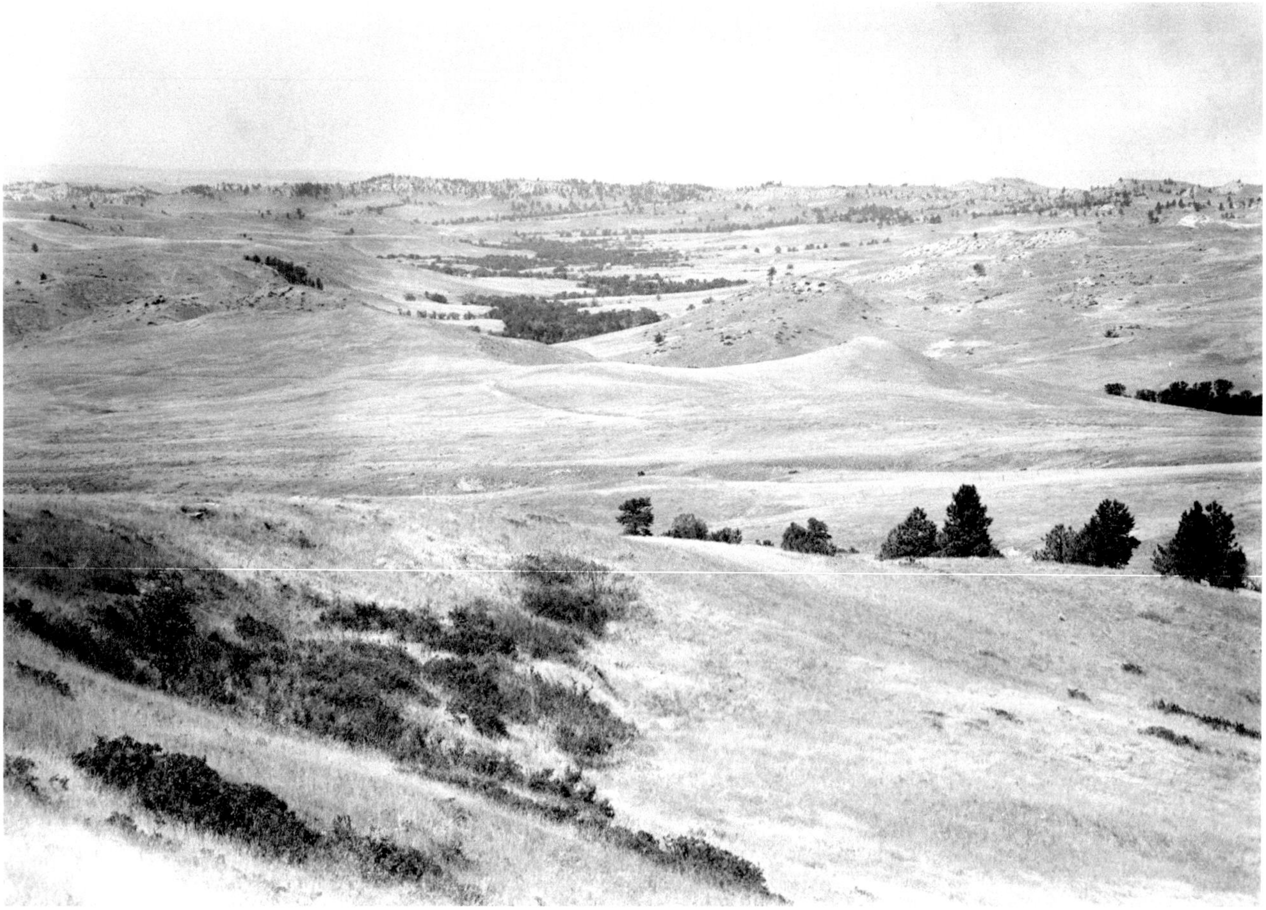

Figure 6.2. Reno Creek, August 18, 1962, looking west. Courtesy of Big Horn County Historical Museum.

CHAPTER 7

The Morass

As the first decade of the twentieth century was closing, Walter Camp remained busy trying to confirm details of Custer's last fight. In September 1908 and August 1909, he traveled to the battlefield on extended research trips with companions who included several battle survivors. Chief among them was Sgt. Daniel Kanipe (often Knipe), who in 1876 had served as a messenger from Custer to the pack train, a fortunate assignment that ensured his survival. More important, he passed the site of what became known as the Morass at least three times: once on Custer's initial advance down Reno Creek; second, on his own ride back to the pack train; and, finally, on his return ride from the pack train toward the site of the Reno-Benteen defense.

Numerous battle survivors mentioned the place labeled the Morass as a swampy area where elements of Custer's command paused to water their horses, but until Camp's fieldwork the specific site was largely unknown. Camp was a meticulous researcher as well as a talented photographer and map maker. He used both skills to augment what he learned by walking the field. Up to now, only two historical photographs of the Morass were known to exist, both taken by Camp in either 1908 or 1909 (figs. 7.1 and 7.2). Undoubtedly, his

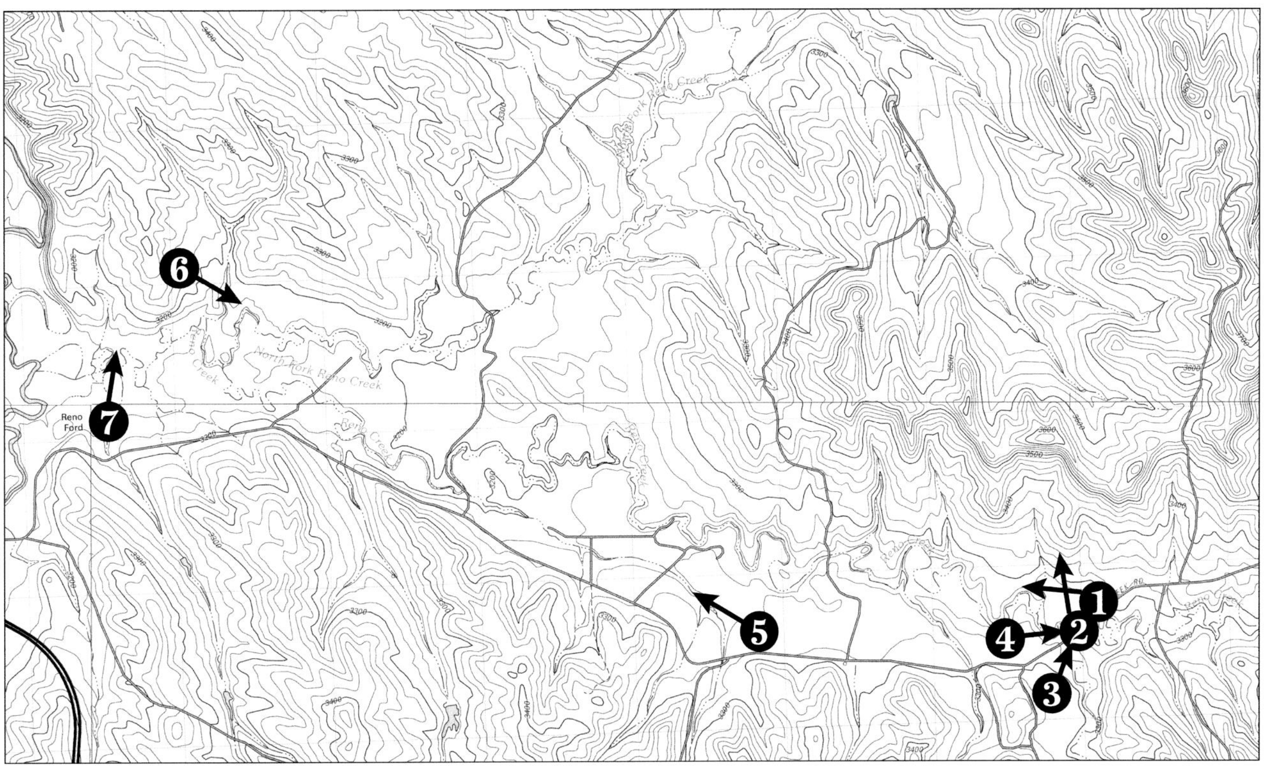

Map 7.1. The Morass, Girard's Knoll, and Reno's first crossing. USGS Quad: Lodgegrass NE Montana (image enlarged). Map by Gary Raham.

1. Fig. 7.8
2. Figs. 7.3, 7.4, 7.5
3. Fig. 7.1
4. Fig. 7.3
5. Fig. 8.1
6. Fig. 8.2
7. Figs. 9.1, 9.3–9.6

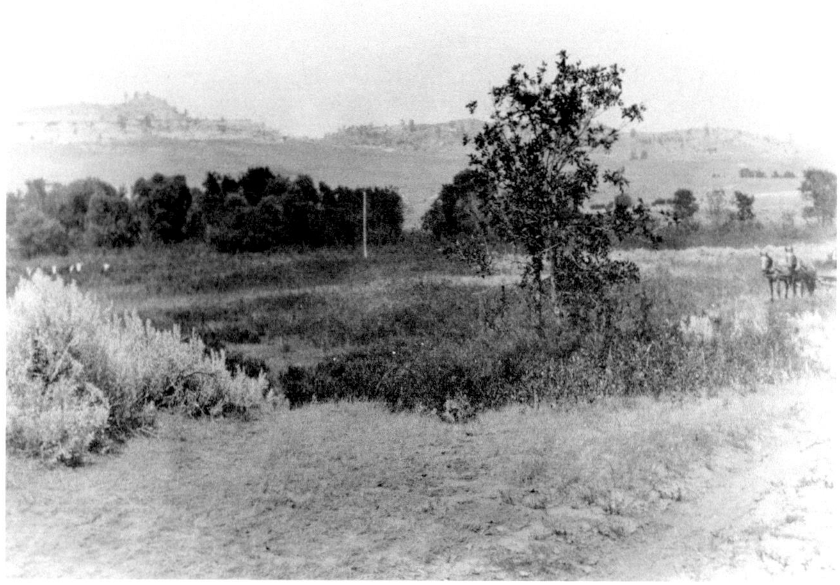

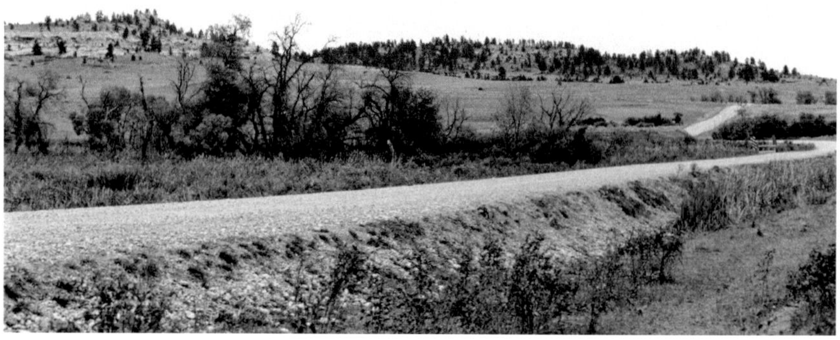

Figure 7.1. (*top*) Photo titled "Morass area along Reno Creek," by Walter Camp, 1908 or 1909. Courtesy of Little Bighorn Battlefield National Monument, no. 11254. (*bottom*) Modern (2000) reshoot. Courtesy of James S. Brust.

source for this identification had been Sergeant Kanipe. His fig. 7.2 appeared in *Where Custer Fell*, and his other, more general view, simply labeled "Morass," was published in the 1998 *Greasy Grass* magazine accompanying an article by Michael Donahue documenting Camp's and Kanipe's relationship.[1]

Today the Morass can be easily located along Reno Creek Road, four to five miles east of the Little Big Horn River. As Camp noted on an undated map he drew, probably on one of his trips with Kanipe, the Morass is where the South Fork of Reno Creek meets the Middle Fork to create the swampy area. Today the two forks meet just south of a modern bridge carrying the roadbed, which stands well above the trail that existed in Camp's day or likely

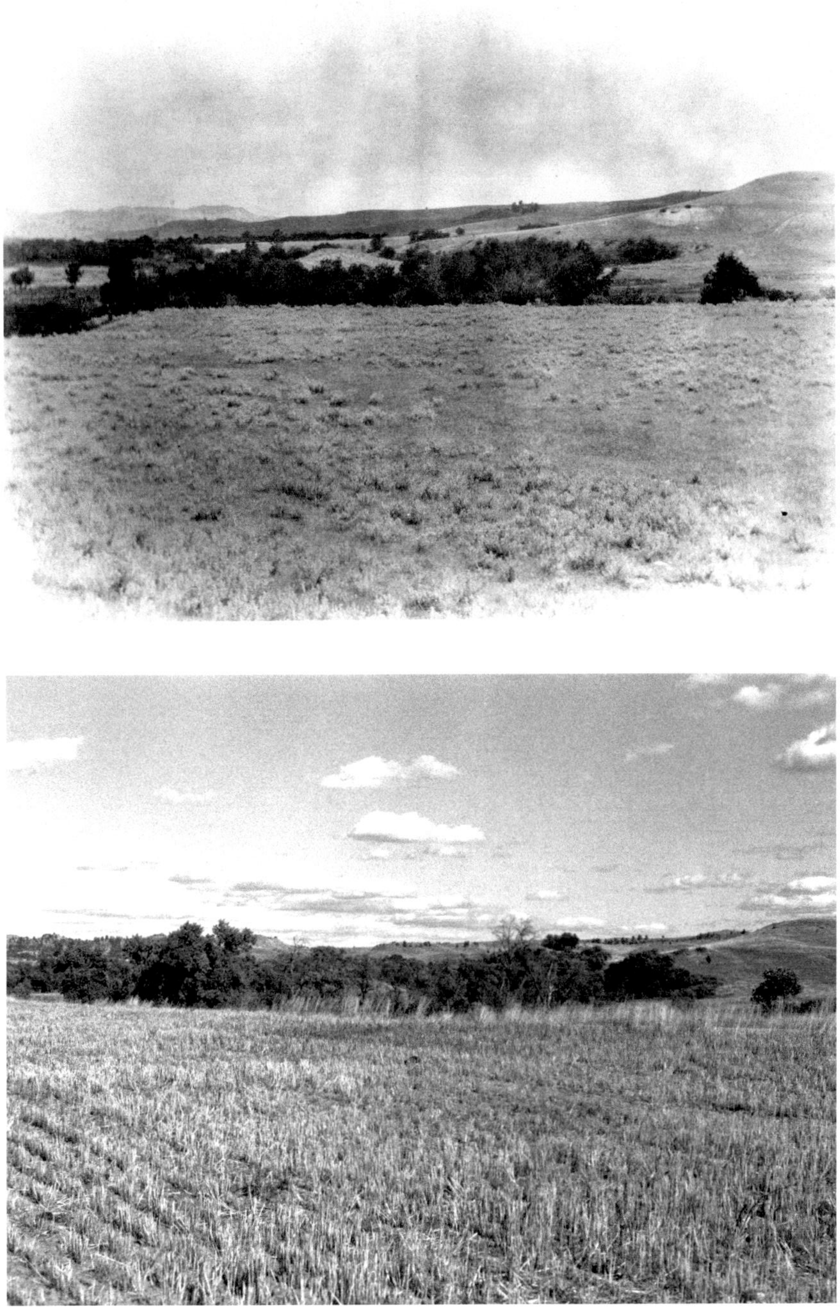

Figure 7.2. (*top*) Camp photo of the Morass, ca. 1908–1909. Courtesy of Little Bighorn Battlefield National Monument, no. 11253. (*bottom*) Modern (1999) reshoot. Courtesy of James S. Brust.

even more than sixty years ago when Roahen photographed the scene. Today's Reno Creek Road, which is visible in figure 7.1, has clearly been raised much higher, undoubtedly for flood reasons.

In the early 1960s when Roahen took his three images (figs. 7.3, 7.4, and 7.5), the area was quite dry, as evident in his photos. In figure 7.3, George Osten (foreground) and William Bellingham are running their metal detectors over the creek bed. Vegetation is much greater as well. Compare that to modern figure 7.6, a 2012 photo, which essentially matches Roahen's images. The now merged Reno forks are flowing through the area.

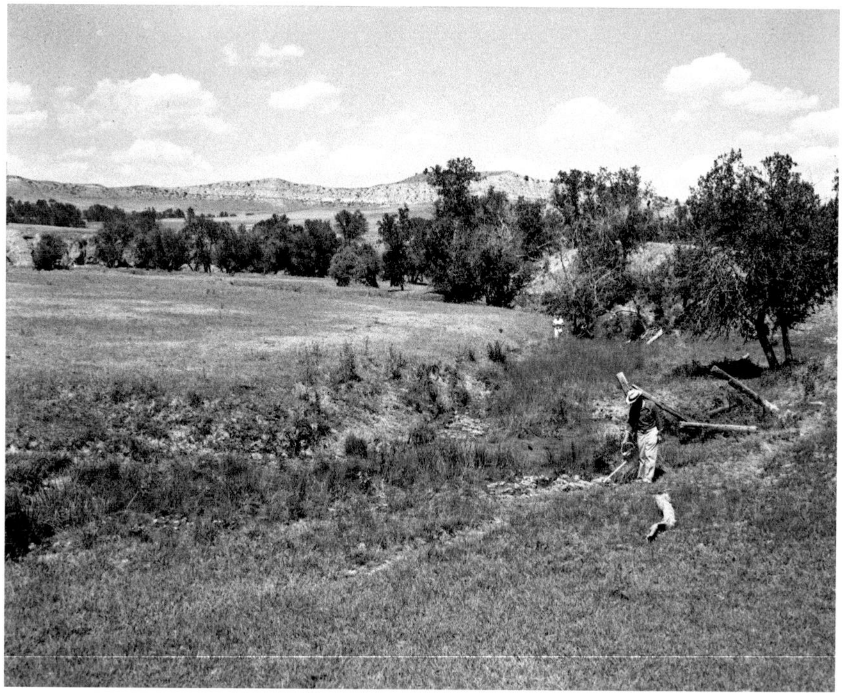

Figure 7.3 Morass with metal detector. George Osten, foreground; William Bellingham, background. Courtesy of Big Horn County Historical Museum.

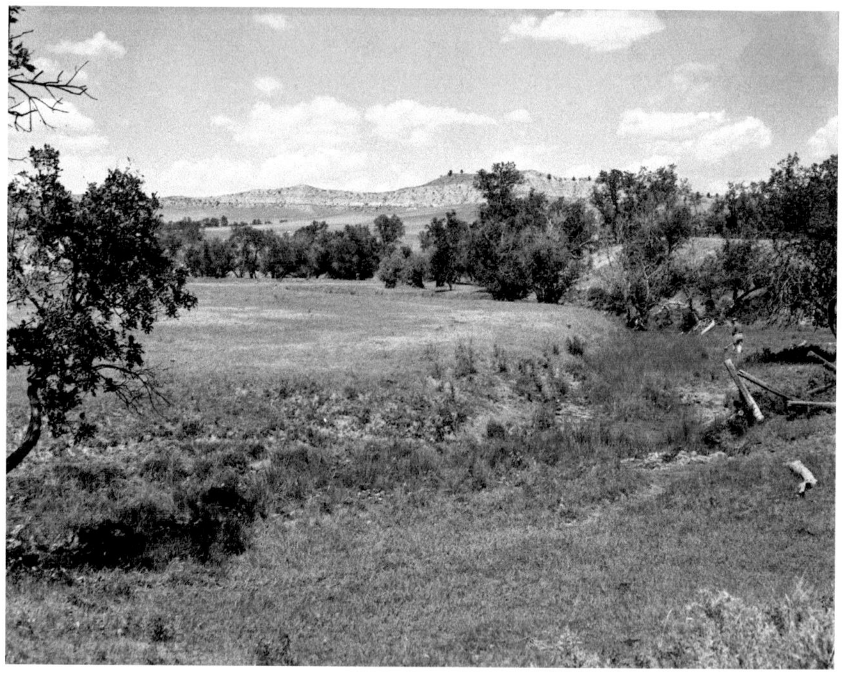

Figure 7.4. Morass with another metal detector, variant of fig. 7.3, probably taken at the same time although only Osten is visible in the creek bed. Courtesy of Big Horn County Historical Museum.

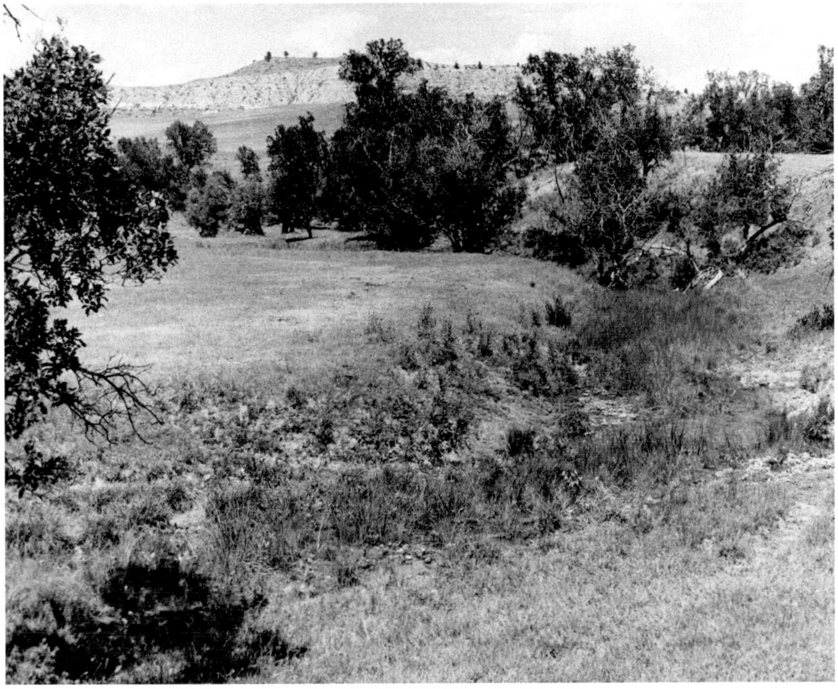

Figure 7.5. Another variant of fig. 7.3, although neither of Roahen's friends can be seen. Note how high the berm is on the east compared to modern fig. 7.6. Courtesy of Big Horn County Historical Museum.

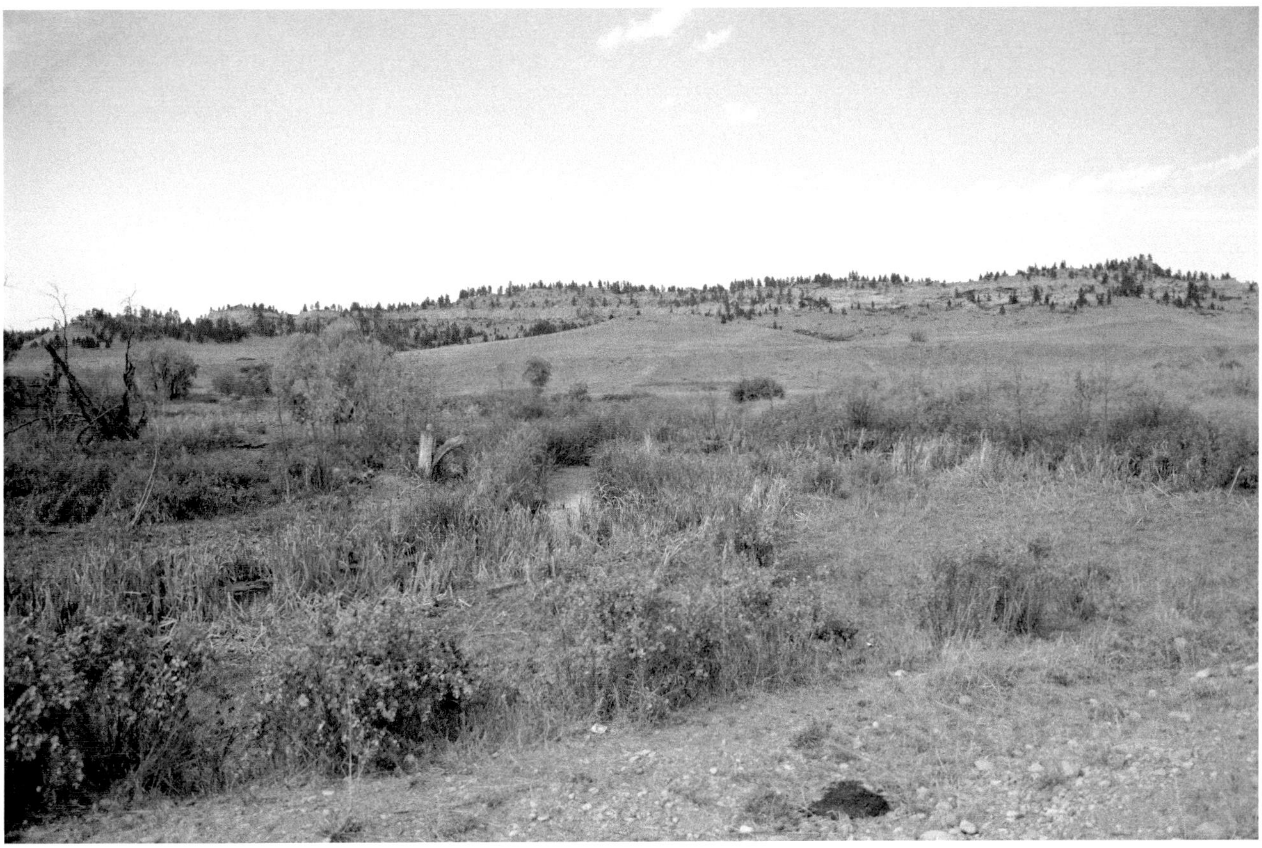

Figure 7.6. 2012 counterpart to Roahen's figs. 7.3, 7.4, and 7.5.

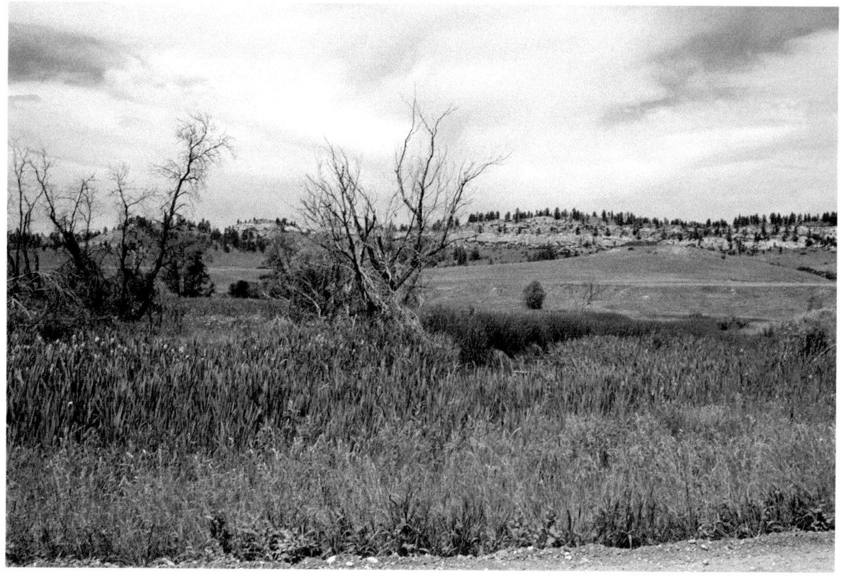

Figure 7.7. This photo from June 30, 2003, reveals how weather can dramatically alter the appearance of the Morass.

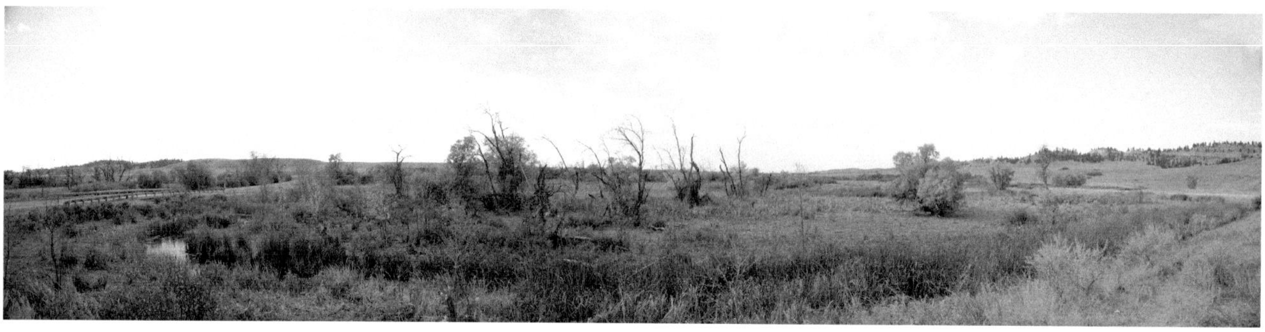

Figure 7.8. 2012 panorama of the Morass, looking from the berm on its east to the west, down Reno Creek toward the Little Big Horn River; created by combining several images taken from atop the now lower berm.

Figure 7.7 offers another view of the same area, from 2003; at that time, the area resembled more of the swampy body of water that historical accounts suggest the 7th Cavalry found in 1876. Also significant, in modern figure 7.6 the berm that appears on the right side of Roahen's photos has been substantially reduced in size. The lower roadbed in the 1960s might account for some of that, but in 2012 it was impossible to find an angle that raised the berm to the height seen in Roahen's trio of images.

Figure 7.8 is a panorama taken in 2012, looking from the berm from east to west, down Reno Creek toward the distant Little Big Horn River. The modern bridge across the creek splits the Morass in half.

CHAPTER 8

Girard's Knoll

It seems incontestable that, as the 7th U.S. Cavalry moved down Reno Creek, at some point scout Fred Girard (sometimes Gerard) yelled to General Custer from a high knoll, "There go your Indians, running like devils!"[1]

Which knoll along that route Girard actually stood on remains in dispute today. A second issue concerns how far up Reno Creek the 7th Cavalry was from the Little Big Horn River: three quarters of a mile, several miles, or somewhere in between. Related to the debate about Girard's Knoll are two other questions: where is the actual location of another landmark, today referred to as the Lone Tepee, and how many tepees were viewed by the passing command?

As the 7th Cavalry descended Reno Creek, troopers observed heavy clouds of dust a couple of miles in front of their advancing columns and believed the Indians were fleeing. Girard rode to the top of a nearby knoll, which may or may not have been a short distance from the Lone Tepee site, and yelled his alert to Custer. Girard's warning and his observations convinced Custer to alter his plans. He issued orders, either personally or through his adjutant, Lt. W. W. Cooke, for Major Reno to take his three companies, cross the Little Big Horn River, and attack the fleeing Indians. Supposedly, Reno was told that his attack force would be supported by the rest of the command, but exactly what that meant Custer never made clear to his subordinate. Reno undoubtedly expected Custer to follow as a reinforcing force behind him; instead, Custer moved north along the bluffs above the river, "in support," and into history.

As for Girard's location, his visit to the knoll and his yell to Custer all occurred in a fleeting moment when everyone was more focused on fleeing Indians, not where a single scout happened to be standing. That the actual locations of the two sites should remain mired in debate is not a surprise.

Tom Bookwalter, a Dayton, Ohio, attorney, is the modern researcher with the most expertise on the subject. In a 2009 article for the Little Big Horn Associates *Research Review*, Bookwalter pointed out how unreliable most researchers' estimates of the distance from the Little Big Horn River to the Lone Tepee have been, ranging from three-fourths of a mile to six and one-half miles. Earlier, in his classic booklet *The Search for the Lone Tepee*, published in 1983, he had concluded that the landmark was "located on the north bank of Reno Creek one mile west of the junction of the Middle and South Forks which is approximately three and one-half miles in a straight line east of the mouth of Reno Creek."[2] Many battle students accept Bookwalter's conclusion, shared with his coauthor, Ray Meketa, but it still lacks universal agreement.

In his 2009 article, Bookwalter summarizes these other theories, but in the end he reaffirms his belief in the location he cited in 1983.

Interestingly, Roahen's collection at the Big Horn County Historical Museum contains no photos of the Lone Tepee site. Roahen presumably photographed such a site, but, if so, the images remain to be discovered, either in private collections or in the holdings of another museum. Nonetheless, Bookwalter's research remains pertinent to locating another landmark on Custer's approach to the Little Big Horn—Girard's Knoll.

In his publications, Bookwalter places Girard's Knoll directly above his Lone Tepee site several miles from the mouth of Reno Creek. But other researchers locate it closer to the Little Big Horn, as Roahen's photos suggest. The qualification is necessary, because no photo in his collection actually is marked "This is Girard's Knoll." Several reveal the vicinity as well as the knoll that Roahen and his friend, George Osten, believed was the correct site.

Roahen's figure 8.1 was taken about a mile west of the Morass on a knoll that provides a turnout for vehicles from Reno Creek Road. From that site one has a superb view of the Reno Creek valley to the west and northwest as well as the bluffs above the creek closer to the river. Portions of the Reno-Benteen Defense Site also can be seen in his photo.

To shoot other photos, Roahen went to the other side of the valley onto the bluffs below the Company H position at the end of the Reno-Benteen acreage protected by the National Park Service. In his collection are three images, all of which show portions of the Reno Creek valley as well as a finger that descends from whatever knoll the photographer was standing on at the time. Because the three Roahen images overlap, I created a panorama of them, figure 8.2. No markings appear on those three images to indicate what they depict, but Hardin resident Dennis Fox owns a personal copy of one of the three photographs. On its reverse appears, in Roahen's pencil handwriting, "Girard's Knoll." That suggests that Roahen shot the photo from what he believed was Girard's knoll, but from which specific high point has not yet been determined.

Because this land is privately owned, during this project we did not venture closer to the edge of the bluffs. Fortunately, two earlier researchers, William W. Boyes and Keith McDougall, had crossed that land in the late 1960s, and Boyes summarized their findings in the Summer 2009 *Research Review.*[3] He noted that none other than George Osten had placed the Lone Tepee much closer to the Little Big Horn, perhaps three quarters of a mile. Furthermore, in a conversation they had on October 12, 1976, Osten told him, "There has to be two lone tepees because I can't believe experienced cavalry officers, some of whom spent their entire military careers on the plains, could be so danged wrong—or even worse—would lie or fabricate such figures as high as five or six miles back."

Boyes also cites the theories of McDougall, another long-time Little Big Horn Associates member-researcher who also believed in two lone tepee sites. Boyes and McDougall walked from the Reno battlefield south along

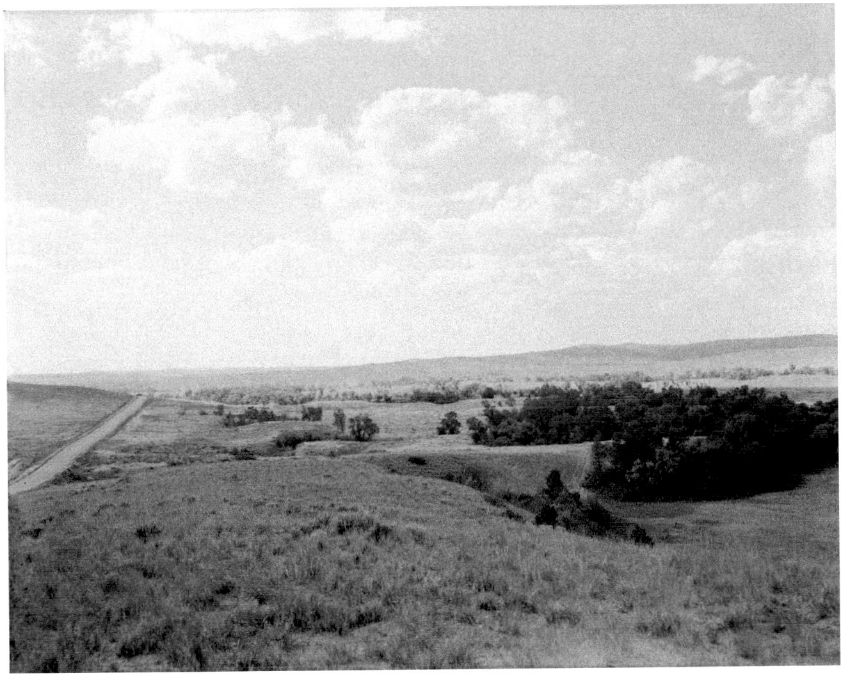

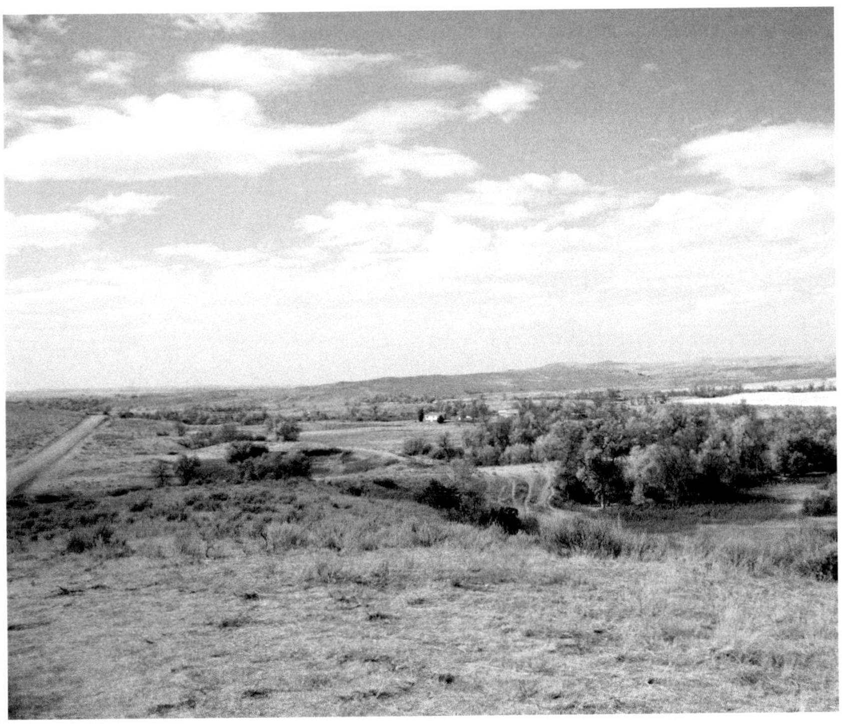

Figure 8.1. (*top*) Looking northwest at Girard Knoll from Reno Creek Road. Courtesy of Big Horn County Historical Museum. (*bottom*) Modern reshoot.

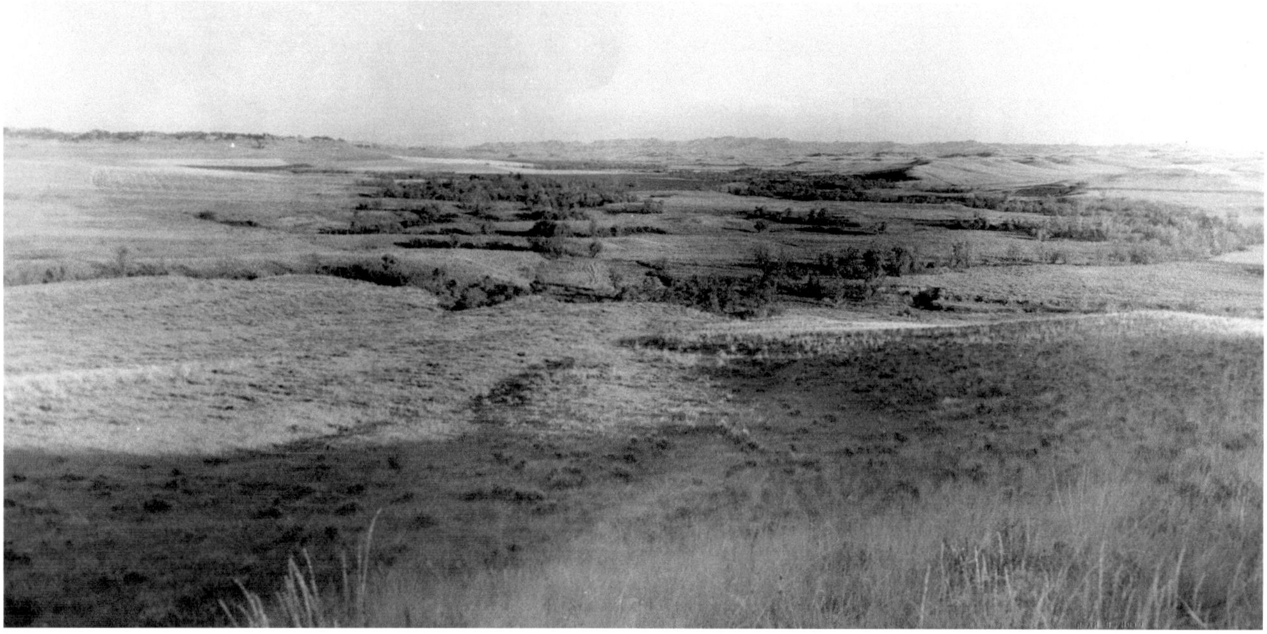

Figure 8.2. Panorama of three Roahen originals, looking east back up Reno Creek, probably taken from the lowest of the three knolls overlooking Reno Creek that are visible in figs. 8.3 and 8.4. Courtesy of Big Horn County Historical Museum.

the bluffs toward Reno Creek. Those bluffs are visible in modern figures 8.3, 8.4, and 8.5. When the two men neared the southern end of the bluffs, well past the Park Service fence and on private land overlooking Reno Creek and its northern tributary, McDougall told Boyes, "Now we look for the lesser of three knolls." Boyes wrote that the three knolls, visible in the modern photos, were right in front of them.

As they stood on what they believed to be Girard's Knoll, they decided that the Lone Tepee site had to be close enough to enable Girard to call out to Custer, "There go your Indians, running like devils."

Before the two men lay the flats along Reno Creek and its junction with its north fork. It matched Girard's own statement that his knoll was where some lodges, containing the bodies of dead Indians, stood. His knoll was reportedly 40–50 yards from a lone tepee or tepees. More important, behind the two men was "a cleft in the bluffs" that afforded them an unobstructed view of what had been the site of the main Indian encampment. In his article, Boyes recalled that Girard had reported his knoll as a mile to a mile and a quarter from the Little Big Horn River. If the knoll and a lone tepee had been three miles or more back up Reno Creek, Boyes believes the high terrain and river bluffs would have blocked any view of the encampment.

Any historical consensus on their distance from the river and their specific locations seems unlikely, so debate over the exact location of these two landmarks undoubtedly will continue. Still, we should note that both Roahen and Osten believed in this near-river location, so much so that Roahen wrote "Girard's Knoll" on the back of a copy of his photo that Dennis Fox now owns.

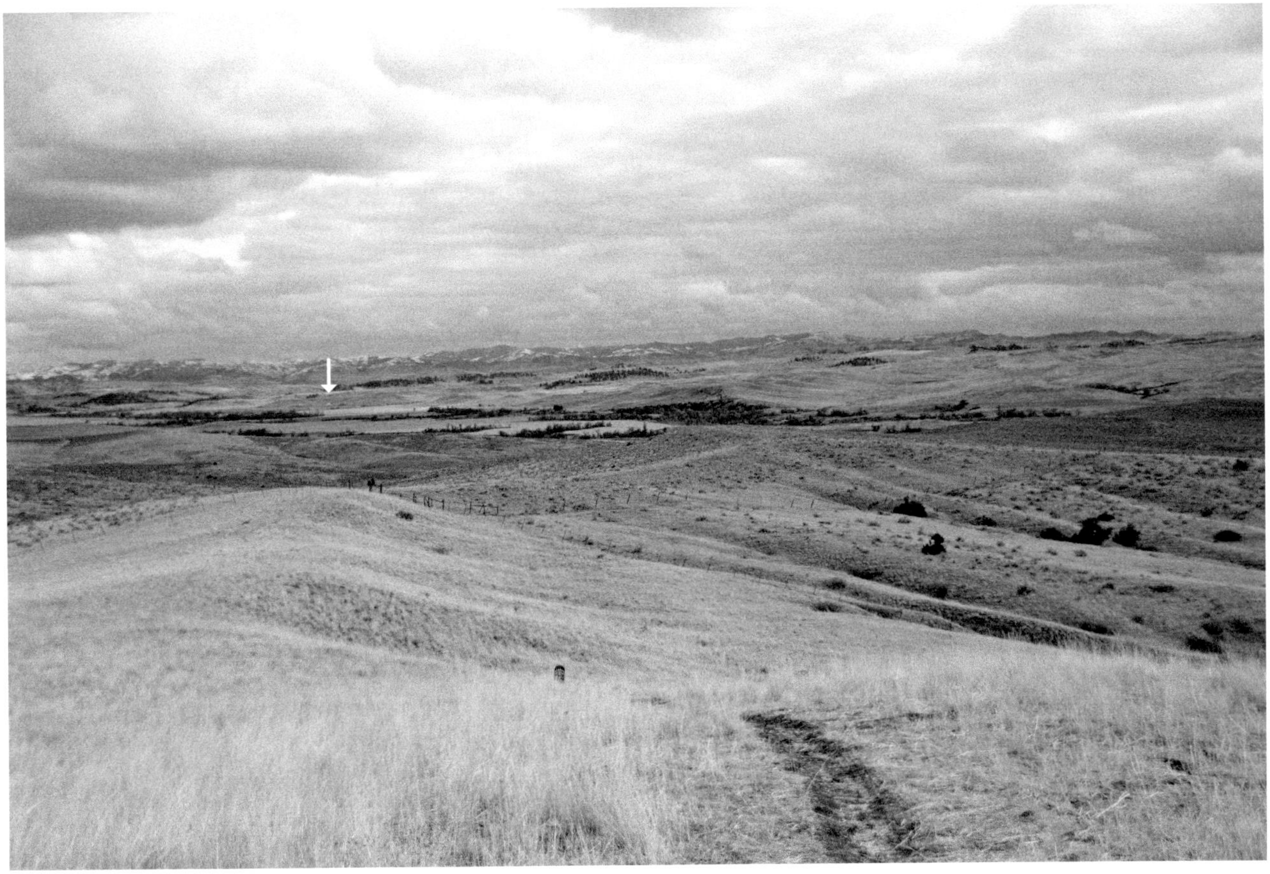

Figure 8.3. This 2012 photo, taken from the southern end of the Company H position, shows the gate down the slope at the end of the Park Service property. If one looks directly across the valley above that gate, one can see the white house and metal barn visible in the foreground of modern fig. 8.1.

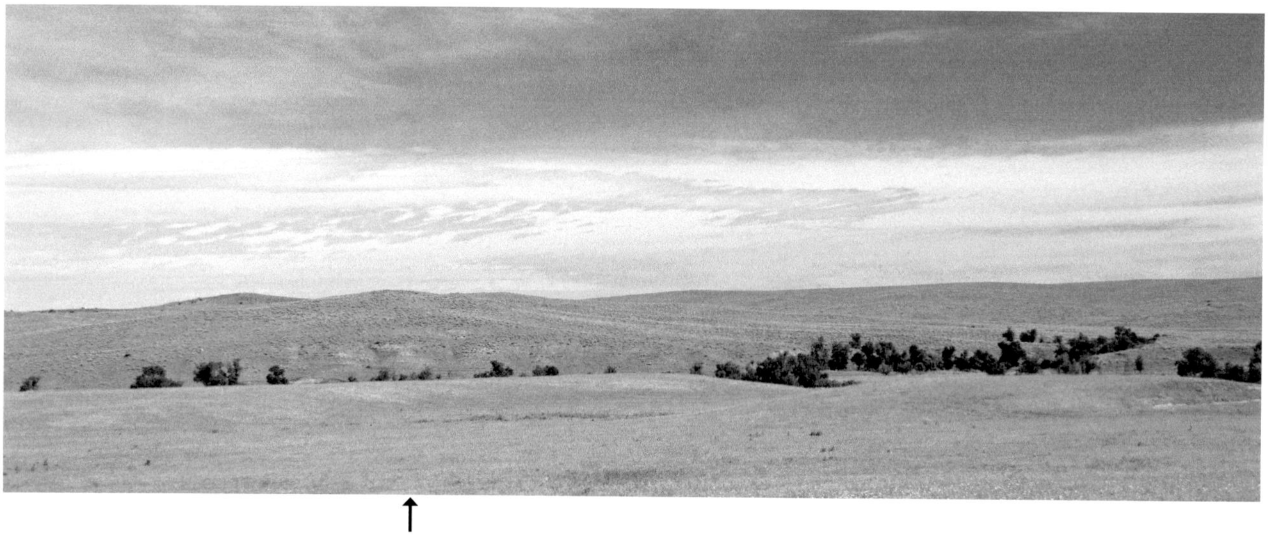

Figure 8.4. Girard's Knoll (2013). The three high points that Keith McDougal and William Boyes discussed as possible sites for Girard's Knoll can be seen in this photo. The nearest finger bluff, visible from the knoll in the middle of the photo and stretching toward the creek on the right, is likely the one in Roahen's photographs.

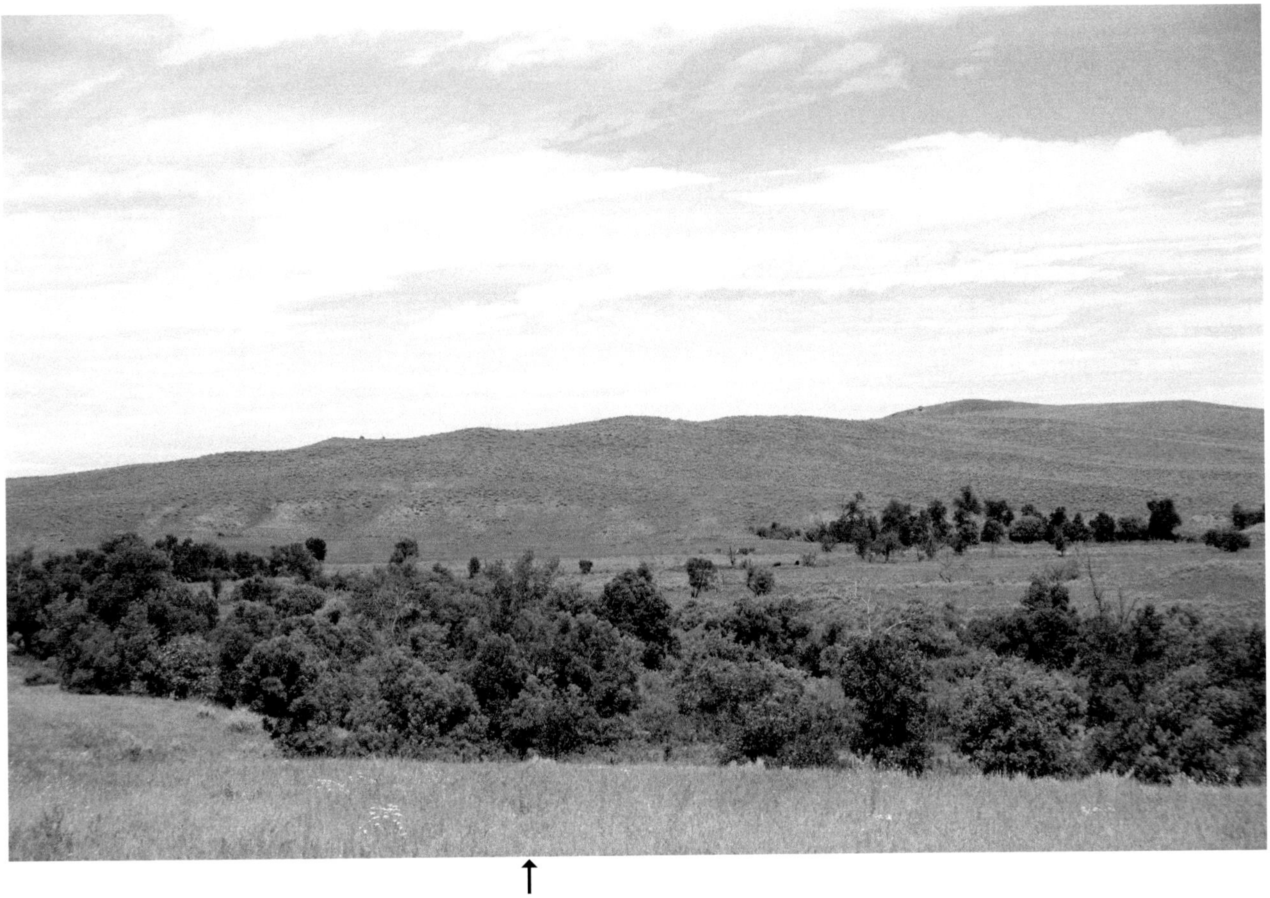

Figure 8.5. Girard's Knoll (2012), different angle.

CHAPTER 9

Major Reno's First Crossing

Researchers encounter a familiar problem when they turn to the subject of Major Reno's first crossing of the Little Big Horn River: where did that event actually take place? None of the historic photographers working between 1877 and the original arbitrary cutoff date of 1926 used for the book *Where Custer Fell* had taken photographs of what seemingly should have been a familiar site; early maps differed about the location—including the original 1891 USGS map and its 1908 printed counterpart. Additionally, such researchers as Henry Weibert and Thomas Bookwalter had provided only approximations for where they believed Reno's troops had crossed to go into battle.

Late in that book project a Roahen photograph (fig. 9.1) surfaced. Owner Dennis Fox had bought it in 1999 at a used bookstore in Billings, along with three other Roahen-identified images. In 2001, Fox accompanied the authors to the site to make the modern image that was published in *Where Custer Fell* and is again here.

Fox's copy of this photo was titled across the top as "Reno's First Crossing" and hand-dated "9/23/70." That likely placed it among the last the then elderly Roahen shot of the battlefield. The photo shows the Little Big Horn River near the mouth of Reno Creek, looking northeast from a ridge that used to be part of the Weibert ranch. Pencil lines on the photo itself indicate access to the river through a dry ravine. We were uncertain who owned the photo originally, although it may have been one of Roahen's friends, George Osten or William Bellingham.

On the back of that photo is inscribed the notation "See Sergeant O'Neil and Young Hawk." O'Neil, a private in Company G, and Arikara scout Young Hawk later gave accounts of the crossing episode. On one occasion, O'Neill referred to it as "a dry ravine" and on another as "an old dry creekbed"; in his account Young Hawk termed it "the mouth of a dry coulee."[1]

In Roahen's 1970 image, Reno Creek itself can be seen in the middle distance, a little downstream of the area shown and indicated by its name and an arrow. High banks rise on either side of the dry ravine itself. Pencil lines indicate that the ravine could be easily accessed from either bank and at its mouth. Additionally, an arrow points to a tree in the ravine, and an inscription at the bottom of the photo includes the words "Burkman blazed tree." Pvt. John Burkman worked as Custer's striker but was assigned to the pack train on the day of the battle. Burkman lived in Billings in his later years and frequently visited the battlefield. When he blazed the tree is unknown, but that story remains at least a strong legend among Custer buffs. More important, the

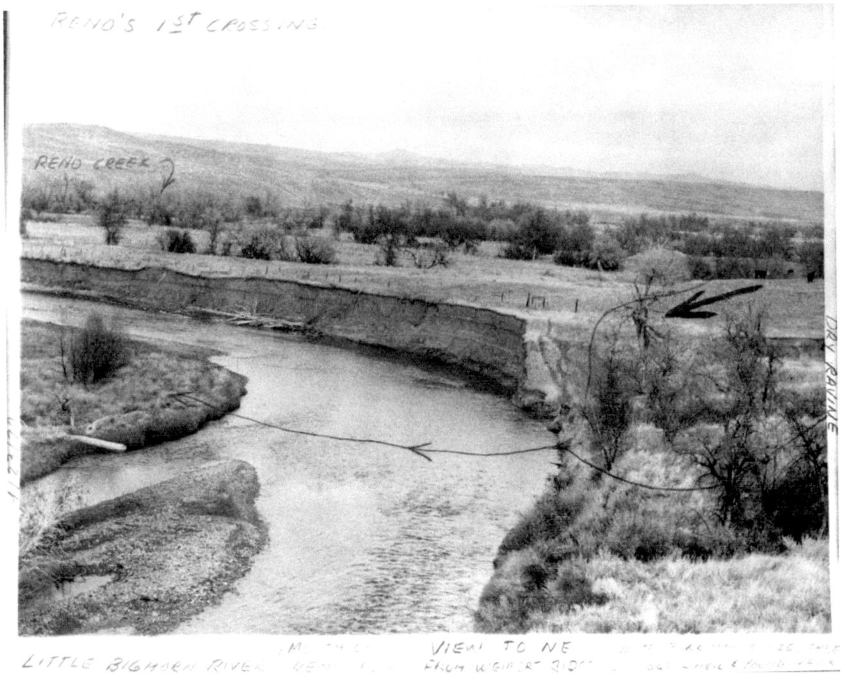

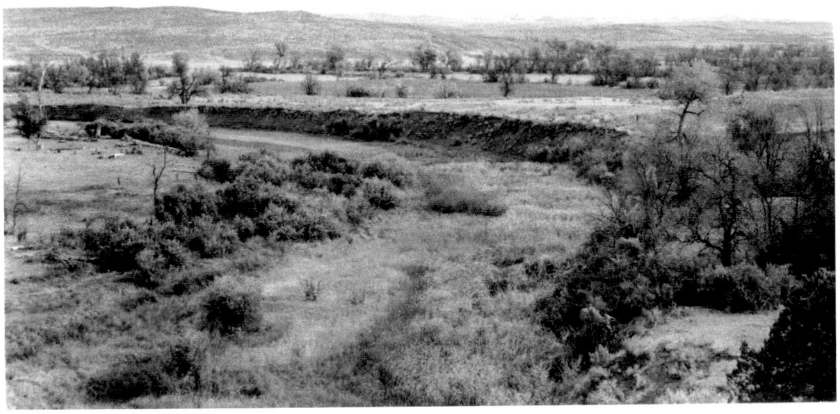

Figure 9.1. (*top*) Reno's first crossing, Roahen's 1970 original. Courtesy of Dennis Fox. (*bottom*) First crossing area (2001). Courtesy of James S. Brust.

tree still stands and does have unusual markings on it. A photo of the blazed tree taken in 2001 is included here (see fig. 9.2).

Roahen's collection at the Big Horn County Historical Museum includes several other images of the site of Reno's first crossing (figs. 9.3–9.6). Clearly all were taken on a different occasion than September 1970. For one thing, in the 1970 photo a heavy cloud cover dominates the sky, whereas the earlier images were taken on a day of sunshine and blue skies. Too, the water level in the river is significantly different.

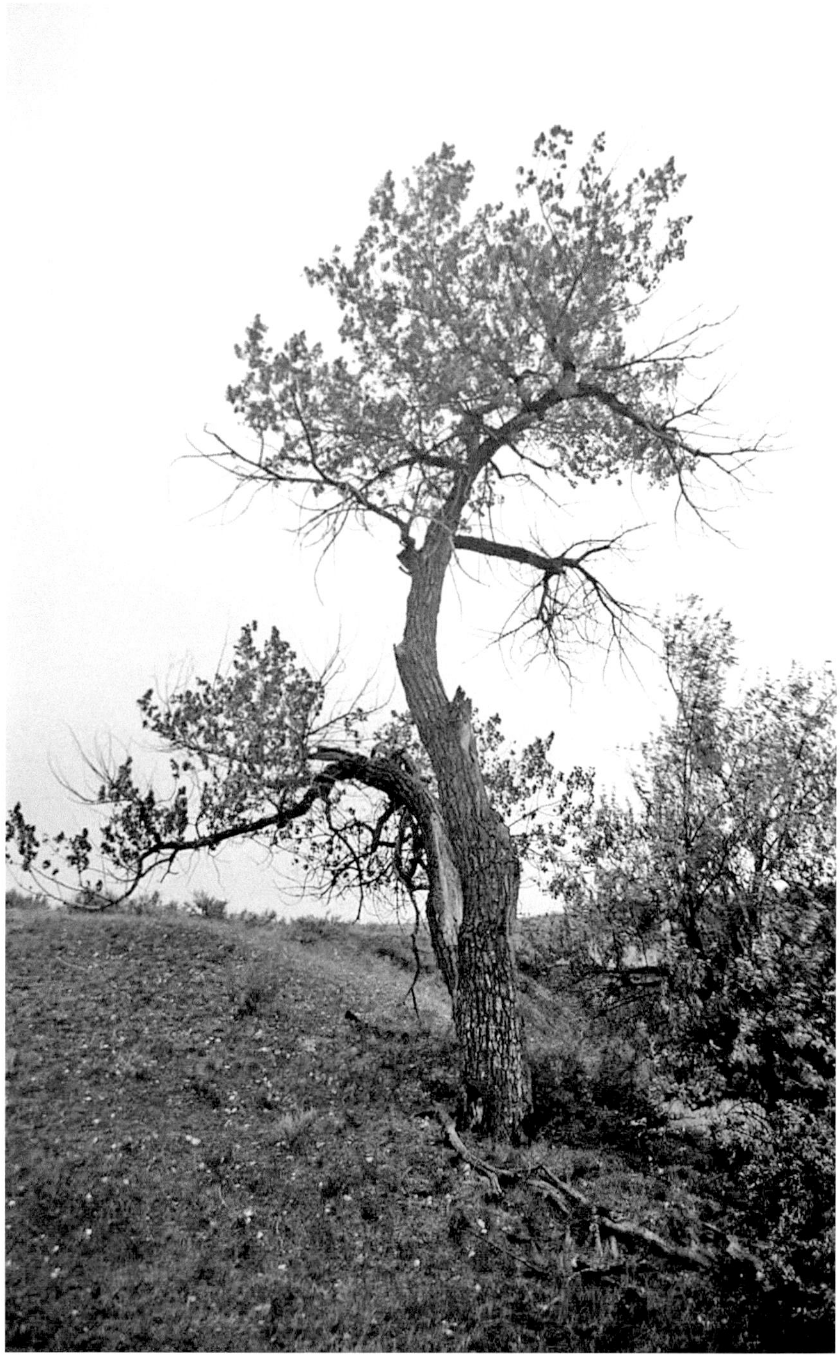

Figure 9.2. Burkman Tree (1985).

Another substantial difference can be noted by comparing Jim Brust's 2001 reshoot (fig. 9.1) to my own reshoots of 2012 and to Roahen's 1970 and earlier photographs: by 2000, the river course had changed, making that loop no longer part of the active stream. The little island in Roahen's 1970 original appears as a raised area in the 2001 Brust image.

Even in the eleven years between Brust's image and my own taken in the fall of 2012, the old river bed has changed that much more. Today, as the modern

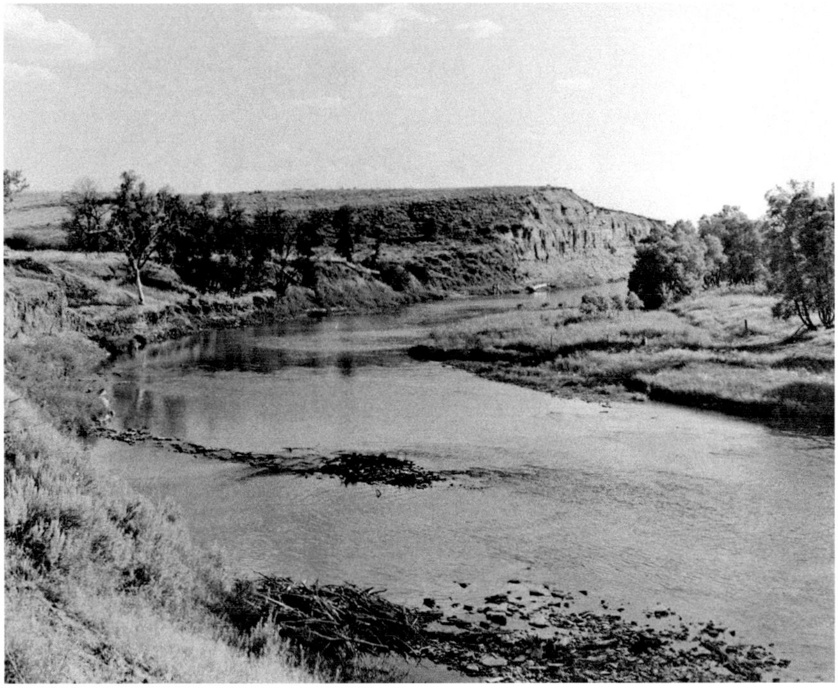

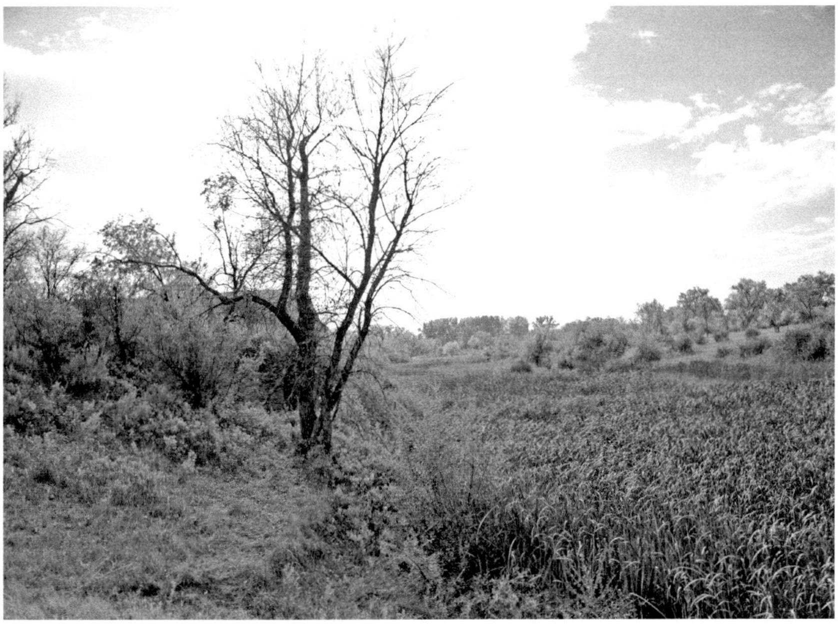

Figure 9.3. (*top*) Reno's first crossing looking south up the Little Big Horn River, with blazed tree mid-left center. Courtesy of Big Horn County Historical Museum. (*bottom*) General vicinity of Reno's first crossing, looking south up Little Big Horn River (2012).

photographs in figures 9.3, 9.4, and 9.7 document, grasses and reeds choke the channel, although some backwater is still visible at different points. But the old dry ravine access point remains. This additional photographic evidence and the background we now have about Roahen himself as a Little Big Horn researcher leave little doubt today. Major Reno and his command crossed the Little Big Horn at this point in 1876 and headed down the valley into battle.

Figure 9.4. (*top*) Looking north down the Little Big Horn toward the battlefield. Courtesy of Big Horn County Historical Museum. (*bottom*) 2012 reshoot.

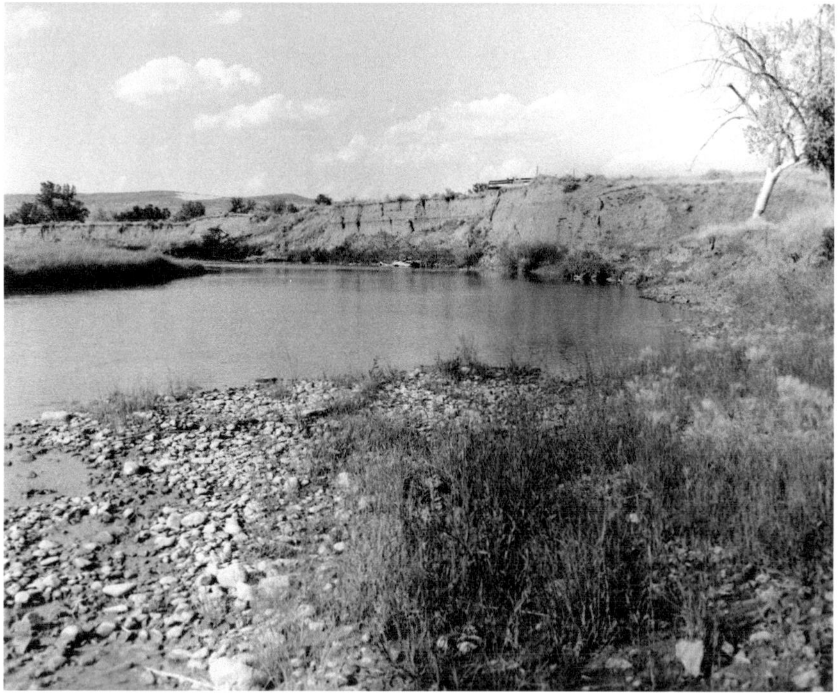

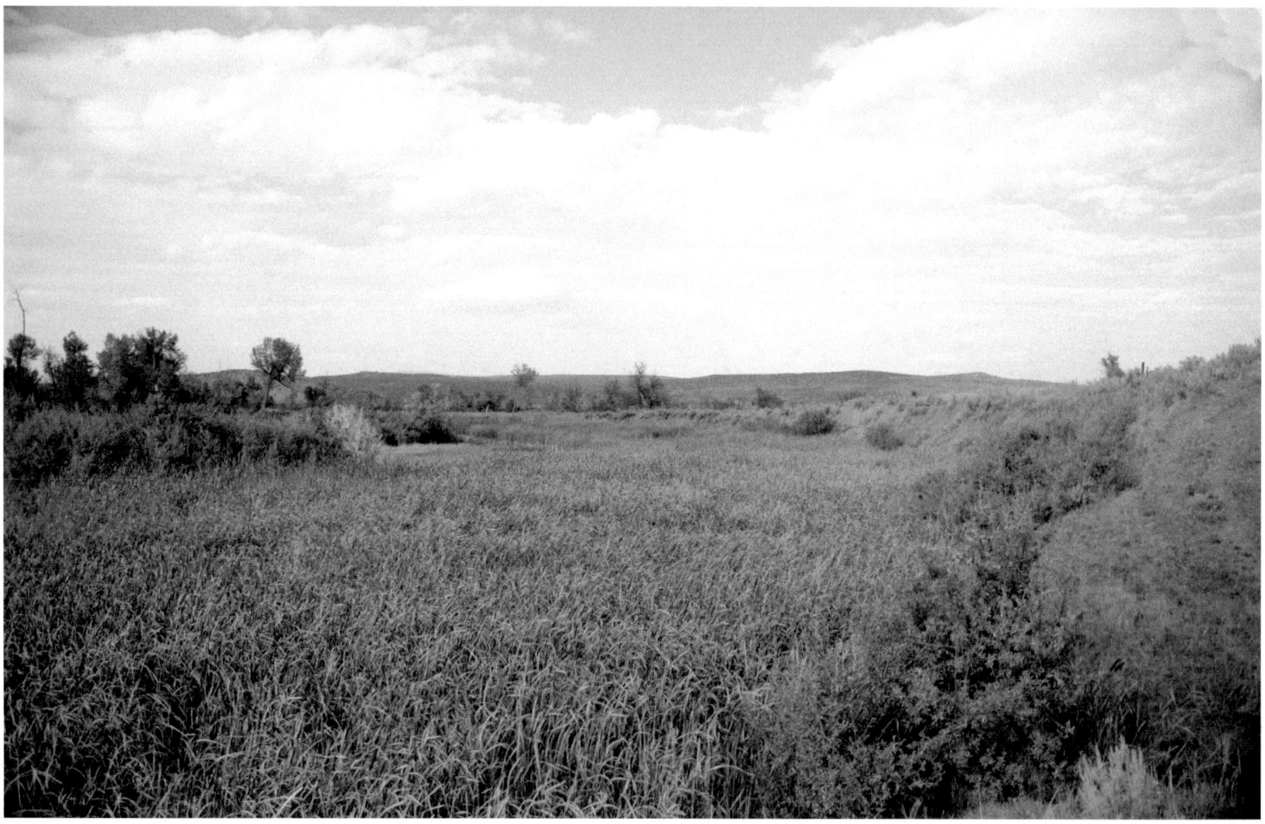

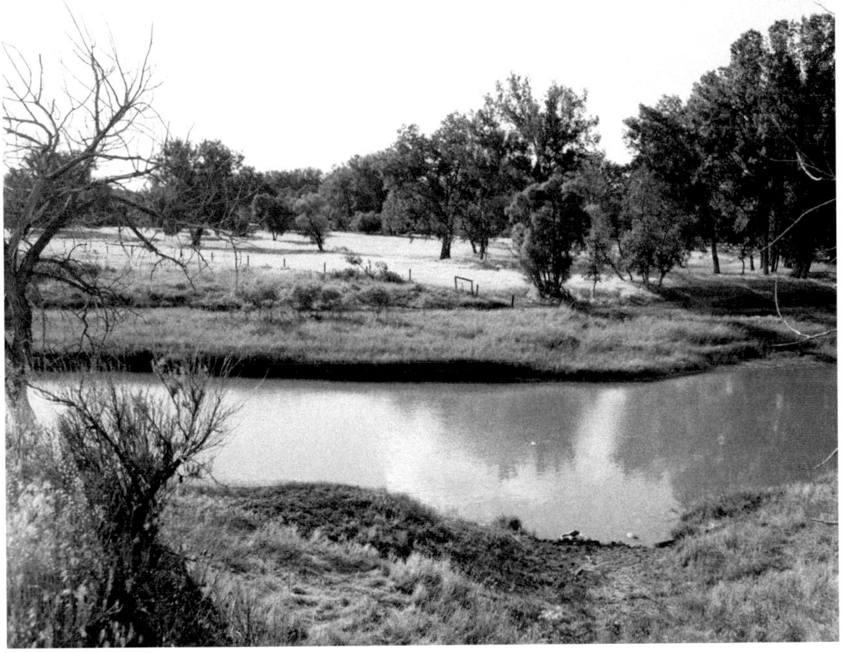

Figure 9.5. Looking west toward the valley plain. Courtesy of Big Horn County Historical Museum.

Figure 9.6. Reno's first crossing, looking west, likely a variant of fig. 9.5. Roahen stepped around to the other side of the tree to shoot this one. Courtesy of Big Horn County Historical Museum.

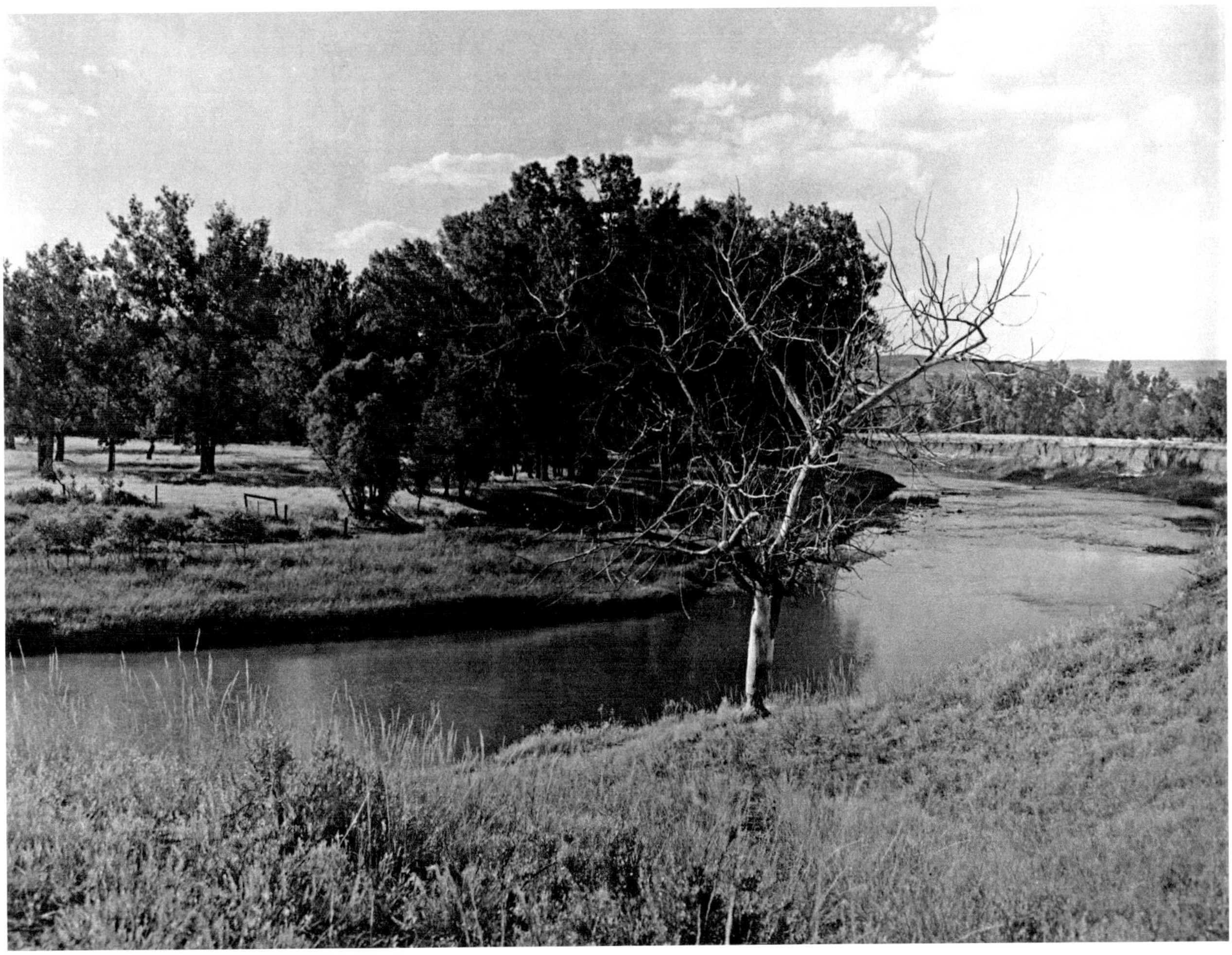

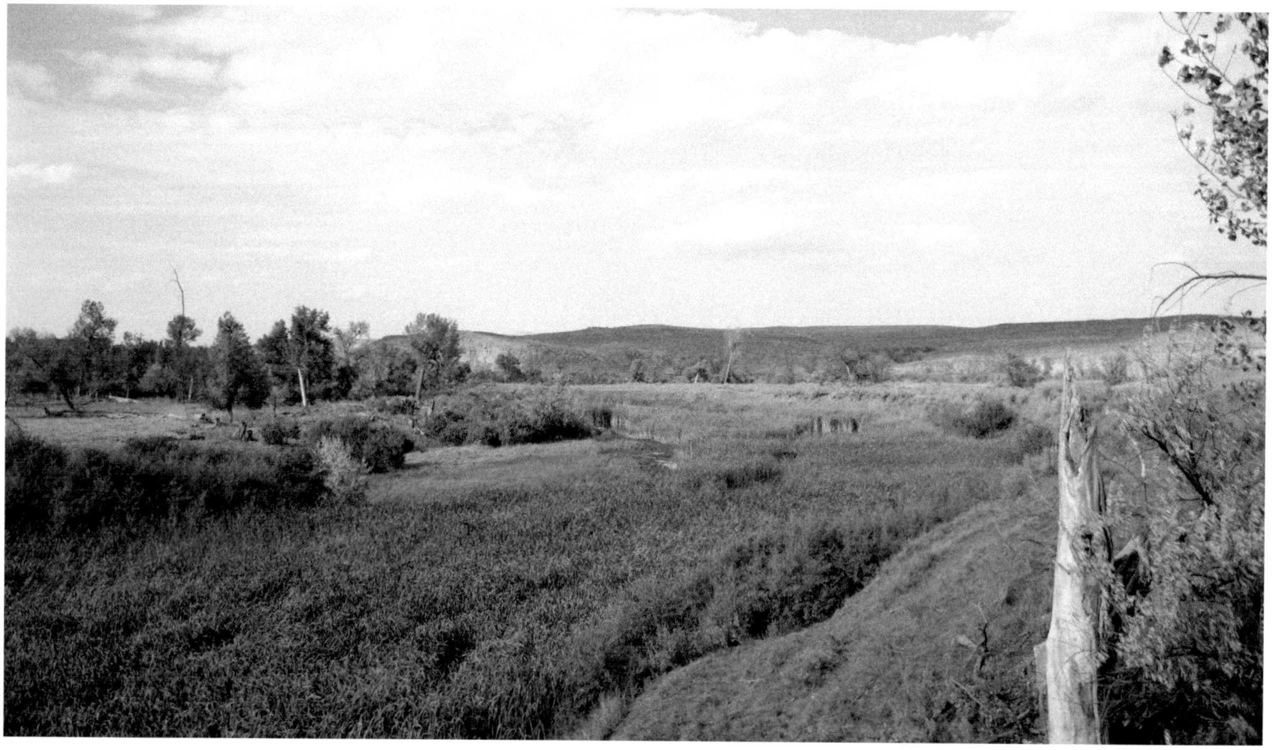

Figure 9.7. General vicinity of area seen in figs. 9.5 and 9.6 (2012).

CHAPTER 10

Reno's Advance Down the Valley

In 1951, for the seventy-fifth anniversary of the battle, Kenneth Roahen climbed into an airplane and soared above Custer battlefield to shoot aerial photos of the main battlefield and the Reno-Benteen area, including where Reno advanced down the valley toward the Indian encampment in the vicinity of today's Garryowen, Montana. He later marked up a series of the Reno-Benteen advance photos with arrows that depict the route he believed the Reno battalion followed in its charge toward the village (five were included in the Roahen collection, but one is not reproduced here, because of its overlap with the others). The route he shows is significant, because he has the three cavalry companies hugging the tree line along the Little Big Horn River as they advance. If anything, this is an indirect route toward the village. Most battle maps show Reno's advance out in the middle of the valley, first approaching and then paralleling the modern interstate highway and railroad.

Roahen's route matches up with one suggested by 1st Sgt. John Ryan in his memoirs. Ryan states that Capt. Thomas H. French, commander of Company M, ordered him to take ten men off the company right and skirmish underbrush and bullberry bushes along the river bank. The soldiers were making certain Indians were not hiding behind the troops as they turned toward the village. In other words, Reno's three companies first hugged the river in coming down the valley, then turned sharply toward their eventual skirmish line at today's Garryowen site, passing the timber where they would later take refuge.[1]

Such an interpretation proposes that Reno's troops actually retreated along the same route they had followed in their advance to their attack. That could mean that Reno did not just flee the timber as if he were a madman. Instead, he might have known where he was going, toward the river and a crossing of sorts he had previously seen in that direction. The historical record, however, especially testimony at the 1879 Reno court of inquiry, provides little or no support for such a theory. Nonetheless, Roahen's series of photographs makes it apparent that he believed events in the valley unfolded in that way. Given his friendship with George Osten, Superintendent Luce, and other researchers of that period, it seems apparent that a river approach by Reno had support among them.

Roahen's figure 10.1 documents his belief that Reno's troops stayed near the river bank as they traveled down the Little Big Horn Valley. If so, they would have been moving at an angle to the center of the Indian camp rather than directly toward it. Roahen's notes say that Reno marched down river "on the right-hand side," or the west side of the river valley, as shown in this photograph.

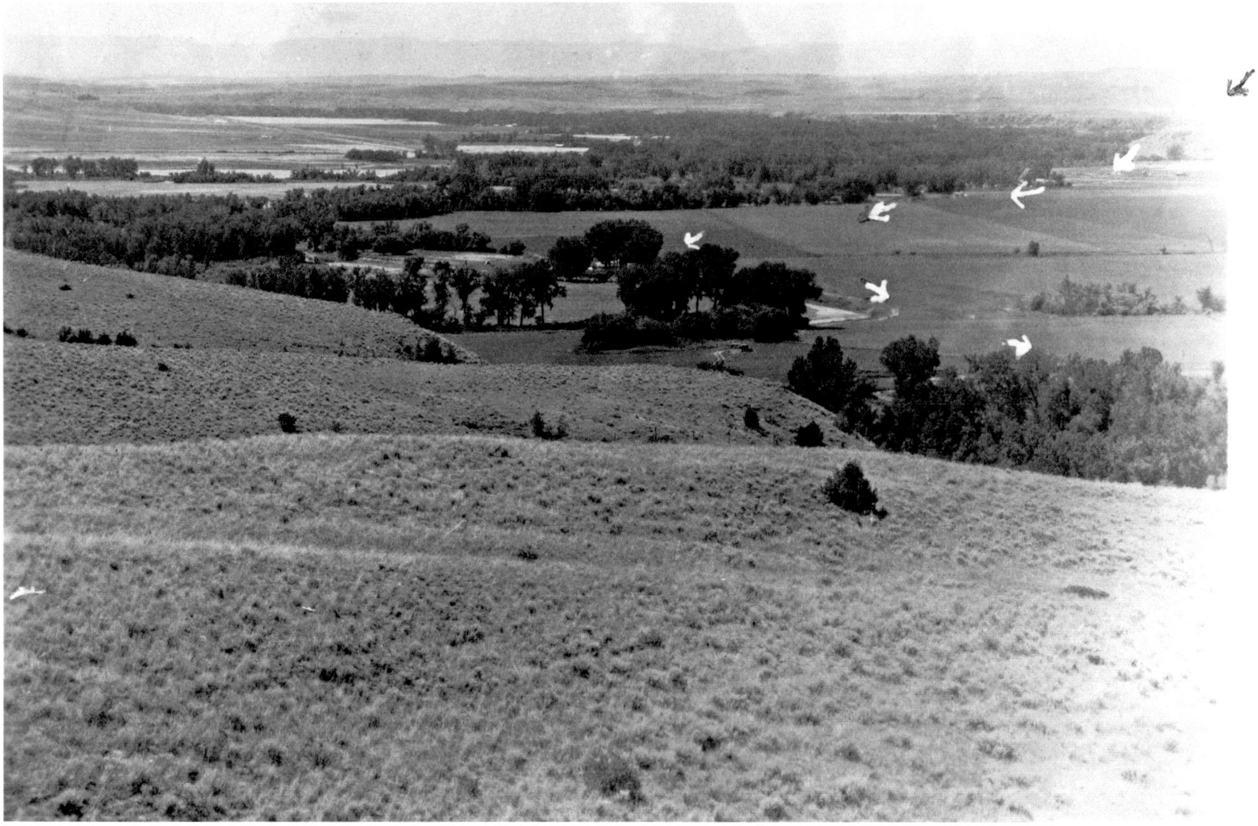

Figure 10.1. Reno approach into the valley, No. 1. Courtesy of Big Horn County Historical Museum.

Figure 10.2 shows the troop line moving away from the river and out past what would become Highway 87, the north-south road in this image that predates the modern Interstate 90. Roahen's handwritten notes say the troops went across what is now a ranch as far as "a small bunch of trees with white house to the right of Road X, then to what is now Garryowen (elevator)." The retreat crossing would be in the foreground to the right of the bluffs but cannot be seen in this photo, which was taken years before Interstate 90 was constructed parallel to Highway 87. Note the east-west dirt road, referred to by Roahen and indicated by the fourth arrow from the left, which extends from the tree line in the photo's mid-center toward the benchlands. It still exists today but no longer crosses the interstate highway. The farthest point on the upper third of the photo (what Roahen labeled "X") marks the Denny ranch complex, now owned by the Custer Battlefield Preservation Committee.

The final two photographs in this series, figures 10.3 and 10.4, are actually variants of the same location, with each offering slight differences in Roahen's apparent thinking. Roahen's handwritten notes say, "Reno's men then moved from what is now the house to what is now known as Garryowen—X elevator and then into heavy timber arrows depict route."

Both begin with an arrow line that turns at the Denny ranch and then advances toward the timber by way of the Garryowen area. Today many researchers would not place the original skirmish line as far north as Roahen's arrow positions it in the upper middle third of the photos. The retreat

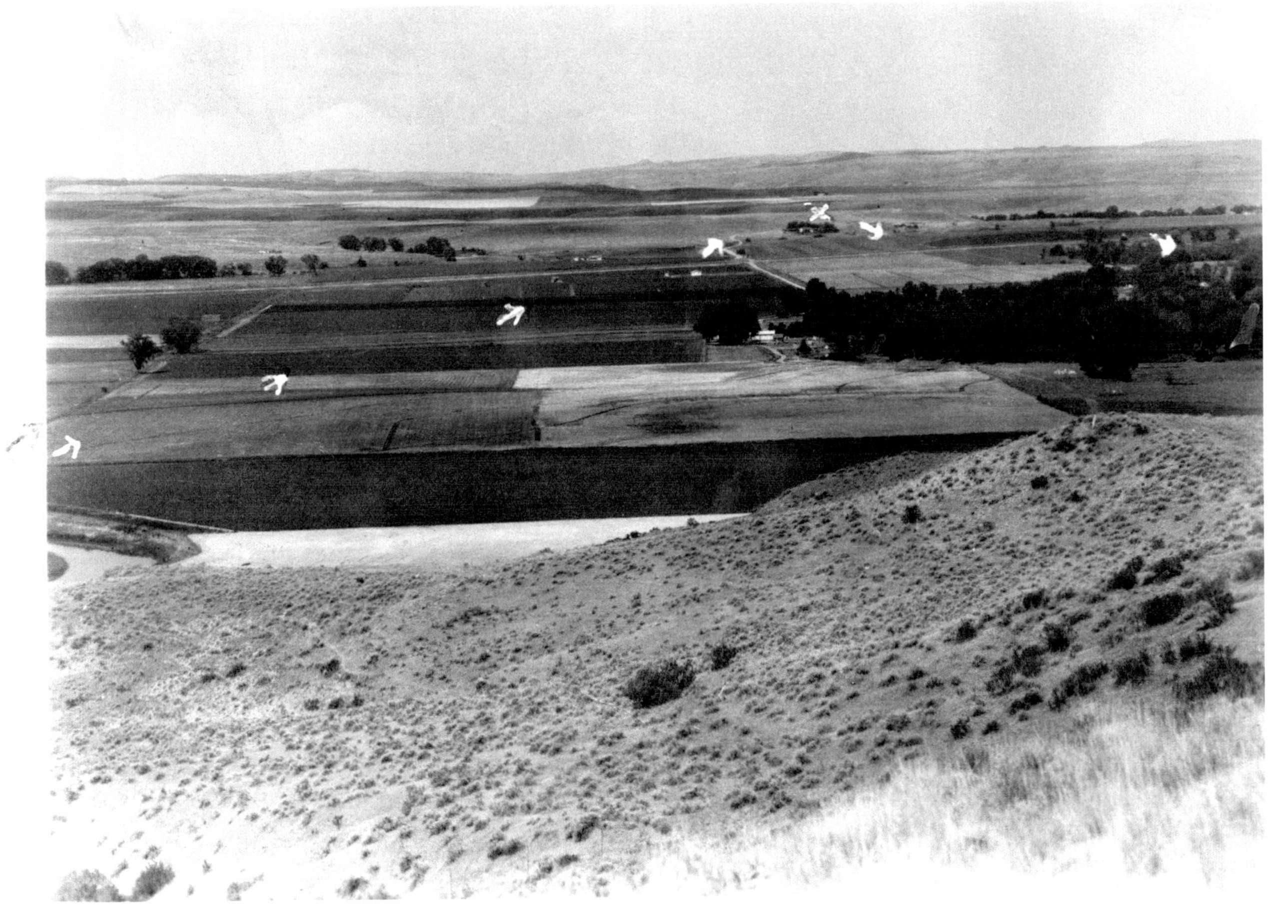

Figure 10.2. Reno valley sequence, No. 2: troops move away from river past road. Courtesy of Big Horn County Historical Museum.

arrows also seem too widely scattered, even for a military line that may have been well stretched out while fighting the Indians from the timber. No arrow in either photo marks the timber's specific site.

Figure 10.3 shows the left edge of the tree line and the modern Bird In Ground family property. Many historians believe at least some of Reno's troops rode parallel to the trees and then turned at the Bird In Ground ranch before streaming toward the retreat crossing, marked in both photos by the triangle of arrows just below the bluffs and at the Little Big Horn River. I made no attempt to duplicate these aerial images, but for similar views from the ground see chapter 13.

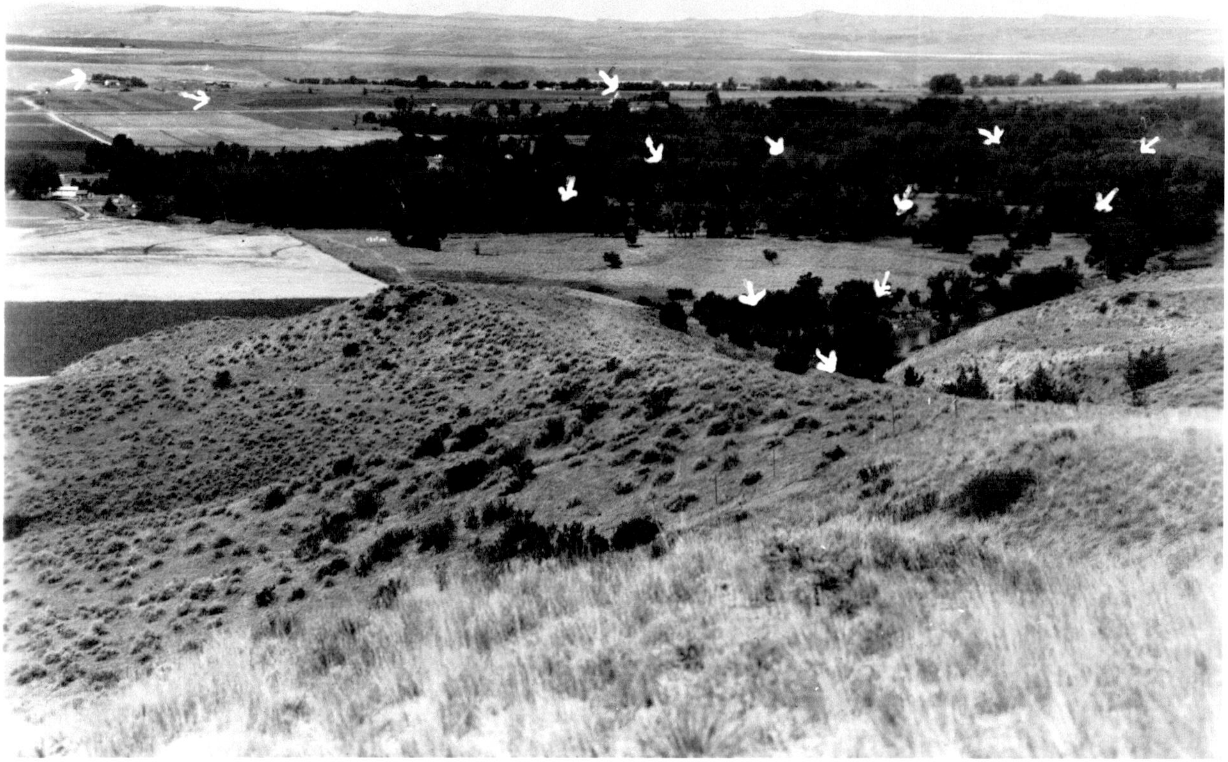

Figure 10.3. Reno valley sequence, No. 4: troops move from Denny ranch through timber toward the retreat crossing. Courtesy of Big Horn County Historical Museum.

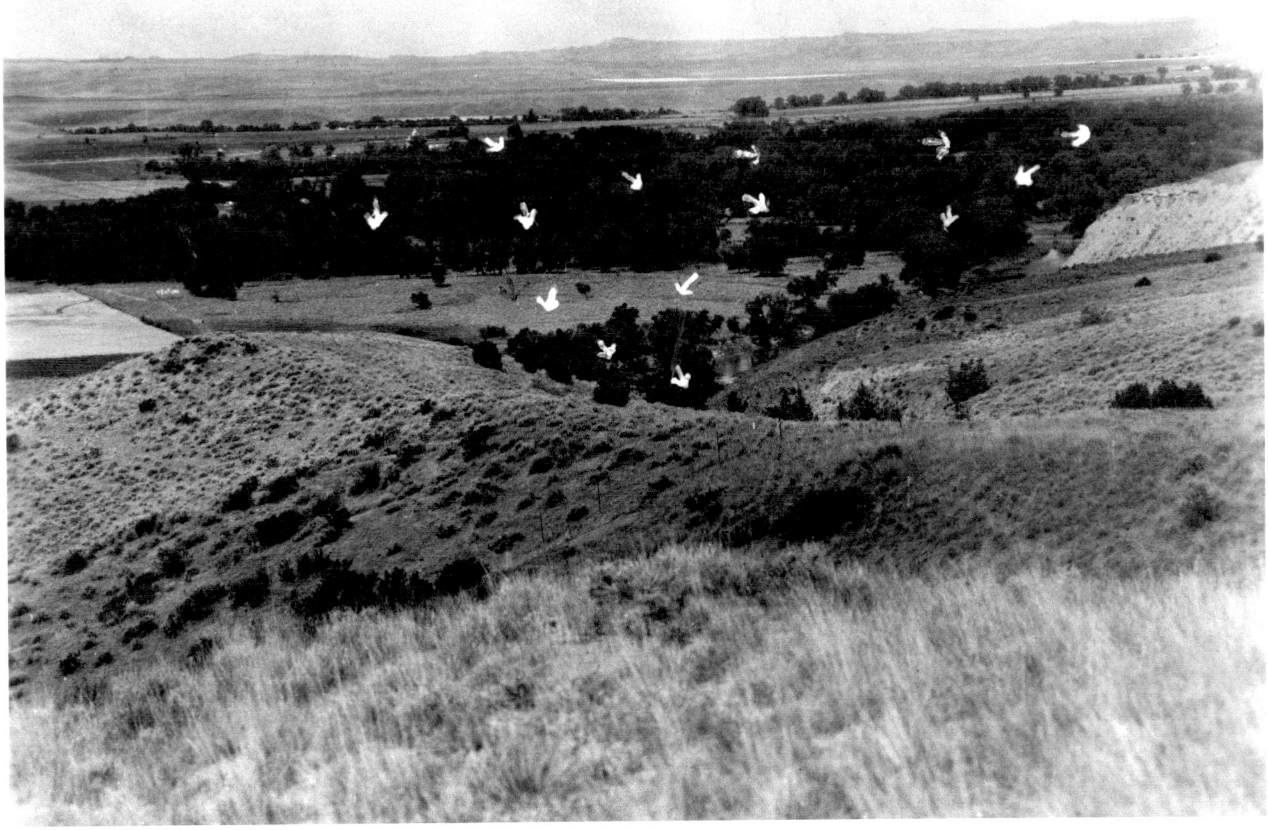

Figure 10.4. Reno valley sequence, No. 5; variant of fig. 10.3. Courtesy of Big Horn County Historical Museum.

CHAPTER 11

Reno Valley Fight and Retreat Crossing

The town of Garryowen, Montana, today is privately owned by one individual, Chris Kortlander. The town hall, such as it is, is housed in a commercial complex of buildings Kortlander owns, including a gasoline station and convenience store, a Subway restaurant, a trading post–like store, and Kortlander's Custer Battlefield Museum. In addition, a U.S. postal facility operates next to Subway. But in 1876 the Garryowen vicinity was at the southern edge of the Indian encampment on the Little Big Horn River and witnessed the opening scene of the Custer battle, when the battalion of Maj. Marcus A. Reno charged the Indian village, only to be forced to go to ground in a dismounted skirmish line.

Garryowen

Today the area of the Little Big Horn Valley looks nothing like it did in 1876. Not only have agricultural, ranching, and railroad interests altered the landscape, the Little Big Horn River through its periodic floods continues to create new channels and leave old ones abandoned. What most dramatically influenced the area's present appearance was construction in the 1970s of Interstate Highway 90. That included locating an overpass and exit at Garryowen, effectively destroying the scene of Reno's skirmish line.

Since 1868, the land has been considered part of the Crow Tribal Reservation. In 1895, the Chicago, Burlington and Quincy Railroad established a tiny watering station on the Little Big Horn River. It served U.S. Army troops and handled supplies and mail for delivery to nearby forts and homesteads. It was called Garryowen after the marching song of George Custer's 7th Cavalry. The land was later sold by the tribe and the federal government to private citizens.

By the fiftieth anniversary of the battle in 1926, the town of Garryowen remained privately owned but mostly consisted of a small store that serviced area ranchers. About a month before the anniversary, workmen were constructing an irrigation ditch just east of Garryowen, essentially along Reno's retreat route, and unearthed a nearly complete set of skeletal remains (no skull was ever found). Because it was accompanied by several bullets and buttons, authorities assumed these were the remains of a 7th Cavalryman killed in 1876. Because fourteen of Reno's men were never accounted for after the battle, accurate identification of the man was impossible.

However, on the eve of the anniversary celebration, the sponsoring Custer Memorial Association decided to hold a reburial service, with full military honors, for this long-lost unknown soldier of the Battle of Little Big Horn. A

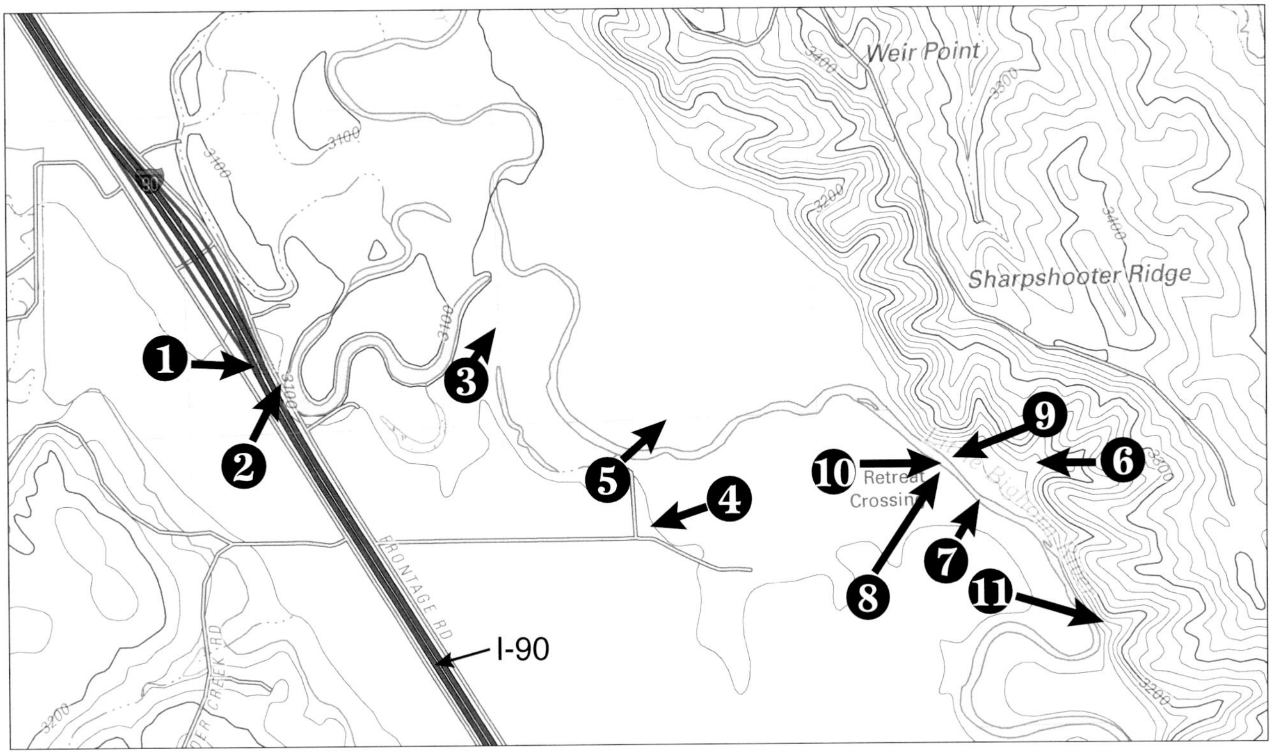

Map 11.1. Reno valley fight and retreat crossing. Map by Gary Raham.

1. Fig. 11.1
2. Figs. 11.3–11.6
3. Figs. 11.9–11.15
4. Fig. 11.17
5. Fig. 11.19
6. Figs. 11.20, 11.21, 11.22
7. Fig. 11.24
8. Fig. 11.23
9. Fig. 11.28
10. Figs. 11.29, 11.30
11. Fig. 11.25

plot of land was set aside for the burial site and donated to Big Horn County. A concrete tomb was constructed in front of A. G. Carter's Garryowen store to hold the remains of the dead soldier. Interment was delayed a day until June 26, 1926, to assure a fitting ceremony was conducted for the man. The event included a symbolic burying of the hatchet between white and Indian. Participants included retired Brig. Gen. Edward S. Godfrey and White Bull, both battle survivors.[1]

In 2012, Kortlander put the town, his museum, and the commercial complex up for sale, but an auction scheduled for that August was abruptly cancelled, according to news accounts. Disclosure documents indicated that Kortlander, despite the historical record of 1926 news accounts, could neither confirm nor deny that a body was actually buried in the tomb on the premises.[2]

In the Roahen museum collection are six photographs of the Garryowen area. One is a Garryowen historical sign (fig. 11.1). To the right of the historical sign in the distance is Weir Point, marked by the saddle between the two peaks. That landmark is important for matching up a modern reshoot of any historical photo taken in the Little Big Horn Valley. Nevertheless, the modern figure 11.1 photo cannot match the historical image for one obvious reason—the commercial complex and museum block the view toward the bluffs. The tomb of the unknown cavalryman is to the right of the sign, as seen in figure 11.2.

To shoot his other five images, Roahen simply walked south on what is today's frontage road east of Interstate 90. The general area where he shot all these photographs is about halfway between the modern gas station and the long defunct Reno Battlefield Museum, a fort-like log structure. Figure 11.3

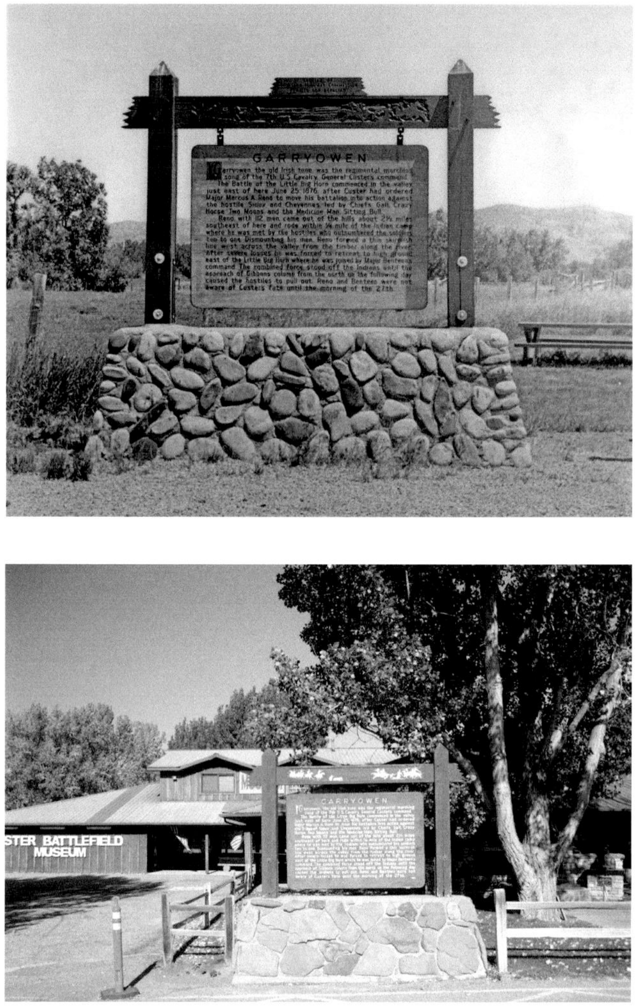

Figure 11.1. (*top*) Garryowen sign, looking east. Courtesy of Big Horn County Historical Museum. (*bottom*) 2012 reshoot.

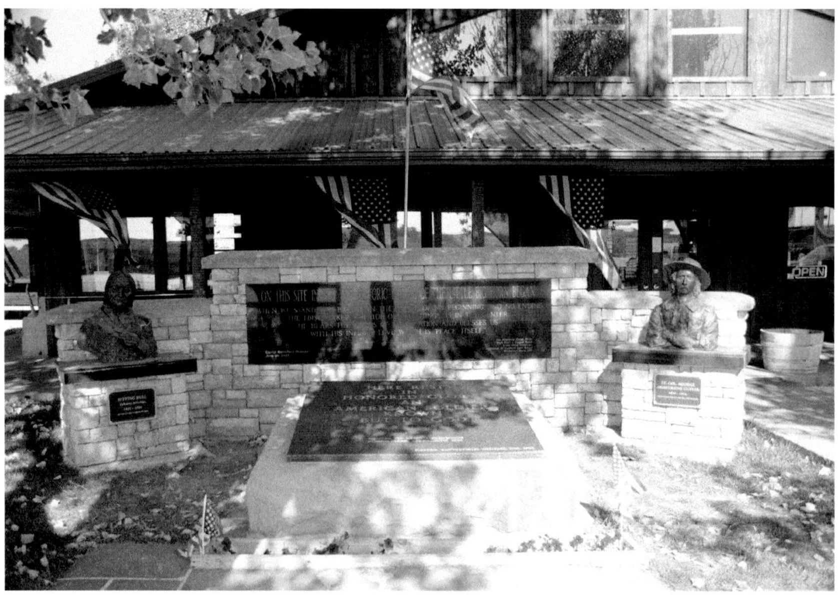

Figure 11.2. Garryowen trooper burial site (2012).

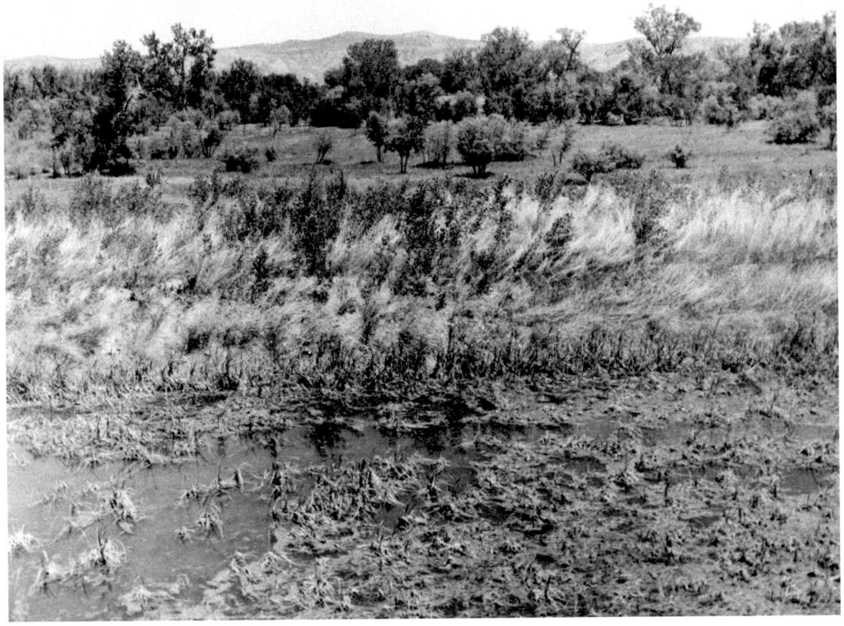

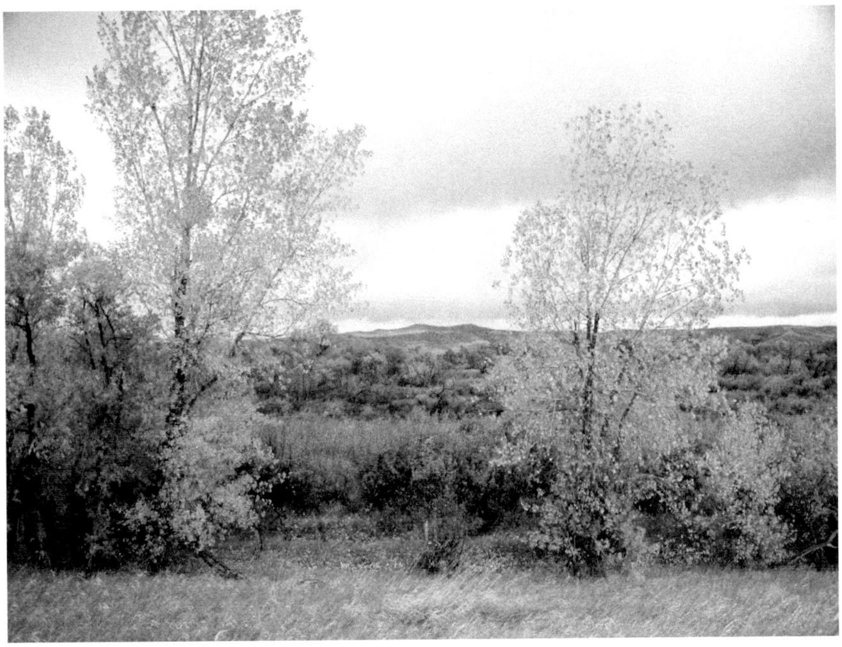

Figure 11.3. (*top*) Looking east across river to Weir Point. Courtesy of Big Horn County Historical Museum. (*bottom*) 2012 reshoot.

looks east across former channels of the Little Big Horn River to Weir Point on the distant bluffs. At the time Roahen shot these photos, likely in the 1960s, the frontage road did not exist; U.S. Highway 87, then the primary road through the area, would have been behind him. It is possible he stood on what is now the Interstate 90 roadway.

Figure 11.4 purports to show the railroad dam that cut off the channel and left it a backwater today. More important, in an enlargement of Roahen's original photo, just to the right of the white house in his photo's mid-center and up on the eastern bluffs, the Reno-Benteen historical monument

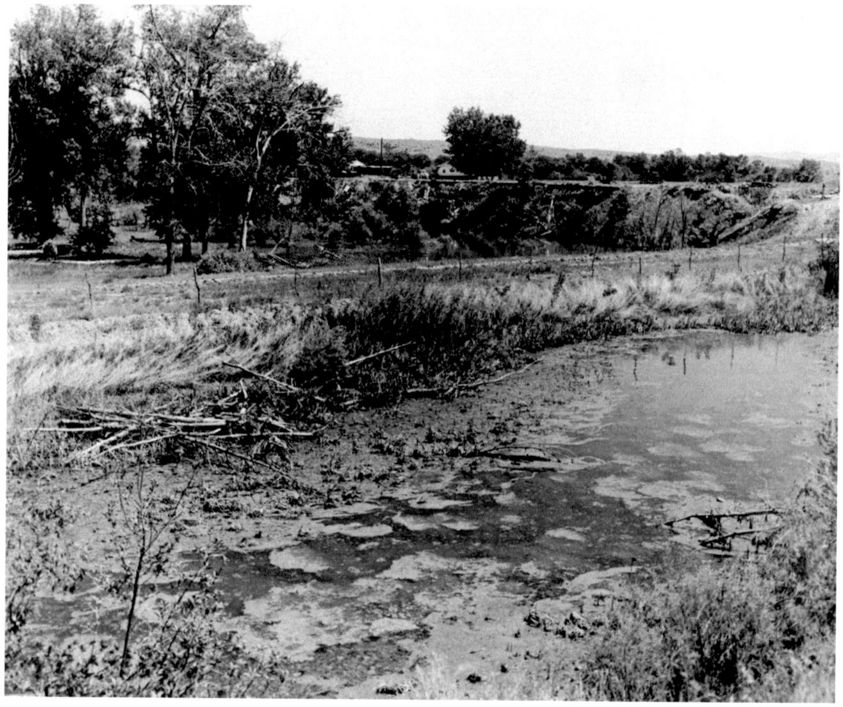

Figure 11.4. (*top*) Railroad dam against loop toward Reno Monument in distant background to the east. Courtesy of Big Horn County Historical Museum. (*bottom*) 2012 reshoot.

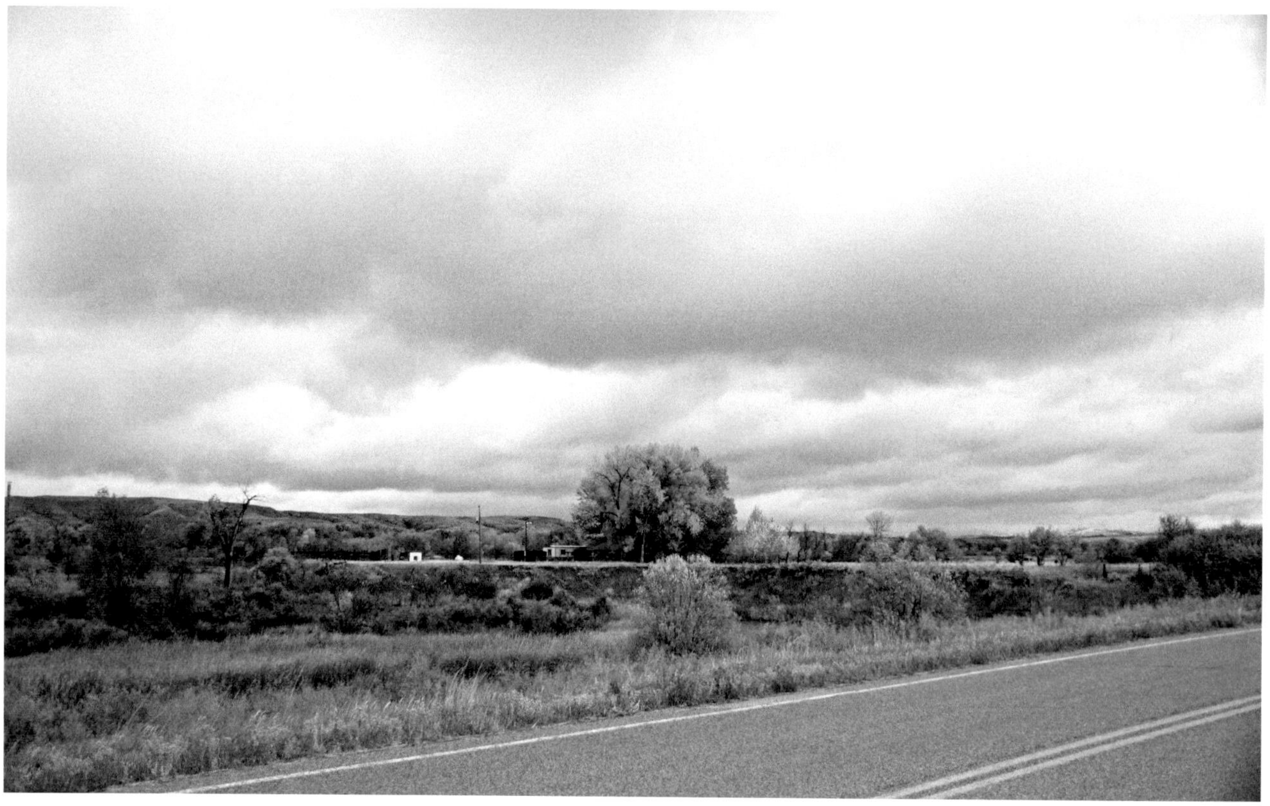

can be made out. The modern figure 11.4 photo was taken just in front of the fence that blocks access to the I-90 roadway. The pavement in the foreground is the frontage road. In an enlargement of this photo, the Reno monument can be seen to the right of the white shed, just to the left of the middle utility pole.

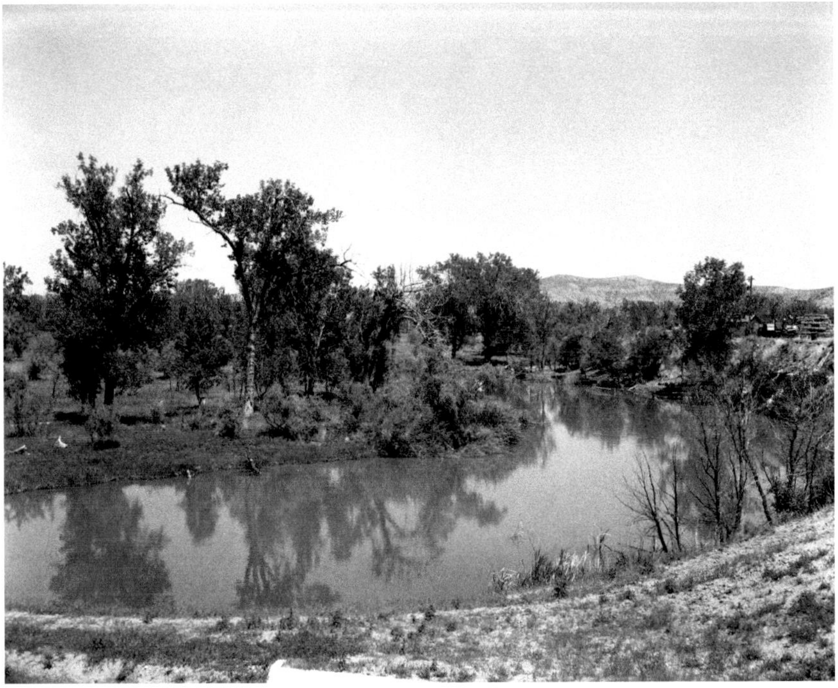

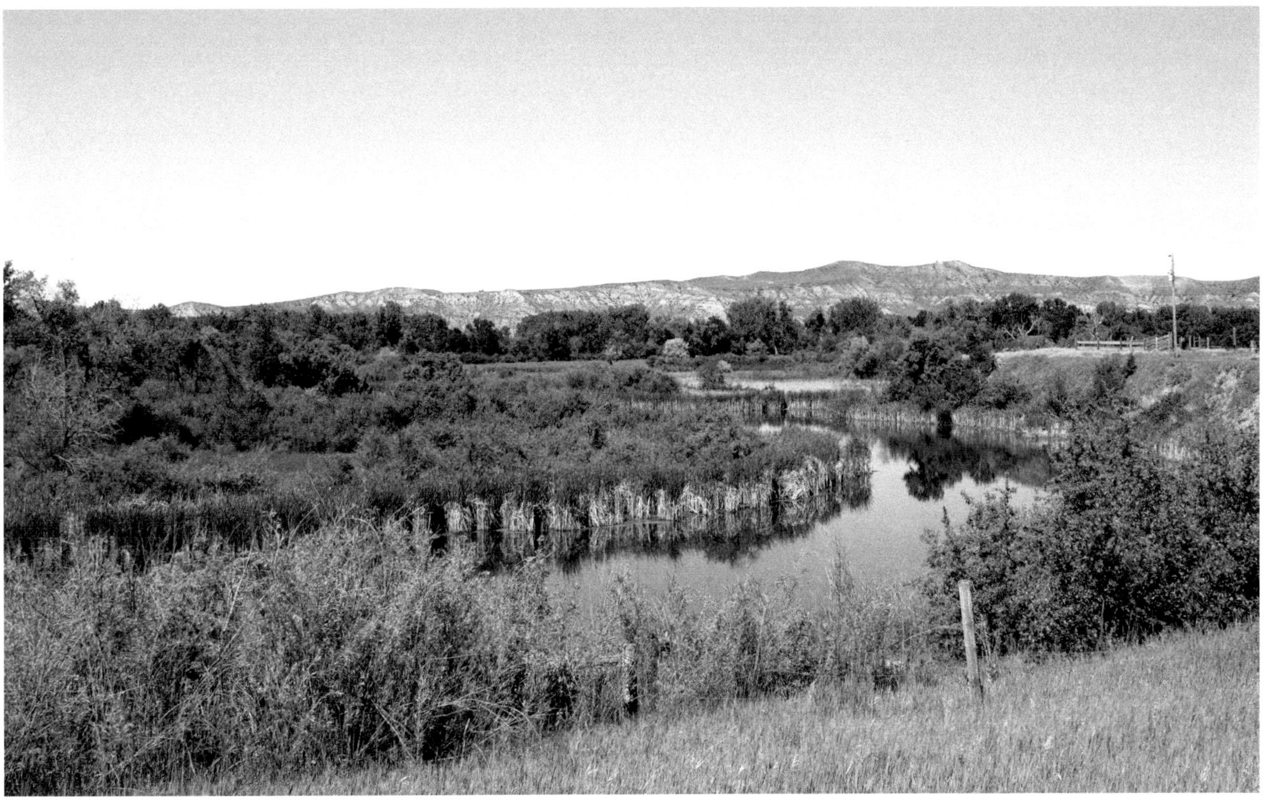

Figure 11.5. (*top*) Garryowen loop. Courtesy of Big Horn County Historical Museum. (*bottom*) 2013 reshoot.

Looking east, figures 11.5 and 11.6 are similar to these other images, although both were taken closer to an old river meander, the Garryowen Loop. Figure 11.5 shows Weir Point's saddle and peaks on the right. The modern figure 11.5 photo is a general match for both of these Roahen images and is distinct in a couple of ways. The river bend was more heavily covered with taller trees when

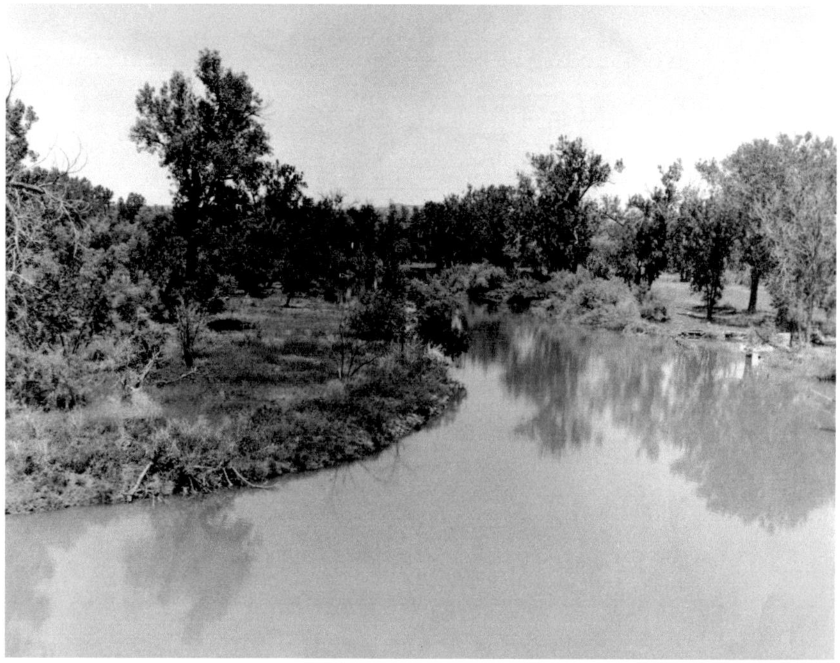

Figure 11.6. Original Little Big Horn River channel bed looking east toward Weir Point; variant of fig. 11.5. Courtesy of Big Horn County Historical Museum.

Roahen made his photograph compared to the modern image. Too, a wider section of the distant bluffs to the north of Weir Point is easier to see today.

Figure 11.7 offers a different perspective from the other photographs in this group. Roahen walked down the driveway of what today is private property next to the old river channel at Garryowen. That allowed him to shoot across not only the river channel and the dam of his day but also, as we can see in the paired modern image, the area of today's frontage road and I-90. Figure 11.8 provides a more complete modern perspective showing the old channel, dam, and modern gas station at Garryowen.

The figure 11.7 pairing offers a significant contrast between today, with the interstate, and Roahen's day, before the interstate. For example, the modern shot shows the overpass at Garryowen with a commercial trailer truck and pickup truck traveling on the bridge. In Roahen's photo, a grove of trees appears in that much lower landscape and extends left, or west, toward the old grain mill. Another grove of trees stands on the site of the old mill. The Burlington Northern and Santa Fe Railway line still runs on the same tracks west of today's interstate, where the train cars can be seen in Roahen's photo. The tracks may not be visible in the modern photo to readers less familiar with this area.

Finally, on the left of the modern image, just west of the interstate roadbed, stand two taller utility poles with a third shorter one behind them. Just to the left of that shorter pole, a dirt track comes off the high benchland. That same track appears on the mid-left of Roahen's image. It appears about halfway between the tallest utility pole and the last railroad car. Close study of Roahen's photo indicates that construction crews must have used considerable fill through Garryowen to build the highway roadbed up to match the level of the old dam and thereby lessen the threat of flooding from the river today.

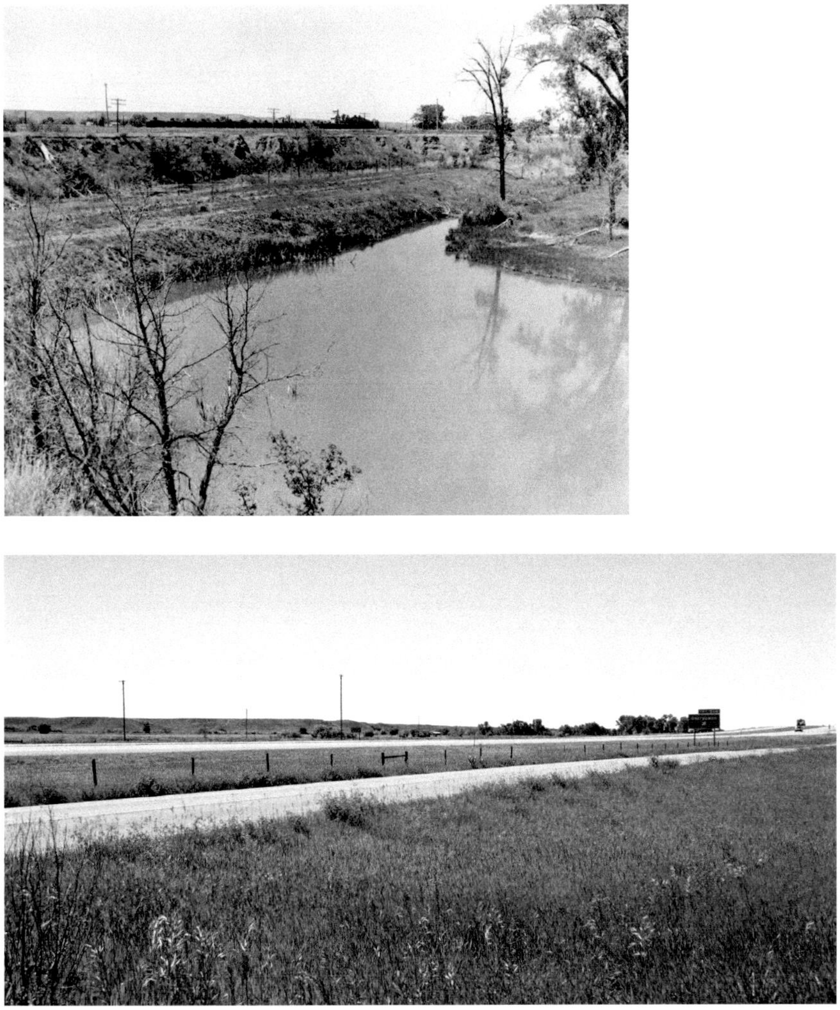

Figure 11.7. (*top*) Little Big Horn River's original bed. Courtesy of Big Horn County Historical Museum. (*bottom*) 2013 reshoot, the river now dammed.

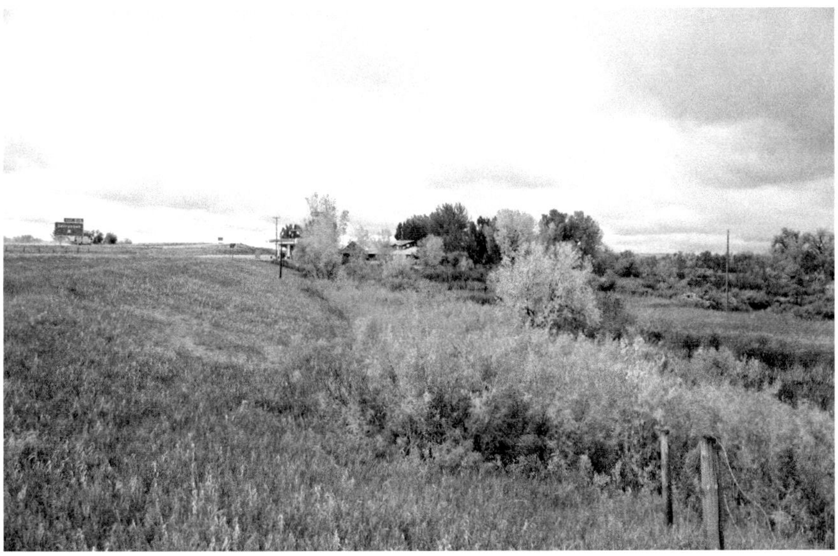

Figure 11.8. Looking toward Garryowen complex (2012), providing added perspective for the modern fig. 11.7 image.

Charley Reynolds's Memorial Marker on the Valley Floor

Custer's chief scout, Charley Reynolds, has been described as "somewhat mysterious, though a dashing figure and crack shot."[3] Roahen's friend George Osten had significant interest in Reynolds, who during the timber episode fought on the far right of the line and was killed in action when Major Reno's battalion dashed for the river bluffs. Numerous eyewitnesses described Reynolds's death. Later, Philetus Norris, a friend of Reynolds and the second superintendent of Yellowstone National Park, claimed to have retrieved the scout's remains, yet the site was not well marked.[4]

In 1908, a four-inch pipe and a brass plate were placed near the timber to mark the site where Reynolds died. In 1926, Custer writer-researcher Earl A. Brininstool installed a painted and lettered cross, wired to a taller iron pipe, at the site. Several amateur photographs document this memorial to Reynolds, and one of them, drawn from the Edward S. Godfrey Collection at the U.S. Army Military History Institute, was published in *Where Custer Fell.*

Twelve years later, on August 17, 1938, a group of dedicated battle students of that generation—led by Osten—placed a new memorial at the site, a granite marker with a brass plaque. The group photo taken during the dedication of the marker (fig. 11.9) includes a who's who of early Custer battle researchers and students, notably Brininstool, Dr. Charles Kuhlman, and Fred Dustin. Albert W. Johnson was a well-known Indian wars researcher from Minnesota. Robert S. Ellison was instrumental in saving large portions of the Camp materials after the latter's death. Ellison donated his own materials as well as Camp's to the Lilly Library at Indiana University. The photographer was Mrs. Ellene Marsh, Brininstool's daughter.

It appears that they erected the new stone marker as a replacement for the earlier cross. However, because the marker interfered with plowing, local ranchers later relocated it some distance away next to an irrigation ditch. The original spot faded from memory. In the early 1990s, Jason Pitsch, whose family had owned the property for decades, and Glen Swanson again moved the Reynolds marker, this time back to what they believed was its original location in front of the timber fight line and some 200 yards from the 7th Cavalry's far right edge. They relied on historical photos to make their determination.[5]

Roahen's photographs (figs. 11.10–11.15) clearly support the Pitsch-Swanson relocation as accurate for the Reynolds marker. This location also matches the placement of the 1926 cross photograph.[6] Roahen's photographs also were likely taken before the marker was moved by the local ranchers. In all his photographs, the marker seems to be in its original location, including figure 11.15, which shows Osten painting the metal protective fence around the marker, apparently in 1966. In that photo Osten appears much older than in the 1938 group image. Also, the base of the stone shows no indication of having been cut off for any move, unlike its appearance today.

In the mid-1990s, Jason Pitsch told me that in the early 1950s his father and grandfather had cleared the site of the timber fight itself, which was heavily brush-covered, for farming and ranch use. The spacious arena-like field behind

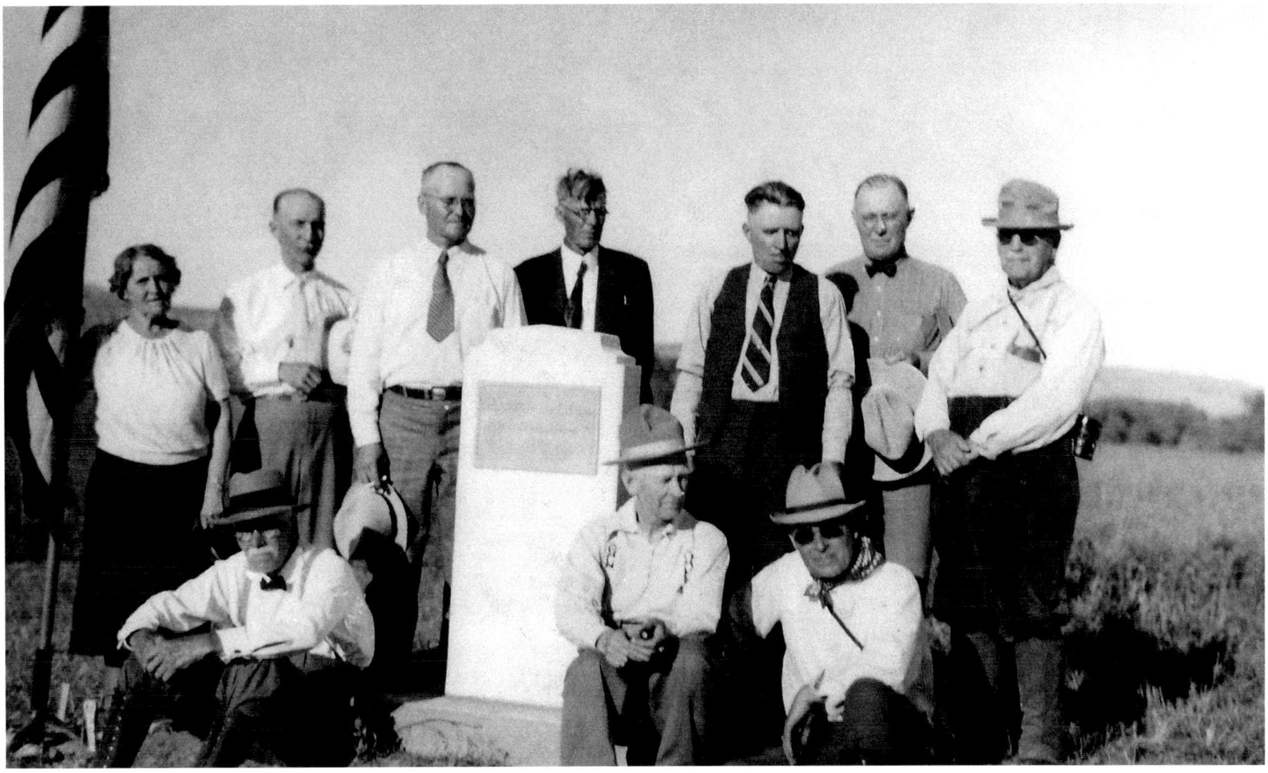

Figure 11.9. Charley Reynolds marker group, August 17, 1938: (*seated, left to right*) Albert W. Johnson, E. A. Brininstool, Robert S. Ellison; (*standing, left to right*) Mrs. Brininstool, George Osten (the day's chairman), Charles E. Reynolds (grandnephew of Reynolds), Dr. Charles Kuhlman, N. J. Hogan (grandnephew of Reynolds), Monte Robertson, Fred Dustin. The photographer was Mrs. Ellene Marsh, daughter of the Brininstools. Courtesy of Lilly Library, Indiana University, Bloomington, Indiana.

the marker today is actually much smaller than it would have been in 1876, for portions of the land have been lost to floods over the years.[7]

In figure 11.10 we can see the Reno monument on the eastern bluffs, which are in the background just to the right of the right rear pipe protecting the marker from farm equipment. Trees prevented a suitable reshoot of this image. On the rear of this picture, Roahen wrote that the marker is west of the Little Big Horn River and only a short distance from the new highway south of the Garryowen store. Presumably he was referring to Highway 87, not I-90. He further wrote that the marker was located in a grain field that at the time of the battle had been a wooded area. That could mean the photograph was taken after the Pitsch family cleared the timber area but before they moved the marker. Figure 11.11 is a variant of figure 11.10. Figure 11.12 is a broader view of the Reynolds marker, looking toward the southeast. Note the shorter marker in the modern image.

Figure 11.13, taken east toward Weir Point, is significant for Roahen's reference to Osten, whom he credits with the marker's placement in that spot. Roahen matched the 1938 group photo (fig. 11.9) when he shot this, although the year is unknown. Note that the field appears to have been cleared, and the bank of an irrigation ditch can be seen in the foreground. In the modern image of this pair, the ditch is not apparent and only a small depression can be seen on the ground covered with tall grasses. Notice how close the tree line marking the current channel of the Little Big Horn River is.

Figure 11.14 differs in that it looks west toward then Highway 87 and where the modern interstate highway will later be built. This pair of photographs

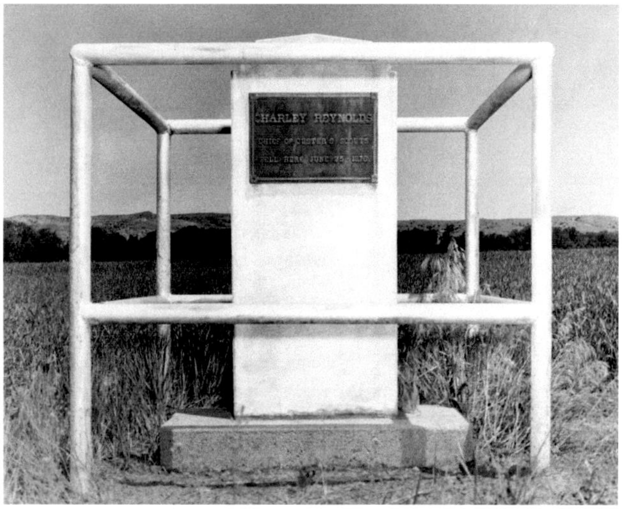

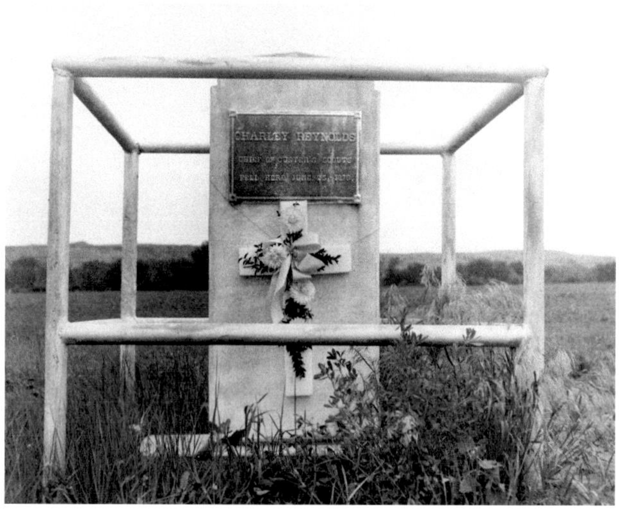

Figure 11.10. (*left*) Reynolds marker on bluff, looking east. Courtesy of Big Horn County Historical Museum.

Figure 11.11. (*right*) Reynolds marker, variant of fig. 11.10. Courtesy of Big Horn County Historical Museum.

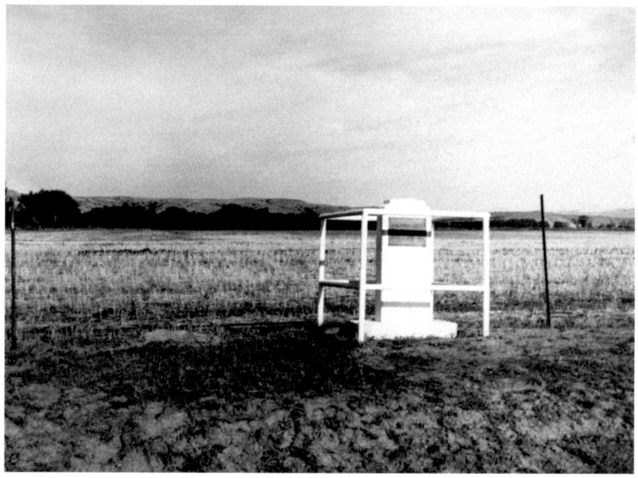

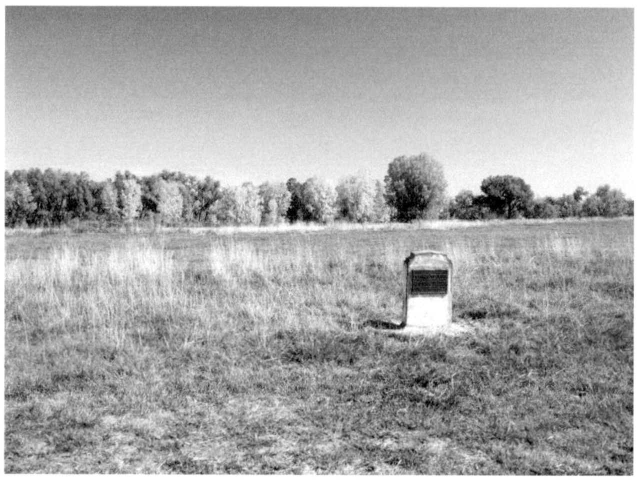

Figure 11.12. (*top*) Reynolds marker in field. Courtesy of Big Horn County Historical Museum. (*bottom*) 2012 reshoot; note the shorter marker.

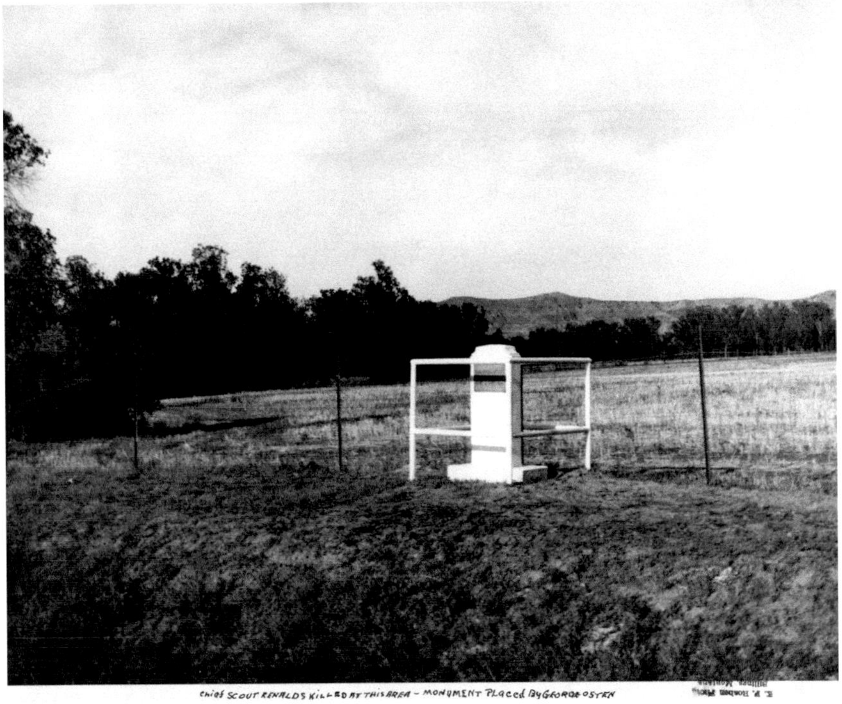

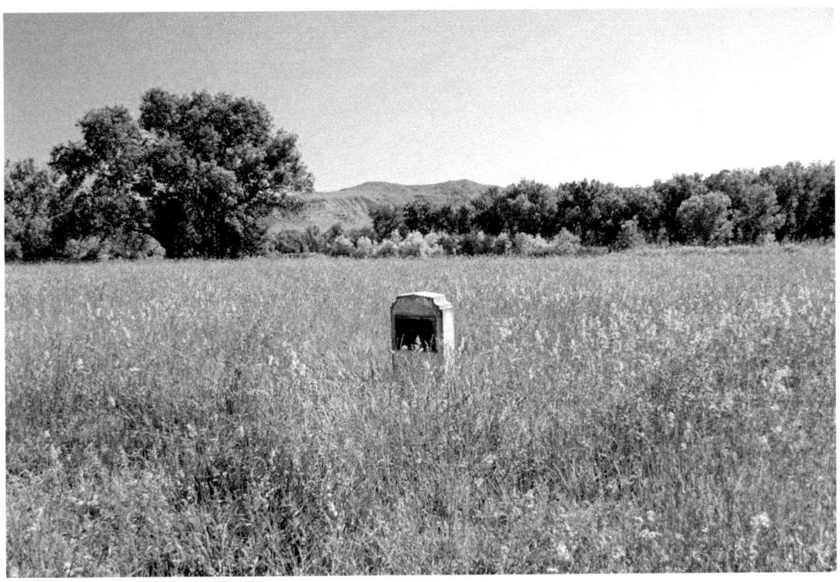

Figure 11.13. (*top*) Reynolds marker, east toward Weir Point. Courtesy of Big Horn County Historical Museum. (*bottom*) 2013 reshoot.

documents the significant impact on the scene made over the years by ranching. The irrigation ditch and vegetation in the background have moved much closer to the Reynolds marker. After Pitsch and Swanson moved the marker to this location, they did not put up any protective fence. Today the marker is vulnerable to being bumped by cattle that graze in the field. Note the truck passing on the I-90 in the modern photo's background.

Undoubtedly, Roahen shot figure 11.15 at a different time from the rest of his Reynolds marker photographs. The fencepost behind Osten does not match the position of those in earlier images. If the Reynolds marker were moved at the same time in the 1950s that the timber area was cleared for

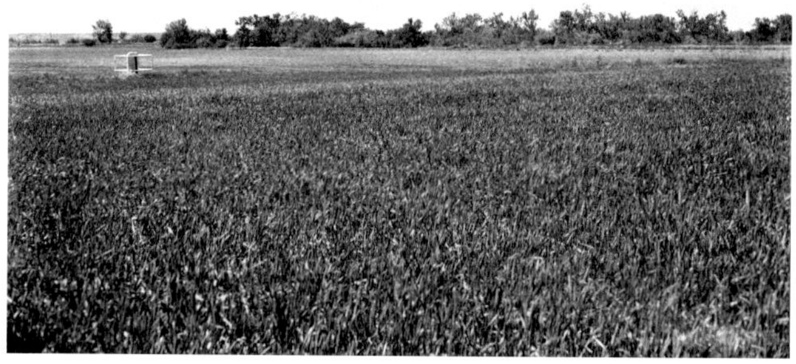

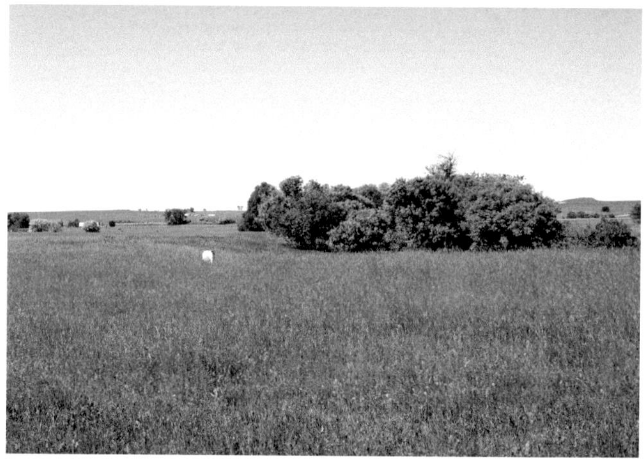

Figure 11.14. (*top*) Reynolds marker looking west. Courtesy of Big Horn County Historical Museum. (*bottom*) 2013 reshoot.

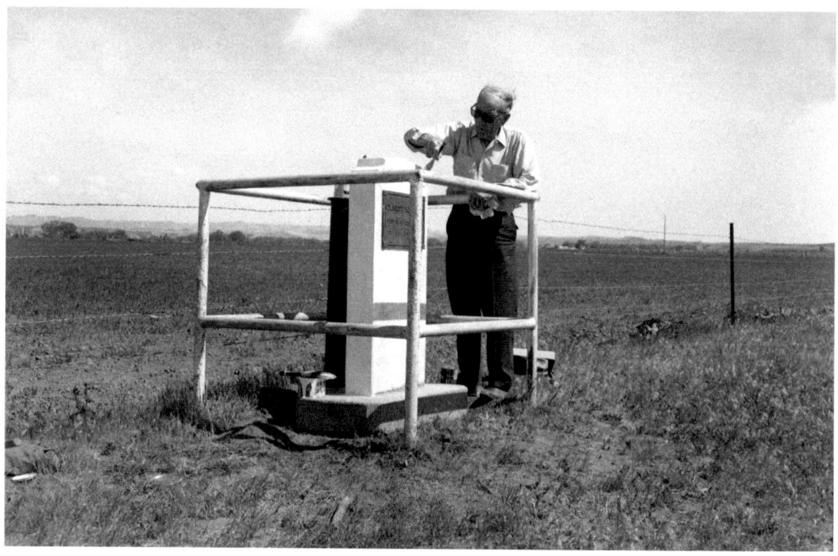

Figure 11.15. Reynolds marker, 1966, with George Osten painting. Courtesy of Big Horn County Historical Museum.

ranching, the 1966 date here also seems questionable. We know Swanson and Pitsch returned it to this position in the mid-1990s, but the actual date of its first move is unknown.[8] Inasmuch as Osten looks considerably older in this photo compared to the 1938 image, we can assume that Roahen took this image much later.

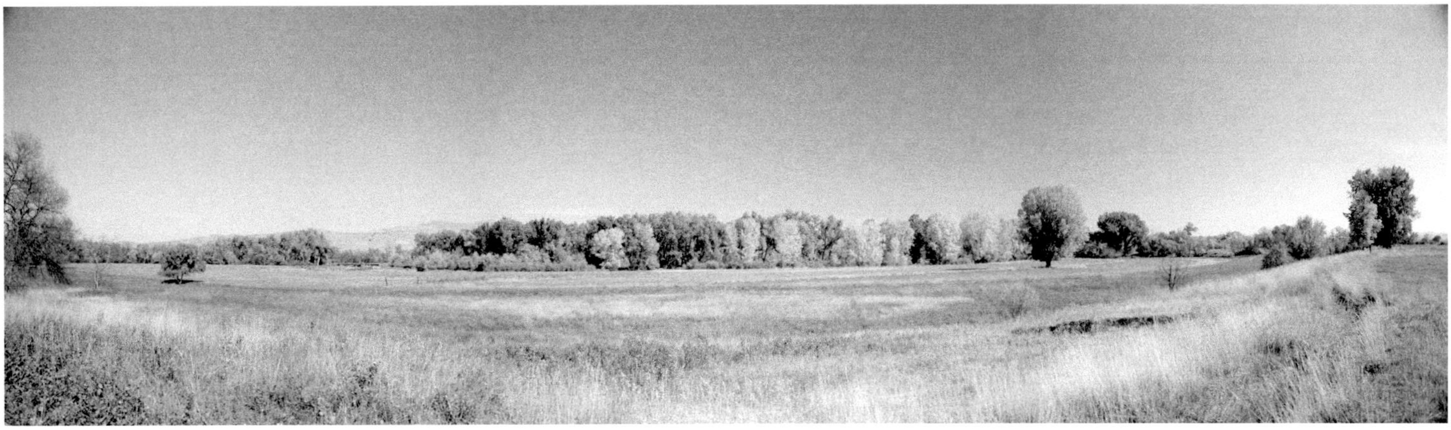

Figure 11.16. Panorama of the cleared timber area (2012).

Lt. Donald McIntosh

First Lt. Donald McIntosh, commanding Company G, accompanied Major Reno into the Little Big Horn Valley. As the troops retreated from the timber, warriors knocked McIntosh from his horse and killed him. His body reportedly was buried where he fell, and a marble marker was erected at the site in 1890, replacing a wooden headboard that originally designated the spot. However, at some point the marker was removed because it interfered with agriculture. It was relocated to a spot alongside an adjacent access road. Unfortunately, no record had been made of its original location.

In *Where Custer Fell*, two photos showed that original site, one of which had been taken about 1912 by photographer Elsa Spear. Many years later, in the mid-1990s, Jason Pitsch and Glen Swanson again relied on photographic evidence to reposition the McIntosh marker in its original spot. A 1998 comparison photo in *Where Custer Fell* indicated that they had correctly moved the marker back to the center of a field. Both of those images showed the bluffs to the southeast at the base of which runs the Little Big Horn River.

When Roahen took his photograph of the McIntosh marker (fig. 11.17), it was not in its original location but in a spot near the intersection of the access road that today takes one back to the Reno Retreat Crossing and the former driveway to the Jason Pitsch house. This site has its own Little Big Horn history; it was where the unknown soldier's remains were discovered in 1926, a few weeks before the fiftieth anniversary. Instead of the McIntosh marker that appears in the Roahen image, today a Weibert family historical marker inside the fence commemorates the 1926 discovery of the remains (fig. 11.18).

The modern figure 11.17 photo proved difficult to shoot as a match for Roahen's because of heavy vegetation around the fenced-in plot. The driveway

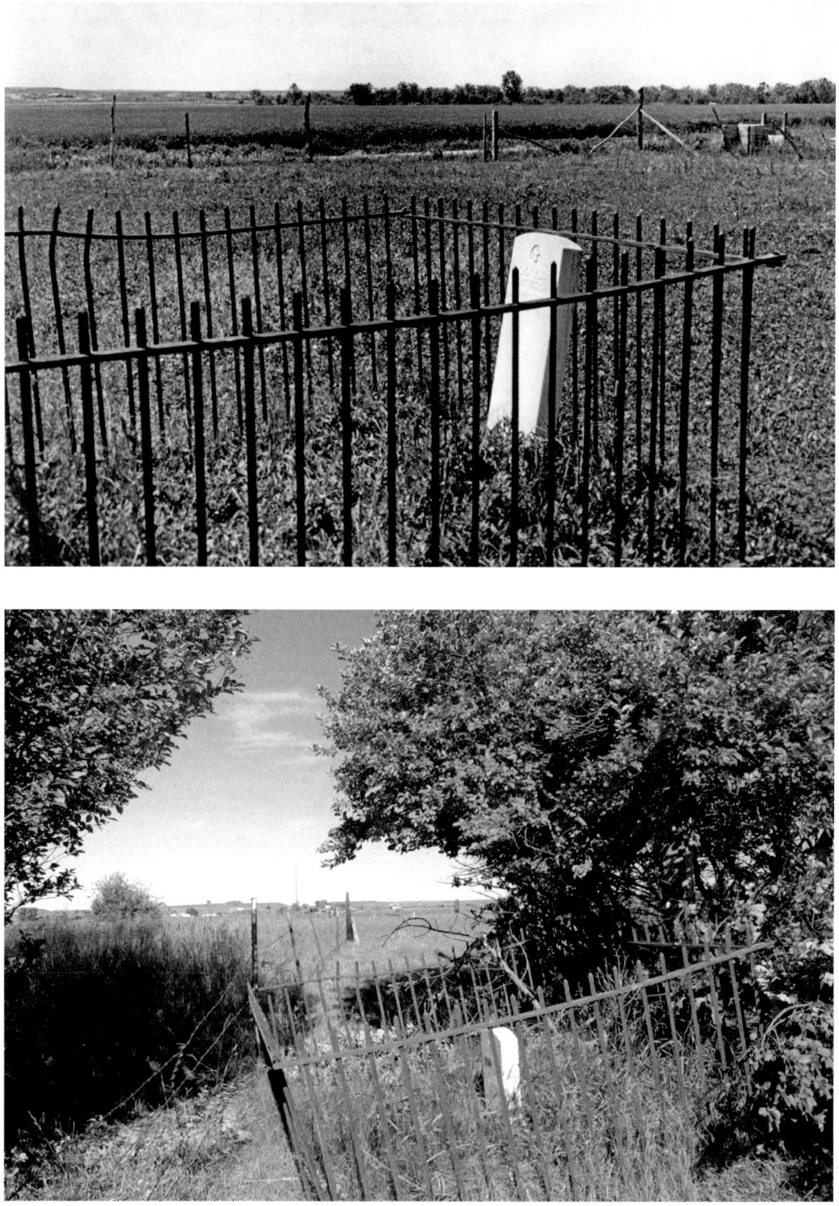

Figure 11.17. (*top*) Donald McIntosh marker. Courtesy of Big Horn County Historical Museum. (*bottom*) 2013 reshoot.

into the Pitsch property, visible in Roahen's photo, is obscured by brush and grass behind the fence on the far side. Also, the ground around the fencing on the left has slumped, giving it a different appearance than in Roahen's period. The Weibert marker is set in the middle instead of toward the north end of the enclosure.

Fortunately, the fence itself can be lined up with Roahen's original. On the modern photo's far side, the top few inches of the fence's left are bent, as in Roahen's. Additionally, in the distance in Roahen's photo, outbuildings for the Sam Denny ranch, now owned by the Custer Battlefield Preservation Committee, can be seen. In my photo, modern buildings stand in their place. Also, in the middle distance, just before the sky touches the benchlands, appears the now defunct Reno Battlefield Museum, which stands about 150 yards south of the Garryowen gasoline station.

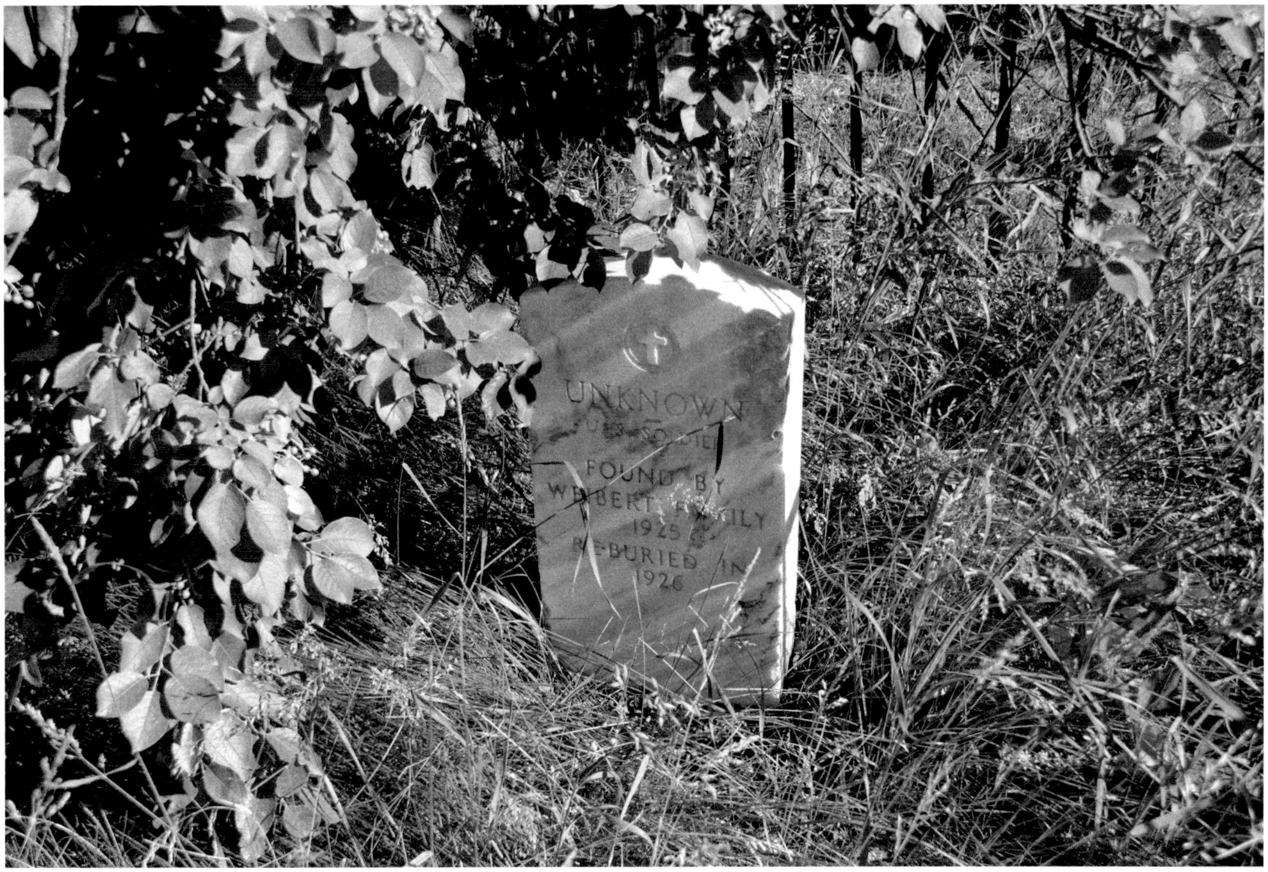

Figure 11.18. Weibert family historical marker (2013).

Weir Point, East from the Pitsch Family Driveway

Figure 11.19 is undated, which made it difficult to match up. The effort required the assistance of several friends, who either reviewed the image or accompanied me to the site. Hardin resident Dennis Fox and Park Service seasonal ranger Michael Donahue immediately pinpointed a former Pitsch family homestead as the likely site. Three friends, James Brust, Kevin Galvin, and Cliff Hamby, assisted me in locating a more exact spot one Sunday morning in June 2013. We encountered two problems almost at the start. The Little Big Horn River has carved new channels in that vicinity, and the cottonwoods along the river banks stand much taller than in the early 1960s, when Roahen likely photographed Weir Point. Additionally, we knew that Roahen had elevated himself, by standing on a ladder or perhaps in the back of his truck.

After our group generally lined up a possible location, Galvin, a retired British Army officer, took command of the situation. He directed Brust to position his rental car in a field near a bend in a driveway that took visitors to the former Jason Pitsch house. The photo site along the Pitsch driveway is about 150 yards north of the main east-west dirt road that leads to the point of Reno's retreat crossing. The Custer Battlefield Preservation Committee, which now owns the property, had the house demolished a few years ago. Galvin quickly mounted the vehicle, asked for my camera, and, over the next few minutes, snapped off a half dozen photographs. I later merged two of them into the

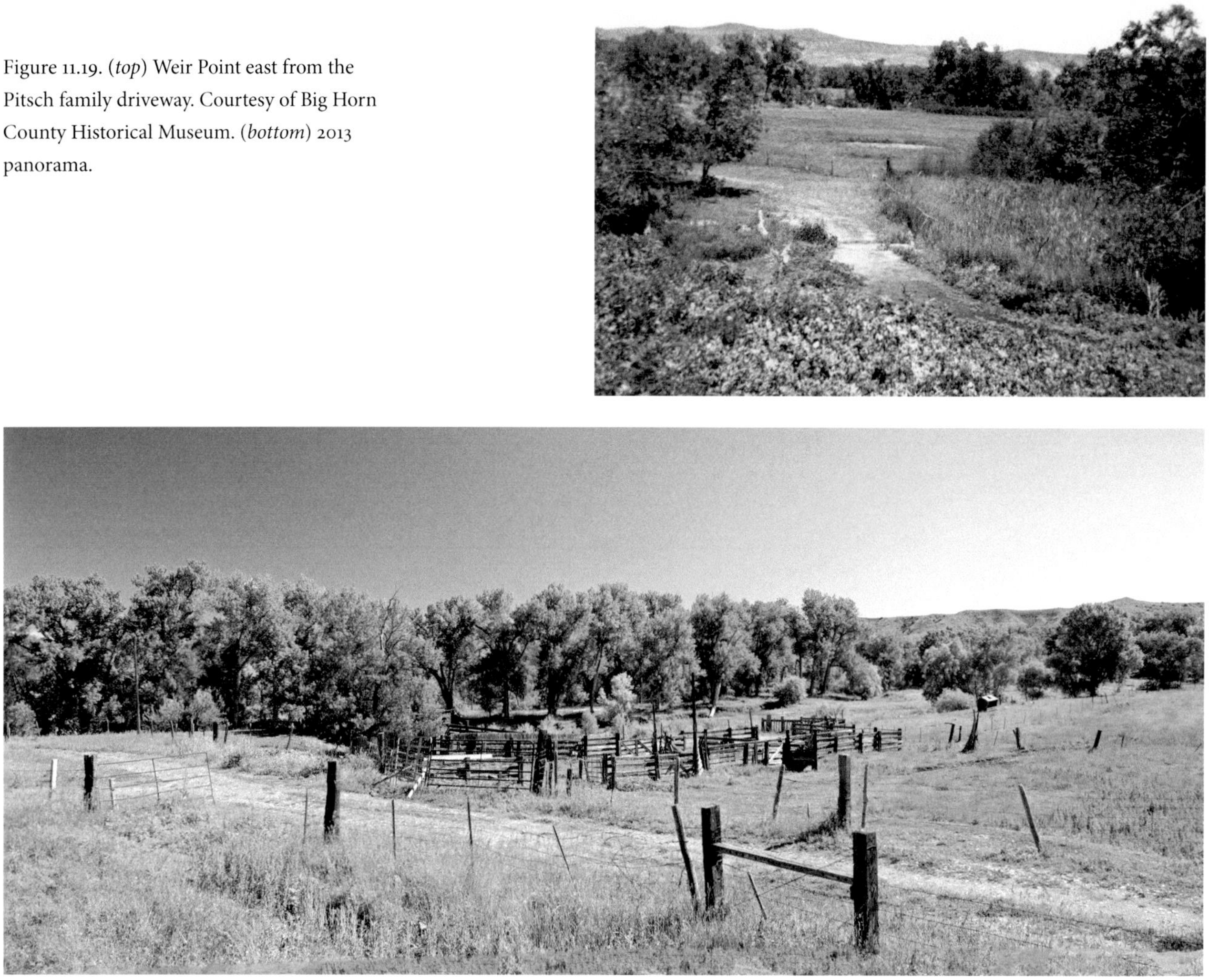

Figure 11.19. (*top*) Weir Point east from the Pitsch family driveway. Courtesy of Big Horn County Historical Museum. (*bottom*) 2013 panorama.

single panoramic image seen here. Even from the car's roof, Galvin was unable to see Weir Point over the trees on the modern photo's left. The site also has been significantly impacted by not only the Pitsch family's ranching and farming activities but also the river changes. The merged image serves to provide a greater perspective of the site's location.

In Roahen's photo, Weir Point quite obviously is over the trees to the left of the corral. Another noteworthy point is the knob on the bluffs to the right of the grove of trees in the photo's mid-right. In the modern panorama, Weir Point cannot be seen, but the knob can be. To locate it, note the shack to the far right of the corral. The knob is just above the shack and the grove of trees behind it. A sharper knoll to the right along the bluffs can be seen on the panorama's far right. Just below that feature a small portion of the river can be spotted. The river channel runs behind the trees that line its bank.

Reno Retreat Crossing

The modern site of Reno's retreat crossing is generally accepted as accurate today. At numerous times in the post-battle period, 7th Cavalry survivors visited the battlefield and pointed out this site as the place where Reno's panicked command splashed across the Little Big Horn River and climbed the bluffs. The most notable reunion occurred in 1886 on the battle's tenth anniversary, a visit that was well documented by D. F. Barry, a Bismarck, Dakota Territory, photographer. In fact, he was close friends with Dr. Henry R. Porter, who had survived the valley fighting, escaped across the river at that site, and earned plaudits for his care of wounded soldiers and civilians in the joint command of Major Reno and Captain Benteen on the bluffs.[9]

By the time Roahen first visited the site, probably in the early 1930s, he would have been just one more battle student viewing a well-established historic landmark. Two of his images, figures 11.20 and 11.21, are variant shots from the mouth of the retreat ravine, which served as the primary escape route for the 7th Cavalrymen racing for the top of the bluffs in 1876. These photos look west across the river toward the general vicinity of the various paths Reno's men traveled in escaping the warriors in the valley. Though no modern photos match these two, Roahen's figure 11.22, which is matched, is similar to them. He took it inside the ravine's mouth, just on the inside of the fence marking the park boundary line. Today the retreat crossing acreage is owned by the Custer Battlefield Preservation Committee.

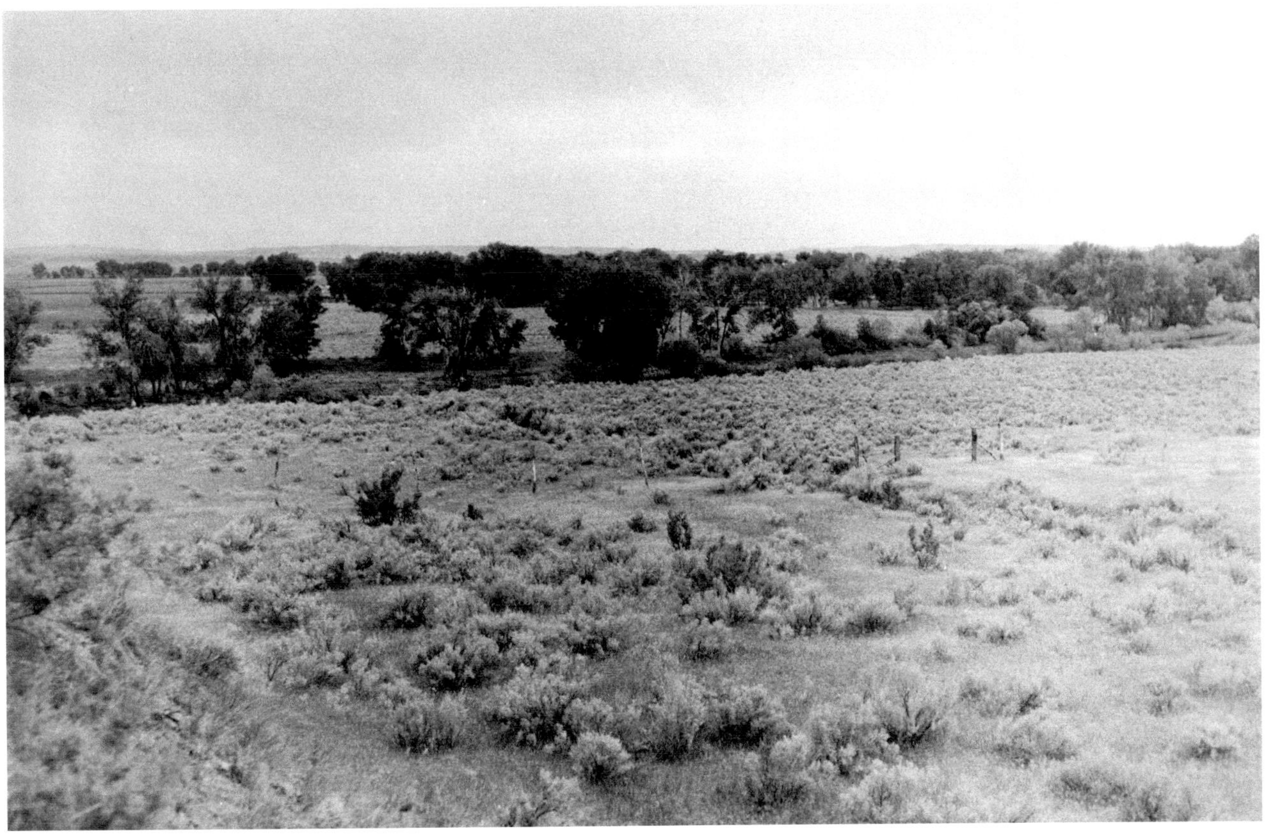

Figure 11.20. Reno retreat crossing, looking west across the east side of the river. Courtesy of Big Horn County Historical Museum.

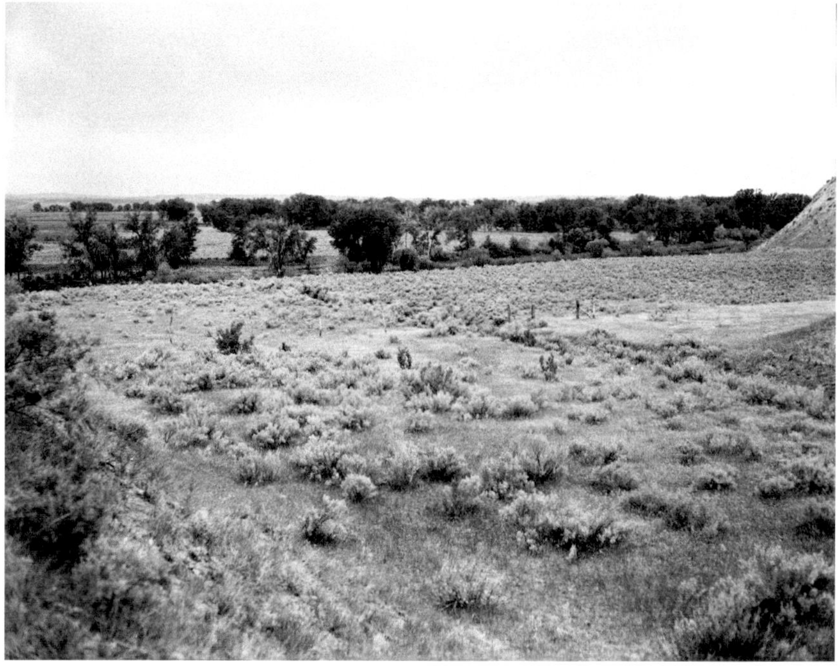

Figure 11.21. Retreat crossing plain. Courtesy of Big Horn County Historical Museum.

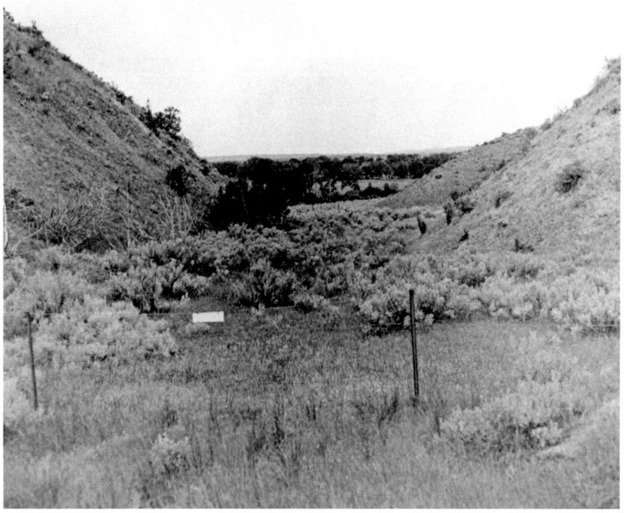

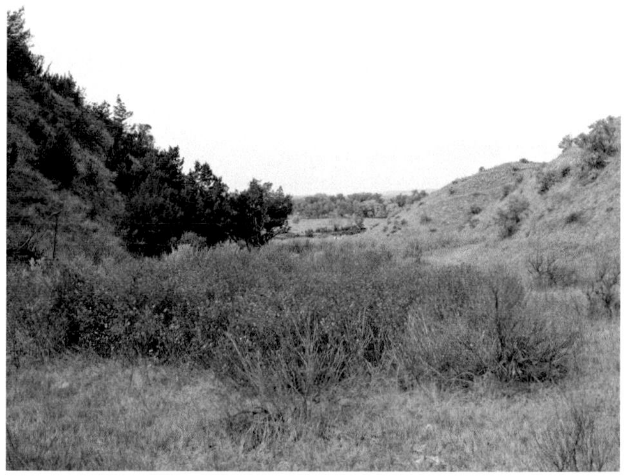

Figure 11.22. (*left*) Reno retreat ravine opening. (*right*) 2012 reshoot.

The modern photo in figure 11.22 was taken on the river side of today's park boundary fence. It reveals how similar the modern mouth of the ravine remains to what is seen in Roahen's photograph from sixty or seventy years ago. In its background is the flat plain leading to the river crossing site. The trees in both Roahen and modern photos are on the valley, or west, side of the river.

Not surprisingly, Roahen shot images looking up and down river from his perch on the west bank of the Little Big Horn River. His figure 11.23 photo looks north from the crossing downstream toward Medicine Tail Coulee. The matching modern photo indicates how little the river's appearance has changed in this vicinity since Roahen took his undated photos. His west bank is much smoother, whereas the 2012 image reveals the ravaging caused by floods, including the most recent in 2011.

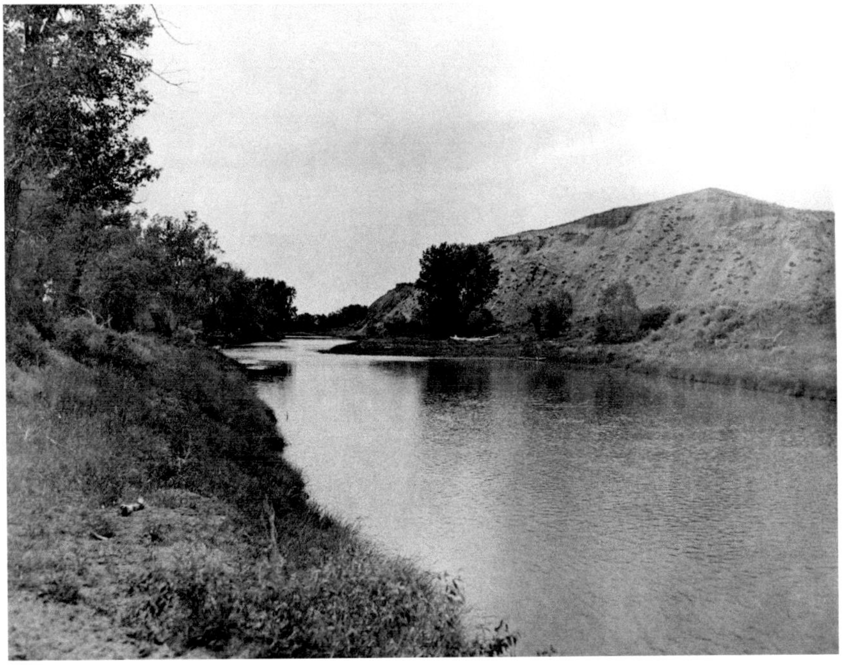

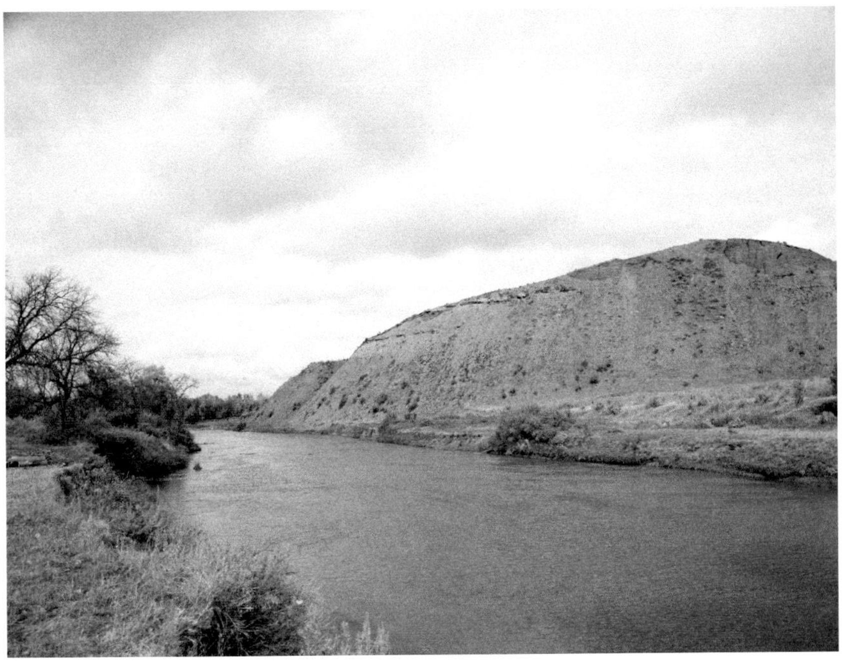

Figure 11.23. (*top*) Looking north at the narrow point of the Reno retreat crossing. Courtesy of Big Horn County Historical Museum. (*bottom*) 2012 reshoot.

Having aimed his camera to the north, Roahen next pointed it south, or upstream, toward the area of Reno's first crossing (fig. 11.24). This photograph proved more revealing than simply being a shot of that river area immediately south of the retreat crossing. In walking the river banks on the west side of the Little Big Horn, I quickly realized that his photograph more likely focused on what he believed to be Water Carriers Ravine. The story of Water Carriers Ravine is well documented in the Little Big Horn literature—how soldiers made their way down to the east bank, retrieved water for their thirsty comrades on top of the bluffs, especially the wounded, and made their way back up

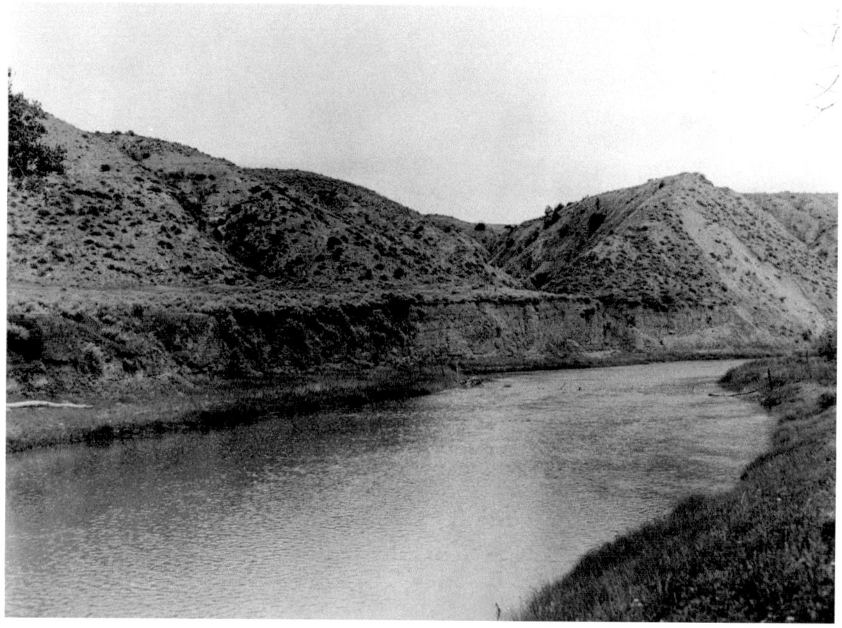

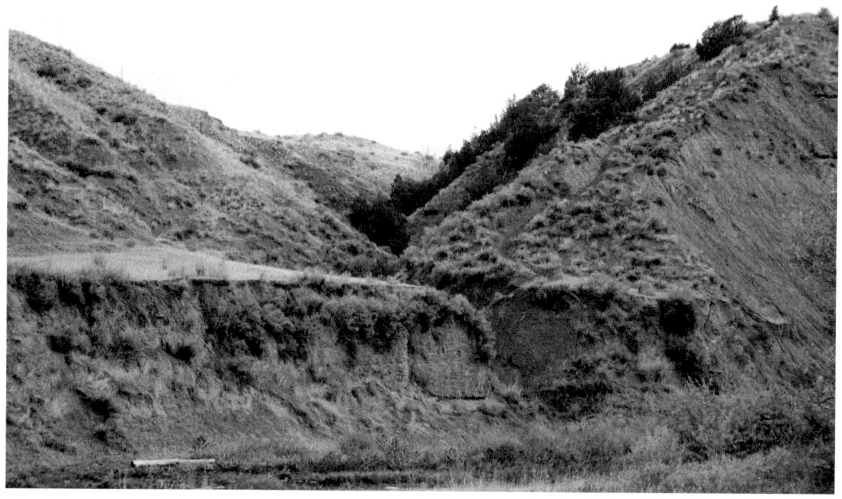

Figure 11.24. (*top*) Retreat crossing looking southeast toward Water Carrier's Ravine. Courtesy of Big Horn County Historical Museum. (*bottom*) 2012 reshoot.

the rugged banks of the deep cut, all while under severe fire from the Indians.

What has been less certain is the specific ravine they used, inasmuch as at least three come off the high ground and provide access to the river. In *Where Custer Fell*, we included a section of unmatched photographs whose original locations we could not determine. One of those photographs was titled "Slaper in water detail ravine" (fig. 11.25). Pvt. William C. Slaper, Company M, was one of the courageous troopers who braved the Indian fire to retrieve the precious water. On the occasion of the fiftieth battle anniversary in June 1926, Slaper, among the soldier survivors in attendance, was photographed in the ravine, although the photographer's identity is unknown. Because of the uncertainty about which route or routes the water carriers followed to make their way to the river bank, the Slaper photograph is potentially of great historical

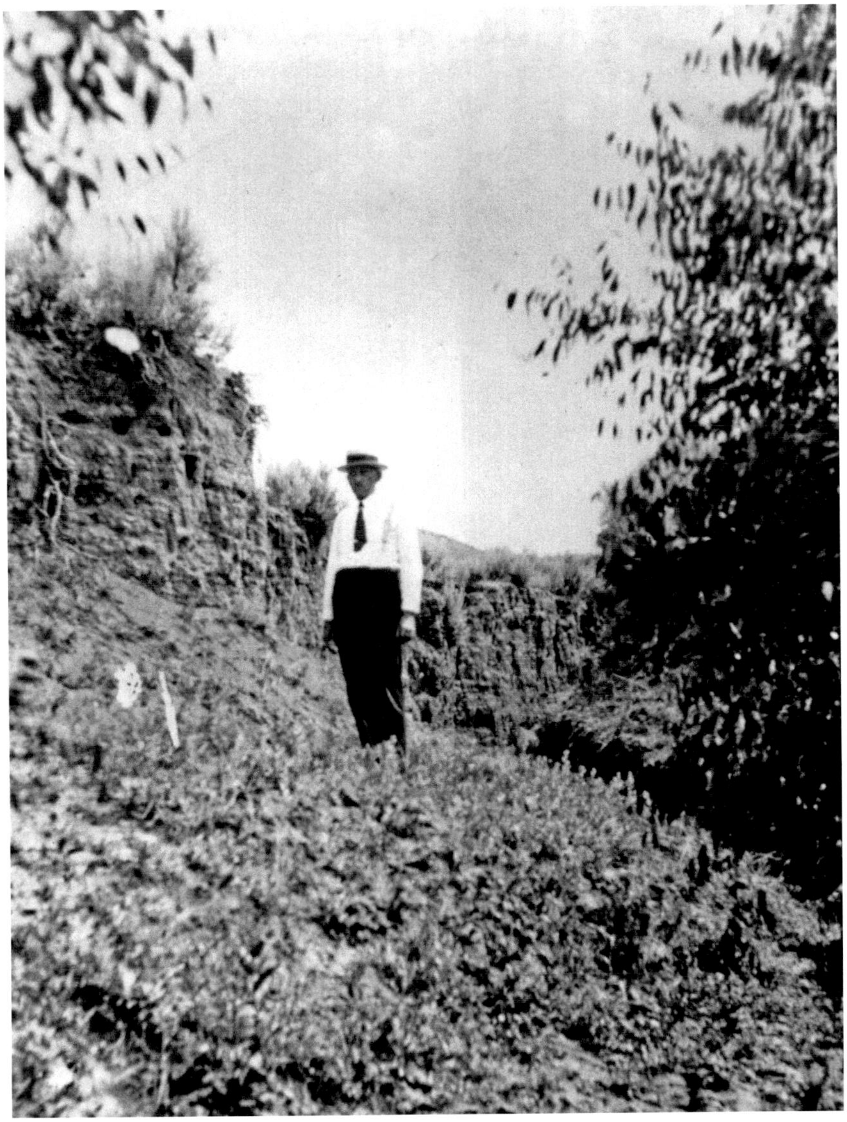

Figure 11.25. "Slaper in water detail ravine." Courtesy of Little Bighorn Battlefield National Monument.

significance. It depicts a surviving participant in the historic episode posing in the ravine he said he used. My colleagues and I made several strenuous hikes up and down the various gullies that appeared as possibilities, but we could never settle on a proper match.

In early October 2012, while reshooting Roahen's Reno Retreat Crossing photographs, I marched to a spot on the west bank opposite the ravine that my colleagues and I had earlier deemed the most likely site. I shot numerous images and include three here (modern fig. 11.24 and figs. 11.26, 11.27).

Modern figure 11.24, which looks east across the Little Big Horn, provides the best view inside the ravine. Erosion has altered its appearance since 1926 and rounded the steep sandstone walls that appeared behind Slaper. We cannot tell how far from the river the ex-soldier was actually standing. If the 1926 photograph marks the site, Slaper likely stood high on the left-side slope of the mouth, while his photographer companion remained below him, perhaps on the grassy riverside bench similar to the one seen in the modern photographs.

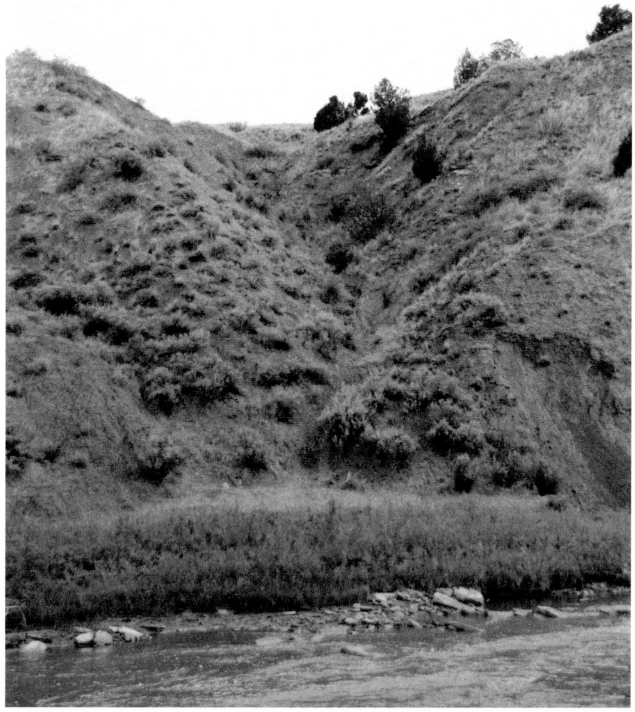

Figure 11.26. Opening of Water Carriers Ravine (2012).

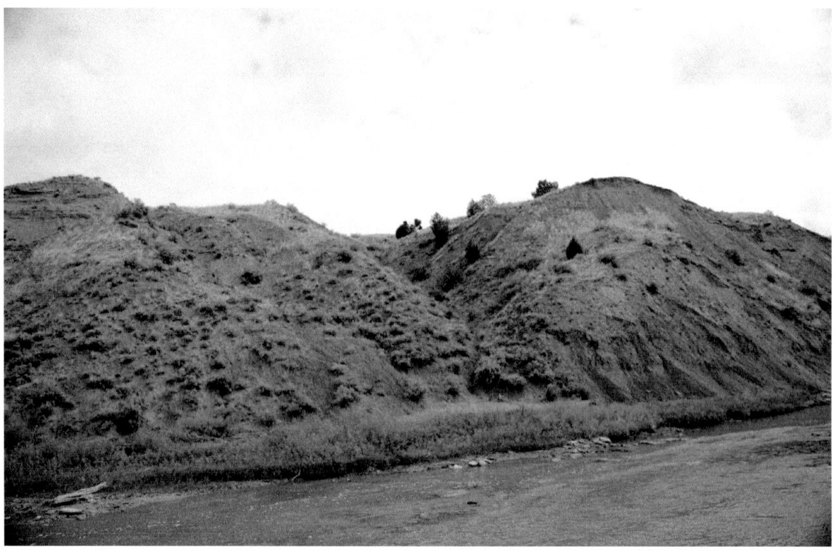

Figure 11.27. Wide view of Water Carriers Ravine (2012).

Unfortunately, no Roahen images of the inside of the ravine from the same vantage point are known to exist. Still, in the absence of any other readily understood purpose for Roahen's photograph, figure 11.24 suggests that the ravine's opening was his focus. His series of historic photographs alongside the modern images may not provide the definitive proof we would like, but they offer us the best evidence that at least one battle survivor thought this spot was where he carried out the most courageous deeds of his career.

Another side-issue involving the retreat crossing area concerns the death and burial of 2nd Lt. Benjamin Hodgson, who was serving as Major Reno's adjutant on June 25, 1876.[10] The historical record generally agrees that Hodgson was badly wounded and unhorsed while attempting to cross the river. Almost as soon as he crawled out of the river with assistance, he was shot a second time and instantly killed on the flats below the bluffs.

Today a marble military grave marker bearing Hodgson's name stands on a slight rise above the river. No doubt the lieutenant was killed in that vicinity, but whether he was buried there or on the top of the bluffs has been another topic of endless discussion among Little Big Horn researchers. Capt. Thomas McDougall's often inconsistent statements seemingly supported the notion that Hodgson's body was recovered and buried in the defensive site on the bluffs.

After examining various historic accounts, my coauthors and I concluded in 2005 that a bluff-top burial for Hodgson seemed highly unlikely. Our historical research convinced us that, regardless of the true location of Hodgson's initial burial, some sort of marker (perhaps a wooden stake) was placed beside the river near his death site. In 1886, General Godfrey reported that such a marker stood there at that time. We further speculated that over time that marker disappeared and led to confusion about his actual burial site.

In 1910, the government erected four markers on the battlefield for Lts. Henry M. Harrington, James E. Porter, and James G. Sturgis, as well as Hodgson. Considerable mystery has surrounded the deaths of the first three officers. Despite how well documented Hodgson's death site at the river had been, his 1910 marker was set up on the bluffs, far above where he actually fell (fig. 11.28). In *Where Custer Fell*, we published a 1916 L. A. Huffman photo that showed this spurious marker in place on a bluff below Sharpshooter Ridge. It overlooked the retreat crossing, about halfway between the Park Service gate and the Reno-Benteen Defense Site and its modern parking lot. Superintendent

Figure 11.28. (*left below*) Hodgson marker with tall vegetation. Courtesy of Big Horn County Historical Museum. (*right below*) 2012 reshoot.

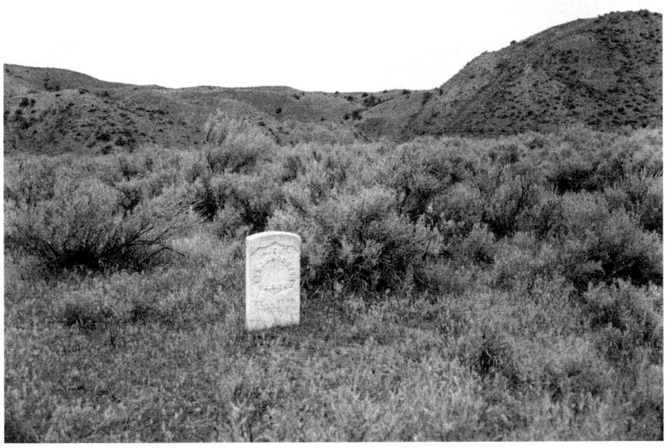

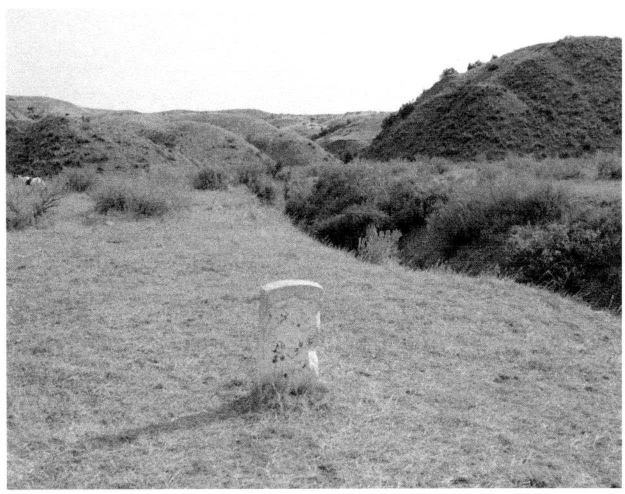

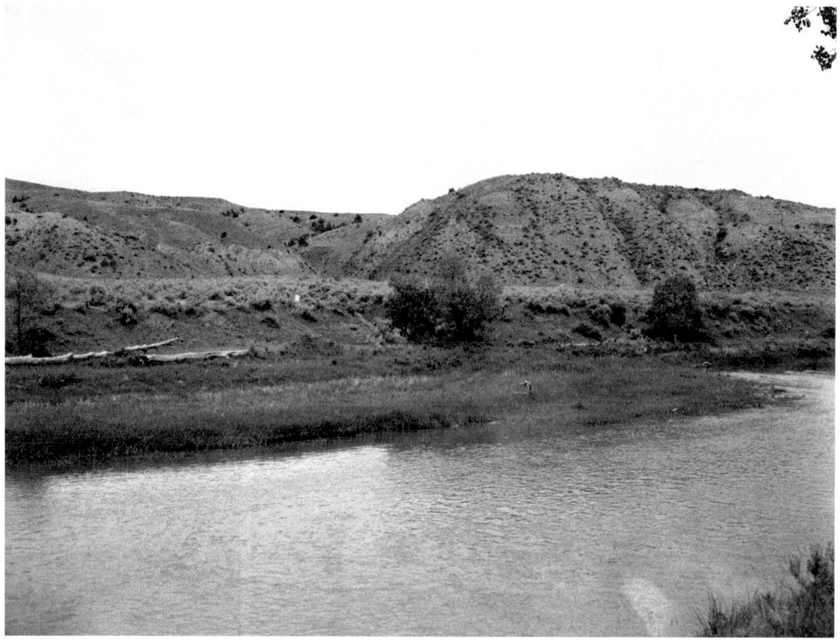

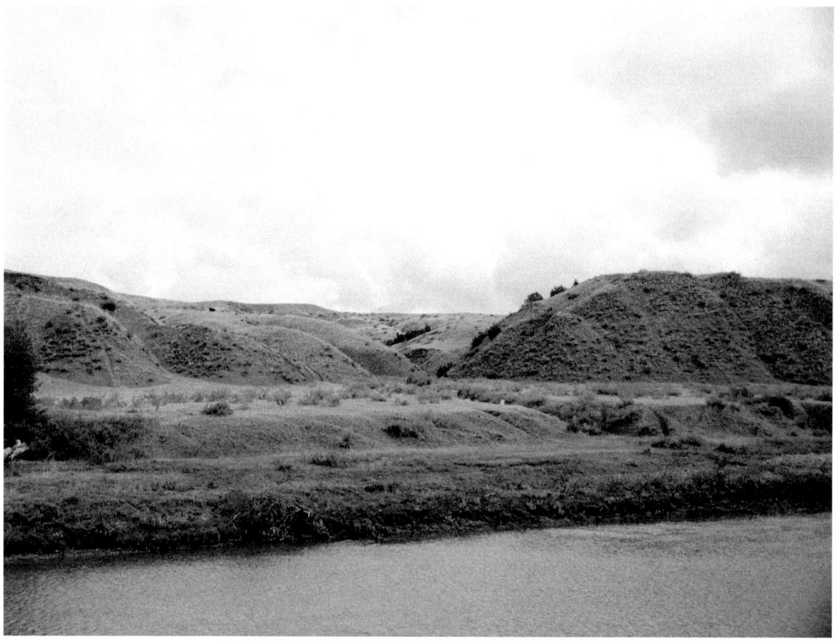

Figure 11.29. (*top*) Retreat crossing with Hodgson marker. Courtesy of Big Horn County Historical Museum. (*bottom*) 2012 reshoot.

Luce later reported that in 1939 he moved the marker from that location and reinstalled it beside the river near Hodgson's apparent actual death site. Inasmuch as Luce did not assume his office until 1941, his move of Hodgson's marker undoubtedly occurred some time later than 1939.

By the time Roahen took his undated photograph, Luce had completed the marker's move and little doubt then existed about the site's accuracy. The only important differences between Roahen's photograph and its modern match are the deep cut now visible on the flatland beside the marker and less vegetation surrounding the marker.

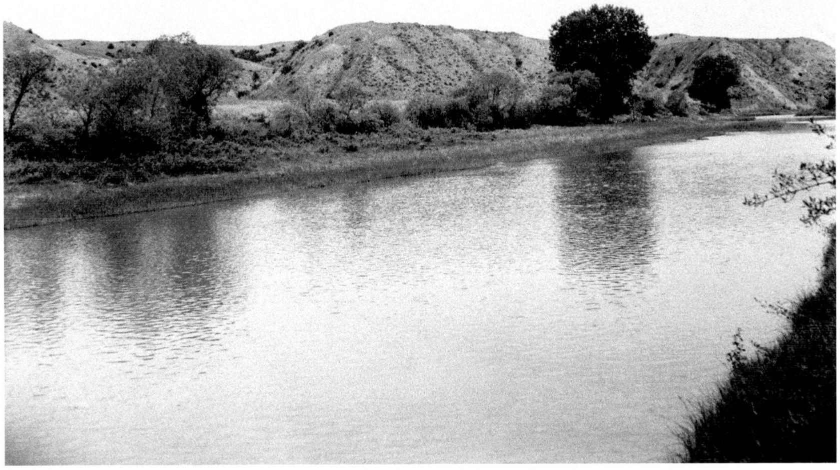

Figure 11.30. Retreat crossing with trees, a variant of fig. 11.29. Courtesy of Big Horn County Historical Museum.

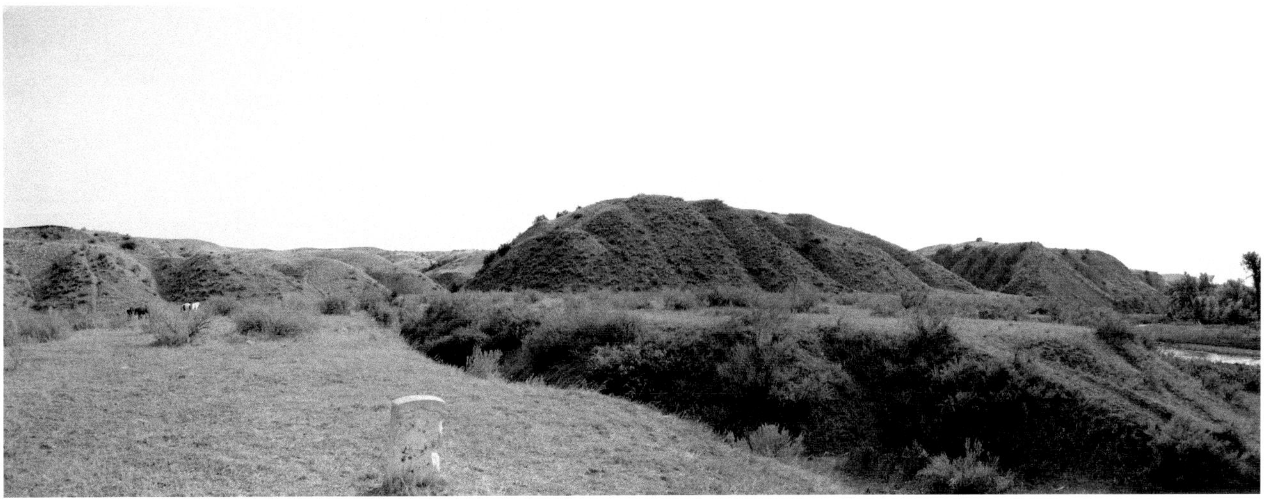

Figure 11.31. Reno retreat plain, 2012 panorama.

CHAPTER 12

Aerial Photos of the Reno Retreat Crossing

Roahen most likely took his series of aerial photographs of the Reno Retreat Crossing during the seventy-fifth battle anniversary in June 1951, when he arranged to fly over the battlefield. Figure 12.1 purports to show the 7th Cavalry's retreat route across the Little Big Horn, but as a single line it might be misleading. Undoubtedly, after fleeing the timber area, the soldiers arrived at the crossing by multiple routes. Many accounts say they rode around the edge of the bend of the river across the modern Bird In Ground family property. If so, they likely would have arrived at the river from that location along the line Roahen drew on his photo.

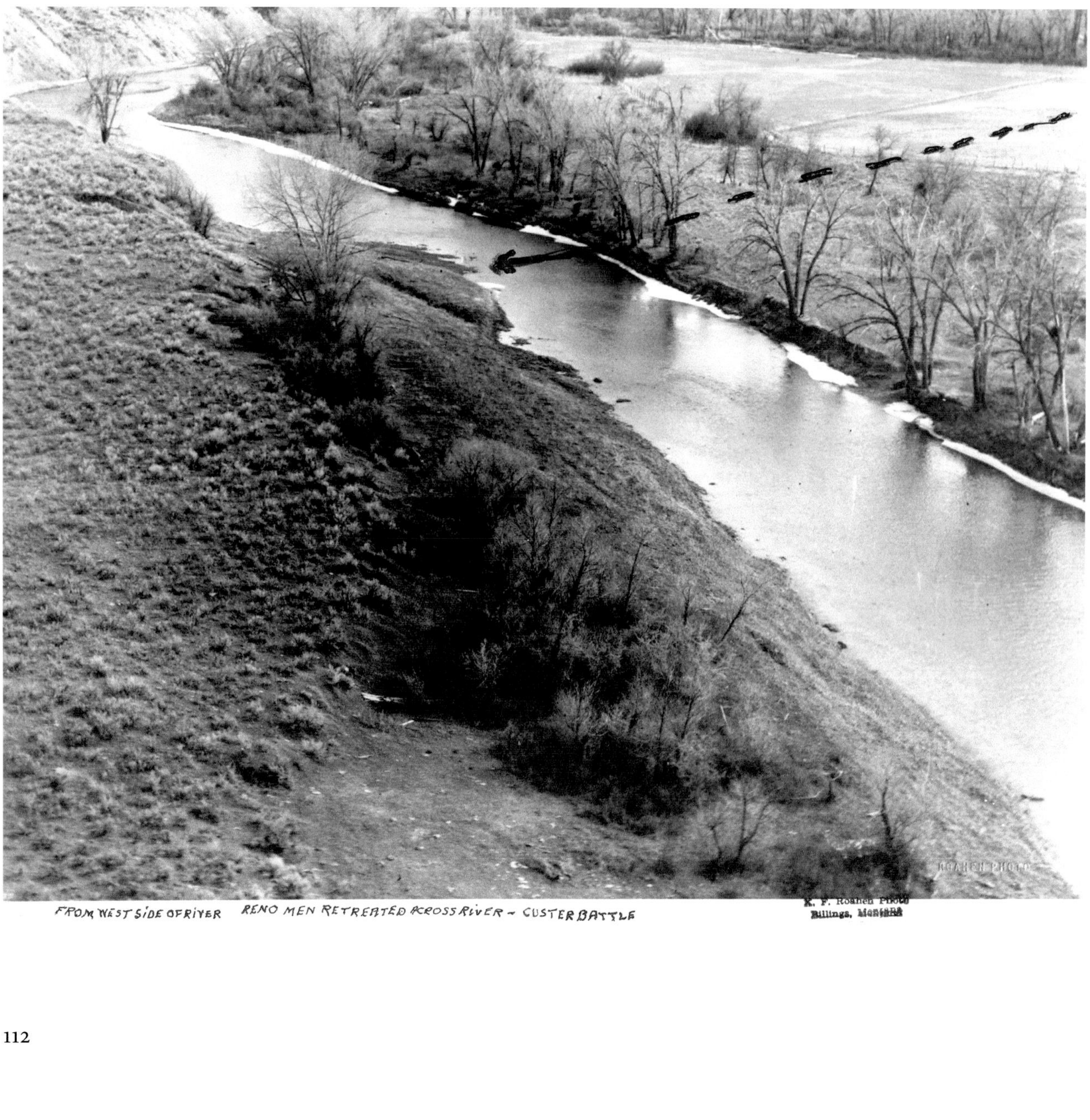

Figure 12.1. Reno retreat crossing route, as supposed by Roahen. Courtesy of Big Horn County Historical Museum.

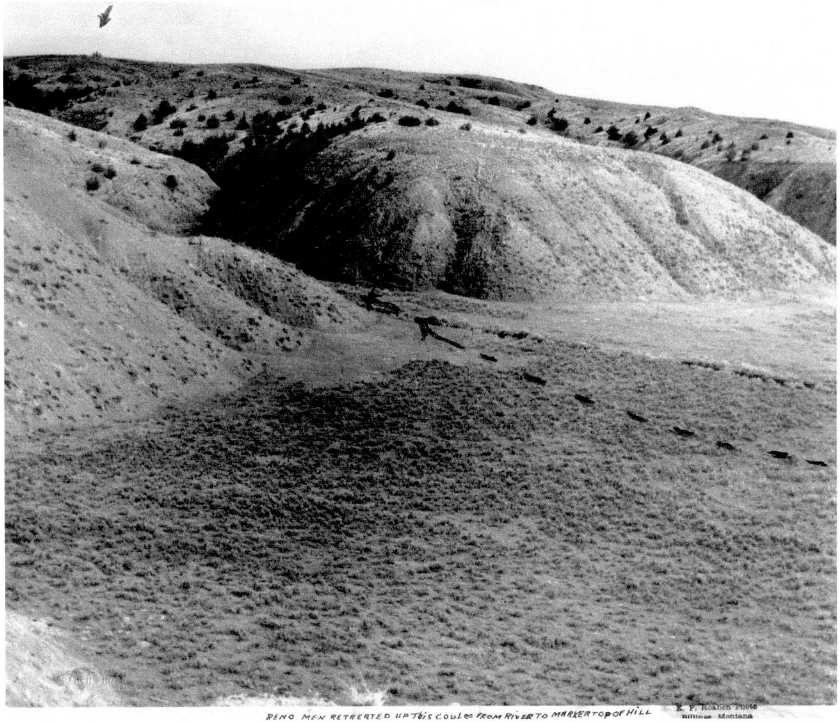

Figure 12.2. Reno retreat route up bluffs, per Roahen; arrow indicates Reno Hill monument. Courtesy of Big Horn County Historical Museum.

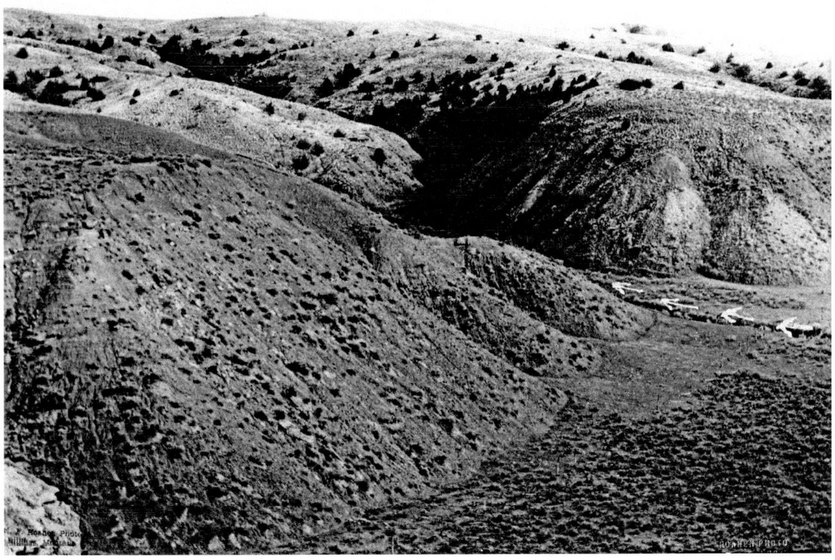

Figure 12.3. Another suggested Reno retreat route up bluffs. Courtesy of Big Horn County Historical Museum.

Figures 12.2 and 12.3 are variants of the same view. Figure 12.2 shows more of the plain the troops had to traverse after crossing the river. From the bluffs Indians reportedly shot down at them. Figure 12.3 may provide a slightly better look inside the rugged retreat ravine used to climb the bluffs. Both photos provide a glimpse of the monument on Reno Hill, designated by Roahen's arrow in figure 12.2.

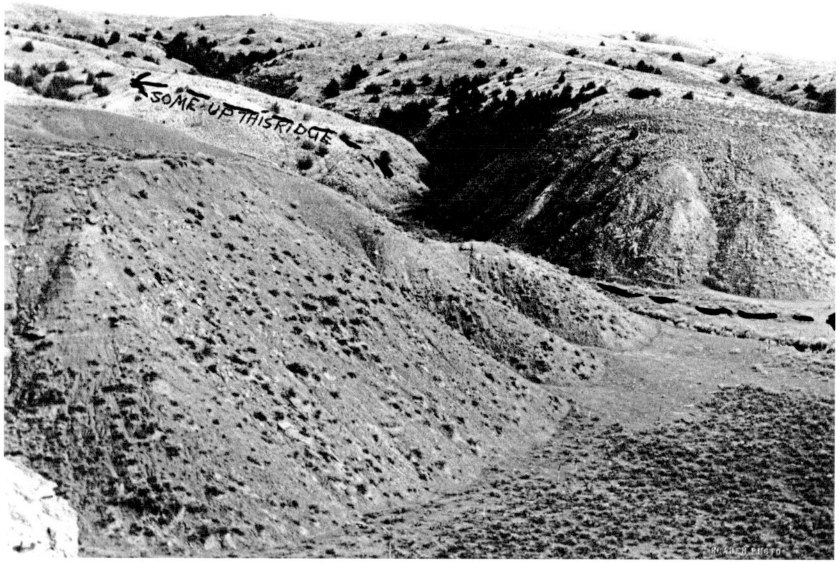

Figure 12.4. Doctor DeWolf's unfortunate route as outlined by arrows. Courtesy of Big Horn County Historical Museum.

Figure 12.4 is important for Roahen's handwritten remark beneath the arrows that "some up this ridge," indicating the one climbed by Dr. James DeWolf and others, who unfortunately ran into warriors and were killed (see chapter 14). In this series of photos, Roahen is revealing his traditional side in telling the Little Big Horn story. Few would disagree with him.

CHAPTER 13

Reno-Benteen Defense Site

By late in the afternoon of June 25, 1876, Lt. Col. George Armstrong Custer was dead. By that point, the action at the Little Big Horn had bypassed him. The historical story would focus more fully on survival efforts by remaining members of his 7th U.S. Cavalry Regiment, commanded by Major Reno and assisted by Benteen, the senior captain. For the next twenty-four hours their soldiers would endure continued onslaughts by the Indian warriors.

That phase of the battle began by at least 4 P.M. that Sunday.[1] Demoralized troops of Reno's command had fled from the valley in chaos under Indian fire to the steep river bluffs. When they reached the top, they numbered only seven officers and eighty-four enlisted men. Their Indian scouts had scattered. A few may have been fighting in the valley below; others were driving off ponies captured from their enemies. The 7th's military predicament gravely worried Reno himself and his subordinates. His battalion's total casualties numbered some forty men killed and thirteen wounded. Fifteen or more men remained missing; many would turn up either later that day or the next. In the valley, warriors looted the army's dead, killed the wounded, and occasionally fired upon survivors huddled on the bluffs.

Reno wondered about Custer's whereabouts. Additionally, he was concerned about the rest of their comrades, including Captain Benteen's battalion as well as the pack train under Captain McDougall. Reno's men haphazardly controlled the high ground, but his barely defensible position made the command's military situation precarious. Soldiers on the west manned a picket line on the downward slope of the bluffs above the river. The army's only surviving medical officer, Dr. Henry Porter, organized a makeshift hospital station for the wounded in a swale that eventually would be protected from Indian firing by the herd of horses and mules.

Fortunately, about 4:20 P.M. Benteen and his men appeared near the Little Big Horn ford at Reno Creek. For the first time he viewed the Little Big Horn Valley, but the sight must have shocked him. He undoubtedly expected the fighting to have ended by the time he arrived. Two messengers sent from Custer, one to McDougall and one to Benteen earlier that afternoon, had suggested that the Indians were running. A combat-experienced officer, Benteen could tell that was not true. Benteen later claimed he had spotted Reno's surviving soldiers on a hilltop about a mile away. He quickly headed in their direction.

Benteen found Reno agitated. Trumpeter John Martin, standing nearby, recalled that Reno blurted out to Benteen either "For God's sake, Benteen,

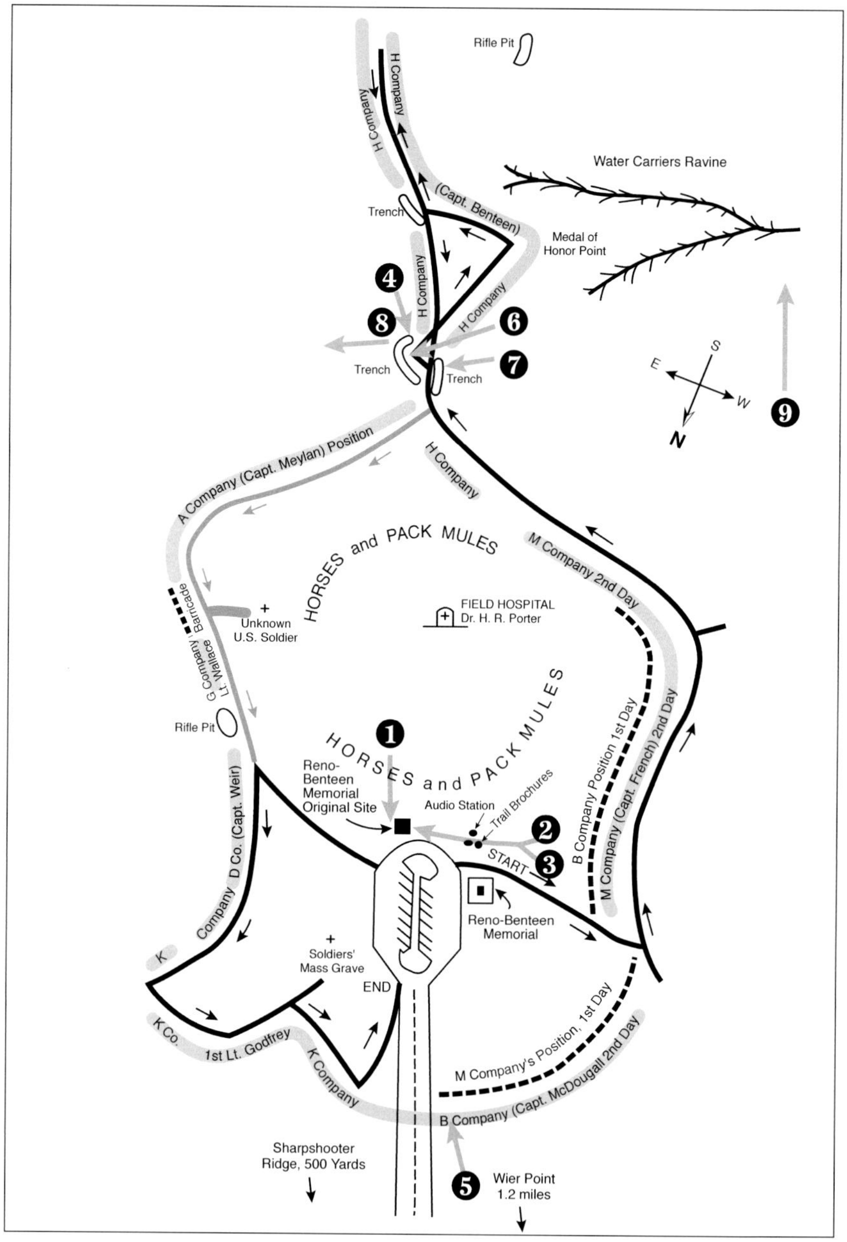

Map 13.1. Reno-Benteen defense site. Map by Gary Raham.

1. Fig. 13.1
2. Fig. 13.2
3. Fig. 13.5
4. Figs. 13.6–13.9
5. Fig. 13.10
6. Figs. 13.11, 13.14
7. Fig. 13.12
8. Fig. 13.13
9. Fig. 13.15

halt your command and help me. I've lost half my men" or "Well, I have lost about half of my men, and I could do no better than I have done."[2]

Although Benteen had shown Reno Custer's written message to bring the packs, the two officers stayed in place. Some of their men reported hearing firing to the north. The two officers' controversial failure to move promptly toward Custer has stirred historical debate ever since. One theory holds that Benteen so hated his commanding officer that he was unconcerned about the fate of Custer and, absurdly, all of his men. At that time, however, the captain would have had no grasp of Custer's true situation. Reno, for his part, remained dispirited as a result of his rout in the valley. He, too, would have lacked any insight into the nature of Custer's predicament. Still, their critics argue that protocols of military orders obligated the two men to comply immediately with Custer's written directive to Benteen. Despite that order and the firing to the north, the two senior officers preferred to stand fast, apparently awaiting the extra ammunition carried by the pack train and expressing concern for their wounded.

At one point, Reno, inexplicably, felt compelled to return to the river's edge, either to retrieve the body of his dead adjutant, Lieutenant Hodgson, or at least to confirm his fate. Reno's absence left Benteen in temporary command of their troops on the hill. He set about organizing the defensive position, adding his own men to Reno's along the skirmish line. Two mules carrying ammunition soon arrived, followed by the rest of the pack train about 5:15 P.M.

During this period, Capt. Thomas Weir, perturbed by his superiors' failure to move north toward the sounds of the guns, headed in that direction on his own. Without orders, Weir's own Company D followed their leader. About fifteen minutes later, Benteen departed with Companies H, K, and M. Eventually Reno himself set off with the remaining troops, their movement slowed by the wounded and the pack train.

A mile and a half ahead stood a high elevation, today designated Weir Point. Weir and Benteen positioned their companies around its slopes. Three miles to the front, bands of Indians scurried about and occasionally fired toward the ground. That action puzzled the soldiers, who still had no idea that they were watching Custer's demise. Soon the Indians were seen riding rapidly toward the troops on Weir Point. Reno and Benteen opted to return to their original, more defensible position on the bluffs.

Back within their lines, the command established an elliptical defensive perimeter on the crest of ridges that today are referred to as the Reno-Benteen Defense Site. In the center, Doctor Porter operated his field hospital, now protected on its open east side by the picketed horses and mules. On the river side to the west, the high bluffs offered reasonable security, but the gentler slopes on the east provided the soldiers with far less cover. Benteen's Company H manned the high ridge on the south perimeter. On the east, Capt. Myles Moylan's Company A defended the swale housing the hospital and corral for the animals. Next to A was Company G under Lt. George Wallace. Company D followed, with K and M in that order on the northern perimeter. McDougall's company secured the high bluffs facing west toward the Little Big Horn River.[3] More men guarded the northern perimeter, the direction from which the Indians likely would attack. The regiment's position was far from impregnable. On the north was a high bluff with a rounded point, later known as Sharpshooter Ridge. It offered the Indians open lines of fire into the cavalry's positions. Pinned down, the soldiers on the bluffs were too far from the village to threaten its inhabitants.

The Indians fired on the troops until dark. Fortunately, Reno and Benteen commanded as many as 367 men: fourteen officers, 339 enlisted, and fourteen scouts or other civilians. They built up makeshift breastworks with ammunition and food boxes and sought protection as best they could. Before the firing ceased at dark, another six men would be killed and twenty-one wounded.

During the night, Custer's whereabouts dominated whispered conversations. Some of the officers and senior enlisted men, such as 1st Sgt. John Ryan of Company M, had fought at the Washita River nearly eight years earlier. After that battle, controversy swirled over whether Custer had abandoned Maj. Joel H. Elliott and eighteen other soldiers by withdrawing from the captured Indian encampment without ascertaining the fate of the major's missing detachment. In 1876, no man on Reno Hill could have grasped the truth—that Custer and 209 of their comrades already lay dead on their own battlefield four miles to the north. Later, in his report, Reno expressed the command's belief that "the awful fate that did befall him never occurred to any of us as within the limits of possibility."[4]

For numerous reasons, history has treated Reno unkindly for his actions at Little Big Horn. Some claim he thought about abandoning his wounded and slipping away in the darkness for the Powder River depot at the Yellowstone River. Others, including Lieutenant Godfrey and Captain French, criticized the major for failing to provide leadership that night. Benteen, however, credited Reno with being cool and collected.[5] In 1879, two mule packers testified at the Reno court of inquiry that the major was drunk both during the afternoon fight as well as that night on the bluffs. Lt. Winfield S. Edgerly, for one, said that if Reno had been drunk he would have been removed from command. The 7th Cavalry's survivors certainly slept fitfully, if at all, the night of June 25.

About 3 A.M. on June 26, the Indians resumed their firing on the soldiers' weakly defended positions. Relying on bushes, stones, and depressions for cover, they edged ever closer to the army's lines. Indian snipers from Sharpshooter Ridge and elsewhere picked off soldiers who came into view. Other warriors launched unsuccessful forays to overrun segments of the defensive perimeter.

On the south, Benteen's Company H was most seriously threatened by such encroachments. Benteen demonstrated his bravery and leadership by countercharging the Indians. The surprised warriors retreated and never again seriously challenged the soldiers on the bluffs.

On the northern perimeter, warriors manning Sharpshooter Ridge clearly held the advantage, pointing their weapons directly at the heart of the 7th Cavalry's defensive line. First Sgt. Ryan reported several men were killed or wounded by warriors firing from this high ground on both days of the siege. Fortunately, he was armed with a Sharp's carbine outfitted with a telescopic sight, which he had had specially made for himself in Bismarck. He stated: "This rifle cost me one hundred dollars. I fired a couple of shots until I got the range of that group of Indians, and then I put in a half dozen well directed shots in rapid succession into that group, and the Indians soon scampered away from that point of the bluff and that ended the firing from the Indians in that memorable engagement, and the boys set up quite a cheer."[6]

By late in the morning, thirst posed a serious problem, especially for the wounded under Porter's care. Soldiers, carrying camp kettles, canteens, and

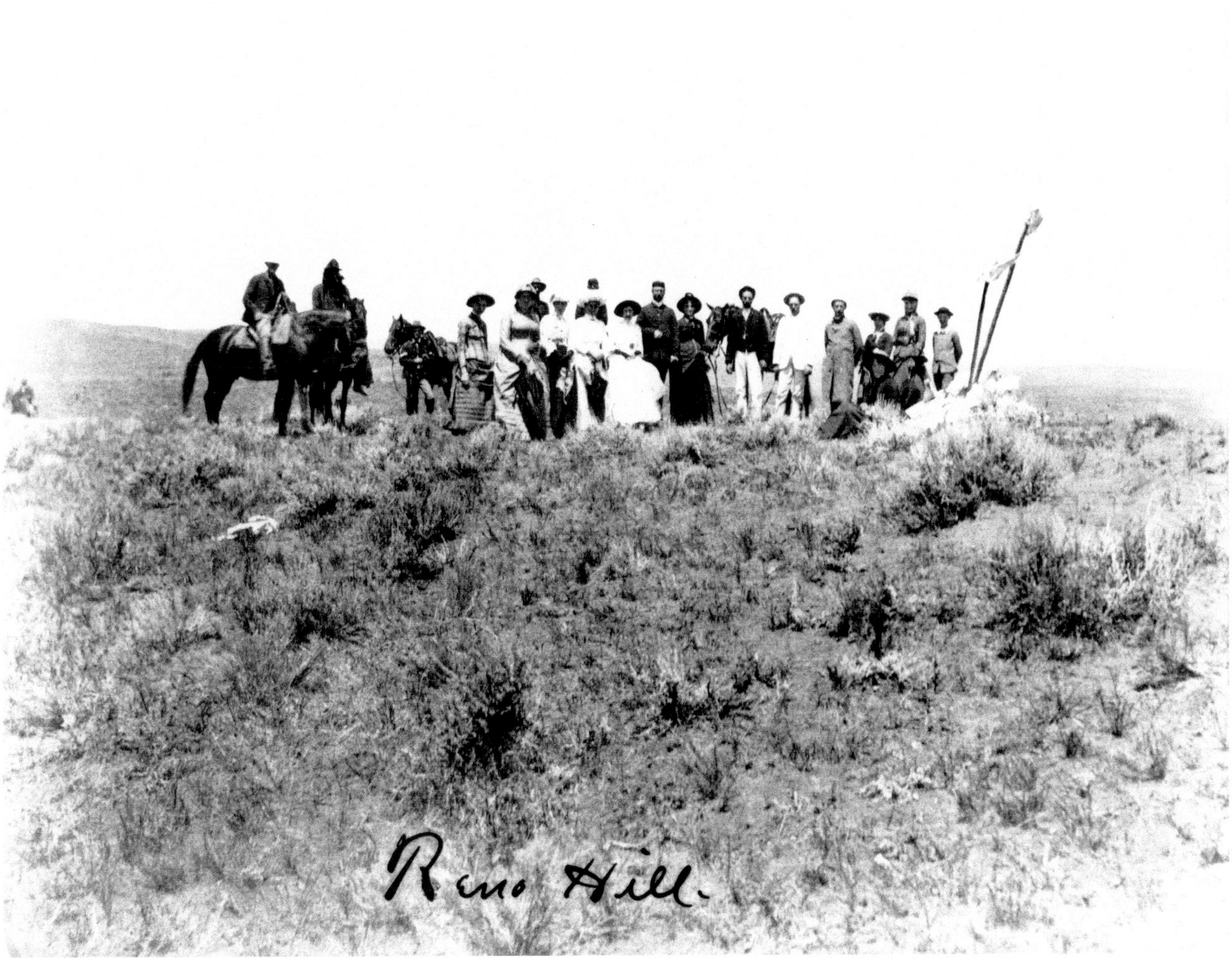

Figure 13.1. Visitors at the Reno-Benteen Defense Site on the tenth anniversary of the battle. Photo by D. F. Barry, courtesy of Little Bighorn Battlefield National Monument, no. 6042.

pots, slipped down a ravine under enemy fire to the river's edge. There they filled their receptacles with water, then climbed up the steep slopes to the safety of the defensive perimeter. Nineteen men were later awarded the Medal of Honor.

About midday, Indian firing slackened. By late afternoon, the warriors were pulling back. Reno contemplated sending scouts out to try to link up with General Terry, but the riders soon returned. Soon the soldiers watched an awe-inspiring sight from atop the bluffs, as an lengthy line of warriors accompanied by their families abandoned the valley, making their way with loaded travois toward the southwest. Four of Reno's men, including Lt. Charles DeRudio, had been missing since the valley fight twenty-four hours earlier but climbed safely up the bluffs. The Battle of the Little Big Horn had ended. The enemy had left the 7th Cavalry in control of the battlefield, but no one claimed victory. Custer remained missing. Reno's two days of fighting had cost fifteen men killed and fifty-six wounded. Five of the wounded would later die.

In 1886, during the tenth anniversary observance at Custer Battlefield, photographer D. F. Barry captured on film a group of visitors posed on the north end of the site of the Reno-Benteen defense (fig. 13.1). On its far right appeared

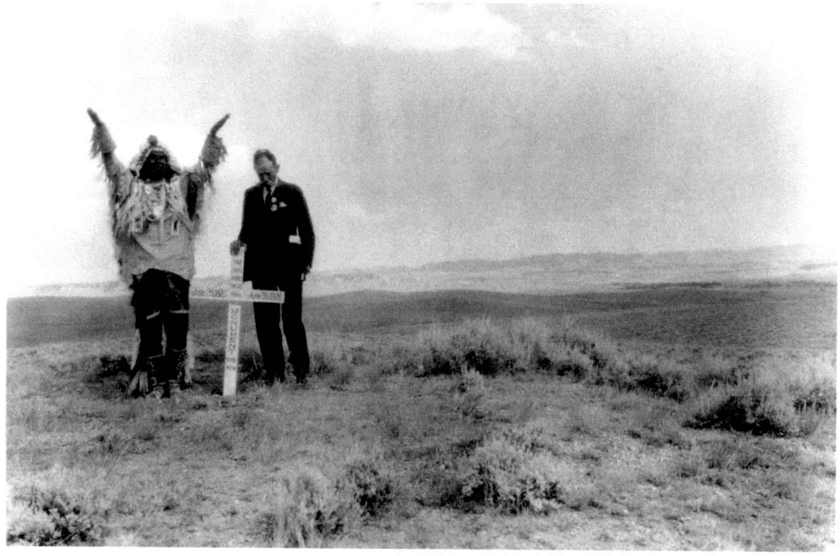

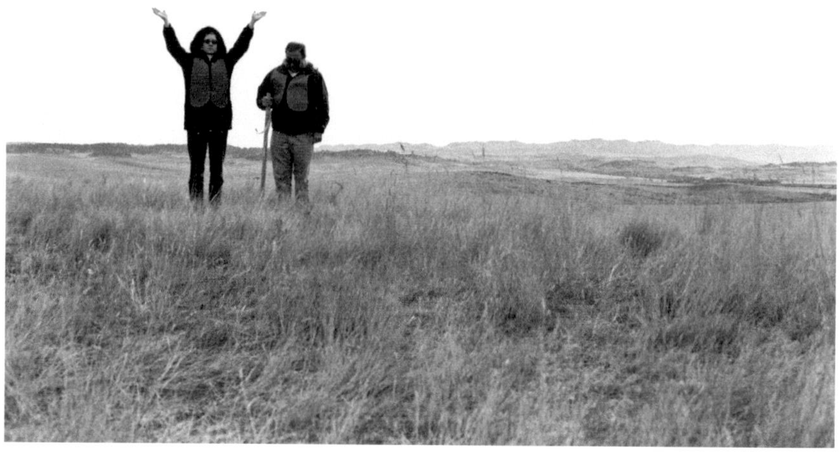

Figure 13.2. (*top*) Gen. Edward S. Godfrey and White Man Runs Him placing a cross at the site of a proposed marker at the Reno-Benteen Defense Site, 1926. Photo by Edward L. Wisherd, courtesy of Edward S. Godfrey Collection, U.S. Military History Institute. (*bottom*) Cricket Bauer Pohanka and Sandy Barnard, 2000. Courtesy of James S. Brust.

what may have been an early primitive marker for the site, although its origins, history, and fate remain unknown. For more than fifty years after the battle, no permanent monument marked the area where the 7th Cavalrymen had successfully defended themselves.

In 1926, on the occasion of the fiftieth anniversary, a new effort was made to commemorate their actions. A 1926 photograph by Edwin L. Wisherd (fig. 13.2) shows battle survivors Edward S. Godfrey and White Man Runs Him standing by a cross that bears the inscription "This cross marks the site for a proposed monument to the 7th Cav., June 26, 1876." Also on view in figure 13.2 is James S. Brust's modern reshoot, showing Cricket Bauer Pohanka and me.

It still took several years to gain congressional approval for a monument because many people, especially Mrs. Libbie Custer, the general's widow, opposed honoring the long-dead major, whom she blamed for her husband's death. Finally, on August 14, 1929, a monument was erected on the Reno-

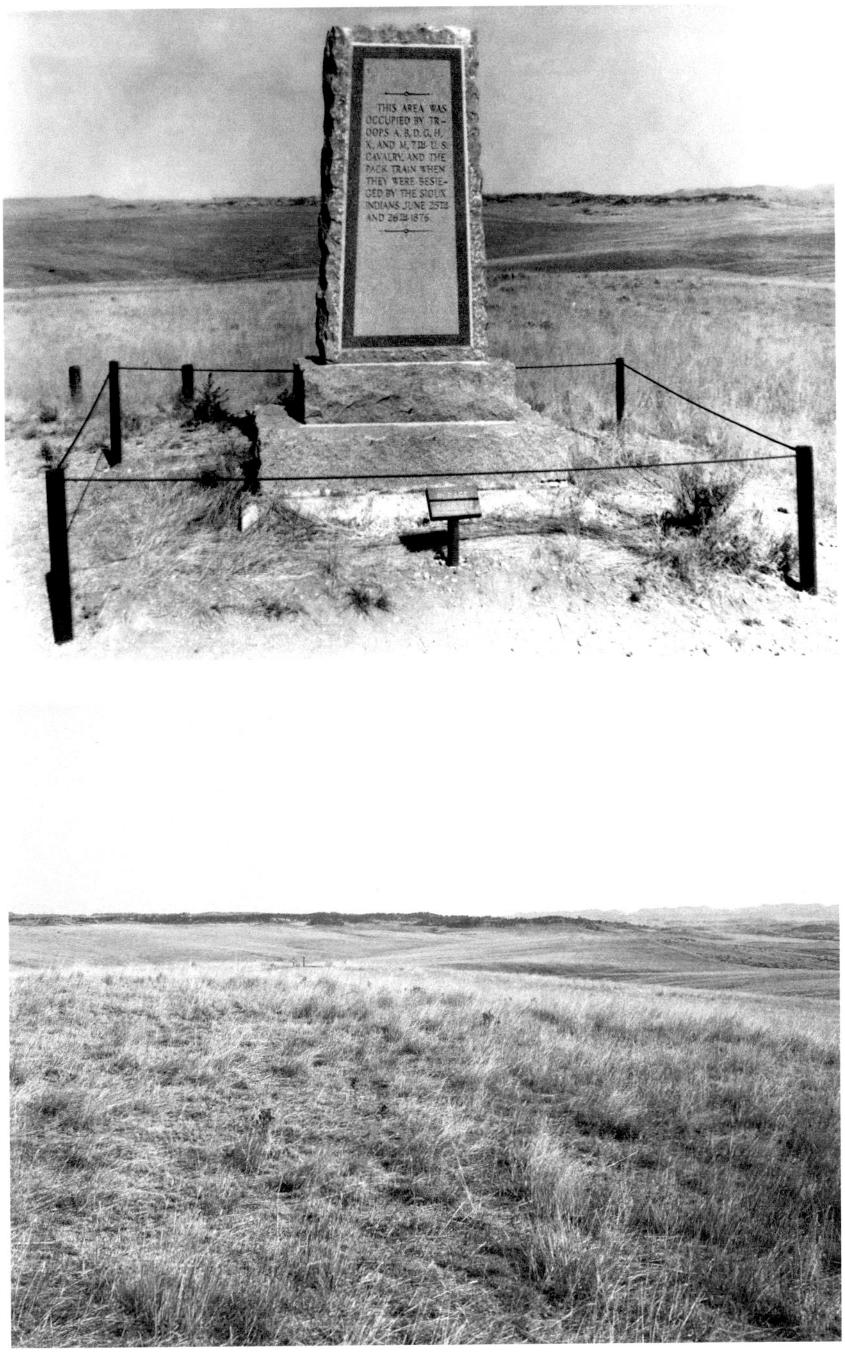

Figure 13.3. (*top*) Reno-Benteen monument, with protective fence, July 31, 1963. Courtesy of Big Horn County Historical Museum. (*bottom*) 2012 reshoot of the same spot.

Benteen ridges, one that still stands. It states, "This area was occupied by troops A, B, D, G, H, K, and M, Seventh U.S. Cavalry, and the pack train when they were besieged by the Sioux Indians June 25th and 26th 1876." Of note, Reno's name is absent from the monument. In August 1930, the Crow Tribe sold the government the Reno-Benteen battlefield, which administratively was taken over by the battlefield's superintendent.

The monument's subsequent history remains just as interesting. Although it still stands on the general site, it is no longer at either the original location of the 1886 primitive marker or the place where Roahen's figure 13.3

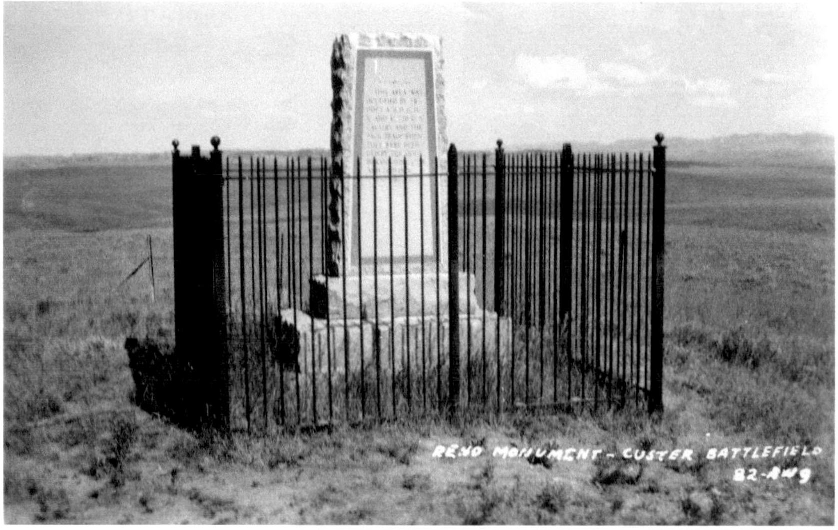

Figure 13.4. "Reno Monument—Custer Battlefield, 82-RWG," real photo postcard. Image attributed now to photographer Robert Whitney Griffing. Courtesy of James S. Brust.

and a 1940s-era postcard, "Reno Monument—Custer Battlefield, 82-RWG" (fig. 13.4), show it. In 2005, the latter photograph was published in *Where Custer Fell* as photographer and date unknown. The photograph may now be attributed to a photographer named Richard Whitney Griffing (1907–63), according to the initials RWG that appear in the lower right corner. Roahen issued a similar view. What is not clear is whether Griffing relied on a Roahen image or vice-versa, or if both copied a common source for the postcard view. The accompanying text in 2005 noted that the fence remained around the marker until 1963. Roahen's figure 13.3 image is dated July 31, 1963, which means he took the photo soon after the fence was removed.[7]

In the fall of 1965, as part of a series of improvements at the battlefield, the parking loop at the Reno Benteen Defense Site was reconstructed. That necessitated removing the monument from its historical site to a new location, out of the way and closer to the edge of the western bluffs. That is where it sits today, without any fencing around it. The modern photograph in figure 13.3 shows the area where the historic marker originally stood.

Another Roahen image, figure 13.5, bears no date, but likely Roahen took it while standing in front of the Reno-Benteen monument at its original location and looking west into the Little Big Horn Valley. The matching 2013 photo captures the relocated Reno-Benteen memorial in its current position, just to the west of the parking lot. On the far right of both photos, the deep cut in Weir Point can be seen to the north.

The Reno-Benteen battlefield has always been a popular location for study by historical researchers, probably because the numerous 7th Cavalry survivors provided a rich trove of historical documentation about the events on the bluffs in June 1876. Since the mid-1950s, researchers have relied heavily on evolving technology to uncover new details about the fighting. Two early historians who made significant use of metal detectors on the field were Don G. Rickey, who became park historian in July 1955, and a Roahen friend and collaborator, Colorado researcher and author Jesse W. Vaughn. In 1956, Rickey

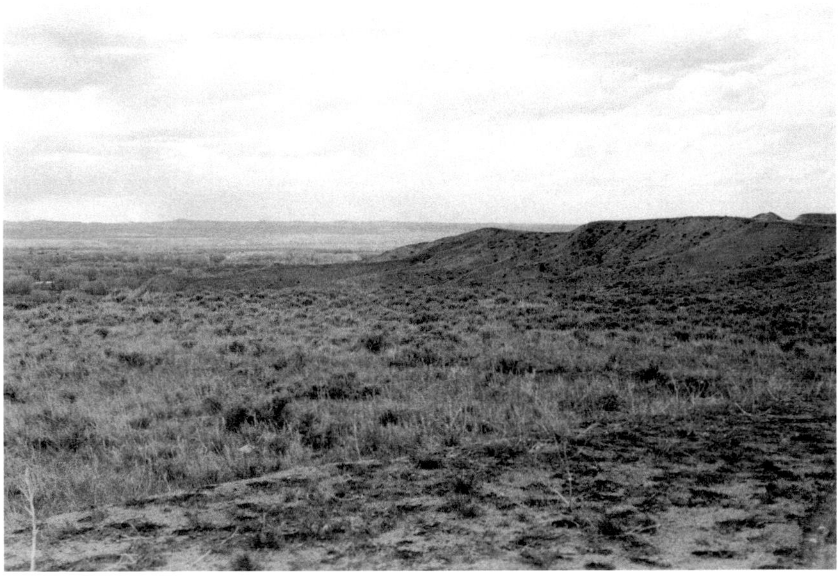

Figure 13.5. (*top*) From Reno-Benteen monument, looking west toward river. Courtesy of Big Horn County Historical Museum. (*bottom*) 2013 reshoot, showing new monument location.

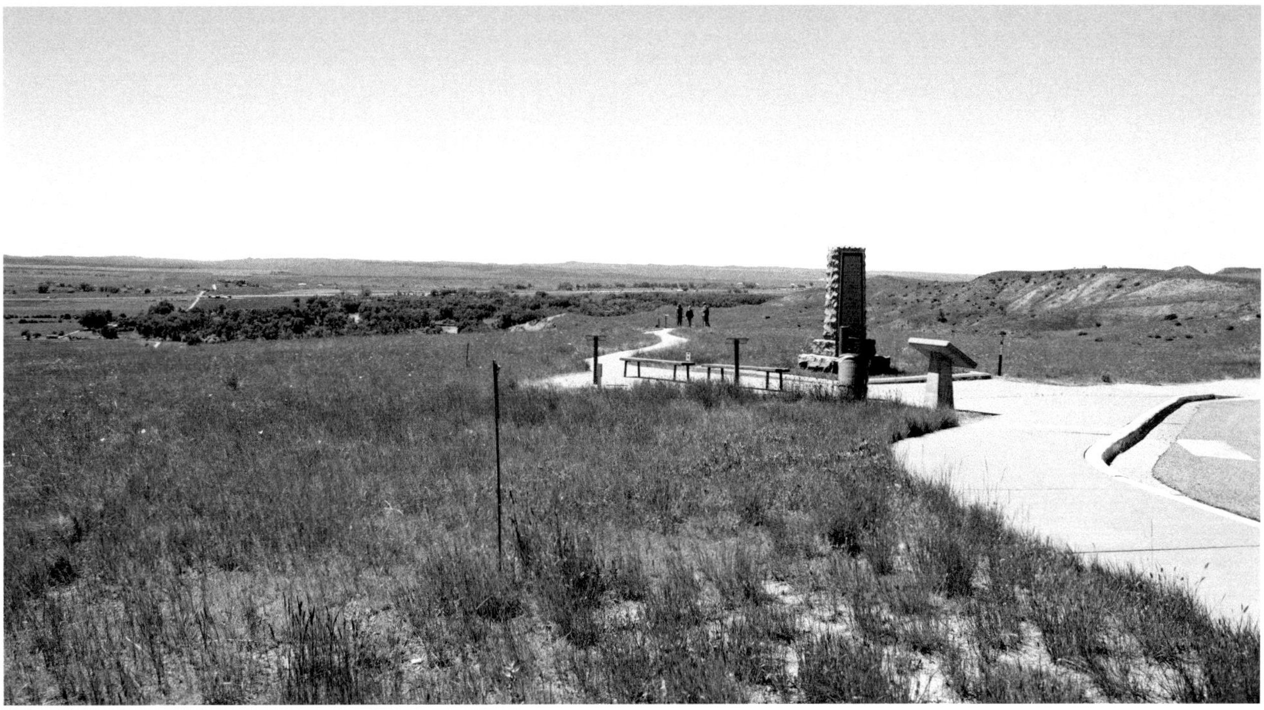

and Vaughn began a systematic scan of the greater battlefield and worked the historic site until 1959. According to archaeologist Douglas D. Scott, the two men focused their attentions on a metal detector survey of the Reno-Benteen site in 1956: "They found and marked with wooden stakes a variety of artifacts, mostly army carbine cartridge cases found in linear arrangements along the presumed arm perimeter. Rickey and Vaughn also located nails and what they believed were pieces of human bone." They also searched the ridges south and east of the Reno-Benteen battlefield.[8]

Through photographic evidence in the Roahen collection, we know the Billings photographer accompanied the two men on one or more of their

Figure 13.6. (*top*) Reno rifle pits, facing hospital. Courtesy of Big Horn County Historical Museum. (*bottom*) 2012 reshoot.

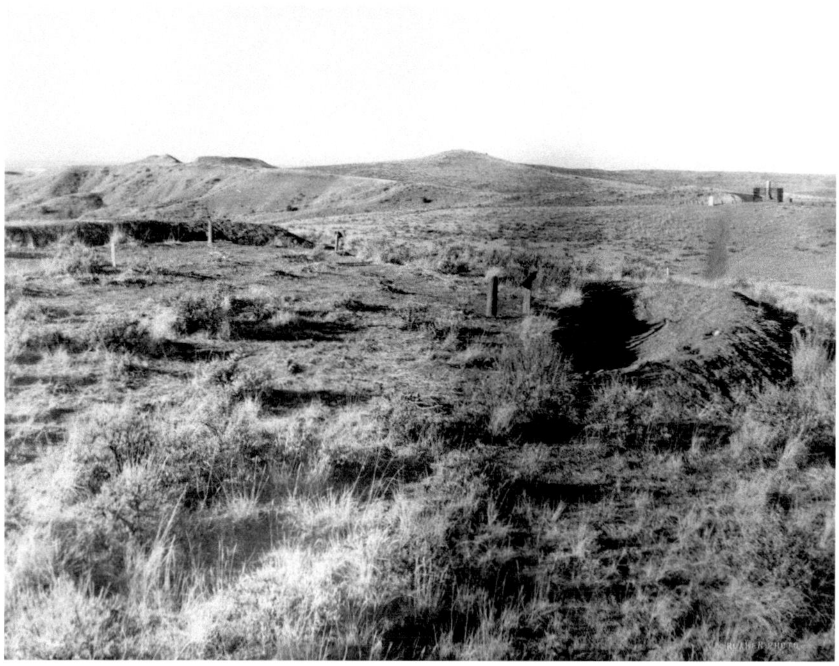

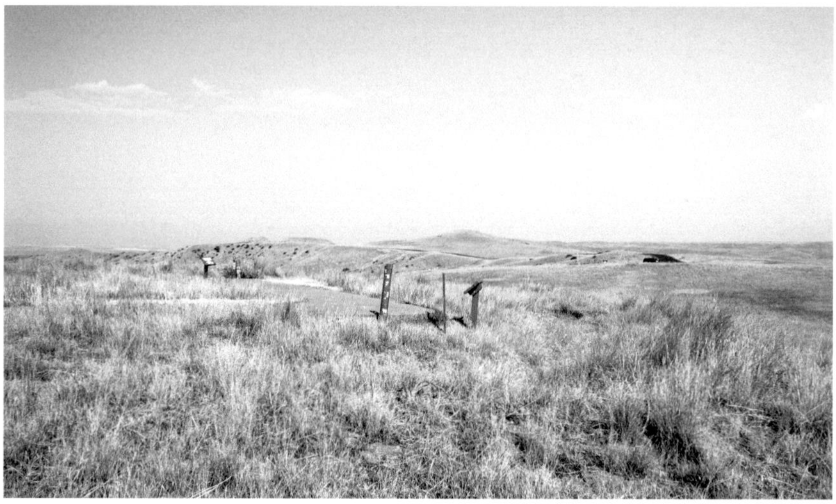

expeditions, which would have begun a year after Roahen's retirement from the government. Also in 1958, archaeologist Robert Bray launched what was the first professional archaeological investigation within the Little Big Horn park. In his 2013 book, Scott, who in the mid-1980s began conducting his own series of archaeological investigations at Little Big Horn, summarized Bray's fieldwork well. Bray's efforts would have overlapped those of Rickey and Vaughn. In the Big Horn County Historical Museum's Roahen collection is a series of photographs of Bray's excavations of three burial pits, two on the north end of the Company H position, which remain partially hollowed out today, and one in the hospital swale center.

Roahen's figure 13.6 image, which he labeled "Rifle pits—Reno retreat from west of river," shows what appear to be two recently excavated entrenchments on the north end of the Company H position, overlooking the hospital swale.

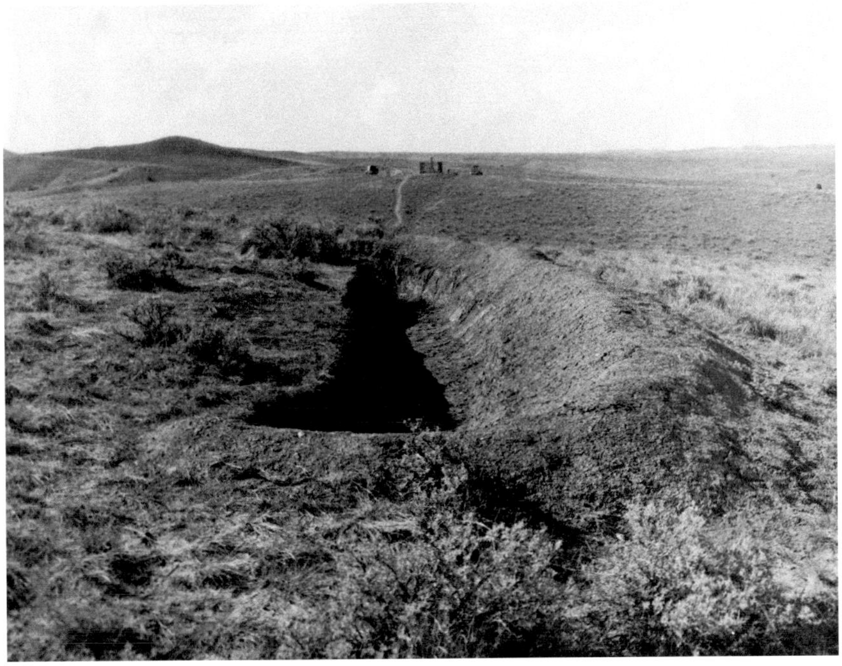

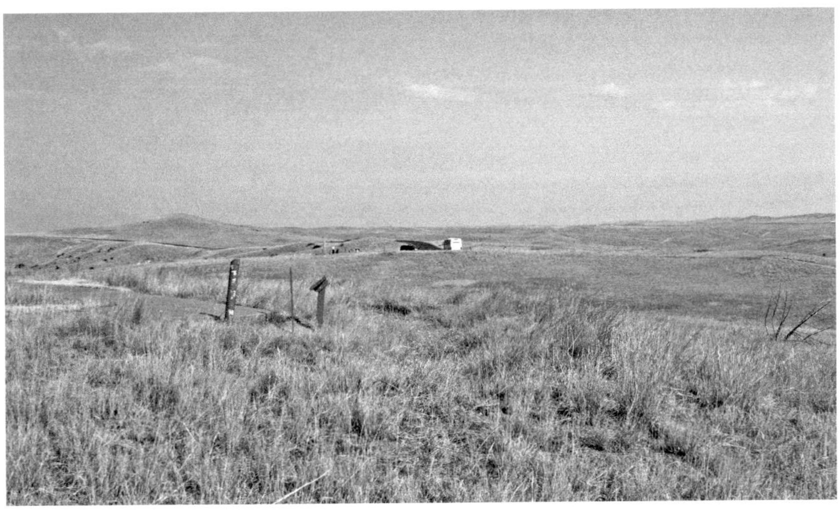

Figure 13.7. (*top*) Reno rifle pit and area. Courtesy of Big Horn County Historical Museum. (*bottom*) 2012 reshoot.

That suggests that Roahen photographed Bray in 1958 while he was working in the field, or soon thereafter.

The figure 13.7 variant images show only the eastern entrenchment, and figure 13.8 looks into the western entrenchment. All three photo pairs include the historic monument in the background, enclosed by its fence in its original location south of the parking area. All of them also show Sharpshooter Ridge in the background. In figure 13.8, Weir Point is visible in the distance. In the modern photos, the burial pits appear less distinct, showing the effects of weathering and grass and the presence of other brush.

The final Roahen photograph in this grouping is figure 13.9, which was printed from a color negative in his collection. It shows the third Bray excavation at a site in the hospital swale. Given the apparent freshness of the excavation, it, too, was likely taken in 1958 during the Bray project or soon after.

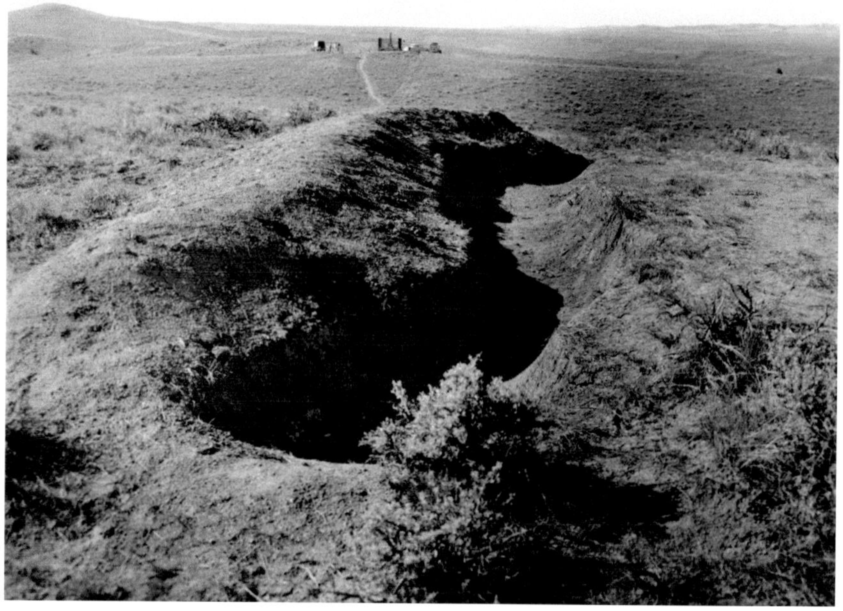

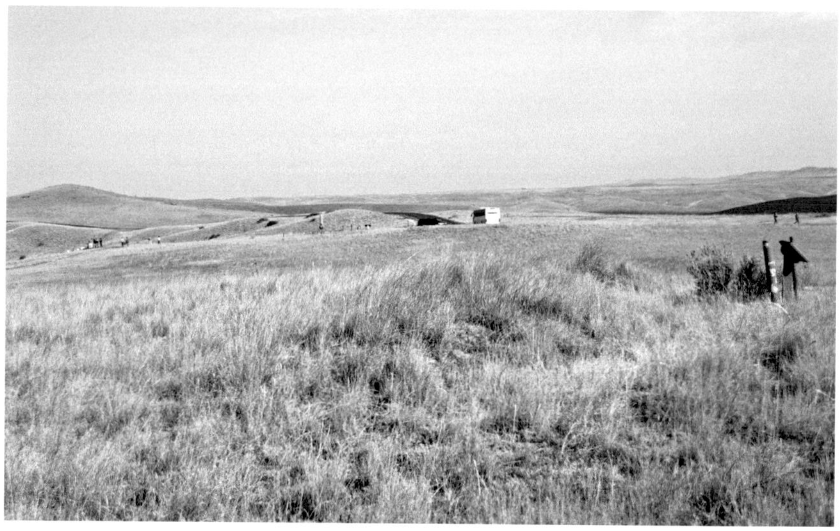

Figure 13.8. (*top*) Reno rifle pit facing Little Big Horn River. Courtesy of Big Horn County Historical Museum. (*bottom*) 2012 reshoot.

It also provides a close-up look of the old dirt trail that is a continuation of what is now the modern battlefield roadway. The modern counterpart photo, which is not an exact match, was taken from atop the Company H ridgeline. It shows the burial site marked today by a historical marker. The old dirt track can be seen outlined by the lighter-colored grass up near the top of the slope.

Related to this series of images is figure 13.10, which shows the old battlefield road entering a much smaller parking lot at Reno-Benteen. The monument remains in its original spot; the dirt track is clearly visible running up the slope to the Company H northern end, where two of Bray's entrenchment excavations were located. The modern view reveals how much wider today's roadway and parking lot are; the monument is on the right of the photo in the position where it was moved in 1965.

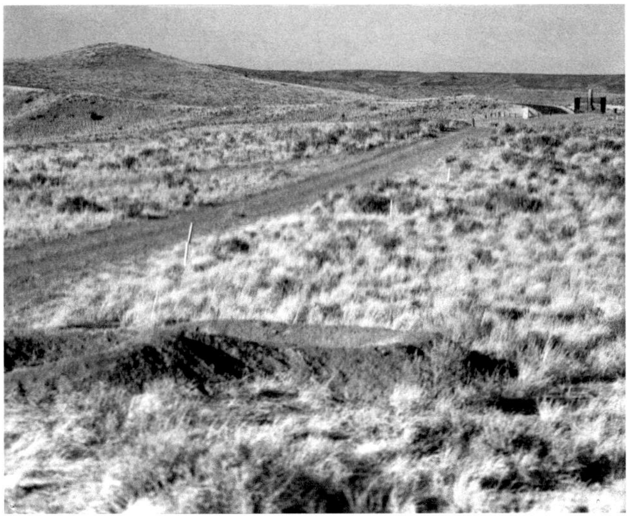

Figure 13.9. (*top*) From rifle pit looking toward old Reno marker site. Courtesy of Big Horn County Historical Museum. (*bottom*) 2012 reshoot.

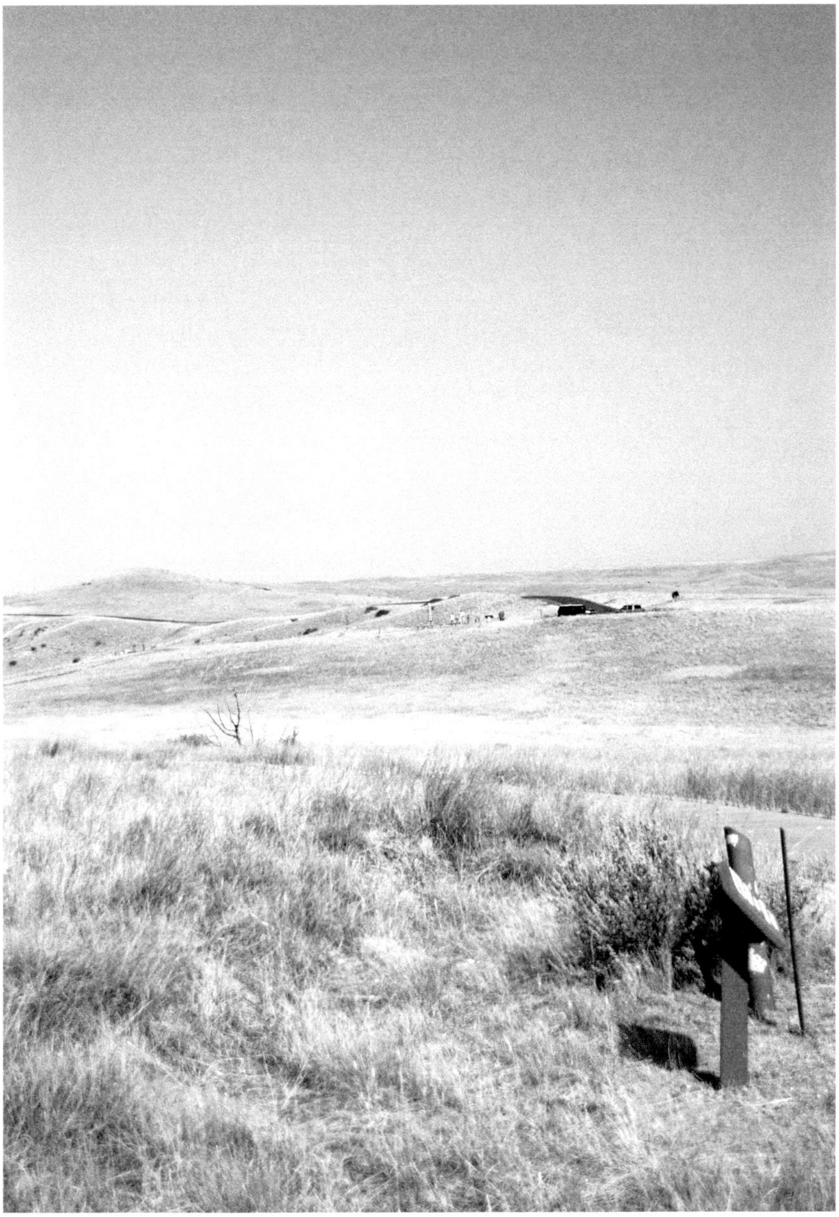

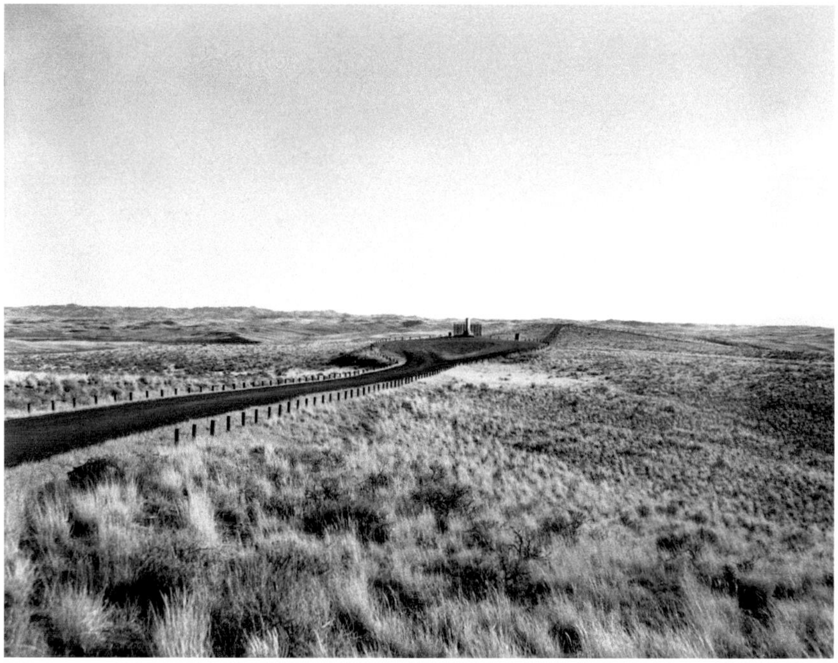

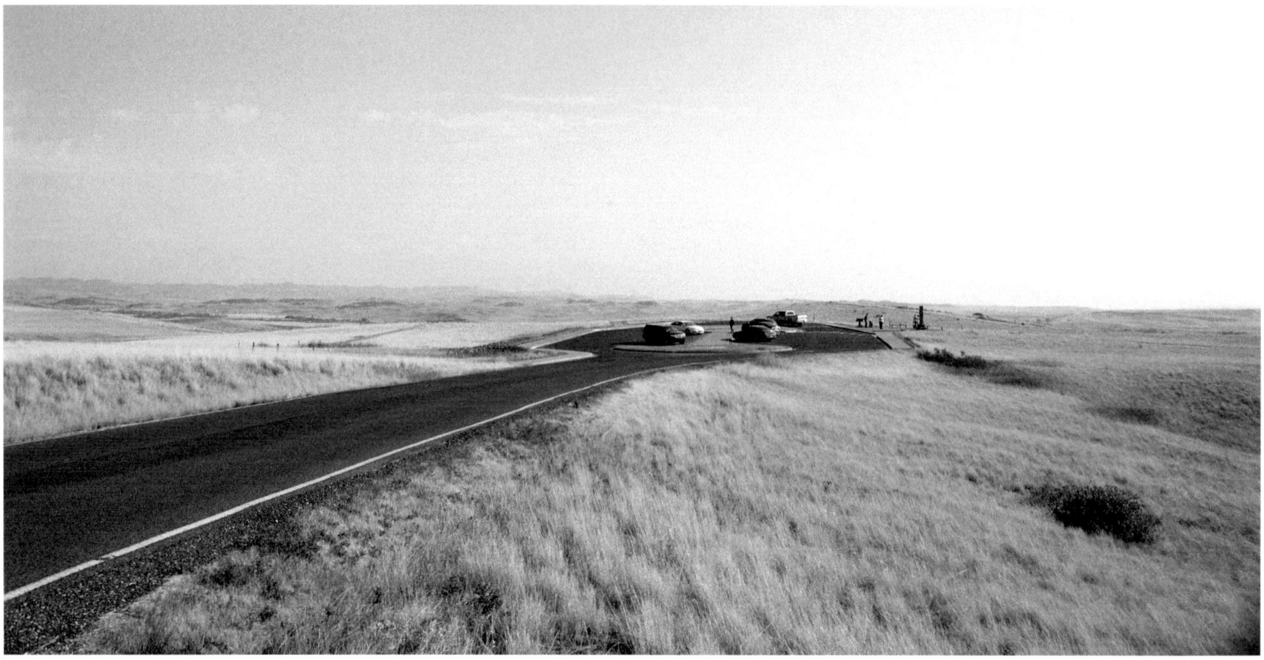

Figure 13.10. (*top*) Old road to the Reno-Benteen battlefield. Courtesy of Big Horn County Historical Museum. (*bottom*) 2012 reshoot.

Battlefield historian Rickey transferred to a new assignment in 1960, but three years later he published his classic *Forty Miles a Day on Beans and Hay: The Enlisted Soldier Fighting the Indian Wars.* Before he departed, he allowed Roahen to capture him portraying an enlisted soldier in a series of photographs, two of which are included here. In figure 13.11, Rickey is firing a Springfield carbine from the eastern entrenchment on the Company H position. Prairie grasses are now beginning to cover the wall of the entrenchment, suggesting the photograph was taken a year or two after Bray completed his fieldwork. The second image, figure 13.12, is similar, except that Rickey is firing from the

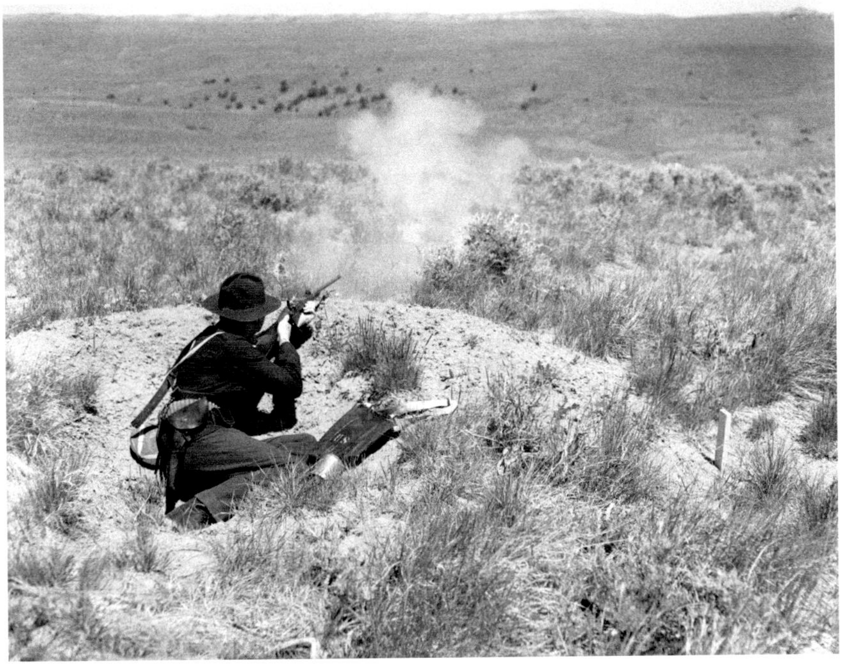

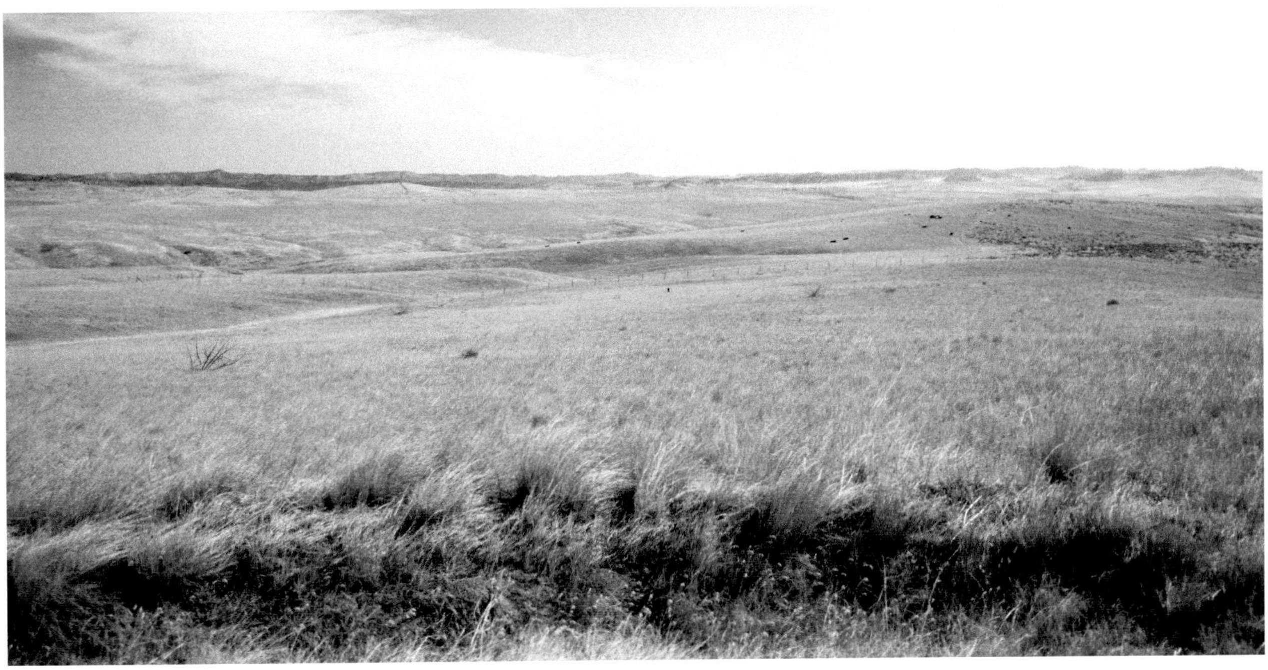

Figure 13.11. (*top*) Don Rickey firing east from rifle pit. Courtesy of Big Horn County Historical Museum. (*bottom*) 2012 reshoot.

western burial pit toward the Reno Retreat Crossing. The light-colored bluff in the distance of this photograph overlooks the retreat crossing. In both modern counterparts the pits are more heavily covered with vegetation. In modern figure 13.12, the retreat crossing is located in the grove of trees below the bluffs on the left of the photograph.

Roahen obviously accompanied Rickey and author Vaughn in 1956 when they were surveying the Reno-Benteen field. Roahen's figure 13.13 image, which dates from 1956, shows the two men on the eastern slope, a short distance down from the eastern entrenchment. Their metal detector can be seen

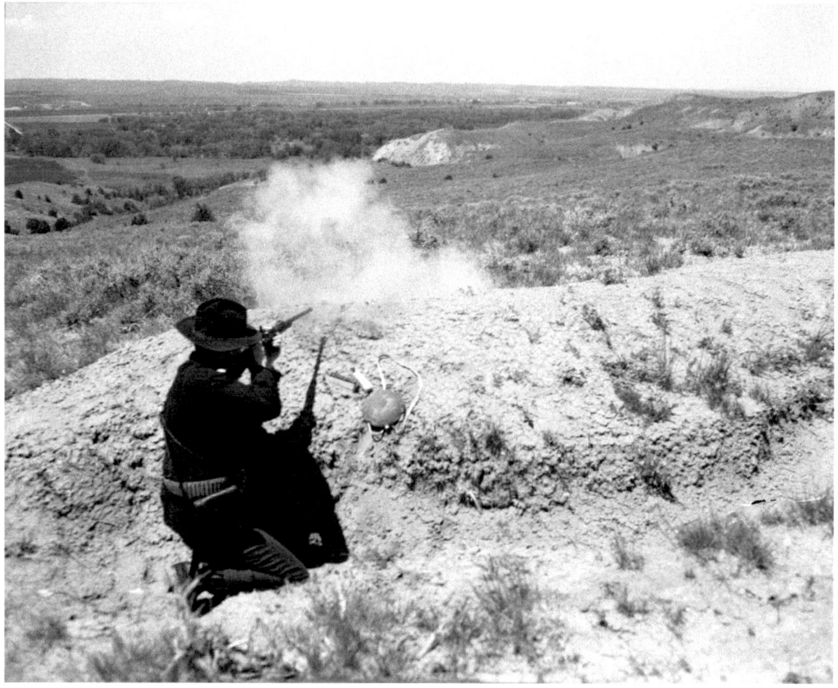

Figure 13.12. (*top*) Rickey firing north. Courtesy of Big Horn County Historical Museum. (*bottom*) 2012 reshoot.

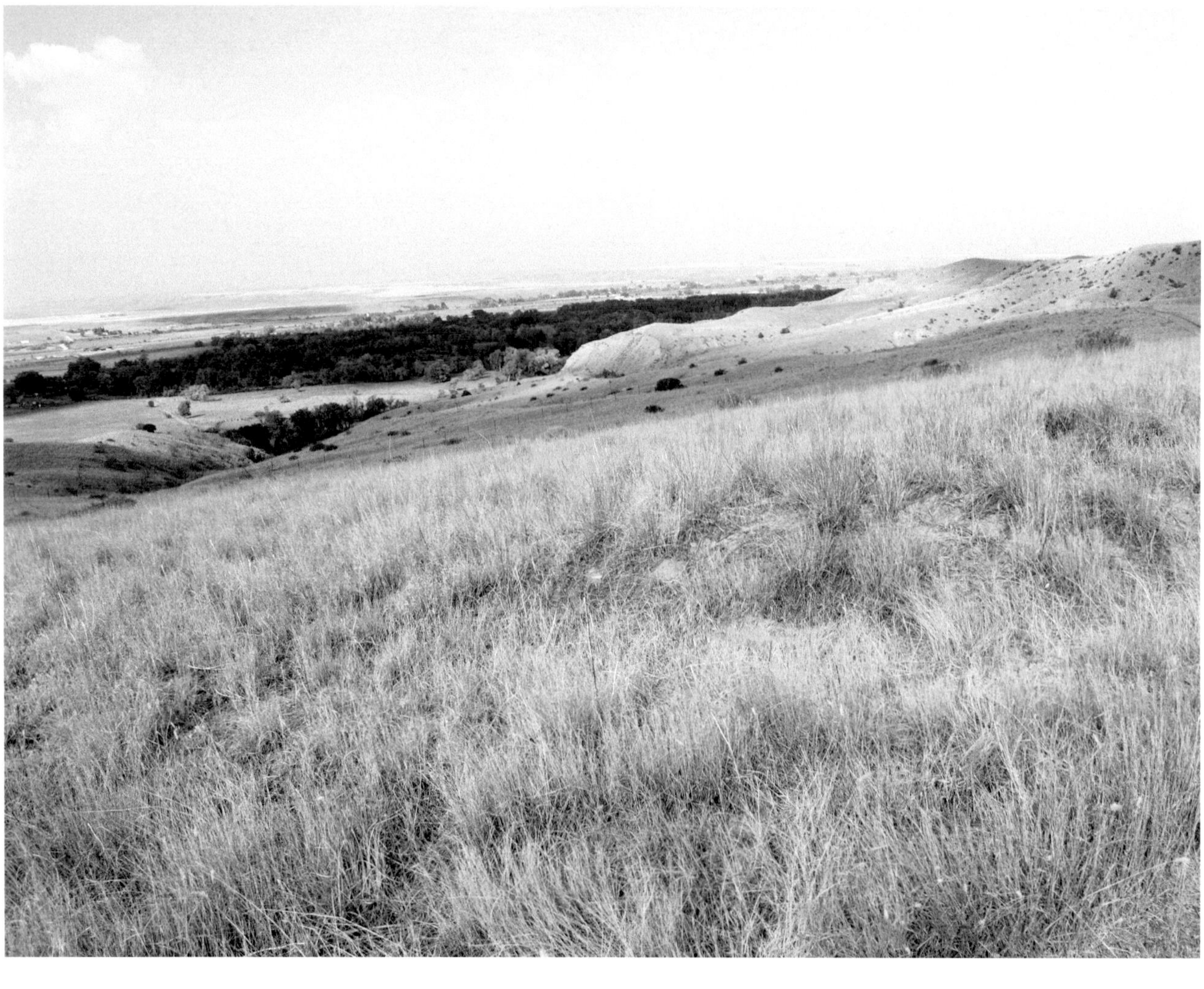

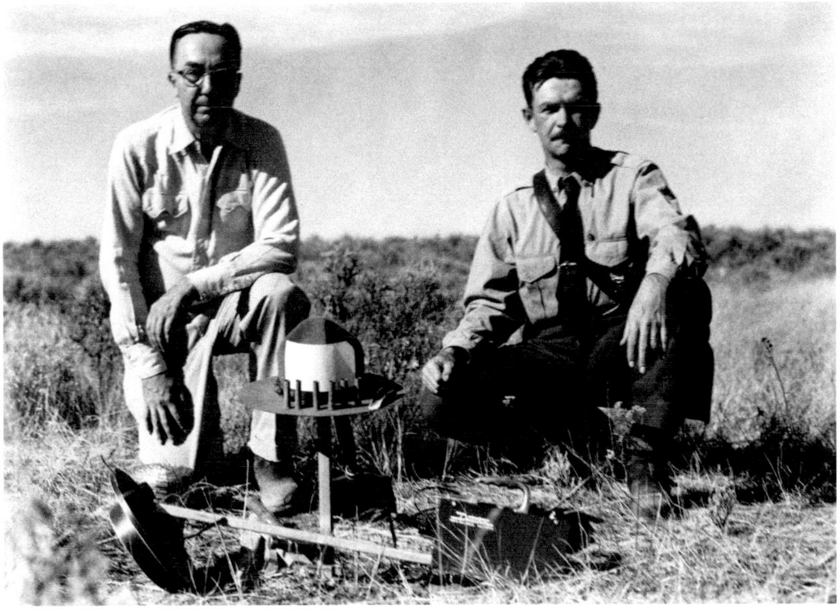

Figure 13.13. (*top*) Jesse Vaughn (*left*), Don Rickey (*right*), and metal detectors. Courtesy of Big Horn County Historical Museum. (*bottom*) 2013 reshoot.

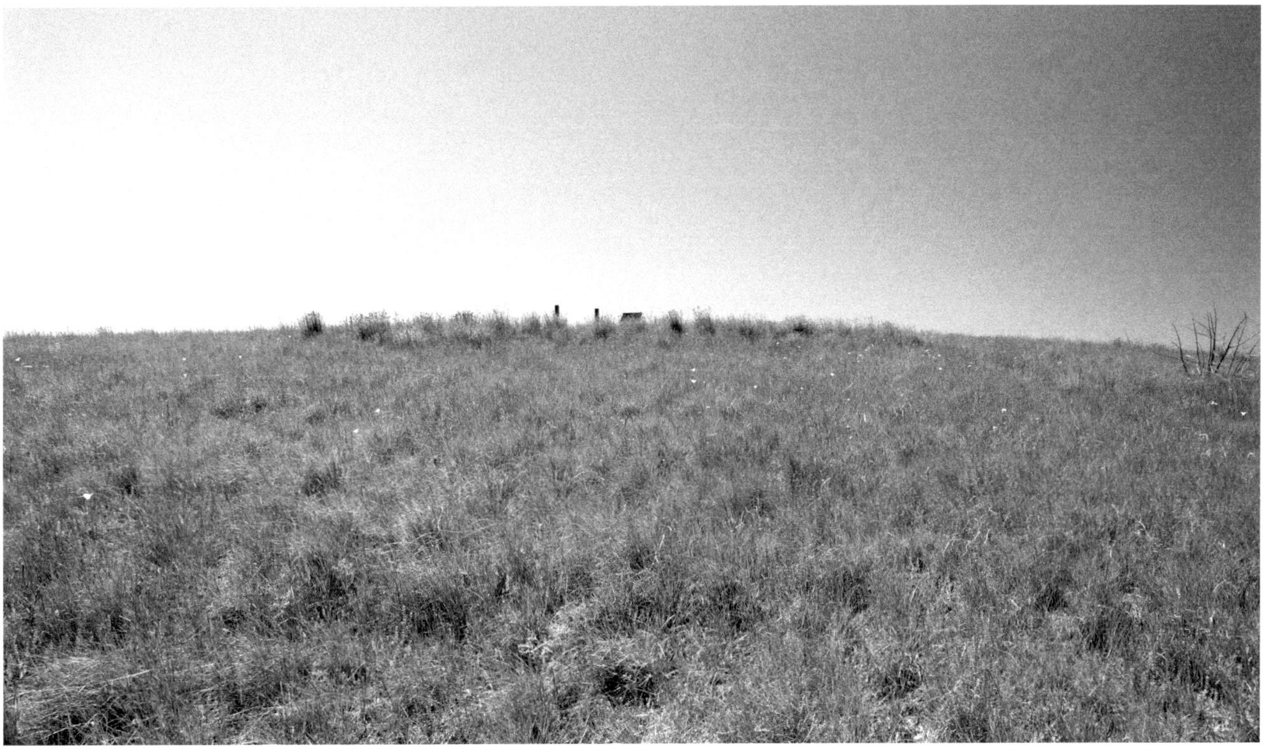

on the ground in front of them. They have placed a half dozen cartridge cases on the brim of Rickey's Park Service hat. The modern reshoot shows historic and warning signs to tourists on top of the hill by the entrenchment. Figure 13.14 is related to figure 13.13; it shows the two men posing inside the eastern entrenchment. Vaughn is holding his metal detector. Given the amount of vegetation and the height of the sagebrush, this photo may have been taken as early as 1956, the first year Vaughn and Rickey collaborated and two years before Bray's excavations.

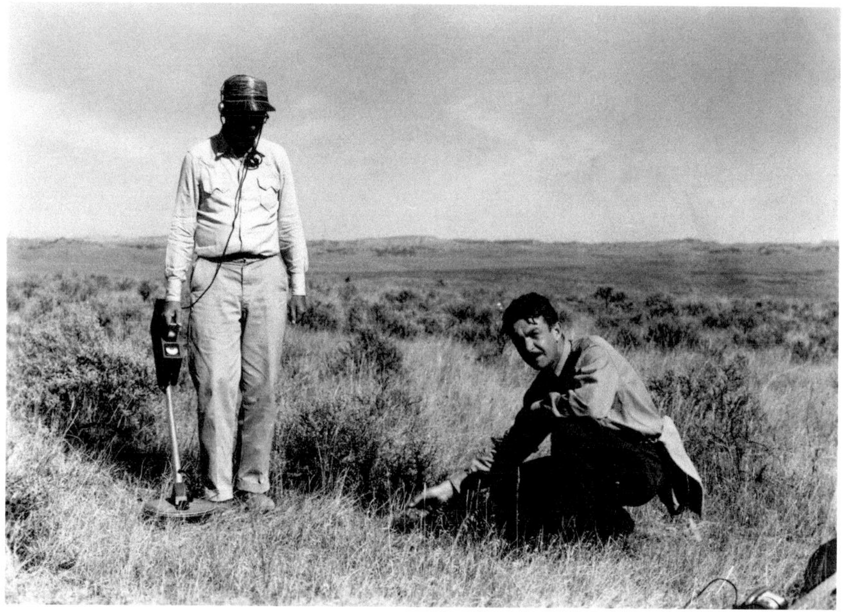

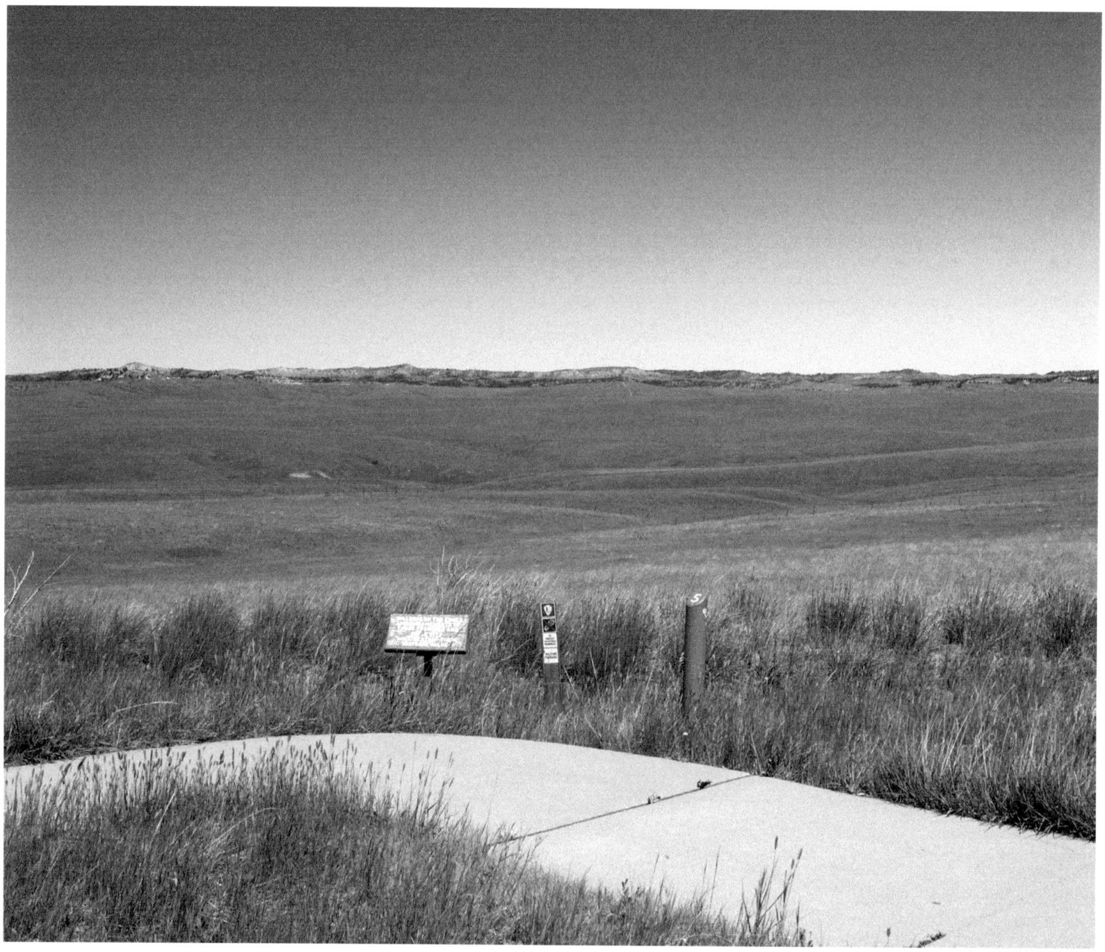

Figure 13.14. (*top*) Vaughn and Rickey in the field, ca. 1950s. Courtesy of Big Horn County Historical Museum. (*bottom*) 2013 reshoot.

Finally, Roahen turned his camera onto the area of the Reno valley fight. Figure 13.15 is a panorama of the valley fight area created by merging three related Roahen images. Precisely when Roahen took these photos is unknown,

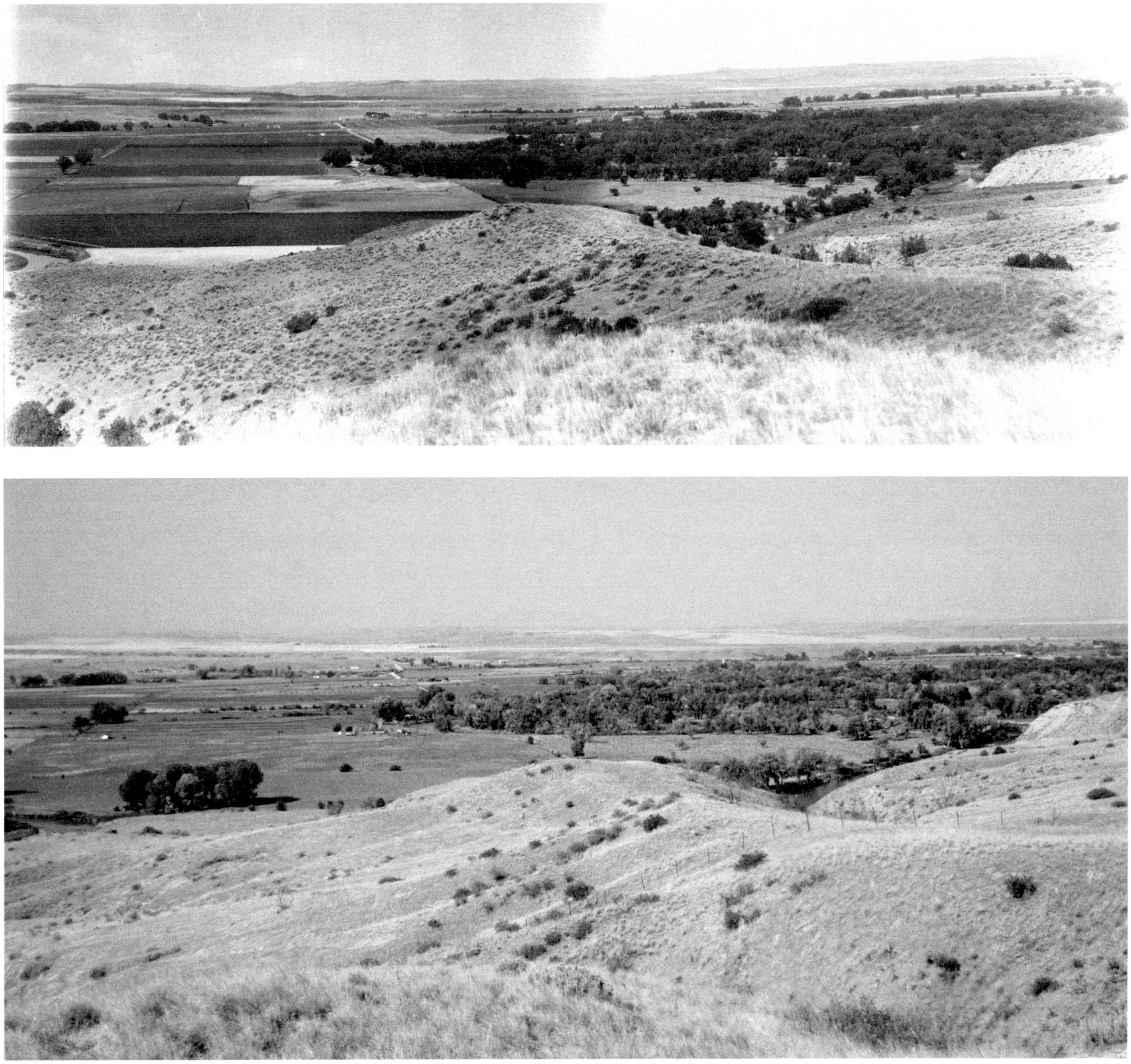

Figure 13.15. (*top*) Panorama of Reno valley fight area created from three Roahen images. Courtesy of Big Horn County Historical Museum. (*bottom*) Panorama of Reno valley fight area created from four modern reshoots.

but it would have been long before Interstate 90 was built through the valley. The access road to the Reno retreat crossing can be seen in the left center of the panorama, running east to west. Old Highway 87 runs through the center of the photo. To match this panorama of Roahen's original photographs, four modern reshoots were merged to form a single image. The biggest difference between the two panoramic shots is the presence of I-90 and a few new buildings. Except for slight changes in the amount of vegetation in the valley, the two scenes are remarkably similar, despite the sixty years or so between our day and Roahen's.

Figure 13.16 is looking up the Little Big Horn River, or south. Though Roahen obviously took this photograph back-to-back with the three in the panorama, the computer could not align it with the others. It, too, is pre-I-90. Again, the modern photo is similar to Roahen's.

Figure 13.16. (*top*) Looking upriver before construction of Interstate 90. Courtesy of Big Horn County Historical Museum. (*bottom*) 2012 reshoot.

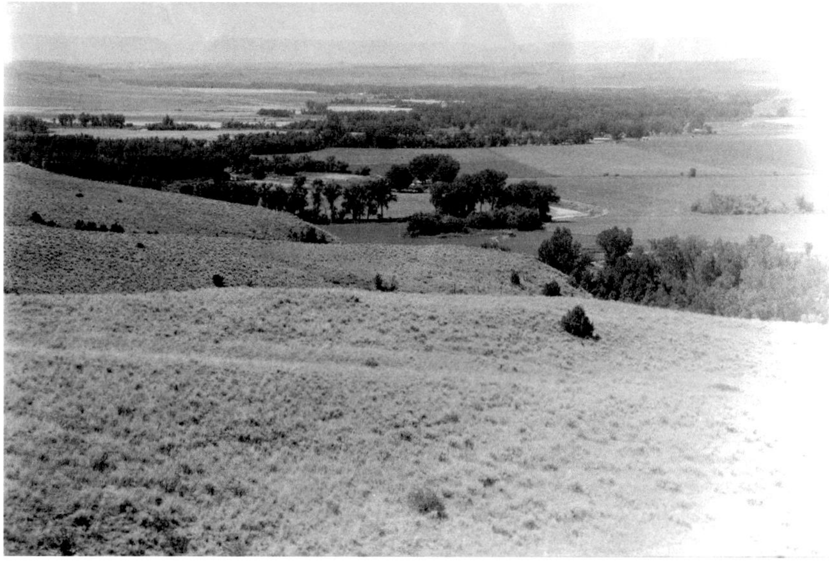

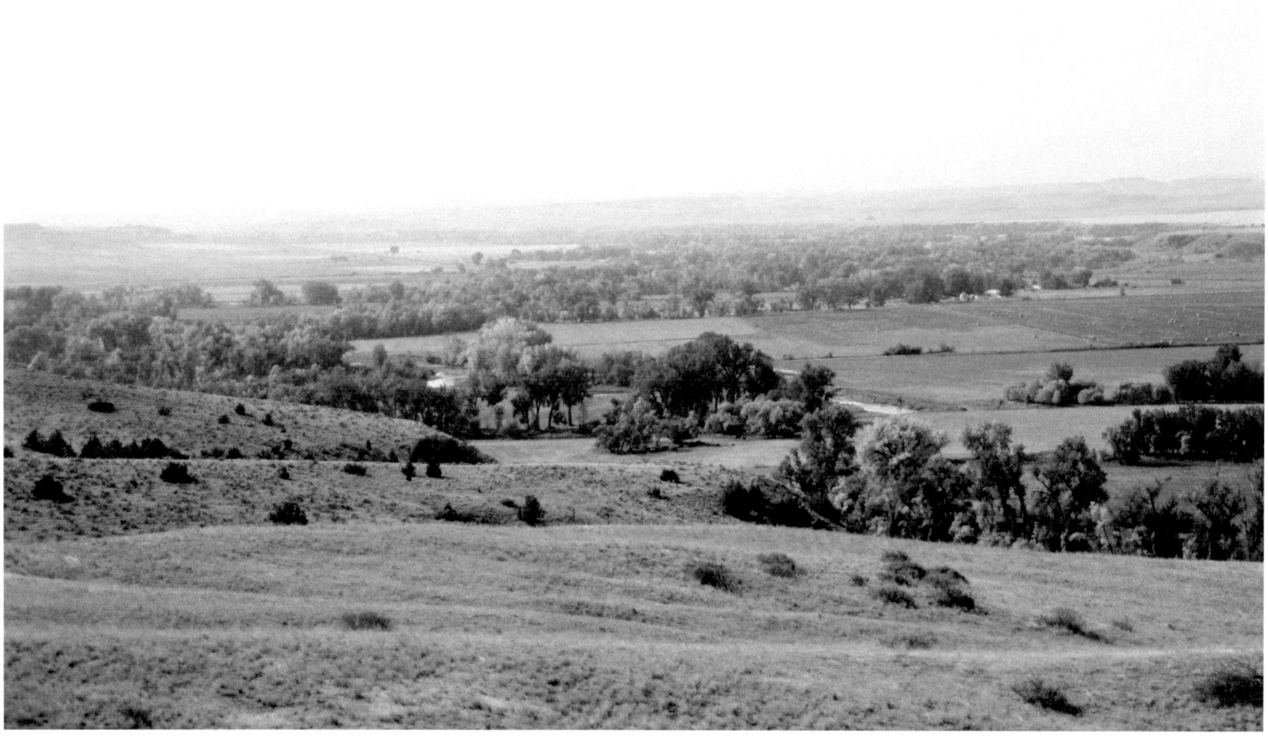

CHAPTER 14

Weir Point to Medicine Tail Coulee

Historians generally consider the Weir Point episode one of the more important during the Little Big Horn fighting. Yet surprisingly Roahen's collection of photographs at the Big Horn County Historical Museum does not contain any that were taken from that site itself, either north toward the main Custer battlefield or back south to the Reno-Benteen battlefield. The collection does contain a few images looking toward the vicinity of Weir Point as well as others that show landmarks on the long slope below that location toward Medicine Tail Coulee.

When Dr. James DeWolf, a civilian contract surgeon accompanying the Reno command, retreated across the Little Big Horn River, he followed the wrong finger bluff to the top, one slightly more to the left, or north, of the main ravine used by the majority of his comrades (see fig. 12.4). Unfortunately for him, warriors who had crossed elsewhere were there waiting for him. In

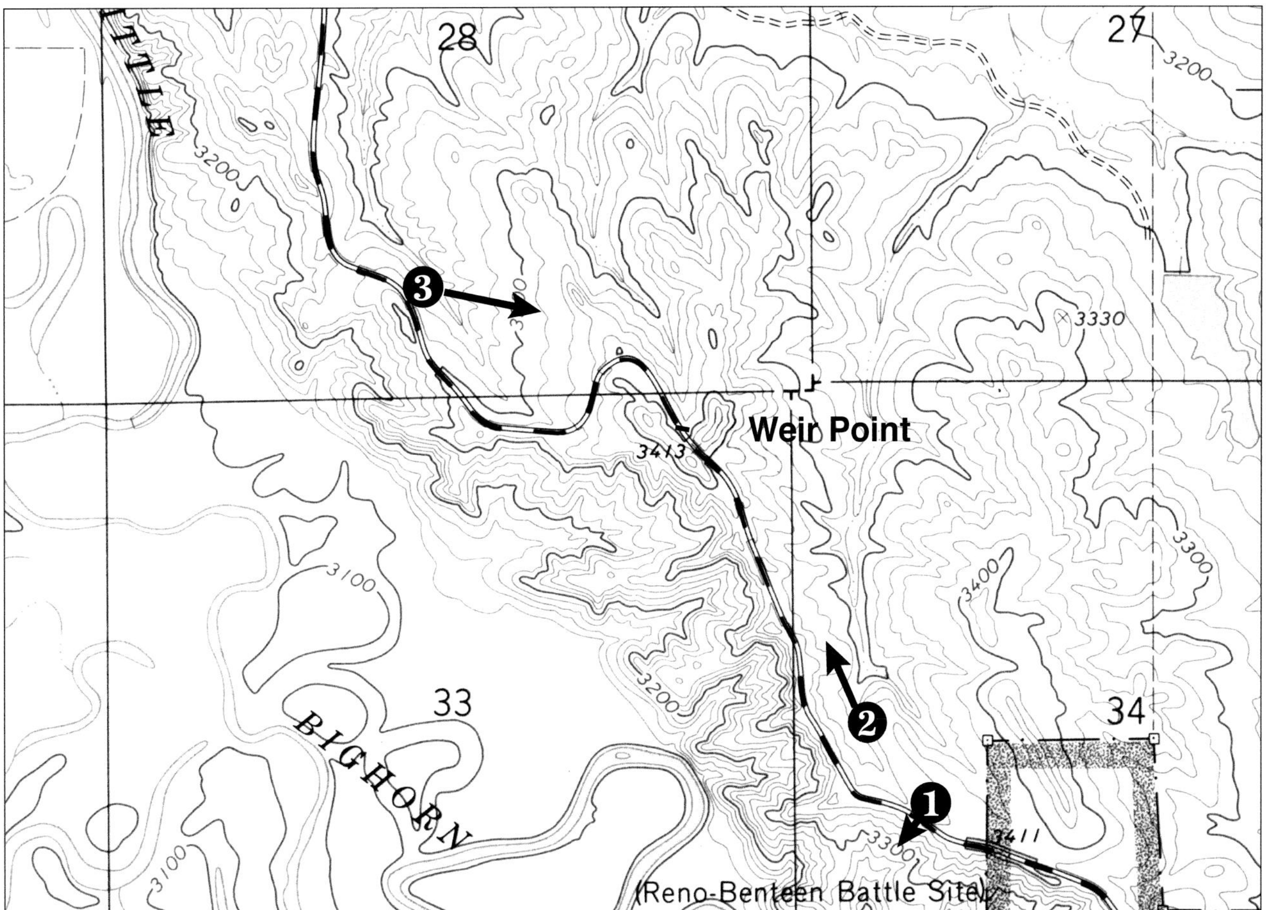

Map 14.1. Weir Point vicinity. Based on the 1967 USGS topographical map. Map by Gary Raham.

1. Figs. 14.1, 14.2
2. Fig. 14.3
3. Fig. 14.4

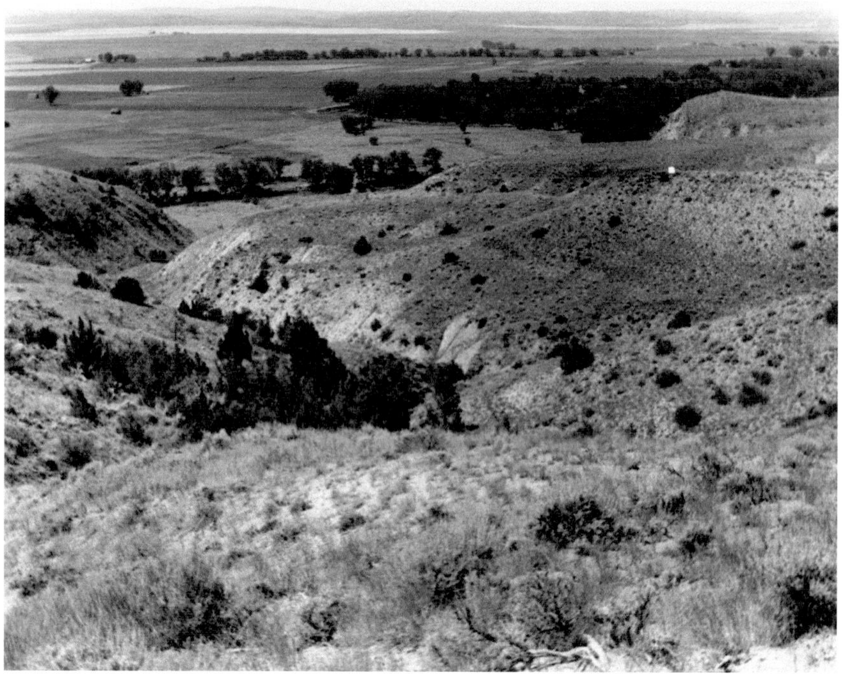

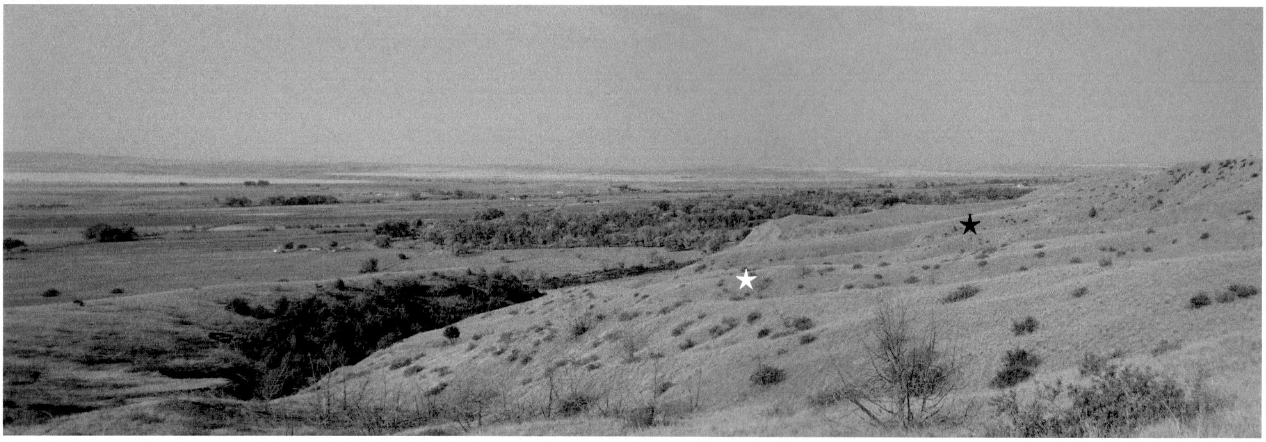

Figure 14.1. (*top*) DeWolf marker in the Reno retreat area. Courtesy of Big Horn County Historical Museum. (*bottom*) Modern panorama (2012). Open star indicates the knoll Roahen cited. Closed star is above DeWolf's marker and another soldier's, both of which stand on a different knoll to the right.

1890, when an army detachment commanded by Capt. Owen Sweet formally erected the memorial markers on the battlefield, one was placed at that site for DeWolf. In *Where Custer Fell*, we included several historical photos and modern reshoots of the DeWolf marker, but none was as difficult to match as Roahen's undated photograph in figure 14.1.

The difficulty arose because Roahen appears to have used a Liquid Paper–like substance on his photograph to enhance the DeWolf monument. If he did so, he marked the wrong rounded knoll. To put his photograph in perspective, for the modern figure 14.1 image I merged two of my photographs. The open star indicates the knoll that Roahen cited. The closed star is above DeWolf's marker and another soldier's, which stand on a different knoll to the right. Clearly, Roahen cited the wrong knoll.

In figure 14.2, taken from a different vantage point, Roahen aimed his camera at the area of the retreat crossing but also picked up the DeWolf marker.

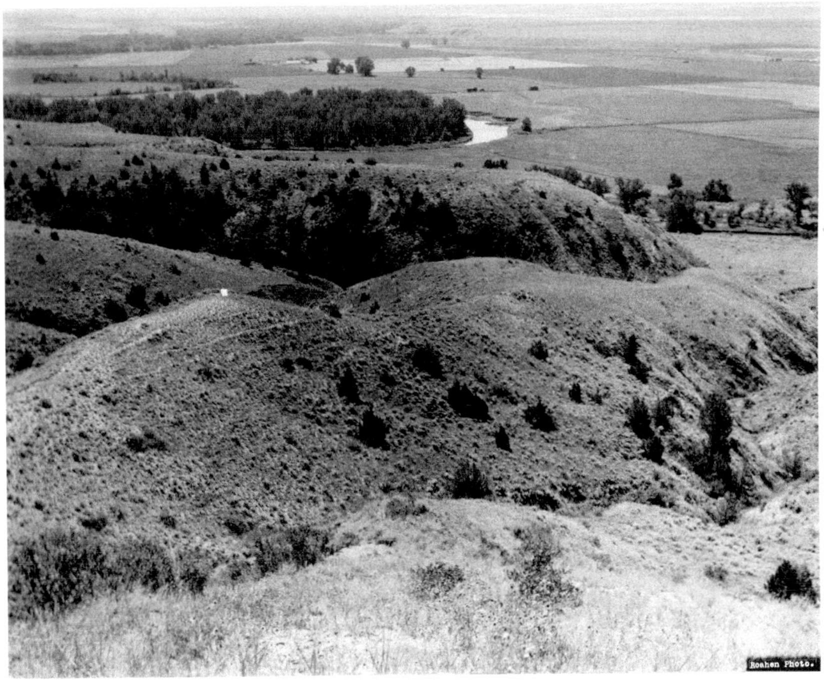

Figure 14.2. (*top*) Retreat crossing and the DeWolf marker, showing more trees in 1876. Courtesy of Big Horn County Historical Museum. (*bottom*) 2012 reshoot.

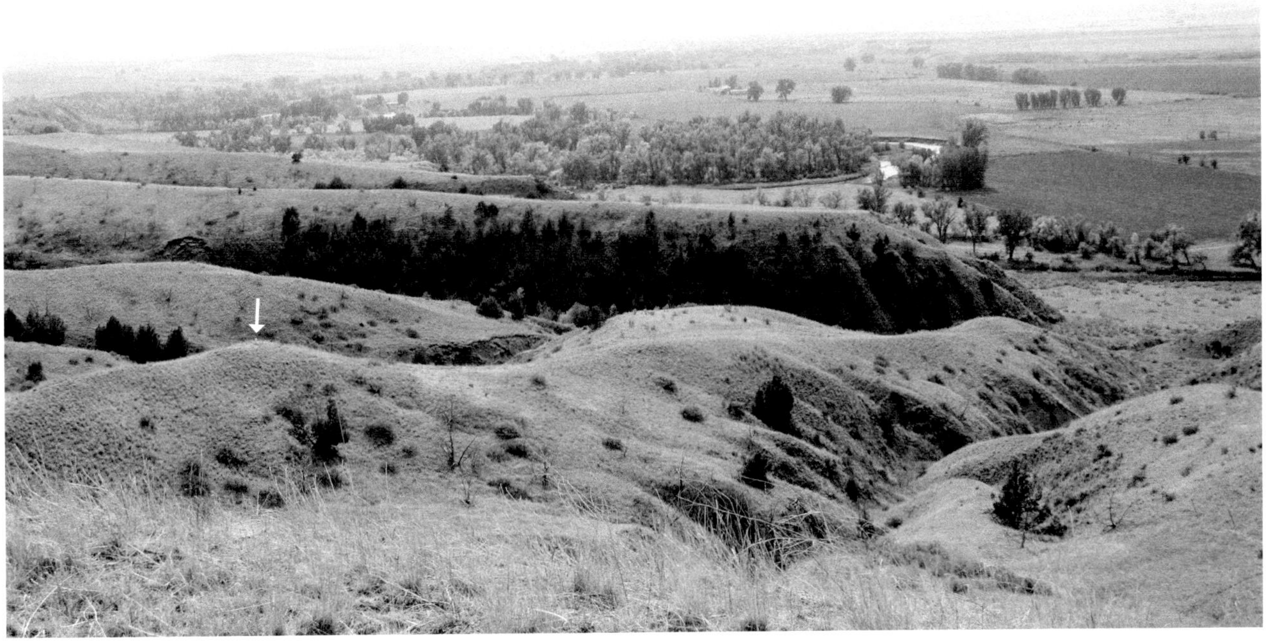

Again, he appears to have used some substance to better indicate the marker's location, but in the modern image DeWolf's marker is on the left. The marker to the right of DeWolf's has long been associated with Pvt. Elihu Clear, who is often cited as DeWolf's orderly killed with him. Clear likely was not the doctor's orderly, but he was killed in the fighting. Historical accounts vary about where his death occurred, suggesting several sites from the timber to the river to the bluffs.[1]

Roahen's correspondence makes clear that he enjoyed a close professional relationship with author Jesse W. Vaughn of Windsor, Colorado. Frequently Vaughn

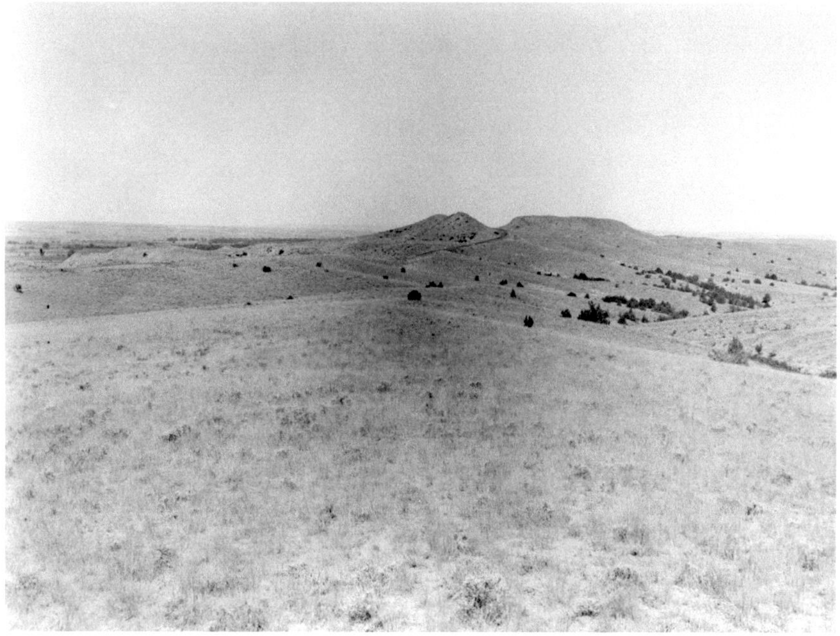

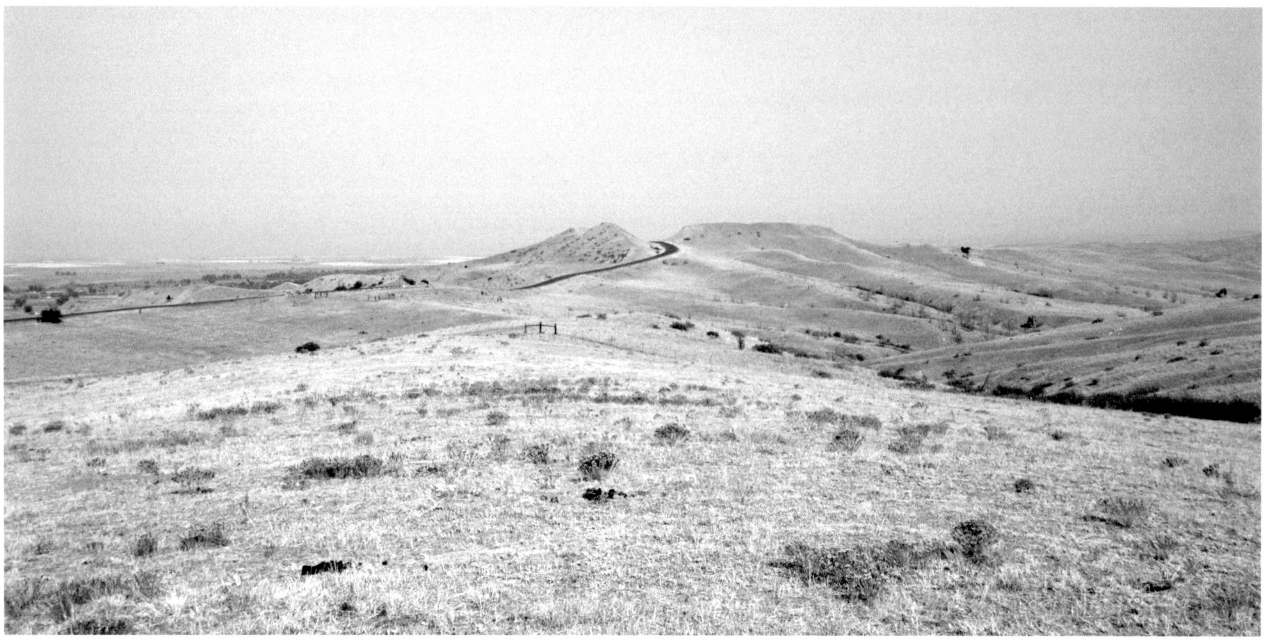

Figure 14.3. (*top*) Weir Point from below Sharpshooter Ridge, taken at author J. W. Vaughn's request. Courtesy of Big Horn County Historical Museum. (*bottom*) 2012 reshoot.

asked him to shoot specific photographs of Little Big Horn or other battlefields for his books. Figure 14.3 shows one of those requested images, taken on the slope between the battlefield road, seen to the left, and Sharpshooter Ridge, out of sight to the right. In the background Weir Point with its distinctive cut dominates not only Roahen's image but also its modern counterpart.

In 1876, Reno's troops never moved farther north than the lower reaches of what would be named Weir Point. Although they probably viewed what proved to be the final action on Last Stand Hill three miles ahead of them, they actually looked past a landmark feature that today's battle students realize significantly impacted the final fight of George Custer—the wide and dry

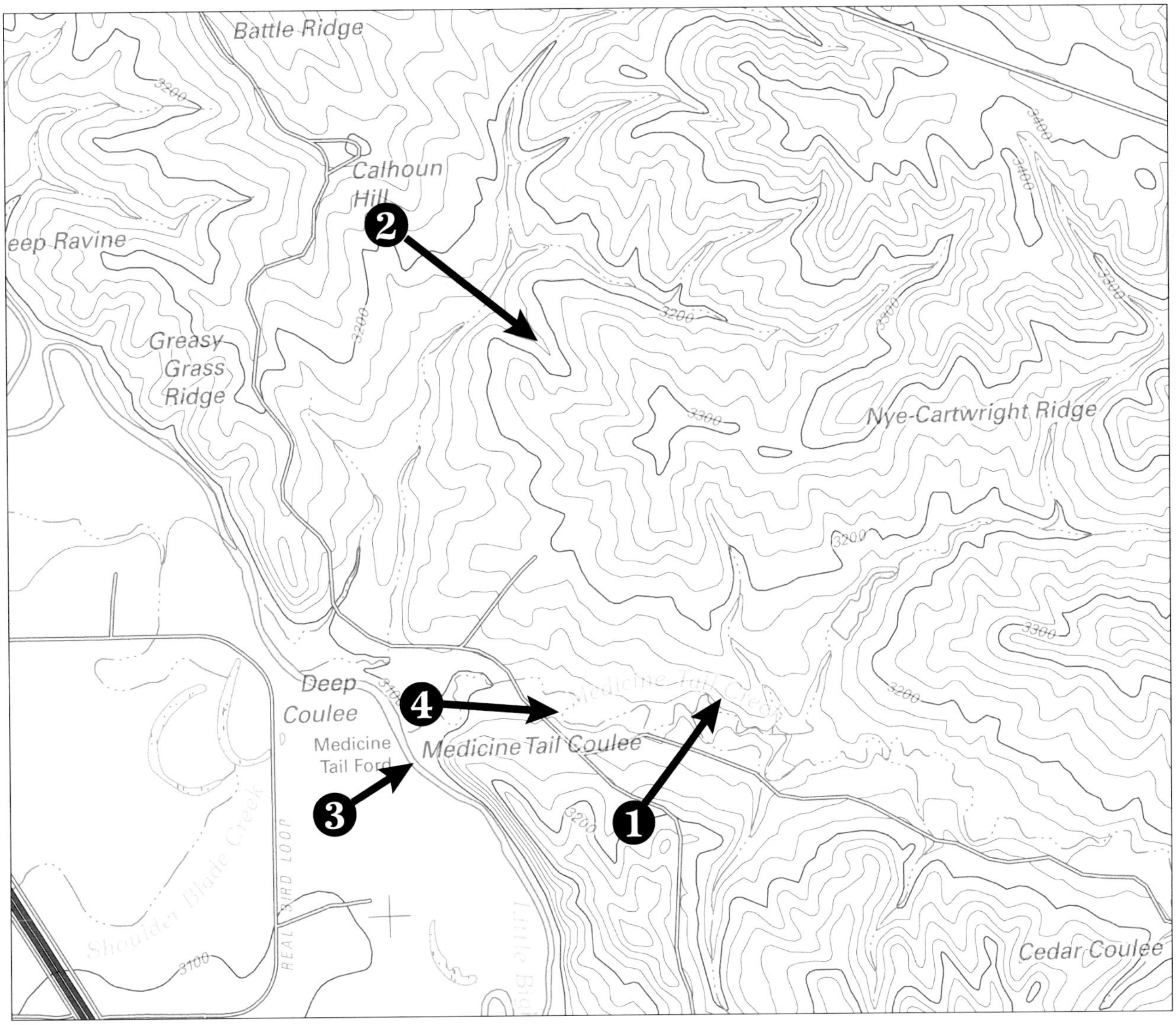

Map 14.2. Medicine Tail Coulee vicinity. Map by Gary Raham.

1. Figs. 14.5, 14.6
2. Figs. 14.7, 14.8
3. Figs. 14.9, 14.10, 14.15–14.17
4. Figs. 14.11, 14.13, 14.14

stream today known as Medicine Tail Coulee. The evidence and theoretical possibilities that surround Custer's movement away from what would became known as the Reno-Benteen Defense Site to Medicine Tail Coulee are often contradictory.[2] In the vicinity of Sharpshooter Ridge, Custer dispatched Sgt. Daniel Kanipe of Company C with verbal orders for Captain McDougall on the back trail to hasten the pack train's advance. Soldiers who encountered Kanipe later recalled that the sergeant gave them the clear impression that all was well with the 7th Cavalry. Ten to fifteen minutes after Kanipe's departure, trumpeter John Martin was sent back with a message hastily scrawled by adjutant W. W. Cooke—Custer's famous last message—calling for Benteen to come quick and bring up the ammo packs. Many battle students believe Martin departed somewhere in a depression now labeled Cedar Coulee that led down from the high ground of Weir Point to the broader valley of Medicine Tail Coulee. That, in turn, provided a natural avenue of approach to the Little Big Horn River and the village on the west side.

On the back trail, Martin encountered Boston Custer, the youngest member of the Custer clan, who was riding overland from the pack train intent on joining his older brothers, George and Capt. Thomas W. Custer. When Martin later found Benteen, the captain likely misinterpreted both the message and the trumpeter's demeanor, believing that by the time he would reach the scene of the fighting with his own battalion and the slow-moving pack train all the action would be over.

Battle students disagree on what happened after Custer entered Medicine Tail Coulee. Did he head his whole column westward toward the river and the northern end of the village? Did he or his commanders decide not to cross because the village appeared empty and, instead, head the troops north? Because Custer had divided his command into two battalions, did just one battalion of two companies, probably commanded by Capt. George Yates, head for the river where it was repulsed?

An older theory, now largely rejected, had Custer himself attempting to lead his troops across the river, only to be fatally wounded. A common scenario for today holds that some troops were engaged prior to reaching the river, causing Custer to deploy all or part of his remaining command onto the heights north of Medicine Tail Coulee. Since the early 1990s, according to a theory advanced by historical archaeologist Richard A. Fox, Custer noticed hundreds of noncombatants fleeing north out of the village. That drew him northward in an attempt to find another crossing and capture the refugees, much as he had done successfully eight years earlier at the Battle of the Washita.[3]

Today, many researchers hold that, while Yates was involved in the advance toward the Little Big Horn River, Capt. Myles Keogh led his battalion over high ground to the north, where numerous .45–55 shell cases have been discovered. In 1943, Superintendent Luce himself found some 150 expended shells on a ridge just over a half mile north of Medicine Tail Coulee. Inasmuch as they were found three to four yards apart along a 100–150-yard-wide line, Luce concluded that a brief dismounted action occurred there involving at least a portion of Custer's soldiers. The so-called Luce Ridge (today often referred to as Traditional Luce Ridge) may, in fact, mark the site of the first significant firing by Custer's troopers.

In the 1920s, local rancher Joseph Blummer had made a similar discovery on another ridge within a half mile of Luce Ridge where the crest that overlooks the Medicine Tail Coulee ford angles northwest toward Custer's own final battlefield. Subsequent exploration on that site by Col. Elwood L. Nye and Ralph G. Cartwright yielded about one hundred expended cartridges. Ever since, that ridge has been viewed as a significant battlefield landmark, labeled Nye-Cartwright Ridge.

From this ridge, Calhoun Hill lies a half mile northwest and is where one of the regiment's significant battle lines would be established. Today's students theorize that soldiers, likely Captain Keogh's battalion, engaged warriors who were harassing the column as the soldiers moved northward to their final battleground.

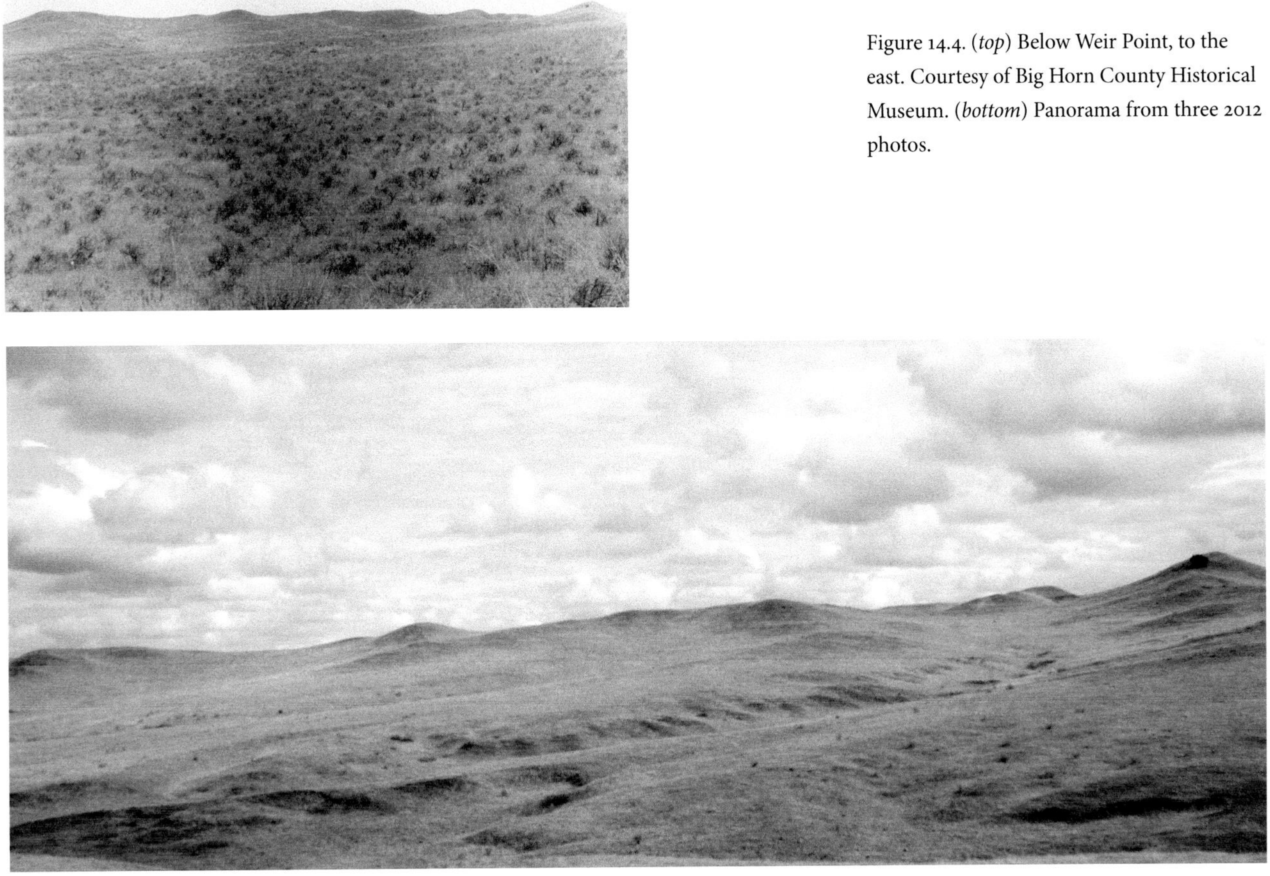

Figure 14.4. (*top*) Below Weir Point, to the east. Courtesy of Big Horn County Historical Museum. (*bottom*) Panorama from three 2012 photos.

Throughout the 1940s to the mid-1950s, Luce remained close friends with photographer Roahen. Not surprisingly, Roahen frequently focused his camera on this general vicinity. The Hardin photo collection contains images of several areas of interest below Weir Point down to Medicine Tail Coulee. They are among the more puzzling images in the collection. What was Roahen's purpose in shooting each of these scenes?

Figure 14.4, showing the knolls looking east on the downslope below Weir Point, may suggest part of an answer. This one appears to have been photographed at the request of J. W. Vaughn. Also in 1956, Vaughn arranged for John Stands In Timber, a Northern Cheyenne historian who gathered information from warriors in the battle, to visit the battlefield with him and Don Rickey. Stands In Timber clearly placed action in the vicinity of the Luce and Nye-Cartwright Ridge sector. Whether Roahen, now retired from the government, accompanied them is unknown, but as a friend of Luce, Rickey, and Vaughn he would have been familiar with these theories. Historical accounts indicate that Captain Weir advanced beyond the high point that now bears his name. If so, Roahen may have been photographing Weir's forward point.

Figure 14.5. (*top*) Bluffs above Medicine Tail Coulee, possibly toward Luce Ridge. Courtesy of Big Horn County Historical Museum. (*bottom*) 2012 reshoot.

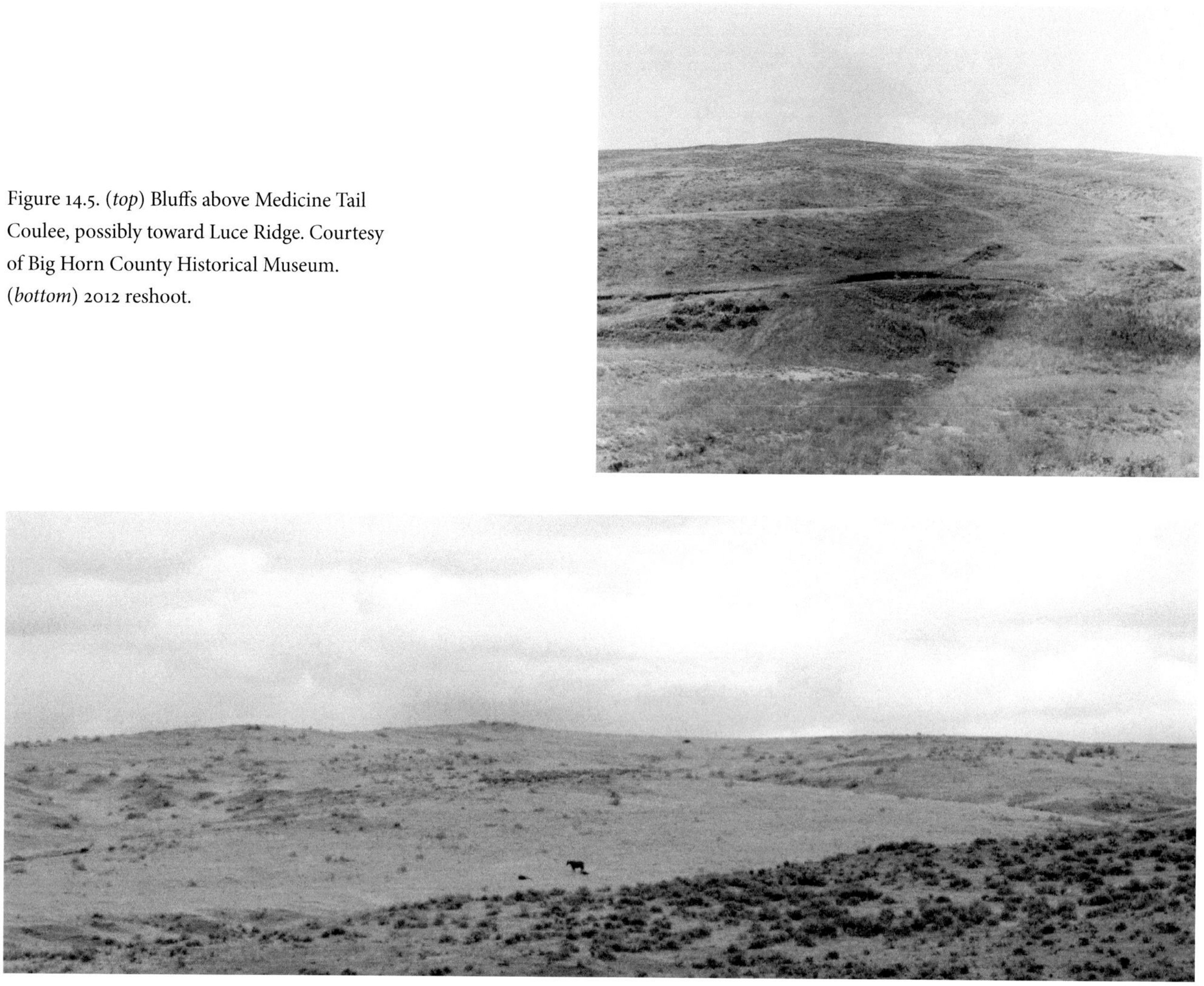

The Roahen photographs in figures 14.5 and 14.6 are overlapping images of the ridgeline to the north, up and across from the south side of Medicine Tail Coulee. Possibly, Roahen was seeking to include so-called Luce Ridge and the area where Custer rode to the high ground after exiting Cedar Coulee. That would include the route he had followed from Sharpshooter Ridge, past Weir Point on the east and down the coulee to the upper reaches of Medicine Tail Coulee. Certainly Roahen and his friends knew of the many accounts that had Custer meeting his youngest brother, Boston, about where the regiment entered Medicine Tail from Cedar Coulee. Custer, upon hearing what Boston had to say about the whereabouts of the regiment's elements on the back trail, rode to the high ground north, across and above Medicine Tail Coulee. That area, Traditional Luce Ridge, would have afforded Custer a better view away from the tunneling effect of the coulee itself. From atop the ridge, one enjoys a great view of all the surrounding area of this portion of the battlefield.[4] According to Bruce Liddic, Traditional Luce Ridge would have been off to the right and out of the photo in figure 14.5. Figure 14.6 appears to be a longer-range shot of what was captured more closely in figure 14.5.[5]

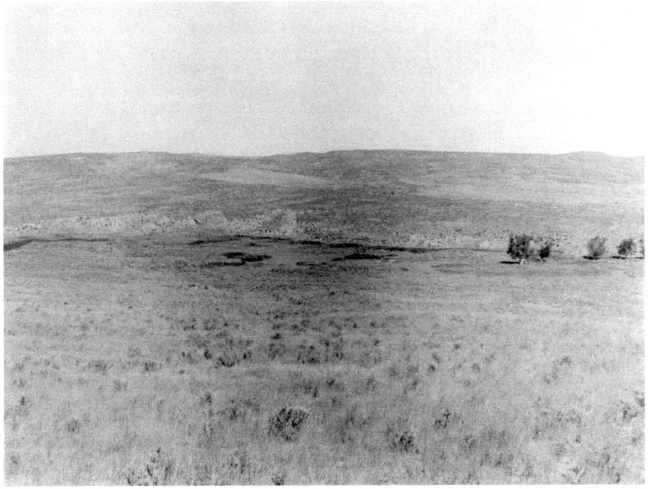

Figure 14.6. (*top*) Looking across Medicine Tail Coulee to the south, possibly toward Luce Ridge. Courtesy of Big Horn County Historical Museum. (*bottom*) 2012 reshoot.

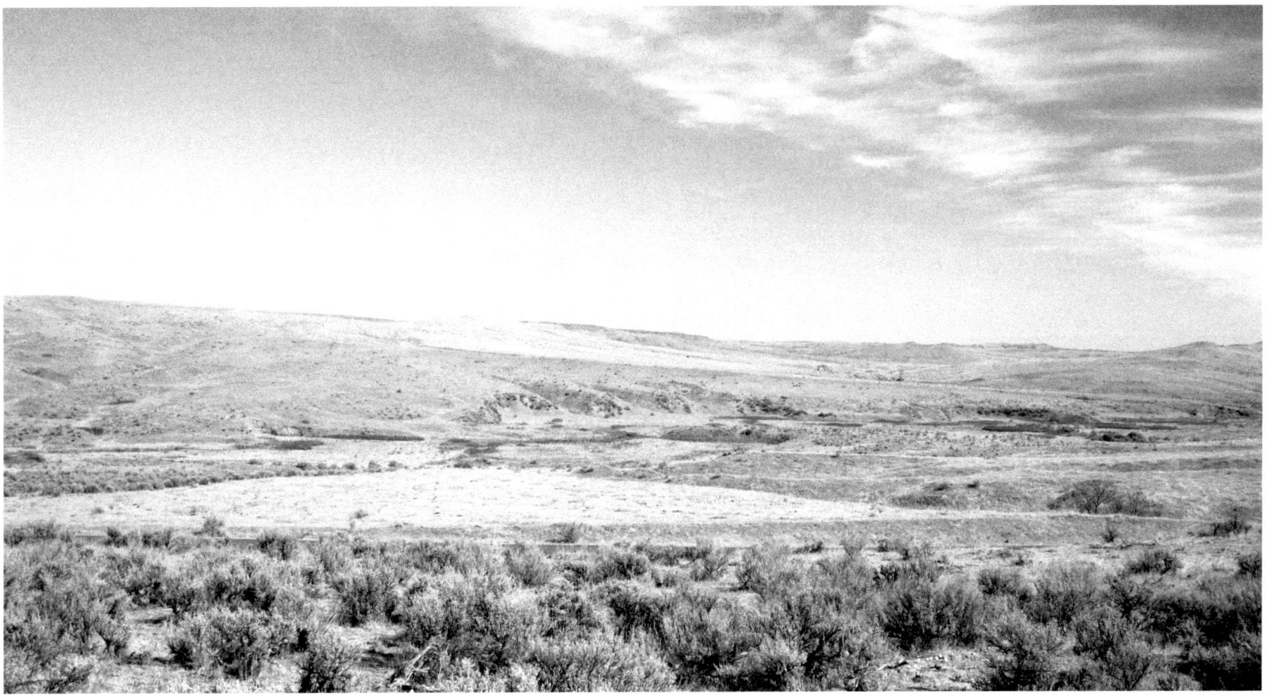

Roahen's figure 14.7 image was taken from the vicinity of Medicine Tail Coulee, but its exact site could not be reliably determined. The 2012 counterpart was taken from the slope of Calhoun Hill. Though it generally looks the same, thanks more to the versatility of modern camera lenses, it is not precise.

In figure 14.8, Nye-Cartwright Ridge can be seen in the upper middle of the photograph about where the road track is visible. Traditional Luce Ridge would be off the photo, about where the tracks end. Liddic said that Traditional Luce Ridge is right above Medicine Tail Coulee, at a right angle, and provides a view toward the Reno-Benteen battlefield in one direction and then to the west or straight down to what is known as Ford B at the end of Medicine Tail Coulee. However, in his day Roahen was unlikely to have made such a differentiation and would have known only the traditional site.

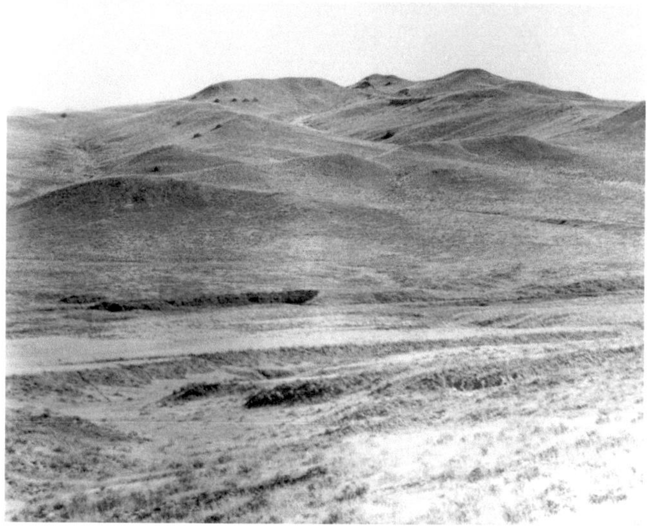

Figure 14.7. (*top*) Slopes of Weir Point. Courtesy of Big Horn County Historical Museum. (*bottom*) 2012 reshoot.

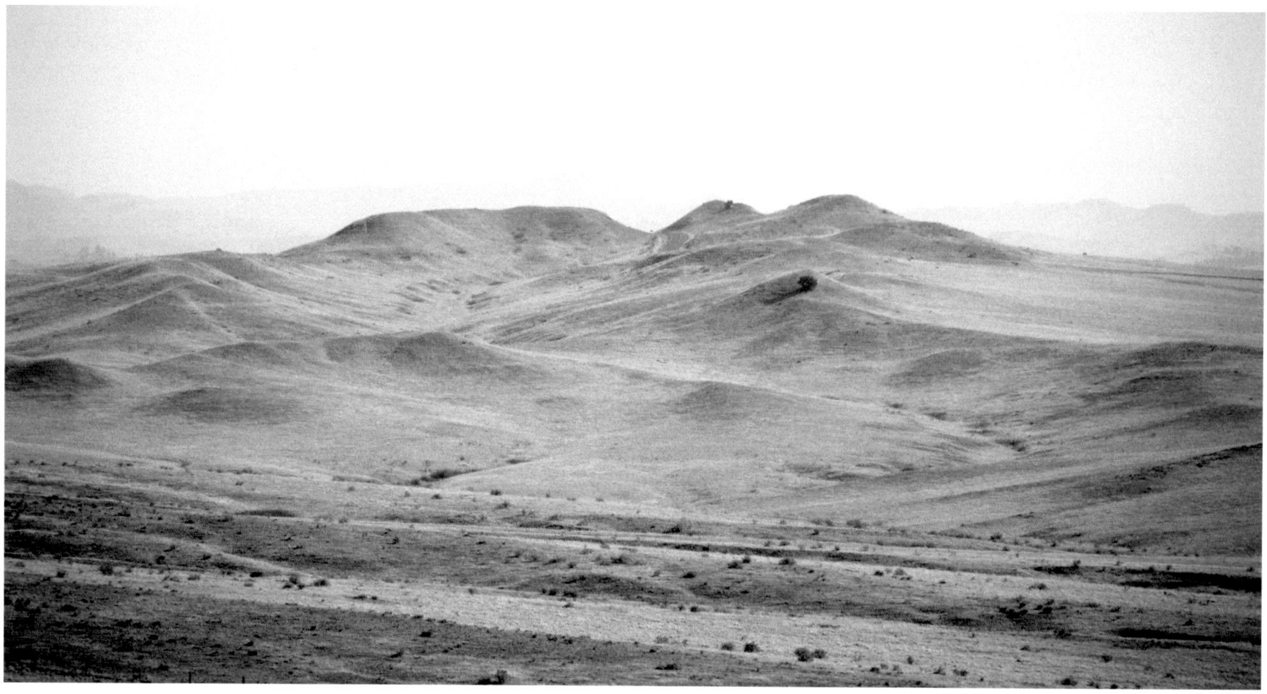

Many of today's visitors to Little Bighorn Battlefield National Monument drive along the battlefield tour road down the slope from Calhoun Hill and through Medicine Tail Coulee. Likely, they barely notice a dead tree snag that has stood for years in the coulee, just to the left of the road before it begins its long rise toward Weir Point (fig. 14.9). In Roahen's photograph of Medicine Tail Coulee (fig. 14.10, dated July 29, 1961), which he shot from the west bank of the Little Big Horn River, where the coulee joins the Little Big Horn, he actually captured the tree in full life. It appears just to the right of the black arrow Roahen drew on that image. In another Roahen photograph (fig. 14.11), it is even more visible on the right, above a finger bluff. For that one, he stood on the river's east bank, focusing on the high ground above the coulee to the east. The tree is missing in the modern counterpart photo.

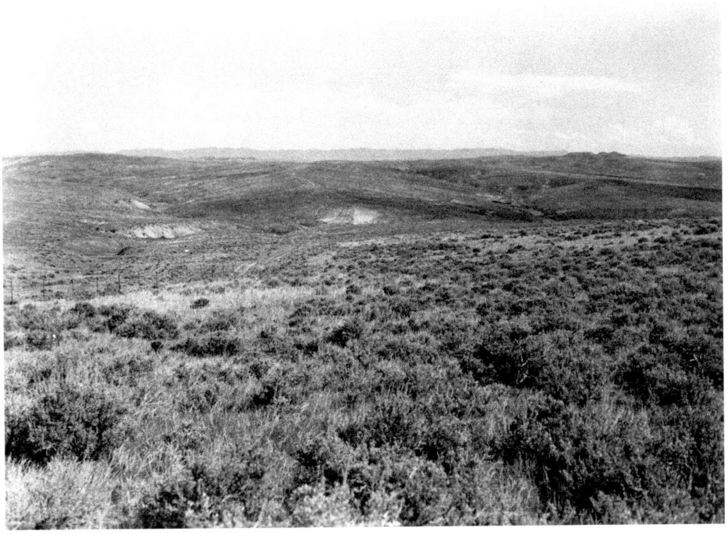

Figure 14.8. (*top*) Nye-Cartwright Ridge. Courtesy of Big Horn County Historical Museum. (*bottom*) 2012 reshoot.

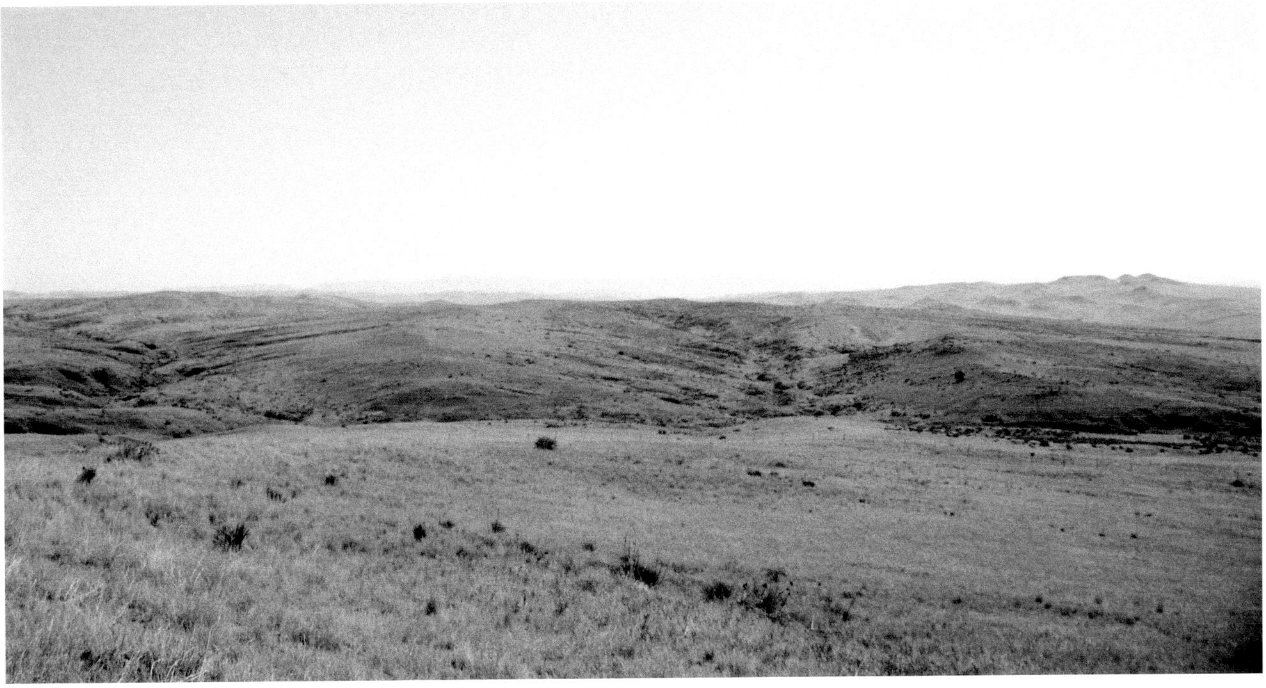

Since the tree appears as just one more object in Roahen's photographs, he undoubtedly gave little thought to its presence. But that tree, or its remnants in death, now looms more important as a result of a National Park Service–sponsored survey conducted in September 2011 along a 1.75 kilometer segment of the Little Big Horn River that forms the national monument's southwest boundary.[6] The scientists' conclusion: "The tree is potentially significant, as it could be a 'witness' to the Battle of Little Bighorn in 1876." It could be, they added, the same tree documented on the 1876 Kill Eagle map contained in the battlefield's collection and published in author Michael Donahue's study of battle maps, *Drawing Battle Lines*.[7] They also stated that "this lone cottonwood 'witness' tree was at least 25-years-old at the time of the battle in 1876 . . . assuming a death date of 1970."

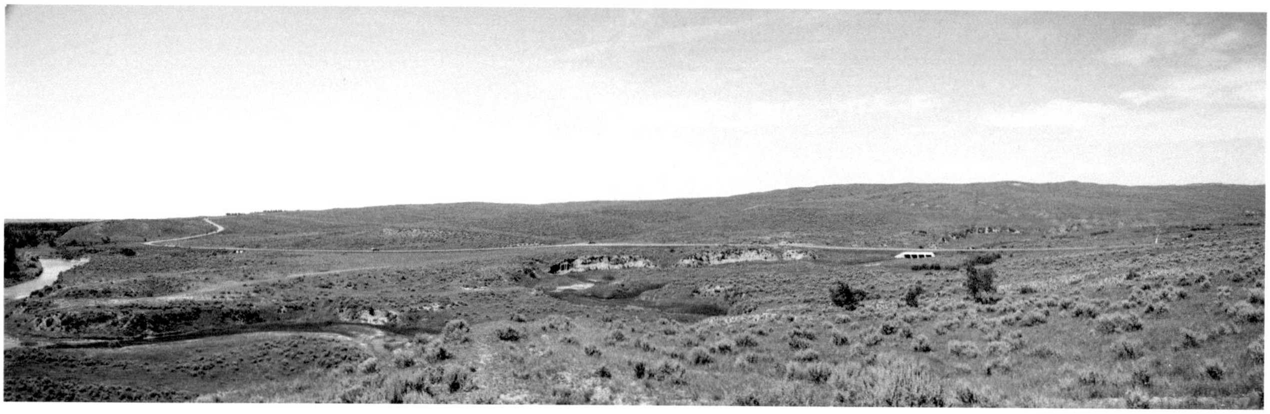

Figure 14.9. Medicine Tail Coulee, modern panorama.

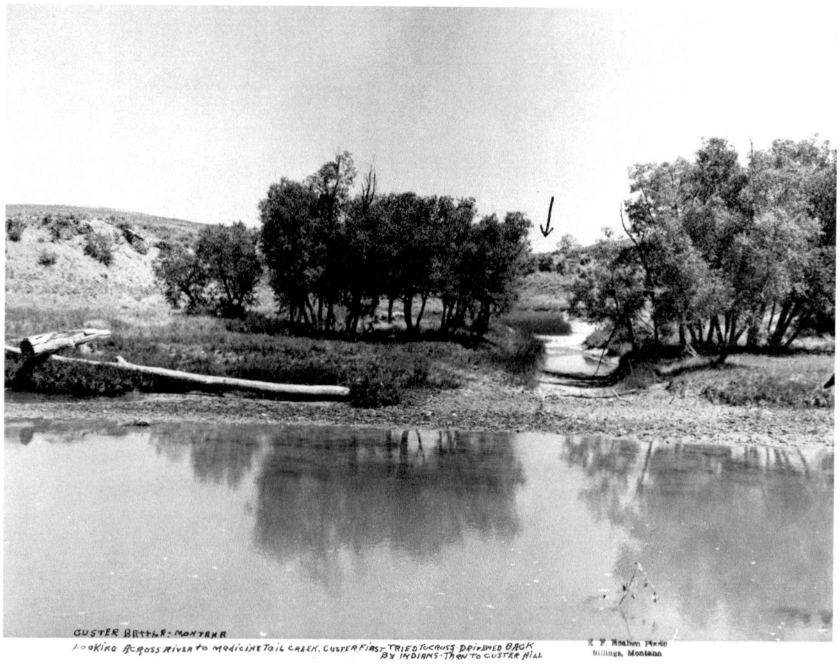

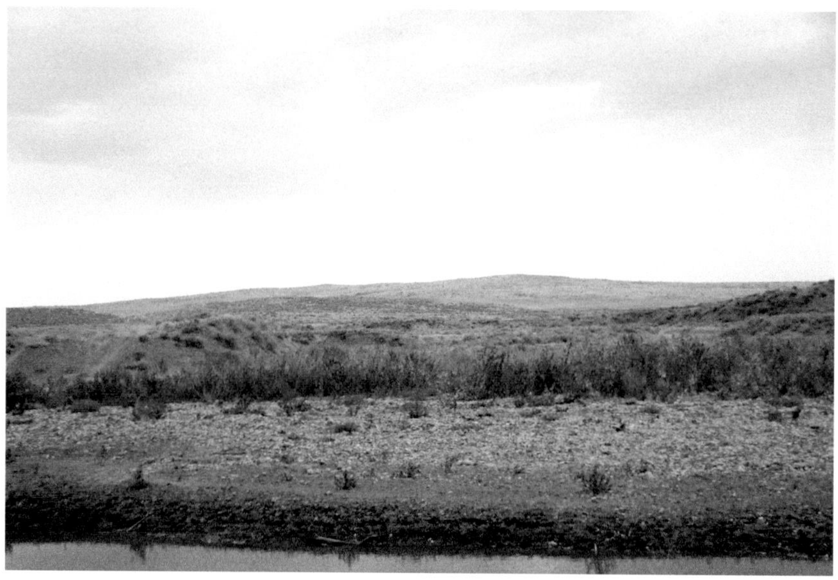

Figure 14.10. (*right*) Junction of Medicine Tail Coulee and Little Big Horn River, looking east, July 29, 1961; arrow indicates tree. Courtesy of Big Horn County Historical Museum. (*bottom*) 2012 reshoot.

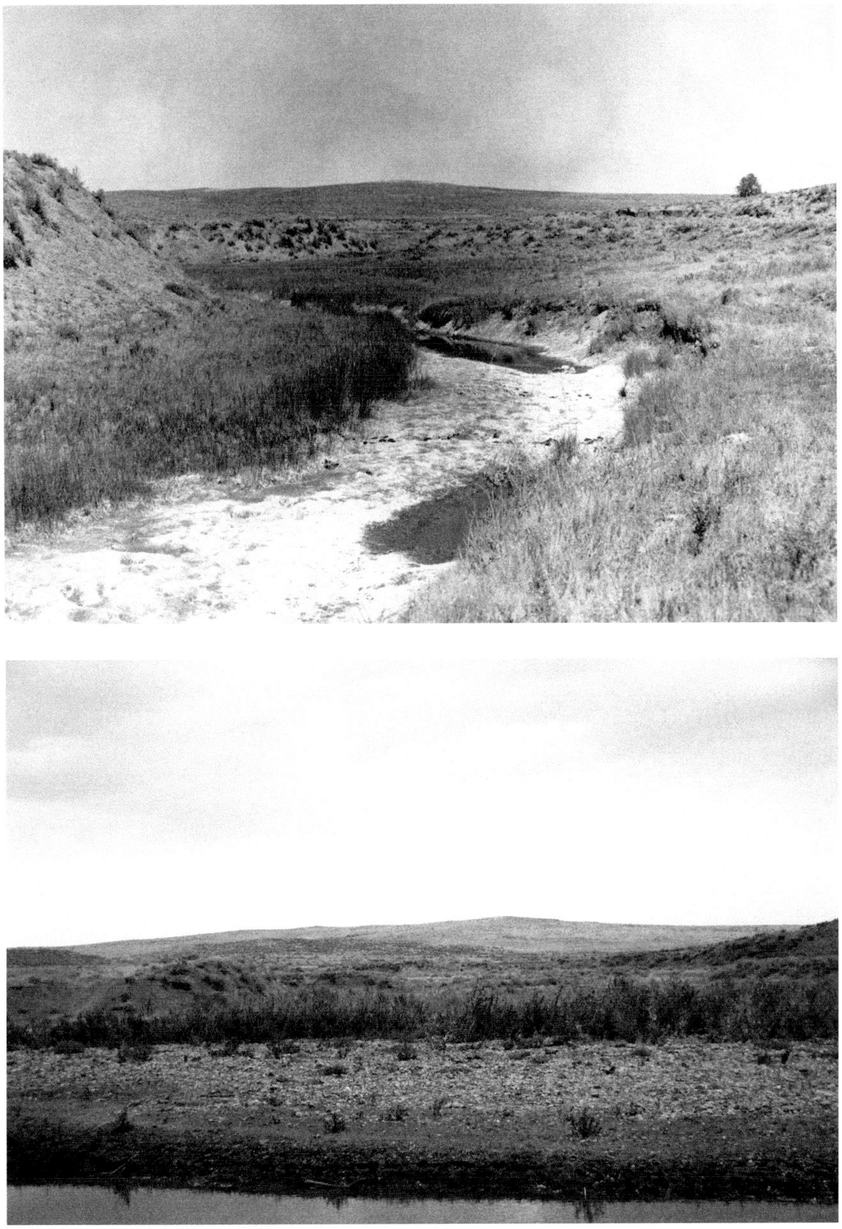

Figure 14.11 (*top*) Looking east up Medicine Tail Coulee, with "witness tree." Courtesy of Big Horn County Historical Museum. (*bottom*) 2012 reshoot.

After the study was published in October 2012, a photograph in my collection, shot on June 24, 2007 (fig. 14.12), revealed that the tree was still alive that year. A more recent 2013 image (fig. 14.14) confirmed that it had died since then. With that information, Gregory T. Pederson, the study's lead author, said that their conclusion about the tree's longevity might have to be revised.[8]

According to the Pederson team's fieldwork, conducted in September 2011, sixty-five trees were sampled in the river bottoms below the main Little Big Horn battlefield. Their germination age ranged from 1878 to 1961. The scientists stressed, however, that those should be viewed as minimum ages. Each tree could be two to fifteen years older. They found numerous cottonwoods in the bottoms that appeared even older, perhaps predating the Little Big Horn battle, but they were so rotted that effective core samples could not be

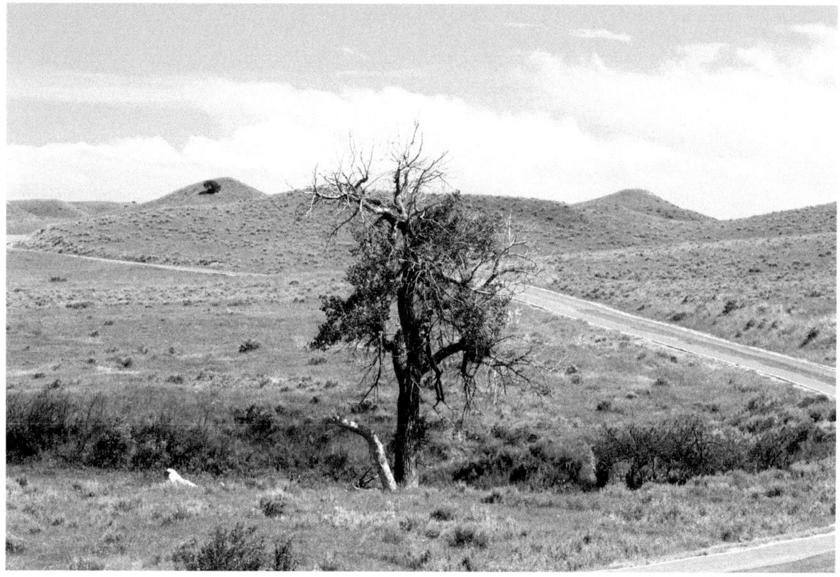

Figure 14.12. Custer battlefield "witness tree," June 24, 2007.

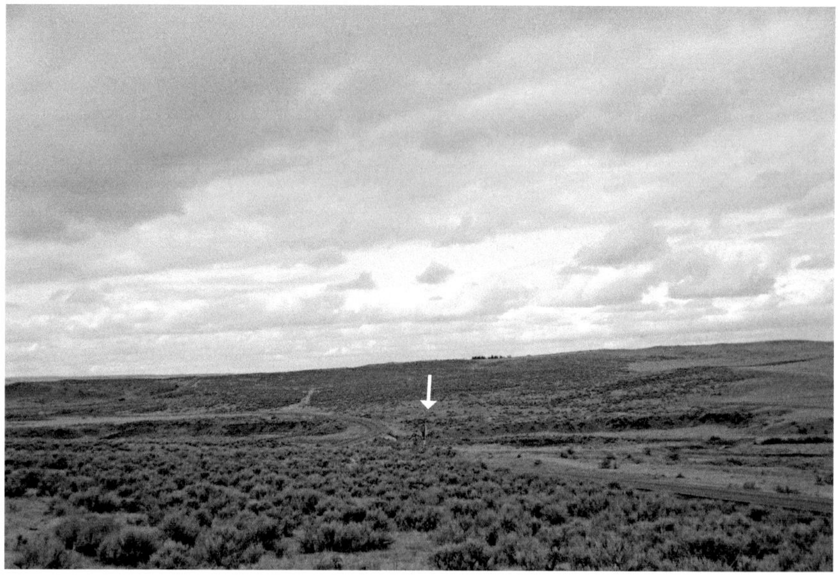

Figure 14.13. "Witness tree" in distance, October 2012.

withdrawn from them for testing. According to the report, "It is likely, however, [that] trees older than 135 years of age do exist since a small number of large individual trees are present, but have extensive rot prohibiting sampling."

Of interest, in 1876 cottonwood trees were less common here than two species of willows. The Pederson report also notes that historic photographs of the Little Big Horn show far fewer trees than can be seen today. Current stands date to two primary periods, ca. 1880–1900 and ca. 1900–25. The majority of them were established between 1890 and 1910 and the youngest in 1961. Few cottonwoods have taken root since the 1930s, despite recurring floods that should have encouraged their growth. The study cites several possible causes, including "historical changes in human land use and fire use, climate, and/or a significant reduction in mammalian (i.e., beaver, bison, horse) tree-harvest/damage activity since the nineteenth century."

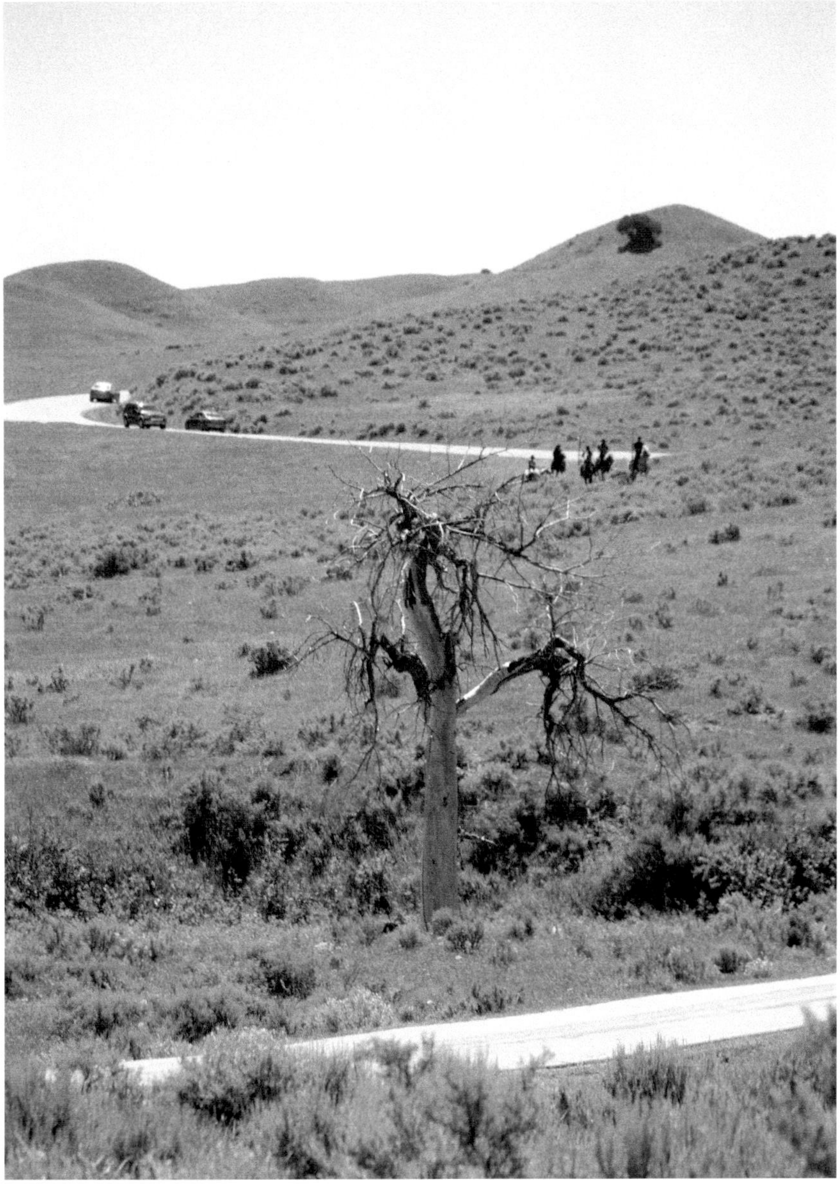

Figure 14.14. "Witness tree," June 25, 2013.

Even though the dead tree in Medicine Tail Coulee stood outside park property, Pederson's team took samples from it, because of the possibility that it could be the one shown on Kill Eagle's map. The core sample from that tree provided age estimates that originally supported the theory that it was alive in 1876. According to information provided by the battlefield, "this now dead 'witness' tree was documented to have been alive into the early 1970s." The study concludes: "Using a successful core from the base of the tree, and assuming a death date of 1970, yields an establishment date estimate of 1851. This would imply the lone cottonwood tree was at least 25 years old at the time of the battle in 1876, and is likely the tree documented in the 1876 Kill Eagle map."

Though Park Service information suggested that the tree died sometime after 1970, the more recent June 2007 photograph indicates that it remained alive for at least thirty-seven years after that date. Backdating the tree by 120

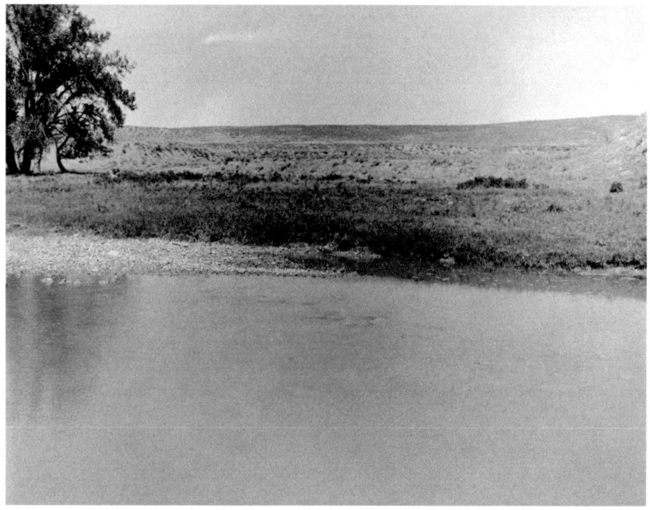

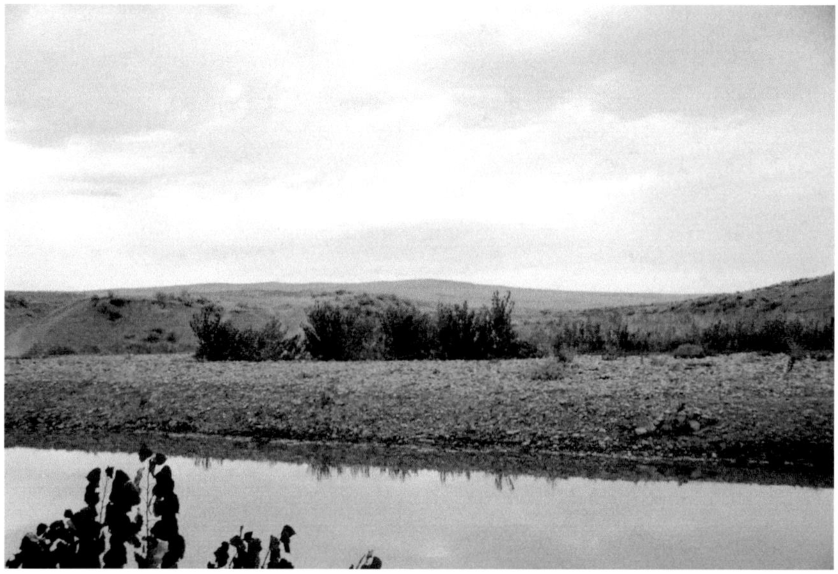

Figure 14.15. (*top*) Across Little Big Horn River to the main battlefield and Medicine Tail Coulee, July 20, 1961. Courtesy of Big Horn County Historical Museum. (*bottom*) 2012 reshoot.

years or so would mean that it established itself well after 1876, as did many of the riverside trees. However, inasmuch as the report indicates the difficulty in determining the exact age of any tree and that some in the river bottoms may be 135 years or older, the Medicine Tail Coulee tree's true age raises some tantalizing possibilities. Pederson indicated that assigning a wider range for determining the age of the trees might mean the Medicine Tail Coulee snag was present in June 1876.

During his career Roahen likely shot numerous photos of the junction of the coulee and the river. On July 20, 1961, he took the figure 14.15 image while standing on the west bank of the river at the coulee. He faced his camera toward the eastern hills beyond the river. The modern images in figures 14.10 and 14.15 provide good views of that area east of the river today.

Another Roahen image (fig. 14.16), also from the river's west bank, was taken about 1,000 yards south of the coulee's junction and is looking north toward

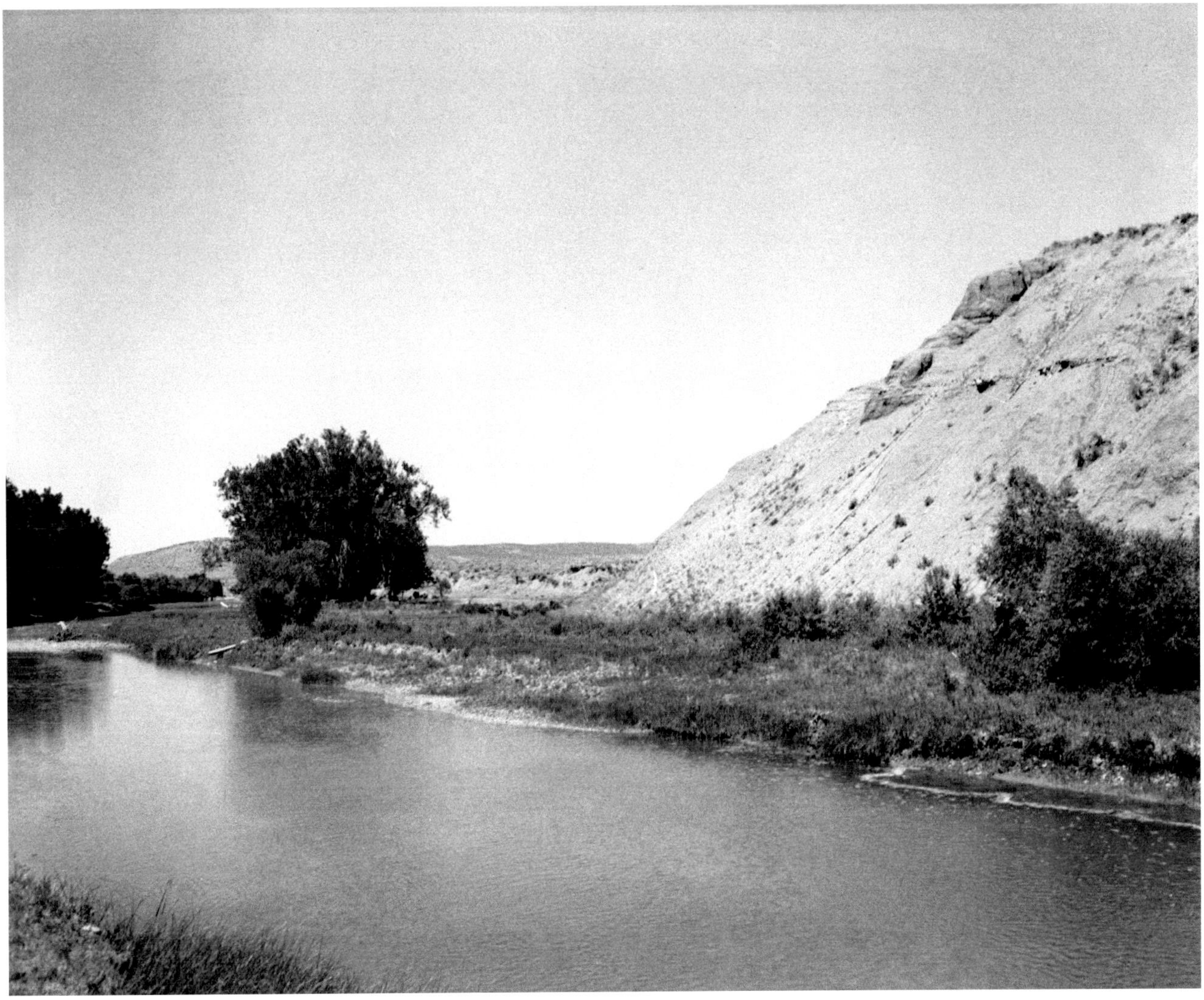

Figure 14.16. Across Little Big Horn River, looking north toward mouth of Medicine Tail Coulee. Courtesy of Big Horn County Historical Museum.

the mouth of Medicine Tail Coulee. I did not match that image, but some of the area it shows can be seen in the modern images of figures 14.10 and 14.15.

Roahen shot two similar views while standing on the west bank and looking south up the Little Big Horn River, merged here in figure 14.17 and matched with a single modern photo.

Figure 14.17. (*top*) Panoramic view looking south from the west bank of the Little Big Horn River at Medicine Tail Coulee. Courtesy of Big Horn County Historical Museum. (*bottom*) 2012 panoramic reshoot.

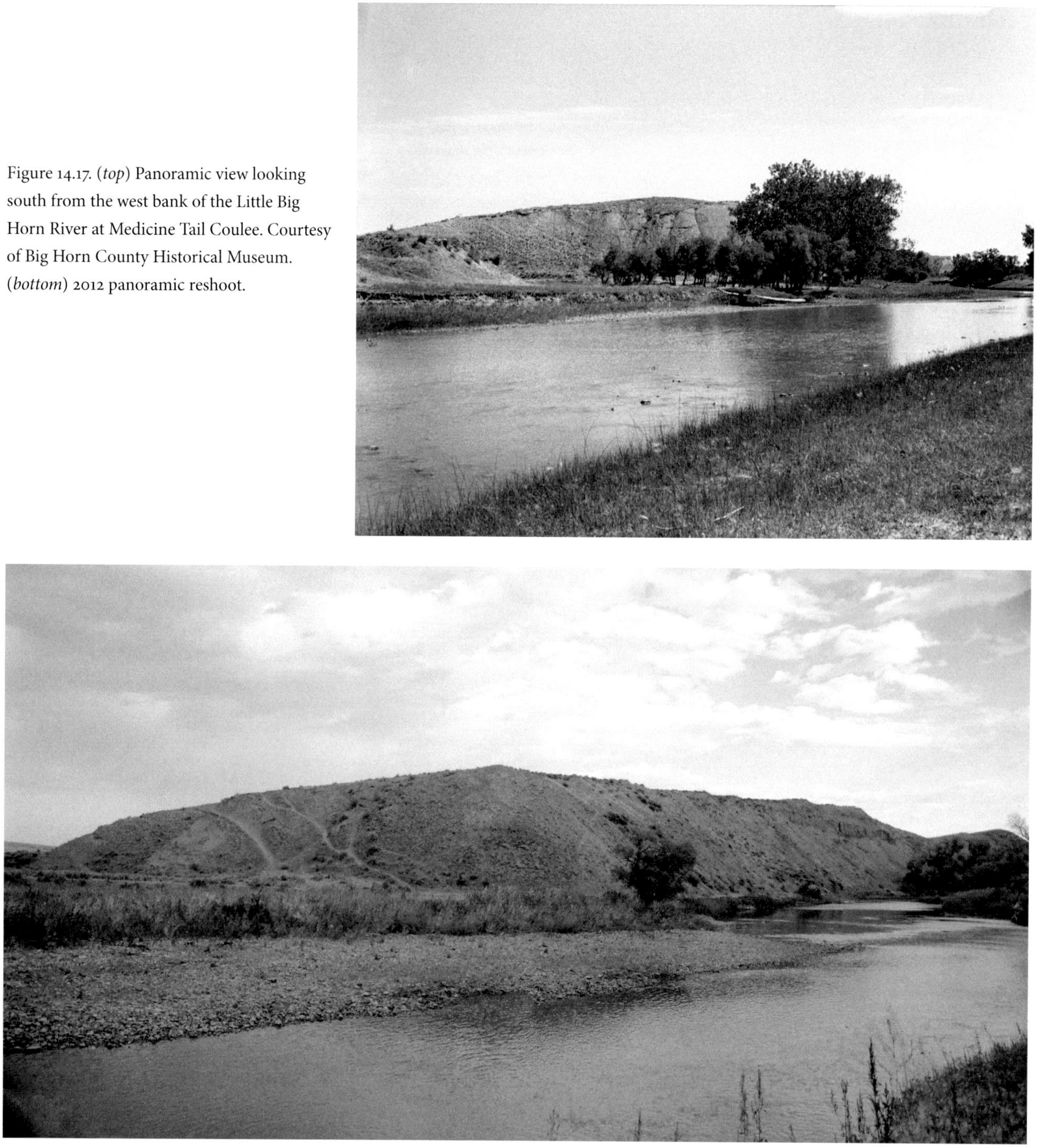

CHAPTER 15

Calhoun Hill, Finley-Finckle Ridge, and Battle Ridge

Calhoun Hill and Finley-Finckle Ridge are tied together not only by their proximity but also by the story of the struggle on June 25, 1876, on the main Custer battlefield. Twenty-three markers are placed along a ridge running south-southwest from Calhoun Hill, fifteen of them positioned on a lower elevation not far from where the park road moves through the boundary fence. That ridge is designated as both Calhoun Ridge and Finley-Finckle Ridge. Another eight markers, hidden from the road, are scattered west-northwest along a swale, dubbed Calhoun Coulee, leading from the flank

Map 15.1. Calhoun Hill, Finley-Finckle Ridge, and Battle Ridge. Based on the 1967 USGS topographical map. Map by Gary Raham.

1. Fig. 15.1
2. Figs. 15.2, 15.3
3. Figs. 15.4, 15.5

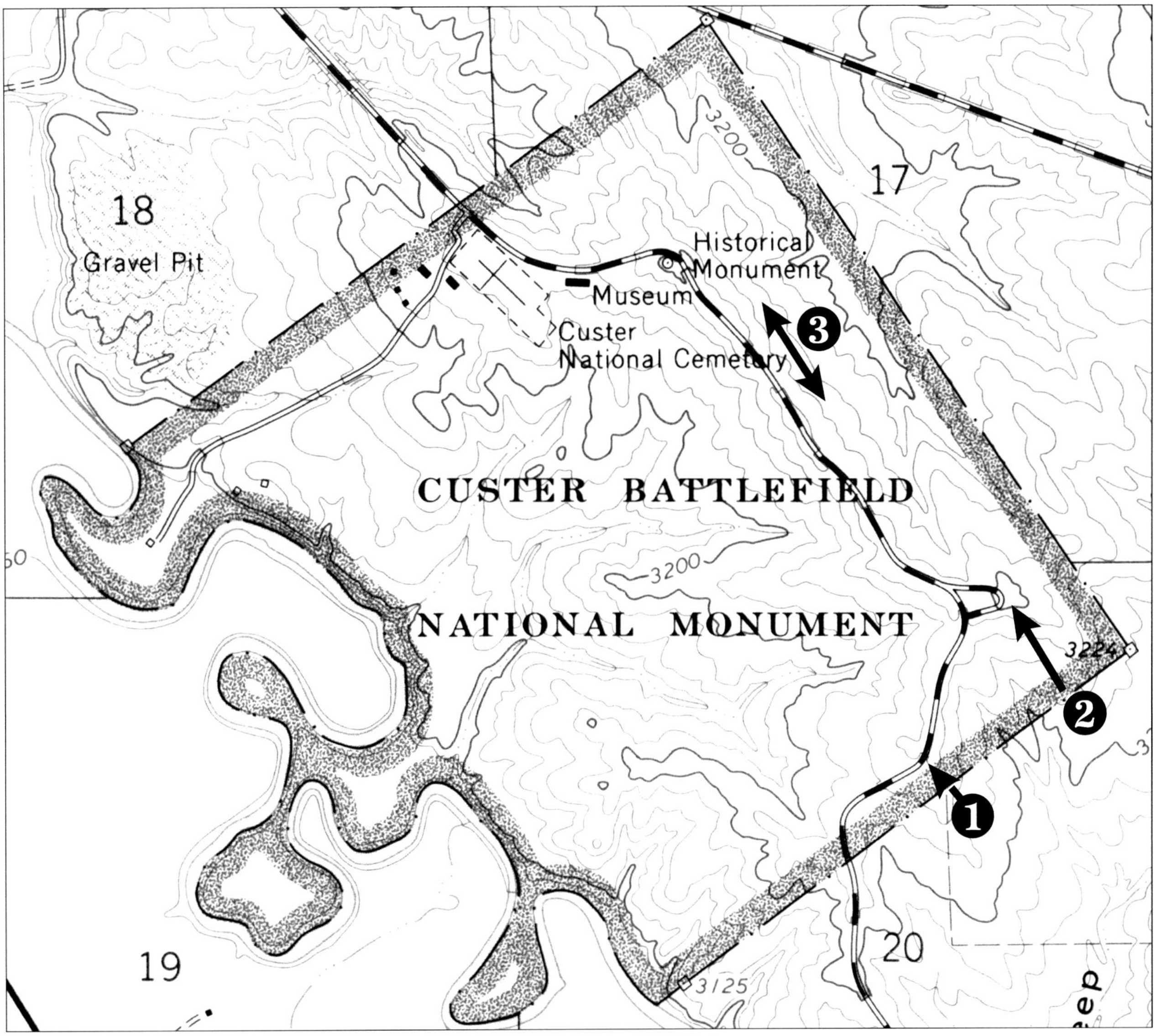

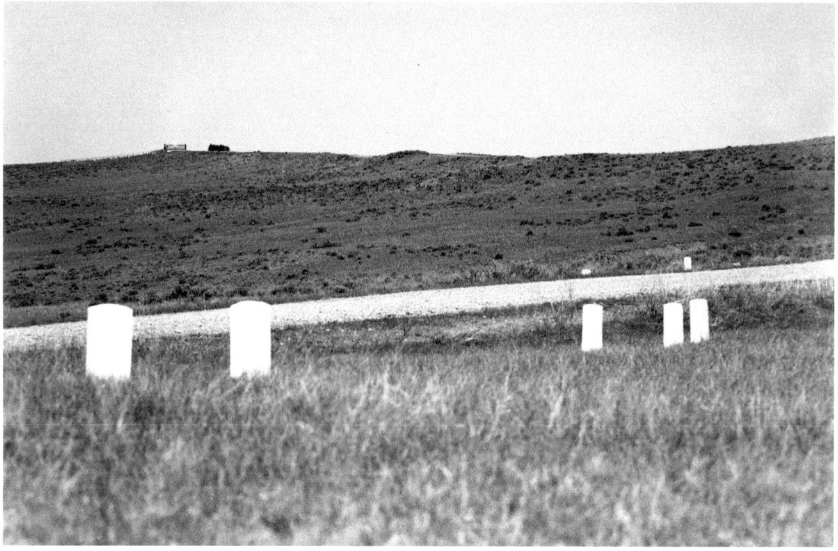

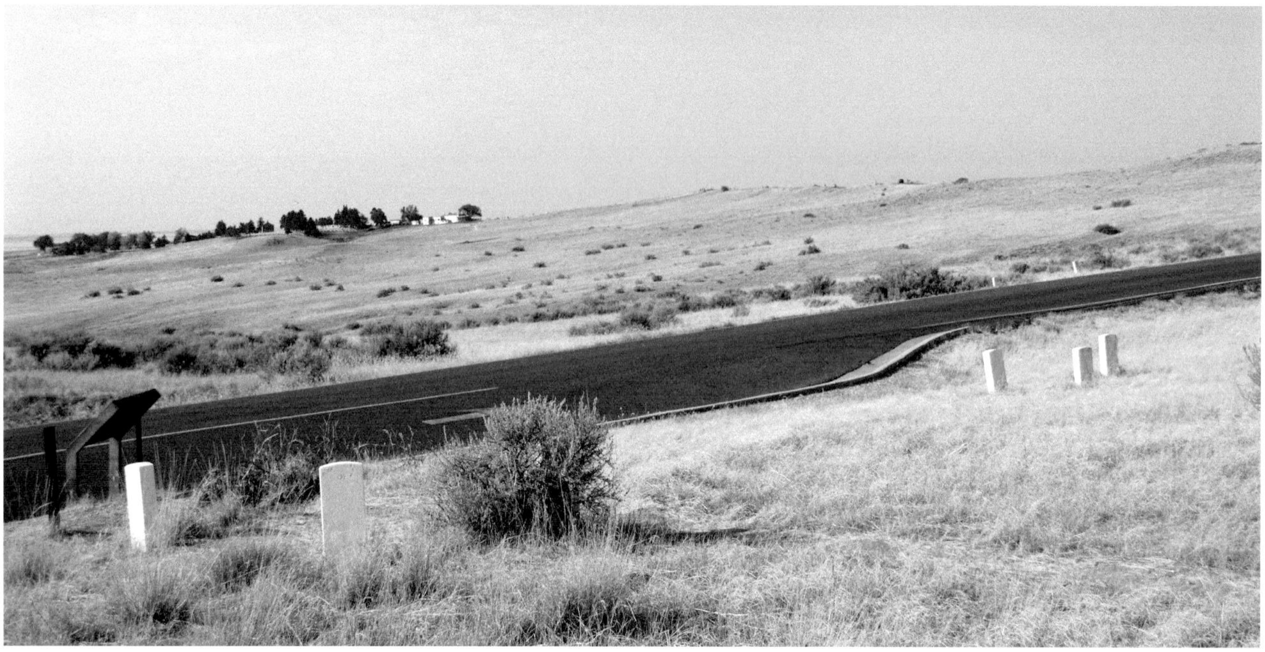

Figure 15.1. (*top*) Six markers, looking north across to Last Stand Hill. Courtesy of Big Horn County Historical Museum. (*bottom*) 2012 reshoot.

of the main ridge toward Deep Ravine. The area obviously was the scene of extensive fighting during the Custer portion of the Little Big Horn battle.

The name Finley-Finckle Ridge comes from two Company C sergeants, Jeremiah Finley and August Finckle, whose original burial places on the battlefield were pointed out by Sgt. Daniel Kanipe on a visit to the battlefield in 1909 with Walter Camp.[1] According to modern theories of the action, Company C had deployed onto the ridge from Calhoun Hill itself, or nearby. Unfortunately for the members of Company C, the Indians reacted decisively and soon washed over the position. That action would prove disastrous for not only the men on Calhoun Hill but Custer's entire command.

Roahen's undated photograph in figure 15.1 shows markers on Finley-Finckle Ridge, but as was true in researching and photographing the battlefield for our earlier book some markers are missing here. The rightmost marker across the road is Finckle's, but other historic photos show a third marker to the left of the two visible in Roahen's; that appears to be missing in his photograph. Today the third marker is hidden behind the big bush visible in the modern counterpart photo.

Note the two groups of three markers apiece in the foreground of the modern figure 15.1 photo. The leftmost marker either was missing when Roahen took his photo or, more likely, he chose not to include it. In 1995, when my coauthors and I were reshooting other historic images for the earlier book, we discovered that the middle marker of the grouping on the right was missing. Later, the Park Service confirmed that the original marker's base was still present. In 2000, a new marker was erected in that grouping.[2] Obviously, when Roahen took his photo, that middle marker was in place.

The earlier research led to the conclusion that Sergeant Finley's marker was among the trio on the left. In Roahen's figure 15.1, which is missing the far left marker, Finley's stone is the leftmost. In the modern shot, Finley's marker is to the left of the sagebrush, which is hiding the rightmost marker of that threesome—on Little Bighorn Battlefield, markers either come or go or Mother Nature hides them.

Calhoun Hill remains one of the more distinctive battlefield features and among the most studied, not only because of its location at the southern end of Custer Ridge (the main battle ridge) but also because surviving soldiers were impressed with the evidence that indicated Calhoun and his men had fought valiantly on the hill and its vicinity. As noted in *Where Custer Fell*, "The amount of expended ammunition, evidenced by the shell cases of Springfield carbines, the pattern of those cases on the ground, and the location of the bodies indicated a degree of tactical cohesion not apparent elsewhere on the battlefield."[3]

Additionally, Calhoun Hill stands out as a defensive position, a half mile from the slightly higher Custer Hill/Last Stand Hill. The crest of Calhoun Hill is slightly bowl-shaped and would have provided some coverage for Lt. James Calhoun's besieged troopers. The rear of the hill descends to a depression that runs some 300 yards to the northwest to a point where the majority of Capt. Myles Keogh's Company I was found. Today that depression has been designated Horse Holders' Ravine, a place where Company L's horses were likely concealed under the control of the No. 4 trooper of each set of four in the company. Eventually, the Indians' superior numbers and firepower began to have a telling effect on the Calhoun and Keogh soldiers. The horses were stampeded, taking with them the reserve ammunition for each trooper. Both General Godfrey and the Hunkpapa war leader Gall believed that proved decisive in the fight for Calhoun Hill.

Early historic photos from the 1890s by the likes of Christian Barthelmess and F. Jay Haynes are different in composition from Roahen's in figures 15.2 and 15.3. The Barthelmess and Haynes photos show four markers, which remain in place today. By the time Roahen shot his undated photographs,

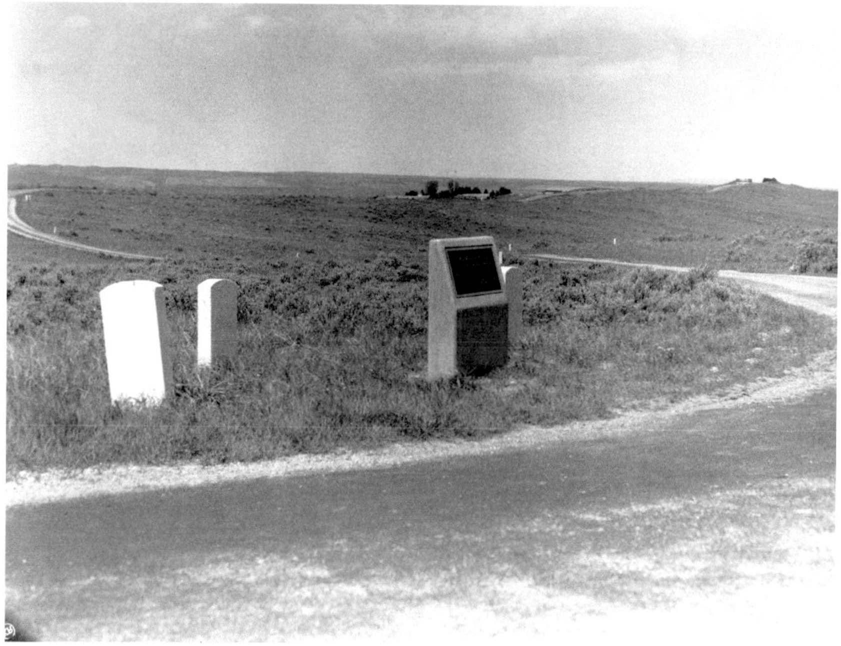

Figure 15.2. (*top*) Calhoun Hill north to Last Stand Hill. Courtesy of Big Horn County Historical Museum. (*bottom*) 2012 reshoot.

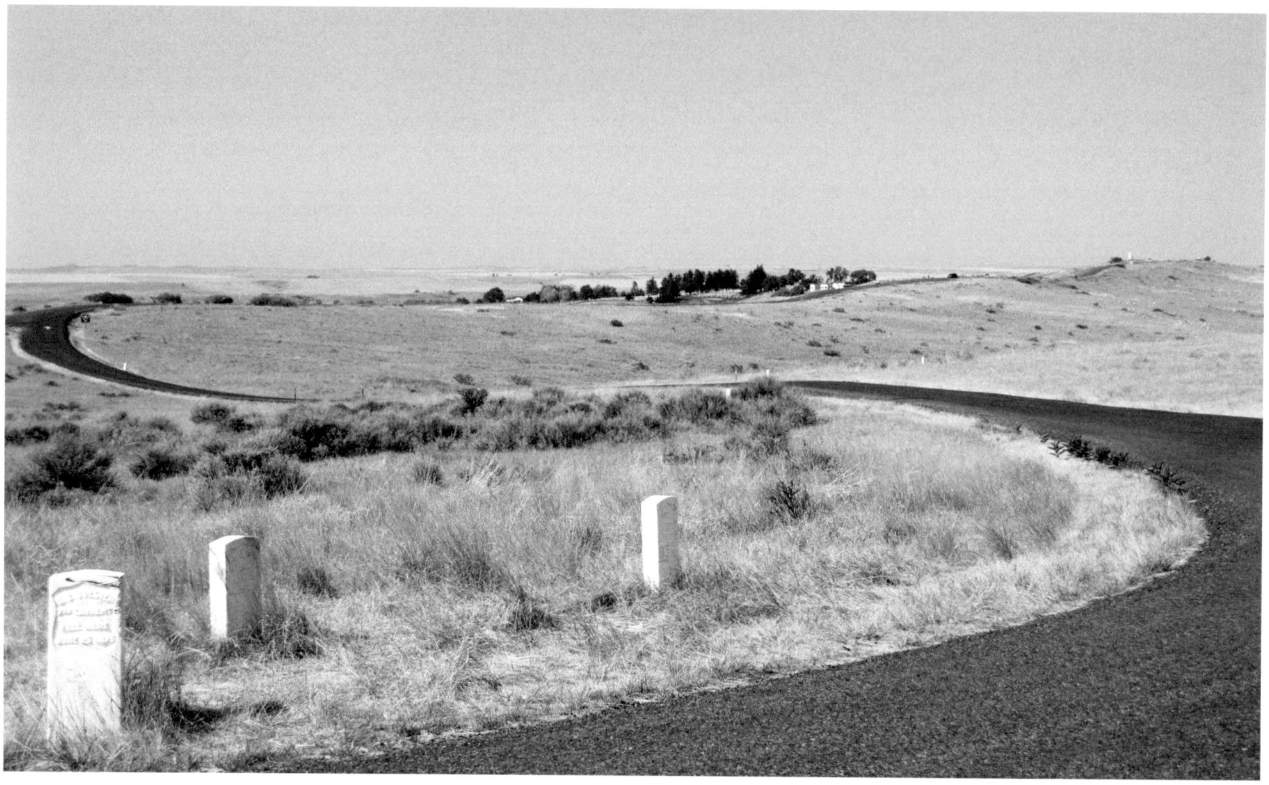

the modern loop of road had been wrapped around the top of Calhoun Hill. As many photographers before him, he aimed his camera toward distinctive landmarks, Last Stand Hill and the even more distant Stone House and Custer National Cemetery. In his figure 15.2 photo, Roahen captured three of the stones at the top of the circle. The third one in this photo is mostly hidden by the historic stone post, which is missing in the 2012 reshoot. Figure 15.3,

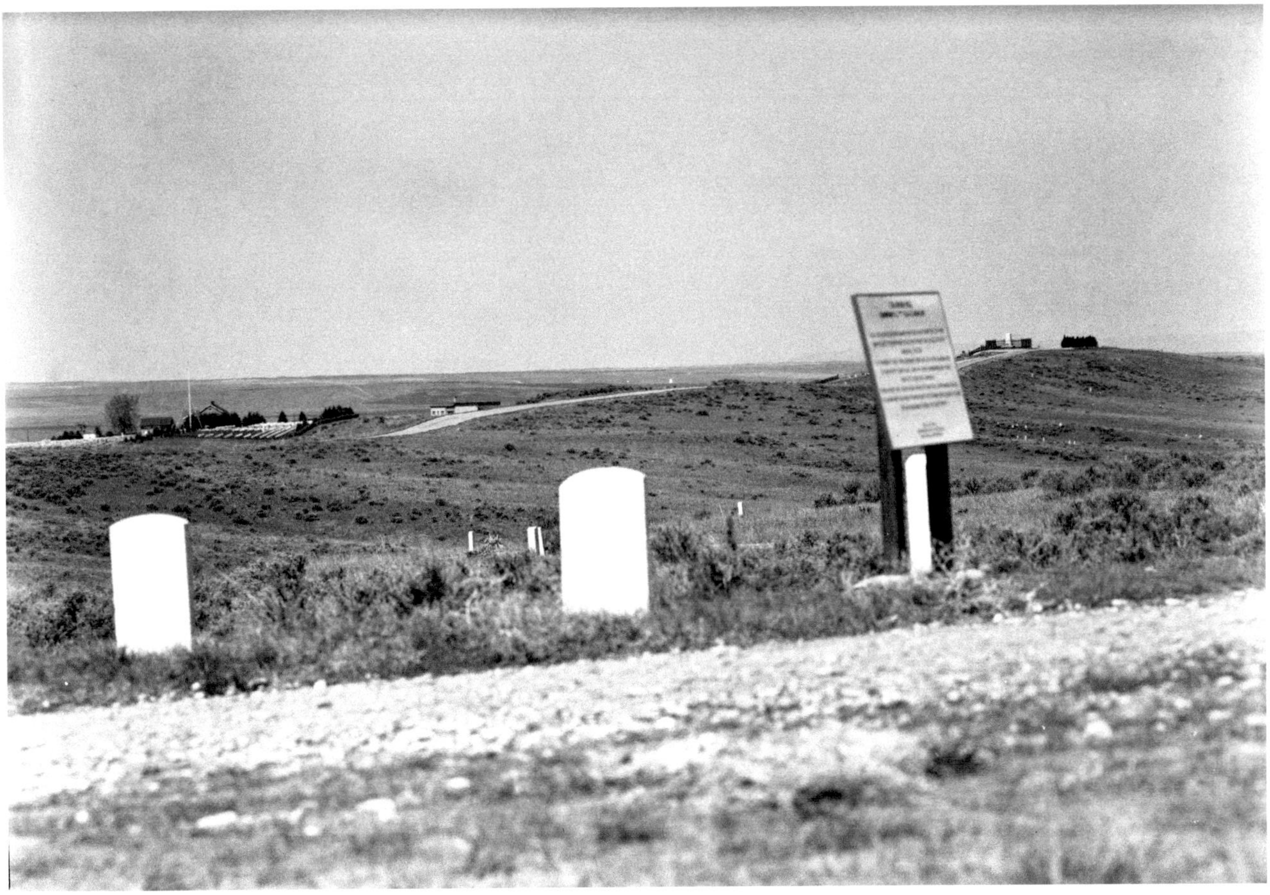

Figure 15.3. Calhoun Hill with sign. Courtesy of Big Horn County Historical Museum.

a variant of figure 15.2, clearly was taken much earlier, based on the significant difference in historical markers. Additionally, the roadway remains covered in stone compared to apparent asphalt in the later photograph. At least two of the four markers are hidden, one by the center stone and another by the historic marker.

Along Battle Ridge, the distance between Calhoun Hill and the place where Custer fell, Last Stand Hill, is only about half a mile, but of course that landform provides the Little Big Horn story's central arena of action. Sometime before the 1951–52 construction of the Visitor Center, Roahen carried his camera and ladder about 120 yards from today's crosswalk on Last Stand Hill and shot two photos. One (fig. 15.4) provides a wide view looking south toward Calhoun Hill and captures U.S. Highway 212 on the east and the Little Big Horn River bottoms on the right. In the far background are Weir Point and the more distant Wolf Mountains. For his other image (fig. 15.5) Roahen turned around and shot north back toward Last Stand Hill, which appears on the right. The photo also captures the Stone House and its surrounding trees on the left. Given the size of those trees and the absence of the Visitor Center or any signs of its construction in the area next to the cemetery below Last Stand Hill, we can date this photo to the late 1940s, if not earlier. The Park Service's long-term plans call for building a new center for tourists in a different location and demolishing the 1950s-era Visitor Center. Roahen's figure 15.5

Figure 15.4. (*top*) Battle Ridge Road, looking south to Calhoun Hill. Courtesy of Big Horn County Historical Museum. (*bottom*) 2013 reshoot.

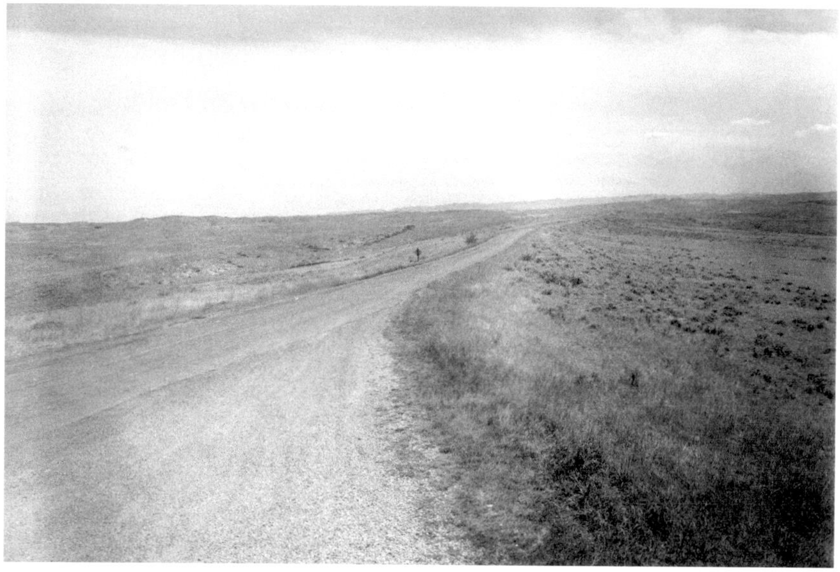

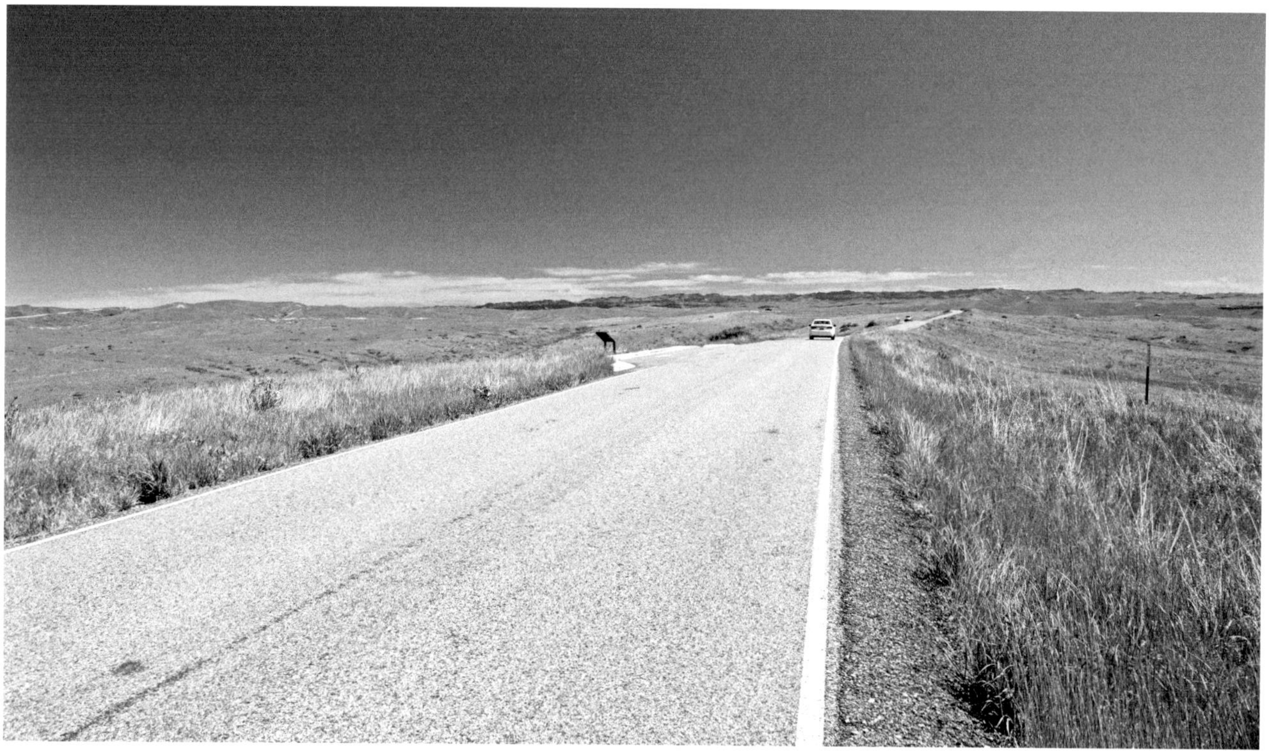

photo would be one of several that could aid the park in restoring the site to its pre-1951–52 appearance.

Both Roahen photos also reveal the changes in the Battle Ridge landscape. For example, the battlefield tour road appears to be made of gravel covered with oil. Figure 15.4 shows a cutout with a historical marker on the left or east side. Figure 15.5 reveals the effects of extensive road building or improvements to the tour road over the years. The modern figure 15.5 image, taken in June 2013, includes a berm of piled-up dirt on the left that did not exist when Roahen took his photo.

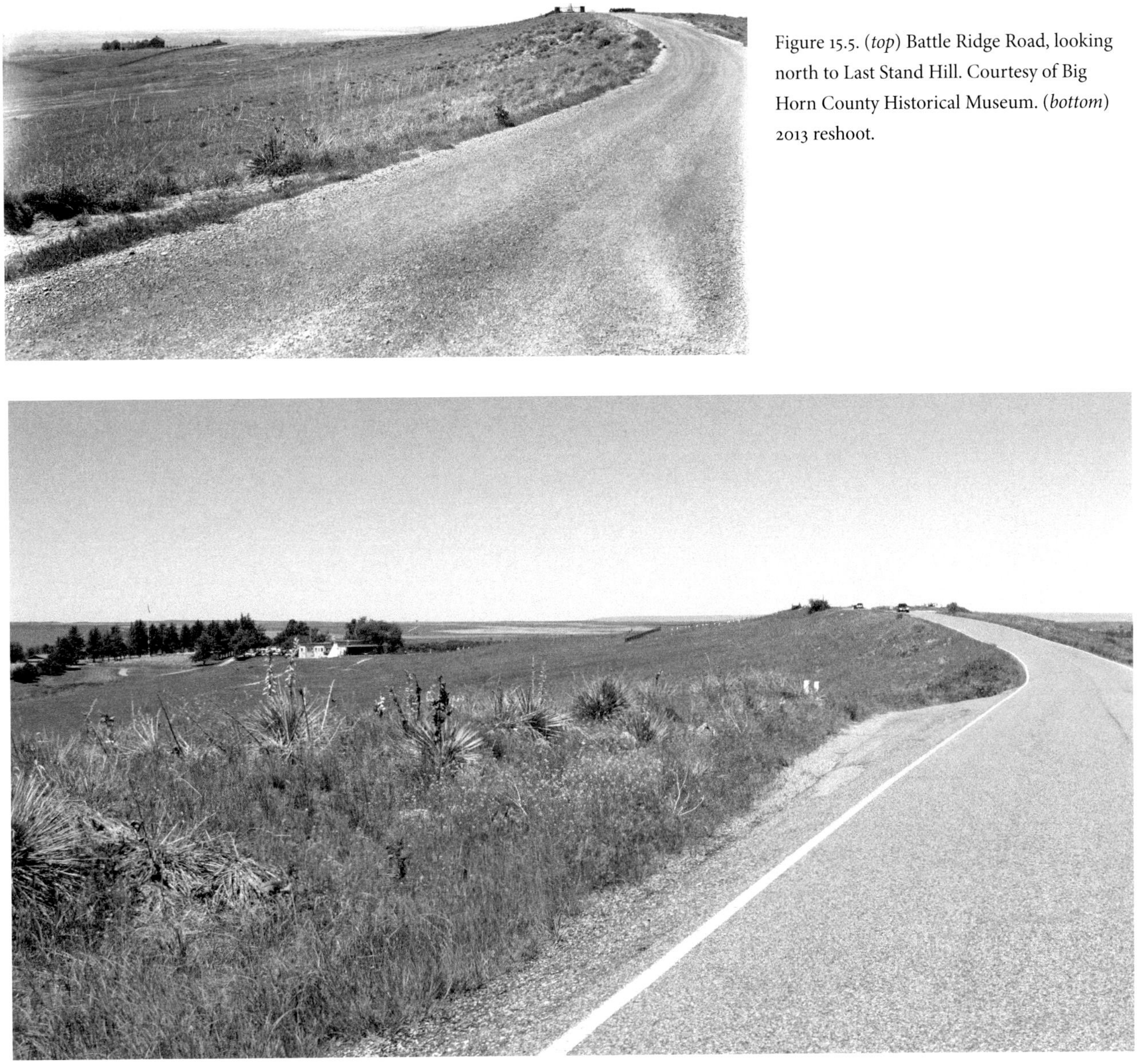

Figure 15.5. (*top*) Battle Ridge Road, looking north to Last Stand Hill. Courtesy of Big Horn County Historical Museum. (*bottom*) 2013 reshoot.

CHAPTER 16

Keogh Sector

Map 16.1. Keogh sector. Based on the 1967 USGS topographical map. Map by Gary Raham.

1. Fig. 16.1
2. Fig. 16.2
3. Fig. 16.3
4. Fig. 16.4

Standing by the marker for Capt. Myles W. Keogh, commander of Company I, one gains a sense of the evolving pattern of fighting on the Custer battlefield. Except for the markers on Last Stand Hill itself, a visitor here will find the largest number of marble stones raised as memorials to individual soldiers and civilians who fell in 1876. A small cluster of markers in Horse Holders' Ravine are just beyond Calhoun Hill and point toward the Keogh group. Around Keogh's stone are eighteen more. About thirty more are scattered in a far-flung pattern northwestward toward Custer Hill. From that

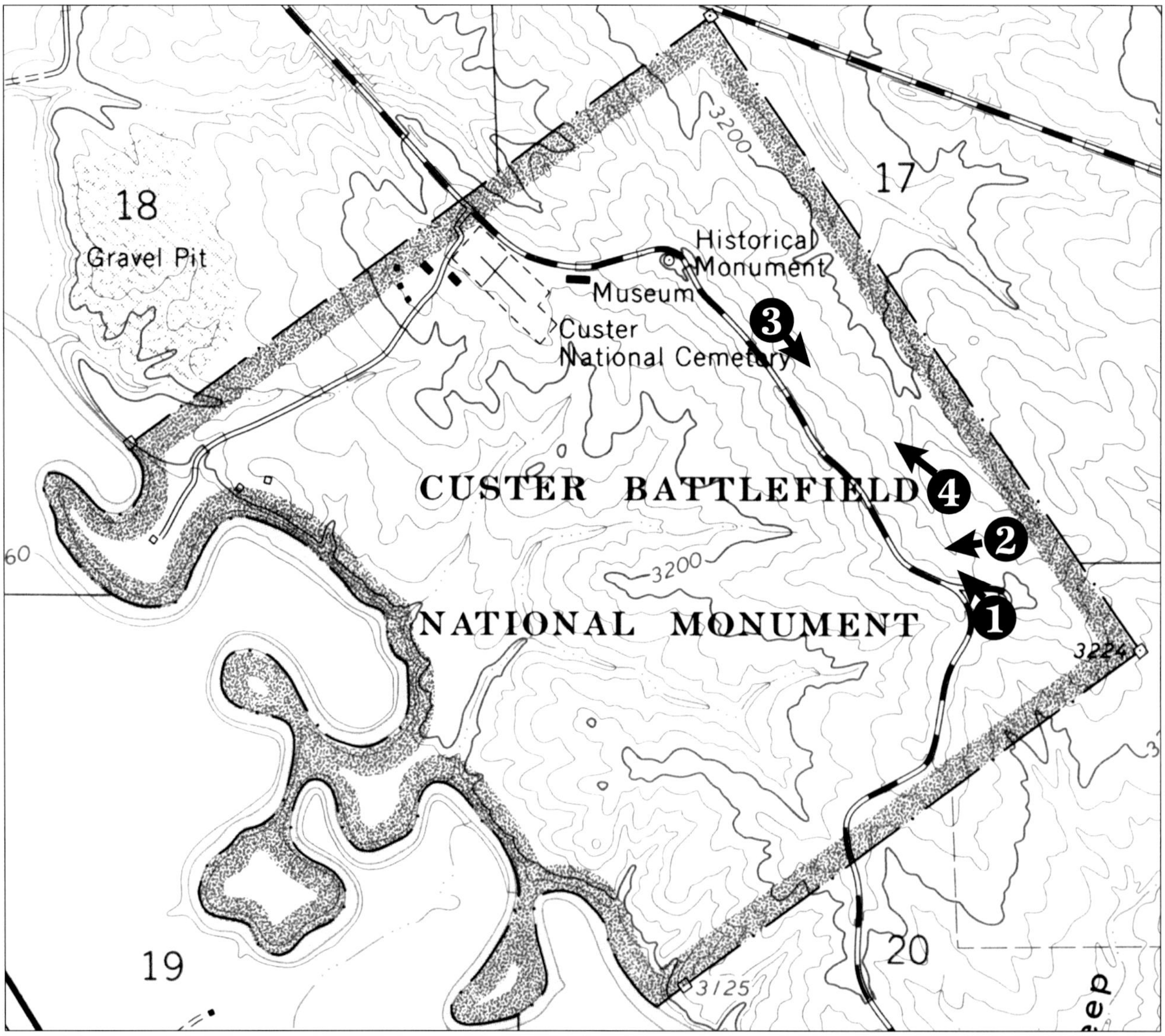

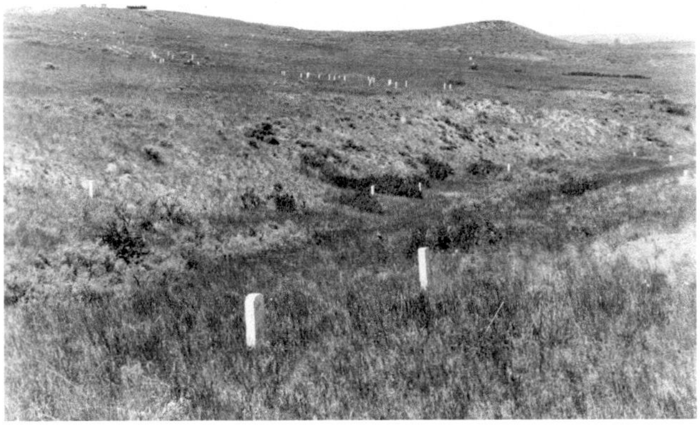

Figure 16.1. (*top*) Horse Holders' Ravine, looking north. Courtesy of Big Horn County Historical Museum. (*bottom*) 2012 reshoot.

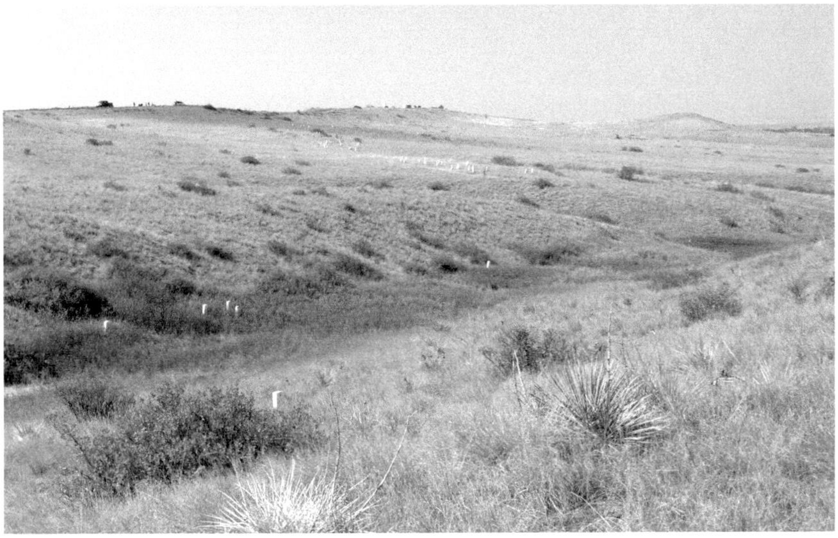

vantage point, one senses the rout and the panic that followed as survivors of Calhoun's and Keogh's commands streamed toward their commander on top of the high ground before them, only to fall short. Or, if you look southeastward from Last Stand Hill toward Keogh, the markers could suggest that men were fleeing from that point toward the captain's position, perhaps in a panicked attempt to escape. Most modern thinking leans toward the former interpretation of the marble markers, which were set in place in 1890. That area of the eastern side of Battle Ridge has been a favorite target for many photographers over the years. So it was for Ken Roahen during his career.

Lining up a reshoot of Roahen's figure 16.1 image, taken from the east slope of Horse Holders' Ravine, past the Keogh sector to Last Stand Hill, was surprisingly difficult. Differences in vegetation have significantly changed the area's appearance since Roahen photographed it, probably in the 1950s, and have obscured several markers, including one in the right foreground. Sometimes that issue works to our advantage. In the modern reshoot, for example, a middle marker can be seen between the two mid-center markers on the ravine's far slope. In Roahen's photograph, a bush covers that marker. Differences in the placement of several other markers in the ravine also are apparent.

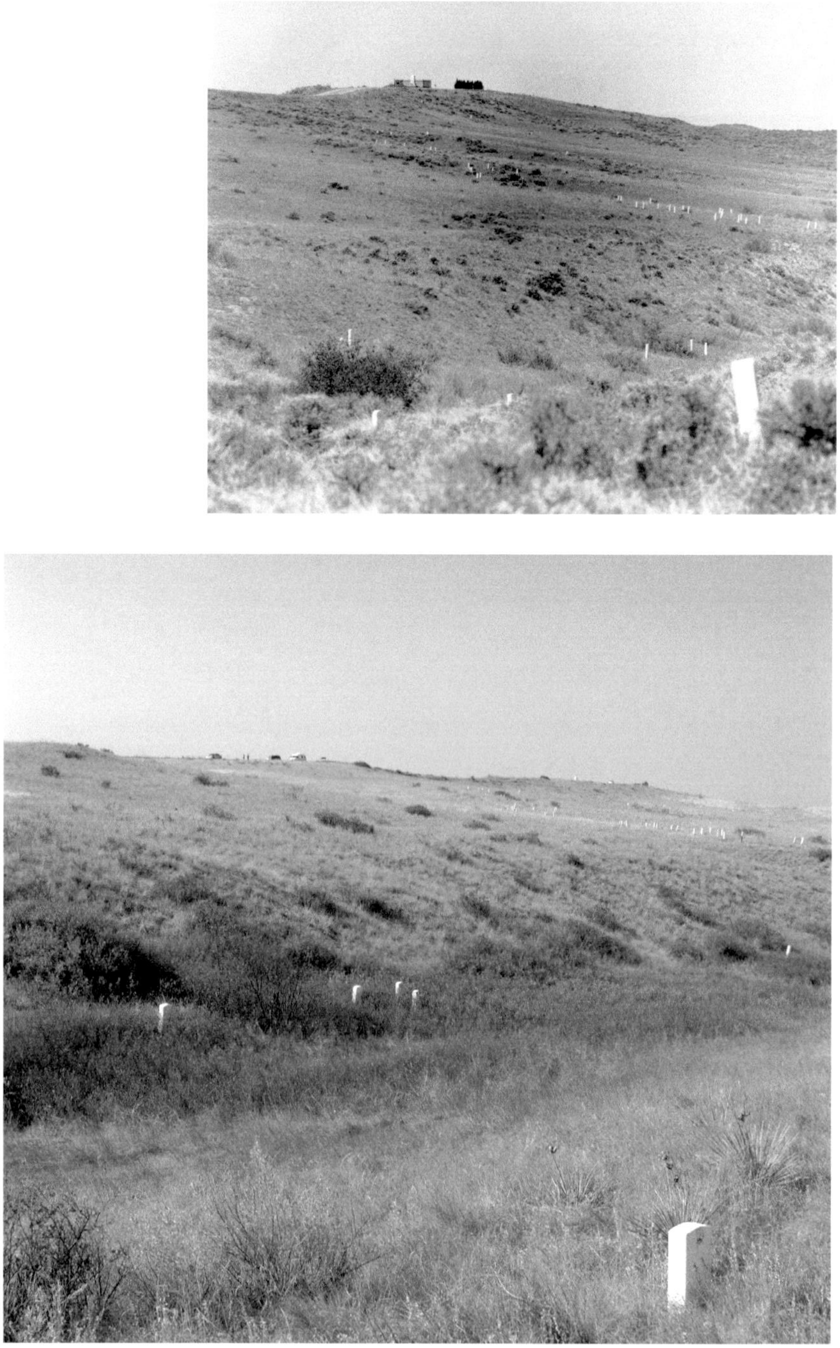

Figure 16.2. (*top*) Looking northwest from Keogh to Last Stand Hill's water tank. Courtesy of Big Horn County Historical Museum. (*bottom*) 2012 reshoot.

Figure 16.2, again taken from the east slope but some distance to the right or northeast of figure 16.1, presented similar problems. Additionally, we do not know what specific lenses were attached to Roahen's cameras, which results in significant differences in perspective. Two markers on the ravine floor toward the left appear to be missing from the modern image and were not located amid the brush. Roahen's image provides a wonderful close-up of the rear of Custer Hill and the fenced-in monument, suggesting this photo is pre-1963, the year the fence was removed. Trees still surround the area of the water tank on Last Stand Hill.

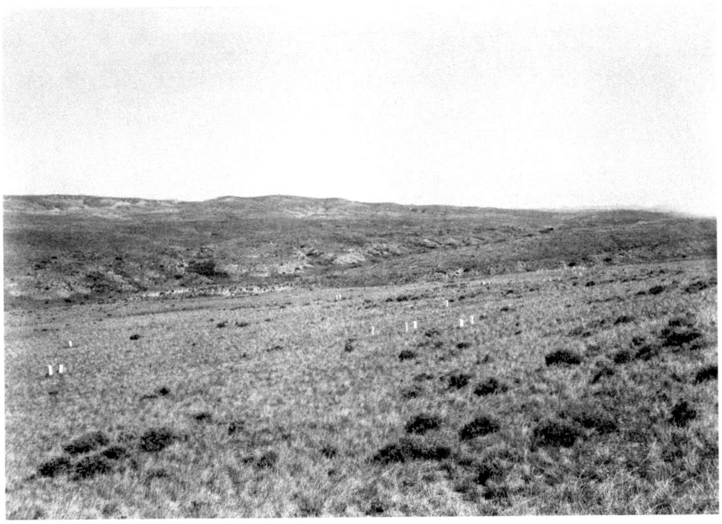

Figure 16.3. (*top*) Looking southeast back to the Keogh sector. Courtesy of Big Horn County Historical Museum. (*bottom*) 2012 reshoot.

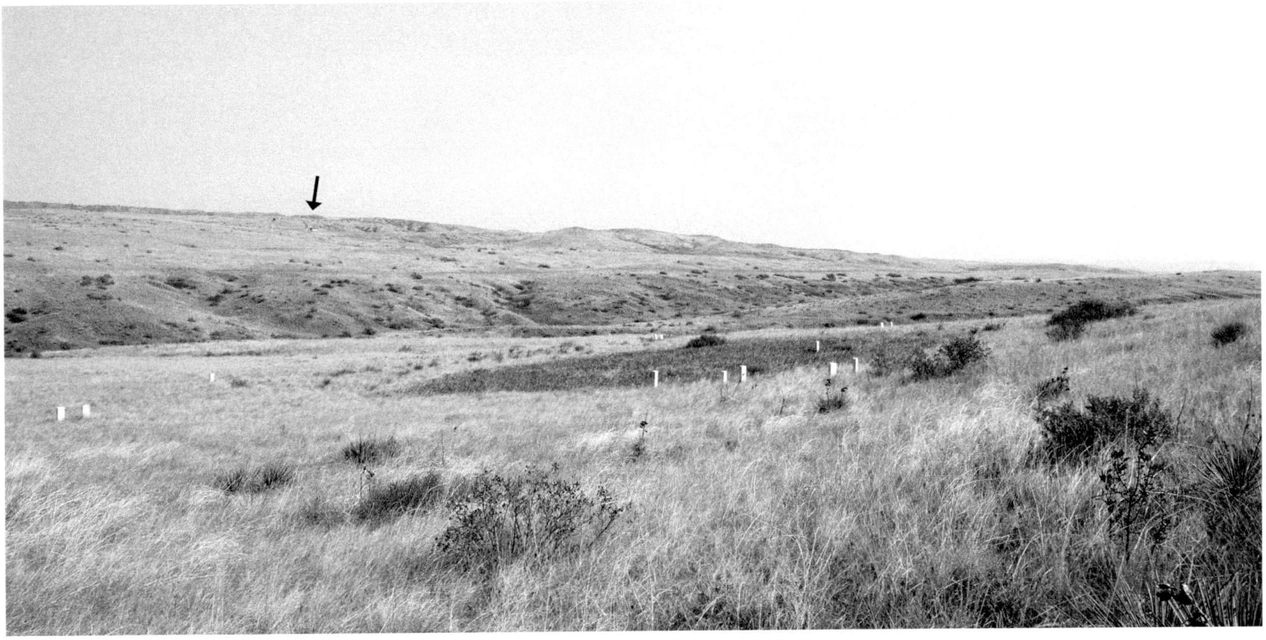

Roahen's figure 16.3 photograph is looking from the area below Last Stand Hill back to the Keogh sector. The modern reshoot matches up quite nicely with his image, except that it lacks any view of the Keogh grouping. To achieve his view of the entire field back to Keogh, Roahen obviously mounted his handy stepladder. The foreground markers make it quite apparent that he was standing above them. On the photo's left, about a third of the way across his image, can be seen the V-shaped cut that U.S. Highway 212 passes through. The modern image captures a truck moving northwest on the highway. The cut itself is visible in the photo some distance behind the truck.

Roahen's figure 16.4 photo shows the eighteen markers of the Keogh sector itself. In the 2012 reshoot, Keogh's own stone is indicated by the placement of an American flag at its base. In Roahen's photo, Keogh's marker is standing in the center, the fifth from the left. At the top right of his photo we can see the

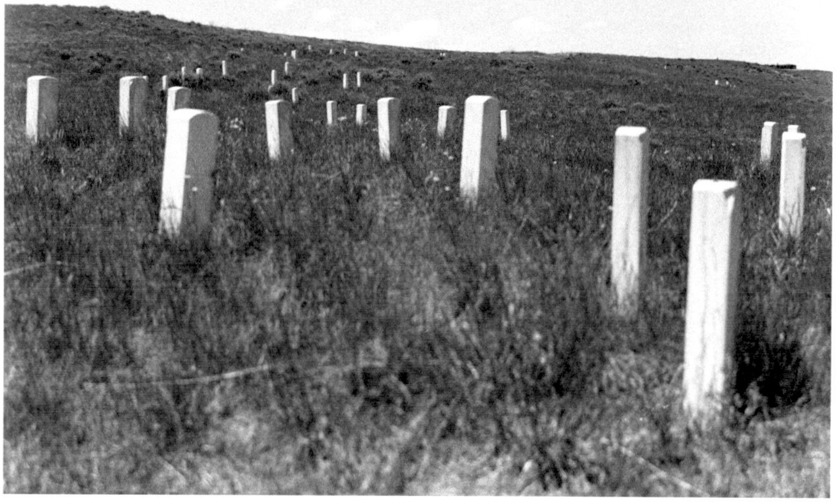

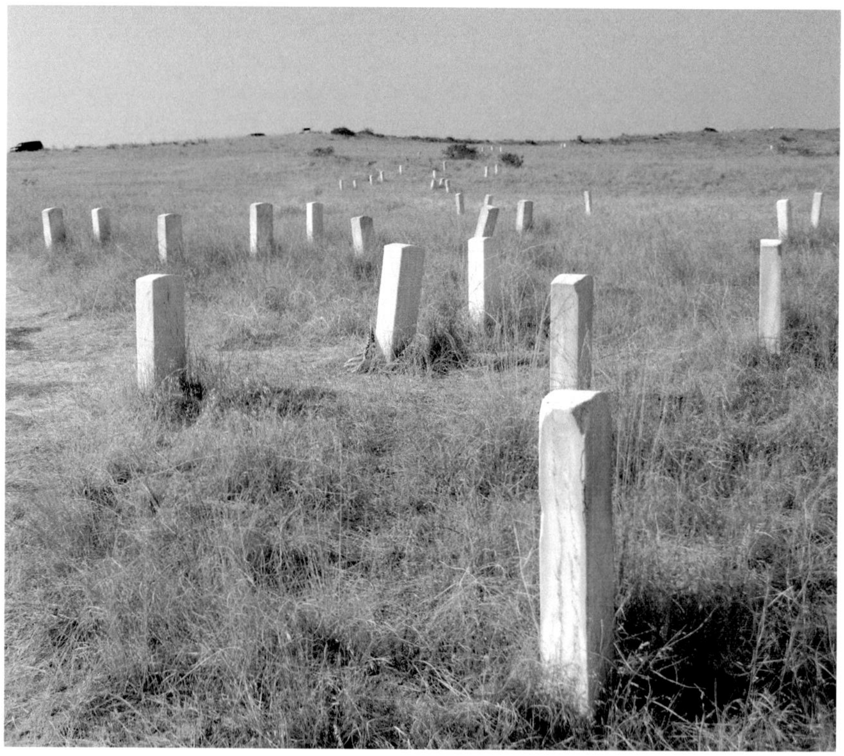

Figure 16.4. (*top*) Looking northwest from Keogh to Last Stand Hill. Courtesy of Big Horn County Historical Museum. (*bottom*) 2012 reshoot.

trees lining the water tank area. Although the monument on Custer Hill is not clear, a portion of its pinnacle is visible to the left of the trees, although it is darkened. In the modern reshoot, the top of today's very white monument on Custer Hill can be made out on the far right. It is in line with the first, or closest, marker of the three on the photo's bottom far right.

CHAPTER 17

Below Custer Hill

One of the undeniable reasons for the public's continuing fascination with the Little Big Horn battle—an abundance of catchy names for its landmarks—goes beyond its historical interest or importance. For example, just as Gettysburg National Military Park in Pennsylvania has its Devils Den, Little Big Horn has the Crow's Nest, the Morass, and the Lone Tepee. Where Gettysburg has the Wheatfield, Little Big Horn has Weir Point. Gettysburg features Pickett's Charge, and Little Big Horn offers the Reno Retreat Crossing.

Map 17.1. Below Custer Hill. Map by Gary Raham.

1. Fig. 17.1
2. Fig. 17.2
3. Figs. 17.3, 17.4
4. Fig. 17.5
5. Fig. 17.6
6. Fig. 17.7
7. Fig. 17.8
8. Fig. 17.9
9. Fig. 17.10
10. Figs. 17.11, 17.12, 17.13
11. Figs. 17.14, 17.15

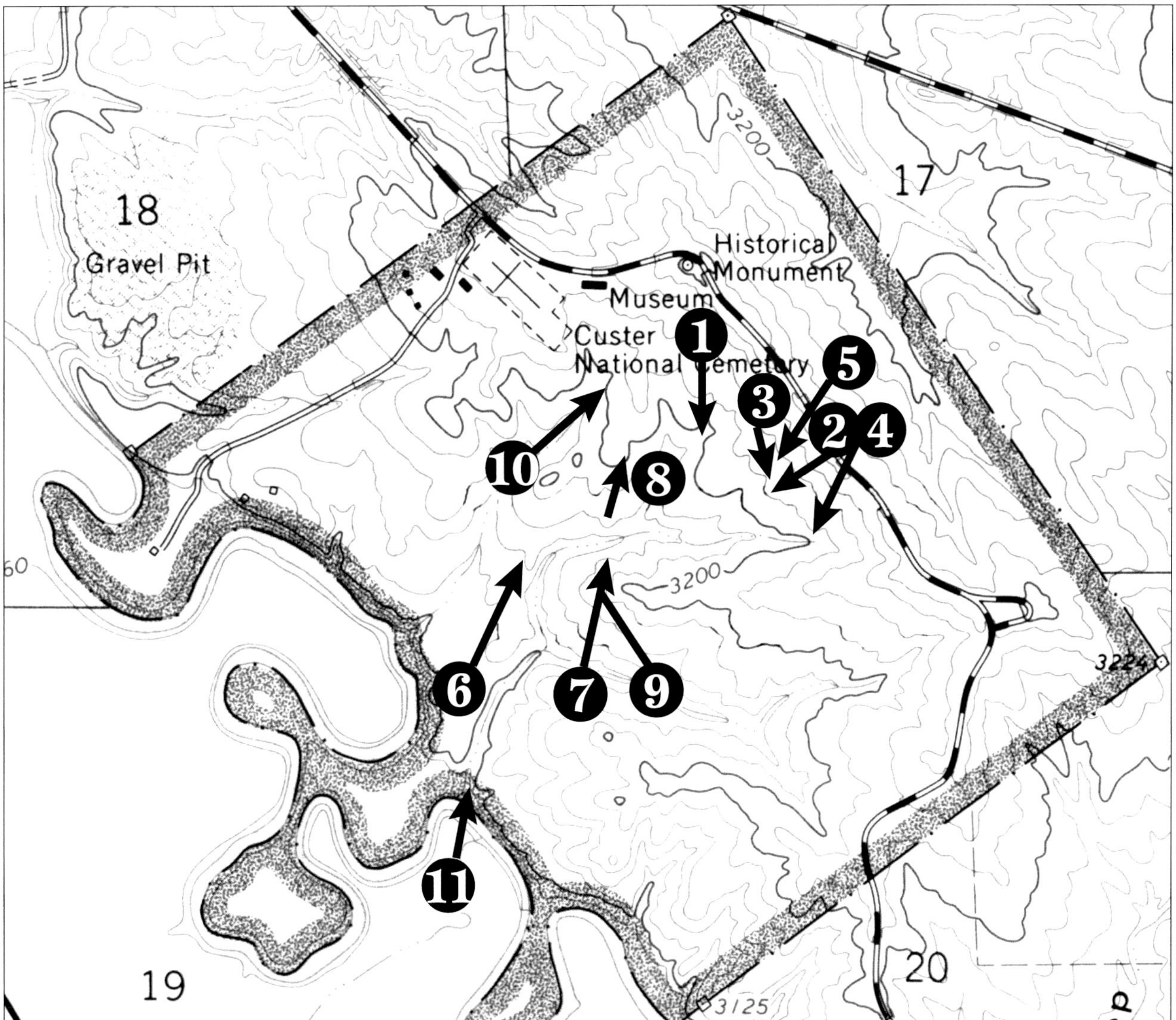

On the main Custer field are located still more fascinating labels for its historical events. We have already looked at Medicine Tail Coulee, Finley-Finckle Ridge, Calhoun Hill, Horse Holders' Ravine, and Battle Ridge, and shortly we will review Custer Hill, or Last Stand Hill. Before doing so, we should note that many of the thousands of tourists who labor up the steep incline of Custer Hill and gaze out upon the slopes before them, with glimpses of the Little Big Horn River glistening amid the trees in the valley below, may miss the significance of two of the more fascinating features on the main battlefield—the so-called South Skirmish Line and Deep Ravine. In fact, during the archaeological projects of the 1980s, no subject was of greater interest to the news media representatives who flocked to Little Big Horn, especially in 1985, than the possibility that in Deep Ravine dig crews might discover the remains of twenty-eight troopers of Custer's Company E who have been missing in action since 1876.[1]

As we wrote in *Where Custer Fell*, "In the historiography of a battle markedly characterized by disputed theories and contradictory evidence, few aspects are as subject to varying interpretation as the events that transpired on the so-called South Skirmish Line and in Deep Ravine." The narrow head of the ravine sits some 700 yards southwest of Custer Hill, and the general drainage area itself runs about another 700 yards through an ever-broadening and deepening gash in the rolling landscape to a mouth that opens abruptly above the Little Big Horn River itself. To feel the historical tension and isolation of Little Big Horn, walk to the end of the path that leads down from the Visitor Center and stand over the sharp drop into the ravine. It is a location that offers stark beauty in its appearance and provides a sense of isolation from the world; as we stated in 2005, it remains both "mysterious and sinister."

How and why the Company E troopers came to fight there remains among the more hotly debated mysteries of the Little Big Horn. Besides the number of men whose bodies were discovered in the ravine itself, other men lay along or near what is the modern path to the Visitor Center. The burial parties generally believed the majority of the dead had been members of Company E, including its first sergeant, Fredrick Hohmeyer. Surprisingly, no marble markers stand in the ravine itself. Instead, some fifty markers stand between the lip of the ravine and the basin below Custer Hill in what some consider a structured defensive deployment of this company.

This apparent skirmish pattern led early researchers to conclude that the path of the dead men represented a "south skirmish line." Today researchers view such a scenario as less likely. If it were a defensive line, it was poorly positioned below the surrounding high ground. Also, given the distance to be covered along the modern path, too few soldiers from Custer's command would have been involved in defending that rugged arena. Although the skirmish line defenders might have been visible to their comrades on top of Last Stand Hill, the folds and rises of the landscape would have given these isolated troopers only glimpses at best of the whereabouts of other soldiers.

Historical accounts differ on what the bodies and later the markers represented in that vicinity. Archaeological evidence developed in the 1980s confirmed that some soldiers fought and died along the line but could not reveal why they had chosen that point to make a stand. Was it a defensive line, or were they moving to or from Custer Hill?

The large number of Company E men reportedly found in Deep Ravine also leads to many questions. Had they made a final rush from Custer Hill only to be trapped in the ravine? Had they attempted to cut off the northward flight of noncombatants from the Indian village in the valley only to be repulsed, trapped, and forced to fight in that vicinity? Considerable historical evidence exists to suggest a detachment, if not a full company, deployed past the modern cemetery ridge toward a crossing in the valley where women and children were hiding at a point north and west of Cemetery Ridge. The soldiers never could cross the river to capture the noncombatants, for warrior strength either had grown too strong in that area or too few soldiers were available to complete the deployment. One or more soldiers and likely civilian news reporter Mark H. Kellogg were killed in this engagement. Eventually survivors pulled back to the vicinity of the modern cemetery, where they may have been scattered, some of the men racing for Last Stand Hill and the rest fleeing toward Deep Ravine.

Indian accounts tell of a group of soldiers who had gathered in the "big basin" below Custer Hill and were attacked by the Cheyenne Suicide Boys—young warriors who had vowed to gain honors or die in battle. Their charge inspired other warriors to join them, and the resulting pressure overwhelmed the soldiers, who may have been from Company E. About that same time, Calhoun's and Keogh's men were being shattered, leaving Custer with only one intact company, Capt. George Yates's Company F, which likely had been bloodied in the swirling action. Company F's survivors would rally around their regimental commander, George Custer, in a final defense for the 7th Cavalry.

Perhaps not surprisingly, the greatest number of Roahen photographs of any one area capture scenes below Custer Hill and the vicinity of Deep Ravine and South Skirmish Line. He appears to have taken some of these images in response to requests by author J. W. Vaughn, others for Superintendent Luce. In many cases, the landmark photographs overlapped, but in ways that suggest that not all the photos were taken at the same time. Often Roahen's broad subject can be determined but not his main point of focus or purpose for a specific image.

Figure 17.1 captures Deep Ravine and Greasy Grass Ridge to the south from the vicinity of Last Stand Hill. These two photographs were taken on the slope on the left side of Last Stand Hill, about 30 yards from the fencing enclosing the individual marble markers. On the far right are the markers along the trail that outlines the South Skirmish Line today. Also, on the mid-right, portions of Deep Ravine can be seen as well as the point where it drops off at the Little Big Horn River. The high ground from the photos' left to right, meeting at the Deep Ravine cut, is Greasy Grass Ridge.

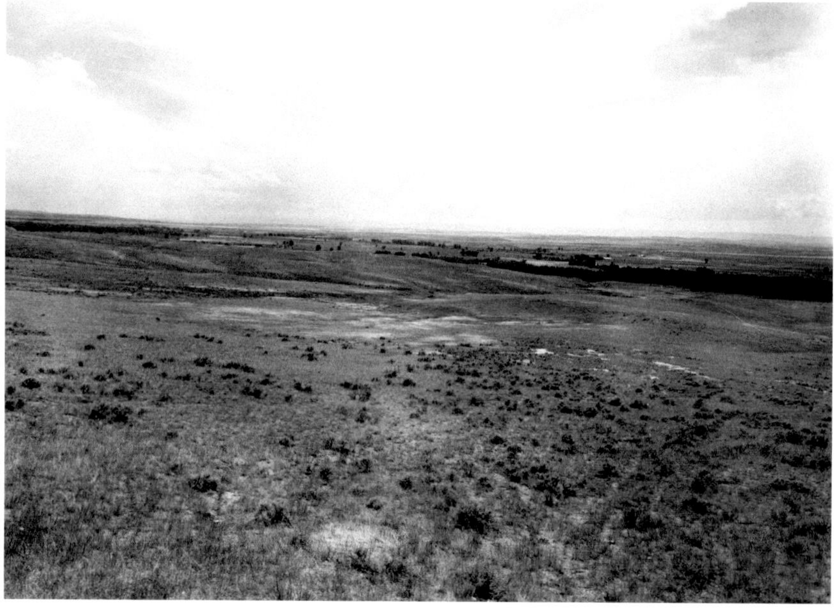

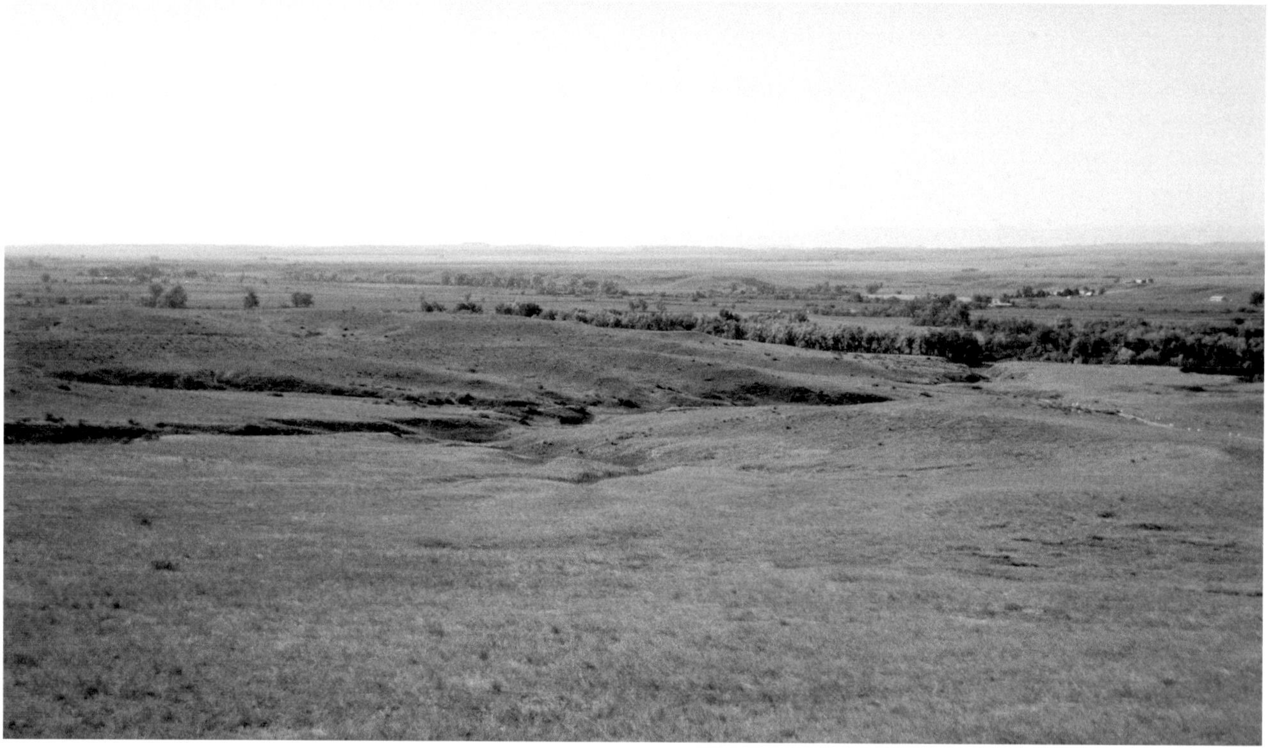

Figure 17.1. (*top*) Looking southwest toward Deep Ravine and Greasy Grass Ridge from Last Stand Hill. Courtesy of Big Horn County Historical Museum. (*bottom*) 2012 reshoot.

Figure 17.2 is looking southwest toward Deep Ravine and Greasy Grass Ridge. These images provide a significant view of Deep Ravine, from its upper reaches below the Battle Ridge roadway to its mouth above the Little Big Horn River. The high ridge along the left to the middle is Greasy Grass Ridge. Though we can only speculate about the date of Roahen's photograph—sometime between the late 1940s and early 1960s—the modern image taken in the fall of 2012 documents how little this area of the battlefield has changed in those sixty to seventy-five years.

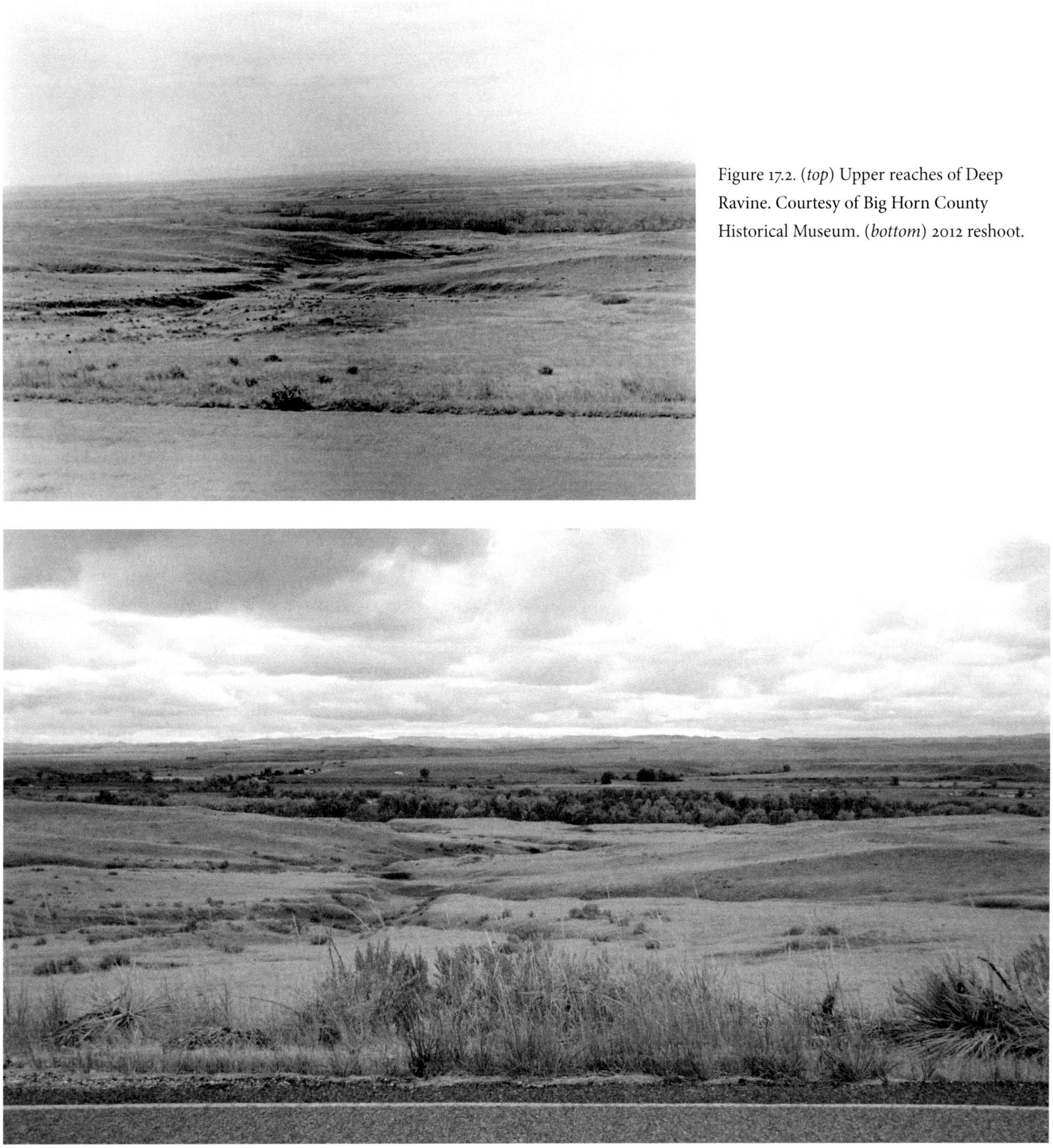

Figure 17.2. (*top*) Upper reaches of Deep Ravine. Courtesy of Big Horn County Historical Museum. (*bottom*) 2012 reshoot.

Roahen's figure 17.3, looking west from Battle Ridge toward Deep Ravine, figure 17.4, looking west across Deep Ravine to Greasy Grass Ridge and a bit of Calhoun Coulee, and figure 17.5, looking southwest to Greasy Grass Ridge vicinity, are all variant views related to figure 17.2. All show different portions of Deep Ravine and Greasy Grass Ridge as well as Calhoun Coulee. After shooting in this area, I merged two of my modern photos to create figure 17.6, a panorama matching the area seen in the three Roahen shots.

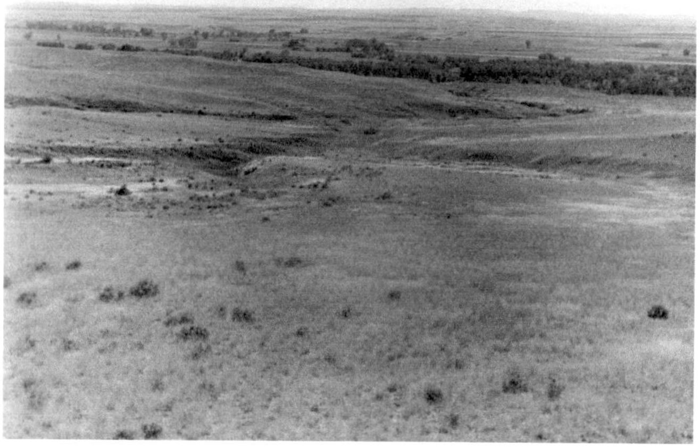

Figure 17.3. Looking west from Battle Ridge toward Deep Ravine. Courtesy of Big Horn County Historical Museum.

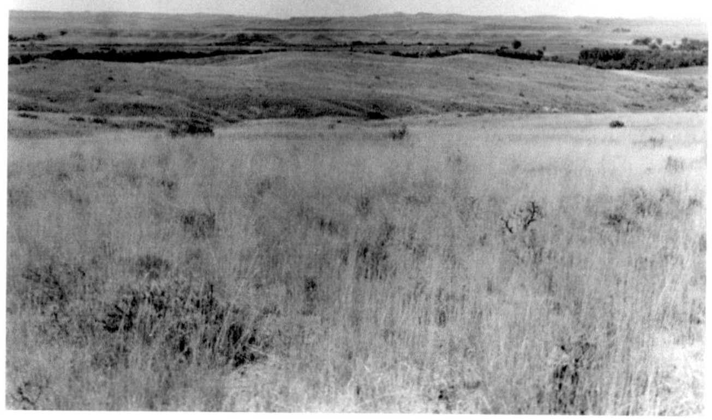

Figure 17.4. Variant of fig. 17.3, looking west across Deep Ravine to Greasy Grass Ridge and a bit of Calhoun Coulee. Courtesy of Big Horn County Historical Museum.

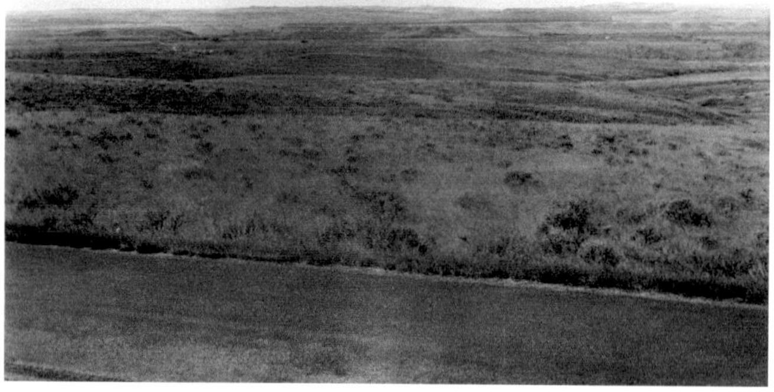

Figure 17.5. Looking southwest to the Greasy Grass Ridge vicinity. Courtesy of Big Horn County Historical Museum.

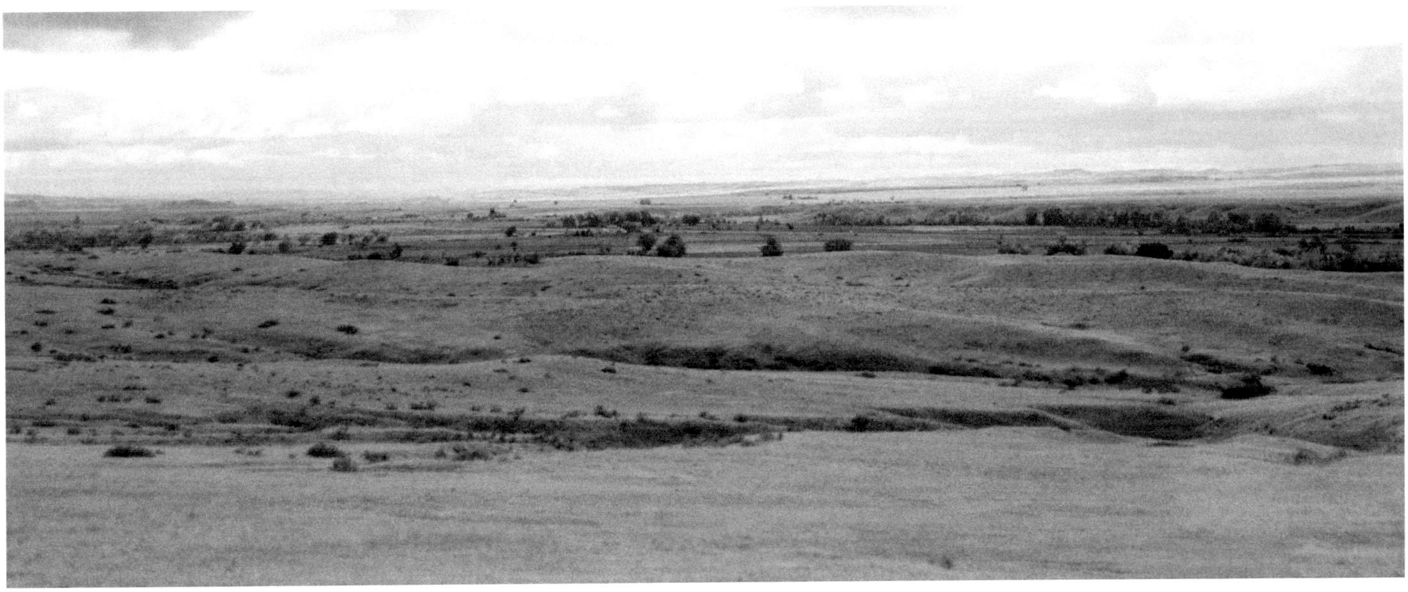

Figure 17.6. Modern panorama matching Roahen's figs. 17.4, 17.5, and 17.6.

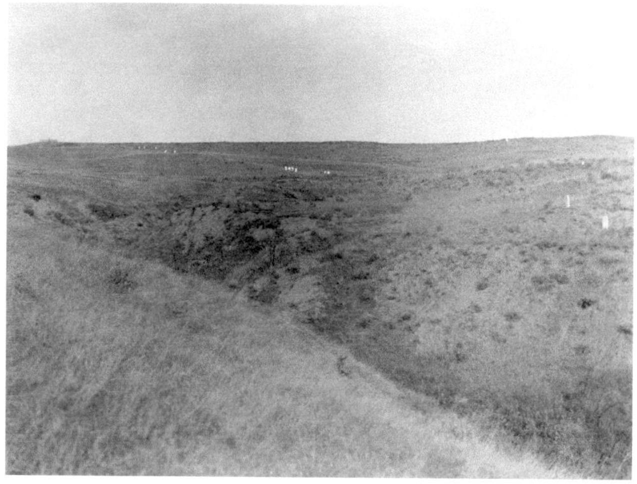

Figure 17.7. (*top*) Looking northwest from elbow in Deep Ravine to Last Stand Hill. Courtesy of Big Horn County Historical Museum. (*bottom*) 2012 reshoot.

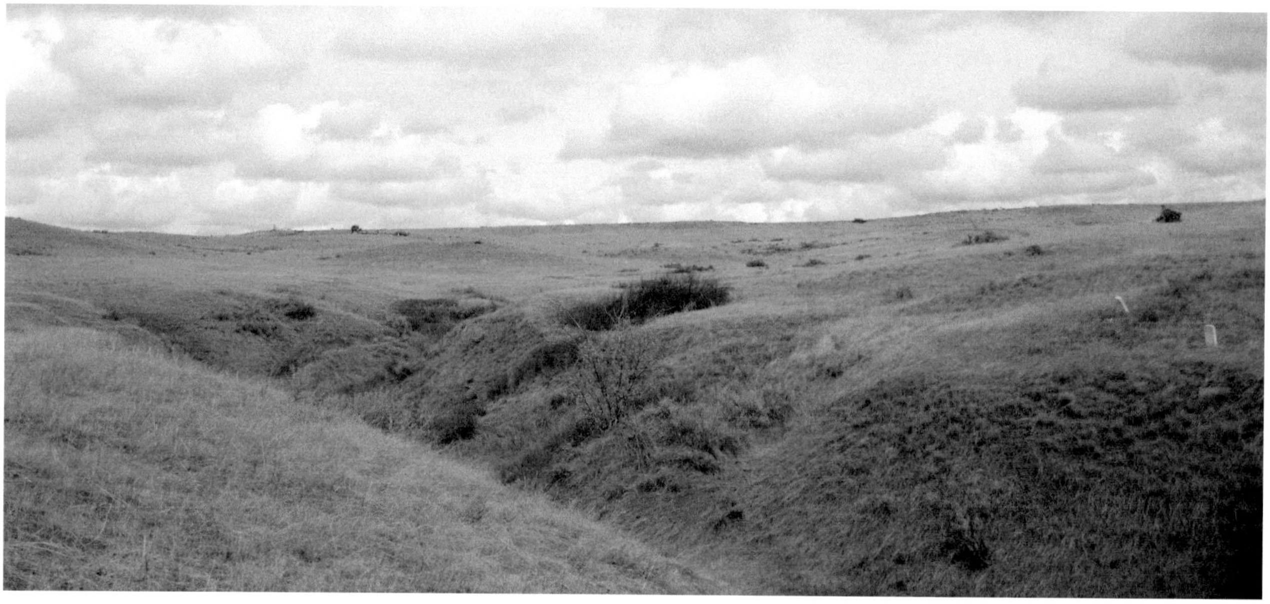

I cannot state with certainty when Roahen took his figure 17.7 image, which looks northwest from the elbow in Deep Ravine to Last Stand Hill. A best guess would be between the late 1940s and the early 1960s. Whether Roahen realized the significance of the site he was capturing here is also absent from the historical record. On the left of his photograph, Deep Ravine completes its sharp bend to the left en route to its overlook at the river. The modern shot, taken in the fall of 2012, shows that the bend and the straightaway running toward the camera remain largely intact.

In the summer of 1996, geophysical remote sensing studies were conducted in this vicinity of Deep Ravine in an effort to unravel the mystery surrounding the twenty-eight or so individuals of Company E believed to have been buried in the ravine.[2] Ground-penetrating radar and magnetometry, at the time state-of-the-art equipment that sent electronic pulses into the earth, disclosed an anomaly in the soil. Archaeologist Douglas Scott explained at the time that such equipment was generally used in geophysics to locate oil fields

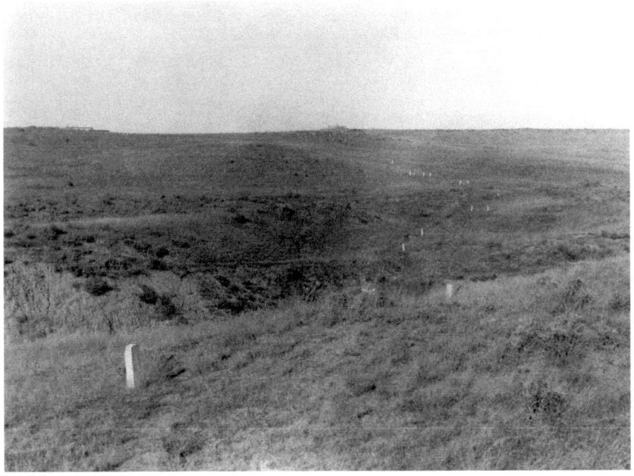

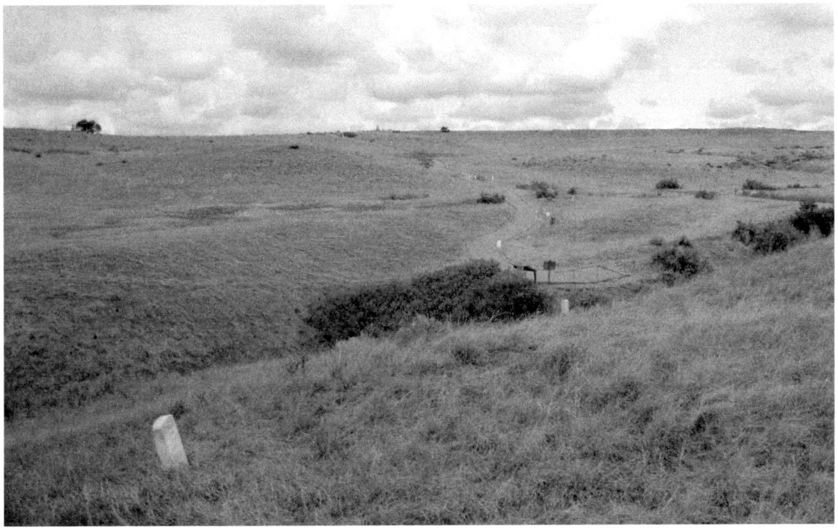

Figure 17.8. (*top*) Looking northeast from Deep Ravine across the South Skirmish Line to Last Stand Hill. Courtesy of Big Horn County Historical Museum. (*bottom*) 2012 reshoot.

or mineral-bearing rock for mining, not to find small historic objects or bone in a ravine on a historic battlefield. Scott downplayed rampant public speculation that the site marked where the missing Custer troopers had been buried, noting that the equipment would more likely indicate changes in soil composition, such as where a pit may have been dug or soil filled in.

In 1998, Scott stated, "At this point, it could be nothing more than a natural change of soil, but it will give us some place to focus on for the future." However, the Park Service has never authorized such a follow-up project. Significant cost would be incurred in shoring up the ravine's walls because of its normally high water table. Scott said the potential historical knowledge to be gained by such a project would not offset the likely destruction of the ravine itself as a historical resource. Although Scott himself is now retired from the Park Service, he stated anew in the summer of 2013 that nothing since the late 1990s has changed his view of the matter.[3]

The undated Roahen image in figure 17.8, looking northeast from Deep Ravine across the South Skirmish Line to Last Stand Hill, captures what for many students of the Little Big Horn battle is an iconic view of the historic field.

In the foreground, you have the drop-off point where visitors first encounter Deep Ravine, one of the great features on the field. Today, for environmental reasons, the Park Service blocks the trail there, but many people have ventured beyond the trail's end and explored the depths of the ravine and its surrounding area. Next, we have the line of markers that outline what can be considered either the South Skirmish Line or simply a tourist trail to the ravine. In the distance are the markers on Last Stand Hill. On the photo's left appears the modern Visitor Center, whose presence helps narrow this image to the period between 1952 and the early 1960s. Narrowing it still further is difficult. The apparent absence of trees behind the 7th Cavalry monument might suggest that Roahen took this photograph in 1963, or soon thereafter. However, the ten-foot fence, removed in 1963, still surrounds the monument.

Figure 17.9 confirms for us how little has changed along the South Skirmish Line in the area below Last Stand Hill. The marker placement between Roahen's image and a 2012 reshoot shows an almost perfect alignment. The significant change, of course, is the modern trail's serpentine-like appearance as it makes its way down to Deep Ravine from the Visitor Center, which would be beyond the photo's left side.

Figure 17.10 is a classic view of the walls of Deep Ravine with the 7th Cavalry monument highly visible on the right top of the image. Roahen's photo likely was taken much earlier than that in figure 17.8 and other Roahen images of this portion of the battlefield. No sign of the Visitor Center, or even its construction, is visible on the left of the photograph. Too, note how straight the walls of the ravine appear, whereas in figure 17.8 they have obviously slumped and are more similar to the modern image in figure 17.10. Even so, the marker arrangement between the two photos is closely matched.

Three Roahen photographs are almost identical: figure 17.11, looking north from the South Skirmish line to Last Stand Hill; figure 17.12, showing Last Stand Hill and the South Skirmish Line; and figure 17.13, a view from the South Skirmish Line to Last Stand Hill. The South Skirmish Line area below Last Stand Hill dominates the center, and in the distance is the ridge where the modern Visitor Center sits. From the absence of the Visitor Center or any sign of its construction, we can conclude that these photographs were likely taken in the 1940s. Trees still appear behind the monument on Last Stand Hill. Each of the modern reshoots shows an excellent alignment with its historical counterpart. The match for figure 17.13 was created by merging two modern photographs, both taken in 2013.

Roahen's photograph in figure 17.14, looking northeast from the west bank of the Little Big Horn River toward Last Stand Hill, is dated July 29, 1961. Inasmuch as vegetation in both this and Roahen's figure 17.15 image appears similar, we can conclude that the two were taken at the same time. The modern figure 17.14 photo was taken on September 29, 2012, by local rancher Glen Elhard, whose family owns the property. Making our way to the actual photo site proved difficult, in part, because recent floods had altered the river's course in that vicinity. With my camera in hand, Elhard volunteered to cross a deep

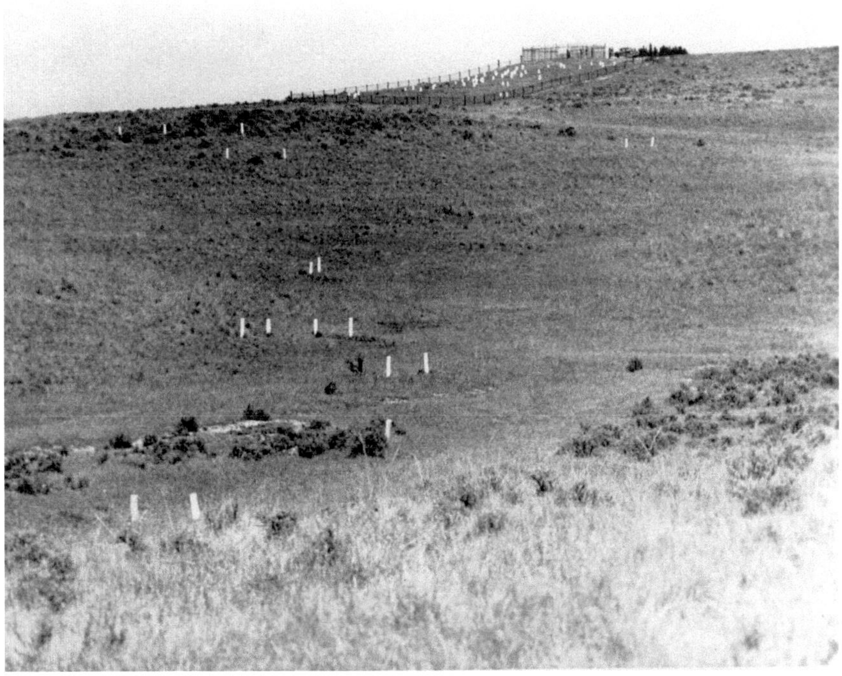

Figure 17.9. (*top*) Looking northeast to Last Stand Hill from the South Skirmish Line. Courtesy of Big Horn County Historical Museum. (*bottom*) 2012 reshoot.

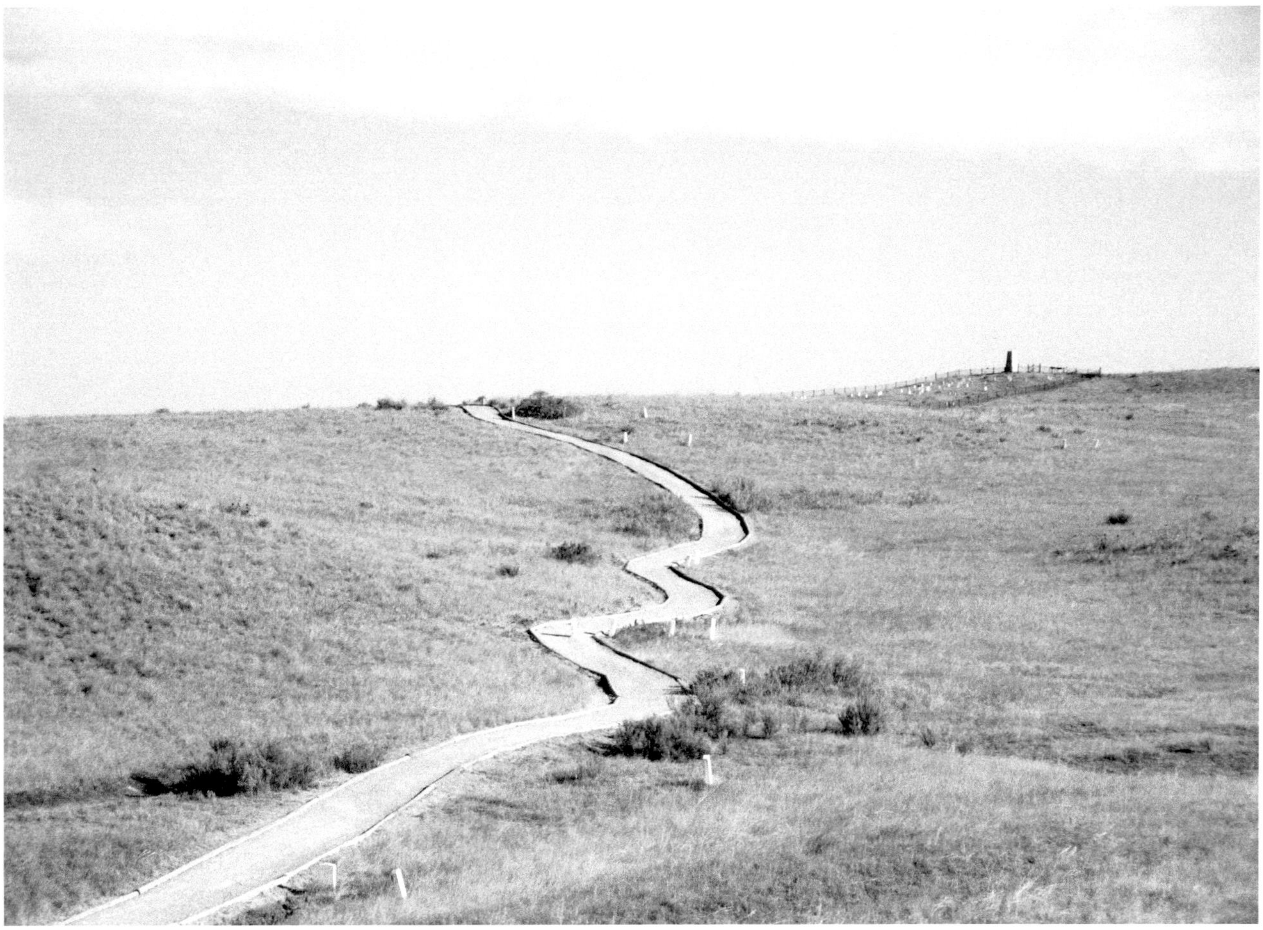

Figure 17.10. (*top*) Deep Ravine walls, looking north toward Last Stand Hill. Courtesy of Big Horn County Historical Museum. (*bottom*) 2012 reshoot.

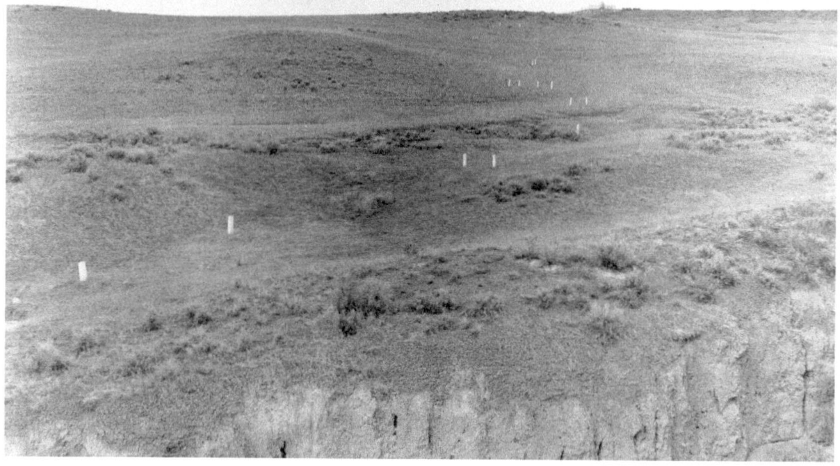

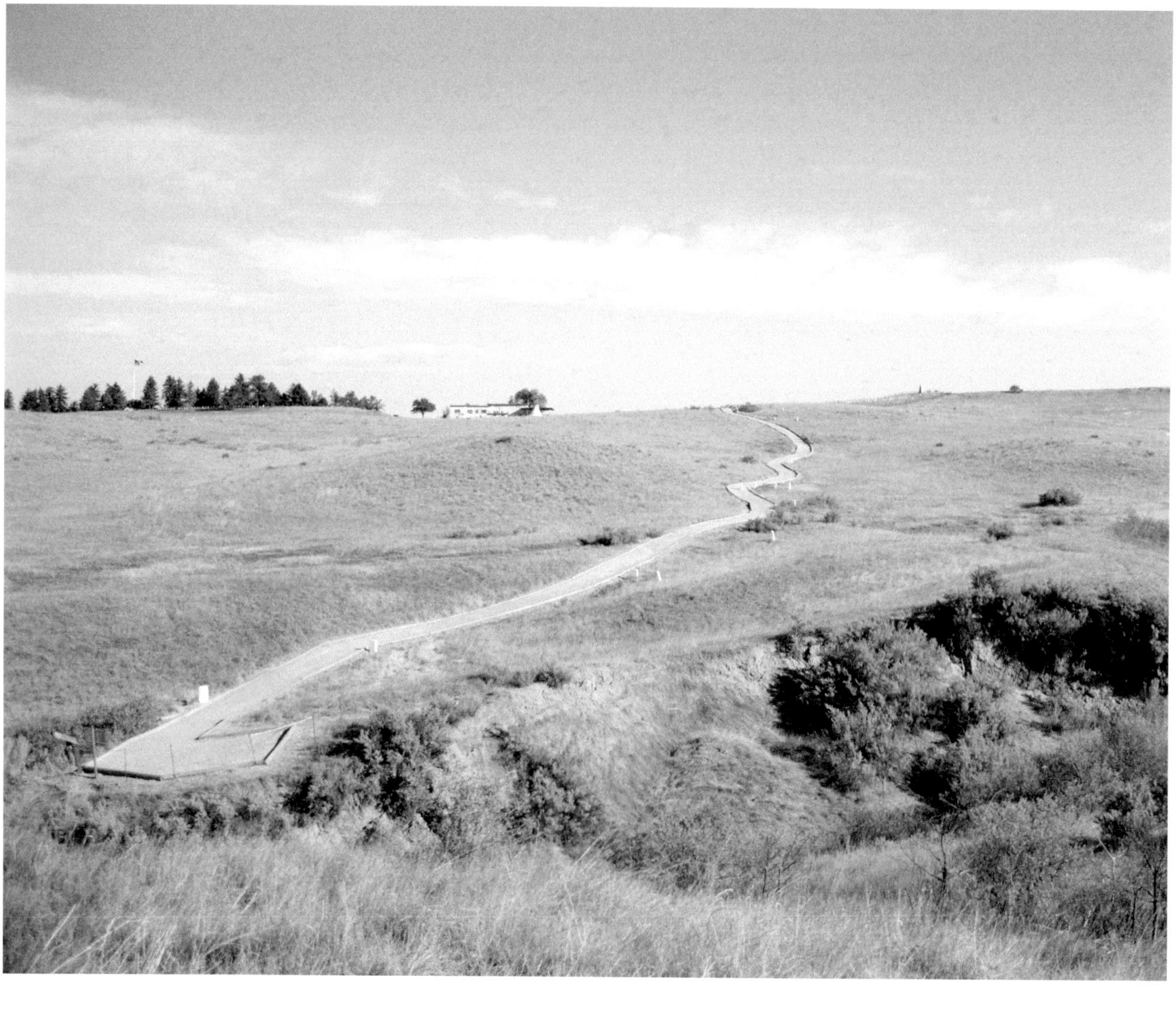

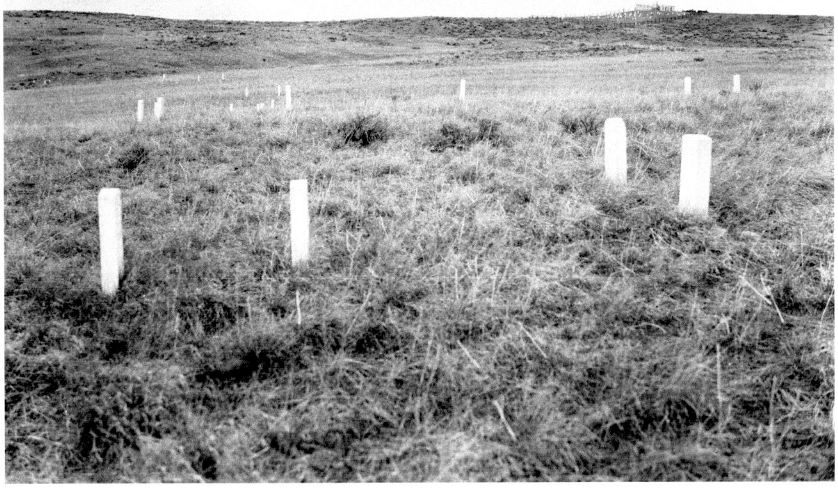

Figure 17.11. (*top*) Looking north from the South Skirmish line to Last Stand Hill. Courtesy of Big Horn County Historical Museum. (*bottom*) 2012 reshoot.

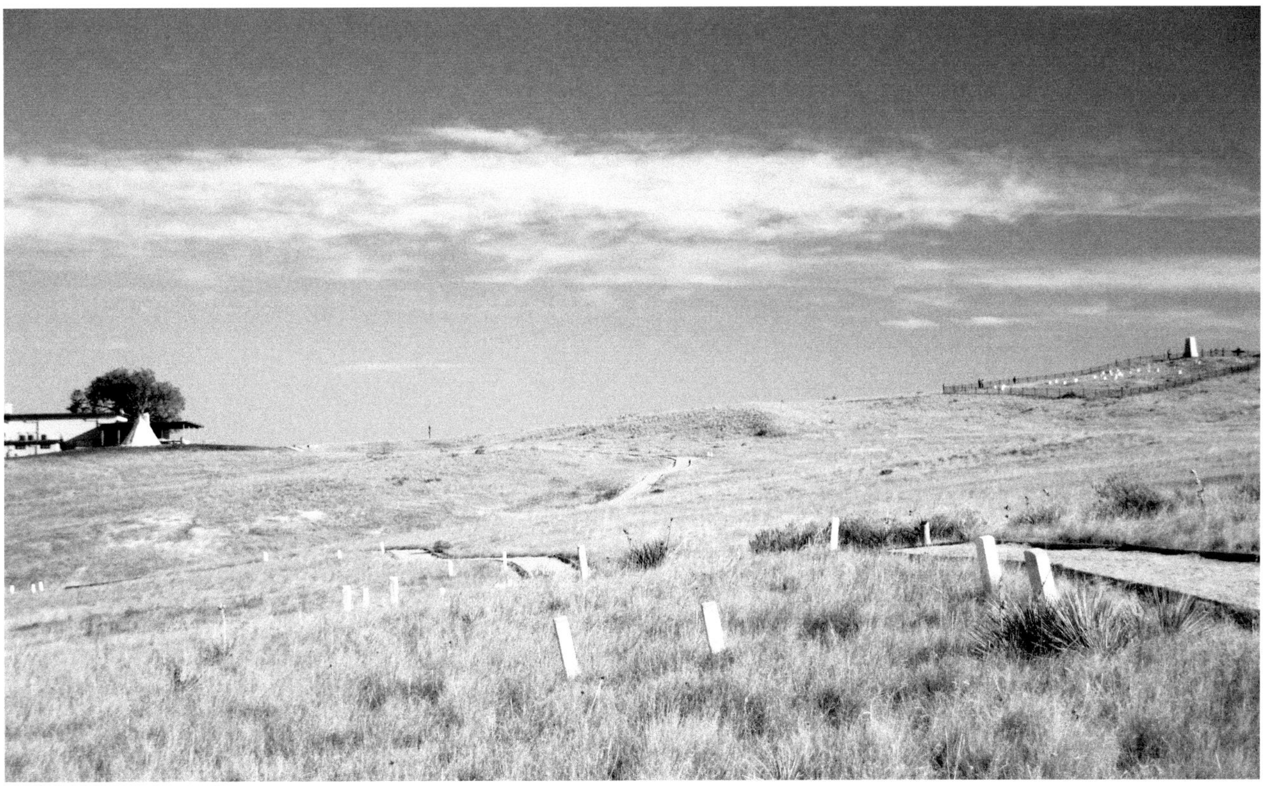

tributary on a beaver dam to locate and photograph the site. He reported that the vegetation next to the river was heavy and made it difficult to determine exactly where Roahen himself had stood.

Figure 17.12. (*top*) Variant of fig. 17.11: Last Stand Hill and South Skirmish Line. Courtesy of Big Horn County Historical Museum. (*bottom*) 2013 reshoot.

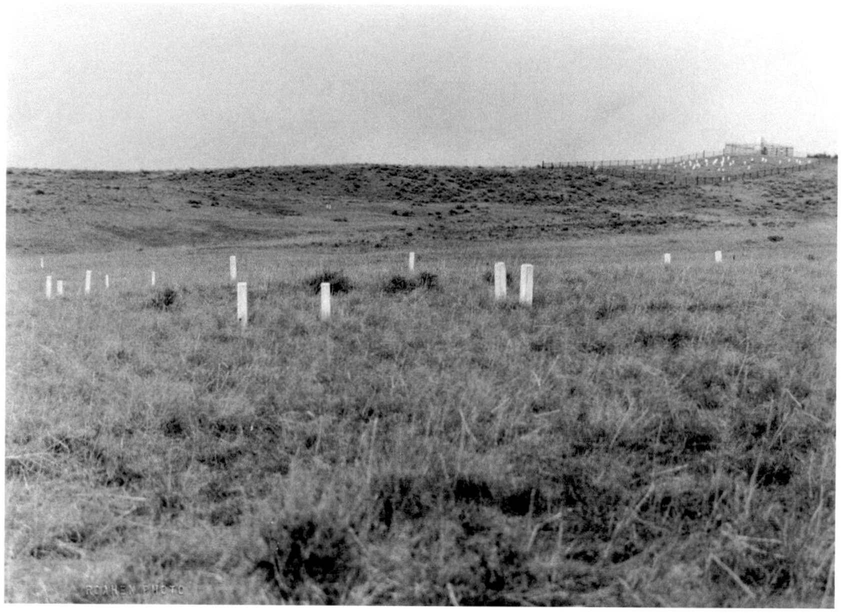

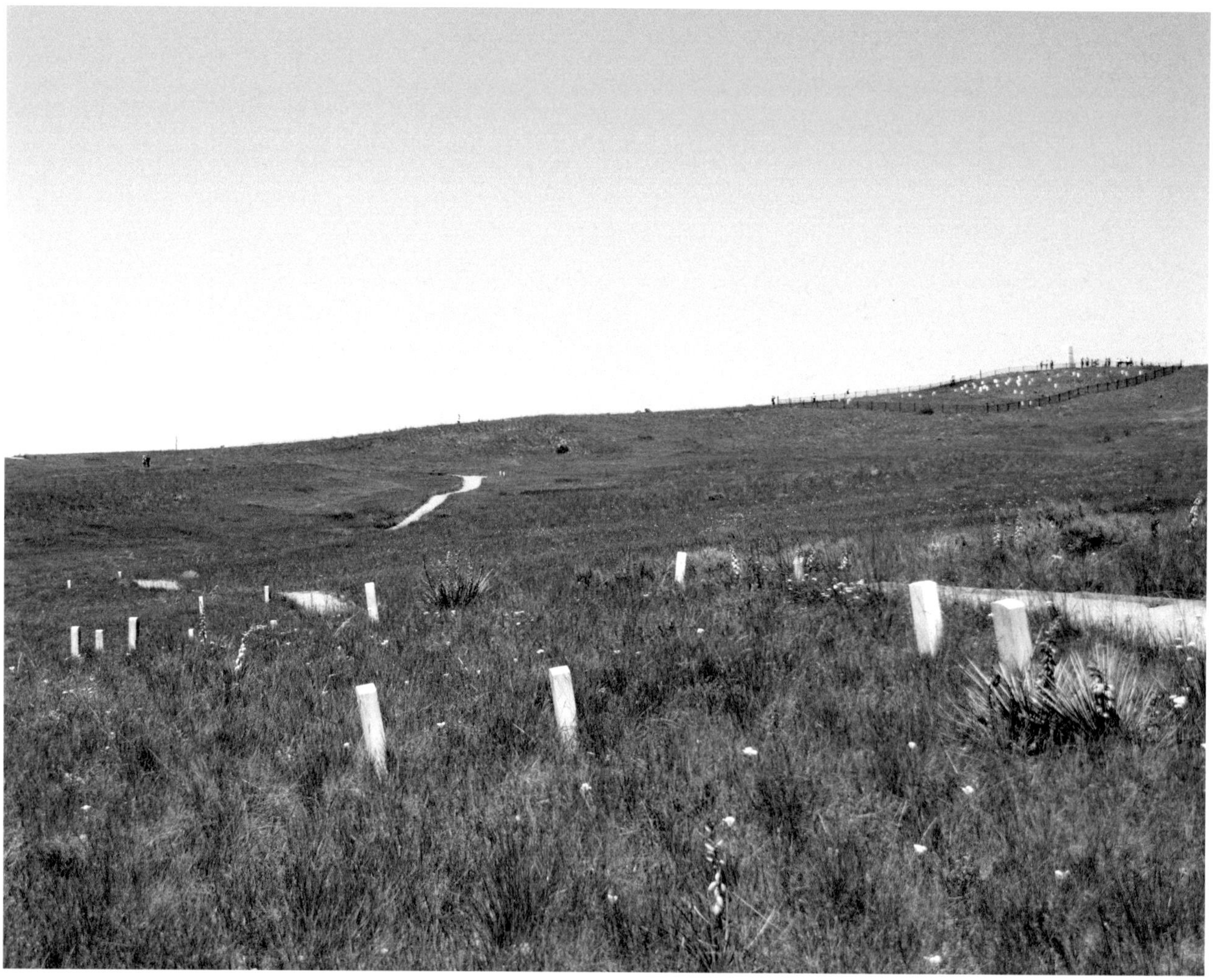

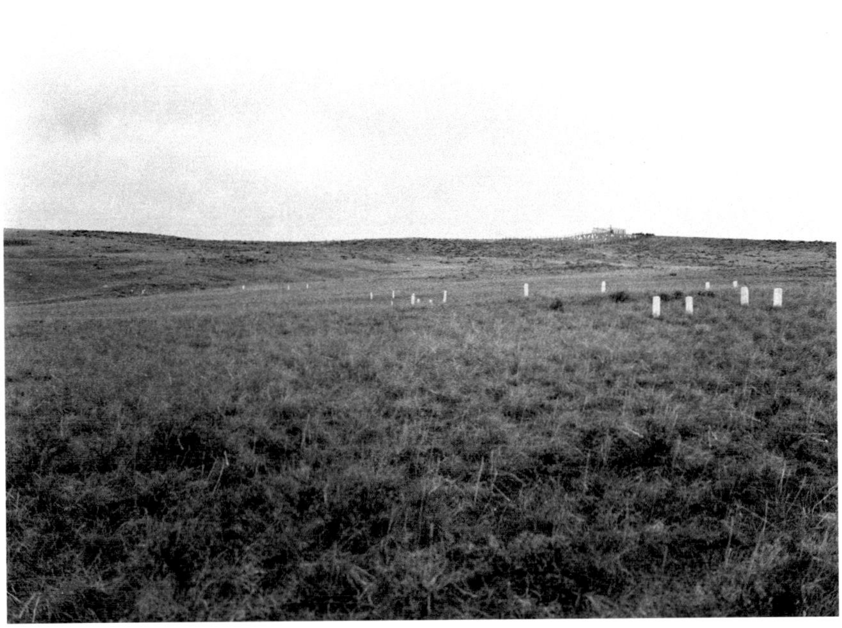

Figure 17.13. (*top*) South Skirmish Line to Last Stand Hill. Courtesy of Big Horn County Historical Museum. (*bottom*) 2013 reshoot.

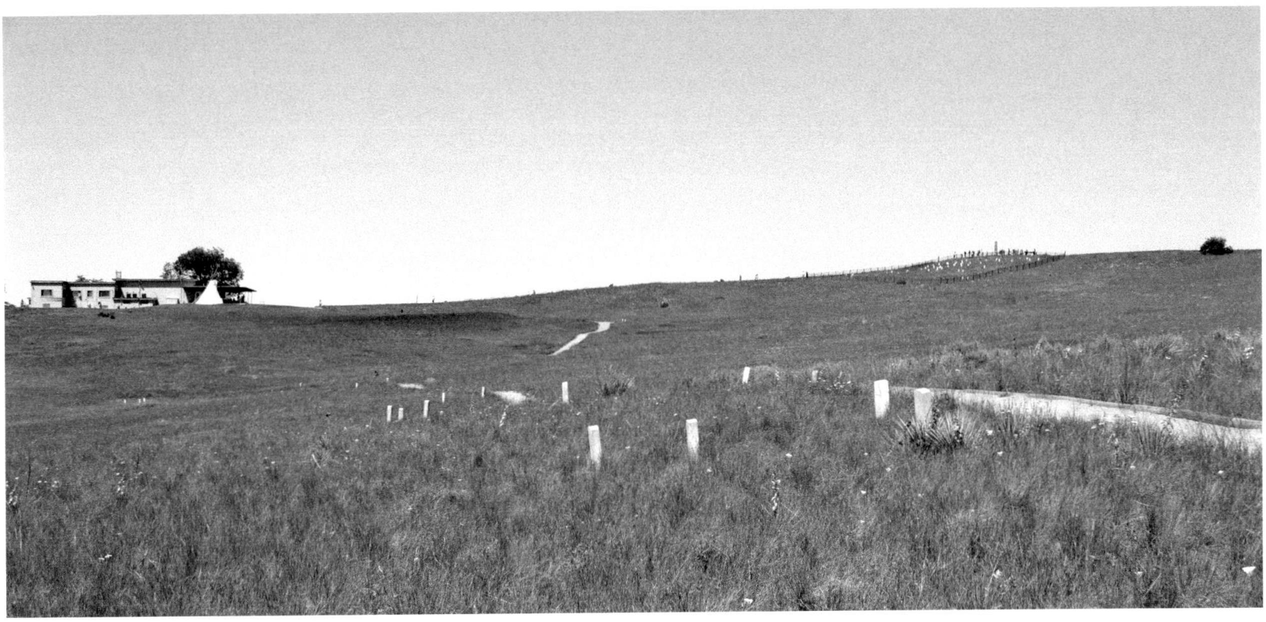

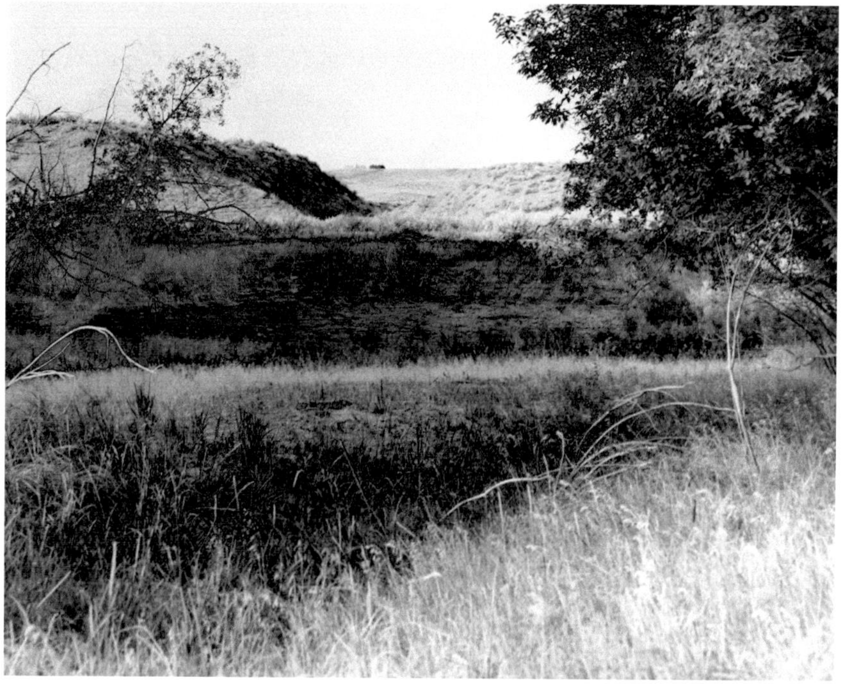

Figure 17.14. (*top*) Looking north across river up Deep Ravine, dated July 29, 1961. Courtesy of Big Horn County Historical Museum. (*bottom*) This 2012 reshoot also matches fig. 17.15.

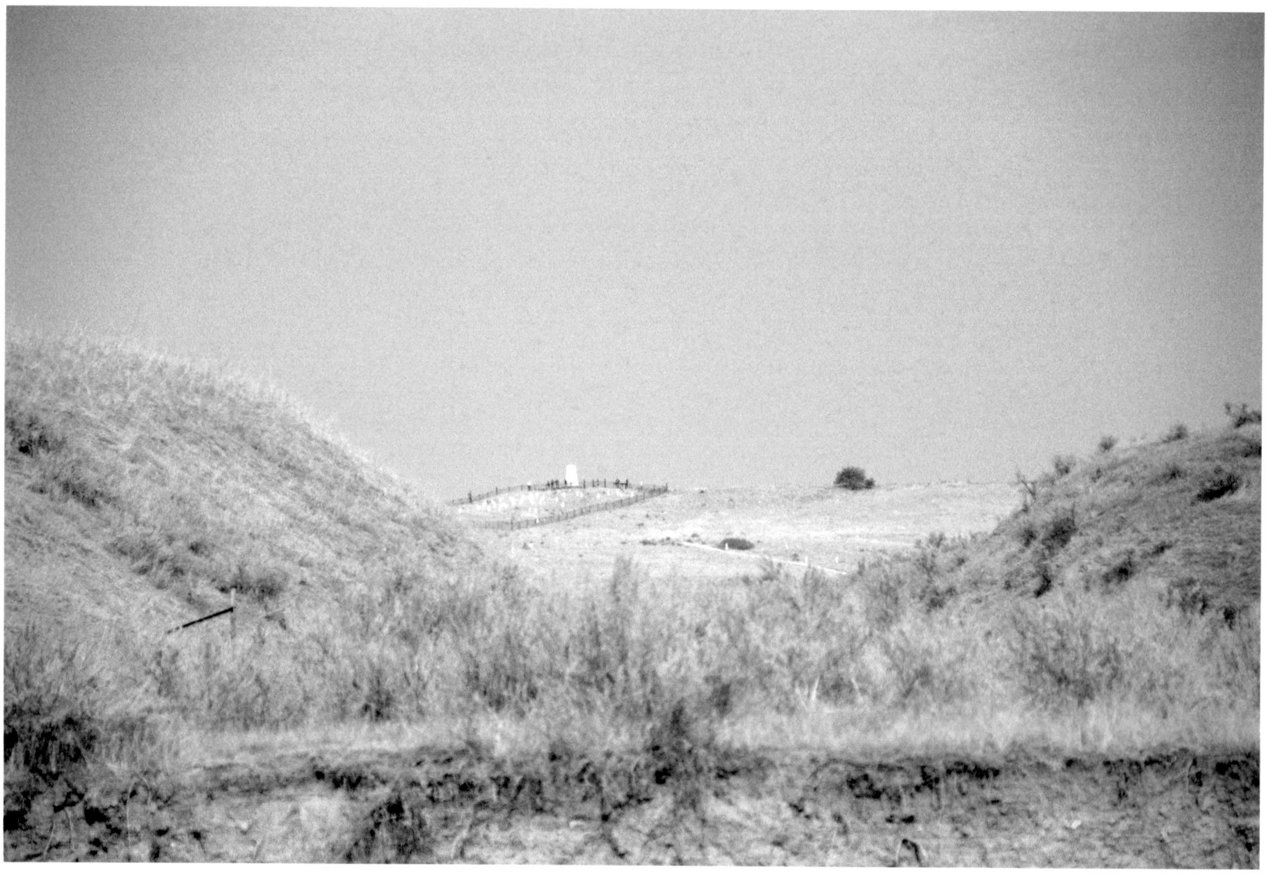

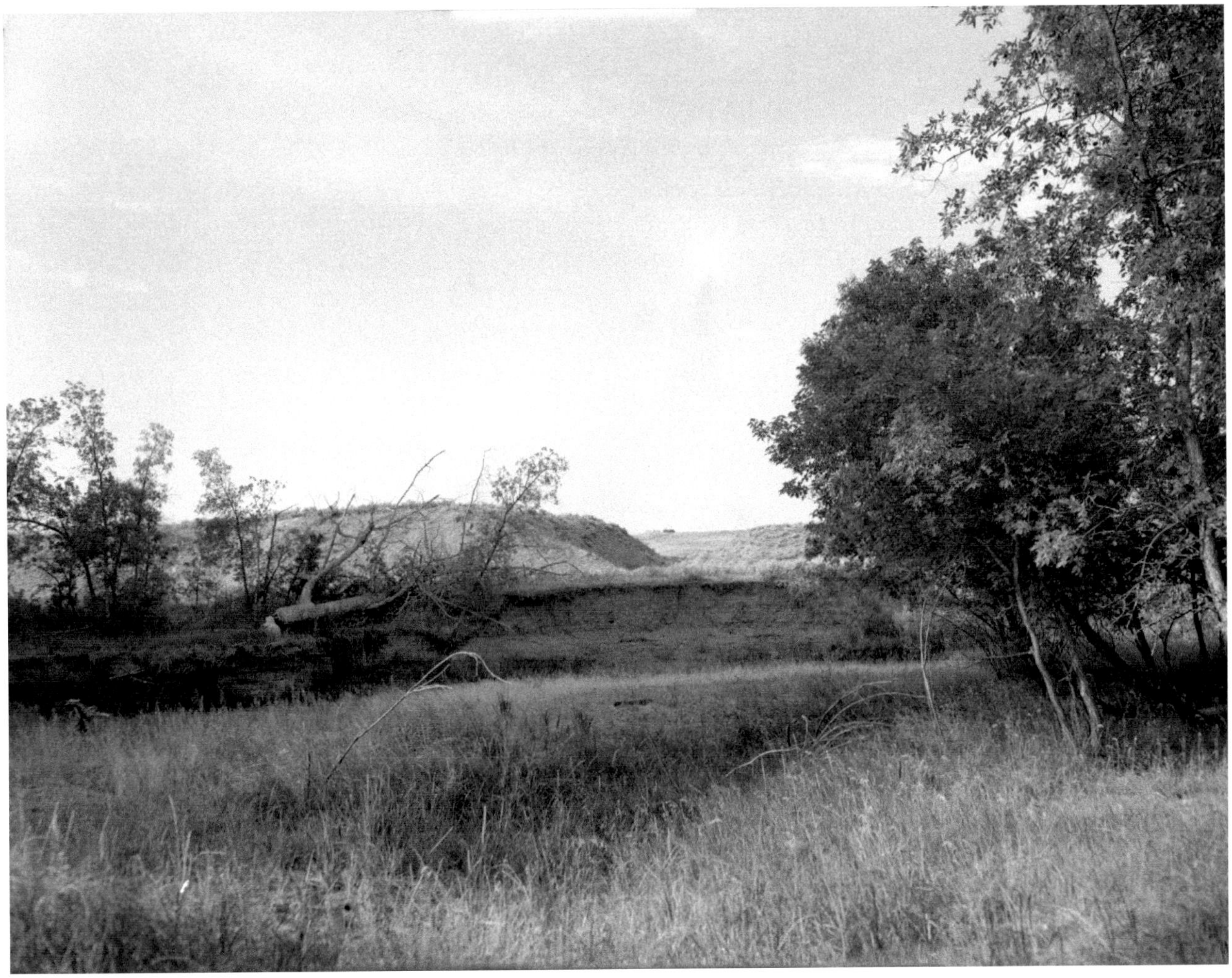

Figure 17.15. Looking northeast toward Last Stand Hill from the west bank of the Little Big Horn River opposite the mouth of Deep Ravine. Courtesy of Big Horn County Historical Museum.

CHAPTER 18

Last Stand Hill

Near the end of the iconic 1941 film *They Died with Their Boots On*, Errol Flynn, as Custer, a saber in his hand, stands on a flat plain. Bodies of dead cavalrymen are stacked around him; behind him, a guidon is blowing in the wind. Custer is about to meet his death gloriously at the hands of Lakota and Cheyenne warriors. Much about the scene, including the saber in Flynn's hand (none was carried by the 7th Cavalry at Little Big Horn), may be wrong, but his portrayal of the doomed Custer stands as a classic. Even a newcomer to the battlefield's history may spot another obvious error—the flat plain. The photograph "The place where Custer fell," as frontier photographer John H. Fouch labeled his 1877 image (fig. 18.1), the first taken of

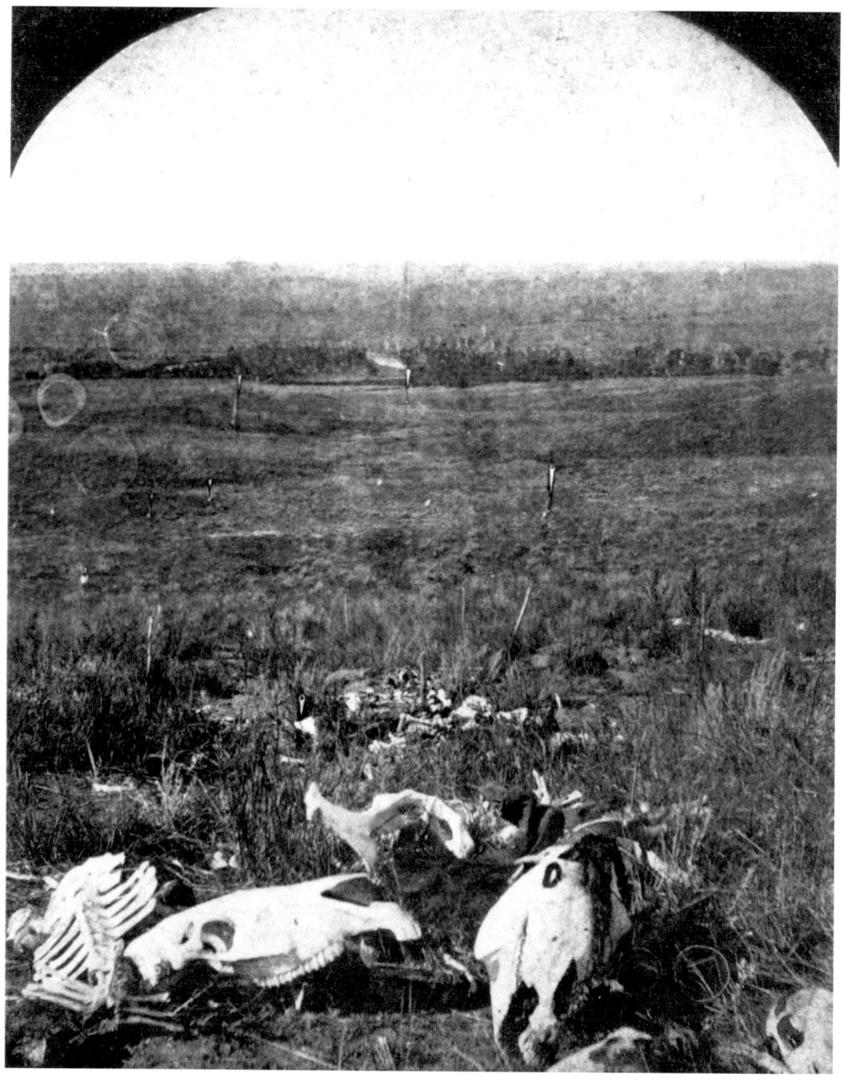

Figure 18.1. John Fouch photo, "The Place Where Custer Fell," 1877. Courtesy of James S. Brust.

the site, reveals a steep-graded hill, not a flat plain. As we noted in *Where Custer Fell*, the hill beckons with the message "'Here it happened.' . . . The enduring sense of place was doubtless a compelling draw to the many photographers whose images provide a visual chronicle of Custer Hill through the decades."[1]

In the early 1930s, the scene clearly engaged Roahen, who would spend some forty-five years photographing the hill and its surrounding countryside. Estimates vary about the number of dead found on the hill, from a low of twenty to forty-five. Lt. Edward S. Godfrey stated that the bodies of forty-two soldiers and civilians and thirty-nine horses were found on the slope.[2] Today fifty-two markers stand on the site, enclosed by an iron fence. Their positions have remained virtually unchanged since their emplacement by Capt. Owen Sweet's detail in 1890. Any extras probably were intended for the Reno-Benteen battlefield.

Besides Custer himself, the bodies of three of his relatives were found on the slope: brothers Capt. Thomas W. Custer and Boston Custer and nephew Harry Armstrong "Autie" Reed. All were initially interred on that ground. Lt. James Calhoun, Custer's brother-in-law and the fifth member of the family to die in the battle, was found with his troops on Calhoun Hill.

Early battlefield observers postulated that Last Stand Hill, or Custer Hill, was the site of a last-ditch stand by Custer's five companies. Too, the presence of so many dead horses led to a widespread belief that the animals had been shot down as breastworks for the besieged troopers and their commander.

The historical record generally reports that Custer himself was found on the crest of the ridge, as shown in Fouch's photograph, and was buried slightly down the slope. His body had been stripped but not severely mutilated or scalped. Custer had bullet wounds in his head and upper torso, either of which could have been fatal.

Most burials on the battlefield were perfunctory at best. Surviving 7th Cavalrymen lacked the necessary tools or the time to give their dead comrades proper burials. Officers received greater attention. Several men left accounts claiming to have buried the Custer brothers; 1st Sgt. John Ryan, Company M, provided the greatest detail: "We wrapped the two bodies in canvas and blankets and laid them side by side in this shallow grave and then covered them with dirt. We took a basket from an Indian travois, turned it upside down, put it over the grave, and laid a row of stones around the edge to keep the wolves from digging them up. That was the best burial of any of the bodies on the field."[3]

Archaeological evidence gathered in the 1980s revealed that the Indians relied on their own firearms as well as those captured from dead cavalrymen. They fired at the soldiers on Custer Hill from numerous positions, including from some 500 yards away along the northward extension of Battle Ridge as well as from came to known as Cemetery Ridge 350 yards below the hill. Other warriors used the terrain to move ever closer to the soldiers.

How long the soldiers resisted is uncertain, but according to Indian accounts the fighting was intense. The outcome for the outnumbered, beleaguered

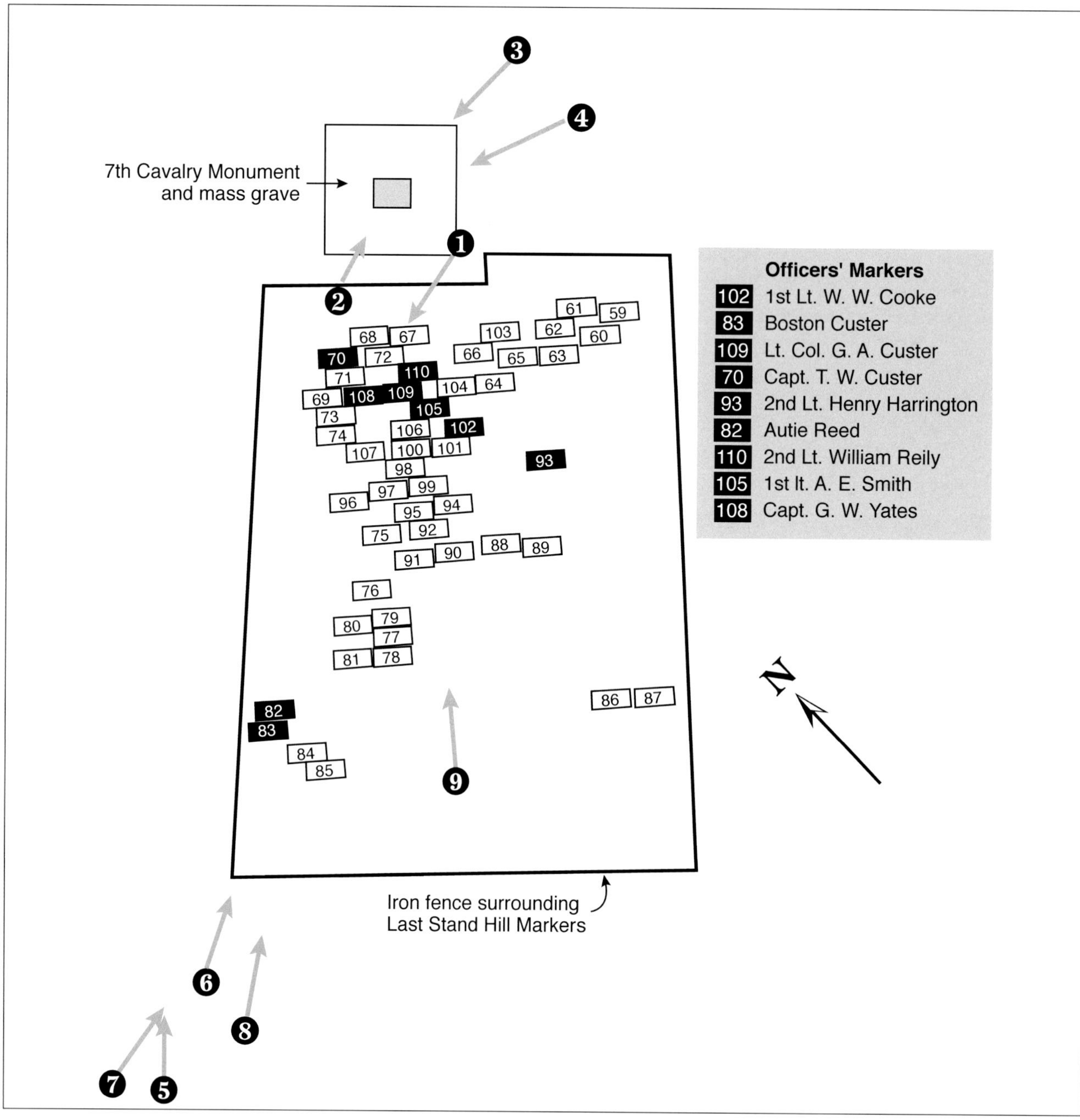

Map 18.1. Custer Hill. Map by Gary Raham.

1. Figs. 18.2, 18.3, 18.8
2. Fig. 18.4
3. Figs. 18.5, 18.6, 18.7
4. Fig. 18.9
5. Fig. 18.10
6. Fig. 18.11
7. Figs. 18.12, 18.13, 18.14
8. Fig. 18.15
9. Figs. 18.16, 18.17

troopers was inevitable. The warriors' final charge swept over the hill, where mostly wounded men were still resisting. Perhaps as many as fifteen soldiers fled toward Deep Ravine and were likely the last to fall.

In *Where Custer Fell* we focused on the first fifty to sixty years of photographs at Little Big Horn in the era long before the Visitor Center was constructed. Not surprisingly, photographers of that period most often aimed their cameras down Last Stand Hill across the South Skirmish Line toward Deep Ravine and, in the distance, the Little Big Horn River. Roahen overlapped that period, arriving in Montana in 1930 and taking his photographs both before and after major changes occurred on the field. His figure 18.2 image is one such photo.

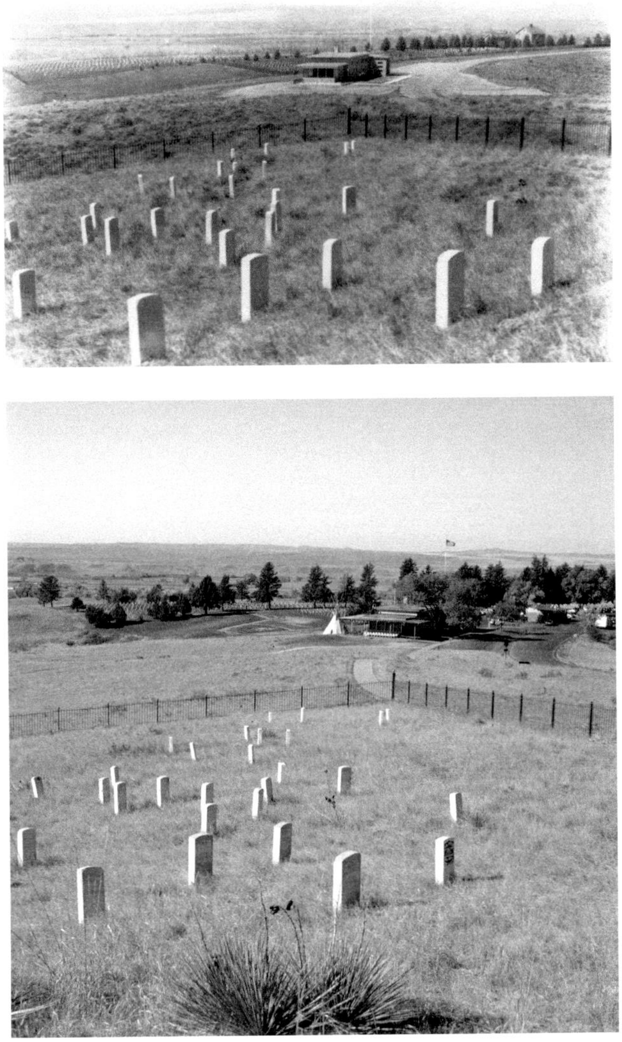

Figure 18.2. (*top*) Last Stand Hill, west to cemetery and Visitor Center. Courtesy of Big Horn County Historical Museum. (*bottom left*) 2013 reshoot.

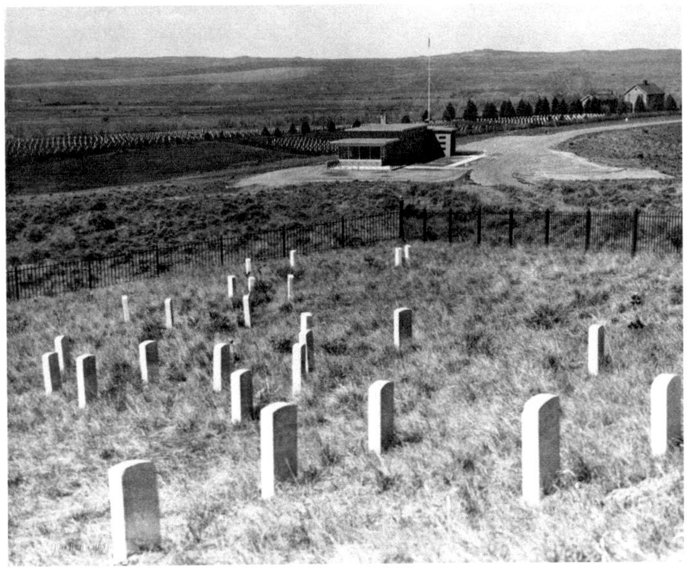

Figure 18.3. Variant of Last Stand Hill to cemetery, Custer stone on right. Courtesy of Big Horn County Historical Museum.

It and figure 18.3 show a view of the Visitor Center, likely just completed in 1952, perhaps before the building was officially dedicated and opened to the public. Note the absence of cars in the parking lot. Roahen's view from Last Stand Hill through the Visitor Center to the cemetery and the area of the Stone House today is probably the most frequently captured modern scene at Little Bighorn Battlefield National Monument.

Roahen's figure 18.4 photograph is dated July 31, 1963, and was taken just after the removal of the ten-foot fence around the monument. The fence was originally erected in 1883. Two changes are obvious between his image and the modern match. The historical marker has been moved forward, and, more significant, the Indian Memorial was constructed in 2003 on the lower ridge behind the 7th Cavalry monument.

The Fetterman burial markers seen in figure 18.5 were emplaced in 1889 and relocated to the National Cemetery about 1930. Inasmuch as Roahen did not arrive in the Billings area until December 1930, it is highly likely that this

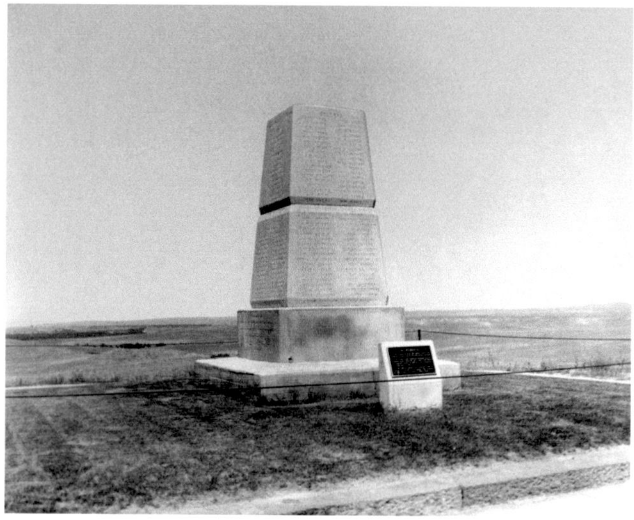

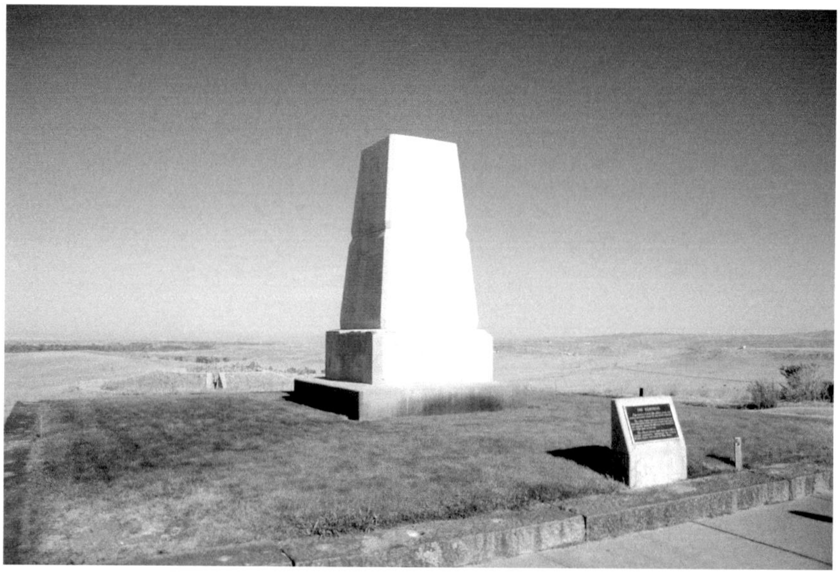

Figure 18.4. (*top*) Custer monument after fence removed, July 31, 1963. Courtesy of Big Horn County Historical Museum. (*bottom*) 2013 reshoot.

image was taken by a different photographer, even though it bears Roahen's imprint. The undated figure 18.6 was likely taken much later, since it offers a much more modern appearance for the Last Stand Hill and Visitor Center/Cemetery area. Similar to it is figure 18.7. Undoubtedly, Roahen stood on a ladder to see over the edge of Last Stand Hill to be able to capture the Visitor Center below. The modern comparison was taken at ground level. The Visitor Center is in view, but not to the extent in Roahen's original.

Roahen's photograph in figure 18.8 may be similar to others he took of the area from Last Stand Hill to the National Cemetery, but it offers one important distinction: this photo obviously was shot before the lot where the Visitor Center now stands was cleared for construction in 1951–52. A comparison of the number of burial markers in both a 1941 aerial photograph by Charles Belden and a 1951 aerial by Roahen himself, as well as figure 18.8, indicates that Roahen's image likely dates from the late 1940s.[4] Roahen's photo also provides a good look at the honeysuckle hedge planted in 1938 around the north and

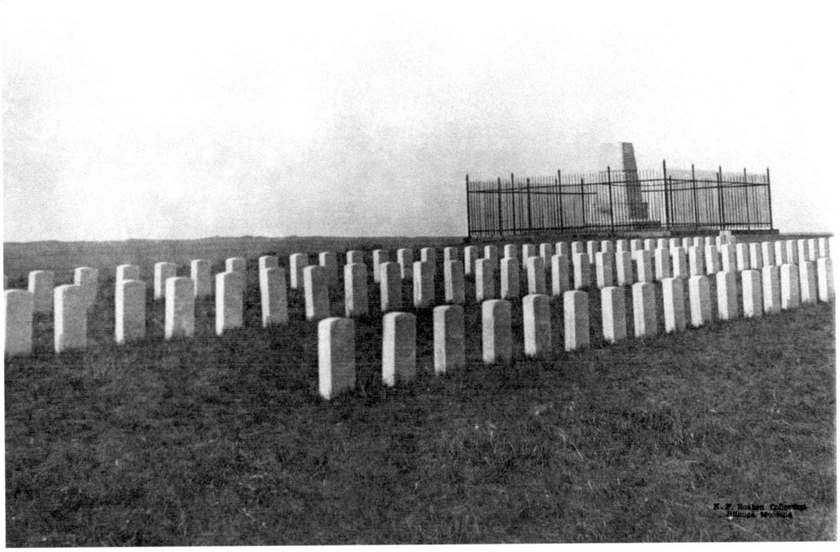

Figure 18.5. Fetterman markers on Last Stand Hill. Likely this is not a Roahen photograph. Courtesy of Big Horn County Historical Museum.

Figure 18.6. Last Stand Hill, more modern appearance. Courtesy of Big Horn County Historical Museum.

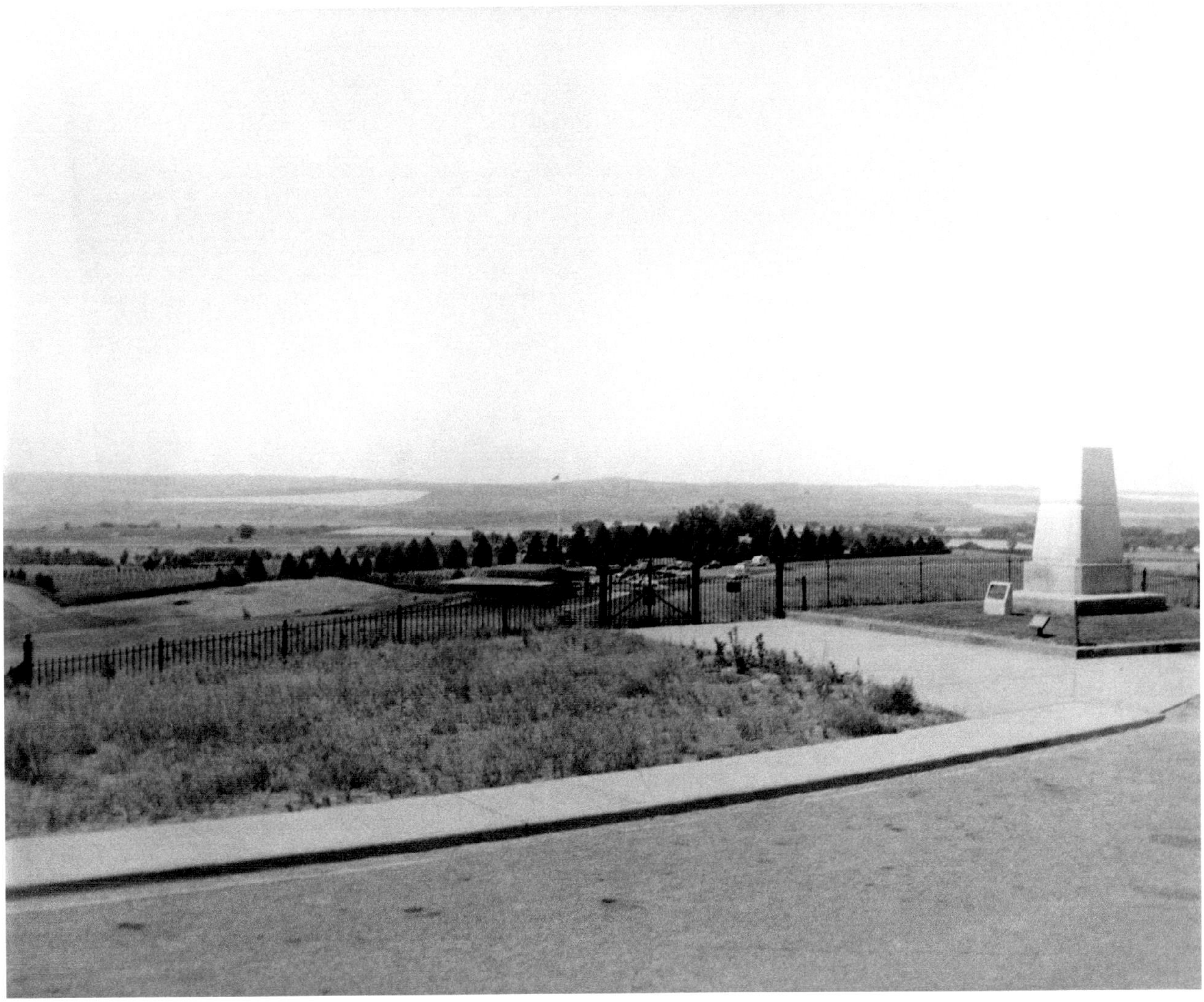

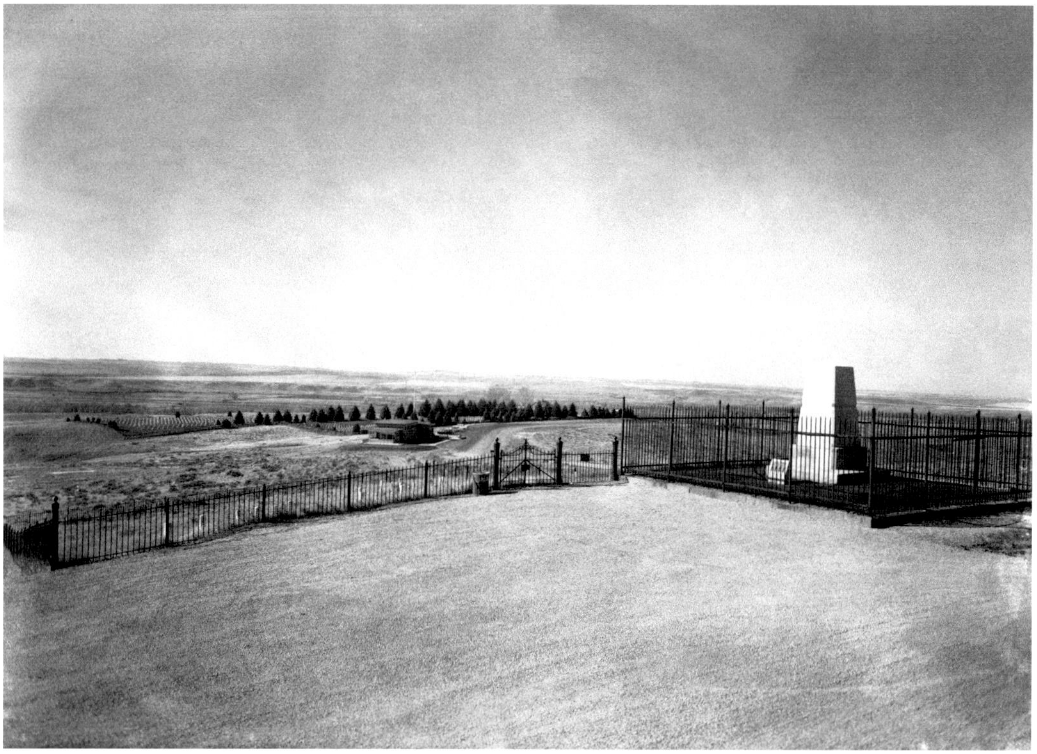

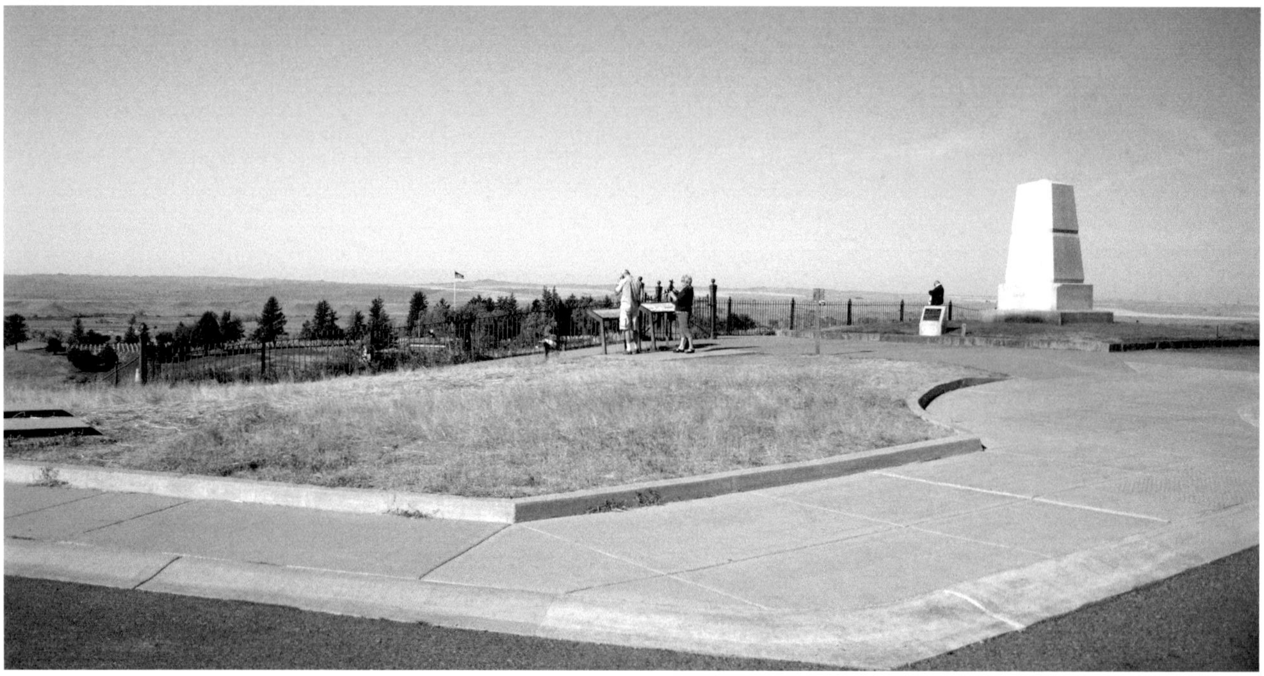

Figure 18.7. (*top*) Last Stand Hill, ca. 1952–63. Courtesy of Big Horn County Historical Museum. (*bottom*) 2013 reshoot.

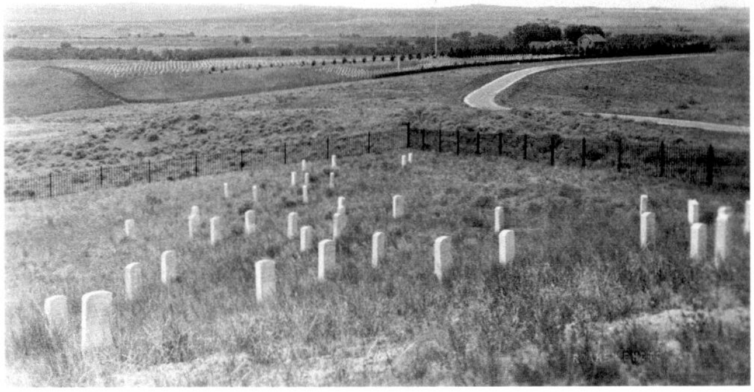

Figure 18.8. (*top*) Last Stand Hill to cemetery. Courtesy of Big Horn County Historical Museum. (*bottom*) 2013 reshoot.

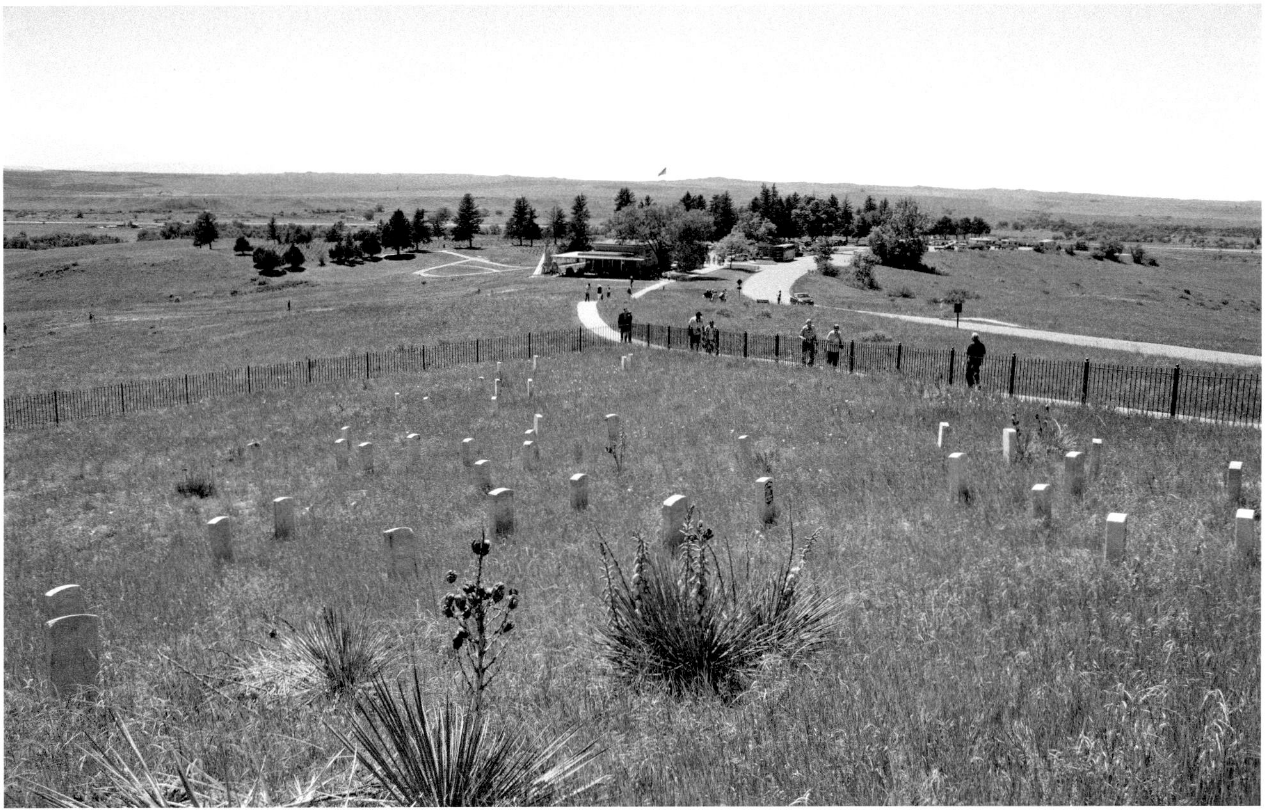

west portions of the cemetery. Also visible is the low fence that was erected around the cemetery in 1891. The modern photo reveals the changes to this area, including the removal of the hedge around the cemetery.

Roahen's photograph of the monument in figure 18.9 is clearly pre-1963, since the fence still surrounds it. The modern shot, taken in June 2013, makes equally obvious how much change has occurred at the Last Stand site. Of course, the fencing has been removed, but the former curbing base still surrounds the monument plot. The ground has been leveled off and replaced by the sidewalk. A new sidewalk runs in front of the grass plot and curbing that were installed in 1975 for the battle's centennial the following year.

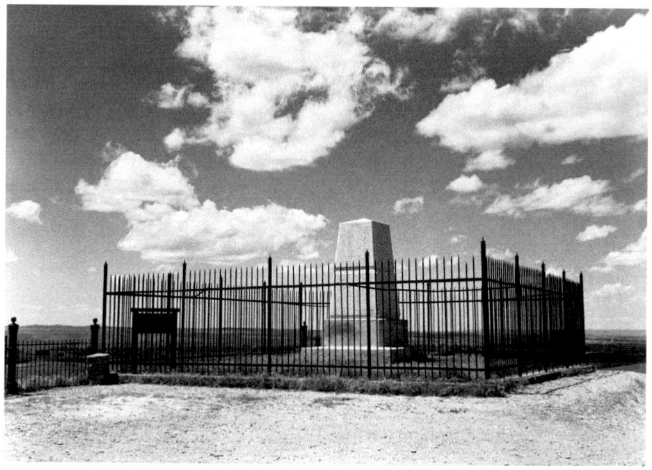

Figure 18.9. (*top*) Last Stand Hill, pre-1963. Courtesy of Big Horn County Historical Museum. (*bottom*) 2013 reshoot.

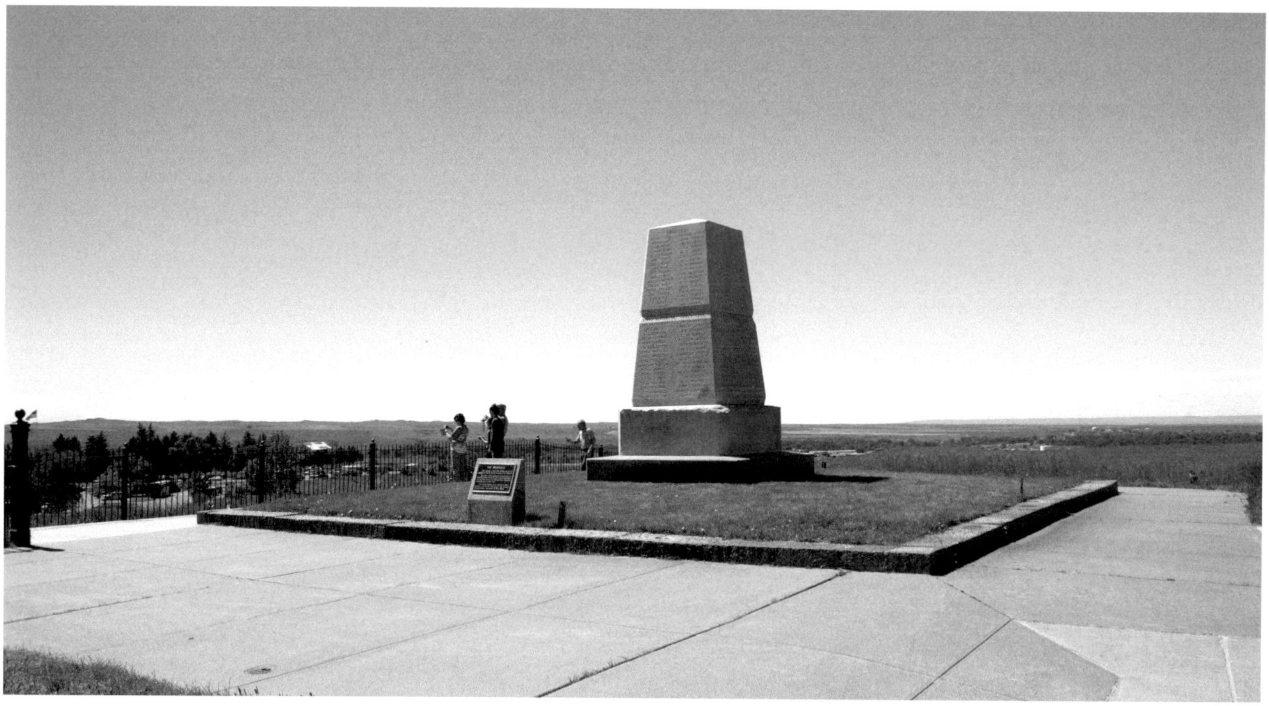

In May 1958, large numbers of Girl Scouts visited Custer Battlefield. Roahen's figure 18.10 photograph shows them making their way to and from Custer Hill, but it raises several questions. The first is easy to answer: did Roahen stand on a ladder to shoot the image? Likely yes. Notice that the young women at the top of the hill have turned the corner toward the monument but remain visible to his camera. Standing on his ladder would seem to be the only way the photographer could have captured the youngsters in his shot.

The second question is more difficult: as we look at the hill, has its north shoulder been extended? In Roahen's image, the surrounding fence is just about at the edge of the hill. In the modern counterpart, several feet of grass-covered ground extend beyond the sidewalk, as if the hilltop had been widened to accommodate the modern sidewalk. Jerome A. Greene, in his battlefield history, pointed out that the battlefield experienced considerable construction

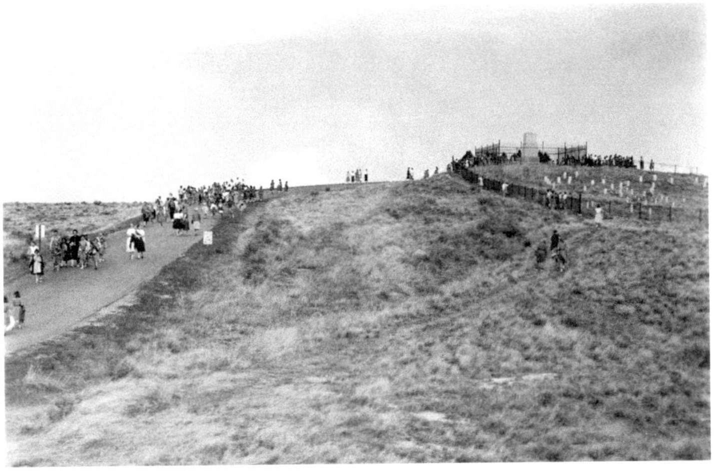

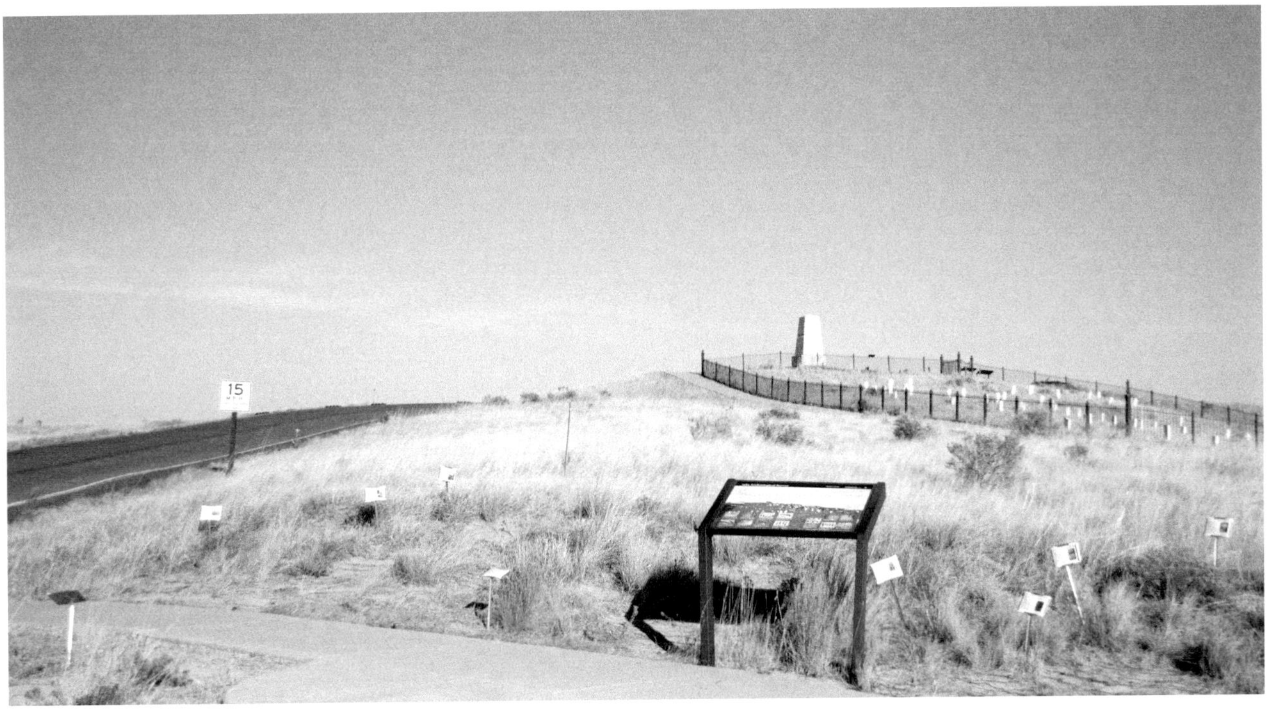

Figure 18.10. (*top*) Girl Scouts on the road to Last Stand Hill. Courtesy of Big Horn County Historical Museum. (*bottom*) 2012 reshoot.

between 1938 and 1940, with at least five major projects completed, drastically altering the field: "For one thing the grading that took place near the monument at the north end of battle ridge likely disturbed and distorted the primary landscape in the area of the monument and Last Stand group."[5]

Greene's statement may explain the hilltop's appearance in Roahen's 1958 photograph of the Girl Scouts, taken some twenty years later. In Roahen's day, no sidewalk existed from the Visitor Center to the top of Custer Hill. In the middle right of the photograph, three girls can be seen walking up a dirt path worn across the grass to the lower section of the fenced-in enclosure. That connects to another dirt path that parallels the fence and leads up to the monument. In the modern photo, the hill appears to have been extended to accommodate the sidewalk installed in 1975. The top east side of the hill fence was moved forward about eight feet to accommodate a sidewalk between the

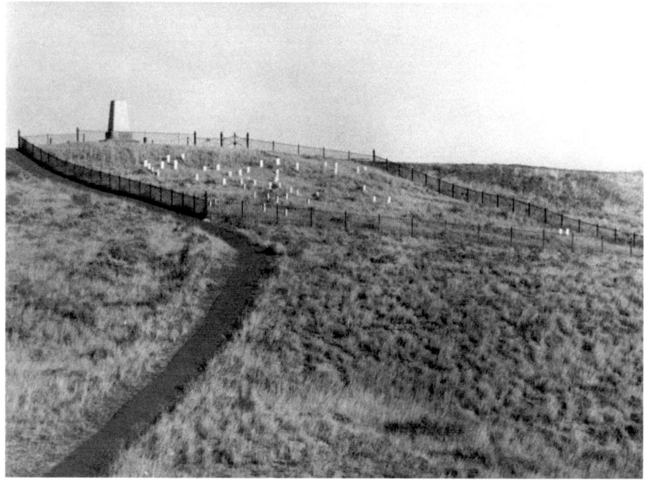

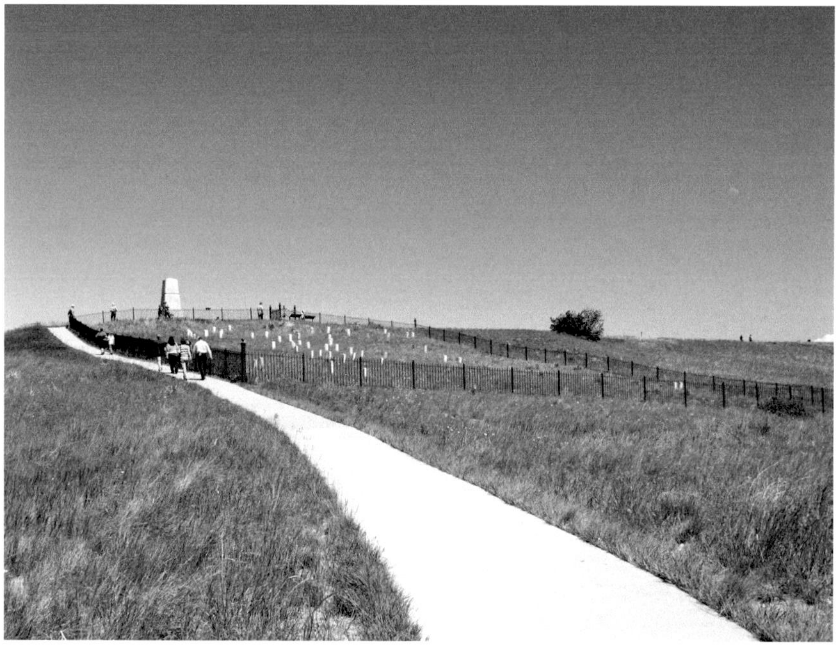

Figure 18.11. (*top*) Last Stand Hill. Courtesy of Big Horn County Historical Museum. (*bottom*) 2013 reshoot.

monument/mass grave area and the upper fence so visitors could view the Custer Hill markers.[6]

Other changes appear in the modern figure 18.10 photo. The battlefield roadway seems straighter than in 1957. In the center foreground, the modern path constructed in the early 2000s leading across the road to the Indian Memorial altered the ground. Various depressions seen in Roahen's photograph seem to have been filled in today, although that may result from heavier grass cover. A close look at the ground itself today revealed only a faint outline of the former depressions.

Though we lack a complete collection of Roahen's photographs of the battlefield, the Big Horn County Historical Museum's large sample provides a solid timeline of the subtle, long-term changes at Little Big Horn. His photograph in figure 18.11 certainly fits that mode. The absence of trees that formerly surrounded the now missing water tank on Last Stand Hill and the lack of the

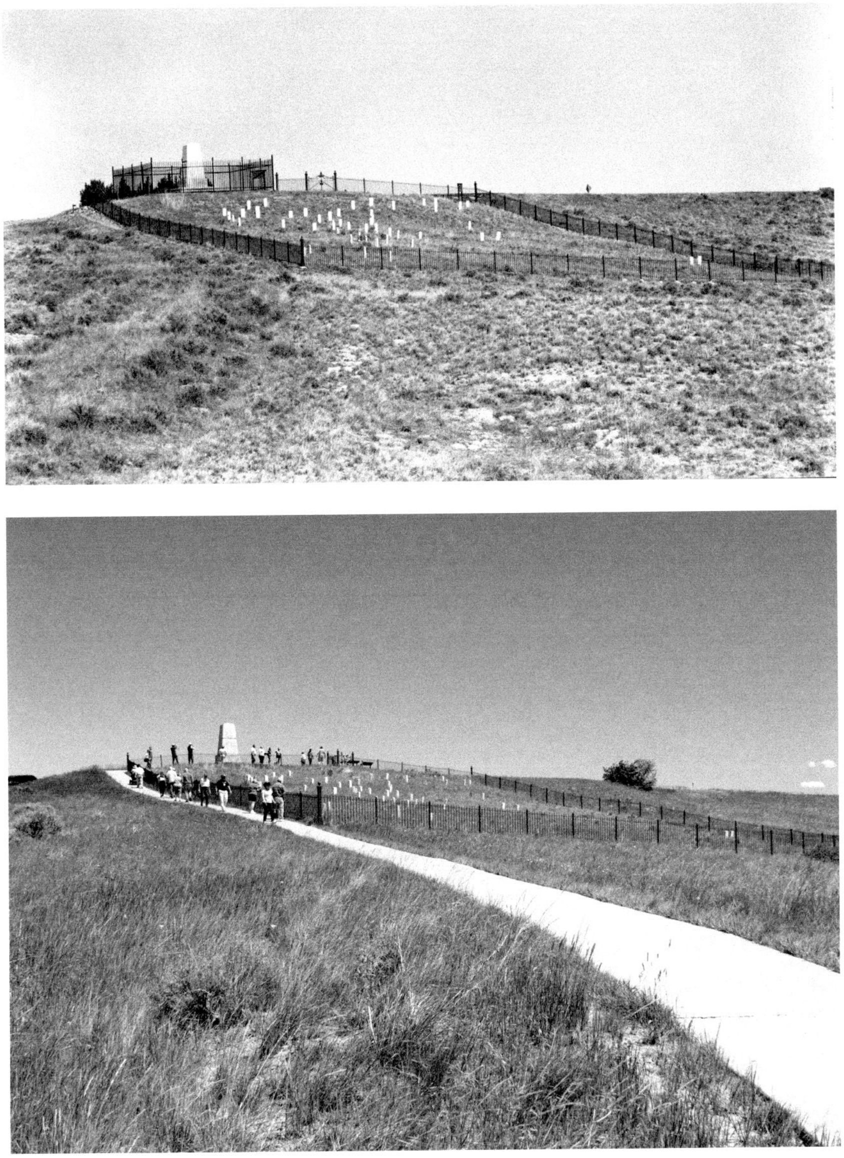

Figure 18.12. (*top*) Last Stand Hill without sidewalk. Courtesy of Big Horn County Historical Museum. (*bottom*) 2013 reshoot.

fence that formerly surrounded the monument itself date this photograph to the post-1963 period. An asphalt walkway comes down the hill to the Visitor Center. Given the composition of the photograph, with Roahen seemingly well above the foreground area (compare the modern shot), he likely stood on his ladder to shoot this image.

Figure 18.12 shows a scene very similar to that in figure 18.11, but it is obvious that the two Roahen photographs were taken some years apart. In figure 18.12, trees can be seen in the background around the water tank, and the taller fence remains in place around the 7th Cavalry monument. No sidewalk is shown in the photo, but the ruts created over the years by many visitors trekking up to Last Stand Hill are easily spotted in the bottom left of the photograph. Both modern photos show a similar arrangement for today's sidewalk. It appears the sidewalk was reconstructed at some point, which eliminated the short angle apparent in Roahen's photo. His image shows a sharper bend to the left than is apparent in the modern images.

Figure 18.13. (*right*) Last Stand Hill, no sidewalk or sign boards. Courtesy of Big Horn County Historical Museum.

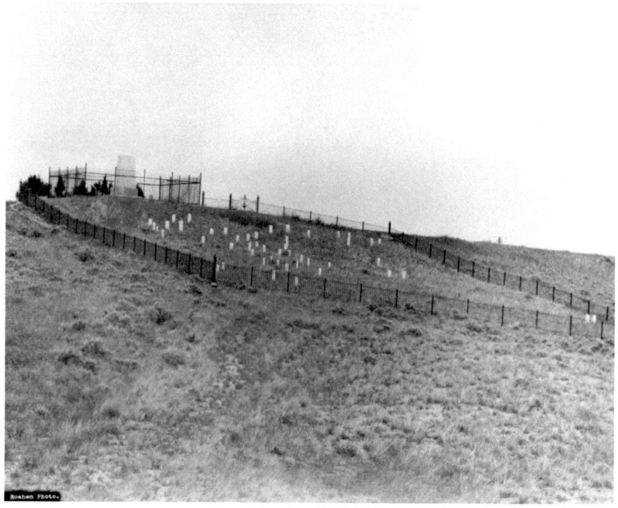

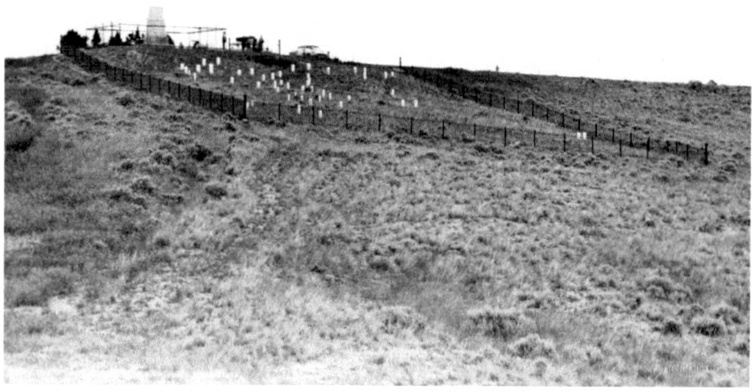

Figure 18.14. (*above*) Last Stand Hill and markers. Courtesy of Big Horn County Historical Museum. (*right*) 2012 reshoot.

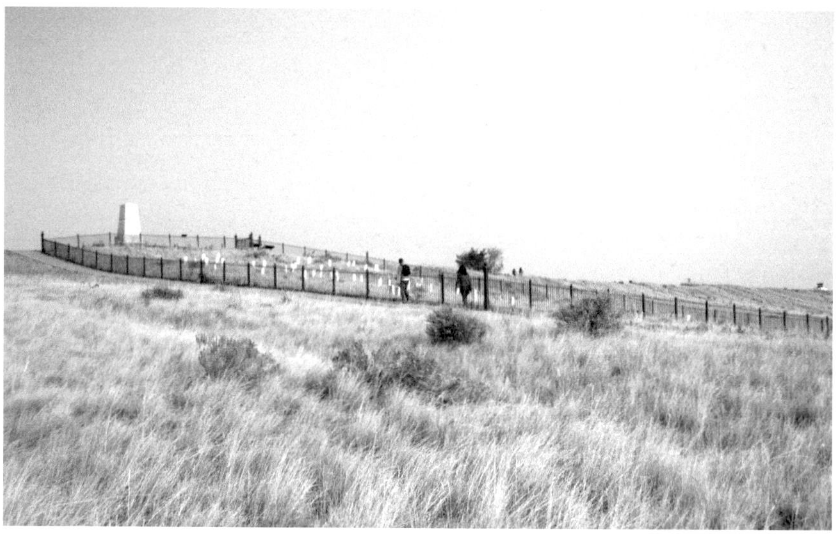

Another Roahen image, figure 18.13, likely taken from almost the same spot as his figure 18.12, possibly at a different time, closely approximates figure 18.12. Thanks to the presence of the hilltop trees and the taller monument fence, we know the photograph was taken prior to 1963. No sidewalk appears in it. Roahen's figure 18.14 shot is yet another view demonstrating his interest in Last Stand Hill. Likely it was taken about the same time as his figure 18.13, for the vegetation in the two images seems to match.

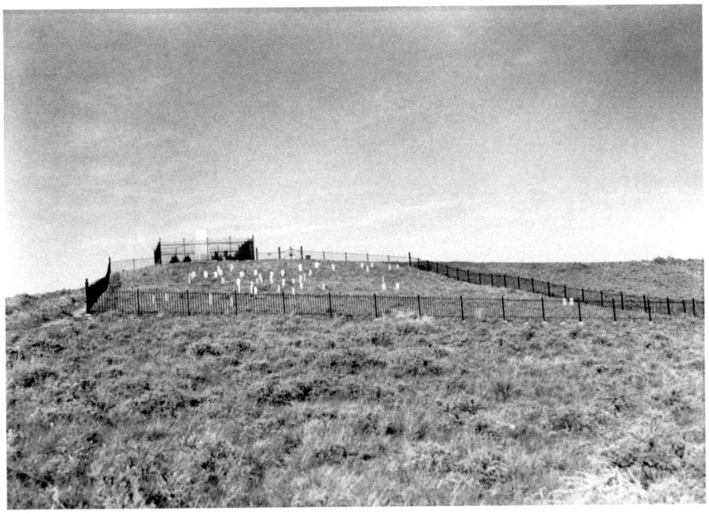

Figure 18.15. (*top*) Last Stand Hill before 1963. Courtesy of Big Horn County Historical Museum. (*bottom*) 2013 reshoot.

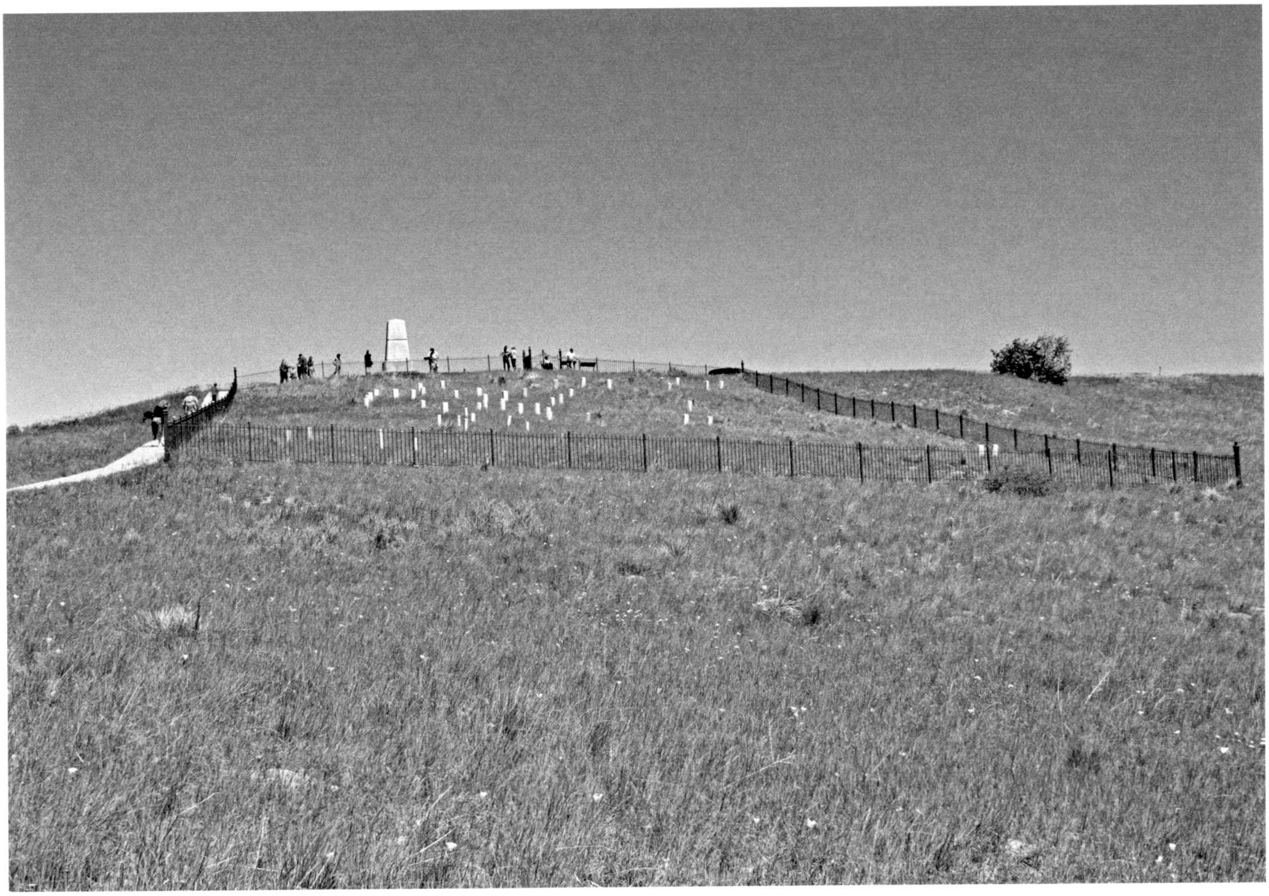

Whether the Roahen figure 18.15 photo was taken about the same time we cannot be sure, but the presence of the trees on the hilltop indicates that it predates 1963. Roahen stood on a small ridge about halfway between the more level ground of the Visitor Center and the bottom of the fenced-in enclosure.

Roahen took the figure 18.16 shot before 1963, from about halfway down the slope within the fenced-in area of Last Stand Hill. Custer's own marker is at the top left of both the Roahen and modern photos, in line with the left side

Figure 18.16. (*top*) Last Stand Hill markers; photo used by Roahen for postcards. Courtesy of Big Horn County Historical Museum. (*bottom*) 2012 reshoot.

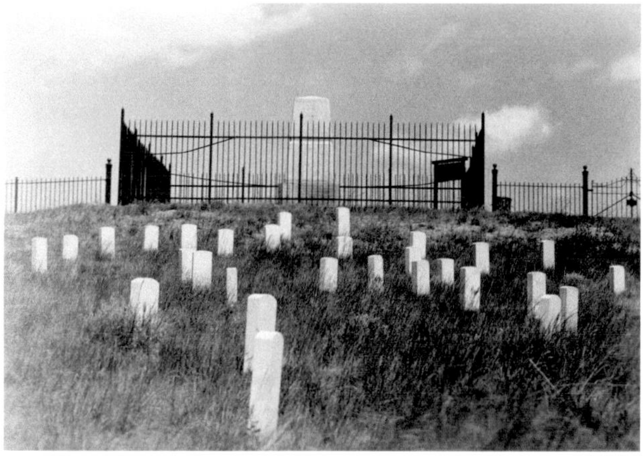

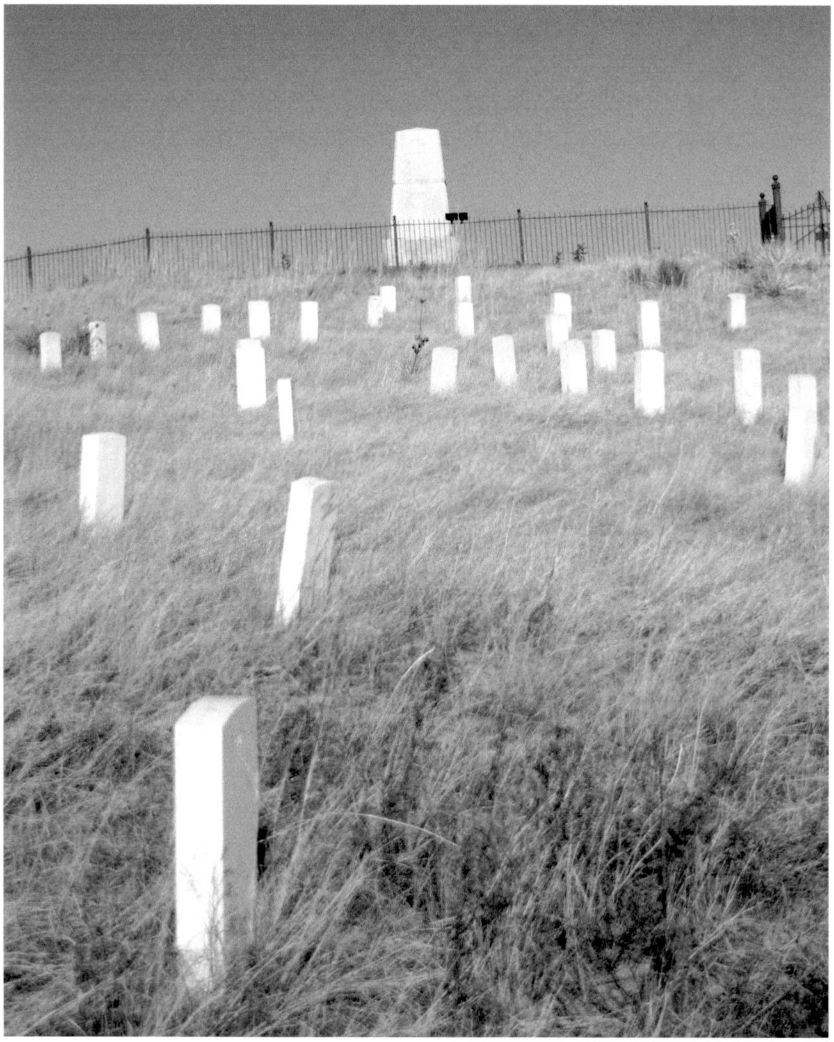

of the 7th Cavalry monument. Although the marker arrangement is about the same in the old and modern images, note the slight change in the position of the enclosure's entrance gate after the monument fence was removed. As noted earlier, in 1975 an eight-foot forward extension was constructed. The gate appears to be in the same location.

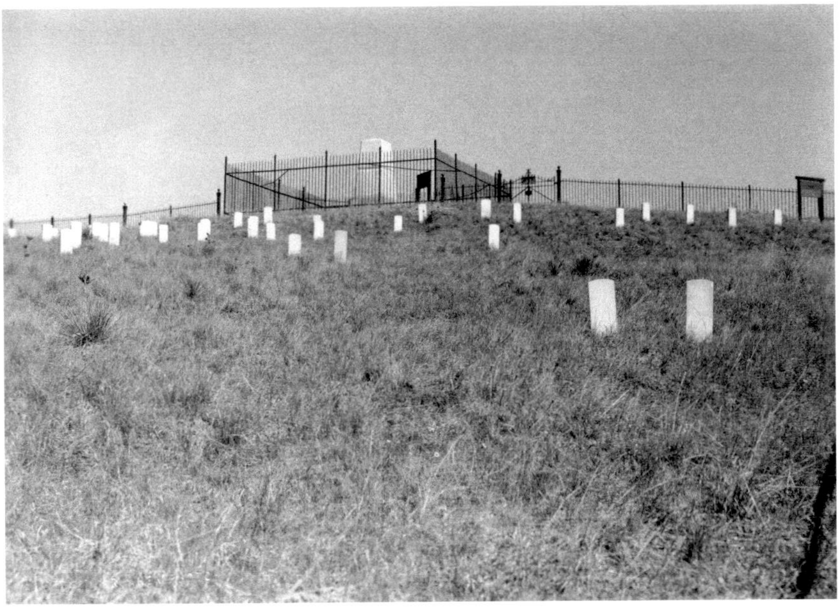

Figure 18.17. (*top*) Last Stand Hill with two sign boards. Courtesy of Big Horn County Historical Museum. (*bottom*) 2012 panoramic reshoot.

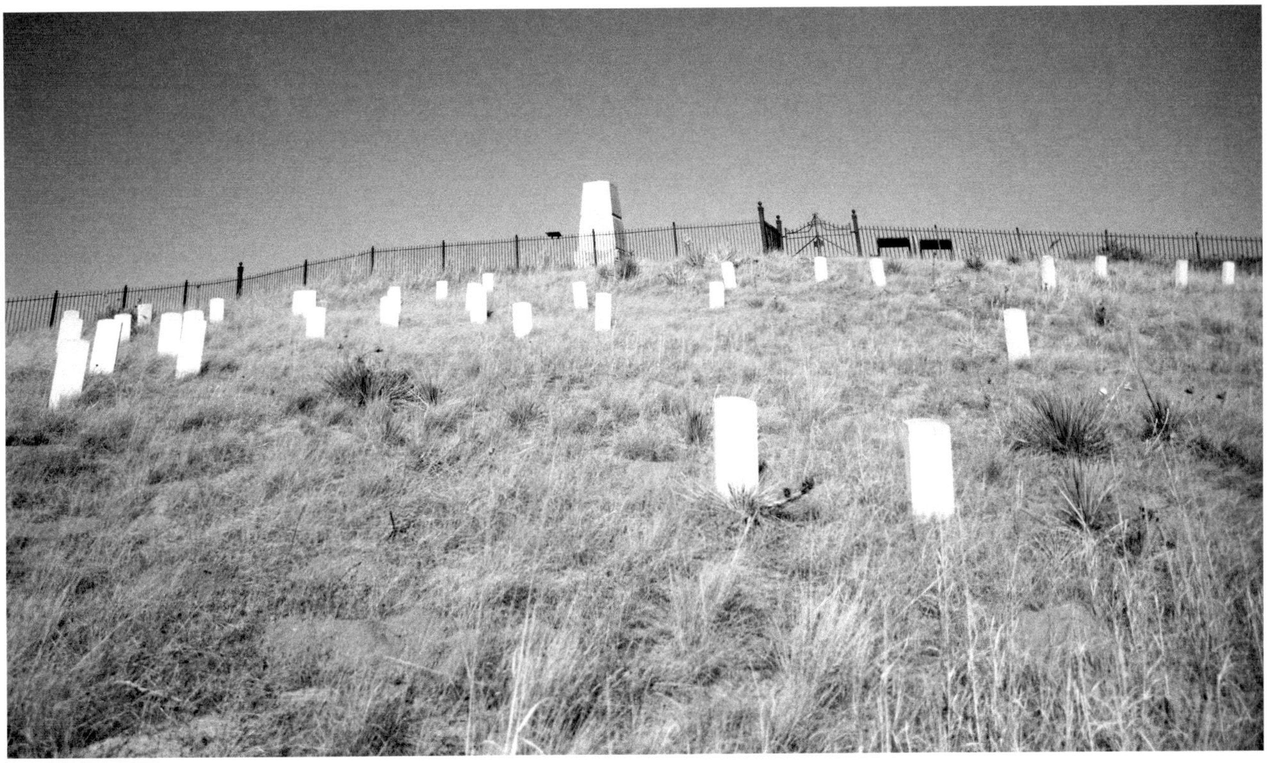

Roahen's figure 18.17 photograph provides a better look at the positioning between the monument fence and the gate into the marker enclosure. Note the two sign boards that appear in his image. One is on the right in the enclosure itself. A second sign sits inside the monument area. In 1975, with the fencing removed, the hillside enclosure was rearranged on its top side to allow for the modern sidewalk that enables tourists to stand between its fence and the curbing around the monument. Undoubtedly the two signs in Roahen's photo were historical markers. In the 2012 photograph, two similar markers can be seen outside the enclosure on the right. Those signs, here and elsewhere on the battlefield, are more recent additions that provide visitors with colorful battle-related images and a narrative text of various segments of the battle.

Little Big Horn researcher James S. Brust provided an image (fig. 18.18) from his personal collection of Maurice Frink historical photographs that shows a close-up of the right-side informational sign visible in figure 18.17 and several other Roahen photographs on Last Stand Hill. The sign states:

> This is Sacred and Hallowed Ground
> Custer's Last Stand
> June 25, 1876
> The marble markers within this enclosure
> note the places where the bodies of
> General Custer and his men were found.

Another Frink photograph (fig. 18.19) from the Brust collection shows the rear of the water tank that once stood on Last Stand Hill. The 20,000-gallon tank lay buried on the northeast side of Last Stand Hill, immediately east of the 7th Cavalry monument. The tank's date of construction remains uncertain, although former historian John Doerner's research placed it about 1911. In April 1941, Superintendent Luce wrote to his superiors that an excavation project on Last Stand Hill had revealed ten horse skeletons. In the early 2000s, Doerner requested permission to mark the site as a horse cemetery. Prior to that, archaeologist Douglas Scott's fieldwork had confirmed the location as a horse cemetery. His study indicated that the water tank had been removed in the early 1950s, although Roahen's photographs of Last Stand Hill suggest it remained after that period. Still, on June 29, 2003, Doerner held a ceremony on Last Stand Hill to dedicate both an interpretive wayside exhibit and a granite marker to pay homage to the 7th Cavalry horses interred there. Brust dates Frink's photograph to 1946, although 1941 remains a possibility.[7]

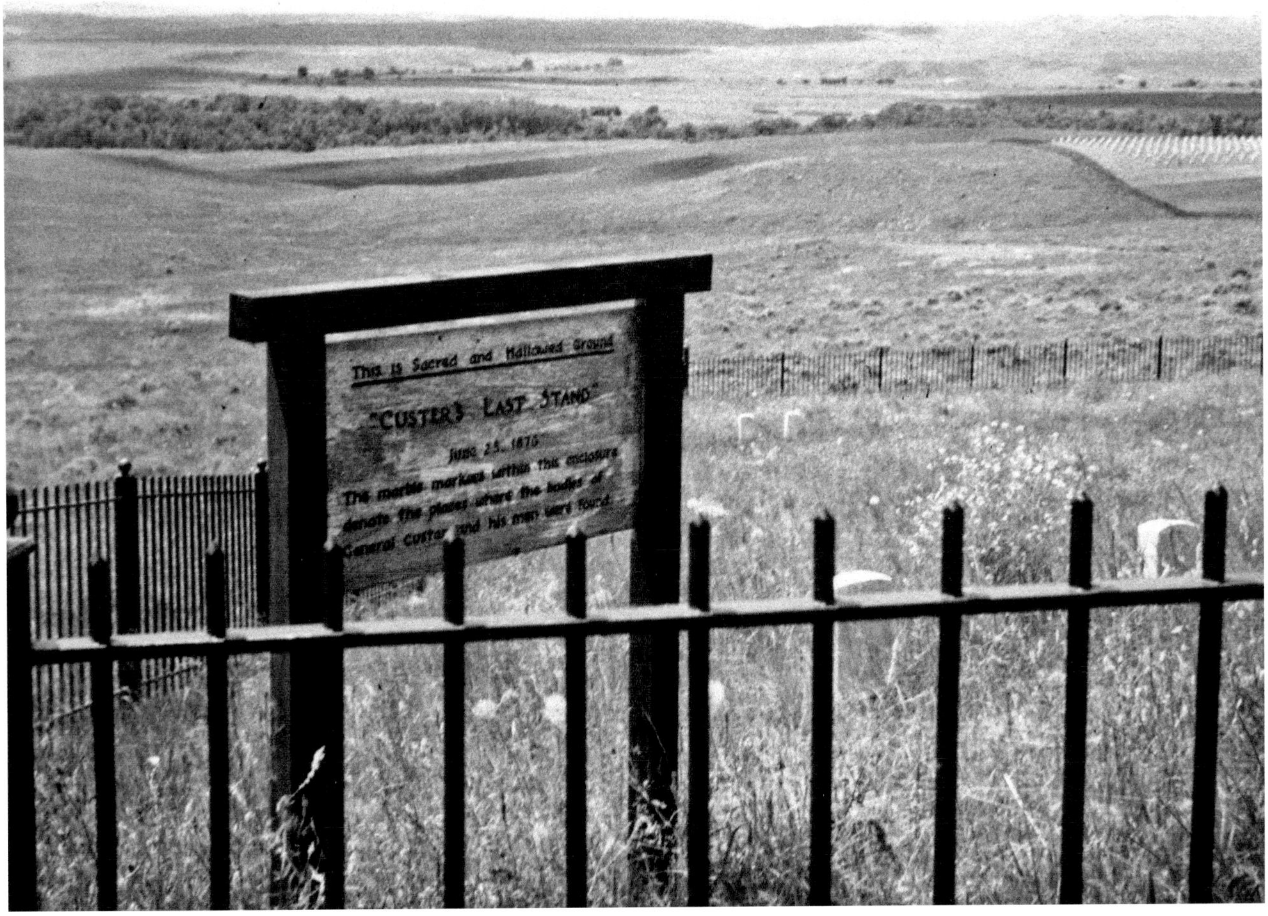

Figure 18.18. Maurice Frink sign, Last Stand Hill. Courtesy of James S. Brust.

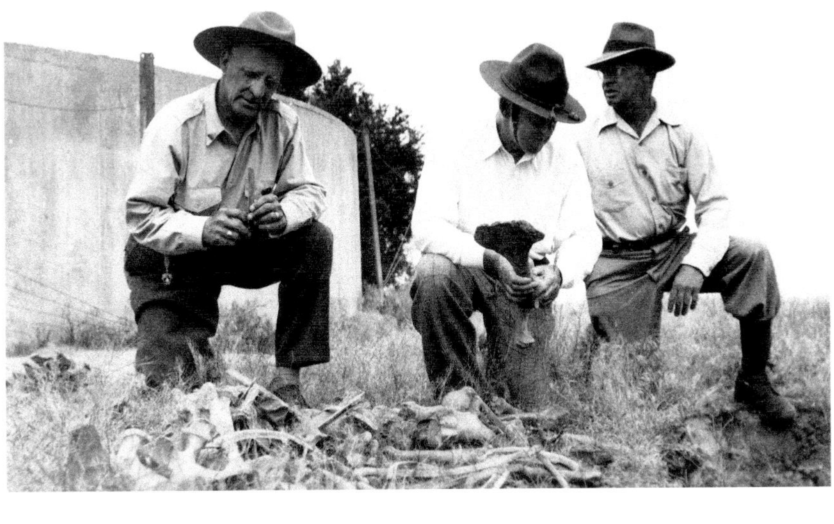

Figure 18.19. (*left to right*) Edward S. Luce, Elwood L. Nye, and Ralph G. Cartwright studying bones behind the water tank, ca. 1941 or 1946. Courtesy of James S. Brust.

CHAPTER 19

Entering the Main Battlefield

Today's Little Big Horn visitors ascend in a nearly straight line from U.S. Highway 212 up the battlefield's access road to its entrance kiosk. Undoubtedly, as they approach the access road off Highway 212, just east of Interstate 90, they probably little notice an old concrete road on the right. But for decades that often winding road served as the primary thoroughfare providing access to the Custer Battlefield. In 1957, today's road was cut more directly from Highway 212 up across several ridges to the battlefield's northwest boundary. Here masonry entrance gateways were constructed to support iron gates. Access from the new gate area to the national cemetery parking lot was gained by a newly constructed short branch road to the right, just inside the park property. From the gate this new entrance road continued straight ahead to the Visitor Center, where visitors found a newly paved parking lot.

Battlefield Main Gate, Then and Now

The now obsolete former gateway was about 100 yards to the right of the access road, or southwest of the new gate, just past the Stone House. Today that site is almost forgotten. If one crosses the lawn between the parking lot and the first set of Park Service quarters, the remnants of the old road inside the former gate quickly become evident along the boundary fence (fig. 19.1). One can spot the former cattle guard that remains in place (fig. 19.2). Past the cattle guard, the old road itself descends west about 900 yards down the ridges (fig. 19.3). Near the river, the now weedy concrete drive turns to right, or north, for about 600 yards to the U.S. highway. Before 1957, visitors who followed this road for those 600 yards turned to the left, or east, to ascend the ridges to the battlefield (for aerial views, see figs. 21.3 and 21.4). Here it branched into three roads which rejoined just before the gate. Today, online images viewable in Google Earth allow the path of the historic road to be traced easily.

Figure 19.4 offers Roahen's well-composed image of the 1957 Custer Battlefield National Monument entrance. Nothing stands between the gate and Custer Hill except the Visitor Center. The modern counterpart photo reveals how much the openness of 1957 has been compromised. To capture the modern scene, it was necessary to step back farther than Roahen stood as well as rely on a wide-angle lens. Today's entranceway has recently been widened to accommodate larger recreational and other modern vehicles. A visitor kiosk stands in the middle where park staff collect entrance fees and pass

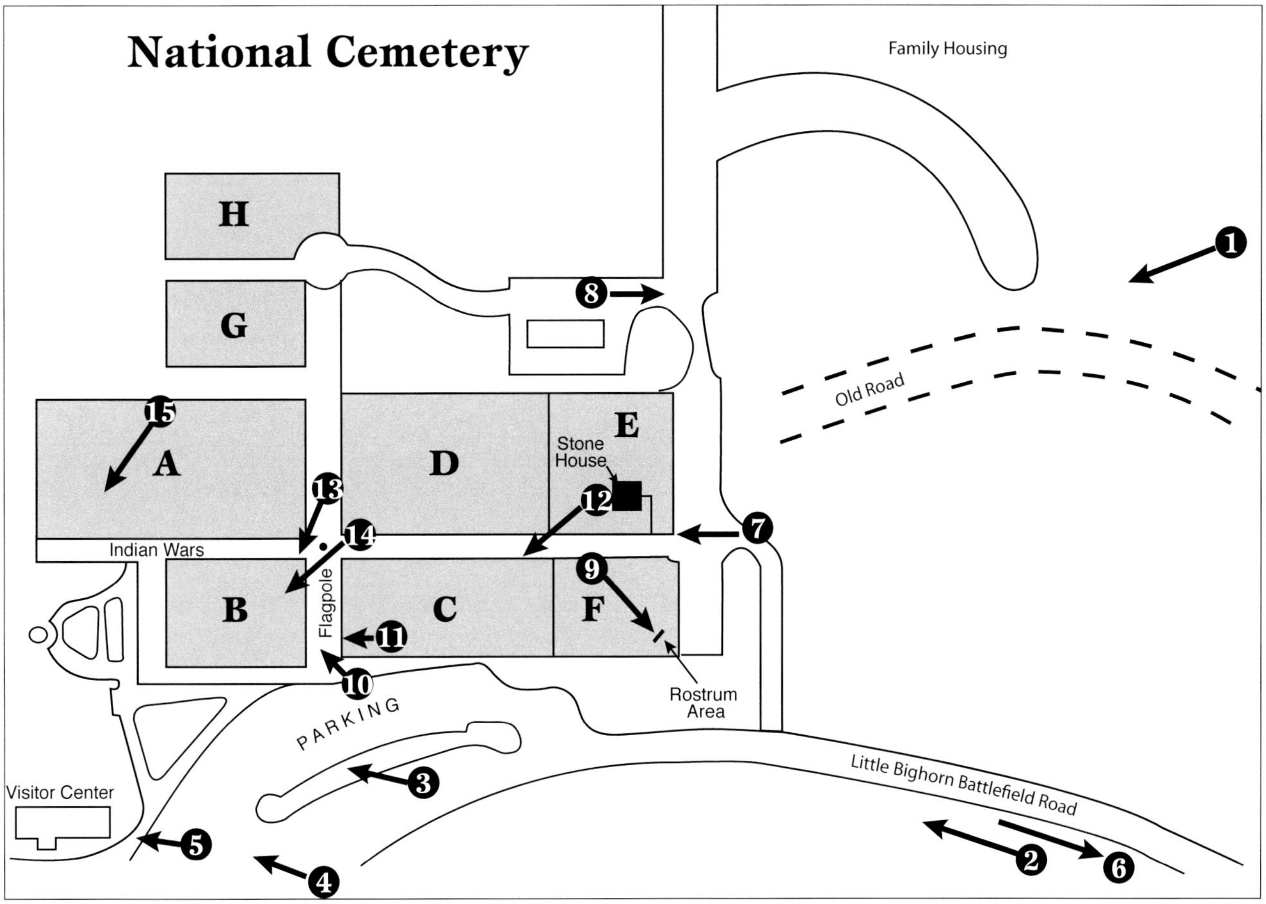

Map 19.1. Stone House, Custer National Cemetery, and vicinity. Map by Gary Raham.

1. Fig. 19.1
2. Fig. 19.4
3. Fig. 19.5
4. Fig. 19.6
5. Fig. 19.7
6. Figs. 19.8, 19.9
7. Figs. 19.10, 19.11, 19.12
8. Fig. 19.13
9. Figs. 19.14, 19.15
10. Fig. 19.18
11. Figs. 19.19, 19.20
12. Fig. 19.21
13. Fig. 19.22
14. Figs. 19.23, 19.24
15. Fig. 19.26

out informational literature. On the far left, Custer Hill is visible, but almost immediately a stand of trees blocks further view of the ridge. Just to the right of those trees recreational vehicles largely block restrooms recently constructed on an island in the center of the parking lot. The Visitor Center itself cannot be seen. The wider modern view provides further context for the gate scene by showing the Stone House and the branch road to it.

Visitor Center Vicinity

Roahen's figure 19.5 photograph was taken in June 1951 on the occasion of the battle's seventy-fifth anniversary. It reveals how much this portion of the battlefield has been altered by the necessity for the Park Service to handle a greater number of tourists compared to the 1950s and to assure their comfort and convenience. In the modern counterpart, the restroom building, a recent addition to the area, blocks much of the left portion of Roahen's image. Trees also prevent us from seeing Battle Ridge in the background, which is more visible in Roahen's shot.

In the past twenty-five years, with more emphasis on protecting the environment, the Park Service has enacted much tighter guidelines on where tourists are permitted to walk on the battlefield. Such restrictions obviously were

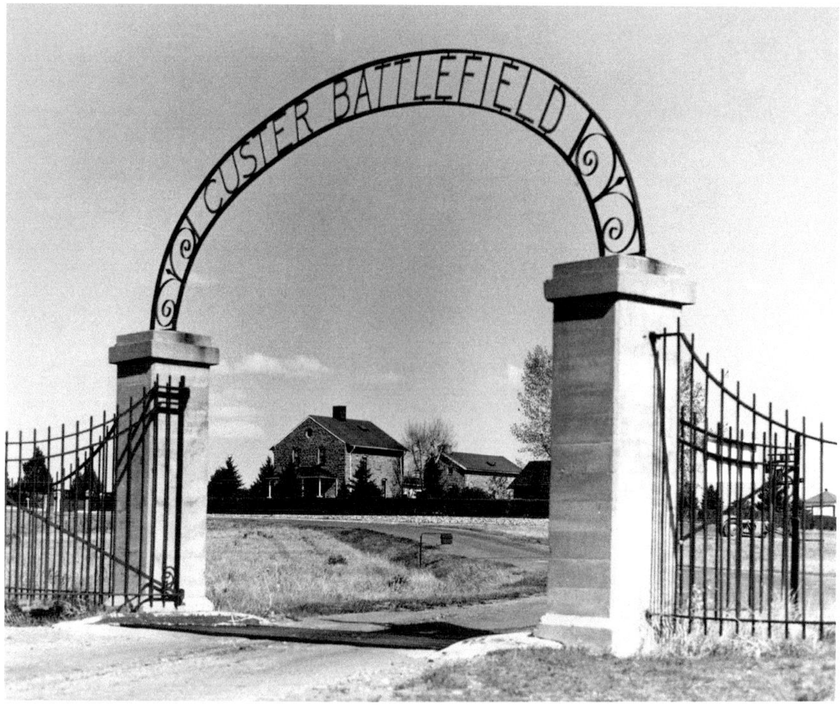

Figure 19.1. (*top*) Original battlefield entrance. Courtesy of Big Horn County Historical Museum. (*bottom*) 2012 reshoot.

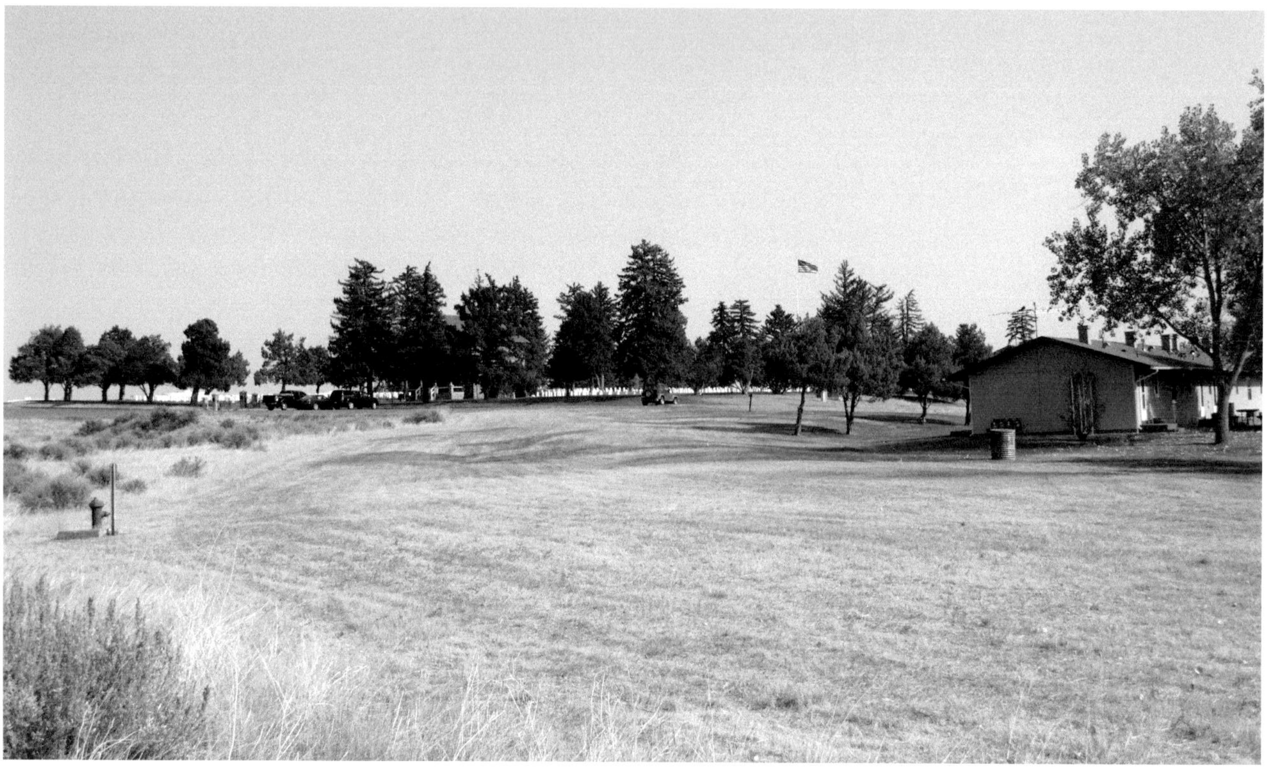

not in force in the mid-1950s. On the left, note automobiles parked on the battlefield, below the ridge that today holds the Indian Memorial. Other vehicles are parked forward of the Visitor Center, which also is forbidden today.

Just as in figure 19.5, Roahen's shot in figure 19.6, which shows Girl Scouts visiting the battlefield in 1958, underscores the changes on today's battlefield.

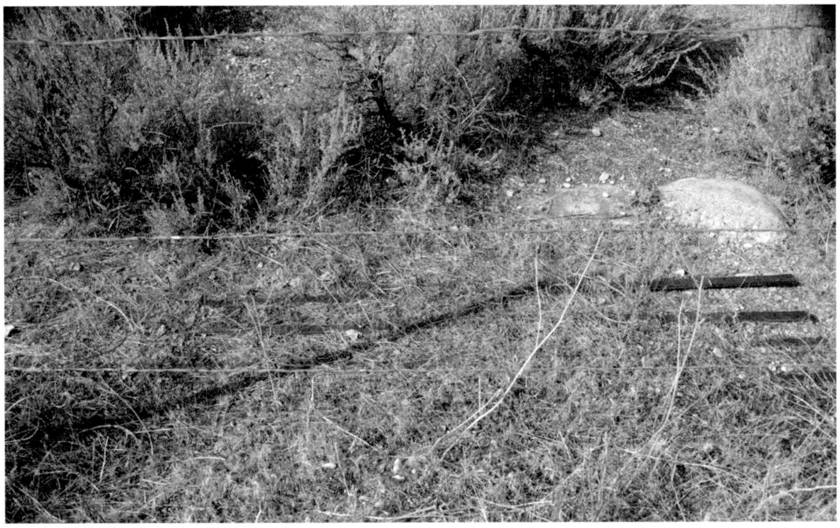

Figure 19.2. Old entrance gate, cattle guard (2012).

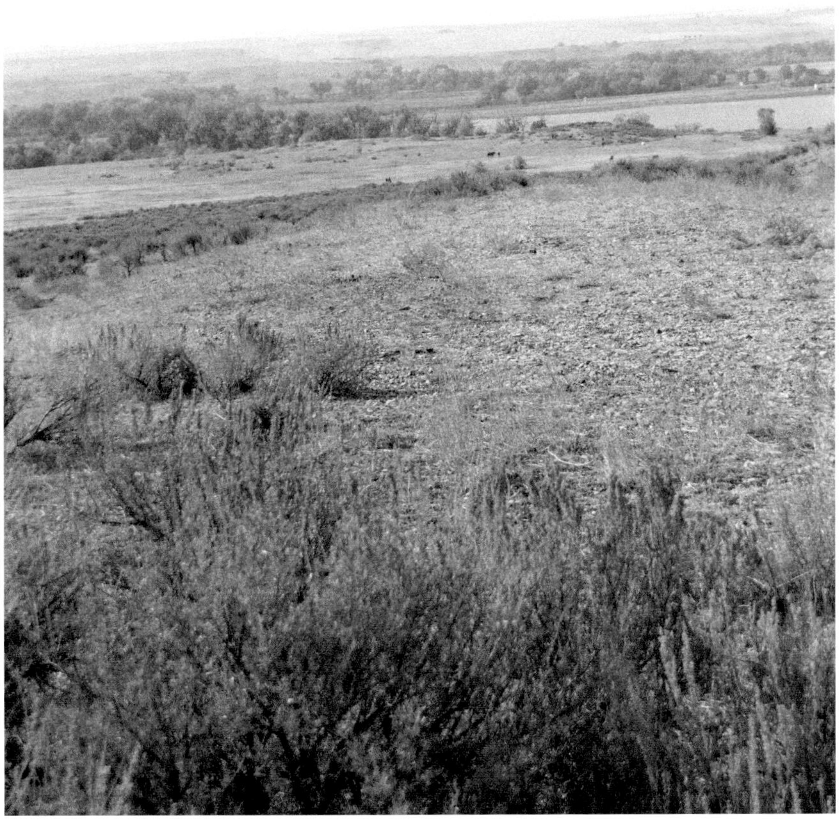

Figure 19.3. Original gate roadway (2012).

Figure 19.4. (*top*) 1957 entrance. Courtesy of Big Horn County Historical Museum. (*bottom*) 2012 reshoot.

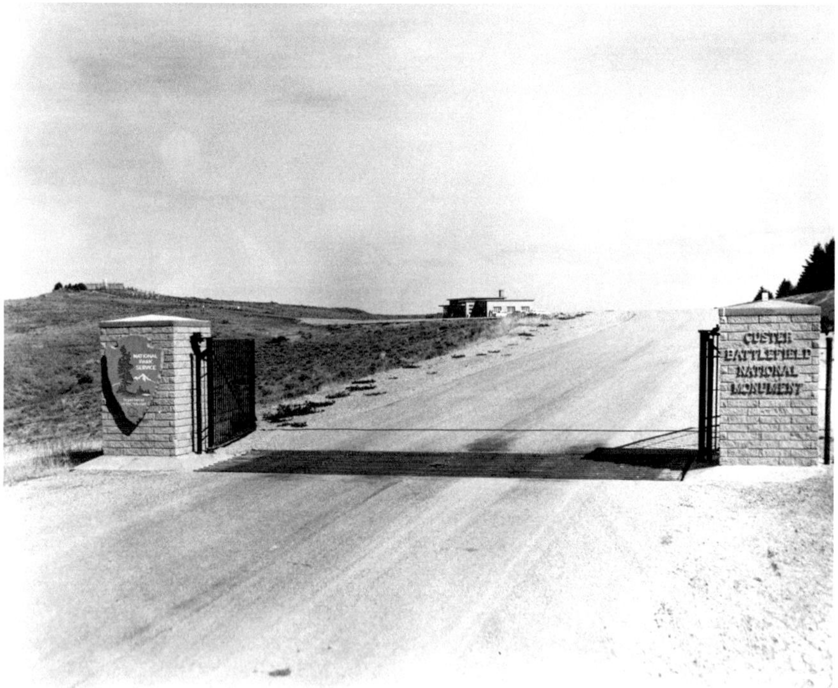

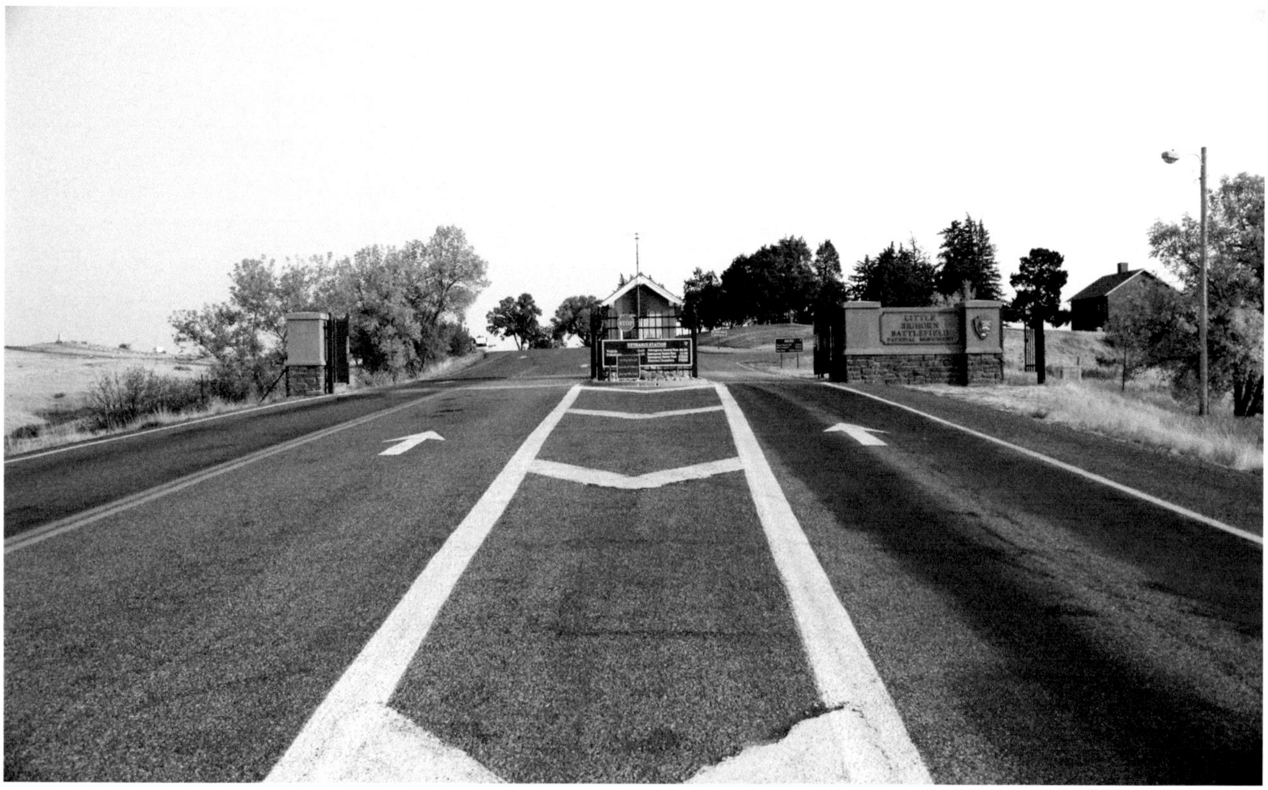

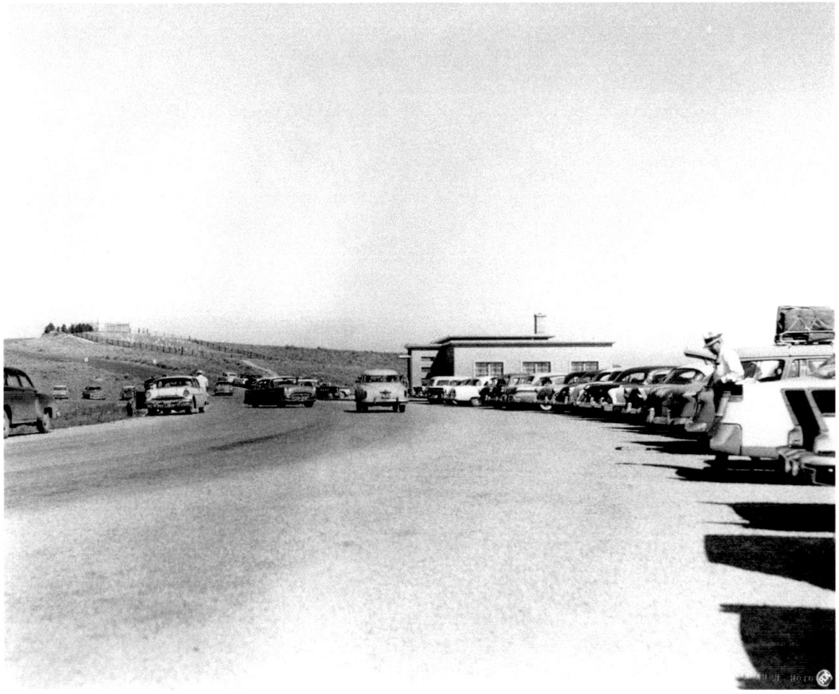

Figure 19.5. (*top*) Parking lot, seventy-fifth anniversary, 1951. Courtesy of Big Horn County Historical Museum. (*bottom*) 2013 reshoot.

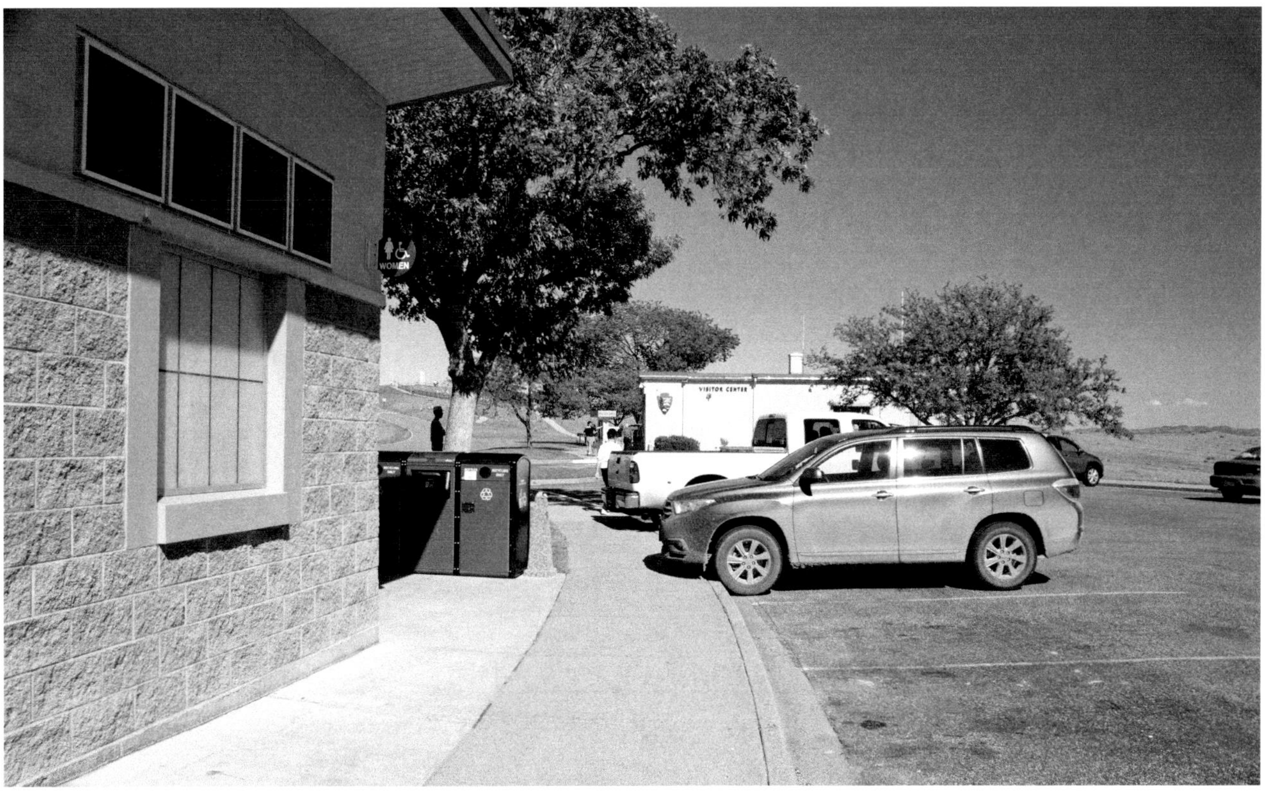

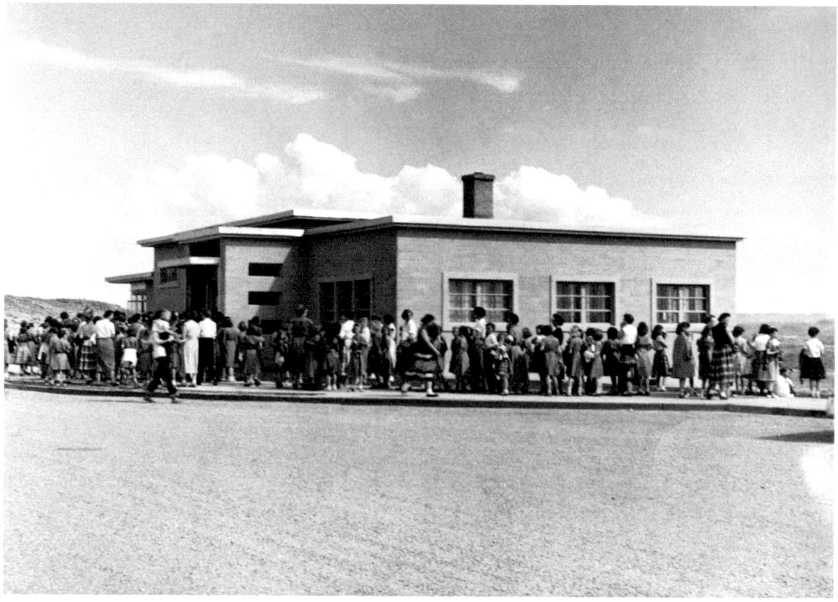

Figure 19.6. (*top*) Girl Scouts at Visitor Center, 1958. Courtesy of Big Horn County Historical Museum. (*bottom*) 2012 reshoot.

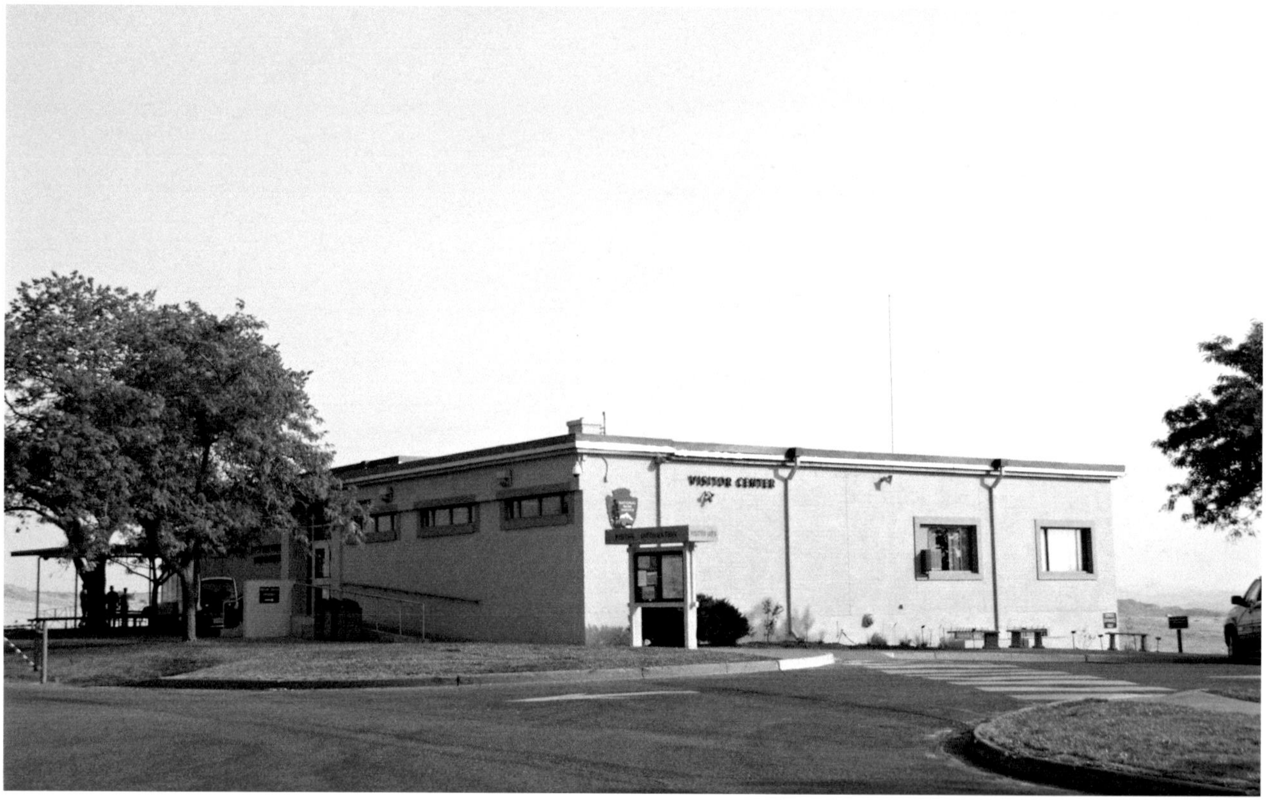

The Visitor Center itself has been altered several times, as has the parking lot's layout. Peeking out on the bottom right of the modern photograph is a corner of the traffic island on which the restrooms sit.

Figure 19.7, again showing the Girl Scouts on their visit in 1958, provides a slightly different view of a portion of the same area. A tree in front of the Visitor Center obscures our view of Last Stand Hill in the modern counterpart.

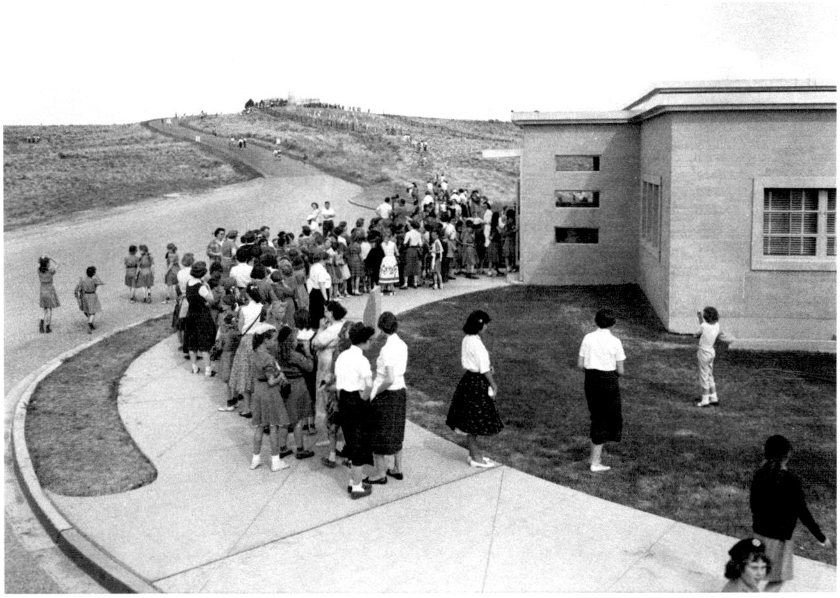

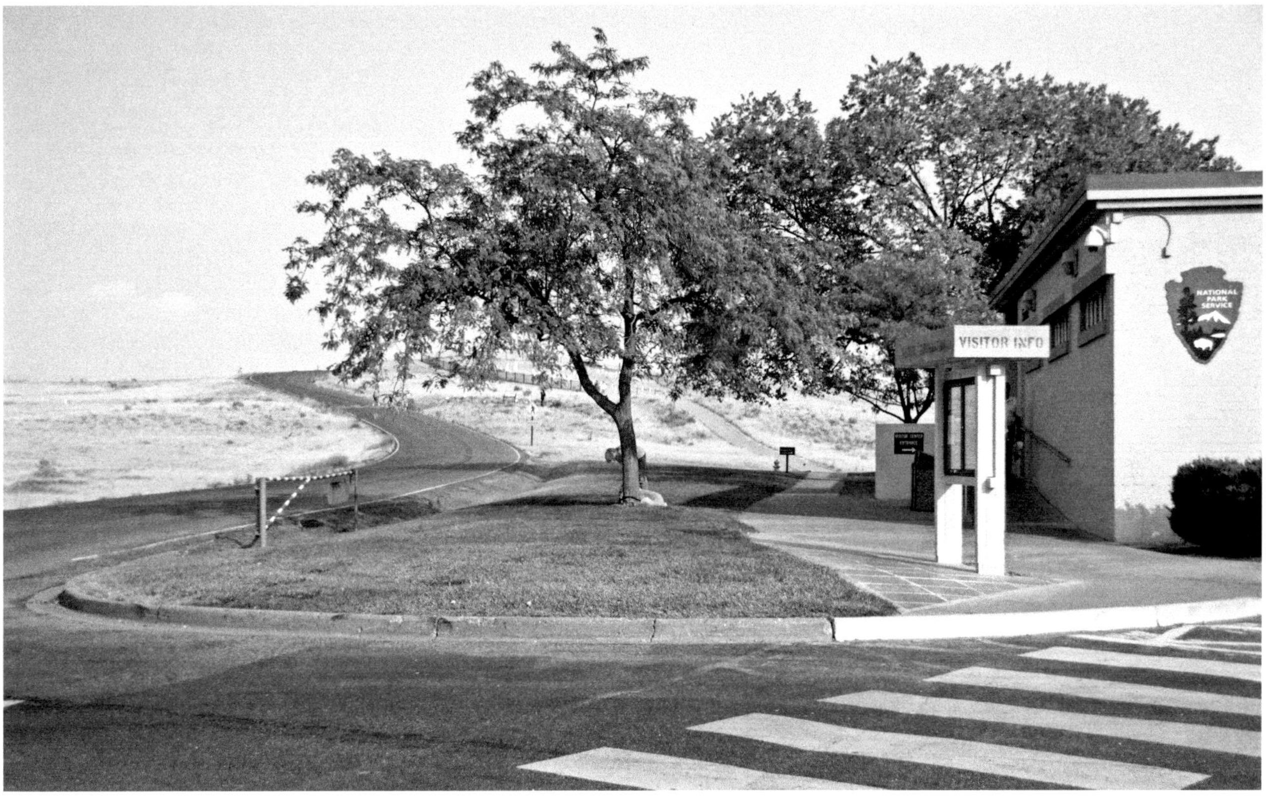

Figure 19.7. (*top*) Girl Scouts and Visitor Center from a different angle. Courtesy of Big Horn County Historical Museum. (*bottom*) 2012 reshoot.

Girl Scouts' 1958 Visit

To shoot his figures 19.8 and 19.9 photos, Roahen mounted his ladder, set up just to the right of the recently constructed entrance road, to capture the Girl Scouts who marched up from the highway below. Both photographs gain significance by providing views of the valley floor prior to construction of both Interstate 90 at its interchange with U.S. Highway 212 as well as the modern commercial zone and Crow Agency buildings, visible in the modern counterpart photos.

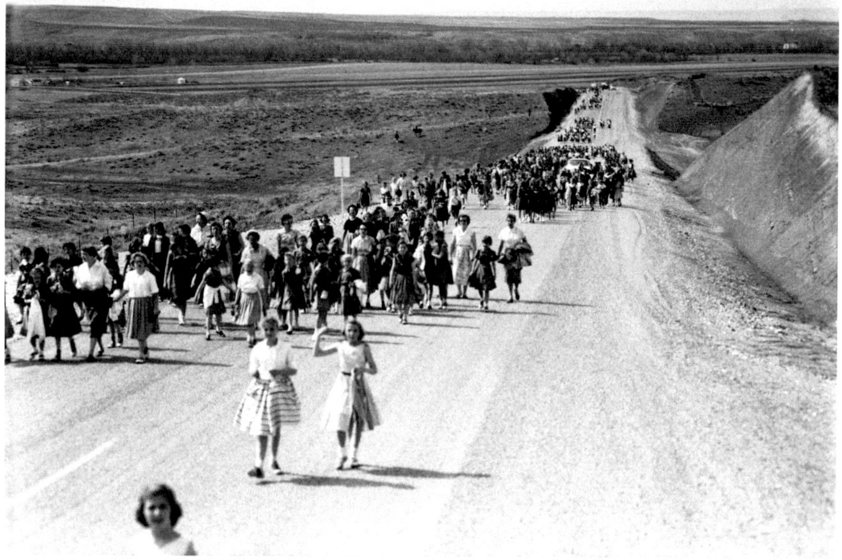

Figure 19.8. (*top*) Girl Scouts marching up the road, before Interstate 90 construction. Courtesy of Big Horn County Historical Museum. (*bottom*) 2013 reshoot.

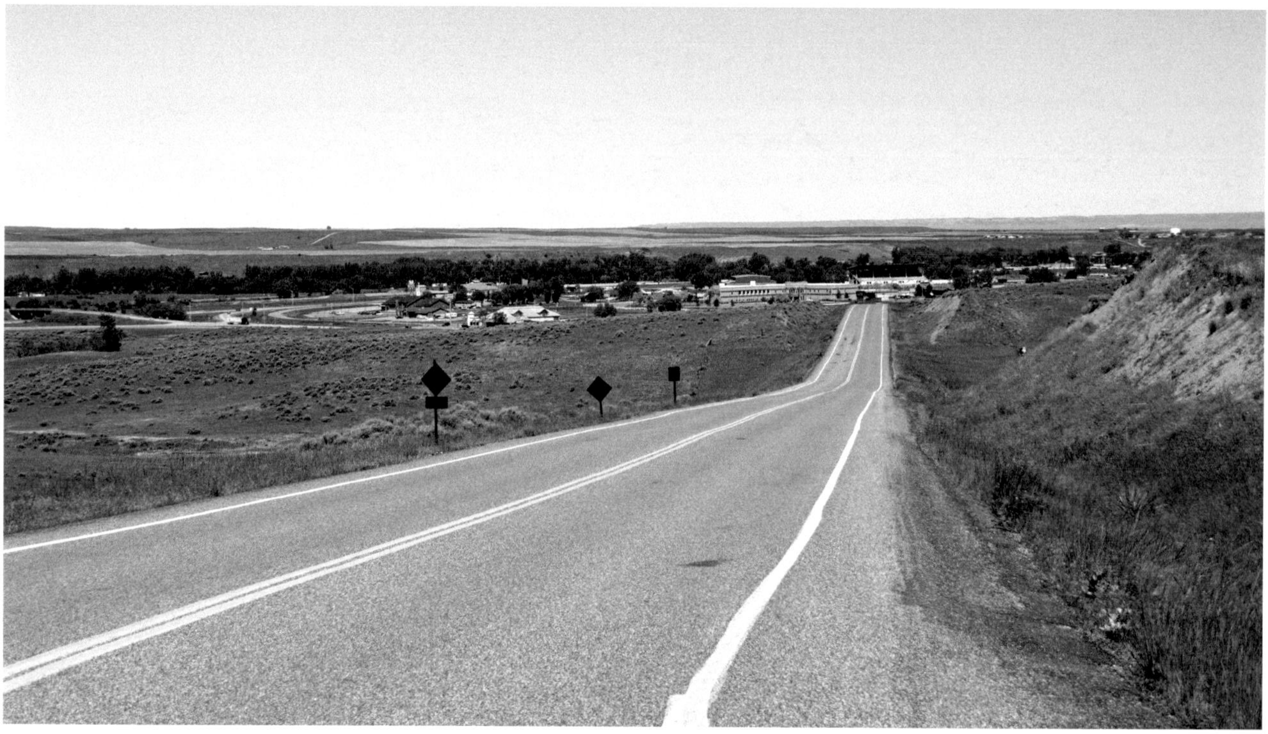

Stone House and Staff Housing

In their battlefield histories, Don Rickey and Jerome Greene document the many changes that have occurred on the historic ground in the more than 139 years since the battle. In 1957, the cemetery road from its gate to the flagpole was reconstructed.[1] Additionally, a concrete sidewalk from the cemetery flagpole to the Visitor Center was constructed. By 1941, sagebrush and other undesirable vegetation had all been removed from the cemetery grounds. Sod replaced the natural plants, and that September 140 evergreen trees were planted.

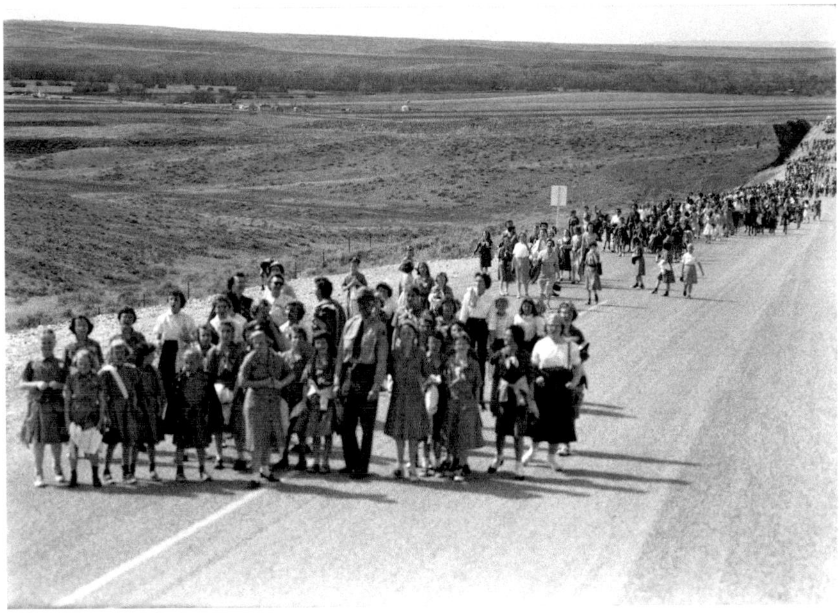

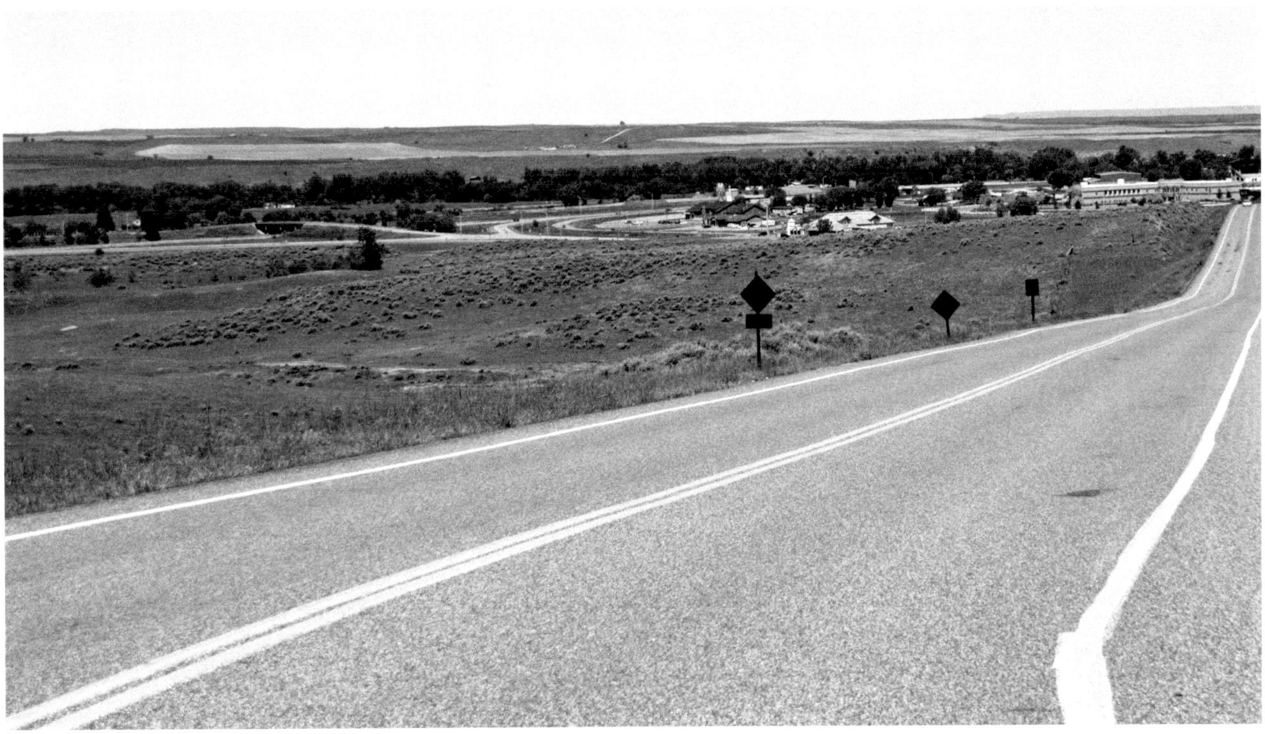

Figure 19.9. (*top*) Variant of Girl Scouts walking up the road. Courtesy of Big Horn County Historical Museum. (*bottom*) 2013 reshoot.

At least three Roahen photographs in the Big Horn County Historical Museum collection document some of these changes in the vicinity of the Stone House, constructed in 1894. Roahen's figure 19.10 photo is undated but, given the height of the trees, he likely shot it in the mid-1940s, if not slightly later. Several of his aerial photographs taken at the time of the seventy-fifth battle anniversary ceremony in 1951 indicate that the trees were taller than they appear in this shot. Also of significance, an "Office" sign hangs on a window

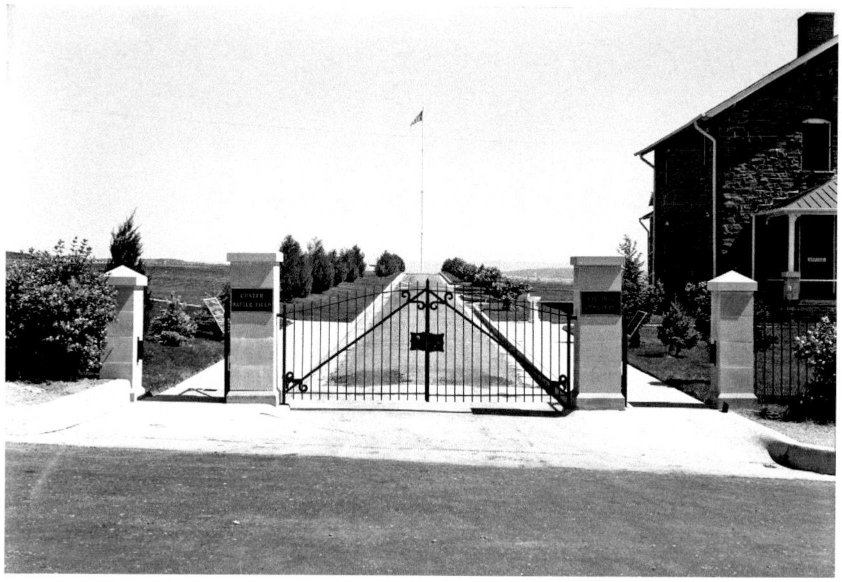

Figure 19.10. (*top*) Cemetery entrance by Stone House. Courtesy of Big Horn County Historical Museum. (*bottom*) 2013 reshoot.

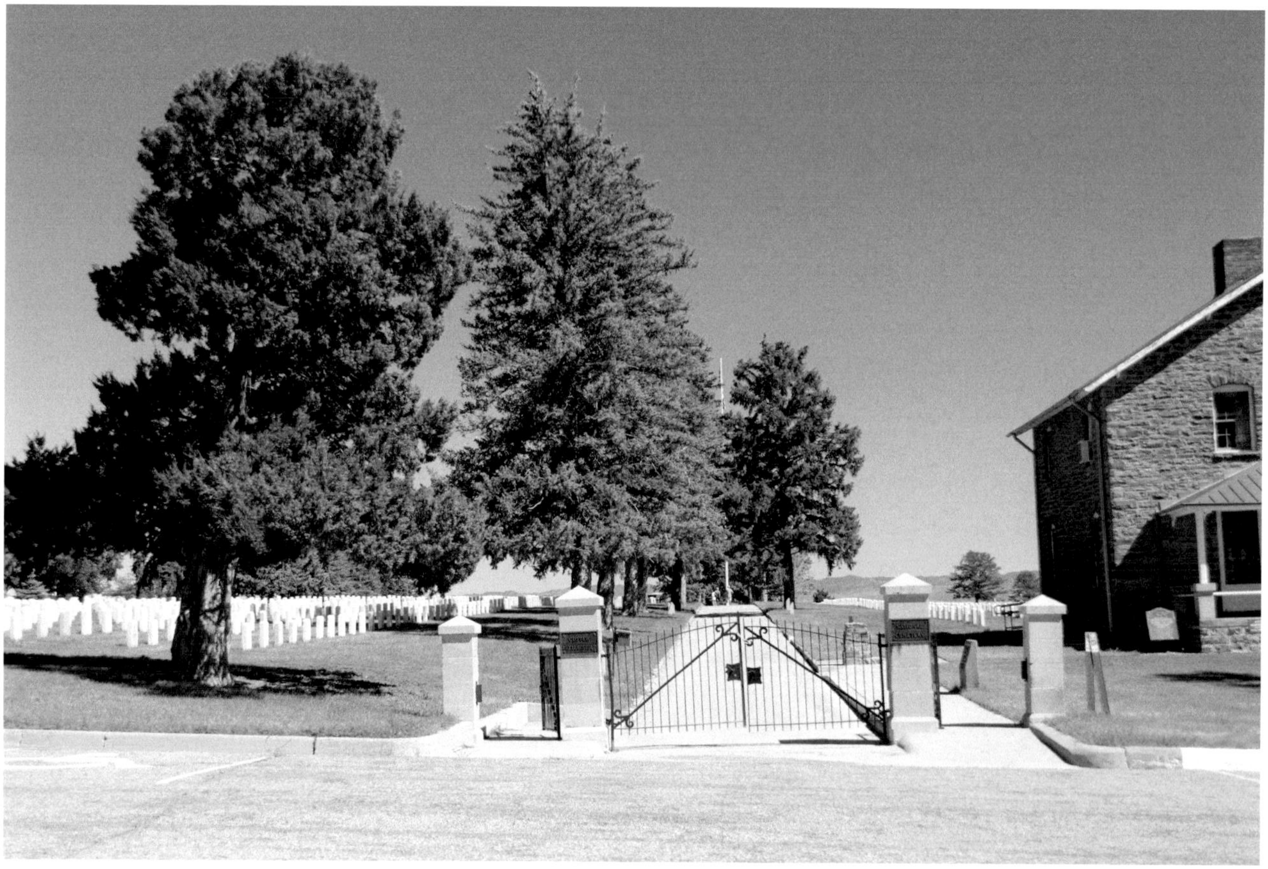

of the Stone House, indicating that the Visitor Center had not yet replaced the former building as the park's new administrative headquarters. Roahen's figure 19.11 photo is also undated, but again the trees appear taller than in figure 19.10.

The vegetation in figure 19.12 again indicates that it was taken later than figure 19.11. In the former, the trees on the left that appear in both images are taller. By the time figure 19.12 was taken, however, some trees on both sides

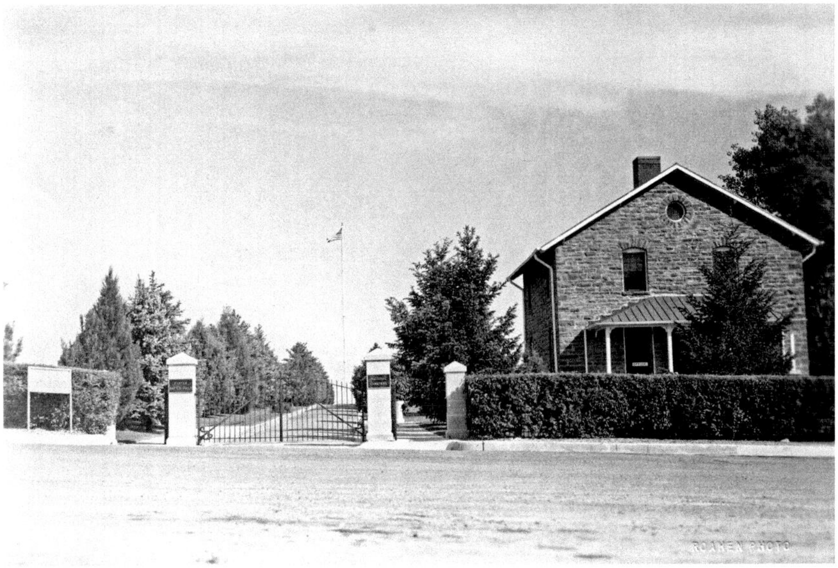

Figure 19.11. (*top*) Stone House front. Courtesy of Big Horn County Historical Museum. (*bottom*) 2013 reshoot.

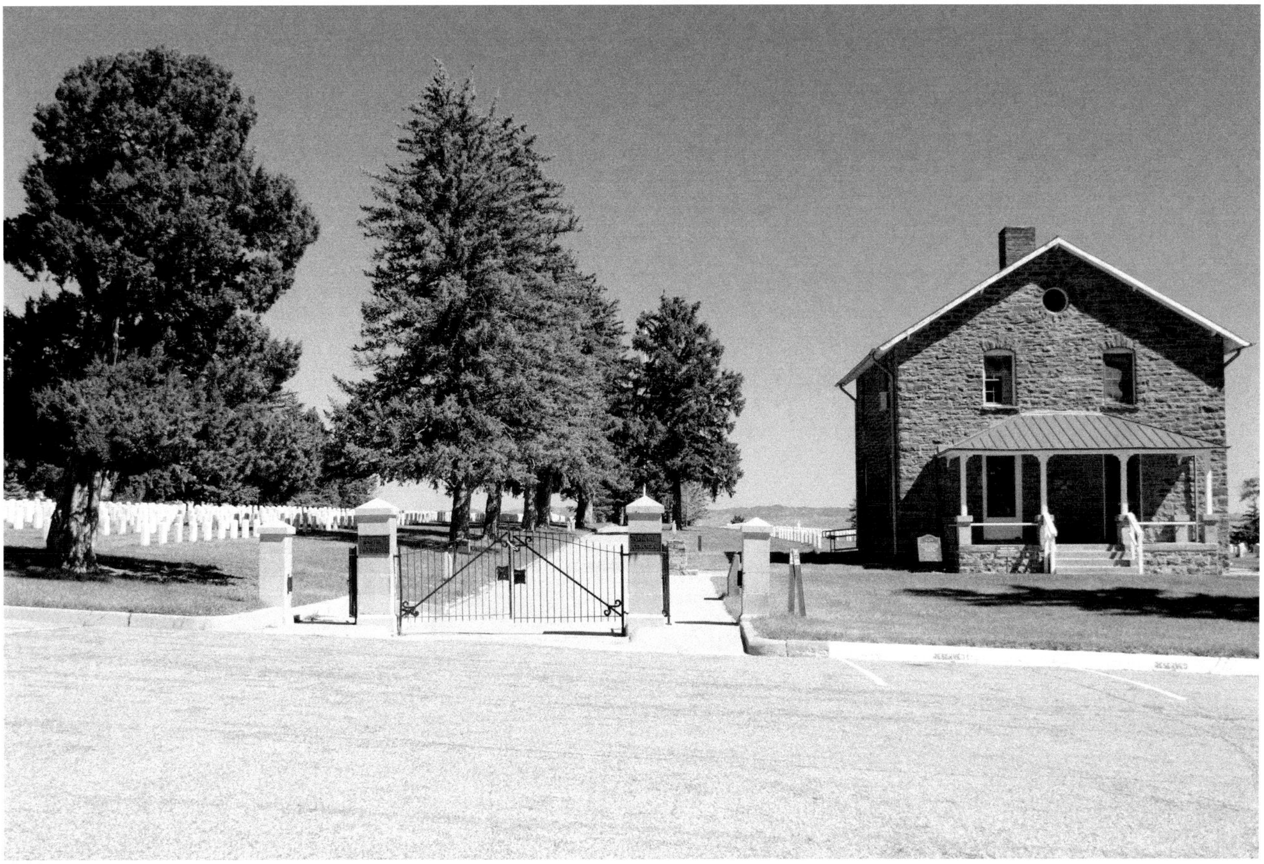

of the concrete walkway had been removed. In Roahen's figure 19.11 image, an arrow sign on the left, reading "Office," points left in the general direction along the road to the now-completed Visitor Center. Finally, we can see two distinctive changes on the right side of Roahen's figure 19.12 shot. The tree on the front lawn of the Stone House appears slightly taller. Additionally, the tallest tree in this series of Stone House/cemetery photographs on the right

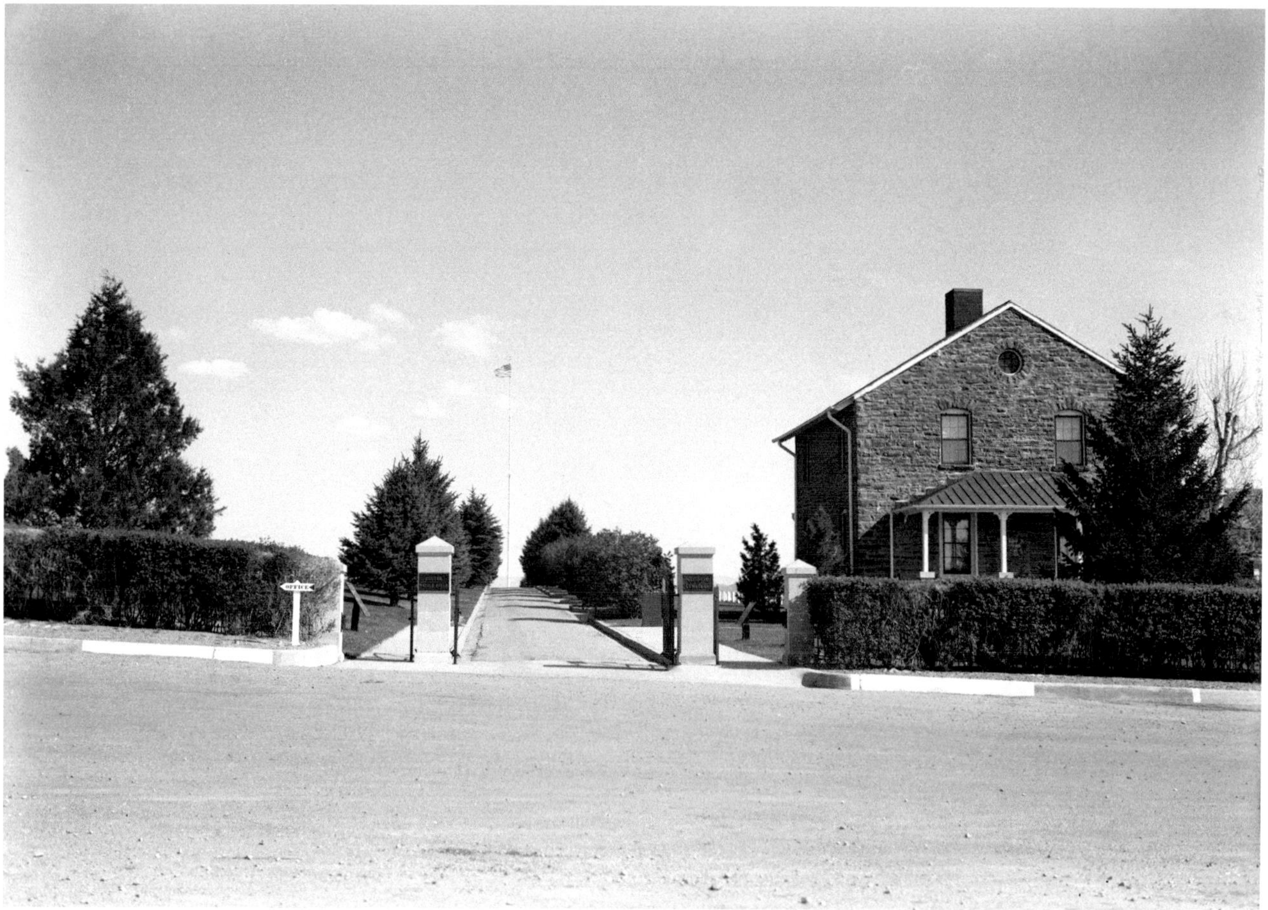

Figure 19.12. Cemetery entrance by Stone House, a later variant of fig. 19.11. Courtesy of Big Horn County Historical Museum.

appears to have died. It has no leaves and has been trimmed below the roofline of the historic structure.

Roahen's figure 19.13 photo shows apparent construction near the Park Service housing area, located below the Stone House parking lot. Roahen probably took this photograph around 1962. Rickey reported that the three single-family houses to the left were completed in 1961. The building on the right is a four-unit apartment building which, along with a maintenance/utility building and a pump house, was constructed in 1962. Construction seems to have been completed on the apartments, but it may be continuing on the other facilities if the muddy area in the foreground is any indication.

Today, all the buildings remain in use by the Park Service, including the apartment building on the right. Although not visible in Roahen's photo or its modern counterpart, the old entrance road ran behind the apartments. Several years ago, the Park Service renovated and expanded the first house on the left. Many of the park's administrative offices, including the superintendent's, that were formerly housed in the Visitor Center were moved to this enlarged facility.

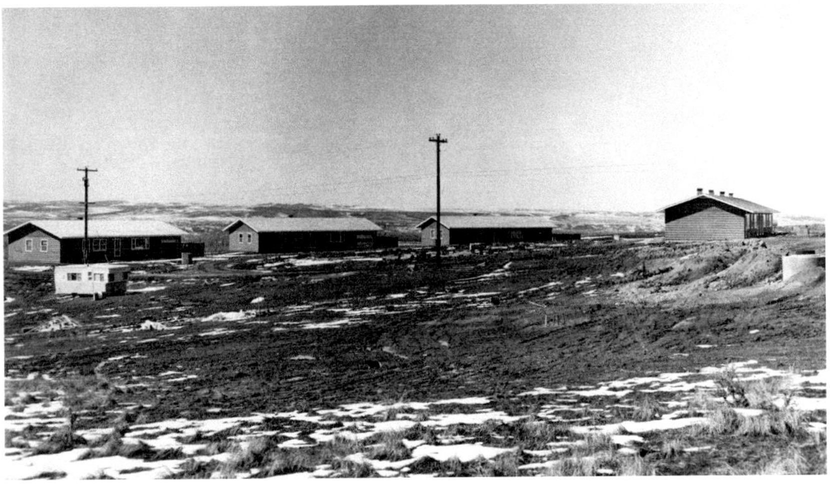

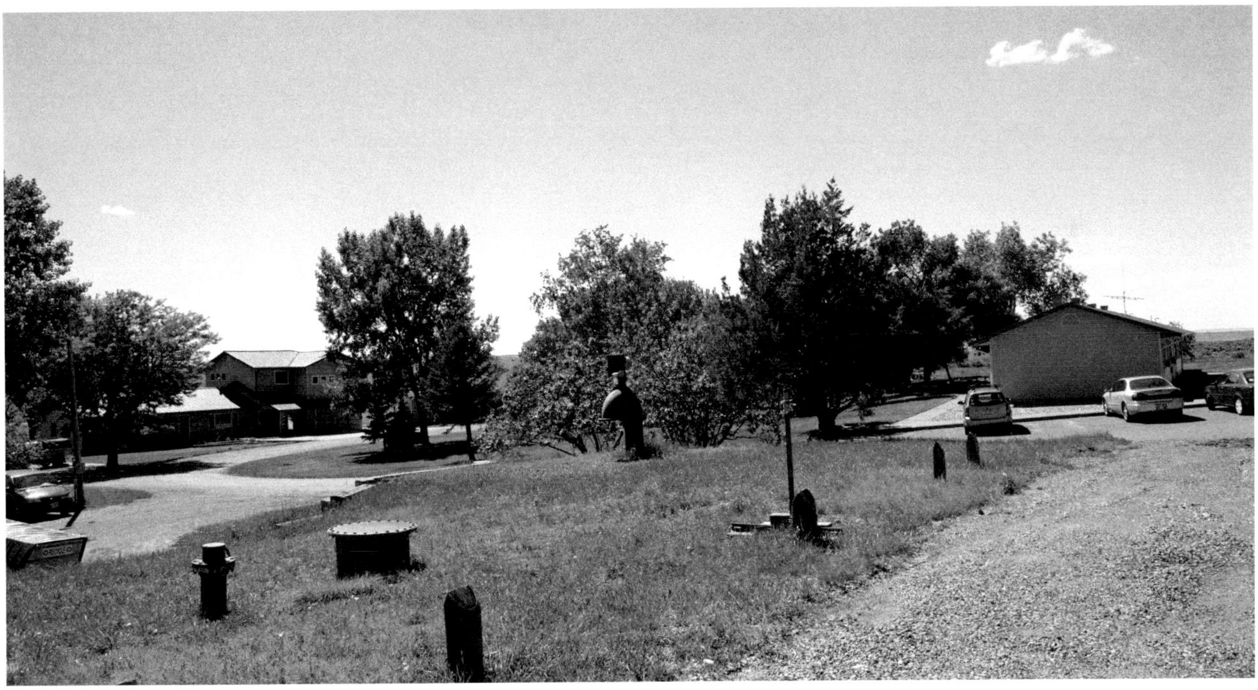

Figure 19.13. (*top*) Family housing construction, ca. 1962. Courtesy of Big Horn County Historical Museum. (*bottom*) 2013 reshoot.

Custer National Cemetery

In 1893, Andrew N. Grover was appointed the first superintendent of Custer National Cemetery. Four years later, he urged that a rostrum for memorial services be constructed, but it would take nearly forty years before the government acted on his suggestion. In 1934, the War Department, which had administrative responsibility for Custer Battlefield, began constructing the long-discussed rostrum in the northwest corner of the national cemetery, an area that was not being used for burials. According to Greene's history, the rostrum measured 14.5 by 23 feet and was built of native stone and concrete, with wooden ceiling and a stone podium.[2] For many years the rostrum was used for ceremonies on Memorial Day and other occasions. In 1965, it was demolished and adjoining sidewalks were removed. This portion of the cemetery's Section F was restored for burial use.

Figure 19.14. (*top*) Speakers' rostrum and crowd, seventy-fifth battle anniversary, June 1951. (*bottom*) 2013 reshoot.

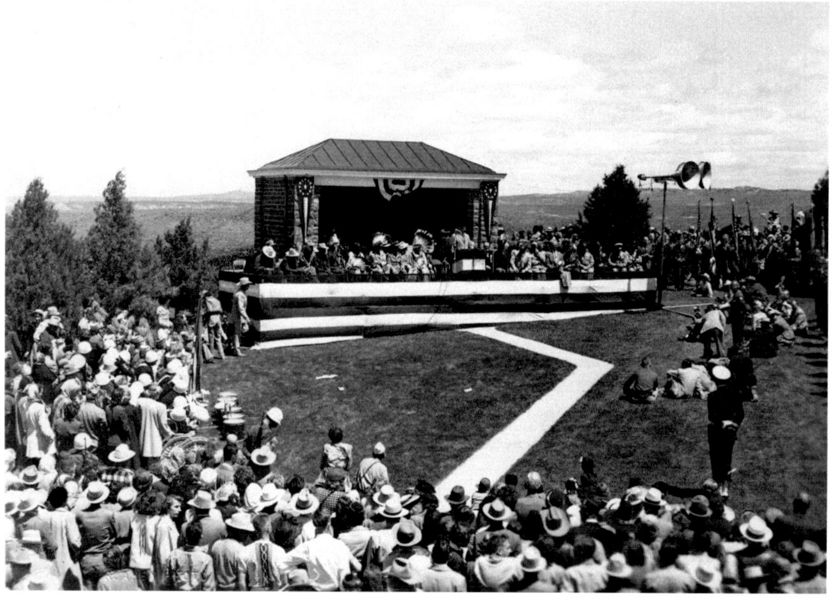

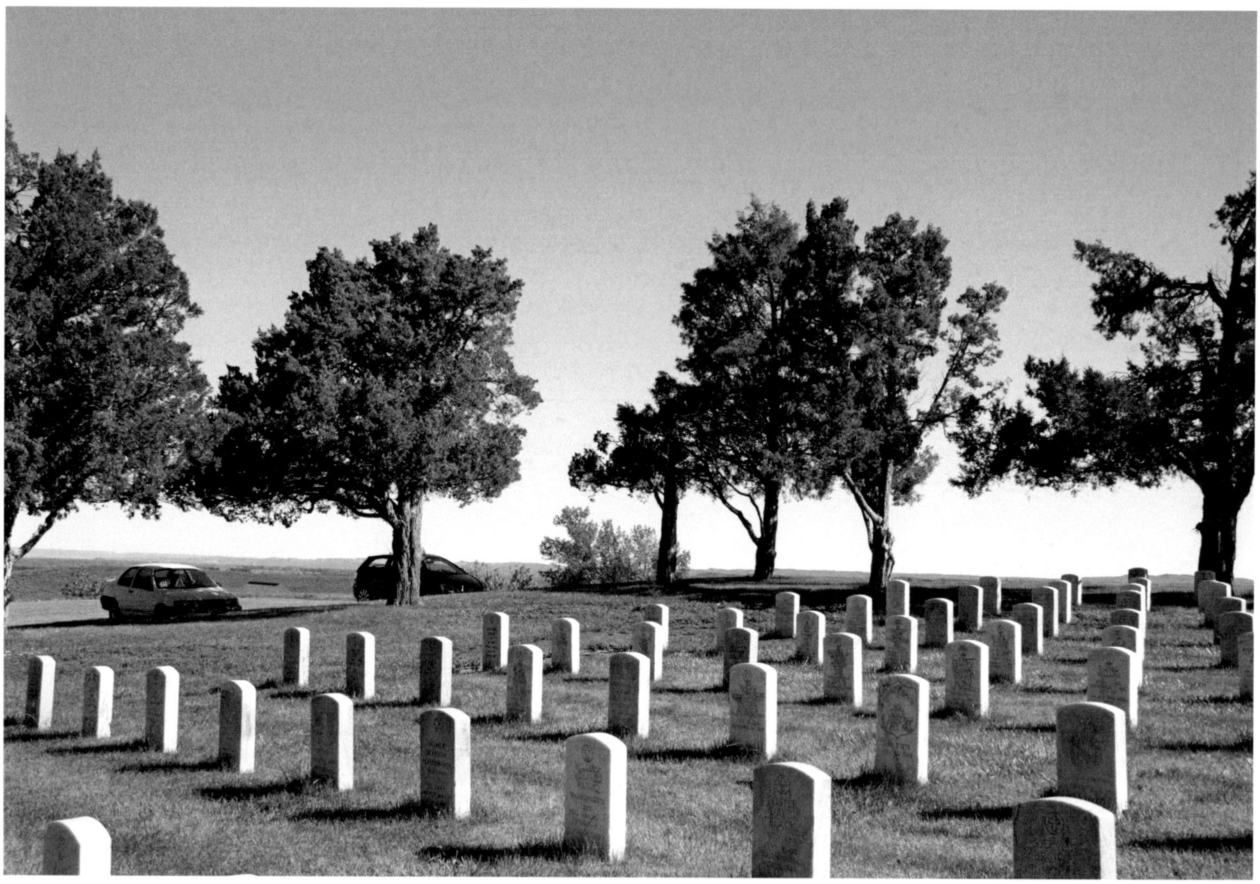

Although it was dedicated on Memorial Day 1935, no photographs of that ceremony are included in the Roahen collection at the Big Horn County Historical Museum. Why Roahen was absent on that occasion is unknown. Inasmuch as it took place during his most active period of Montana service with the U.S. Fish and Wildlife Service, likely his government duties kept him away.

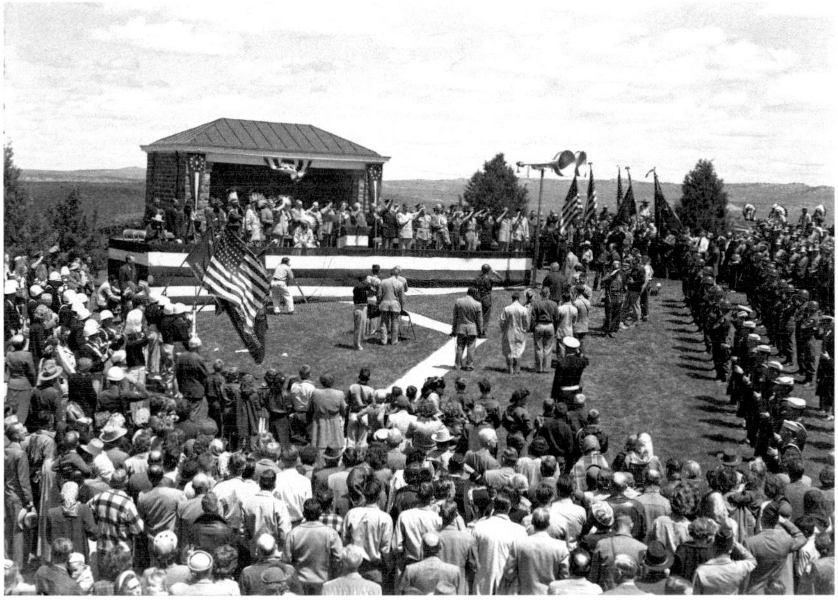

Figure 19.15. (*top*) Seventy-fifth battle anniversary, June 1951, troops saluting. Courtesy of Big Horn County Historical Museum. (*bottom*) 2013 reshoot, arrows indicate edges of rostrum.

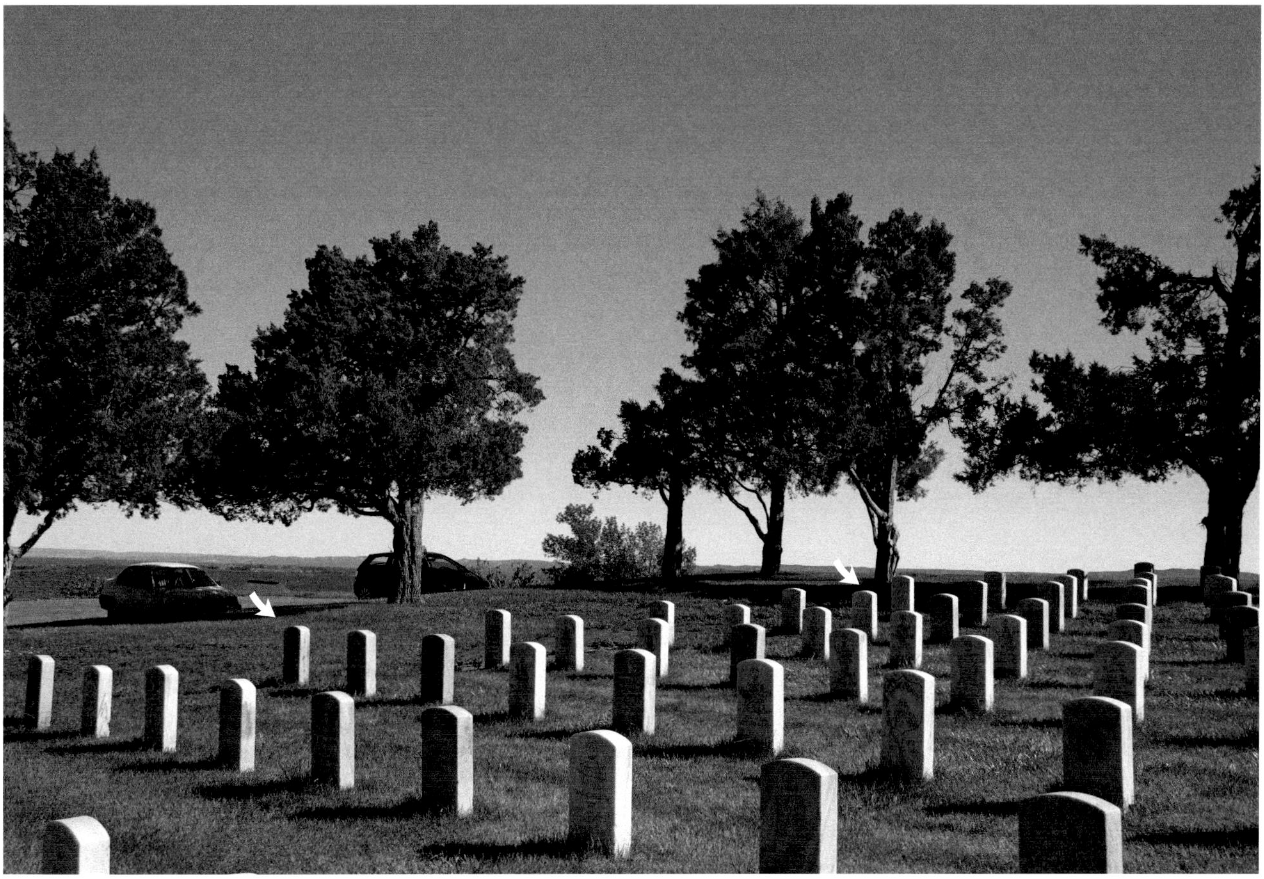

On June 25, 1951, however, on the occasion of the battle's seventy-fifth anniversary, Roahen was very much present, taking historically significant photos from the air and on the ground. His photographs in figures 19.14 and 19.15 provide excellent views of the rostrum and anniversary ceremonies (for his aerial photographs, see chapter 21). These two ground images, taken as he

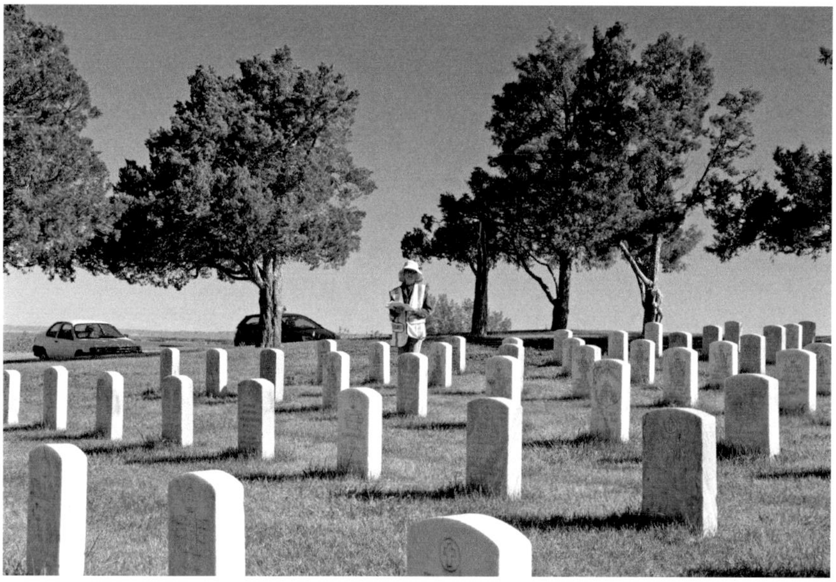

Figure 19.16. This 2013 reshoot matches the turn in the Rostrum path, figs. 19.14 and 19.15. Betty Barnard is in the center of the photograph.

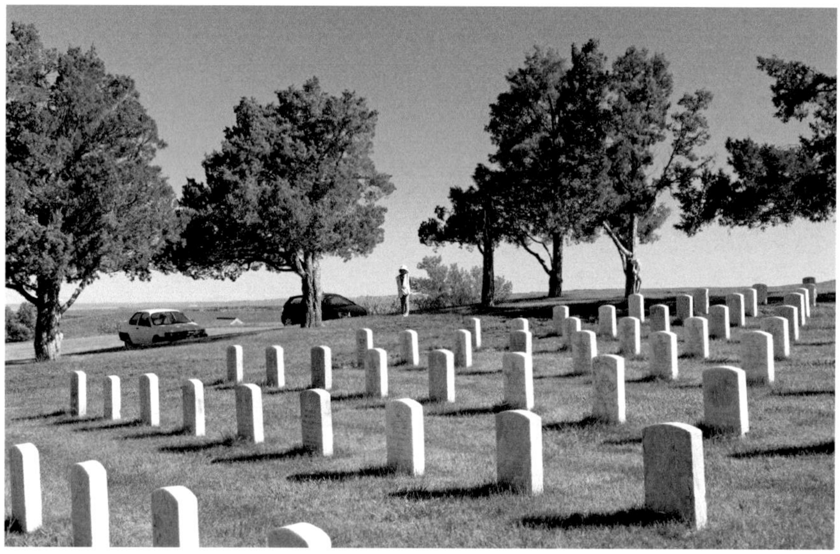

Figure 19.17. This 2013 photo also matches figs. 19.14 and 19.15, with Betty Barnard in rear center.

stood on his ladder, make clear that dignitaries at the ceremonies included a mix of civilians and military leaders as well as numerous American Indians. Figure 19.15 shows the military personnel saluting. On the far left of that photograph, about its middle third, a park ranger can be seen standing at attention. That individual has been identified as historian Robert M. Utley, then a young seasonal ranger at the battlefield. He has long ranked among the significant historians researching and writing about the Battle of the Little Big Horn and the Plains Indian wars.

Both show the general vicinity of where the rostrum stood for thirty years; one of them (fig. 19.15 reshoot) is marked to indicate the edges of the rostrum itself. Two other modern photos provide further information: in figure 19.16, Betty Barnard is standing at the point where the sidewalk from the Stone House (not in view) turned at an angle and ran toward the rostrum itself. In figure 19.17, she is standing in the center of the rostrum area itself.

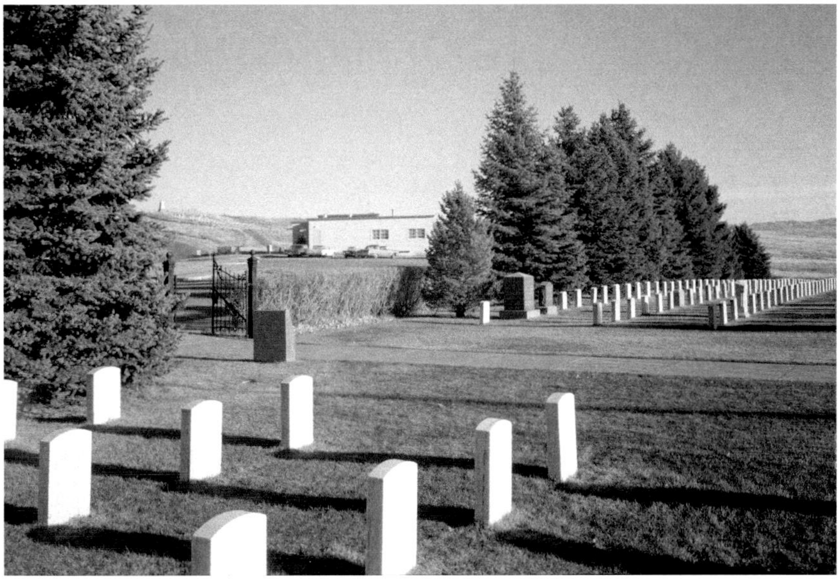

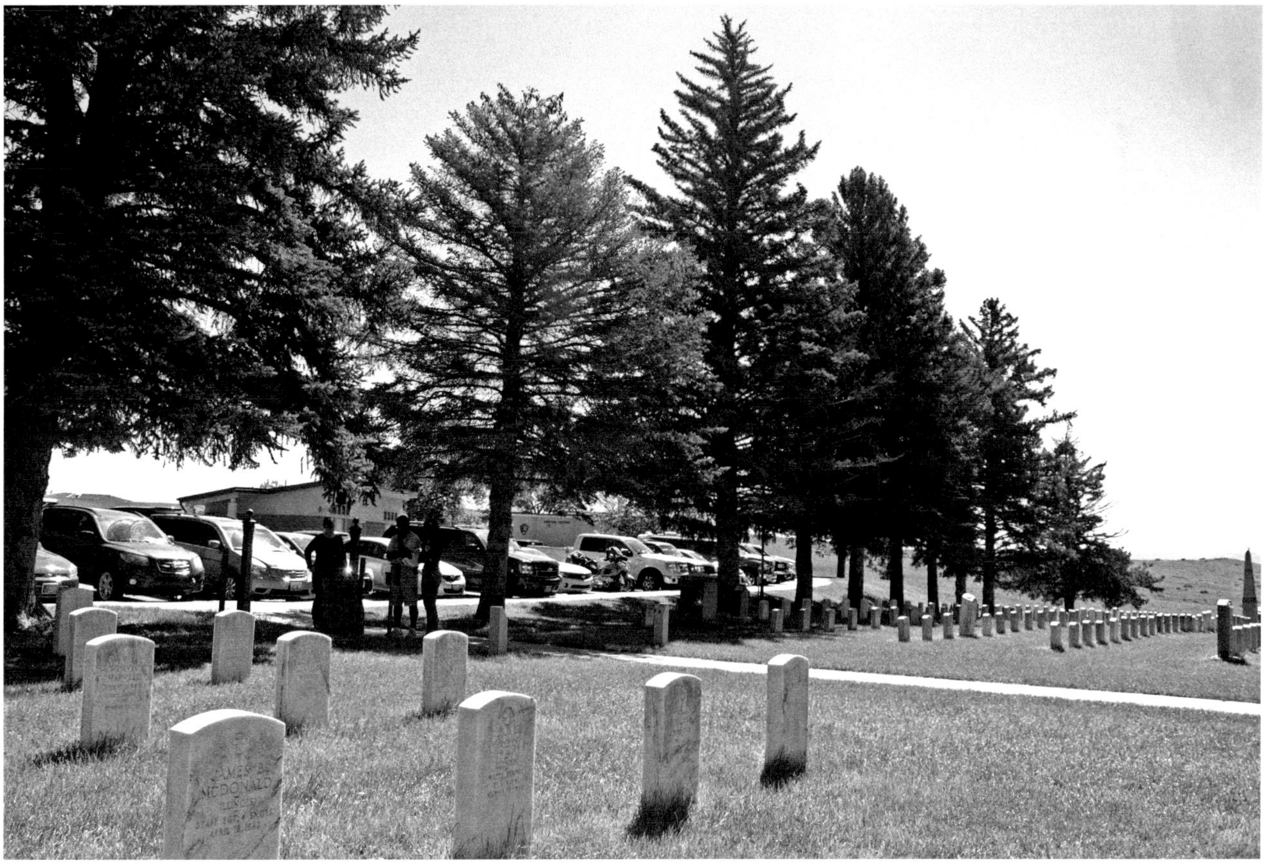

Figure 19.18. (*top*) Custer National Cemetery, main gate; Visitor Center visible in rear. Courtesy of Big Horn County Historical Museum. (*bottom*) 2013 reshoot.

Roahen's figure 19.18 photo not only provides a unique view of the Visitor Center and Custer Hill in the background but also is one of the few available in color. The image he obtained in the 1950s is, however, more difficult to match today. As its modern counterpart shows, much taller trees obscure the scene. Also, the modern restrooms on the parking lot island completely block the view of Custer Hill. Instead, on the photograph's far left, just above

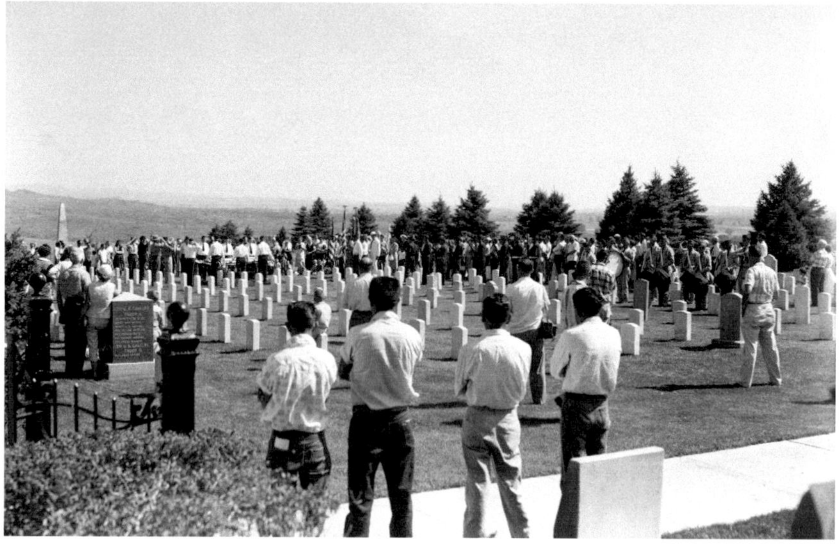

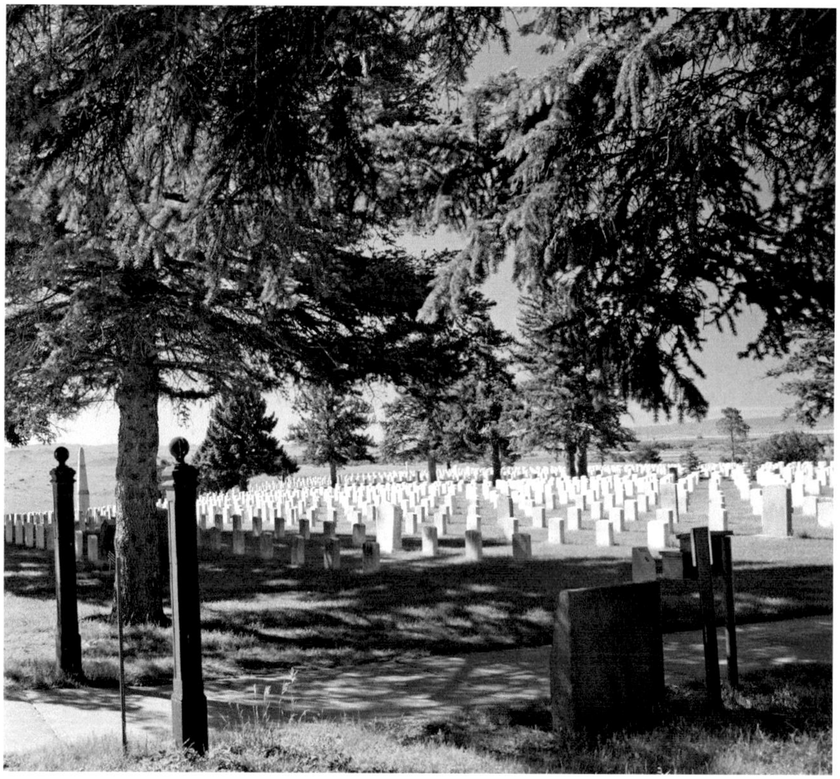

Figure 19.19. (*top*) Crowd watching reburial of 7th Cavalry remains, August 1958. Courtesy of Big Horn County Historical Museum. (*bottom*) 2013 reshoot.

the automobiles in the parking lot, we can make out one side of the Indian Memorial, which was dedicated on June 25, 2003.[3]

Two similar Roahen photographs, figures 19.19 and 19.20, show another view of the cemetery's main gate, taken during a reburial service for 7th Cavalry remains in August 1958. The modern view, taken in June 2013, reveals that the scene remains much the same. The trees are taller, of course, and some markers have either been broken or replaced. The fence itself has been removed, apparently to make access easier for visitors, but the posts and odd-shaped historical marker appear to be the same.

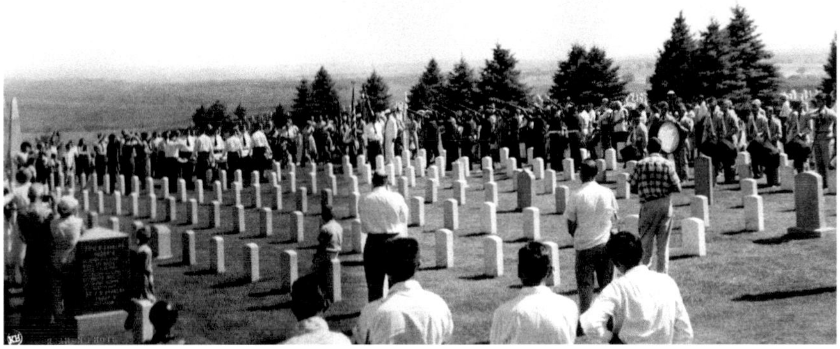

Figure 19.20. Variant of fig. 19.19 reburial ceremony. Courtesy of Big Horn County Historical Museum.

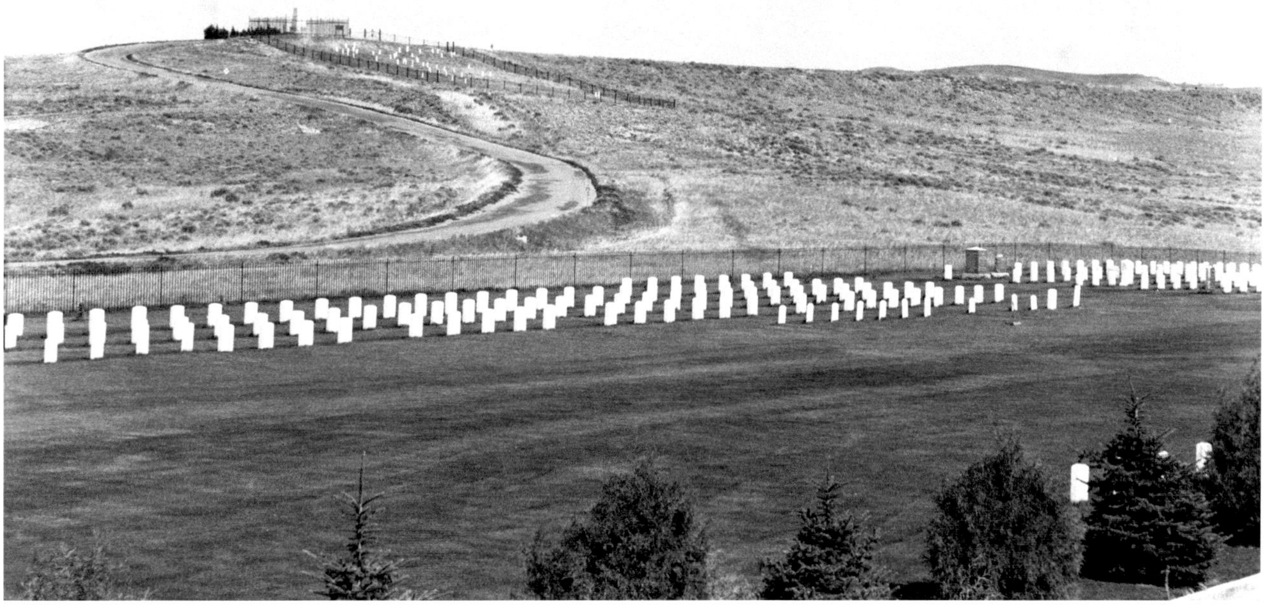

Figure 19.21. Last Stand Hill from Custer National Cemetery, pre-1952. Courtesy of Big Horn County Historical Museum.

Figure 19.21, which looks across Section F of the National Cemetery to Last Stand Hill, is unusual in several ways. For one, Roahen shot it in the late 1940s or quite early in the 1950s; it obviously predates the construction of the Visitor Center in 1951–52. Second, the cemetery's trees are still low-growth and do not obstruct the historic scene. Unfortunately, the modern situation prevented us from reshooting it. Roahen apparently stood on the second floor of the Stone House and shot his photo through an open rear window. In 2012, we faced insurmountable obstacles. The window was essentially locked shut and could not be opened; it was dirty and covered with dead insects, and the

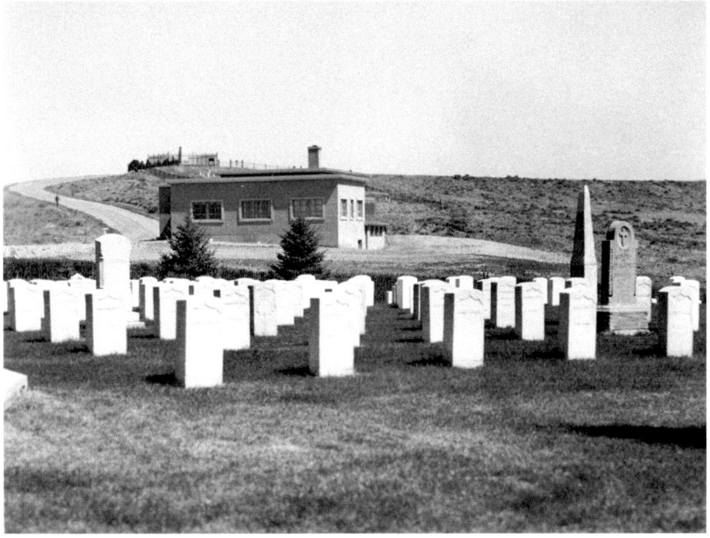

Figure 19.22. (*top*) Custer National Cemetery toward Last Stand Hill. Courtesy of Big Horn County Historical Museum. (*bottom*) 2012 reshoot.

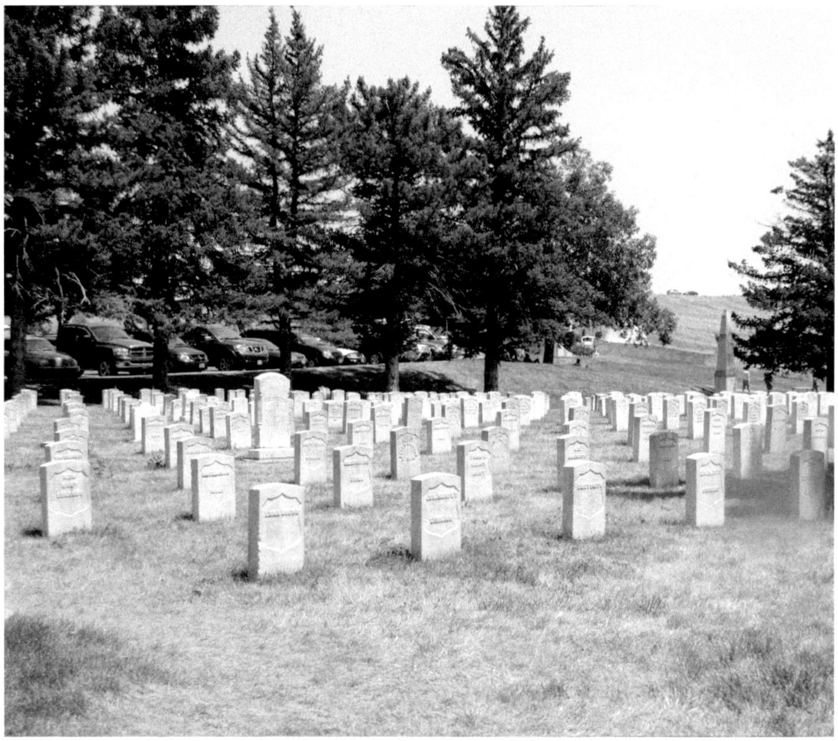

cemetery trees had grown so tall that no view of what had once been an open scene to Last Stand Hill was possible. The Visitor Center and modern restrooms further obscure the modern view.

Inasmuch as the Visitor Center had been completed by the time he took his figure 19.22 shot, we can determine that it is likely from early June 1952 during a quiet moment at the battlefield. No sign of tourists can be seen. On the photograph's right rear, the Fort C. F. Smith Memorial, moved to the cemetery in 1892, stands well above all but two of the other grave markers. On the far left, just a small triangular stone can be seen; it actually is a small part of the base of a large block-like monument that commemorates the 5th Infantry

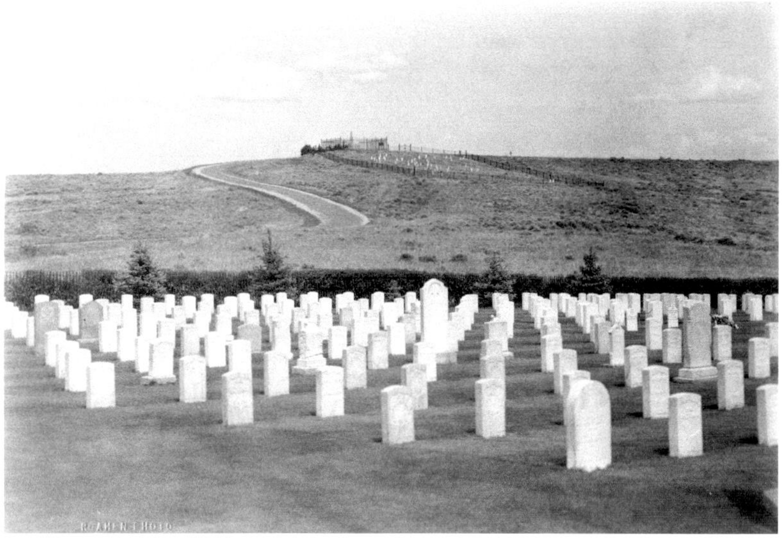

Figure 19.23. (*top*) Wider view of Custer National Cemetery toward Last Stand Hill. Courtesy of Big Horn County Historical Museum. (*bottom*) 2013 reshoot.

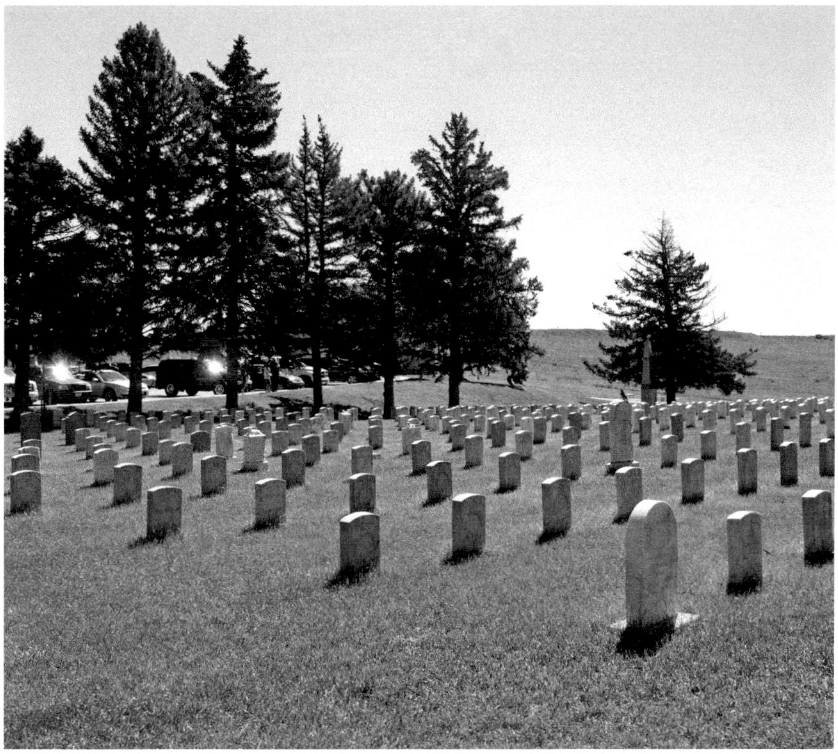

and was moved to the cemetery in 1908. This photograph's modern counterpart is actually a panorama created in 2012. Both the Fort Smith marker and the left-side tall marker remain in their early 1950s positions, but a tall gray marker just in front of the Smith marker on the right has been replaced. More graves fill out the scene. The Visitor Center is mostly blocked by the much taller trees, and the shorter fence that formerly surrounded the cemetery, visible in Roahen's image, is gone today.

Roahen's photo in figure 19.23 is similar to that in figure 19.22, except, of course, that it predates the Visitor Center and is slightly northwest of figure 19.22. The tall stone in the right foreground of figure 19.23 is actually the one

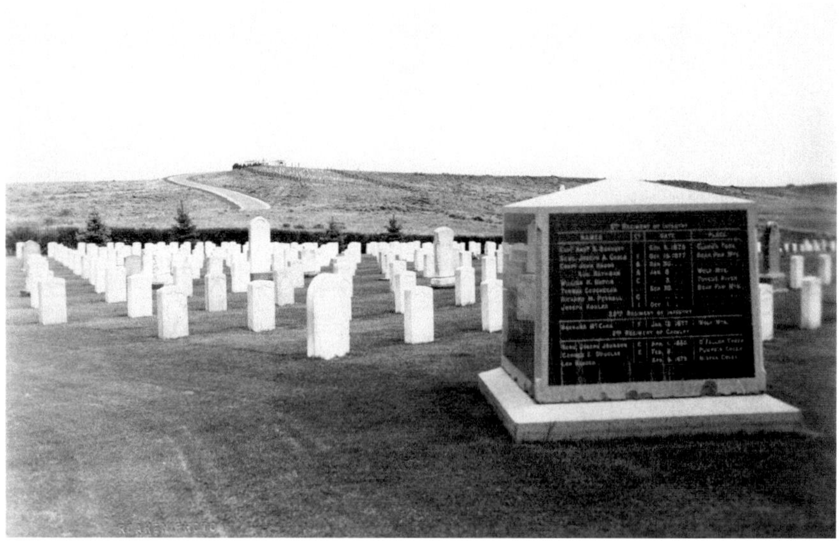

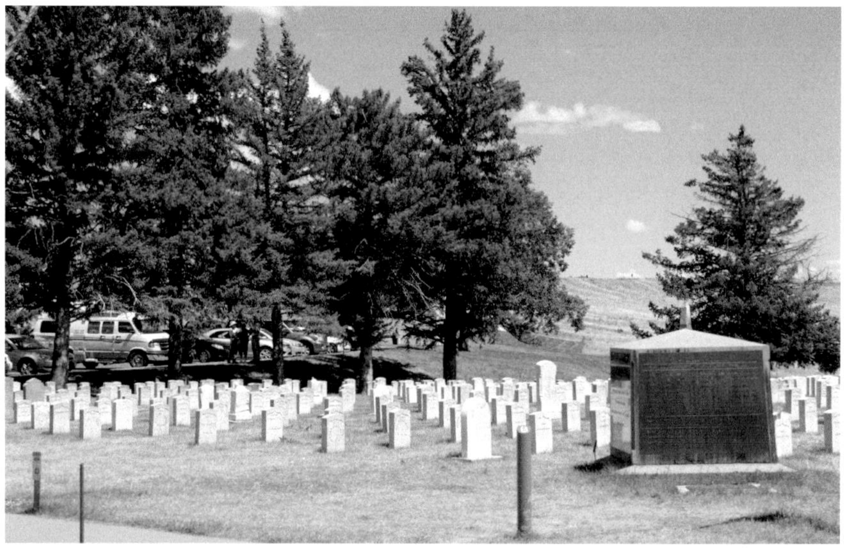

Figure 19.24. (*top*) Custer National Cemetery toward Last Stand Hill, pre-1952. Courtesy of Big Horn County Historical Museum. (*bottom*) 2012 reshoot.

on the far left of figure 19.22. The taller marker in the center of figure 19.23 does not appear in the other photo. The modern figure 19.23 photo was shot wider to include the Fort C. F. Smith marker for perspective. The right-side tall marker is clearly visible today and is the one with a bird sitting on it. Note, though, that the tall marker in the center of Roahen's figure 19.23 photo is missing. Nothing but a stub of a grave marker appears in its place. That site is still flanked by grave markers for children, which are the stones with the lambs on top. Finally, in the left background we can see two gray stones. The one on the left appears to have a masonic symbol on it. Both stones still stand on the far left edge of the modern reshoot.

Roahen photographs in figures 19.24 and 19.25 are virtual twins, albeit nonidentical. The former was taken before the Visitor Center was constructed, the latter after it was built. The two modern matches share a problem: trees and modern vehicles obscure the background, making it impossible to see Custer Hill beyond the Visitor Center.

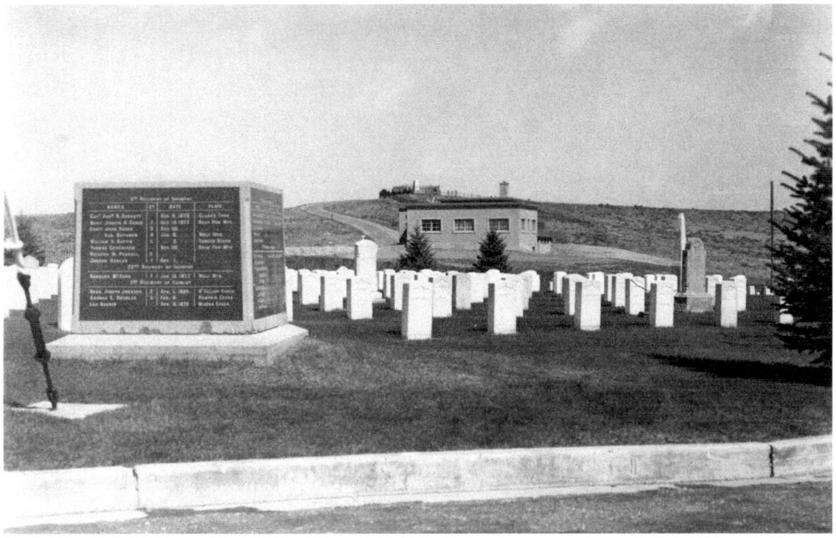

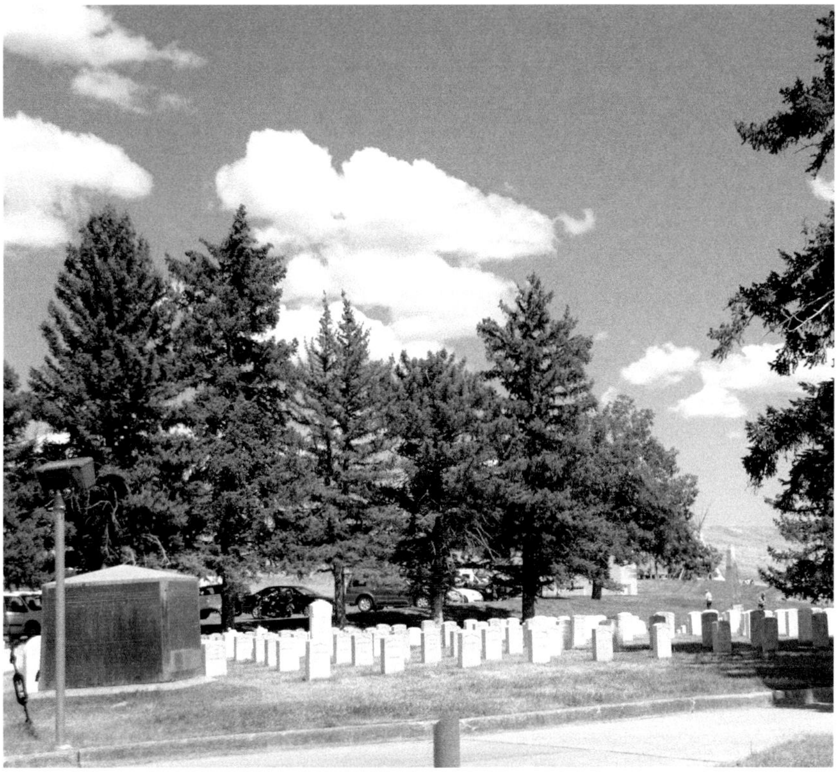

Figure 19.25. (*top*) Custer National Cemetery to Last Stand Hill, post-1952. Courtesy of Big Horn County Historical Museum. (*bottom*) 2012 reshoot.

Roahen did not date his figure 19.26 photo, which initially made determining its exact date difficult. The presence of the Visitor Center indicates a post-1952 image. Trees can still be seen behind the 7th Cavalry monument on Custer Hill, which means we can position this photograph between 1952 and 1963. In recent years, archaeological surveys of the battlefield have added significantly to our knowledge of the battle. One of the first major projects was conducted in June 1958 by archaeologist Robert Bray, who discovered the remains in the casket at the Reno-Benteen battlefield. In his excellent overview of archaeological efforts at Little Big Horn, author-archaeologist Douglas Scott noted that

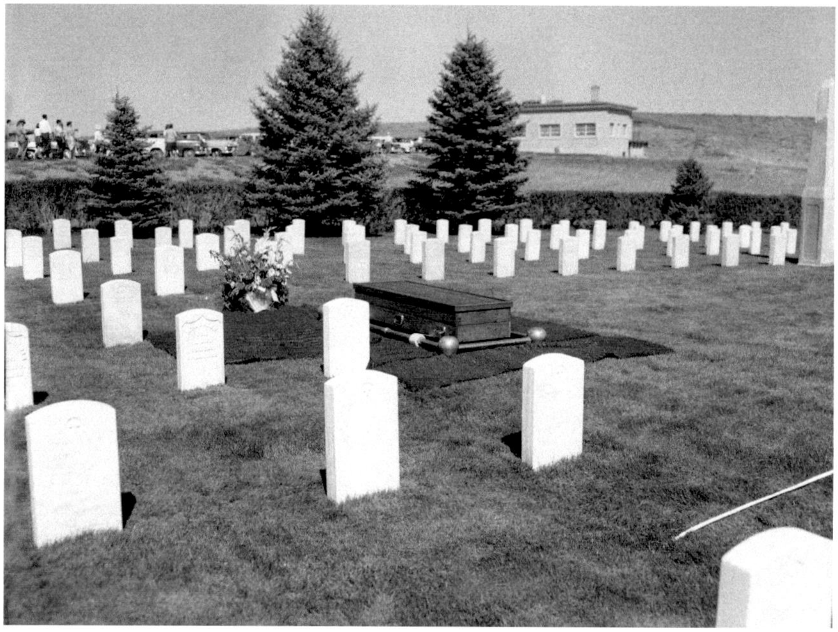

Figure 19.26. (*top*) 7th Cavalry remains about to be reburied, August 1958. Courtesy of Big Horn County Historical Museum. (*bottom*) 2012 reshoot.

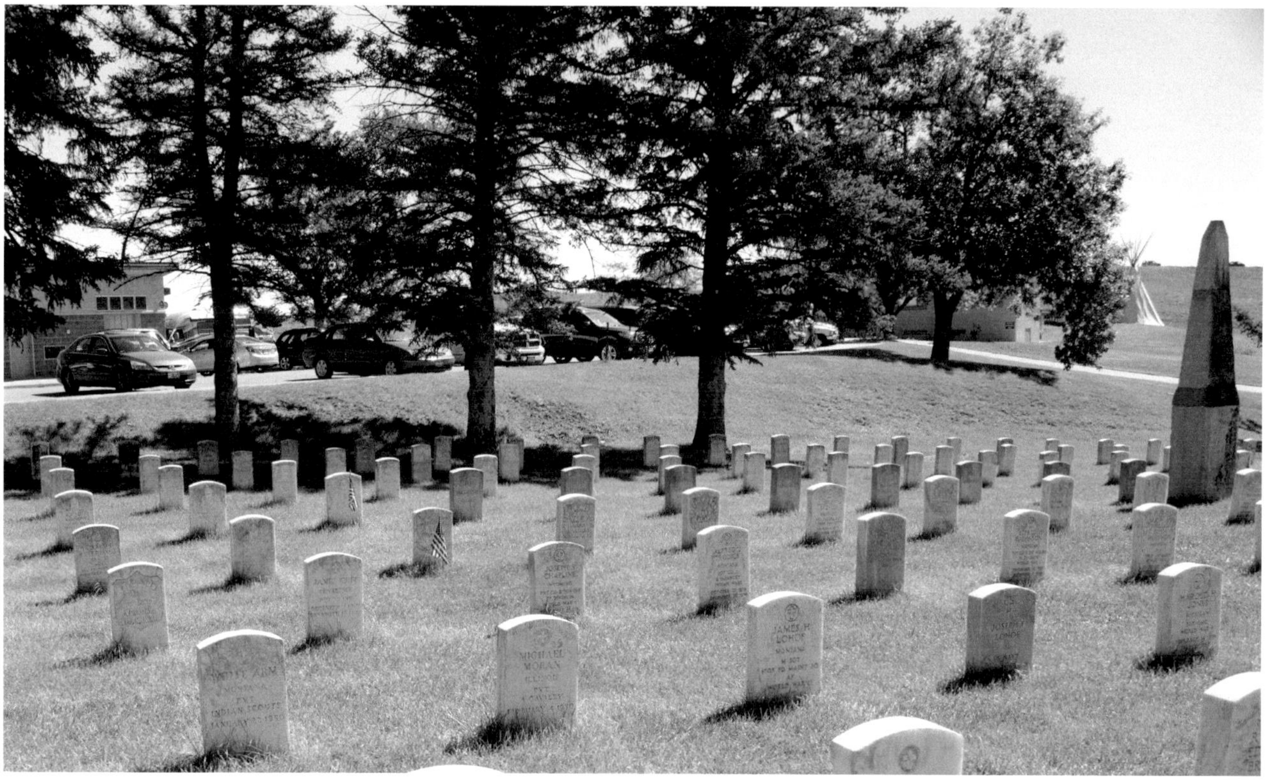

those remains were reinterred in the National Cemetery in August 1958, two months after Bray had recovered them at Reno-Benteen. The modern shot in figure 19.26 shows that the casket in Roahen's photograph was located at the grave whose marker today is engraved "U.S. Soldiers, 7th Cavalry." That stone is the one in the foreground with a small U.S. flag in front of it. Remains from the 1980s and later archaeological projects subsequently have been reburied in this same grave.[4]

CHAPTER 20

Visitor Center Dedication, June 25, 1952

Ever since his arrival in 1941, Superintendent Edward S. Luce had worked tirelessly to obtain funding for the construction of a museum at Custer Battlefield.[1] Over the years, he also acquired a wide variety of collections of historical records and artifacts, including documents from the 7th U.S. Cavalry itself; the letters and diary of Dr. James DeWolf, a battle casualty; and papers of Dr. Thomas B. Marquis, a researcher and long-time friend of the Northern Cheyenne people. However, nothing was more important than the papers and historical materials owned by Mrs. Elizabeth B. Custer, whose will had stipulated that these go to a museum at Custer Battlefield, if and when one were constructed. Luce arranged for temporary quarters for the collection in a bank storage vault at Crow Agency, Montana, and the materials were received in May 1943. Funds for a museum were actually approved in 1939, but construction was delayed by World War II. Finally, in spring 1950, plans were set and a contract was let. On July 17, 1950, a ground-breaking ceremony was held.

By June 25, 1952, the new building had been completed and plans were made for its dedication on what would be the seventy-sixth anniversary of the Little Big Horn battle. Luce had everything well organized, except the weather. Rain began falling in the late afternoon of June 24 and lasted for twenty-four hours. The program had to be shifted inside the museum itself, and chilly, damp weather significantly cut the crowd to about 1,200 people.

Many notable people—military, civilian, and National Park Service—were scheduled to speak. They included superintendent Edmund B. Rogers of Yellowstone National Park; George F. Will, a North Dakota historian; Judge Ben Harwood, a Billings friend of Kenneth Roahen and George Osten; and Ned J. Burns, chief of the Museum Branch of the Park Service, who had prepared the exhibits.

Perhaps the most notable person on the program was Gen. Jonathan M. Wainwright, a World War II hero who presented a Model 1866 Winchester carbine to the new museum. The carbine supposedly had been picked up by a Crow warrior on the battlefield after the fighting and captured from an insurgent Crow warrior by the general's father in 1887. The modern 7th Cavalry was represented by Col. William A. Harris, who had commanded the regiment in Korea. Col. Brice C. W. Custer represented the Custer family. Despite the bad weather, portions of the ceremonies were still held outside. General Wainwright placed a wreath on the base of the 7th Cavalry monument on Last Stand Hill.

Inasmuch as Roahen shot all but one of these photographs inside the building, I reshot only the site of figure 20.3.

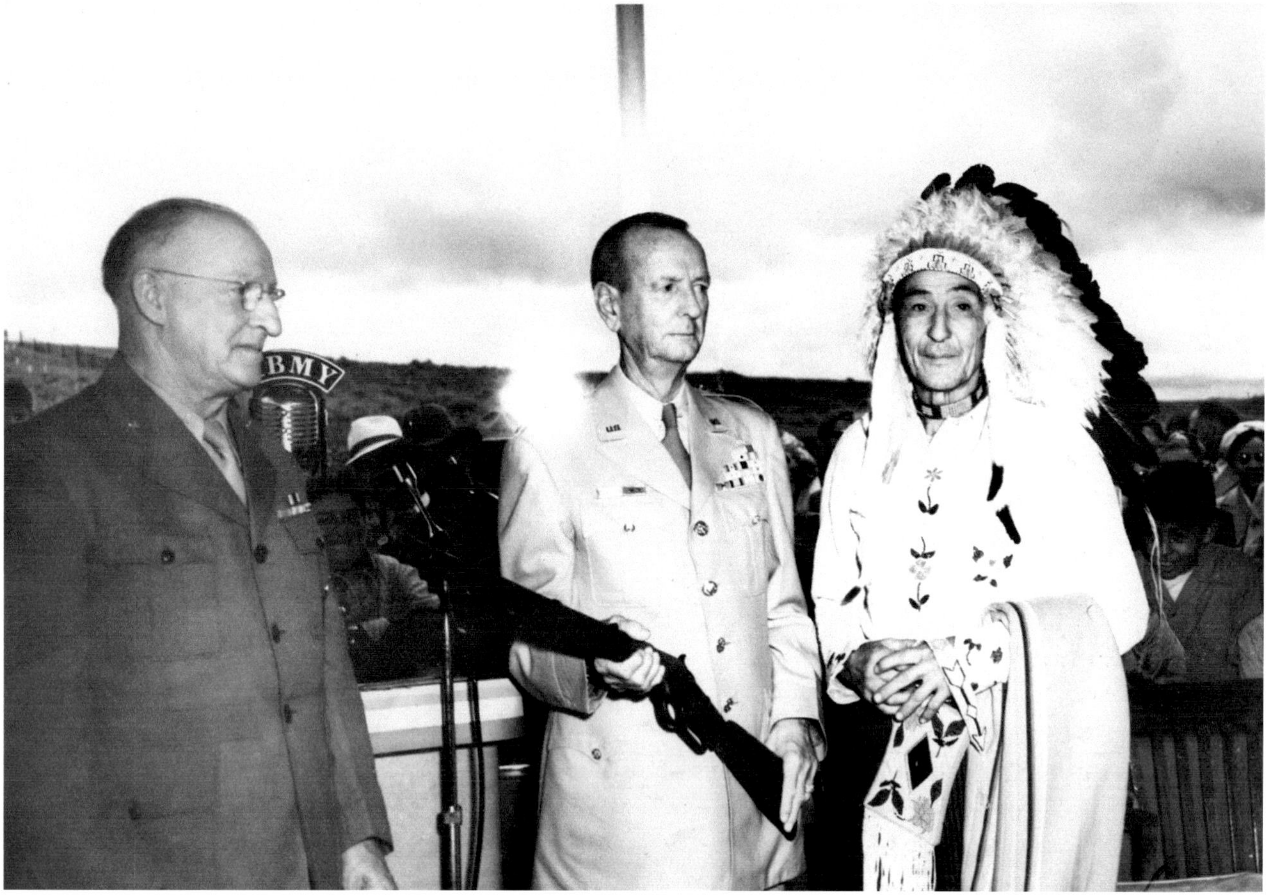

Figure 20.1. Seventy-sixth battle anniversary: (*left to right*) Superintendent E. S. Luce, Gen. Jonathan Wainwright, and Art Bravo, a descendent of Two Whistles, the Crow warrior from whom the general's father had captured the battle relic in 1887. Courtesy of Big Horn County Historical Museum.

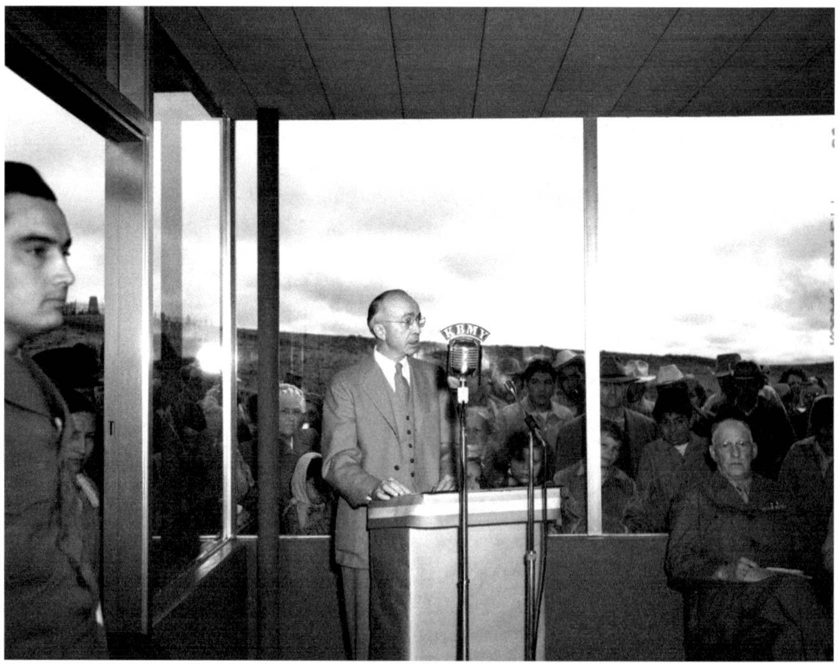

Figure 20.2. Seventy-sixth battle anniversary, Judge Ben Harwood, civilian speaker. Harwood was a friend of Roahen's and George Osten's. On the left is seasonal ranger Robert M. Utley. Courtesy of Big Horn County Historical Museum.

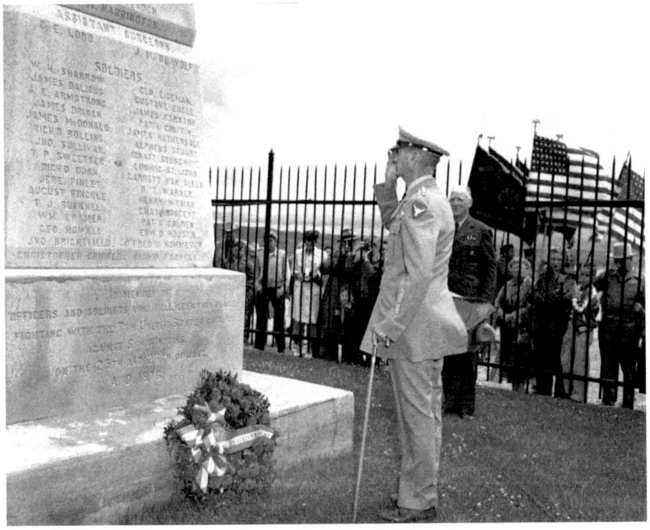

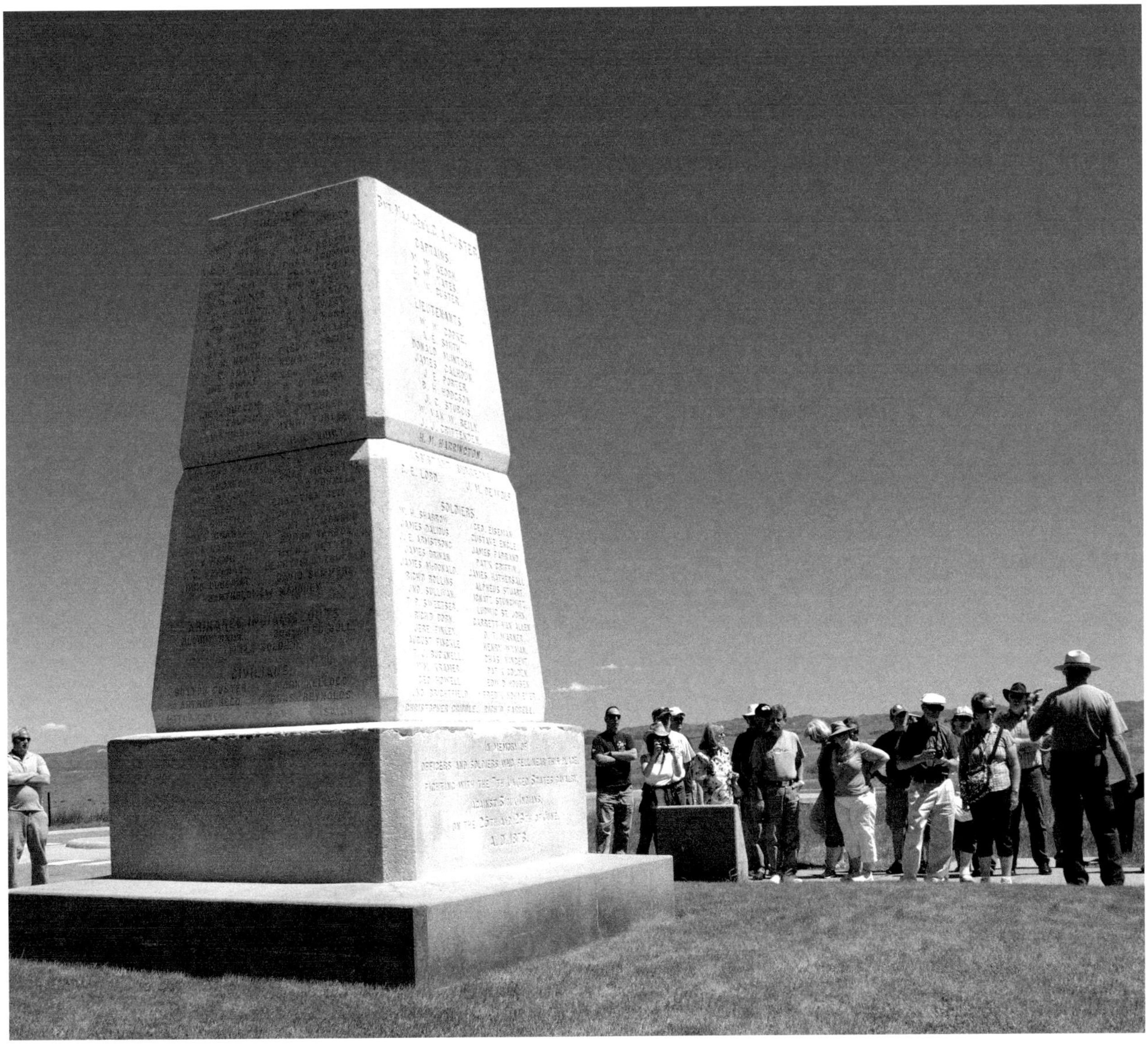

Figure 20.3. (*top*) Gen. Jonathon Wainwright saluting monument. Courtesy of Big Horn County Historical Museum. (*bottom*) The monument in 2013.

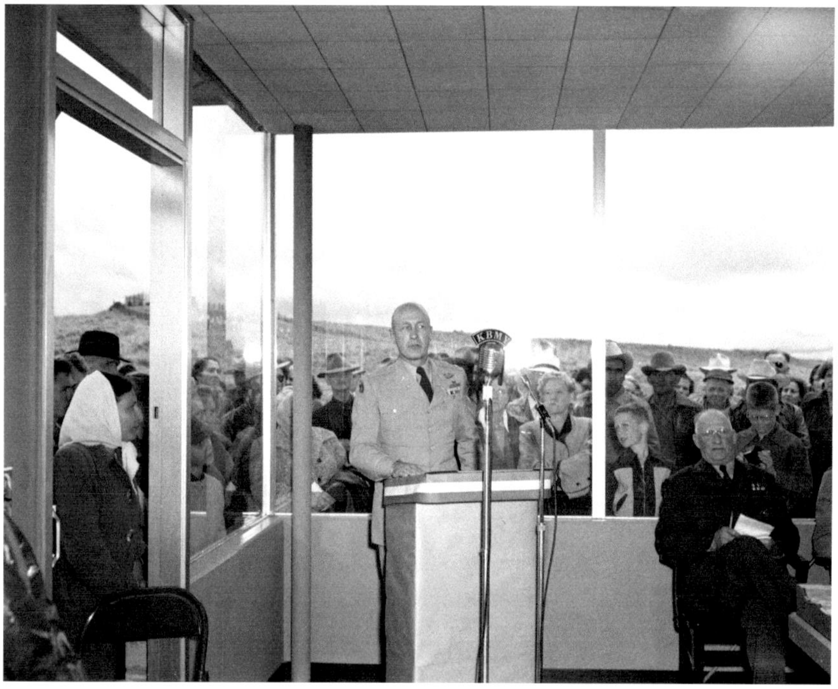

Figure 20.4. Col. William A. Harris, commander of the modern 7th Cavalry. Courtesy of Big Horn County Historical Museum.

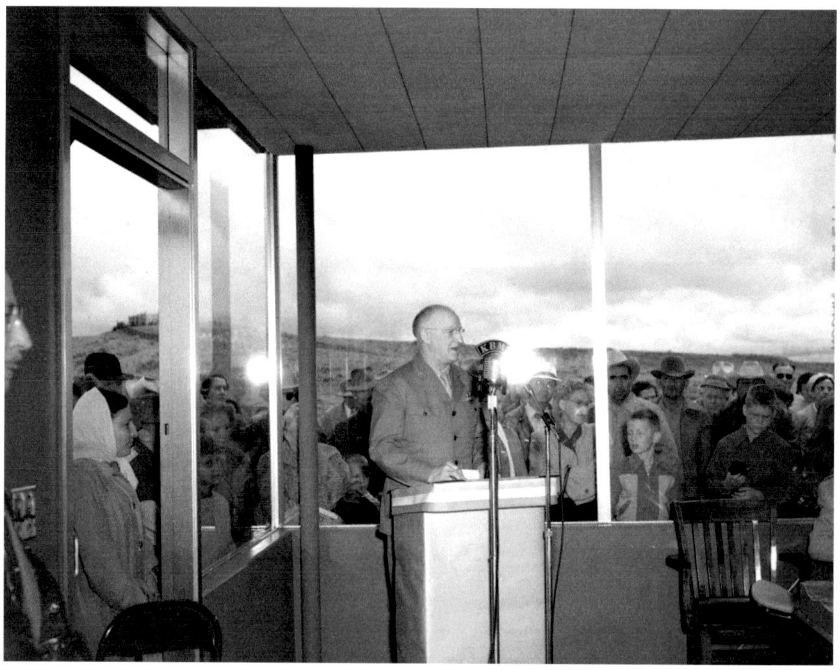

Figure 20.5. Superintendent E. S. Luce. Courtesy of Big Horn County Historical Museum.

CHAPTER 21

Roahen's 1951 Aerial Photos of the Seventy-Fifth Anniversary

In the spring of 1951, plans were made for a special battlefield event to commemorate the seventy-fifth anniversary of the battle at Little Big Horn.[1] The ceremonies were scheduled for 10 A.M. to noon that June 25. Initially large crowds of spectators were anticipated, but cool, damp weather reduced the turnout to an estimated 7,500 people. The main observances were held in the rostrum area of the cemetery. In the key address, Gen. Albert Wedemeyer, son of an Indian wars officer, called for world unity in the face of ever-increasing threats of war. Representing the 7th Cavalry were Col. William A. Harris and M.Sgt. Francis R. Riley. Adm. William Leahy represented President Harry S Truman.

Kenneth F. Roahen must have been visible at every place one could expect on the battlefield. Not only did he shoot numerous photographs on the ground, often while mounted on his ladder, but he also arranged a flyover of the battlefield and took numerous significant images of the historic site.

Roahen's figure 21.1 was taken as his plane passed over Custer Hill and Battle Ridge, neither of which appears in the image. On the right is the still incomplete Visitor Center, which would not be dedicated and ready for use for another year (June 1952). Tourists were parked on the ridges to the southwest below the Stone House. It would still be almost a decade before government housing would fill up the space occupied by the closest cars. Outbuildings at the rear of the Stone House remain. Crowds fill the two sections of the cemetery on the right and beyond the flagpole, known today as Sections C and F (where the rostrum was located). The nearer Section C is about half full of graves. Section B, in the foreground on the right, is notable for the Fort C. F. Smith marker that stands out in the center. A sidewalk that once ran to it has already been removed. In the area closest to Roahen's camera, three buses are parked. In that site today is the amphitheater where programs similar to this one are held. Section A on the left contains the most graves. Section D between it and the Stone House has the smallest number. The area on the photo's far right, where today the majority of the battlefield's public parking is located, consists only of the road to Last Stand Hill.

Figure 21.2 is quite similar in perspective to figure 21.1, although Roahen's plane must have been flying lower. On the right, the new Visitor Center is now out of sight. In the upper third of the photo, the two side roads can be seen joining the main entrance road below the Stone House. In the rostrum area a military color guard and line are more obvious.

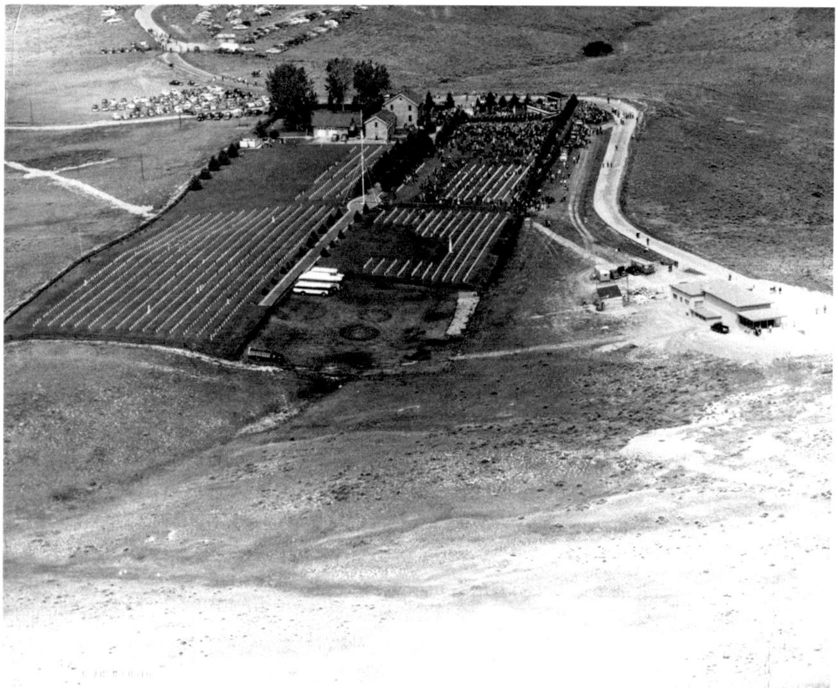

Figure 21.1. Aerial view of the Visitor Center and Custer National Cemetery, seventy-fifth battle anniversary, 1951. Courtesy of Big Horn County Historical Museum.

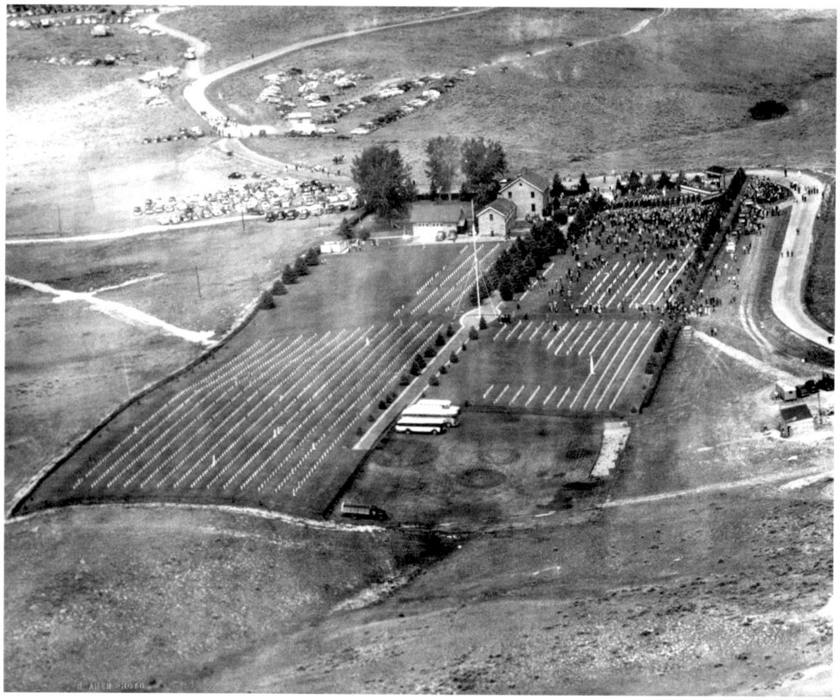

Figure 21.2. Variant aerial view of the Visitor Center and Custer National Cemetery. Courtesy of Big Horn County Historical Museum.

Although showing the primary area of the battlefield and cemetery as in figures 21.1 and 21.2, figure 21.3 offers the view from a different perspective, northwest to southeast. The three sections of the entrance road are more obvious, as are the vehicles parked for the ceremonies below the cemetery ridge. Calhoun Hill can be seen on the mid-upper right of the photograph. Last Stand Hill and Battle Ridge also stand out.

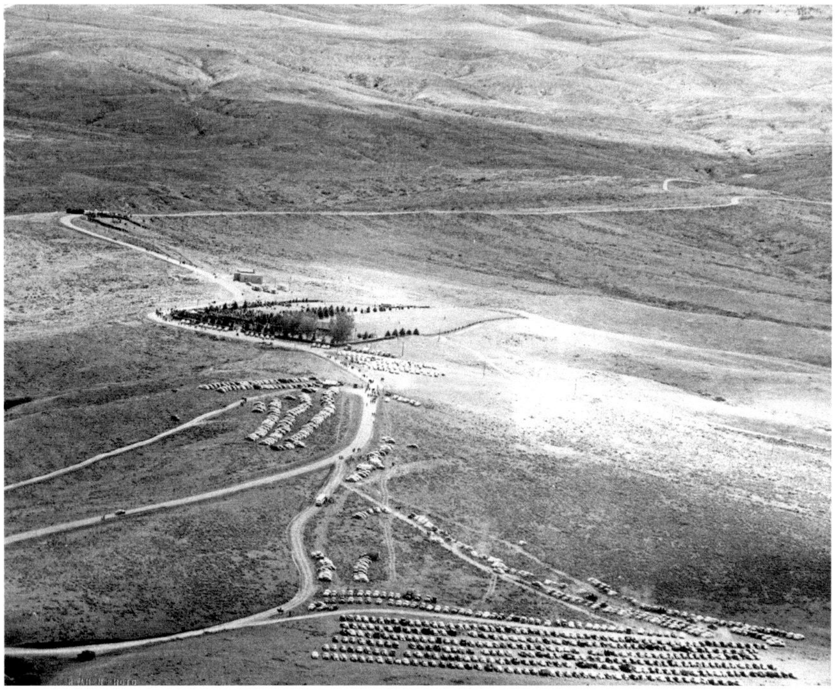

Figure 21.3. Aerial overview of the Visitor Center and Custer National Cemetery, northwest to southeast. Courtesy of Big Horn County Historical Museum.

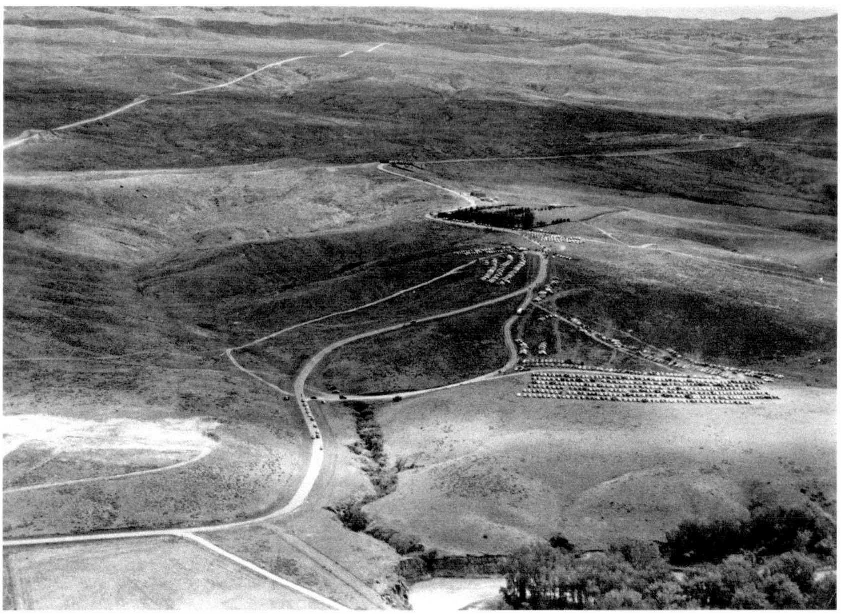

Figure 21.4. Aerial overview and Kellogg Ravine. Courtesy of Big Horn County Historical Museum.

Compared to figure 21.3, figure 21.4 provides a different west-east perspective, but it is also significant in another way.[2] It shows the likely site where Col. John Gibbon discovered the body of *Bismarck Tribune* reporter Mark H. Kellogg on June 29, 1876. In 1876, Gibbon commanded the Montana Column. Along with the remaining Dakota Column under Brigadier General Terry, Gibbon's troops arrived on the battlefield on June 27 and went into camp below the bluffs where the battered remnants of Major Reno's command had been besieged for two days. For the next two days, while Custer's dead were buried and the wounded were cared for, Gibbon had no time to visit the Last Stand Hill area.

On June 28, Gibbon moved his camp north beyond what had been the northern limits of the Indian village. This area was directly below the northern end of today's Little Bighorn Battlefield National Monument. On June 29, while the troops constructed mule litters in the camp to transport the wounded to the waiting riverboat *Far West* at the junction of the Big Horn and Little Big Horn, Gibbon decided to ride up to the scene of Custer's demise. In his own writings, he told of two fords in this area, one of which he and his aides used to cross the Little Big Horn. They then moved up the river's wooded right bank:

> On our left the valley opens out into a grass-covered prairie, fringed on its southern side, and again on its western side, where the stream curves to the north again, with timber and brushwood. Riding along up the stream we come to the point where, after cutting the bluffs skirting it on the north, it turns sharply to the south.
>
> Here the ground commences to rise before us in gently sloping hills separated by little valleys, one of which seems to lead in about the direction we want to take. Just before this valley joins the valley of the river, the bottom has been cut into a gulch some eight or ten feet deep, and this is filled with brushwood nourished by the moisture of the rain-water, which doubtless cut out the gulch. Struck with the fact that this little valley seemed a natural outlet from the scene of the fight, and the possibility that individuals might have sought shelter in the gulch on their way to the timber below, we closely examined the place up to the point where the gulch headed but found no "signs."
>
> As we proceeded up the valley, now an open grassy slope, we suddenly came upon a body lying in the grass. It was lying upon its back, and was in an advanced state of decomposition. It was not stripped, but had evidently been scalped and one ear cut off. The clothing was not that of a soldier, and, with the idea of identifying the remains, I caused one of the boots to be cut off and the stockings and drawers examined for a name, but none could be found. On looking at the boot, however, a curious construction was observed. The heel of the boot was reinforced by a piece of leather which in front terminated in two straps, one of which was furnished with a buckle, evidently for the purpose of tightening the instep of the boot. This led to the identification of the remains, for on being carried to camp the boot was recognized as one belonging to Mr. Kellogg, a newspaper correspondent who accompanied General Custer's column.
>
> Beyond this point, the ground commenced to rise more rapidly, and the valley was broken up into several smaller ones which lead up towards the higher ground beyond. Following up one of these we reach a rolling but not very broken space, the ground rising higher and higher until it reaches a culminating knoll dominating all the ground in the immediate vicinity. This knoll, by common consent now called Custer's hill, is the spot where his body was found surrounded by those of several of his officers and some forty or fifty of his men.[3]

In figure 21.4, Roahen, probably unknowingly at the time, captured the scene that Gibbon described of his ride to the battlefield, the ravine and the place where the reporter's body was found. The bend in the Little Big Horn River that Gibbon described can be seen near the bottom of the photograph. Emptying into the bend is the ravine that Gibbon ordered his aides to check, but where they found "no signs."

Just beyond the ravine, about where the old entrance road splits into three avenues, is the possible spot where he found Kellogg. As Gibbon stated, beyond this point the ground commences to rise more rapidly. He rode up the left-hand coulee toward the highest ridge, which today holds the modern entrance road constructed in 1957. The coulee itself was filled in, except for a culvert to allow water to pass through, to accommodate the new roadbed.

Gibbon and his party continued to ride up the main passage of that ever rising coulee, or "the valley . . . broken up into several smaller ones," to the point where it turns right, "until it reaches a culminating knoll dominating all the ground in the immediate vicinity"—Custer Hill. En route, Gibbon would have found that the main coulee branches off at various points into what he refers to as "several smaller ones [valleys]," which aim directly at the area of the Stone House itself. The very last one would have taken Gibbon's party by a ridge on their left where the Indian Memorial was constructed straight to the top of Custer Hill.

Why was Kellogg killed so far away from the command, and why was he still fully clothed when Gibbon discovered his body on June 29? In my biography of Kellogg, *I Go with Custer*, I subscribed to theories put forth by archaeologist Richard A. Fox in his 1993 book, *Archaeology, History and Custer's Last Stand*, that Custer's left wing, consisting of Companies E and F or portions thereof, pushed forward from Last Stand Hill through the modern cemetery ridge and toward the valley floor, if not to the floor itself. Indian women and children were known to have fled north and may have taken refuge in old river beds in that area. Custer's goal may have been to seize the noncombatants as hostages. In November 1868 at the Battle of the Washita against the Cheyenne village, such a strategy had worked well for him. He forced the warriors, who likely outnumbered him as at the Little Big Horn in 1876, to hold their fire and to remain at a distance from the army's lines.

Kellogg, despite his status as a civilian journalist, was armed and willing to fight in 1876. He likely had accompanied Custer's men on the advance toward the river. When the soldiers encountered resistance from warriors, they retreated to the vicinity of Custer Ridge, but not before suffering casualties. One of those casualties was the newsman, who was shot off the mule he had been riding. Initially his body remained in range of the soldiers' carbines firing from what would become Cemetery Ridge. That would have given a warrior little time to mutilate Kellogg's body, beyond cutting off an ear and scalping the reporter. Such a warrior would have been unable to remove Kellogg's clothing or boots. In time, the fighting moved away from the dead newspaperman. After the battle ended, his body was so far out of the way from the rest of the command that no Indians, warriors or noncombatants, returned to the site to complete their plunder of Kellogg's body.

In 1951, Roahen probably was unaware of the significance of the site in the foreground of his photograph. In his day, researchers gave little thought to Kellogg's demise and assumed that the marker for the reporter on the east side of Battle Ridge was accurate. Nonetheless, this image is an excellent example of the great value that photographs can provide as evidence in studying historical events.

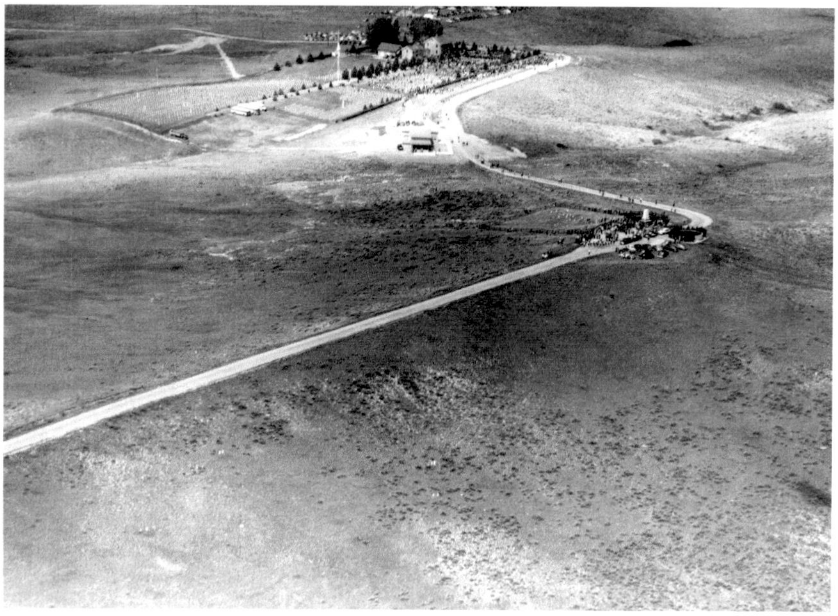

Figure 21.5. Aerial overview and Last Stand Hill. Courtesy of Big Horn County Historical Museum.

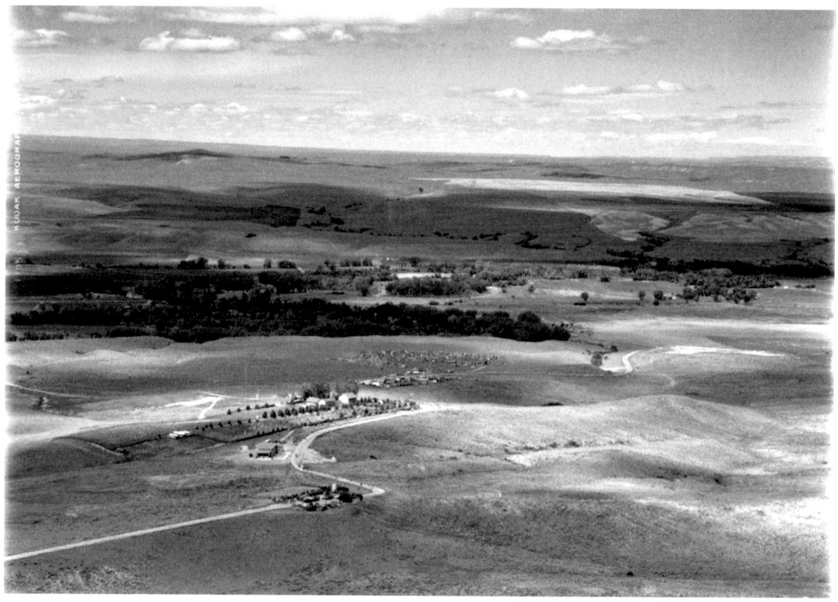

Figure 21.6. Aerial overview looking west over Last Stand Hill. Courtesy of Big Horn County Historical Museum.

In figure 21.5, we are looking at Battle Ridge and Last Stand Hill, with the Visitor Center and National Cemetery in the background. Roahen's plane would have been flying either parallel to Battle Ridge or approaching it from the east. Figure 21.6 provides a wide westward view of the Last Stand Hill area as well as the National Cemetery ridge. Both this image and figure 21.4 provide an excellent view of the high ridge just to the north of the 7th Cavalry monument where the Indian Memorial was constructed in the early 2000s. Equally important, we also can see the coulee Gibbon would have ridden up to complete his journey on June 29, 1876, to view the site of Custer's last stand. Note, too, the finger ridge off the northwest corner of the cemetery. Six years later, the Park Service would construct its new entrance road across that ridge, after filling in the open coulee through which Gibbon would have ridden.

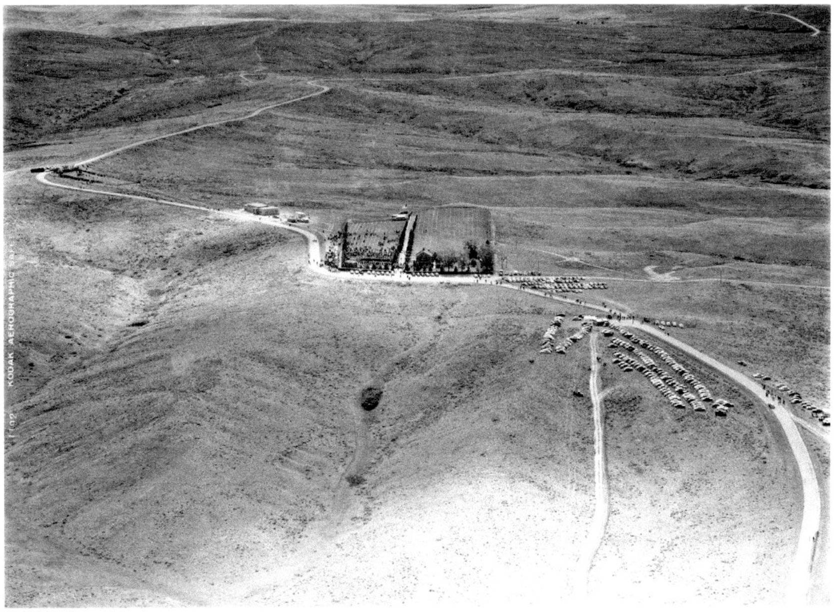

Figure 21.7. Aerial overview looking west to east of the Stone House. Courtesy of Big Horn County Historical Museum.

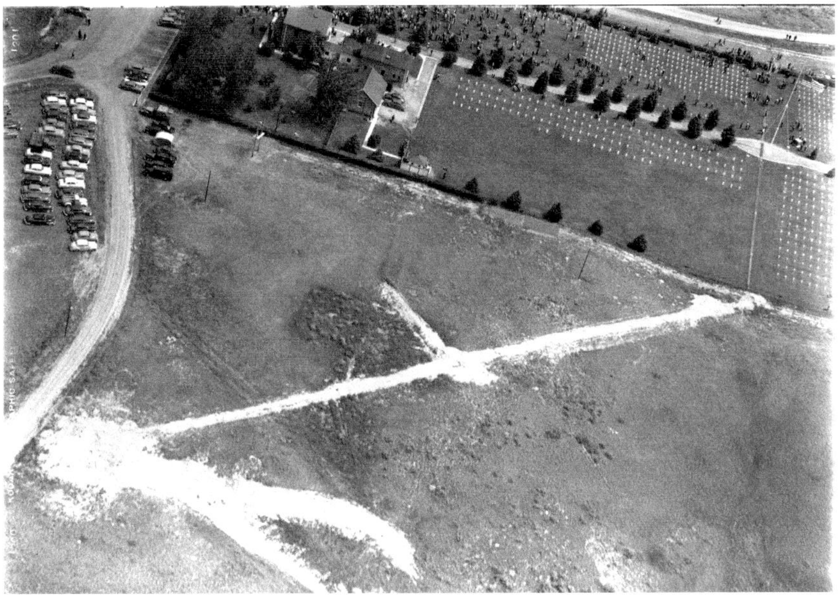

Figure 21.8. Aerial overview of the battlefield's maintenance area. Courtesy of Big Horn County Historical Museum.

Figure 21.7 provides a straight west-to-east view of the main battlefield area. In the lower left corner, the Gibbon trail through that coulee, which would be filled in 1957 for the new entrance road, can be seen. In the upper left corner we can see the loop around Calhoun Hill, and the main road begins its drop from Battle Ridge toward Medicine Tail Coulee. In the top right we can see the battle road leaving Medicine Tail and beginning its climb toward Weir Point and the Reno-Benteen battlefield beyond. Figure 21.8 is significant in providing a close view of the area where in time the Park Service would build its maintenance facilities, essentially in the triangular area below Sections D and E of the cemetery.

Figure 21.9 is essentially a variant of figure 21.8. Roahen's plane was flying a little higher, which enabled him to capture more of the cemetery area.

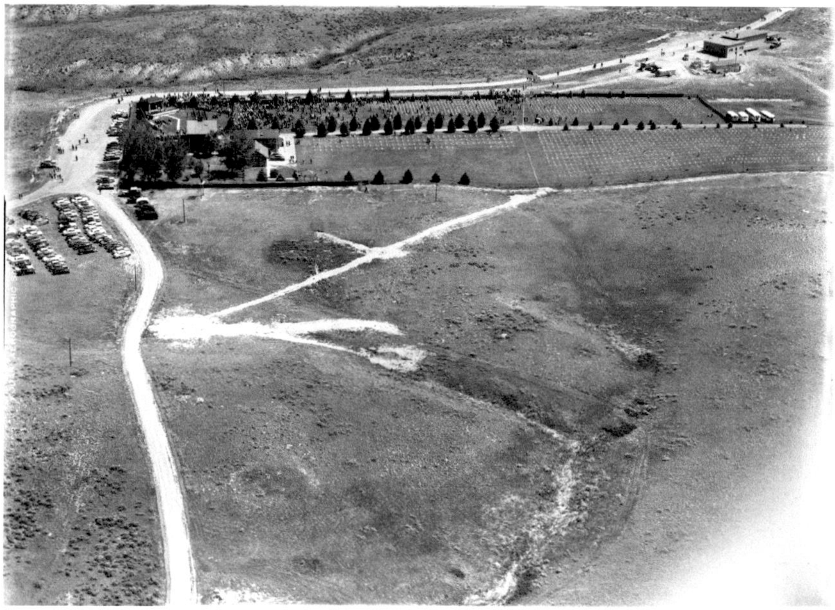

Figure 21.9. Aerial overview of Stone House and the new Visitor Center. Courtesy of Big Horn County Historical Museum.

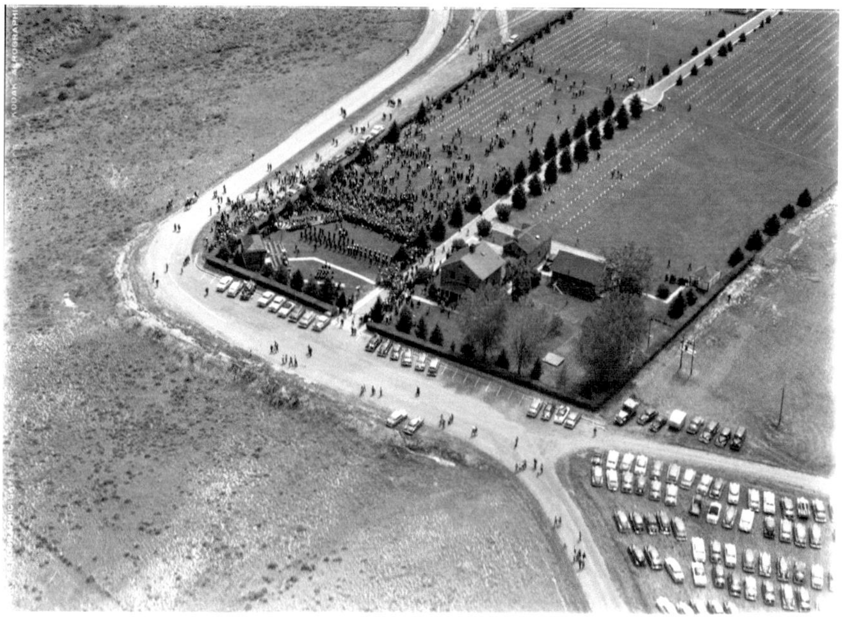

Figure 21.10. Aerial close-up of Stone House. Courtesy of Big Horn County Historical Museum.

Additionally, the upper left area where all the cars are parked is the general vicinity of today's apartment complex used for housing Park Service employees.

In figure 21.10 we have an excellent close-up of the Stone House complex of buildings as well as a view of the rostrum area. Note the sidewalk that extends across the cemetery road from the Stone House's front sidewalk and turns at an angle toward the rostrum. That sidewalk was later removed, and the former rostrum area today has been used for burials as the cemetery's Section F. Readers familiar with the layout of the modern parking lot in front of the Stone House will note how level the 1950s parking area and road appear near the right turn by the cemetery. Today that turn is separated from the entrance road by a small man-made ridge. A newer branch road leads from the modern entrance kiosk area past the end of the ridge into the Stone House parking lot.

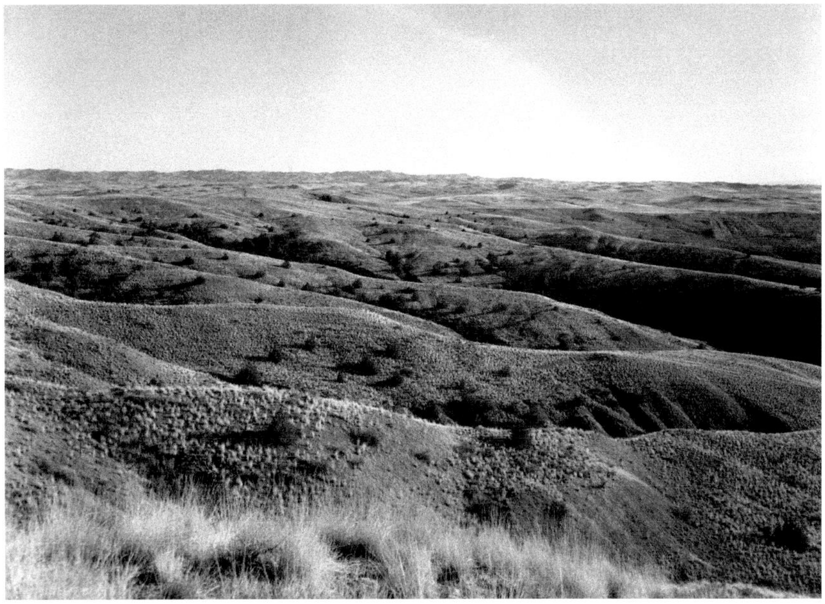

Figure 21.11. Aerial view of bluffs to Reno-Benteen Defense Site. Courtesy of Big Horn County Historical Museum.

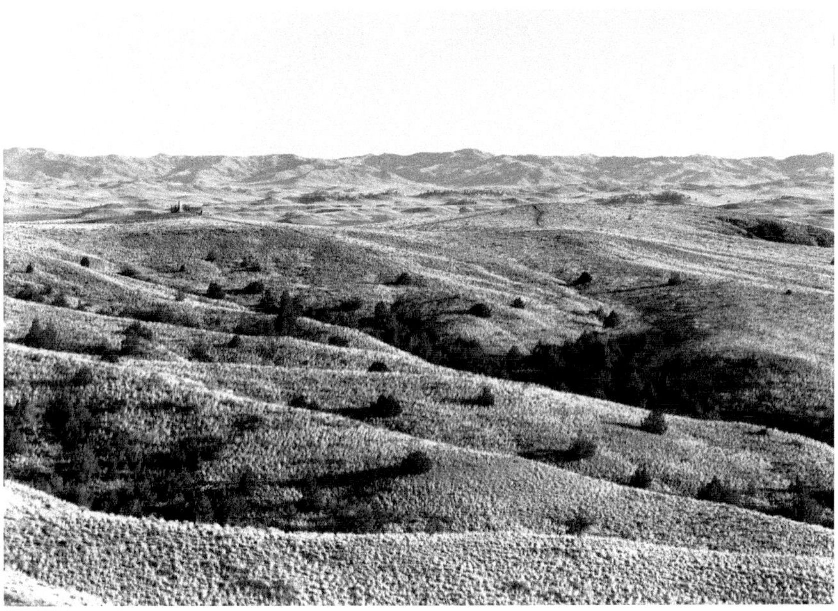

Figure 21.12. Another aerial view of bluffs to Reno-Benteen Defense Site. Courtesy of Big Horn County Historical Museum.

It seems likely that Roahen took advantage of his flight in June 1951 over the main battlefield to shoot figures 21.11 and 21.12, of the Reno-Benteen site. Of these two variants, figure 21.11 was shot at a slightly greater distance. The two photos are significant because they show the Reno-Benteen monument prior to its move in 1965. A high fence that was not removed until 1963 surrounds the monument. Even if these two photographs were not shot at the time of the 1951 anniversary, they certainly date to that decade.

Notes

Preface

1. Thackeray, "Photo Collection Donated"; see also Beaumont, "Kenneth F. Roahen." Much of what follows is taken from these news stories or from my interview with Mrs. Ooley on October 3, 2012, at the Big Horn County Historical Museum (hereafter Ooley interview).

2. According to correspondence between Roahen and Luce, they relied on a gentleman's agreement about crediting the images to the former. But after Luce's retirement subsequent National Park Service administrations did not maintain accurate records about the photographer's identity for many of Roahen's images.

3. Kenneth F. Roahen letter to Conrad L. Wirth, undated, Kenneth F. Roahen Collection, U.S. Fish and Game Service, Shepherdstown, West Virginia (hereafter KFRFWS). According to the context of the letter, Roahen likely wrote it in 1963. Wirth served as the National Park Service director from 1951 to 1964.

4. In the Civil War, Custer attained the rank of major general of volunteers. In the postwar army, his official rank as an active duty officer was lieutenant colonel, but in that period officers were frequently addressed by the highest rank they had attained during the war. Thus, it is proper to refer to Custer as a general, even for 1876.

1. Researching the Custer Battlefield Story

1. U.S. Fish and Wildlife Service, "Kenneth Roahen."

2. See Brininstool, *Troopers with Custer*; Graham, *Custer Myth*; and Kuhlman, *Legend into History*.

3. See Rickey, *History*, for a lengthy summary of Luce's role at the battlefield during his tenure as superintendent.

4. Nichols, "CBHMA Marks Its 50th year," 3. The CBHMA predated the Little Big Horn Associates, another group of Custer researchers, by some fifteen years, but both organizations have produced solid research on the various battles and campaigns of 1876 into 1877. Many members, in fact, have held membership in both groups. A third organization that has produced outstanding research on the battle is the Custer Association of Great Britain, founded in 2000. All three organizations consist of individuals with a common fascination for the life and times of George Armstrong Custer, the Battle of the Little Big Horn, the Plains Indian wars, the culture of the tribes involved, and their leaders.

5. My on-the-scene encounter with what was then called the Custer Battlefield National Monument began on July 29, 1980, when my family and I made our initial visit to the site. Since then, I have written biographies of such Custer associates as reporter Mark H. Kellogg, 1st Sgt. John Ryan, and Maj. Joel H. Elliott. Other writings have concerned such individuals as Custer's close friend, actor Lawrence P. Barrett, and Custer researcher Walter M. Camp. In the 1980s, I handled public relations for the National Park Service during archaeological projects at the battlefield, which led to two books, one of which, *Digging into Custer's Last Stand*, remains popular in its third edition today. In the 1990s, I engaged in a decade-long photo history project of Custer Battlefield/Little Bighorn Battlefield with coauthors James S. Brust and the late Brian C. Pohanka, which led to the award-winning *Where Custer Fell*. For twenty-three years I edited *Greasy Grass* magazine, the annual research journal published by the Custer Battlefield Historical and Museum Association.

6. Brust et al., *Where Custer Fell*, ix.

7. Ibid., x.

2. Roahen Biographical Sketch

1. "U.S. Game Agent for Montana Retires after 30 Years," *Billings (Montana) Gazette*, January 2, 1955 (hereafter, "U.S. Game Agent Retires").

2. Bragg, "Green with Envy."

3. "Poachers' Sport: Kill the Game Agent," *Billings (Montana) Gazette*, February 9, 1964 (hereafter, "Poachers' Sport").

4. Cashmere Precinct, Chelan, Washington, World War I Draft Registration Cards, 1917–18, Ancestry.com.

5. Roahen, Daniel L., obituary, *Great Bend (Kansas) Tribune*, October 5, 1932.

6. Central Kansas Integrated Family Tree Database 120108, Ancestry.com.

7. Kansas State Census Collection, 1855–25, for 1895, Ancestry.com.

8. "West from Ohio," *Great Bend (Kansas) Tribune*, August 8, 1937.

9. Roahen, Daniel L., obituary, *Great Bend (Kansas) Tribune*, October 5, 1932.

10. "West from Ohio," *Great Bend (Kansas) Tribune*, August 8, 1937.

11. Kenneth F. Roahen letter to unknown family members, August 27, 1960, KFRFWS.

12. This and later comments by Elaine Ooley taken from Ooley interview.

13. "Poachers' Sport."

14. Roahen letter, August 27, 1960, KFRFWS.

15. Kansas City, Missouri, City Directory, 1910, U.S. City Directories, 1821–89, Ancestry.com.

16. 1910 United States Federal Census, Great Bend, Ward 4, Barton, Kansas, Ancestry.com; Wichita City Directory, 1910, U.S. City Directories, 1821–89, Ancestry.com. According to the document, he boarded at 425 N. Emporia Ave.

17. "Roahen-Moses," *Great Bend (Kansas) Tribune*, December 27, 1910.

18. 1910 U.S. Census, Ancestry.com.

19. Cashmere Precinct, Chelan, Washington, World War I Draft Registration Cards, 1917–18, Ancestry.com.

20. U.S. Department of Veterans Affairs, BIRLS Death File, 1850–2010, Ancestry.com. Interestingly, Roahen's obituary, published January 10, 1976, in the *Billings Gazette*, claimed that for a time he had been a partner in a Ford automobile dealership in Wenatchee, Washington.

21. Roahen letter, August 27, 1960, KFRFWS.

22. Burnett, Frances, obituary, *Great Bend (Kansas) Tribune*, February 27, 1946.

23. U.S. City Directories, 1821–89, Chelan County, Washington, 1914–15, Ancestry.com; "U.S. Game Agent Retires."

24. "U.S. Game Agent Retires"; "Colorful U.S. Game Agent Retires after 30 Years," *Great Falls (Montana) Tribune*, January 2, 1955.

25. His date of birth is given as December 10, 1875, or nearly a full year before his parents actually married. That would seem to be in error. Ernest E. Roahen, Certificate of Death, 3–10–1923, Missouri State Board of Health, Bureau of Vital Statistics. His address was given on the document as 120 Huntington Rd. Elsie died of colon cancer on October 21, 1949. She was born on July 31, 1880. Elsie Leigh Roahen, Certificate of Death no. 33983, filed November 5, 1949, Division of Health of Missouri.

26. Roahen letter, August 27, 1960, KFRFWS.

27. According to several records available through Ancestry.com, including the 1940 U.S. Census, Richard Roahen had been born February 6, 1905, in Missouri, and likely Kansas City. He continued to teach well into the 1970s, if not later. According to the Social Security Death Index, he did not die until May 1, 1994, in Emporia, Kansas. He served two years in the army, from January 1944 to January 1946. His son was also named Richard.

28. "Roahen Summoned by Father's Death," *Billings (Montana) Gazette*, January 3, 1932.

29. Central Kansas Integrated Family Tree Database 120108, Ancestry.com.

30. "U.S. Game Agent Retires."

31. "Poachers' Sport"; this news article along with "U.S. Game Agent Retires" and "Colorful U.S. Game Agent Retires after 30 Years," *Great Falls (Montana) Tribune*, January 2, 1955, are the basis for the Chicago-era discussion here and on the next page.

32. Peoria, Illinois, City Directories, 1929 and 1930, U.S. City Directories, 1821–89, Ancestry.com. In 1929 they lived at 237A Moss Ave., and he had his office at the Federal Building, Room 404. The 1931 Peoria directory also lists them living there, but the information was undoubtedly gathered in 1930 for publication in 1931. Other sources clearly indicate that Roahen and his new wife had moved to Billings, Montana, in December 1930.

33. Novak Family Tree, Ancestry.com.

34. World War I Draft Registration Cards, 1917–18, Ancestry.com; also, 1910 U.S. Census, and Chester Gouker, Social Security Death Index, Ancestry.com.

35. Decatur, Illinois, City Directories, 1909, 1911, 1921, 1923, and 1925, U.S. City Directories, 1821–89, Ancestry.com.

36. Gouker himself appears to have remained unmarried for a considerable period. By the late 1950s, city directories for Decatur, Illinois, and Middletown, Ohio, show him married to a Pearl Gouker. As noted earlier, his death was recorded in Missouri in March 1964. Decatur, Illinois, City Directories, 1955 and 1957, and Middletown, Ohio, 1955, U.S. City Directories, 1821–89, Ancestry.com. His draft card lists his contact person as his mother, Ida, who was still in Illinois. By then he himself was living in Austin, Texas, although his occupation was not listed. Chester A. Gouker World War II draft Card, 1942, Ancestry.com.

37. Roahen letter to R. W. Caldwell, November 27, 1931, KFRFWS.

38. Roahen letter, August 27, 1960, KFRFWS.

39. "Poachers' Sport."

40. Undated, untitled draft, ca. 1954, KFRFWS.

41. Kenneth F. Roahen draft, June 16, 1954, KFRFWS.

42. "Poachers' Sport." Much of the following section is based on details from this article by Chuck Rightmire; also, undated, untitled draft, ca. 1954, KFRFWS.

43. "U.S. Game Agent Retires"; Becker, "Goose Heaven."

44. Becker, "U.S. Wars."

45. The four-page draft document is in KFRFWS. In it, Roahen outlines several of his episodes along the rivers and marshes in this period in Illinois. The U.S. Fish and Wildlife Service Archives at the National Conservation Center in Shepherdstown, West Virginia, has published a soft-bound booklet, *Assault Cases against Agent and Deputy Wardens*, covering the period from 1918 to 1964. It is undated and lacks page numbers but is organized according to state. The Roahen report for March 3, 1925, is in the Illinois section.

46. "U.S. Game Agent Retires."

47. "Poachers' Sport"; Kenneth F. Roahen, witness affidavit, June 23, 1954, Billings, Montana, Federal Court.

48. Kenneth F. Roahen draft, June 16, 1954, KFRFWS.

49. Kenneth F. Roahen, letter to J. P. Landuska, Chief, Branch Game Management, Washington, D.C., June 21, 1954, KFRFWS; undated, untitled draft, ca. 1954, KFRFWS.

50. Kenneth F. Roahen draft, June 16, 1954, KFRFWS.

51. Undated, untitled draft, ca. 1954, KFRFWS.

52. Letter from Charles Perry to Roahen, January 15, 1955, KFRFWS; Kenneth F. Roahen letter to Paul Quick, Assistant Regional Director, U.S. Fish and Wildlife Service, Portland, Oregon, January 28, 1955.

53. Letter from E. L. Paynter to Roahen, January 18, 1955, KFRFWS.

54. "Poachers' Sport."

55. Ibid.

56. Billings, Montana, City Directories, 1933, 1935, and 1937, U.S. City Directories, 1821–89, Ancestry.com.

57. See Greene, *Stricken Field*. This book offers significant background on Luce's personality as well as his administration at Custer Battlefield National Monument.

58. Noyes, "Federal Agent," 12. The association referred to by Utley in the article seems to be the Custer Battlefield Historical and Museum Association, but that organization was not founded until 1953. More likely, the association running the sales outlet in the late 1940s was the Yellowstone Library and Museum Association, which opened a modest sales outlet at the Custer Battlefield in 1943, offering only postcards and a battlefield pamphlet. See Nichols, "CBHMA Marks Its 50th Year," 2–11.

59. Kenneth F. Roahen letter to 20th Century Photo Color Service, Boise, Idaho, October 1, 1963, KFRFWS.

60. Letter from J. Edgar Hoover to Roahen, August 3, 1961, KFRFWS.

61. Roahen letter, August 27, 1960, KFRFWS.

62. Kenneth F. Roahen letter to Paul Quick, Assistant Regional Director, U.S. Fish and Wildlife Service, Portland, Oregon, January 28, 1955.

63. Kenneth F. Roahen letter to Superintendent Thomas Garry, July 14, 1963, KFRFWS.

64. Kenneth F. Roahen letter to Conrad L. Wirth, undated, KFRFWS.

65. Author's telephone interview with B. William Henry, January 23, 2013.

66. Author's interview with Richard Upton, December 27, 2012. Upton also visited Roahen at his home on Lewis Ave. in Billings and bought several of his Indian photos. See Upton, "Custer Adventure," 10.

67. "Roahen," *Billings (Montana) Gazette*, January 10, 1976, 8-A.

3. Little Big Horn Battle Historical Background

1. Brust et al., *Where Custer Fell*, 5.

2. Much of the following account of Custer's Little Big Horn campaign is drawn from Brust et al., *Where Custer Fell*, 5–13.

3. Terry to Sheridan, May 16, 1876, National Archives M1495, Headquarters Military Division of the Missouri.

4. Gray, *Centennial Campaign*, 287.

5. 2nd Lt. Winfield Scott Edgerly wrote to his wife on July 4, "We were told that the Indians had undoubtedly discovered our presence as several had been seen on the bluffs and the only thing left for us to do was move on them at once. . . . now all hopes of a surprise were gone." Clark, *Scalp Dance*, 24

6. At the Reno court of inquiry, Captain Moylan testified that Reno, Benteen, Keogh, and Yates were given command of battalions, noting, "Each of these battalions I have named consisted of three companies, except Captain Yates' which was two companies." Nichols, *Reno Court*, 213. Lieutenant Edgerly similarly informed researcher Walter Camp that Custer divided the regiment "into four battalions, Benteen, Reno, Keogh and Yates and had McDougall rear guard for pack train. He took Keogh and Yates with him." Hammer, *Custer in '76*, 54. In *Where Custer Fell* we used the term "battalion" to describe units of two or more companies; other terminology appears in the literature to denote subregimented segments of the command. Though most battle historians, including my coauthors of *Where Custer Fell* and I, assume that Keogh commanded Companies C, I, and L and Yates E and F, the evidence is less than conclusive on that point and subject to interpretation. Earlier in the campaign, Keogh had commanded Companies, B, C, and I and Yates E, F, and L.

7. Gray, *Centennial Campaign*, 296. In Nichols, *In Custer's Shadow*, 184, Joe Sills, Jr., and Ronald H. Nichols determined the total number of men with Reno as 165, 130 of whom were soldiers.

8. Graham, *Custer Myth*, 249; Hammer, *Custer in '76*, 92, 97.

9. Stands In Timber and Liberty, *Cheyenne Memories*, 197–98.

10. Gray, *Centennial Campaign*, 296, gives the loss as forty killed, thirteen wounded, and seventeen abandoned in the timber. Nichols, *In Custer's Shadow*, 383, interprets the loss as thirty-seven killed, ten wounded, and seventeen abandoned in the timber.

11. Two of the more thought-provoking analyses of the Weir Point episode are Taunton, "Enigma of Weir Point," and Sills, "Weir Point Perspective," 45–51.

12. Gray, *Centennial Campaign*, 206, gives a total of twelve killed—thirteen, if one includes Vincent Charley—and forty-one wounded during the two-day siege. Nichols, *In Custer's Shadow*, 384–85, places the loss at fifteen killed and fifty-five wounded. The subsequent deaths from wounds brought the fatalities sustained in the siege to twenty.

13. Taunton, *Custer's Field*, 26

14. Brust et al., *Where Custer Fell*, 13.

4. The Crow's Nest

1. The background on Camp's search is from Liddic, *Vanishing Victory*, 19.

2. See Brust et al., *Where Custer Fell*, 27–28.

3. Graham, *Custer Myth*, 112

4. Weibert, *Sixty-Six Years*, xi–xvii.

5. Hammer, *Custer in '76*, 59–63; Hardorff, *On the Little Bighorn*, 73.

6. Today, as a result of agricultural and railroad interests damming the waterway, the former river channel is a backwater of the Little Big Horn.

7. 1920 United States Federal Census, Ancestry.com.

11. Boyes "Other Lone Tepee," 23; Social Security Death Index, Ancestry.com (original data: Social Security Administration. Social Security Death Index, Master File).

9. 1940 United States Federal Census, Ancestry.com; see also Upton, "Custer Adventure," 10, in which he referred to Osten as a "very quiet and unassuming man."

10. Researcher Bruce Liddic provided me with a letter from his collection written by Owen B. Williams of Sheridan, Wyoming, on November 16, 1974. Both Williams and the recipient, the late Jay Smith, were members of the Little Big Horn Associates. Williams told Smith that a local man, Charley Erlanson, hired Russell White Bear to take him to the Crow's Nest in 1944 for three dollars. "They left Crow Agency on horse back and visited the Crow's Nest where Weibert has his monument and returned to Crow [Agency]." He added: "Also a photographer (professional) out of Billings, KEN ROAHEN photographed from the Crow's Nest in 1930 the Little Bighorn valley and mouth of Reno Creek." Though we might question whether 1930 was accurate, it seems likely that Roahen photographed the backcountry as early as that year or soon thereafter. Williams further described Roahen as "probably pretty feeble by now and . . . an inveterate cigar smoker."

11. Dustin, *Custer Tragedy Events*, 101.

12. Quoted in Hutchins, *Papers of Edward S. Curtis*, 128.

13. Scott, *Uncovering History*, 41.

14. Liddic, *Vanishing Victory*, 20.

5. Walter Camp's Marker on the Divide

1. Hardorff, *Camp, Custer*, 24–26. Much of what follows is based on Hardorff's description of the episode.

2. Ibid., 25.

7. The Morass

1. See Brust et al., *Where Custer Fell*, 28–29; and Donahue, "Knipe's Recollections."

8. Girard's Knoll

1. Stewart, *Custer's Luck*, 324.

2. Meketa and Bookwalter, *Search for the Lone Tepee*, 34.

3. Boyes, "Other Lone Tepee."

9. Major Reno's First Crossing

1. See Brust et al., *Where Custer Fell*, 35–36, for more details about the descriptions provided by Private O'Neil and Young Hawk.

10. Reno's Advance Down the Valley

1. Barnard, *Ten Years with Custer*, 291.

11. Reno Valley Fight and Retreat Crossing

1. For further information on the 1926 ceremonies, see Greene, *Stricken Field*, 61–65.

2. Author's interview with Chris Kortlander, Garryowen, Montana, October 1, 2012.

3. Brust et al., *Where Custer Fell*, 36.

4. For more on Reynolds and his death, see Hardorff, *Custer Battle Casualties*, 150–51; Hardorff, *Custer Battle Casualties, II*, 125–26; Brust, "Adventurous Detour"; and Brust, "Norris Drew."

5. See Brust et al., *Where Custer Fell*, for further information. Note that the marker was initially taller in 1938, as is evident in some of Roahen's photographs. It was initially first in concrete but had been cut off at the ground when the farmers moved it originally. Glen Swanson to James Brust, telephone interview, May 27, 2002. In my telephone interview with him on August 21, 2013, Swanson corrected the date that he and Jason Pitsch moved the marker from the late 1990s to the mid-1990s, ca. 1993–95.

6. Brust et al., *Where Custer Fell*, 36–37.

7. Barnard, *Digging*, 154.

8. In a telephone interview with me, August 21, 2013, Swanson recalled that in the mid-1980s he discussed when the marker was moved with Pitsch's father, who claimed it occurred in the early 1950s. At this late date, with Roahen, Osten, and Mr. Pitsch all dead, we are left with uncertainty. The marker clearly was in its original location when Roahen took this photo. Whether that was in the 1950s or 1966 we do not know.

9. See Brust et al., *Where Custer Fell*, 40–43, for the Barry views of the retreat crossing.

10. See Brust et al., *Where Custer Fell*, 54–57.

13. Reno-Benteen Defense Site

1. Most books dealing with this subject focus on the Custer segment of the Battle of Little Big Horn and may neglect the story of the valley and bluff fights. Readers seeking further information on those aspects of the battle should review the following books: Stewart, *Custer's Luck*; Gray, *Centennial*

Campaign; Utley, *Cavalier in Buckskin*; Larry Skelnar, *To Hell with Honor*; and Donovan, *Terrible Glory*. In great part the discussion in this chapter relies on these works.

2. Martin gave researcher Walter M. Camp two different statements. See Hammer, *Custer in '76*, 101, 105.

3. See Nichols, *In Custer's Shadow*, for excellent maps of troop dispositions on June 25 and June 26 at the site of the Reno-Benteen defense.

4. Stewart, *Custer's Luck*, 413.

5. Ibid.

6. Barnard, *Ten Years*, 298, 300.

7. Brust and Barnard, "Historic Gateway," 29.

8. Scott, *Uncovering History*, 41. See *Uncovering History*, 41–49, for an excellent summary of not only the 1950s work by Rickey and Vaughn but also that of other early surveyors who used archaeological techniques to study the fighting ground.

14. Weir Point to Medicine Tail Coulee

1. Brust et al., *Where Custer Fell*, 59. In that book we concluded that evidence that Clear died next to DeWolf was not strong, but placing his marker next to the doctor gives him greater visibility in the Little Big Horn story.

2. Brust et al., *Where Custer Fell*, 72–79.

3. Fox, *Archaeology, History.*

4. For greater insight into as well as the whereabouts of Traditional Luce Ridge and Luce Ridge, see Trinque, "Elusive Ridge."

5. Bruce Liddic e-mail to author, September 2, 2013.

6. Pederson et al., "Little Bighorn Battlefield."

7. See Donahue, *Drawing Battle Lines*, 138–43.

8. E-mail correspondence between Gregory T. Pederson and author, September 6, 2013.

15. Calhoun Hill, Finley-Finckle Ridge, and Battle Ridge

1. Whether Sergeant Finckle (also Finkel or Finckel) survived the battle has long been debated. Recently the debate has been reignited in Koster, *Custer Survivor.* See also the following articles published in the CBHMA newsletter *Battlefield Dispatch:* George Kush, "Who Was August Finckle" (Spring 2013): 8–9; George Kush, "Rhymes of the Regiment" (Winter 2013): 8; John Koster, "On the Trail of the Custer Survivor" (Winter 2011): 10–11; Michael Donahue, "It's Time to Kick the Dead Horse (Or, the Story of Frank Finkel)" (Summer 2013): 11; Michael Donahue, "It's Important to Cross Your 'T's" (Fall 2013): 11–13; and John Koster, "In My Opinion" (Fall 2013): 8–9. Other related titles of interest are Boyes, *No Custer Survivors*; and Ellison, *Sole Survivor.*

2. Brust et al., *Where Custer Fell*, 92.

3. Ibid., 95.

17. Below Custer Hill

1. See Barnard, *Digging.* I handled public relations for the National Park Service during archaeologically related events in 1985, 1986, and 1989. Twenty-eight seemed to be the most common figure cited for the number of missing troopers, although historical recollections offer a range of between twenty-two and thirty-five. Brust et al., *Where Custer Fell*, 111.

2. Scott, *Uncovering History*, 74.

3. Barnard, *Digging*, 118–19. Scott repeated his belief during a conversation with me in Hardin, Montana, on June 21, 2013.

18. Last Stand Hill

1. Brust et al., *Where Custer Fell*, 126.

2. Graham, *The Custer Myth*, 377.

3. Barnard, *Ten Years*, 304.

4. Brust et al., *Where Custer Fell*, 168–69.

5. Greene, *Stricken Field*, 69.

6. Brust et al., *Where Custer Fell*, 159.

7. Barnard, *Digging*, 182–86.

19. Entering the Main Battlefield

1. Rickey, *History*, 99.

2. Greene, *Stricken Field*, 58, 93.

3. Barnard, *Digging*, 165–87.

4. Scott, *Uncovering History*, 44; Barnard, *Digging*, 51–52.

20. Visitor Center Dedication, June 25, 1952

1. See Rickey, *History*, 31–36, 90–91, 93–94, 105–10.

21. Roahen's 1951 Aerial Photos of the Seventy-Fifth Anniversary

1. Rickey, *History*, 90.

2. This section is based on Barnard, *I Go with Custer*; Fox, *Archaeology, History*; Donahue and Moore, "Gibbon's Route"; and Donahue, "Revisiting."

3. Barnard, *I Go with Custer,* 140.

Bibliography

Archives

Frank L. Anders Papers, OGL 43-5-1, Elwyn B. Robinson Special Collections, Chester Fritz Library, University of North Dakota, Grand Forks.

Walter M. Camp Collection, Brigham Young University, Provo, Utah.

Ralph G. Cartwright Collection, Phoebe Apperson Hearst Memorial Library, Lead, S.Dak.

W. J. Ghent Papers, Library of Congress, Washington, D.C.

Edward S. Godfrey Papers, Library of Congress, Washington, D.C.

Little Bighorn Battlefield National Monument, Crow Agency, Mont.

Record Group 393, Headquarters Military Division of the Missouri, National Archives, Washington, D.C.

Kenneth F. Roahen Collection, Big Horn County Historical Museum, Hardin, Mont.

Kenneth F. Roahen Collection, U.S. Fish & Wildlife Service, Shepherdstown, W.Va.

U.S. Fish and Wildlife Service Archives, Shepherdstown, W.Va.

U.S. House of Representatives, History, Art and Archives website: http://history.house.gov/People.

Elmo Scott Watson Papers, Newberry Library, Chicago, Ill.

Interviews

Author's interview with Chris Kortlander, Garryowen, Mont., October 1, 2012.

Author's interview with Elaine Ooley, Big Horn County Historical Museum, Hardin, Mont., October 3, 2012.

Author's telephone interview with B. William Henry, January 23, 2013.

Author's interview with Richard Upton, December 27, 2012.

Books and Articles

Aadland, Dan. *Women and Warriors of the Plains: The Pioneer Photography of Julia E. Tuell.* Missoula, Mont.: Mountain Press, 2000.

Albright, Peggy. *Crow Indian Photographer: The Work of Richard Throssel.* Albuquerque: University of New Mexico Press, 1997.

Assault Cases against Agent and Deputy Wardens. U.S. Fish and Wildlife Service Archives, National Conservation Center, Shepherdstown, W.Va.

Barnard, Sandy. *Custer's First Sergeant John Ryan.* Terre Haute, Ind.: AST Press, 1996.

———. *Digging into Custer's Last Stand.* Terre Haute, Ind.: AST Press, 1998.

———. *I Go with Custer: The Life and Death of Reporter Mark Kellogg.* Bismarck, N.D.: Bismarck Tribune, 1996.

———. "Ken Hammer, Looking for Walter Camp." *Greasy Grass* 11 (May 1995): 20, 25–29.

———. "Mark Kellogg's Role during the 1876 Campaign." In *1st Annual Symposium, Custer Battlefield Historical and Museum Association, Held at Hardin, Montana, on June 26, 1987,* 9–11. Hardin, Mont.: CBHMA, 1988.

———. *Ten Years with Custer: A Seventh Cavalryman's Memoirs.* Terre Haute, Ind.: AST Press, 2001.

Beaumont, Shelley. "Kenneth F. Roahen Photograph Collection Donated to Museum." *Big Horn County News*, Hardin, Mont., June 7, 2009.

Becker, Bob. "Goose Heaven: Free Corn and Police Guard." *Peoria (Ill.) Star*, April 6, 1929.

———. "U.S. Wars on Ducks' Leggers on the Illinois." *Peoria (Ill.) Star*, undated clipping, KRFRWS.

Bookwalter, Thomas. "The Photographs Described." In R. Norvelle Wathen, *The Custer Battlefield: An Aerial Perspective.* Louisville, Ky.: R. N. Wathen, 1976.

Boyes, William, ed. *Don Rickey Interview with John Stands In Timber*, August 8, 1956. Little Big Horn Associates, 1991.

———. *No Custer Survivors.* Rockville, Md.: WJBM Associates.

———. "The Other Lone Tepee." *Research Review* 23 (Summer 2009): 23–30.

Bragg, Addison. "Green with Envy of Chewers." *Billings (Mont.) Gazette*, undated news column.

Brininstool, Earl A. *Troopers with Custer.* Harrisburg, Penn.: Stackpole, 1952.

Brown, Mark, and William Felton. *The Frontier Years: L. A. Huffman, Photographer of the Plains.* New York: Bramhall House, 1955.

Brust, James. "Adventurous Detour to Battlefield." *Greasy Grass* 10 (May 1994): 8–12.

———. "Curtis Photographs Offer Unique Glimpse of Custer's Crow Scouts." *Greasy Grass* 13 (May 1997): 10–16.

———. "Fouch Photo May Be the First." *Greasy Grass* 7 (May 1991): 2–10.

———. "Into the Face of History." *American Heritage* 43 (November 1992): 104–13.

———. "John H. Fouch, First Post Photographer at Fort Keogh." *Montana: The Magazine of Western History* 44 (Spring 1994): 2–17.

———. "Learning about the Little Big Horn Battle from Photos Old and New." In *8th Annual Symposium, CBHMA, Held at Hardin, Montana on June 24, 1994,* 50–69. Hardin, Mont.: CBHMA, 1995.

———. Letter to the editor. *Montana: The Magazine of Western History* 45 (Spring 1995): 90–91.

———. Letter to the editor. *Montana: The Magazine of Western History* 48 (Spring 1998): 84.

———. "Letting the Photos Speak." In James Hutchins, ed., *The Papers of Edward S. Curtis Relating to Custer's Last Battle,* 161–85. El Segundo, Calif.: Upton and Sons, 2000.

———. "Lt. Oscar Long's Early Map Details Terrain, Battle Positions." *Greasy Grass* 11 (May 1995): 5–13.

———. "Norris Drew Early On-site Map of Battle." *Greasy Grass* 10 (May 1994): 13–15.

———. "Photojournalism, 1877: John H. Fouch, Fort Keogh's First Post Photographer." *Montana: The Magazine of Western History* 50 (Winter 2000): 32–39.

———. "Stanley J. Morrow's 1879 Photographs of the Custer Battlefield." In *9th Annual Symposium, CBHMA, Held at Hardin, Montana on June 23, 1995,* 47–78. Hardin, Mont.: CBHMA, 1996.

———. "Where Was the Timber?" In *11th Annual Symposium, CBHMA, Held at Hardin, Montana on June 27, 1997,* 5–12. Hardin, Mont.: CBHMA, 1998.

Brust, James, and Sandy Barnard. "Historic Gateway to the Custer Battlefield." *Greasy Grass* 24 (May 2008): 26–29.

Brust, James S., Brian C. Pohanka, and Sandy Barnard. *Where Custer Fell: Photographs of the Little Bighorn Battlefield Then and Now.* Norman: University of Oklahoma Press, 2005.

Burnett, Frances, obituary. *Great Bend (Kansas) Tribune,* February 27, 1946.

Carroll, John, ed. *The Benteen-Goldin Letters on Custer and His Last Battle.* New York: Liveright, 1974.

———. *The Custer Battlefield Ghost Picture.* Bryan, Tex.: privately published, 1978.

———. "The Little Big Horn Medals of Honor." *Research Review* 4 (January 1990): 20–32.

Carroll, John, and Byron Price. *Roll Call on the Little Big Horn, 28 June 1876.* Fort Collins, Colo: Old Army Press, 1974.

Cecil, Jerry. "Lt. Crittenden, Striving for the Soldier's Life." *Greasy Grass* 11 (May 1995): 30–36.

Clark, George M. *Scalp Dance: The Edgerly Papers on the Battle of the Little Big Horn.* Oswego, N.Y.: Heritage Press, 1985.

"Colorful U.S. Game Agent Retires after 30 Years." *Great Falls (Mont.) Tribune,* January 2, 1955.

Cowdrey, Mike. "Crows Who Scouted for Custer." *Greasy Grass* 14 (May 1998): 39–44.

Curtis, Edward. *The North American Indian, Being a Series of Volumes Picturing and Describing the Indians of the United States and Alaska,* vol. 3. Cambridge: University Press, 1908.

Darling, Roger. *Benteen's Scout to the Left—the Route from the Divide to the Morass, June 25, 1876.* El Segundo, Calif.: Upton and Sons, 1987.

Dixon, Joseph. *The Vanishing Race: The Last Great Indian Council.* Glorieta, N.Mex.: Rio Grande Press, 1973.

Doerner, John. "Human Bones Discovered during Indian Memorial Construction." *Post Dispatch of the Frontier Army of the Dakota* 17 (July 2002): 1, 14–15.

———. "Seventh Cavalry Horse Cemetery Excavated at Little Bighorn Battlefield." *Post Dispatch of the Frontier Army of the Dakota* 17 (July 2002): 1, 18–19.

Donahue, Michael N. *Drawing Battle Lines.* El Segundo, Calif.: Upton and Sons, 2008.

———. "Knipe's Recollections Help Camp Reconstruct Custer's Final Hours." *Greasy Grass* 14 (May 1998): 2–17.

———. "Revisiting Col. Gibbon's Route." *Greasy Grass* 19 (May 2003): 12–20.

Donahue, Michael, and Michael Moore. "Gibbon's Route to Custer Hill." *Greasy Grass* 7 (May 1991): 22–32.

Dustin, Fred. *The Custer Tragedy Events Leading Up to and Following the Little Big Horn Campaign of 1876.* Ann Arbor, Mich.: Edwards Brothers, 1939 (reprint, El Segundo, Calif.: Upton and Sons, 2011).

Ellison, Douglas. *Sole Survivor.* Aberdeen, S.Dak.: North Plains Press, 1983.

Fleming, Paula, and Judith Luskey. *The North American Indians in Early Photographs.* New York: Dorset Press, 1986.

Frink, Maurice, and Casey Barthelmess. *Photographer on an Army Mule.* Norman: University of Oklahoma Press, 1965.

Fox, Richard Allan, Jr. *Archaeology, History, and Custer's Last Battle: The Little Big Horn Reexamined.* Norman: University of Oklahoma Press, 1993.

———. "West River History." In Charles Rankin, ed., *Legacy: New Perspectives on the Battle of the Little Bighorn.* Helena: Montana Historical Society Press, 1996.

Frost, Lawrence. *The Custer Album: A Pictorial Biography of General George A. Custer.* New York: Bonanza Books, 1984.

———. *General Custer's Libbie.* Seattle, Wash.: Superior, 1975.

Godfrey, Edward. "Custer's Last Battle." *Century Monthly Illustrated Magazine* 43 (January 1892): 358–84.

Graham, William. *The Custer Myth: A Source Book of Custeriana.* New York: Bonanza Books, 1953.

———. *Story of the Little Big Horn, Custer's Last Fight.* New York: Bonanza Books, 1926.

Gray, John. *Centennial Campaign: The Sioux War of 1876.* Norman: University of Oklahoma Press, 1988.

———. "Itinerant Frontier Photographers and Images Lost, Strayed or Stolen." *Montana: The Magazine of Western History* 38 (April 1978): 2–15.

———. "Nightmares to Daydreams," *By Valor and Arms* 1 (Summer 1975): 30–39.

———. "Photos, Femurs and Fallacies—Part II." *(Chicago) Westerners Brand Book* 20 (September 1963): 49–51, 56.

Greene, Jerome. *Evidence and the Custer Enigma: A Reconstruction of Indian-Military History.* Golden, Colo.: Outdoor Books, 1986.

———. *Stricken Field: The Little Bighorn since 1876.* Norman: University of Oklahoma Press, 2008.

Hammer, Kenneth, ed. *Custer in '76: Walter Camp's Notes on the Custer Fight.* Provo, Utah: Brigham Young University Press, 1976.

Hammer, Kenneth, and Ron Nichols, eds. *Men with Custer: Biographies of the 7th Cavalry.* Hardin, Mont.: CBHMA, 1995.

Hardorff, Richard G., ed. *Camp, Custer and the Little Bighorn.* El Segundo, Calif.: Upton and Sons, 1997.

———. *Cheyenne Memories of the Custer Fight.* Spokane, Wash.: Arthur H. Clark, 1995.

———. *The Custer Battle Casualties, Burials, Exhumations, and Reinterments.* El Segundo, Calif.: Upton and Sons, 1989.

———. *The Custer Battle Casualties, II: The Dead, The Missing, and a Few Survivors.* El Segundo, Calif.: Upton and Sons, 1999.

———. *Hokahey! A Good Day to Die! The Indian Casualties of the Custer Fight.* Spokane, Wash.: Arthur H. Clark, 1993.

———. *Lakota Recollections of the Custer Fight.* Spokane, Wash.: Arthur H. Clark, 1991.

———, ed. *On the Little Bighorn with Walter Camp: A Collection of W. M. Camp's Letters, Notes and Opinions on Custer's Last Fight.* El Segundo, Calif.: Upton and Sons, 2002.

———. *Walter M. Camp's Little Bighorn Rosters.* Spokane, Wash.: Arthur H. Clark, 2002.

Hedren, Paul. "Holy Ground: The United States Army Embraces Custer's Battlefield." In Charles Rankin, ed., *Legacy: New Perspectives on the Battle of Little Bighorn,* 189–206. Helena: Montana Historical Society Press, 1996.

———. *With Crook in the Black Hills: Stanley J. Morrow's 1876 Photographic Legacy.* Boulder, Colo.: Pruett, 1985.

Heier, Vincent A. *Little Bighorn.* Charleston, S.C.: Arcadia Publishing, 2009.

Heski, Thomas. *The Little Shadow Catcher: D. F. Barry, Celebrated Photographer of Famous Indians.* Seattle, Wash.: Superior, 1978.

Hoopes, Lorman. *This Last West.* Helena, Mont.: Falcon, 1990.

Hurt, Wesley, and William Lass. *Frontier Photographer: Stanley J. Morrow's Dakota Years.* Lincoln: University of Nebraska Press, 1956.

Hutchins, James, ed. *The Papers of Edward S. Curtis relating to Custer's Last Battle.* El Segundo, Calif.: Upton and Sons, 2000.

Karson, Terry. *L. A. Huffman, Pioneer Photographer.* Exhibition catalogue. Billings, Mont.: Yellowstone Art Center, 1990.

Koster, John. *Custer Survivor: The End of a Myth, the Beginning of a Legend.* Palisades, N.Y.: History, 2010.

Kuhlman, Charles. *Legend into History.* Fort Collins, Colo: Old Army Press, 1977.

Libby, O. G. *Arikara Narrative of the Campaign against the Hostile Dakotas.* New York: Sol Lewis, 1973.

Liddic, Bruce. *Vanishing Victory.* El Segundo, Calif.: Upton and Sons, 2004.

Liddic, Bruce, and Paul Harbaugh. *Camp on Custer: Transcending the Custer Myth.* Spokane, Wash.: Arthur H. Clark, 1995.

Magnussen, Daniel O., ed. *Peter Thompson's Narrative of the Little Bighorn Campaign.* Glendale, Calif.: Arthur H. Clark, 1974.

Marquis, Thomas. *Wooden Leg: A Warrior Who Fought Custer.* Lincoln: University of Nebraska Press, 1931.

Mautz, Carl. *Biographies of Western Photographers.* Nevada City, Calif.: Carl Mautz, 1997.

Meketa, Ray, and Thomas E. Bookwalter. *The Search for the Lone Tepee.* n.p., Little Horn Press, 1983.

Michno, Gregory. *Lakota Noon.* Missoula, Mont.: Mountain Press, 1997.

———. *The Mystery of E Troop: Custer's Gray Horse Company at the Little Bighorn.* Missoula, Mont.: Mountain Press, 1994.

Mitchell, Lynn. "William Richard Cross, Photographer on the Nebraska–South Dakota Frontier." *South Dakota History* 20 (Summer 1990): 81–95.

Montana Historical Society. *F. Jay Haynes, Photographer.* Helena: Montana Historical Society Press, 1981.

Nelson, R. L. "Sergeant Butler's 'Travelling' Marker." *Research Review* 8 (Spring 1974): 5–9.

Neihardt, John G. *Black Elk Speaks.* Lincoln: University of Nebraska Press, 1995.

Nichols, Ron. "CBHMA Marks Its 50th Year." *Greasy Grass* 19 (May 2003): 3.

———. *In Custer's Shadow: Major Marcus Reno.* Fort Collins, Colo.: Old Army Press, 1999.

———, ed. *Reno Court of Inquiry.* Crow Agency, Mont.: CBHMA, 1992.

Noyes, Lee. "Federal Agent Was Renown Battlefield Photographer." *Battlefield Dispatch* (Hardin, Mont.: CBHMA), Winter 2010.

O'Connor, Nancy. *Fred E. Miller, Photographer of the Crows.* Missoula: University of Montana, 1985.

Pederson, Gregory T., Stephen T. Gray, Mark Lesser, and Leslie Allen. "Little Bighorn Battlefield National Monument Riparian Forest Demography: Hydroclimatic Tree-Establishment Conditions and a Search for 'Witness' Trees." Final Report to the National Park Service, rev. October 23, 2012.

"Poachers' Sport: Kill the Game Agent." *Billings (Mont.) Gazette*, February 9, 1964.

Rickey, Don, Jr. *Forty Miles a Day on Beans and Hay: The Enlisted Soldier Fighting the Indian Wars.* Norman: University of Oklahoma Press, 2013.

———. *History of Custer Battlefield.* Billings, Mont.: CBHMA, 1967.

"Roahen." *Billings (Mont.) Gazette*, January 10, 1976, 8-A.

Roahen, Daniel L., obituary. *Great Bend (Kansas) Tribune*, November 5, 1932.

"Roahen-Moses." *Great Bend (Kansas) Tribune*, December 27, 1910.

"Roahen Summoned by Father's Death." *Billings (Mont.) Gazette*, November 3, 1932.

Russell, Don. *Custer's Last.* Fort Worth, Tex.: Amon Carter Museum of Western Art, 1968.

Scott, Douglas D. *Uncovering History: Archaeological Investigations at the Little Bighorn.* Norman: University of Oklahoma Press, 2013.

Scott, Douglas D., and Peter Bleed. *A Good Walk around the Boundary: Archaeological Inventory of the Dyck and Other Properties adjacent to Little Bighorn Battlefield National Monument.* Lincoln: Nebraska Association of Professional Archeologists and Nebraska State Historical Society, 1997.

Scott, Douglas, and Richard A. Fox. *Archaeological Insights into the Custer Battle: An Assessment of the 1984 Field Season.* Norman: University of Oklahoma Press, 1987.

Scott, Douglas, Richard A. Fox, Melissa Connor, and Dick Harmon. *Archaeological Perspectives on the Battle of the Little Bighorn.* Norman: University of Oklahoma Press, 1989.

Scott, Douglas, and P. Willey. *Osteological Analysis of Human Skeletons Excavated from the Custer National Cemetery.* Technical Report 50. Lincoln, Neb.: Midwest Archaeological Center, 1997.

Scott, Douglas, P. Willey, and Melissa Connor. *They Died with Custer.* Norman: University of Oklahoma Press, 1998.

Sills, Joe, Jr. "The Crow Scouts: Their Contribution in Understanding the Little Big Horn Battle." In *5th Annual Symposium CBHMA, Held at Hardin, Montana, June 21, 1991*, 11–18. Hardin, Mont.: CBHMA, 1992.

———. "Weir Point Perspective." In *7th Annual Symposium, CBHMA, Held at Hardin, Montana, on June 25, 1993*, 45–51. Hardin, Mont.: CBHMA, 1994.

———. "Were There Two Last Stands?" In *2nd Annual Symposium, CBHMA, Held at Hardin, Montana, June 24, 1988*, 13–21. Hardin, Mont.: CBHMA, 1989.

Skelnar, Larry. *To Hell with Honor: Custer and the Little Bighorn.* Norman: University of Oklahoma Press, 2000.

Smalley, Vern. "Where Was the Crow's Nest." In *13th Annual Symposium, CBHMA, Held at Hardin, Montana on June 25, 1999*, 77–90. Hardin, Mont.: CBHMA, 2000.

Southwest Parks and Monuments Association. *Custer National Cemetery.* Little Bighorn Battlefield National Monument, Mont.: Southwest Parks and Monuments Association, 1999.

Spear, Elsa. *Bozeman Trail Scrapbook: The Books and Photos of Elsa Spear.* Banner, Wyo.: Fort Phil Kearny/Bozeman Trail Association, and the family of Elsa Spear, 1993.

Stands In Timber, John, and Margot Liberty. *Cheyenne Memories.* Lincoln: University of Nebraska Press, 1967.

Stewart, Edgar. *Custer's Luck.* Norman: University of Oklahoma Press, 1955.

Taft, Robert. *Photography and the American Scene: A Social History, 1839–1889.* New York: Dover, 1938.

———. "The Pictorial Record of the Old West, IV: Custer's Last Stand—John Mulvaney, Cassilly Adams and Otto Becker." *Kansas Historical Quarterly* 14 (November 1946): 361–90.

Taunton, Francis. *Custer's Field: A Scene of Sickening Ghastly Horror.* London: Johnson-Taunton Military Press, 1986.

———. "The Enigma of Weir Point." In *No Pride in the Little Big Horn.* London: English Westerners' Society, 1987.

Thackeray, Lorna. "Photo Collection Donated to Museum." *Billings (Mont.) Gazette*, June 7, 2009.

Tilden, Freeman. *Following the Frontier with F. Jay Haynes, Pioneer Photographer of the Old West.* New York: Knopf, 1964.

Treadwell, T. K., and William Darrah. *Stereographers of the World.* National Stereoscopic Association, 1994.

Trinque, Bruce. "Elusive Ridge." *Research Review* 9 (January 1995): 2–8.

———. "The Fight in Fishing Woman Ravine." In *Custer and His Times*, book 4. Little Big Horn Associates, 2002.

———. "It's About Time." In *17th Annual Symposium of the Custer Battlefield Historical and Museum Association, June 27, 2003.* Hardin, Mont.: CBHMA, 2004.

Tuttle, Jud. "Who Buried Lieutenant Hodgson?" In *4th Annual Symposium CBHMA, Held at Hardin, Montana on June 22, 1990*, 9–16. Hardin, Mont.: CBHMA, 1991.

Upton, Richard. "The Custer Adventure." In *Brian C. Pohanka 26th Annual Symposium, Custer Battlefield Historical and Museum Association, held at Hardin, Montana, June 22, 2012*, 10. Hardin, Mont.: CBHMA, 2012.

———. *Fort Custer on the Big Horn, 1877–1898: Its History and Personalities as Told and Pictured by Its Contemporaries.* Glendale, Calif.: Arthur H. Clark, 1973.

U.S. Fish and Wildlife Service. "Kenneth Roahen, a True FWS Hero." *Historical Happenings*, March 2010.

"U.S. Game Agent for Montana Retires after 30 Years." *Billings (Mont.) Gazette*, January 2, 1955.

Utley, Robert. *Cavalier in Buckskin.* Norman: University of Oklahoma Press, 1988.

———, ed. *The Reno Court of Inquiry.* Fort Collins, Colo.: Old Army Press, 1972.

Watson, Elmo. "Photographing the Frontier." *(Chicago) Westerner's Brand Book* 4 (January 1948): 66.

———. "Way Out West: The Story of Stanley J. Morrow, a Pioneer Photographer in Every Sense of the Word." *Coronet* 5 (April 1939).

Weibert, Henry and Don. *Sixty-Six Years in Custer's Shadow.* Billings, Mont.: Falcon Press, 1985.

Wells, Wayne. "Custer's Arrival Time at the River." In *1st Annual Symposium CBHMA, Held at Hardin, Montana, June 26, 1987,* 76–87. Hardin, Mont.: CBHMA, 1988.

———. "The Fight on Calhoun Hill." In *2nd Annual Symposium, CBHMA, Held at Hardin, Montana, June 24, 1988.* Hardin, Mont.: CBHMA, 1989.

———. "Kanipe, Martin and Benteen." *Research Review* 2, no. 1 (1988).

———. "Little Big Horn Notes: Stanley Vestal's Indian Insights." *Greasy Grass* 5 (May 1989).

Wengert, James W., and E. Elden Davis, eds. *That Fatal Day: Eight More with Custer.* Howell, Mich.: Powder River Press, 1992.

"West from Ohio." *Great Bend (Kansas) Tribune*, August 8, 1937.

Index

Page numbers followed by an f *in italic type indicate figures (photographs); an* m *indicates a map and an* n *indicates an endnote.*

aerial photographs: Reno advance into the valley, 81, 82*f*–85*f*; on seventy-fifth battle anniversary, 229–37, 230*f*–31*f*, 234*f*–37*f*
archaeological surveys, 124–26, 166, 183, 223–24
Archaeology, History and Custer's Last Stand (Fox), 233
Arikara scouts, 74
Army campaign strategy, 33–35

Barnard, Betty, 53*f*, 216, 216*f*
Barnard, Sandy, 53*f*, 120*f*
Barrett, Lawrence P., 239*n*5
Barry, David F., 5, 103, 119
Barthelmess, Christian, 5, 155
Barton County, Kan., 9
battalion composition, 241*n*6
battlefield entrance roadway, 203*f*
battlefield main gate, 200–201, 202*f*–204*f*
battlefield tour road, 126, 144, 192
Battle of the Little Big Horn, 32*m*; casualties, 115, 117–18, 183, 232, 241*n*10, 241*n*12; centennial anniversary, 28, 189; controversy surrounding, 6–7; division of army forces in, 36; extraction of wounded, 232; fiftieth anniversary, 47–48, 86, 106; Indian accounts of, 167, 183–84; scholarship on, 3–4, 29; seventy-fifth anniversary, 81, 112, 205*f*, 214*f*–15*f*, 225, 226*f*–28*f*, 229–37, 230*f*–31*f*, 234*f*–37*f*; survivors of, 3, 6, 61, 87, 103, 106, 120, 122; tenth anniversary, 103, 119*f*
Battle of the Rosebud, 32*m*, 34
Battle of the Washita, 36, 118, 140, 233
Battle Ridge, 139*m*, 153*m*, 157, 161, 230*f*, 234*f*
Battle Ridge Road, 158*f*
Becker, Bob, 19
Belden, Charles, 186
Bellingham, William H., 3, 4, 28, 46, 52*f*, 63, 64*f*, 74
Benteen, Frederick W., 36, 37*f*, 39, 115; Custer's last message and, 140; decision to remain at defense site, 116–17; on Reno's conduct, 118; theories on role of in battle, 7
Big Foot, 38
Big Horn County Historical Museum, 46, 124–26, 135, 192, 214
Big Horn Mountains, 40
Billings Gazette, 9, 12, 20, 23, 28
Biological Survey, 16
Bird in Ground ranch, 83, 112
Bismarck Tribune, 231
Black Hills, 30–31
Blummer, Joseph, 140
Bookwalter, Tom, 67–68, 74
Boyes, William, 47, 68, 70
Bragg, Addison, 9
Bravo, Art, 226*f*
Bray, Robert, 124, 125, 223
Brininstool, Earl A., 3, 48, 94, 95*f*
Brininstool, Mrs. E. A., 95*f*
Broom, Thornhill, 18
Brown, William Carey, 3
Brust, James S., 8, 76, 101, 120, 198, 239*n*5, 242*n*5
burial sites, 124–26, 129, 173, 183; reburial sites, 218, 218*f*–19*f*, 224*f*; of unknown soldier, 86–87, 88*f*, 99, 223–24, 224*f*
Burkman, John, 74
Burkman blazed tree, 74, 74*f*, 77*f*
Burlington Northern and Santa Fe Railway, 92
Burnett, Swan, 13
Burns, Ned J., 225

Caldwell, R. W., 16
Calhoun, James, 155, 167, 183
Calhoun Coulee, 153–54, 169
Calhoun Hill, 139*m*, 140, 143, 144, 153*m*, 153–55, 156*f*–57*f*, 230*f*, 235*f*
Calhoun Ridge, 153. *See also* Finley-Finckle Ridge
Camp, Walter Mason, 3, 4*f*, 5, 43, 46, 47, 48, 61, 94, 154, 239*n*5; divide marker and, 56–58; Morass area, 62*f*, 63*f*
campaign strategy, 33–35
Capone, Al, 14–15
Carter, A. G., 87
Cartwright, Ralph G., 140, 199*f*
cattle guard, 200, 200*f*–204*f*, 203*f*
Cedar Coulee, 139, 139*m*, 142
cemetery. *See* Custer National Cemetery
Cemetery Ridge, 183, 233
cemetery road, 208
Charley, Vincent, 39, 241*n*12
Charlton, M. A., 19–20
Cheyenne Suicide Boys, 167
Cheyenne tribe, 29. *See also* Indian forces
Chicago, Burlington and Quincy Railroad, 86
Chiperfield, Burnett Mitchell, 21–22
Civil War, 33, 239*n*4

Claflin, Kan., 9, 11
Clear, Elihu, 137, 243*n*1
Clear Lake Hunting Club, 20–21
Clifford, Walter, 40
Colorado State University, 6
Company A, 36, 117, 121
Company B, 36, 38, 121
Company C, 36, 139, 154
Company D, 36, 39, 117, 121
Company E, 36, 166, 167, 172–73, 233
Company F, 36, 167, 233
Company G, 36, 99, 117, 121
Company H, 36, 68, 71*f*, 117, 118, 121, 124, 126
Company I, 36, 155
Company K, 36, 39, 117, 121
Company L, 36
Company M, 36, 81, 106, 117, 121
Cooke, W. W., 67, 139
Cooke marker, 184*m*
cottonwood trees, 147–50
Crazy Horse, 31
Crook, George, 33, 33*f*
Cross, William R., 5
Crow Agency, 225
Crow scouts, 36, 43, 44, 50, 58
Crow's Nest, 7, 32*m*, 36, 43–55, 45*f*, 53*f*, 165, 242*n*10; Curtis description of, 50–51; Dustin description of, 49; physical location of, 44–45, 47; Roahen photographs of, 48*f*–52*f*, 54*f*; Roahen's siting of, 46–47; vegetation on, 55*f*
Crow's Nest area, 44*m*
Crow's Nest marker, 43–44, 46*f*
Crow Tribal Reservation, 86
Crow tribe, 121
Curly (Crow scout), 58
Curtis, Edward S., 5, 50
Custer, Boston, 140, 142, 183; marker, 184*m*
Custer, Brice C. W., 225
Custer, Elizabeth B., 225
Custer, George Armstrong, 1*f*, 6*f*, 29, 30*f*, 115, 167; actions at Medicine Tail Coulee, 140; burial of, 183; Crow's Nest and, 44; decision to head north, 36, 38; fort building and, 30–31; Girard's Knoll and, 67; marker, 184*m*, 195; message concerning pack train, 38, 39, 116–17, 139; rank, 239*n*4; Reno on death of, 118; role in campaign strategy, 33–35; theories concerning death of, 7
Custer, Libbie, 120
Custer, Thomas W., 140, 183; marker, 184*m*
Custer Association of Britain, 239*n*4
Custer Battlefield Historical and Museum Association (CBHMA), 4, 26, 28, 47, 239*n*4, 239*n*5, 241*n*58
Custer Battlefield Museum, 86, 88*f*, 225
Custer Battlefield National Monument, 239*n*5; entrance, 200–201, 202*f*–204*f*; environmental considerations at, 201–202. *See also* Little Bighorn Battlefield National Monument
Custer Battlefield Preservation Committee, 82, 100, 101, 103
Custer Hill, area below, 165*m*, 165–81, 168*f*–70*f*, 172*f*–73*f*. *See also* Last Stand Hill
Custer Hill markers, 184*m*
Custer Memorial Association, 86
Custer monument, 185, 186*f*, 187*f*
Custer Myth, The (Graham), 45
Custer National Cemetery, 156, 185*f*, 213–24, 215*f*–16*f*, 220*f*–23*f*; aerial view, 230*f*, 231*f*, 234*f*; entrance, 210*f*, 212*f*, 217*f*; grave markers for children in, 222; honeysuckle hedge, 186, 189
Custer Ridge, 155
Custer Survivor (Koster), 243*n*1
Custer Tragedy, The (Dustin), 48–49

Dakota Column, 33, 34, 40, 231
Davis Creek, 45, 46, 50, 54*f*, 55*f*
Deep Coulee, 139*m*
Deep Ravine, 154, 166–67, 168*f*–70*f*, 169, 174, 180*f*; geophysical remote sensing studies of, 172–73
Deep Ravine walls, 176*f*
Denny, Sam, 100
Denny ranch, 82, 100
DeRudio, Charles, 119
Devil's Den, 165
DeWolf, James, 114, 135–36, 225, 243*n*1
DeWolf marker, 136*f*, 137*f*, 138*f*
Digging into Custer's Last Stand (Barnard), 239*n*5
Divide, The, 55*f*; to Reno Creek, 59–60. *See also* Crow's Nest
Divide marker, 56*f*–58*f*, 56–58
Doerner, John, 198
Donahue, Michael, 62, 101, 145
Drawing Battle Lines (Donahue), 145
duck bootleggers, 14–15, 16–17, 21
Dude Ranch Association, 25–26
Dustin, Fred, 3, 48–49, 94, 95*f*

Edgerly, Winfield S., 118, 241*n*5
Edward S. Godfrey Collection, 94
Elhard, Glen, 174, 177
Elliott, Joel H., 118, 239*n*5
Ellison, Robert, 3, 94, 95*f*
environmental considerations, 201–202
Erlanson, Charley, 242*n*10

Far West (riverboat), 232
Fetterman burial markers, 185–86, 187*f*
field hospital, 39, 115, 116*m*, 117
5th Infantry monument, 220–21
Finckle, August, 154, 243*n*1
Finckle marker, 155
Finley, Jeremiah, 154
Finley-Finckle Ridge, 153*m*, 153–55, 154*f*, 156*f*
Finley marker, 154*f*, 155
firearms safety, 25
flagpole, 201*m*
Flynn, Errol, 182
Ford B, Medicine Tail Coulee, 143
Fort Abraham Lincoln, 32*m*, 33
Fort C. F. Smith Memorial, 220–22, 229
Fort Ellis, 32*m*, 33
Fort Fetterman, 32*m*, 33
Fort Laramie Treaty (1868), 31
forts, 30–31, 32*m*
Fort Shaw, 33
Forty Miles a Day on Beans and Hay: The Enlisted Soldier Fighting the Indian Wars (Rickey), 128
Fouch, John H., 5, 182–83
Fox, Dennis, 68, 70, 101
Fox, Richard A., 140, 233
French, Thomas H., 81, 118
Frink, Maurice, 198
Frink sign, 199*f*
F. R. Moses Mercantile Co., 13
fur smuggling, 23

Gall, 31, 31*f*, 155
Galvin, Kevin, 101, 102
Garry, Thomas K., 26, 27
Garryowen, Mont., 81, 86–93, 93*f*
Garryowen gasoline station, 100
Garryowen historical sign, 87, 88*f*
Garryowen loop, 91*f*
Garryowen trooper burial site, 86–87, 88*f*, 99
geophysical remote sensing studies, 172–73
Gerow, James, 23*f*
Gettysburg National Military Park, 165
Ghent, William J., 3
Gibbon, John, 33, 33*f*, 34, 40, 231–33
Girard, Frederick, 36, 37*f*, 67, 70
Girard's Knoll, 7, 61*m*, 67–73, 69*f*–73*f*; possible sites for, 72*f*
Girl Scout visit, 190, 191, 191*f*, 202, 206*f*–209*f*, 207
Godfrey, Edward S., 39, 39*f*, 40, 47, 87, 94, 109, 118, 120, 120*f*, 155, 183
gold rush, 30–31
Goose Creek encampment, 34
Gouker, Chester A., 16, 240*n*26
Gouker, Olathe Susanne Woodworth. *See* Roahen, Sandae
Gouker, Pearl, 240*n*26
Graham, William A., 3, 45, 48
Grant, Ulysses S., 29, 31
Greasy Grass magazine, 62, 239*n*5
Greasy Grass Ridge, 139*m*, 167, 168*f*, 169, 170*f*
Great Bend Tribune, 12, 13
Great Sioux War, 33
Greene, Jerome A., 190–91, 208
Griffing, Richard Whitney, 122
ground-penetrating radar, 172
Grover, Andrew N., 213

Hamby, Cliff, 101
Hardin photo collection, 141
Harrington, Henry M., 109
Harrington marker, 184*m*
Harris, William A., 225, 228*f*, 229
Harwood, Ben, 26, 28, 225, 226*f*
Haynes, Frank Jay, 5, 155
Henry, B. William, 27–28
Herendeen, George, 58
Hodgson, Benjamin, 109, 117
Hodgson marker, 109, 110*f*
Hohmeyer, Frederick, 166
Hoover, J. Edgar, 25
horse cemetery, 198
Horse Holders' Ravine, 155, 161*f*
Horse Holders' Ravine markers, 160–61
Huffman, Laton A., 5, 109

I Go with Custer (Barnard), 233
Illustrated Weekly, 30*f*
Indiana State University, 7, 94
Indian Crow's Nest, 46. *See also* Crow's Nest
Indian encampment, 34, 88*f*
Indian forces: accounts of battle, 167, 183–84; noncombatants, 36, 38, 167; strength of, 35–36; weapons, 183; withdrawal from battle, 119
Indian Memorial, 185, 202, 218, 233, 234
Indian pony herd, 36
Indian reservations, 31
Indian scouts, 36, 38, 39, 74, 115
Indian Wars, 29–33
Interstate 90, 82, 86, 87*m*, 89, 90, 133
Izaak Walton League, 22

Jardone, W. M., 20
Johnson, Albert W., 94, 95*f*

Kanipe, Daniel, 38, 61, 62, 139, 154
Kellogg, Mark H., 167, 231, 232–33, 239*n*5
Kellogg Ravine, 231*f*
Keogh, Myles W., 36, 140, 155, 160, 167, 241*n*6
Keogh marker, 163, 164*f*
Keogh Sector, 160*m*, 160–64
Keogh Sector markers, 163, 164*f*
Kill Eagle map, 145, 149
Kortlander, Chris, 86, 87
Kuhlman, Charles W., 3, 48, 94, 95*f*

Lakota. *See* Sioux tribe
Lamb-Davis Lumber Co., 13
Last Stand Hill, 156, 157, 172*f*–73*f*, 175*f*, 177*f*–79*f*, 181*f*, 187*f*–88*f*, 192*f*, 219*f*, 230*f*; aerial view, 234*f*; errors in depictions of, 182–83; modern alterations to, 190–93; sidewalk, 193*f*. *See also* Custer Hill
Last Stand Hill historical markers, 197–98
Last Stand Hill markers, 174, 183, 196*f*
Last Stand Hill water tank, 162*f*, 192, 198, 199*f*
Lawyer, George, 20
Leahy, William, 229
Liddic, Bruce, 43, 52, 142, 143, 242*n*10
Life magazine, 25
Lilly Library, 94
Little Big Horn Associates, 47, 67, 239*n*4, 242*n*10
Little Bighorn Battlefield National Monument: archaeological investigation of, 124–26; battlefield tour road, 144; impact of Roahen photography on, 4–6; postcards of, 25. *See also* Custer Battlefield National Monument
Little Bighorn Battlefield Road, 144, 201*m*
Little Big Horn campaign, 32*m*
Little Big Horn River, 74, 77*f*–78*f*, 86, 181*f*; channel bed, 91–92, 92*f*–93*f*; flooding impact, 104; junction with Medicine Tail Coulee, 150, 150*f*–52*f*
Little Big Horn Valley, changes to, 86
Locke, H. R., 5
Lone Tepee, 7, 67–68, 70, 165
Look magazine, 25
Luce, Edward S., 3, 5*f*, 25, 26, 51, 81, 140, 141, 167, 198, 199*f*; Hodgson marker and, 109–10; in museum fundraising, 225; at seventy-fifth anniversary observance, 226*f*, 228*f*
Luce Ridge, 140, 142, 243*n*4. *See also* Traditional Luce Ridge

magnetometry, 172
main gate, 200–201, 202*f*–204*f*
maintenance area, 235*f*
Marquis, Thomas B., 225
Marsh, Ellene, 94, 95*f*
Martin, John, 115, 139–40
McCoy, Tim, 44
McDougall, Keith, 68, 70
McDougall, Thomas M., 36, 38, 39, 109, 115, 117, 139
McIntosh, Donald, 99–100
McIntosh marker, 99–100, 100*f*
Medal of Honor recipients, 56, 119
Medicine Crow, Joe, 26
Medicine Tail Coulee, 104, 146*f*, 235*f*; Custer actions at, 140; Custer movement toward, 139; Ford B, 143; Weir Point to, 135–52; Witness Tree, 144–45, 146*f*–47*f*, 147–49
Medicine Tail Coulee vicinity, 139*m*
Meketa, Ray, 67
metal detectors, 52, 64*f*, 122–23, 129–30
Migratory Bird Treaty Act, 20
Miller, Fred E., 5
Model 1866 Winchester carbine, 225, 226*f*
Montana Column, 33, 40, 231
Montana Historical Society, 57
Moorhouse, Lee, 5
Morass, 7, 61*m*, 61–66, 62*f*–66*f*, 165
Morrow, Stanley J., 5
Moses, Louise A., 12–13
Moses, Reuben H., 12–13
Mountview Cemetery, Billings, 28
Mushbach, George, 22

National Bison Range, 23
National Park Service, 68, 149, 173, 201, 243*n*1
National Park Service survey, 145
Neal, Bruce, 10*f*
Nichols, Ronald H., 241*n*7
Norris, Philetus, 94
North American Indian, The (Curtis), 50
Northern Cheyenne. *See* Cheyenne tribe
Northern Pacific Railroad, 30
Nye, Elwood L., 140, 199*f*
Nye-Cartwright Ridge, 139*m*, 140, 143, 145*f*

O'Neil (private), 74
Ooley, Elaine, 11*f*, 12, 13
Osten, George C., 3, 26, 27, 28, 46, 51, 52*f*, 63, 64*f*, 74, 81, 95*f*, 242*n*9; Girard's Knoll and, 67; importance in battlefield research, 47–48; Lone Tepee site theory, 70; Reynold's marker and, 94, 95, 98*f*
Ozenberger, Elsie L., 14

pack train, 36, 121; Custer's message concerning, 38, 39, 115–16, 139
parking lot area, 126, 201*m*, 202, 205*f*, 236
Paynter, E. L., 22
Pederson, Gregory T., 147, 149, 150
Peoria, Ill., 16–17
Peoria Star, 19
Perry, Charles, 22
Petty, Warren J., 27
photographs: evidentiary value of, 7–8, 40. *See also* Roahen photographs
photographs, panoramic: below Weir Point, 141*f*; cleared timber area, 99*f*; Deep Ravine, 171*f*; Medicine Tail Coulee, 146*f*; Morass, 66*f*; Reno Creek, 70*f*; Reno Creek valley, 54*f*, 55*f*; Reno retreat plain, 111*f*, 136*f*; Reno valley fight, 133*f*; Weir Point, 102*f*
Pitsch, Jason, 94, 97, 98, 99, 101, 242*n*5
Pitsch family homestead, 101
"Place Where Custer Fell, The" (Fouch), 182*f*
Pleasant View Cemetery, Claflin, 14*f*
Pohanka, Brian C., 239*n*5
Pohanka, Cricket Bauer, 120, 120*f*
Popovich, John A., 28
Porter, Henry R., 103, 115, 117
Porter, James E., 109

railroad dam, 89, 90*f*
Ralston, J. K., 28
reburial service, 218, 218*f*–19*f*, 224*f*
Reed, Harry Armstrong "Autie," 183
Reed marker, 184*m*
Ree scouts, 36
Reily, William, 184*m*
Reno, Marcus A., 37*f*, 67; actions prior to battle, 34–36; advance down valley, 38; battlefield marker, 121; on Custer's death, 118; decision to remain at defense site, 116–17; reputation, 118; retreat to timber, 38–39; theories on role of in battle, 7
Reno Battlefield Museum, 87, 100
Reno-Benteen Defense Site, 68, 69*f*, 81, 115–34, 116*m*, 121*f*, 123*f*–34*f*; aerial view, 237*f*; casualties, 117–18; metal detector use at, 122–23; rifle pits, 124*f*–27*f*; visitors on tenth anniversary, 119*f*
Reno-Benteen marker, 89–90, 90*f*, 95, 237*f*; current marker, 120*f*, 120–22, 121*f*–23*f*; original site, 116*m*, 119*f*, 119–20
Reno court of inquiry, 81, 118, 241*n*6
Reno Creek, 7, 46, 53*f*, 54*f*, 55*f*, 59*f*–60*f*
Reno Creek Road, 62*f*, 62–63
Reno Creek valley, 54*f*, 68
Reno Hill monument, 113, 113*f*
Reno retreat crossing, 82–83, 103*f*–107*f*, 103–11, 109*f*–11*f*, 129*f*, 165; aerial photos of, 112–14; with DeWolf marker, 137*f*
Reno's advance down the valley, 81–85; Roahen's arrow lines indicating, 82*f*–85*f*
Reno's first crossing, 61*m*, 74–80, 75*f*, 77*f*–80*f*
Reno valley fight, 87*m*, 133*f*–34*f*; Garryowen, 86–93; McIntosh marker, 99–100; Reynold's marker, 94–98, 95*f*–98*f*; Weir Point, 101–102
Research Review, 67, 68
restroom building, 201
Reynolds, Charles E., 95*f*
Reynolds, Charley, 94–98
Reynolds marker, 94–98, 95*f*–98*f*
Rickey, Don, 51, 122–23, 128, 141, 208; in enlisted soldier reenactment, 128, 129*f*–30*f*; metal detector use, 129–30, 131*f*–32*f*
rifle pits, 124*f*–27*f*
Riley, Francis R., 229
Roahen, Daniel L., 10–11, 11*f*, 14, 14*f*
Roahen, Elsie, 14, 240*n*25
Roahen, Ernest, 12, 14
Roahen, Frances, 12–13
Roahen, Kenneth F., 3, 4*f*, 5*f*, 10*f*, 11*f*, 15*f*, 18*f*, 19*f*, 23*f*, 27*f*, 28*f*; assassination attempts against, 17–22; attempts to bribe, 21; awards and citations, 20, 22, 26–27; birth date, 240*n*25; in CBHMA, 4, 26; childhood, 9–12; as commercial photographer, 25–26; death of, 28; early career, 12–14, 13; education, 12; as federal game agent, 14–15, 16; injuries sustained in the line of duty, 15, 16, 17; marriages, 12–13, 15; military service, 13; as Montana state game warden, 22–23; obituary, 240*n*20; photographic assignments for Fish and Game Service, 24; on photography, 12
Roahen, Richard L., 14, 240*n*27
Roahen, Sandae, 15*f*, 15–16, 18, 28
Roahen, Susan M., 10–11, 14, 14*f*
Roahen photographs: access to battlefield and, 51–52; aerial, 81, 82*f*–85*f*, 230*f*–31*f*, 234*f*–37*f*; area below Custer Hill, 168*f*–70*f*, 172*f*–73*f*; battlefield entrance, 202*f*; Battle Ridge Road, 158*f*–59*f*; Calhoun Hill, 156*f*; credits for, 239*n*2; Crow's Nest, 48*f*–52*f*, 54*f*; Custer monument, 188*f*, 190*f*; Custer National Cemetery, 213*f*, 217*f*–24*f*; DeWolf marker, 136*f*–38*f*; evidentiary value of, 40, 47–48, 233; Finley-Finckle Ridge, 154*f*, 156*f*; Garryowen loop, 91*f*; Girard's Knoll, 69*f*–73*f*; Girl Scout visit, 190, 191*f*, 206*f*, 207*f*; Keogh Sector, 161*f*–64*f*; Last Stand Hill, 183, 191*f*–97*f*; Little Big Horn River channel bed, 92*f*–93*f*; Lone Tepee site and, 67; McIntosh marker, 100*f*; Morass area, 63, 63*f*–66*f*; Nye-Cartwright Ridge, 145*f*; Reno-Benteen Defense Site, 121*f*, 123*f*–34*f*; Reno retreat crossing, 103*f*–107*f*, 109*f*–11*f*, 112*f*–14*f*; Reno's advance

Roahen photographs (*continued*)
down the valley, 82*f*–85*f*; Reno's first crossing, 75*f*, 78*f*, 79*f*; Reno valley fight, 133*f*–34*f*; Reynolds marker, 95*f*–98*f*; of Rickey as enlisted soldier, 128, 129*f*–30*f*; of seventy-fifth battle anniversary, 214*f*–15*f*, 215–16, 226*f*–28*f*, 229–37, 230*f*–31*f*, 234*f*–37*f*; in showing changes at battlefield, 192–98; Visitor Center, 186, 189*f*; Water Carriers' Ravine, 106*f*–108*f*, 107*f*–108*f*; Weir Point, 89*f*, 102*f*; Weir Point to Medicine Tail Coulee, 141*f*–46*f*; Witness Tree, 146*f*–47*f*
Robertson, Monte, 95*f*
Rogers, Edmund B., 225
Rosebud Creek, 35*f*
Rosebud / Little Big Horn divide. *See* Divide, The
rostrum, 214*f*–15*f*, 215; construction of, 213
rostrum area, 201*m*, 229, 236
Ryan, John, 81, 118, 183, 239*n*5

Santa Fe Trail, 9
Saskatchewan Department of Natural Resources, 22
Saturday Evening Post, 25
Scott, Douglas D., 123, 172–73, 198, 223–24
Scott, Hugh, 44, 46*f*, 47
Search for the Lone Tepee, The (Bookwalter), 67
7th U.S. Cavalry monument, 162, 164, 174, 223*f*, 227*f*. *See also* Last Stand Hill
7th U.S. Cavalry Regiment, 6; in campaign plan, 33; division of forces at Little Big Horn, 36; marching song, 86; modern, 225, 228*f*, 229; position prior to battle, 45; in protection of railroad, 30; reburial of remains, 218, 218*f*–19*f*, 224*f*; scholarship on actions of, 29; survivors, 3, 6, 61, 87, 103, 106, 120, 122
Sharpshooter Ridge, 87*m*, 109, 116*m*, 125, 138; Indian forces' use of, 117, 118; Weir Point from, 138*f*
Sheridan, Philip H., 33
sidewalks, 190, 191, 193*f*, 194, 208, 236
Sills, Joe, Jr., 241*n*7
Sioux tribe, 29, 30; Army campaign against, 33. *See also* Indian forces
Sitting Bull, 31, 31*f*, 34
Slaper, William C., 106–107, 107*f*
Smith, Jay, 242*n*10
Smith marker, 184*m*
South Skirmish Line, 166, 167, 173*f*, 177*f*–79*f*
South Skirmish Line markers, 167, 168*f*, 174
speaker's rostrum. *See* rostrum
Spear, Elsa, 5, 99
staff housing, 201*m*, 208–12, 213*f*, 236
Stands in Timber, John, 141
State College of Pullman, Wash., 13
Stone House, 25, 26, 156, 185, 201*m*, 208–12, 211*f*–12*f*, 236*f*
Sturgis, James G., 109
Swanson, Glen, 94, 97, 98, 99, 242*n*5
Sweet, Owen, 136, 183

Taylor, Malissa Douglas, 16
Temple College, 6
Terry, Alfred H., 6, 29, 33, 34, 34*f*, 35, 40, 231
They Died with Their Boots On (film), 182
Thompson, Peter, 56–57
Throssel, Richard, 5
Traditional Luce Ridge, 140, 142, 143, 143*f*, 243*n*4
traffic island, 206
tree longevity, 147–50
Truman, Harry S, 229
20th Century Photo Color Service, 25
Two Whistles, 226*f*

unknown soldier burial site, 86–87, 88*f*, 99, 223–24, 224*f*
Upton, Richard, 27–28, 241*n*66
U.S. Army Military History Institute, 94
U.S. Department of Agriculture Biological Survey, 14
U.S. Department of the Interior, 14
U.S. Fish and Wildlife Service, 14; field agents, 17*f*, 18*f*, 24*f*; patrol boat, 19*f*; Roahen photographic assignments for, 24; on Roahen's service, 3
U.S. Highway 87, 82, 89, 95, 133
U.S. Highway 212, 157, 163, 200
U.S. Military Academy, 6
Utley, Robert M., 216, 226*f*, 241*n*58

Valparaiso University, 6
Varnum, Charles A., 43, 45, 46
Vaughn, Jesse W., 51–52, 122–23, 131*f*–32*f*, 137–38, 141, 167
Visitor Center, 25, 26, 157, 179*f*, 185*f*, 201*m*, 206*f*–207*f*, 211, 217*f*, 223*f*; aerial view, 230*f*, 231*f*, 234*f*, 236*f*; dedication ceremony, 225
Visitor Center path, 166
Visitor Center vicinity, 201*m*, 201–206
visitor kiosk, 200–201, 236

Wainwright, Jonathan M., 225, 226*f*, 227*f*
Wallace, George, 117
War Department, 213
Washington State Game Department, 13
Water Carriers' Ravine, 105–106, 106*f*–108*f*, 116*m*, 118–19
Wedemeyer, Albert, 229
Weibert, Henry, 43–44, 45, 46, 47, 74
Weibert family historical marker, 99–100, 101*f*
Weir, Thomas B., 39, 117, 141

Weir Point, 39, 87, 87*m*, 89*f*, 91*f*, 101–102, 102*f*, 116*m*, 117, 123*f*, 125, 138, 157, 235*f*; to Medicine Tail Coulee, 135–52, 141*f*–46*f*; from Sharpshooter Ridge, 138*f*
Weir Point vicinity, 135*m*
Where Custer Fell: Photographs of Little Bighorn Battlefield (Brust, Pohanka, and Barnard), 5, 7–8, 29, 40, 45, 62, 94, 99, 109, 122, 136, 155, 166, 183, 184, 239*n*5
White Bear, Russell, 242*n*10
White Bull, 87
White Man Runs Him, 44, 46, 47, 50, 51, 120, 120*f*
White Swan Library, 26
Will, George F., 225
Williams, Owen B., 242*n*10
Wilson, M. L., 57
Winchester carbine, 225, 226*f*
Wirth, Conrad, 27, 239*n*3
Wisherd, Edwin L., 120
Witness Tree, 144–45, 146*f*–47*f*, 147–49
Wolf Mountains, 157
Wolf Tooth, 38
Woodworth, William Horace, 16
Wyoming Column, 33

Yates, George, 140, 167
Yates, W. M., 36
Yates marker, 184*m*
Yellowstone Library and Museum Association, 241*n*58
Yellowstone National Park, 94
Young Hawk, 74